Heritage Matters

# MUSEUMS AND BIOGRAPHIES

## STORIES, OBJECTS, IDENTITIES

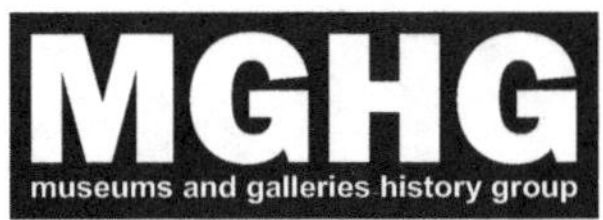


The publication of this book has been made possible by a grant from
The Scouloudi Foundation in association with the Institute of Historical Research

## Heritage Matters

ISSN 1756–4832

*Series Editors*
Peter G. Stone
Peter Davis
Chris Whitehead

Heritage Matters is a series of edited and single-authored volumes which addresses the whole range of issues that confront the cultural heritage sector as we face the global challenges of the twenty-first century. The series follows the ethos of the International Centre for Cultural and Heritage Studies (ICCHS) at Newcastle University, where these issues are seen as part of an integrated whole, including both cultural and natural agendas, and thus encompasses challenges faced by all types of museums, art galleries, heritage sites and the organisations and individuals that work with, and are affected by them.

Previous volumes are listed at the back of this book

# Museums and Biographies

## Stories, Objects, Identities

Edited by

KATE HILL

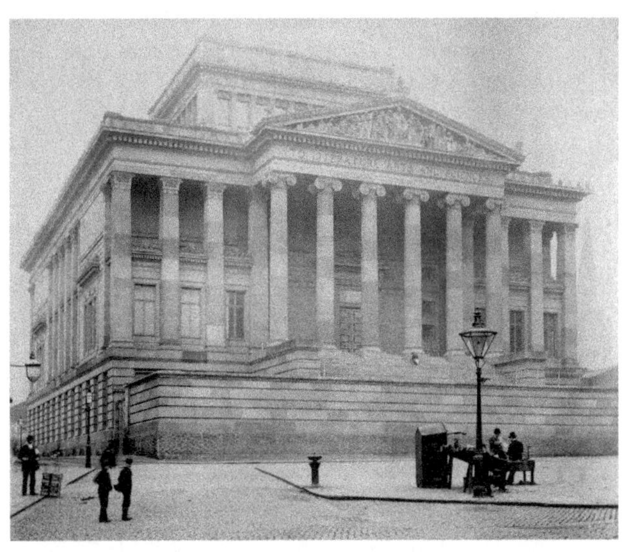

THE BOYDELL PRESS

First published 2012
The Boydell Press, Woodbridge
Paperback edition 2014

ISBN 978 1 84383 727 5 hardback
ISBN 978 1 84383 961 3 paperback

The Boydell Press is an imprint of Boydell & Brewer Ltd
PO Box 9, Woodbridge, Suffolk IP12 3DF, UK
and of Boydell & Brewer Inc.
668 Mt Hope Avenue, Rochester, NY 14620–2731, USA
website: www.boydellandbrewer.com



A CIP record for this book is available
from the British Library

This publication is printed on acid-free paper

# Contents

# Illustrations

The authors and publisher are grateful to all the institutions and individuals listed for permission to reproduce the materials in which they hold copyright. Every effort has been made to trace the copyright holders; apologies are offered for any omission, and the publishers will be pleased to add any necessary acknowledgment in subsequent editions.

# Introduction: Museums and Biographies – Telling Stories about People, Things and Relationships[1]

Kate Hill

'As long as there's a story, it's all right'
Graham Swift, *Waterland* (Swift 2010, 68)

Biographies and museums both lie in a grey area of knowledge and affect; they tell us about what happened, but also form emotionally compelling and satisfying narratives. They mediate the academic and the popular, spanning the physical and imaginary worlds. They are linked by an ability to tell us about ourselves and our world as moving through time, but also serve to immortalise, to freeze in time. Above all, when museums and biographies come together or overlap, what we get is relationships: between people, between people and things, and between people and buildings. Moreover, museums and biographies together highlight questions around how we know and communicate the past, and to what extent our selves are separate from both other selves and the 'object' world. They prompt us to ask how far we can interact with the materiality of the museum to develop our relationship with others, alive or dead, and whether objects can be active agents in those relationships. They suggest questions about identity as process and relationship.

On the other hand, biographies have subjects, while museums have objects. In bringing the two together are we not transgressing some fairly fundamental ways of thinking and understanding the world?[2] Certainly the 19th-century canonical museum was concerned to develop an objective, systematic representation of the world as knowable by the Western subject, while the biography promised to offer an understanding of the subjectivity of the great man; the 'existential and perceptual textures' of that life (Kaplan 1978, 2; Clifford 1978, 42). Both were premised on an understanding of the subject as a rational individual, exerting his will on the world; and simultaneously on an understanding of the world as knowable, separate from the knowing subject, and less likely to be composed of rational individuals (Epstein 1991, 2). Several of the contributors to this volume reflect on this legacy; but what emerges is the understanding that these ways of knowing were historically constructed, and are not necessarily inherent to either the practice of biography or of museology. The challenge of this volume, therefore, is to consider how biography in and of the museum can be used to become more reflexive about the 19th-century inheritance, and to develop new ways of knowing.

1 I am very grateful to Amy Culley for offering comments on this piece. Any errors that remain are, of course, my own.

2 A similar apparent dichotomy between history and biography is explored by Munslow 2003, 3.

Biography is not a new approach for understanding museums and museum displays; contributors to this volume chart the growth of a biographical approach within museums from the 19th century (Booth, Forgan). Museums have frequently been understood in terms of the life-story of the institution (a pre-eminent example is Miller 1973; see also Stearn 1981); while the lives of curators and others have been taken as a correlate of museum history. Kemp's 1990 essay on 'Biography and the Museum' groups a number of significant museum figures' lives together, arguing that such figures reflect their social and intellectual background, and thus provide a rich history which links the museum with its context (Kemp 1990, 263; see also Schadla-Hall 1989). However, such biographical approaches suffer from a 'smoothing out' effect remarked on by several contributors (MacLeod, Abt; see also Lee 2005, 2). Can lives, of people, things and institutions, be seen as messier, more entwined, less coherent, and yet still yield meaning?

Biography has been the subject of much scholarly attention recently, though opinion varies as to whether this interest has been shared by the wider public (Backscheider 1999, xiii; Cowman 2011). But if biography is not necessarily *more* popular than before, it has certainly demonstrated an enduring prominence in popular culture. However, biography is not a static genre, and its form and content, and relationship to scholarship, have developed substantially over the last two or three centuries. Caine singles out the influence of feminist theory, the study of new biographical subjects, the growth of interest in group biography, and the changing conceptualisation of the relationship between life and context as key developments (Caine 2010, chapter 6). In other words, the scholarly study of biography has demonstrated its flexibility and historical constructedness as a form, and the way in which, counter-intuitively, it is not only implicated in the construction of a 'great man', or even 'great woman', approach to history and literature, but can also be instrumental in dismantling this approach and recovering history's 'others' (Epstein 1991, 1; Booth 2004, 10–11; Cowman 2011). It has the capacity to situate individuals within a dense web of relationships, which serves both to limit the autonomy of the individual, and to suggest that individual identities are not the achievement of the individual, but brought into being as a process of interaction (Booth 2004, 4; Clifford 1978, 50). Biography, then, can be a transgressive genre, or one which confirms existing valuations and hierarchies. It maintains affective impact with particularity and detail, and strong narrative sweep (Clifford 1978, 44, 47). Contributors to this collection understand biography in a range of ways, from the more traditional to those informed by recent scholarship.

Museum studies and museum history, similarly, are enjoying prominence at least within the academic world; certain ways of engaging with their own past are more commonly undertaken by museums now than previously, though as commentators to this volume suggest, this is not unproblematic (Rees Leahy, Whitehead). However, there is a consensus that older models of museum history, which told an uncomplicated story of institutional progress – often identified with a particular, charismatic curator, or a series of them – are too celebratory, and not critical or reflexive enough to help museums understand themselves (Alberti 2009, 1). The very figure of the curator him/herself is being unpicked, to understand the ways in which the construction of a professional identity allowed curators to portray themselves as autonomous actors, and to deny the agency of others working within the museum (Teather 1990; Alberti 2009, 124; Hooper-Greenhill 1992, 1994; see also Sandino, this volume). Within museum studies and museum history, attention has recently been paid to questions of agency and meaning production, as well as to the narrative space of the museum (Alberti 2005; 2009; Gosden and Larson 2007). Agents within the museum turn out to be much more multifarious than the individual curator; Actor-

Network Theory and the work of Alfred Gell suggest that the material, in the shape of objects or buildings, can act to shape the museum's development, and the meaning of its displays (Gell 1998; Hetherington 1999). A recent biography of Henry Wellcome's collection suggested that in examining it over time, we are drawn 'away from Wellcome and towards the other people who collected for him. Wellcome's collection, and by extension his life, like all lives, was an emergent, negotiated entity' (Larson 2009, 5). Audiences, also, emerge as much more central to the construction of museum meaning (Kirschenblatt-Gimblett 1998; Hooper-Greenhill 1994; Alberti 2009, chapter 6). In addition, the narrative strategies and spaces of museums have come to be a key concern for scholars of museums (Bal 1992; Silverstone 1989). What sorts of stories can they tell, and how similar are those stories to textual ones?

Biography, then, can offer methodological possibilities to students of museum history; it offers a way of understanding the relationships between people and between people and things, and of plotting the development of museums and things. It can help us to conceptualise an understanding of museums, not as producers of knowledge about a knowable world which is simply transmitted to an audience, but as arenas where relationships produce narratives of various sorts. It can also suggest ways in which museums can tell better stories, which do fuller justice to the complicated histories of things, institutions and people. And museums, perhaps, can help to expand our understanding of what biography is and how it works; if a biography can be narrated in ways other than text, how does that inform our knowledge of the form?

This book arises from a conference of the same title held by the Museums and Galleries History Group in 2009. It became obvious as abstracts for papers came in that this was an extremely popular topic, but at the same time a topic which was being interpreted by contributors in varied and complex ways. Drawing together analyses of representation, material culture and personality, papers cast new light on the study of lives, objects, buildings and displays. Given such a breadth of approaches, the book has been organised into sections, although there is a considerable amount of overlap and many of the chapters are relevant to several sections.

Firstly, then, Individual Biography and Museum History investigates the extent to which individuals have been identified with particular museums, and have even 'become' their museum in some ways. As Kemp has suggested, 'the imprint of individual collectors and administrators looms over many gallery walls' (Kemp 1990, 263). This sense of imprint has attracted those seeking to understand museum history, such as Edward Alexander and his *Museum Masters* of 1983. Such an approach works particularly well for the early years of public museum development, when charismatic figures single-handedly developed the whole museum, from its buildings to its collections to its staff structure to its educational programmes (Hill 2005). They did not have role models for being curators, and did not separate their professional and personal identities. However, as this section demonstrates, this was not the only situation in which particular figures and their lives became strongly identified with the museum. Pontus Hultén, in Stuart Burch's essay, was a 20th-century art curator and a man who cultivated personality as art, who through canny use of bequest continued to influence the Museum of Modern Art in Stockholm after his death. Sydney Pavière, in Laura Gray's essay, was a curator whose innovative collecting practices and confidence with modern art essentially convinced his Museum Committee that if he wanted to do it, it must be a good idea. As Burch suggests in relation to Hultén, this is Bourdieu's distinction in action (Bourdieu 1984). These curators' actions are also clearly linked to a developing sense of professional identity – a curator should shape their museum, but should also remember that their tenure of it is temporary and should not identify themselves too much with it. But in both these cases, curator and museum were complicit in the construction of the myth of a heroic curator who 'became' his museum. Meanwhile, Felicity Bodenstein looks not at curators, but at collectors and donors, who could exercise an equally strong hold over the development and identity of the museum (see also Hill 2005; Alberti 2009). Moreover, the museum in this instance embraced the idea of valorising the individual donor, in a way that illuminates the museum–donor relationship, and highlights that while a professional identity for curators might be crucial, the absence of it could also be significant. Individuals are understood in these institutions as uncomplicated actors who could impose their will on institutions such as museums (though arguably Hultén had a more complex conception of an individual as partly created by his/her own publicity). However, importantly, it is the institution which makes such a myth possible.

The second section, Problematising Individuals' Biographies, takes issue with the extent to which simple and discrete life-stories of individual selves can explain museums and their histories. This might be because we are unable to take their own account of their centrality to a museum at face value, as with Lady Eastlake, examined here by Julie Sheldon. Eastlake constructed an idealised unity in the biographies of herself, her husband, and the National Gallery. Although she did have a public presence as an author, this was not always overt, and in correspondence she relied heavily on ambiguities which suggested she had played a much bigger role in the development of the National Gallery's collection than can be justified. What is maybe more interesting is why so many scholars of art, connoisseurship and collecting have taken her word for it. The answer is probably that this version has more intimacy, interiority and narrative drive than that of a competent professional carrying out his job. Ann Whitelaw's essay also suggests that individual biographies cannot, in fact, be trusted, because they replicate a focus on 'important' (usually male) individuals, which actively conceals the contribution of a broad group of volunteers and others. Neither traditional biography nor feminist re-readings of the genre seem to fit the bill here, because there are in most cases no names or basic biographical details for the people concerned, and their actions do not fit into a mould of 'action'.[3] These chapters remind us that curators are not always to be taken at their own valuation, and that other people have an important role in museums too. Meanwhile Linda Sandino examines the extent to which curators' own biographies and identities are bound up with the history of their institution. Using an oral history approach reveals how individuals constructed their own sense of identity, and thus tends to undermine any idea of biography as the story of an autonomous, integrated self. What this section seems to suggest is that agency in museums is complicated, and individual biography is not always able to do justice to it. While male curatorial agency may work in direct and clear ways, it does not always do so, and such agency is and has been problematic for women. A model of collective or relational agency, including the concept of a professional identity, may be more productive (see Gosden and Larson 2007). Equally, while it is salutary to unpick individual biographies, life-stories which explore the *construction* of identity and narrative, and acknowledge the relational nature of lives, can be useful.

3 But see Cowman (2011) for the argument that a collective biography based on fragments of evidence can be a productive methodology for feminist historians; and also for the argument that such a biography could challenge the ideas about private and public, and about significance, which have shaped women's biographies hitherto.

The third section, Institutional Biographies, aims to examine the extent to which the institution of the museum itself has a biography. Contributors here have examined the legal 'life' of the museum (Abt) as well as its architecture (MacLeod). In the USA, many museums are corporations, with the same legal status as people, and Jeffrey Abt considers both why this might be, and what the implications are for the study of museums. Wallis Miller looks at the particular issues raised by creating a museum devoted to architecture and to a particular architect, and examines the life-story of the Schinkel Museum in various guises to elucidate these issues. Architecture as a practice is hard to convert into narrative, but Suzanne MacLeod suggests that hitherto biography has not been prominent enough in the study of museum architecture. Buildings are seen as the special product of the individual architect and, once built, as achieved and static. MacLeod suggests instead that a complex process continues whereby the building is acted upon and acts on the people who surround it. It is, in other words, part of a process; and therefore part of a story. In other instances, institutions might already be attempting to narrate their own history. Both Helen Rees Leahy and Christopher Whitehead evaluate the extent to which museums can or should practise a form of institutional autobiography, either by restaging exhibitions or by recreating galleries, and ask why such a practice has become more common. For Whitehead, there is a similar sort of self-heroising taking place as could be seen with individual curators. He shows how the biography is constructed in the present and responds to current circumstances. Rees Leahy, by contrast, broadly welcomes the trend to exhibitionary autobiography as giving depth to our understanding of museum displays and spectatorship. This section both imputes an agency to institutions and buildings, and suggests that approaches which acknowledge the complexity and constructedness of biographies can help us understand institutions more fully; but also cautions against the individual actor model of biography being used for such subjects (or objects).

The fourth section is called Object Biographies, and it brings together a number of essays which are interested in using the object biography approach to understand museums more fully. A key inspiration here is Kopytoff's 1986 article which urged the study of objects throughout their lifecycle, in order to fully appreciate the way the object's meaning developed and changed in different situations (Kopytoff 1986; see also Hoskins 1998; and Gosden and Marshall 1999). And of course, this very idea of a 'lifecycle' for objects suggests that it is both possible and meaningful to write their biography. Both Louise Tythacott and Mariana Françozo follow particular objects before and after they enter the museum. For Tythacott's Chinese Buddhist bronze, the classifications imposed on it by the museum fundamentally affected and produced its meaning. Moreover, these museum classifications themselves can be traced to the museum's development, or life, and to the particular interests of the curators and staff who had responsibility for the bronze. Thus object biography is intimately linked to institutional and individual biographies. Françozo, while following a similar methodology to Tythacott, stresses the extent to which this approach can help to give complexity and depth to museum displays. It can illuminate relationships and processes, rather than more static 'facts'. Like Tythacott, Françozo sees object biographies as deeply entwined with institutional and individual biographies. Lucie Carreau and Mark Elliott look at collections of objects, and ask to what extent they may be considered to have a biography. Carreau's chapter explores the nature of the ethnographic collection of a wealthy amateur, and establishes that the reception of such a collection both contributes to the identity of the collector and attempts to sever the collection from its collector, who is seen as a 'contaminating' influence. In fact, as with individual object biographies, the objects, the individual(s) and the institutions are all entangled, and all have to be taken into account. Elliott deals similarly with a collection, but asks how a biographical approach to their understanding might inform current and future roles for the objects within the museum, arguing once more that biographies of people and of things are inseparable. He draws not just on Kopytoff but also on Gell with his reference to the 'cognitive stickiness' of objects and their capacity to act in a 'person-like' way, applying this insight to understand how collections have impacted upon museums and disciplines (Gell 1998). It seems, therefore, as if not only people, groups of people, buildings and institutions have agency, but objects and collections do too.

The fifth section, Museums as Biography, assesses the ways in which museums can produce biographical narratives. The contributors consider literary house museums (Booth), scientists' house museums (Forgan), and the 19th-century Museum of French Monuments as a biography of the nation and its heroes (Stara). For both Alison Booth and Sophie Forgan, while the individuals being portrayed have substantial public presences, the house museum serves largely to create a sense of intimate knowledge about those individuals. The power and attraction of the biographical museum lies in its use of domestic objects and buildings to produce new insights and a sense of intimate contact with the interior world of the biographee (Bryant 2003, 55). In the Museum of French Monuments, by contrast, Alexandre Lenoir sought to engage the empathy of the visitor by turning French history into a dramatic series of stories about artists, men of letters, kings and other leading figures using monumental sculpture. This extended to commissioning monuments to individuals for whom there was no extant historical monument. The text of the museum catalogue was an important part of the narrativisation of French historical sculpture, and here again both the interior and the public life of key figures was examined. All of these examples of biographical museums, then, adhere to a model whereby the 'real' person or persons are to be found in their greatness, or public impact, as well as their interiority and private life; with the latter usually serving to 'explain' the former. These ideas have been challenged within the field of textual biography (though see arguments that this has not been the case in scientific biography, particularly relevant to Forgan's chapter; Shortland and Yeo 1996, 2). Within a museum context, though, biography seems not to have changed much since its 19th-century roots. Most personality museums in Britain were founded around 1900 and in the 1930s (Bryant 2003, 53). A challenge for museums, then, may be to try to expand their methods of narrating lives in such a way that assumptions about public and private significance, the coherence of the individual self, and the inherent nature of genius are not replicated in the way shown here.

The sixth section, on Museums as Autobiography, interrogates the ways in which museums can enable people to tell their own lives in different ways and for different groupings. This is, by and large, a more recent development than the attempt to narrate other people's lives, and has a democratic impulse. However, Nemec's exploration of the genre of 'pure' autobiographical museums indicates that conviction of one's own unique and special contribution could be the impulse behind the foundation of such institutions, as well as a fear that without them the founder's genius would not be properly appreciated, or they might be totally forgotten. For artists of various kinds, it was particularly important to try to document the process of inspiration and creativity in a way that they felt only they could do; they subscribed to the idea of the unique artistic genius. Alternatively, 'ordinary' people might form an autobiographical museum that tied them in to a global, national and local history. De Jong's focus on the use of autobiographical accounts in museums shows more clearly, though, an attempt to democratise history, and to give a voice to ordinary people, along with public space to tell their stories/histories. However, she shows how the very didactic aim of several of the exhibitions she examines, and the exigencies of using video testimony in museums, tends to turn the use of autobiographical accounts more into a rhetorical strategy than an actual democratisation of museum spaces. Crooke, on the other hand, examines a yet more democratic area of museum autobiography, where a community tells its own story. The particularity of the biographical form is important here: the details of what a community has done or experienced, and the ways in which this has played out through time, as well as the way in which the community is linked to specific places, buildings and things, are what makes such an undertaking valuable to that community. It also more or less consciously embraces the constructed nature of autobiography: the community needs and wants to forge a shared story, and this story is 'better', the greater the density of relationships and connections within it. She argues that rather than community or individual autobiographies being utilised by the museum in a didactic way, community groups have become acknowledged gatekeepers of the past, in a way that alters power relationships substantially. For all of the contributors in this section, the question of what is displayed to create a material autobiographical narrative is key. This ranges from scraps and the minutiae of a life for Nemec, to video and audio recordings for de Jong, to photographs for Crooke. These are not conventional museum objects, but are powerful objects with which to tell stories that resonate, and narrative resonance may be the best criterion to evaluate them.

Finally, in the endpiece, Preziosi focuses on issues of immortality, representation and the separation of subject and object, which are of relevance to many of the preceding chapters. Can museums immortalise lives, or make their own and their objects' stories into immortal truth or knowledge? Or is their role in fact to insert stories into the passage of time? Moreover, what is the position of the visitor relative to the object and display – does it tell our story or do we tell it? Preziosi suggests that while we wish to stage this encounter as a finite and straightforward dialogue between subject and object, it overwhelms this frame in many ways. Thus the real and the imagined, the subject and the object, the material and the immaterial, the immortal and the temporal collide in museums, and as visitors we perform a creative or poetic act to both recognise and ignore this collision. Thus he argues that museums are key to understanding the fictiveness and contingency of our world view.

In bringing together museums and biographies, then, we are highlighting the processual, relational nature of museum narratives and knowledge (Gosden and Larson 2007). We want museums to transmit knowledge, to separate us from the material world and inform us about it; but simultaneously we want a subjective, imaginative connection with the immaterial. Biographical narratives both reveal this tension and help to mediate it. This is true for the investigation of museums as much as it is for the experience of visiting them. We can understand museums, their buildings, their objects and collections and their staff by considering them as unfolding through time, rather than as synchronous structures. Not only this, but museum analyses and narratives need to take into account the distributed and inter-related nature of the actors concerned, rather than identifying and celebrating the heroic curator, scientist or author. Through their very widely ranging chapters, the contributors to this volume demonstrate the value of thinking about the stories told in and by museums, and the relationships which make up museums; and suggest new ways of doing and understanding museum biographies.

## Bibliography and References

Alberti, S J M M, 2005 Objects and the Museum, *Isis* 96 (4), 559–71

— 2009 *Nature and Culture, Objects, Disciplines and the Manchester Museum*, Manchester University Press, Manchester

Alexander, E, 1983 *Museum Masters: Their Museums and Their Influence*, American Association for State and Local History, Nashville

Backscheider, P R, 1999 *Reflections on Biography*, Oxford University Press, Oxford

Bal, M, 1992 Telling, showing, showing off, *Critical Inquiry* 18, Spring, 556–94

Booth, A, 2004 *How to Make it as a Woman: Collective Biographical History from Victoria to the Present*, University of Chicago Press, Chicago

Bourdieu, P, 1984 (1979) *Distinction: A Social Critique of the Judgement of Taste* (trans R Nice), Routledge and Kegan Paul, London

Bryant, J, 2003 Homes for Heroes: the rise of the personality museum in Britain 1840–2002, in *Historic House Museums as Witnesses of National and Local Identities* (ed R Pavoni), DEMHIST, Milan

Caine, B, 2010 *Biography and History*, Palgrave Macmillan, Basingstoke

Clifford, J, 1978 'Hanging up looking glasses at odd corners': ethnobiographical prospects, in *Studies in Biography* (ed D Aaron), Harvard University Press, Cambridge MA and London

Cowman, K, 2011 Collective Biography, in *Research Methods in History* (eds L Faire and S Gunn), Edinburgh University Press, Edinburgh

Epstein, W H, 1991 Introduction: contesting the subject, in *Contesting the Subject, Essays in the Theory and Practice of Biography and Biographical Criticism* (ed W H Epstein), Purdue University Press, West Lafayette

Gell, A, 1998 *Art and Agency: An Anthropological Theory*, Clarendon Press, Oxford

Gosden, C, and Larson, F, with Petch, A, 2007 *Knowing Things: Exploring the Collections at the Pitt Rivers Museum 1884–1945*, Oxford University Press, Oxford

Gosden, C, and Marshall, Y, 1999 The Cultural Biography of Objects, *World Archaeology* 31 (2), 169–78

Hetherington, K, 1999 From Blindness to blindness: museums, heterogeneity and the subject, in *Actor Network Theory and After* (eds J Law and J Hassard), Blackwell, Oxford

Hill, K, 2005 *Culture and Class in English Public Museums*, Ashgate, Aldershot

Hooper-Greenhill, E, 1992 *Museums and the Shaping of Knowledge*, Routledge, London

— 1994 Museum Learners as active postmodernists: contextualising constructivism, in *The Educational Role of the Museum*, Routledge, London

Hoskins, J, 1998 *Biographical Objects: How Things Tell the Stories of People's Lives*, Routledge, New York and London

Kaplan, J, 1978 The 'Real Life', in *Studies in Biography* (ed D Aaron), Harvard University Press, Cambridge MA and London

Kemp, L W, 1990 Biography and the Museum, in *The Museum: A Reference Guide* (ed M S Shapiro), Greenwood Press, New York and Westport

Kirschenblatt-Gimblett, B, 1998 *Destination Culture: Tourism, Museums and Heritage*, University of California Press, Berkeley and Los Angeles

Kopytoff, I, 1986 The cultural biography of things: commoditization as process, in *The Social Life of Things: Commodities in Cultural Perspective* (ed A Appadurai), Cambridge University Press, Cambridge

Larson, F, 2009 *An Infinity of Things: How Sir Henry Wellcome Collected the World*, Oxford University Press, Oxford

Lee, H, 2005 *Body Parts: Essays on Life-writing*, Chatto and Windus, London

Miller, E, 1973 *That Noble Cabinet: A History of the British Museum*, Andre Deutsch, London

Munslow, A, 2003 History and Biography: an editorial comment, *Rethinking History* 7 (1), 1–11

Schadla-Hall, T, 1989 *Tom Sheppard, Hull's Great Collector*, Highgate Publications, Beverley

Shortland, M, and Yeo, R, 1996 Introduction, in *Telling Lives in Science: Essays on Scientific Biography* (eds M Shortland and R Yeo), Cambridge University Press, Cambridge

Silverstone, R, 1989 Heritage as media: some implications for research, in *Heritage Interpretation, vol. 2: The Visitor Experience* (ed D Uzzell), Frances Pinter, London, 138–48

Stearn, W T, 1981 *The Natural History Museum at South Kensington*, Heinemann, London

Swift, G, 2010 (1983) *Waterland*, Pan Macmillan, London

Teather, J L, 1990 Professionalism and the Museum, in *The Museum: A Reference Guide* (ed M S Shapiro), Greenwood Press, New York and Westport

# Individual Biography and Museum History

1

# A Show of Generosity: Donations and the Intimacy of Display in the 'Cabinet des médailles et antiques' in Paris from 1830 to 1930

Felicity Bodenstein

In 1929, Jean Babelon, curator and future director of the *Département des monnaies, médailles et antiques*, better known as the *Cabinet des médailles*, claimed that the donations of individual benefactors had been of essential importance to forming an official science of archaeology, contributing to 'constructing an edifice, which otherwise would not be standing today' (Babelon 1929, 6).[1] The metaphoric edifices he was referring to were the disciplines that had been developed to classify and understand the new material regrouped and housed in public archaeology museums; physical edifices such as the *Cabinet des médailles et antiques*.

Who were these benefactors, how should we write about them and how can their biographies contribute to a history of the museum? An administrative entity that displays objects, develops collections and operates scientifically as the *haut lieu* of the discipline of numismatics in France, the *Cabinet des médailles* is also, and perhaps most interestingly, a place where different groups of people cross paths. The network of collectors and researchers, the public (identified, named and studied as a *milieu* through the visitors' book), and the employees themselves provide cases of different social and scientific practices, characterising what we might define as the identity of the institution that we want to portray. By concentrating on the principle of group 'portraits' and by considering the general characteristics of these different *milieux*, we may hope to give this institutional history a more varied and nuanced structure than more classical museum histories. Yet sometimes this essentially prosopographical thinking can blot out the preponderant importance of certain individual actors.

From a methodological point of view I want to adopt two different but – I believe – complementary approaches. Firstly, I intend to briefly introduce the phenomenon of donations as a 'social fact' in the Durkheimian sense (Durkheim 1990): that is to say, a phenomenon with clearly identifiable chronological limits. The archives of the *Cabinet des médailles* show that donations came in from a diverse and large population, over a specific period, and the discourses developed to describe and encourage them show that it was a coercive or contagious phenom-

1 Translation by the author. 'En effet, la collaboration des particuliers à cette œuvre de vaste envergure: la formation d'une science archéologique en quelque sorte officielle, a été un facteur primordial, sans lequel l'édifice aujourd'hui debout risquait de ne jamais voir le jour.'

enon existing independently of strong individual choices, and directly related to social, moral and patriotic values.

However, this sociological perspective tends to negate the significance of the individual actions and choices of benefactors, the singularity of their generosity or the spectacular nature of their intentions, facts which are never fully explicable. In contrast, but not in opposition to this point of view, I would like to examine two specific cases of donations as biographical events. In his introduction to *Art and Agency*, Alfred Gell commented that:

> writers who deal with the sociology of art, such as Berger and Bourdieu concern themselves with particular institutional characteristics of mass societies, rather than with the network of relationships surrounding particular artworks in specific interactive settings. This division of labour is characteristic; anthropology is more concerned with the immediate context of social interactions and their 'personal' dimensions, whereas sociology is more preoccupied with institutions. (Gell 1998, 8)

In trying to understand what individual donations meant to the donor and to the institution of the museum we are at the crossroads of these approaches. Combining them should help us to understand the different motivations that attracted certain collectors to what we might call an economy of giving and its rational and symbolic significance, and to consider how this economy was materialised in the displays dedicated to presenting their gifts.

As the oldest of France's museums, the *Cabinet* was first a royal treasure, a cabinet of curiosities, and became a museum dedicated to numismatics and archaeology; it had been housed in the *hôtel de Nevers* since 1741 in the buildings of the *Bibliothèque nationale de France* on the rue de Richelieu (Sarmant 1994) (Fig 1.1). Henri Labrouste reinstalled it provisionally in 1865 in new rooms that had been initially designed as reserves for the printed books department. It then moved a third and last time in 1917 to its current location on the rue de Vivienne, in the wing constructed by Jean-Louis Pascal, architect of the Library between 1875 and 1913 (Bodenstein 2009a; 2010). The 1865 reinstallation was largely motivated by three factors; the lack of space for the collections and the dilapidated state of the building were endemic problems, but the sense of urgency was due to a conditional clause related to one of the most magnificent donations the department was ever to receive. Indeed, in 1862, the Duke Honoré d'Albert of Luynes (1802–1867) offered his entire collection of coins and antiquities to the *Cabinet des médailles*, at that time in France second in value only to the Campana collection which had just been bought by the State, and which is today housed in the Louvre. In return for his generosity, he asked that it always be presented to the public in its entirety and in a specifically dedicated and separate display area.

Restrictive display conditions were still a relatively new phenomenon in 1862, but as donations multiplied it became an issue of increasing importance and the department quickly expanded to include another new room in the 1870s, named the *Salle des donateurs*. Here, in recognition of their gifts, donors' names were inscribed in golden letters. The display cases, containing a very mixed display of antiquities of all kinds and ages, were crowned, as it were, by a kind of genealogy of benefactors beginning chronologically with the uncle of Louis XIV, Gaston Duke of Orleans (Fig 1.2).

The phenomenon of donations to the *Cabinet des médailles* will be used here to examine links between civil society and the public museum during an extremely important period in the devel-

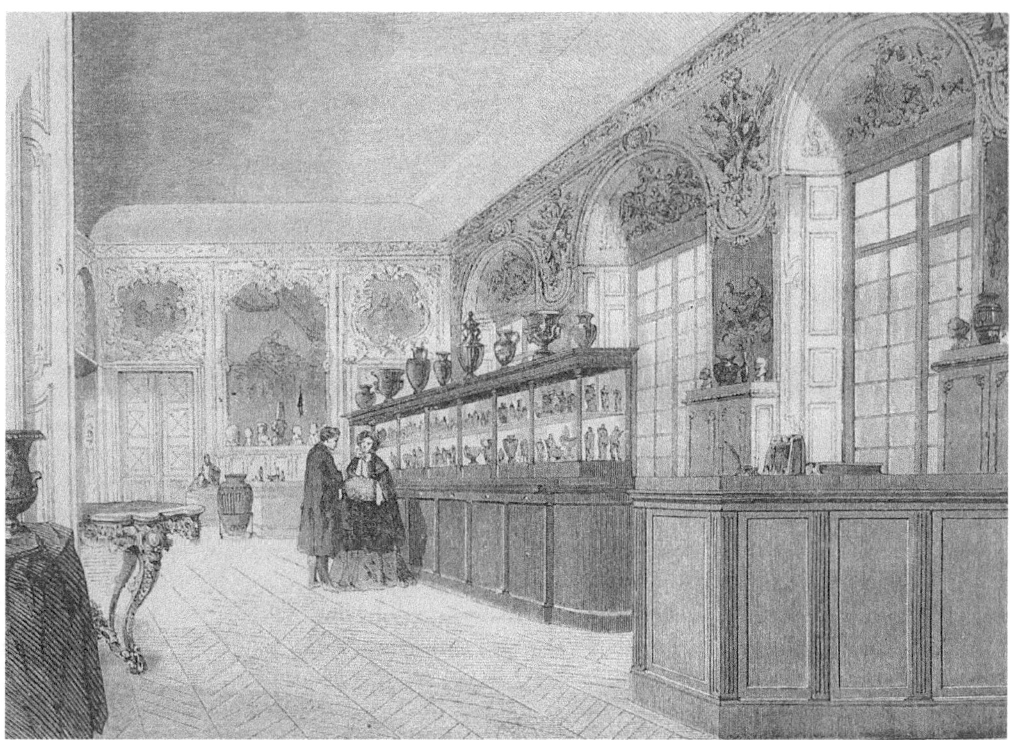

Fig 1.1.
'Le Cabinet des médailles à la Bibliothèque impériale. Dessin de Thérond'

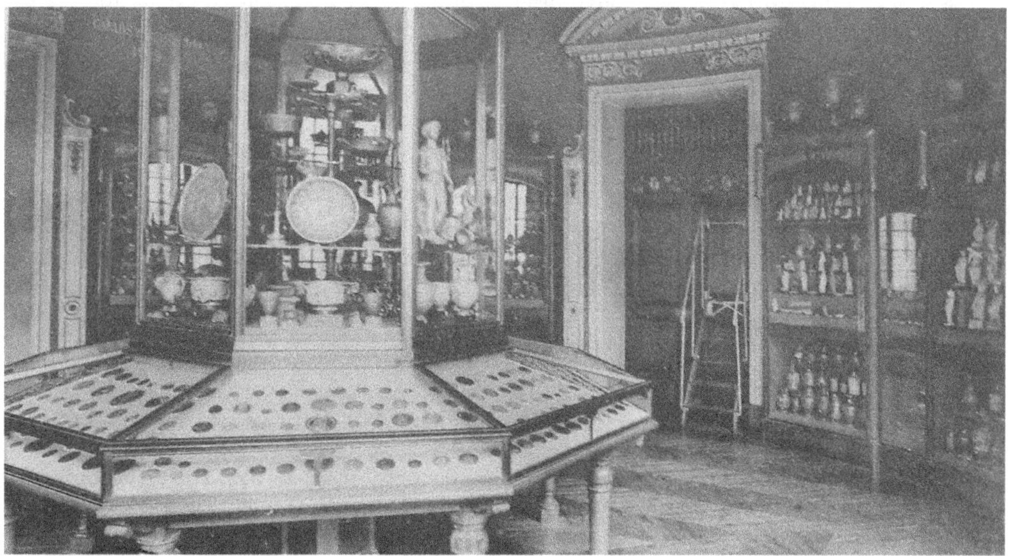

Fig 1.2.
'La Salle des donateurs', Cabinet des médailles, 1907

opment of museum holdings in general and of the *Cabinet*'s holdings in particular. The transfer from private collections into the public sphere was a vital stage in the evolution of archaeology and numismatic sciences but in the *Cabinet* it also conditioned the particular character of its display and gave it the intimate character so often described by those who worked there or visited its exhibition spaces. If the Louvre was often referred to as the *palais populaire* (Trabaud 1878, 275), the *Cabinet de France* was a museum of intimacy. One of its own curators wrote in 1906: 'when one penetrates it, one rather has the impression of being in the home of some welcoming collector who allows you to see his treasures and hold them so you may fully profit from them' (Foville 1906, 312).[2] This impression was indeed largely due to the fact that much of what the visitor could find there represented and was presented as the accumulated wealth of a private amateur or collector.

In his general study of donations in France between 1800 and 1940, Jean-Luc Marais described the gift to the museum as a new phenomenon characterised by the militant positivist intentions of its benefactors. He also claims that, proportionately to other public institutions in the 19th century, it was the museum that had most benefited from the generosity of private citizens (Marais 1999, 382–5).[3] As one of the oldest of France's museums, the *Cabinet des médailles* provides us with the rule and the exceptions that confirm this observation. The collections of this originally royal cabinet go as far back as Henri IV and it received some of its most generous donations well before the 19th century: it was the bequest of Louis XIV's uncle Gaston Duke of Orleans in 1661 that allowed it to become Europe's richest monetary collection. Again, a century later, in 1765, the magnificent legacy of Count Caylus made it France's first public collection of Greco-Roman antiquities. However, one might add that these collections did not receive any special treatment in terms of their display. We only know that Caylus' collection was kept for the most part out of the way of the general public in a room above the cabinet that could be visited only upon request. It was first and foremost considered of interest as a study collection for scholars. Such donations as these, though of great importance, were isolated events and Caylus' gift was later interpreted by Clément de Ris and other early historians of collections as the first in a long line of great and generous presents made to the French nation by its most worthy men (Long 2007, 32); his donation was to become a traditional reference for a small army of 19th-century benefactors.

In the case of the *Cabinet*, the unprecedented wave of donations that led to the rapid expansion of its holdings during the second half of the 19th century can be easily illustrated statistically. We have exact figures concerning the museum's holdings from 1794 onwards, when huge numbers of objects confiscated during the Revolution or brought back from other countries as trophies by the revolutionary army began making their way into its collections, leading the museum's keepers to begin a systematic record of entries. As observed by Laclotte (1989, 10) for

2 Translation by the author. 'Le Cabinet de France est un musée d'intimité.'; 'Lorsqu'on y pénètre, on se croirait plutôt chez un collectionneur accueillant, qui montre libéralement ses trésors et nous les laisse tenir dans la main pour que nous en jouissons à loisir.'

3 385: 'Nous n'évoquerons que par allusion les musées dont les collections pour une part énorme sont dues aux dons ou aux legs des collectionneurs, des conservateurs, des artistes et de leurs descendants. Il est quelques autres domaines où les libéralités jouent un rôle important, mais moins continûment.'; 382: 'Car les donateurs veulent agir. Si une très petite minorité se contente de vouloir partager avec d'autres des satisfactions esthétiques, la grande masse veut, par son don, infléchir les comportements de ses concitoyens, améliorer les institutions existantes, convaincre.'

the Louvre, these show that, outside of a few medals of revolutionary heroes, next to no donations were made to the museum before 1830. Throughout the 1830s, figures slowly began to rise and in 1838 the record book, which up until then had indifferently included a chronological list of all acquisitions, exchanges and the exceptional gift, was physically divided into three books. Between 1838 and 1970, three registers were kept to separately record acquisitions, exchanges and donations. Since 1970, due to the very small number of entries for all three categories, especially donations and exchanges, they have been recorded together. A basic head-count reveals a rise in donations from the end of the 1840s onwards, slowly at first, and exponentially from 1860 to 1914, with figures levelling out in the 1930s, then falling, to even out at a steady level after World War II. In 1931, Jean Babelon rightly observed what he called the end of the age of collector and amateur cabinets (Babelon 1931, 75).

Indeed, larger personal donations have since become rare and patronage in general has been replaced by the more impersonal group donation, often made by associations of benefactors, but whilst museums such as the Louvre began to have their own *Société d'amis*, most of which were created around 1900, the network of benefactors around the *Cabinet* never formed an official group until very recently, when a society was formed to save the museum from closure.[4] Though donations have been scarcer since the 1950s, exceptional gifts from private collectors still occur, notably the rich collection of Greek coins donated by Marie Delepierre in 1966. The relative absence of donors in recent decades has of course, as elsewhere, led the institution to seek out new benefactors such as banks and other private companies, a trend that is indicative of the disappearance of the close personal relationships that formerly united the donor with the museum and its curators.

Interestingly, in France the historiography dedicated to the emergence of public museums has paid relatively little attention to the importance of the contributions made by individual collectors to public museums, and this despite the fact that two-fifths of the 600 museums founded before 1914 were due to the gift of some individual benefactor (Georgel 1996, 24). However this is in part due to the fact we have just underlined; donations were indeed insignificant in establishing museum collections during the first decades of the 'age of museums' and were eclipsed by the spectacular revolutionary moment that so famously founded such institutions as the *Muséum du Louvre* on the basis of former royal collections, confiscations and acquisitions.

The age of donations began later, and we can pinpoint the emergence of a general attitude to, and active promotion of, donations quite precisely to around 1848. At this point, France saw a sharp rise in liberalities which was observed again by Laclotte (1989, 14) in the case of the Louvre – they concerned all of the museum's departments and were offered by a very varied group of personalities, but most especially archaeologists and travellers. The same situation may also be observed in the case of the *Cabinet des médailles*. For the first time, curators began to develop a discourse that described and sought to encourage donations. In May 1848, Philippe-Auguste Jeanron, who had just been named director of national museums, signed a law to help facilitate the acceptation of donations to museums. Similarly, the first text concerning donations received by the *Cabinet des médailles* was written in 1849 by one of its employees, Anatole Chabouillet (1849, 337). Although a man far removed from socialist sympathies, his general tone is very much coloured by the political upheavals and ideas that accompanied the foundation of the Second Republic:

4 See http://www.cabinetdesmedailles.net/.

> The successive additions made to public museums are amongst the developments that have caused the most keen excitement and curiosity amongst archaeologists. Every object that finds its place in a national repository becomes the property of all; everyone may delight in it, study it, comment upon it; it belongs to everyone, as it belongs to the State; this is a kind of Communism that may in no way be considered as dangerous and which every truly liberal mind should herald.[5]

Yet the decisive impulse driving this new policy was led by a handful of dedicated benefactors, who began making their first gifts to the *Cabinet des médailles* and to the Louvre at the same time in the 1840s and 1850s, and we find the same names attached to some of the most precious entries made during these decades in both museums (Nieuwerkerke 1869, 29–31): the Duke of Luynes, Félicien de Saulcy (1807–1880) and Hippolyte de Janzé (1790–1865). Their contemporaries clearly interpreted their gifts as important stages in the democratisation of cultural wealth. Indeed, they themselves wanted to change the often negative image that society had of the miserly collector. When Bonnaffé (1878, 9) wrote his *Causeries sur l'art et la curiosité,* he described the discrepancy between the public image of collectors, society's perception of them and the benefit that had been gained from their work, largely of course through their generosity to public institutions.

> Purveyors of our public collection, museum founders whose names are Du Sommerard and Sauvageot, you who have provided entire rooms in the Library and in the Louvre: Lacaze, Lenoir, Hennin, de Luynes and in 50 provincial museums. Pioneers of modern archaeology, you have given life back to 20 industries and made Paris into the centre of universal curiosity, my dear brothers, be modest. The historian will pass you by, the philosopher raise his shoulders, the artist will accuse you of acting like a bourgeois speculator and the man of the world will call you a collector of trinkets; only the doctor will raise his hat to you hoping to have you soon as his client.[6]

Jean de Witte (1808–1889), a Belgian antiquarian and numismatist who made several important donations to the *Cabinet* in the 1880s, rejected the idea of egotistical accumulation often attached to collecting and considered himself to be part of the first generation that clearly understood the necessity of uniting in one place the greatest possible number of similar objects, of organising them in series and developing typologies as the only means of gaining greater knowledge of the

5 Translation by the author. 'Les accroissements successifs des musées publics sont au nombre des faits qui excitent le plus vivement la curiosité des archéologues. Chaque objet qui vient se ranger dans un dépôt national devient aussitôt la propriété de tous; chacun peut en jouir, l'étudier, le commenter; il est à tous du moment qu'il appartient à l'État; c'est là un communisme qui n'a rien de dangereux et dont tous les esprits vraiment libéraux se réjouiront.'

6 Translation by the author. 'Pourvoyeurs de nos dépôts publics, fondateurs des musées Du Sommerard et Sauvageot, vous qui avez ouvert au Louvre et à la Bibliothèque les salles Lacaze, Lenoir, Hennin, de Luynes, et doté cinquante musées de province, pionniers de l'archéologie moderne qui avez ressuscité vingt industries et fait de Paris le centre de la curiosité universelle, collectionneurs mes confrères soyez modestes. L'historien passera encore à côté de vous sans vous apercevoir, le philosophe haussera les épaules, l'artiste vous traitera de bourgeois spéculateurs, l'homme du monde de 'bibelotiers'; seul, le médecin vous tirera son chapeau, espérant bien avoir prochainement votre clientèle.'

past. He believed with Luynes and Saulcy that only large national museums could become the material expressions of one of the founding principles of archaeology as famously expressed by Edouard Gerhard: 'Monumentorum artis quis vidit, nullum vidit, quis millia vidit, unum vidit' (Schnapp 2004, 174).[7]

The archives of the department document the contagious effect of these ideas: they contain letters sent from every corner of the country, and from many Frenchmen residing abroad; letters from members of the old aristocracy and from upper class bourgeoisie; from men designating themselves as archaeologists or antiquarians but also from secondary school teachers, soldiers, priests and farmers, all formulating the same desire. Indeed, in a sense, they each reformulated in their own way the proclamation made by the Duke of Luynes in 1862. He stated: 'I love my country. I wish for my collections to be in its possession, that they may be profitable to all' (Huillard-Bréholles 1868, 112).[8] So, indeed, from the 1860s onwards, far from being a sentiment reserved to a few highly cultivated benefactors, the desire to give for the further advancement of the historical sciences was generally perceived as an element of patriotic duty and its expression quickly became totally commonplace, exacerbated by growing nationalism under the Third Republic.

For their part, the curators of the *Cabinet des médailles* did all they could to encourage benefactors to donate all or parts of their collections, an effort that often meant accepting sometimes very constraining conditions for their display. Indeed, one may suppose that the department owes some of its donations to the fact that collectors felt that their objects were less likely to disappear into different anonymous series here than in the Louvre. Furthermore, the turn of the century saw Ernest Babelon (Bodenstein 2009b) – director of the *Cabinet des médailles* from 1982 to 1924 – and more especially his son – Jean Babelon, who carried on his father's legacy in the department – firmly reject the tendency that was expressed by curators of other museums: the desire to stem the influx of donations which seemed to be of little value, or of an all too heterogeneous character. Jean Babelon rightly sensed that such attitudes spelt the end of a golden age of donations. It was this disposition which allowed the *Cabinet* to accept such collections as the Guérin donation as late as 1948. It included many small disparate pieces, which the donor had specifically asked be kept on show together. We find everything from black figure vase fragments to Egyptian figurines mounted on pedestals of varying sizes and shapes, giving the display a picturesque effect. However, it is quite improbable that any other important Parisian institution would have accepted such conditions for display in the middle of the 20th century. Jean Babelon refused to consider any donation as possibly cumbersome; on the contrary he believed it was a tradition that gave museums the quality of living organisms. He ridiculed those collections, which to his mind lacked all charm and those museums that would have you go from 'the room of vase handles to that of locks or hinges' (Babelon 1931, 78).[9] He was placing himself in stark

7 Quoted by Schnapp, 2004: 'He who has seen only one object, has seen none at all, but he who has seen a thousand has seen one'.

8 Translation by the author. 'J'aime mon pays. Je désire que mes collections lui soient acquises et qu'elles puissent dès maintenant servir à tous.'

9 Translation by the author. 'garder à nos musées d'Europe leurs traditions et leurs titres de noblesse, c'est sauvegarder leur qualité d'organismes vivants'; 'où l'on me fera passer de la salle des anses de vases à celle des entrées de serrures'.

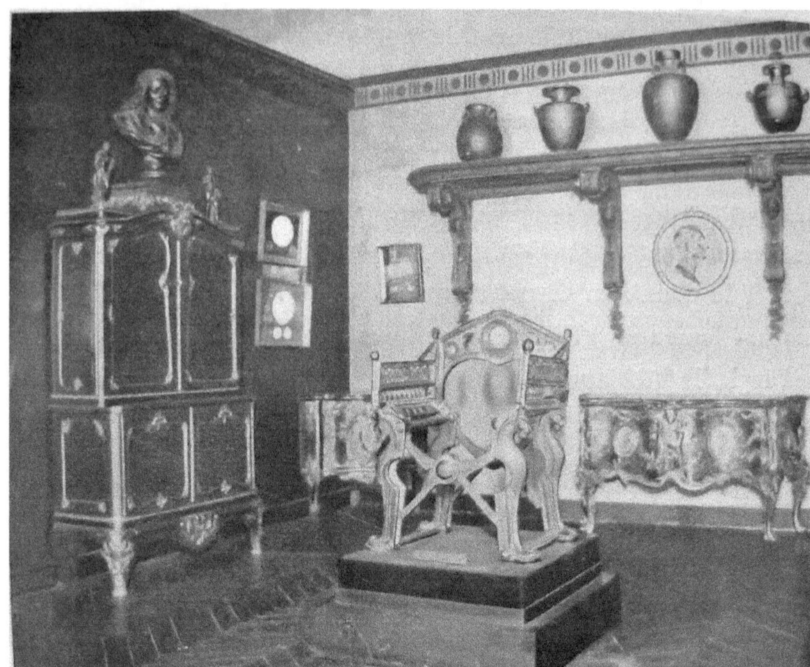

FIG 1.3. 'LA SALLE RENAISSANCE', CABINET DES MÉDAILLES, 1907

opposition to his colleagues who in the 1930s had begun claiming the need to purify displays of the dead weight of mediocre objects often accompanying more important pieces in whole collections (Reinach 1931, 13–19).

Jean Babelon was of course expressing his nostalgia for a tradition related to the presentation of private collections at the end of the 19th century – and whose relation to the development of museum display needs to be more fully explored. The 1880s saw the publication of such works as Charles Blanc's *Grammaire des Arts décoratifs, decoration intérieure de la maison* (1882) or Spire Blondel's *L'art intime et le goût en France: grammaire de la curiosité* (1889). Both of these texts provide classifications of objects as elements of decorative schemes. They both explicate a mode of collecting and display that Blondel called *l'art intime* which he defined as the art of collecting curiosities: objects of small dimensions such as precious enamel works, miniatures, boxes, fans, and medals that enchant the owner by providing him with the exquisite familiarity of beauty. He explained the aim of the amateur who establishes a careful juxtaposition of objects of different shapes and types in order to attain perfect beauty and harmony. The diversity of their types was key to producing their sensuous effect, yet his ability to master this art was considered to stem from his moral self and intellectual capacity (Blondel 1889, 5). The displays in the *Cabinet des médailles* may in many cases be interpreted as institutional celebrations of this *art intime*, usually considered only in the context of the private sphere. It may be observed in the presentation of donated objects but also in the general display, as it had been practised by its donors and as was applied by its curators.

If we consider the contents of a display case entitled *Objets divers, figurines, tessères de theatre ou de jeux en os et en ivoire* and detailed in the 1889 guide to the collections (Babelon 1900,

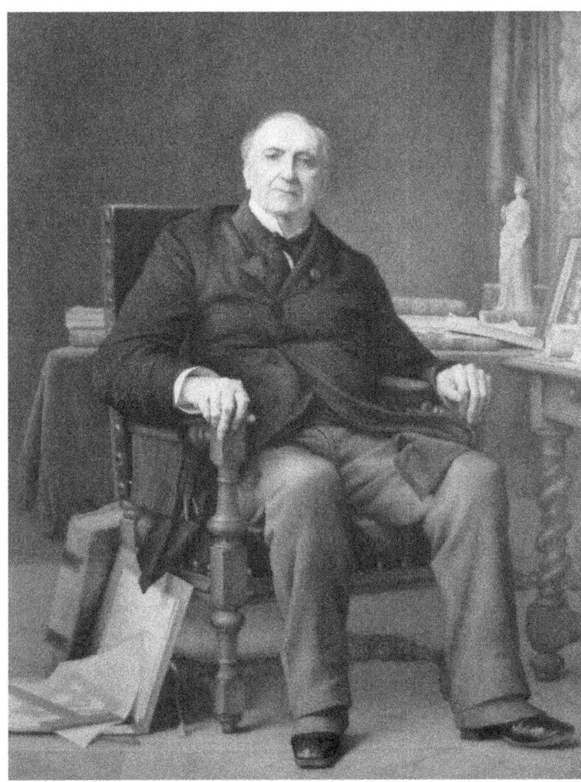

Fig 1.4.
'Alfred Armand (1805–1888)', print by Bouthelié, after Alexandre Cabanel's 1883 portrait

107), we see that the only objects directly listed are those from well-known collectors and that, indeed, no other connection may sensibly be established between them. It describes a medley of Etruscan figurines from M. Charles de Férol; a fragment of a comb from Eugène Piot; a Hermes from Priape given by Vattier de Bourville and a crouching lion from Charles Lenormant. What was in fact on display was not so much a narrative relating to a particular civilisation or artistic technique, not an evolution of style or form, but rather the quality of their discernment as collectors and donors. In the same *Salle de la Renaissance*, where only a minority of objects may be said to date from the Renaissance, one could find some rather odd arrangements of objects, in particular a presentation of Greek vases on a shelf made from 18th-century consoles, salvaged during the destruction of a series of rooms in the library 20 years earlier (Fig 1.3). The historian and novelist Georges-Gustave Toudouze (1906, 357) described the happy juxtaposition of the ancient and the modern to be met with in the *Cabinet des médailles* as the pleasure that the eyes gained from gazing simultaneously on beautiful Roman portraits, medallions by Germain Pilon (1528–1590) and by David d'Angers (1788–1856), all of them framed, as it were, by on one side a triptych representing a Bacchanal from Bourges cathedral and on the other two Byzantine triptychs. In order to interpret the rather disconcerting organisation that one finds described in the guide book of the *Cabinet des médailles*, we may consider the principle of the bibelot that the 19th-century novelist Paul Bourget related to the concept of the museum at this time, in writing about the Goncourts as private collectors. He described them, indeed, as 'men of the museum, and as such modern' and went on to define the *bibelot* – a word which may be translated as trinket, though the translation does not render its historical meaning – as 'that minuscule fragment of a work of art, that can be placed on the corner of a table or console, that can be something from the Far East, from the Renaissance, a little of the French middle ages and a bit of the eighteenth century' (Watson 1999, 21–2).[10] Thus defined by Paul Bourget, who we know to have visited the *Cabinet* on several occasions and to have been acquainted with Ernest Babelon, the cultural phenomenon of the *bibelot* seems to perfectly embody an over-riding relationship between the public and the private collection and indeed *fin-de-siècle* society as a whole at a time that saw even the most modest homes succumbing to the fashion for over-crowded displays of heteroclite objects – often small bronzes and other cheap copies of art-works that were available due to new reproduction techniques. When observing strategies of display for smaller objects in the museum from this period, one certainly has the impression that there is a transfer of aesthetic principles and attitudes between the private and public realm and, in view of the consistent contribution of individual collectors to the museum, we might suggest that it is the world of the collectors that may be more influential to the dispositions of objects in the museum than vice versa.

Having thus considered the general evolution of donations to the *Cabinet*, it is interesting to consider some of the personal motivations which drove so many to leave what was sometimes a life's work in the hands of the *Cabinet*'s curators. When we consider the portraits of donors such as Carlos de Beistegui and Alfred Armand[11] we find that they had themselves portrayed in intimate proximity with objects from their collection, illustrating the extent to which these defined the identity of their owners (Fig 1.4). Yet the act of donation provides the collection with supplementary biographical significance. In his study of the anthropology of giving, Alain Caillé writes that the gift confirms the idea that the link between the giver and the receiver is more important than the object itself. His description of the social phenomenon of the gift of donation lets it appear as an ideal subject for studying the interrelation between individual and collective action:

> The paradigm of the gift precisely claims not to analyse the creation of social ties from the bottom up in a way that considers each individual separately – nor from the top down – from a social totality that always exists over everything, but rather it takes its starting point in the middle, horizontally beginning with those ties that relate actors to each other transforming them into social actors. (Caillé 2000, 19)[12]

10 Quoted by Watson, 1999, translation by the author. 'Les frères Goncourt ont été des hommes de musée, et en cela des modernes, dans toute la force du mot, car cet esprit de dilettantisme et de critique s'est développé chez nous à ce point qu'il a étendu le musée bien au delà des collections publiques et privées, en l'introduisant dans le moindre détail de l'ameublement et en créant le bibelot. Le bibelot, – ce minuscule fragment de l'œuvre d'art, qui met sur un angle d'une table de salon quelque chose de l'extrême Orient et quelque chose de la Renaissance, un peu du moyen âge français et un peu du XVIIIe siècle.'

11 *Portrait de Carlos de Beistegui (1863–1953)*, by Ignacio Zuloaga, musée du Louvre; *Alfred Armand (1805–1888)*, by Alexandre Cabanel, 1883, musée d'Orsay.

12 Translation by the author. 'Le paradigme du don ne prétend justement analyser l'engendrement du lien social ni par en bas – depuis les individus toujours séparés -, ni par en haut – depuis une totalité sociale

This is also very much the general aim of Bruno Latour's actor-network theory which might also quite ideally be applied to the question of the action of donors to one museum as a social group (Latour 2007). In order to give a very small impression of how one might go about this, in our case we will try to consider what information we have about why these donations were made and how it might be interpreted biographically and socially in relation to the donor. No simple pattern emerges for the reasons are as different as the individuals themselves. However, having looked at how donations came about and having collected the important mass of biographical texts – most often necrologies – written by curators and scholars in homage to the *Cabinet*'s benefactors, it appears that donations may first and foremost be analysed as important biographical events and as markers of personal relationships, gestures that radically modify how the lives and actions of benefactors are characterised by the contemporaries and by posterity.

None of the donations given to the *Cabinet* were richer and indeed more poignant than that of the Duke of Luynes received in 1862 (Aghion and Avisseau-Broustet 1994; 1996; Bodenstein 2009c). As an avid archaeologist and an even more passionate numismatist, he had made regular donations to the department since 1846. In 1850 he even drafted a report describing the state of the department, so one might say that outside of its employees, few people knew the collections and the problems faced by the museum better than he did. Of aristocratic origins and lifestyle, yet a firm believer in the future of a democratic society, the Duke's generosity was later interpreted by his biographers as the means he had found to justify the property and wealth that was his family heritage, having established for himself a personal code of conduct that he had noted in a private booklet entitled *Devoirs des riches - The Duties of the Rich Man* (Huillard-Bréholles 1868, 9). His liberalities touched on every aspect of social life, and numerous institutions benefited from his wealth over his lifetime. The decision to donate his entire collection of antiques seems to have been taken after a series of adverse events robbed him of his desire to have them magnificently displayed in his castle at Dampierre. His collection was very much the result of a lifetime of scholarly pursuits generally based on, or related to, the objects in his collection. One of his most cherished projects since the 1830s had been the renovation of the family castle at Dampierre in the countryside outside of Paris (Ockman 1982). He intended to install his antiquities magnificently there in a gallery to be conceived especially for its display by the architect Félix Duban and to be decorated by, amongst others, Jean-Auguste-Dominique Ingres. However, the project was put on hold when the famous painter stormily abandoned his half-finished oil frescoes, and so the collections of the Duke remained in his *hôtel particulier* in Paris, rue Saint-Dominique. It was his wife's death, however, that provided the decisive blow; only a few short months after her passing, he declared that he had lost all interest in the study of his objects and preferred to make them available to the nation, as long as they be presented together in one part of the *Cabinet des médailles*. An entire room has since been dedicated to his collections and to his memory in each of the reinstallations of the museum in respectively 1865 and 1917 (Fig 1.5). By contrast, the display of his collections in the castle of Dampierre would have produced a very different effect, framed by this richly and colourfully decorated gallery, boasting high ceilings covered in neo-classical and neo-renaissance decors and elegant display cases designed by Félix Duban, the whole presentation presided over by a recreation of the chryselephantine Athena of

en surplomb et toujours déjà là –, mais en quelque sorte depuis son milieu, horizontalement, en fonction de l'ensemble des interrelations qui lient les individus et les transforment en acteurs proprement sociaux.'

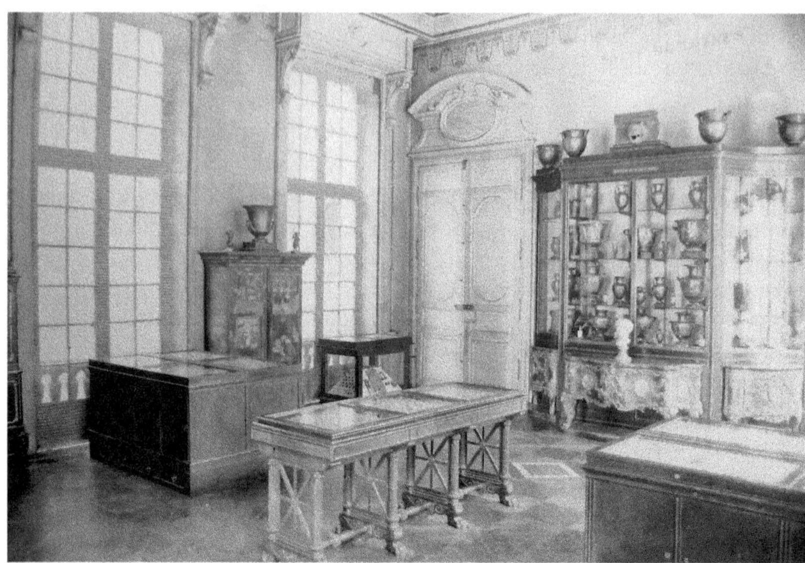

FIG 1.5. 'SALLE DE LUYNES', CABINET DES MÉDAILLES, N.D.

the Parthenon (Shedd 1986). For Thomas de Luynes (1996, 152), the decors designed by Duban referred to the ancient aristocratic history of the family, the solemnity of the 'Grand Siècle' and the marvels of the Greco-Roman civilisation. It would have placed his collection and its display in the context of more ostentatious collecting practices of antiquities such as the gallery of James-Alexandre de Pourtalès-Gorgier in Paris, also installed by Félix Duban (Boisset 2005). Instead, in the *Cabinet des médailles,* the collection maintained an intimate quality in the vein of what one might expect in a personal study cabinet, as it would have appeared during the lifetime of the Duke in his Parisian hotel.

The Duke continued to complete his collections even after his donation, making another exceptional gift in 1865, offering what is today one of the *Cabinet*'s most precious pieces: the so-called sword of Boabdil. The director of the department later recounted how just a couple of years before his death the duke ceremoniously handed the sword over to him, declaring: 'Monsieur Chabouillet, I surrender my arms to you' (Huillard-Bréholles 1868, 119).[13]

As a legacy, the gift to the museum could also become a form of biographical reinvention. Perhaps the best illustration of this is the bequest made to the *Cabinet* in 1908 by the German archaeologist living in France, Wilhelm Froehner (Hellmann 1992). Certainly one of the most taciturn figures in the small world of archaeology, Froehner had suffered from the deep disappointment and humiliation of being let go from his position at the Louvre in 1870 as a result of the Franco-Prussian war. The inventory of his collection that he kept meticulously up to date begins the very same year; and according to one of his biographers, his passion for collecting was to become the unique flame of interest in an otherwise rather solitary life (Cumont 1931). Indeed, his relationship with his collection was very much like that of a jealous lover; he himself wrote: 'My collection is virgin, I do not put it on show' (Babelon 1936, ii). He never published any of

13 Quoted by Huillard-Bréholles, translation by the author. 'Monsieur, je vous rends les armes'.

the pieces in it and seemed to take pleasure in possessing objects that had never been devalued by their diffusion. They were his realm and clearly a kind of *ersatz* for the collections and scholarly circles from which he had been excluded and from which he excluded himself. However, a few acquaintances had the privilege of visiting him and sometimes peeking into the crimson velvet-lined boxes in which he carefully kept his objects stored away. One of these was Ernest Babelon, who brilliantly directed the *Cabinet* from 1895 to his death in 1924 and with whom he frequented the famous Bixio lunches along with Paul Bourget, Samuel de Pozzi, Saint-Saëns and others. For financial reasons, Froehner sold his collection of coins in 1909, retaining only his small antiquities whose principal archaeological merit lay in their inscriptions, whilst his library and correspondence went to his hometown, Weimar, in Germany. Froehner had deliberately kept his collection far from the world to be revealed only through his bequest at the time of his death. His collections, unknown to a world of scholars who he had violently criticised throughout his lifetime, were to be discovered as an extension of his self through his donation which might be described as a kind of *bouquet final*. Froehner had obviously orchestrated this situation to give the revelation of his collections greater impact and perhaps even to impress those whom he felt had betrayed him. The Louvre of course was not to benefit from his generosity; it was the *Cabinet des médailles*, an institution where he had experienced no professional disappointments and amongst whose curators he counted a close personal friend, that was to claim the privilege of his collection.

Outside of these major donations, many smaller, sometimes of themselves insignificant gifts, sought above all to confirm a social link or to attest to an affiliation of interest and affection. In 1926 the famous amateur of old books, manuscripts and artistic medals, Seymour de Ricci, made an isolated present to the *Cabinet*, declaring it to be a homage in memory of his friend Froehner and desiring it to be exhibited alongside the objects of his collection. Generally it is true to say that the names of those who gave single elements of their collections, such as a modest coin or a cut gem, understood their gifts as markers, symbols of a social position and of shared scientific aspirations. They also formed the social networks that defined the identity of the *Cabinet des médailles et antiques* and confirmed its importance in scholarly circles, a phenomena described by Marais (1999, 311) in more general terms as applying to most institutions benefiting from liberalities.

By first considering donations as an essential phenomenon in the life or biography of our museum, and secondly its role in the lives of the benefactors themselves, we see that donations greatly contributed to restructuring the *Cabinet*'s scientific mission and social purpose. Indeed, during the second half of the 19th century, it sought with much effort to meet the modern requirements of specialised republican museum culture by conducting major cataloguing and inventory campaigns and producing guides and didactic material. However, its curators sought to preserve the long tradition of aristocratic antiquarianism that seemed to define its prestigious royal past. In this context donations indeed provided the means to accumulate complete series and specialised collections. Inversely, benefactors were also attracted by the museum's reputation and contributed in turn to confirming its historical identity as the intimate cabinet of elite (if not elitist) antiquarian ambitions as aspired to by men who considered themselves, and who were considered to be, of taste, patriotic duty and learning. It was the discreet and intimate character of the museum that gave the visitor the impression that he (or very rarely she) was not in a public collection, but, as Toudouze had put it, in the 'private collection of the French state' (Toudouze 1906, 356).

## Bibliography and References


Aghion, I, and Avisseau-Broustet, M, 1994 Le duc de Luynes, archéologue, historien, homme de sciences et collectionneur, *La revue de la Bibliothèque nationale: Le cabinet des médailles* 3, 12–19

— 1996 Le duc de Luynes: un esprit encyclopédique, in *Tous les savoirs du monde, encyclopédies et bibliothèques de Sumer au XXIe siècle* (ed R Schaer), Flammarion, Paris, 327–38

Babelon, E, 1900 *Guide illustré au Cabinet des médailles et antiques de Bibliothèque nationale: les antiques et les objets d'art*, E Leroux, Paris

Babelon, J, 1929 *Choix de bronzes et de terres cuites des collections Oppermann et de Janzé*, G Van Oest, Paris et Bruxelles

— 1931 Musées ou cabinets d'amateurs?, *Musées*, Cahiers de la République des lettres et des sciences et des arts XIII, Paris

—1936 *Collection Froehner. Inscriptions grecques*, Ed des Bibliothèques Nationales, Paris

Bodenstein, F, 2009a Le Musée du Cabinet des médailles. Éclectisme et historicisme au début du XXe siècle, *Revue de la BnF* 32, 83–92

— 2009b Ernest Babelon, 1854–1924, *Dictionnaire critique des historiens de l'art actifs en France de la Révolution à la Première Guerre mondiale* (eds p. Sénéchal and C Barbillon) [online], available from: http://www.inha.fr/spip.php?article2177 [5 December 2010]

— 2009c Luynes, Honoré d'Albert (duc de), 1802–1867, *Dictionnaire critique des historiens de l'art actifs en France de la Révolution à la Première Guerre mondiale* (eds P Sénéchal and C Barbillon) [online], available from: http://www.inha.fr/spip.php?article2425 [5 December 2010]

— 2010 Le Salon Louis XV à la Bibliothèque nationale de France: l'archéologie et la reconstitution d'un lieu d'histoire (1865–1913), *Livraisons d'histoire de l'architecture* 19, Septembre, 7–17

Blondel, S, 1889 *L'art intime et le goût en France: grammaire de la curiosité*, C Marpon & E Flammarion, Paris

Boisset, O, 2005 Les antiques du comte James-Alexandre de Pourtalès-Gorgier (1776–1855): Une introduction, *Collections et marché de l'art en France 1789–1848*, PUR; INHA, Rennes, 187–206

Bonnaffé, E, 1878 *Causeries sur l'art et la curiosité*, A Quantin, Paris

Caillé, A, 2000 *L'anthropologie du don, le tiers paradigme*, Desclée de Brouwer, Power

Chabouillet, A, 1849 Note sur les dons faits au département des médailles et antiques de la BN ainsi que sur les acquisitions principales opérées depuis deux années par le même établissement, *Revue archéologique* 6, 337–51

Cumont, F, 1931 Préface, *Souvenirs de Froehner recueillis par la Comtesse de Rohan-Chabot*, s e, Paris, 3–17

Durkheim, D, 1990 (1895) What is a Social Fact, in *Mapping the social landscape: readings in sociology* (ed S J Ferguson), Taylor & Francis, Oxford, 37–43

Foville, J de, 1906 II Les Antiques, *Le Musée*, 309–58

Gell, A, 1998 *Art and Agency: An Anthropological Theory*, Clarendon Press, Oxford

Georgel, C, 1996 Collections privées/collections publiques: un dialogue permanent, in *Les musées de province dans leur environnement* (ed L Vadelorge), Cahiers du GRHIS, PUR, Rouen, 23–30

Hellmann, M-C, 1992 Wilhelm Froehner, un collectionneur pas comme les autres, 1834–1925, in *L'anticomanie. La collection d'antiquités aux XVIIIe et XIXe siècles* (eds K Pomian and A Laurens), EPHE, Paris, 251–64

Huillard-Bréholles, J-L-A, 1868 *Notice sur M. le duc de Luynes*, H Plon, Paris

Laclotte, M, 1989 *Les donateurs du Louvre*, Réunion des Musées Nationaux, Paris

Latour, B, 2007 (2005) *Changer de société, refaire de la sociologie*, La Découverte, Paris

Long, V, 2007 *Mécènes des deux mondes, les collectionneurs donateurs du musée du Louvre et de l'Art Institute Chicago 1879–1940*, PUR, Rennes

Luynes, T de, 1996 Duban à Dampierre, in *Félix Duban, les couleurs de l'architecte* (ed B Foucard), Gallimard, Paris, 150–54

Marais, J-L, 1999 *Histoire du don en France de 1800 à 1939, dons et legs charitables, pieux et philanthropiques*, PUR, Rennes

Nieuwerkerke, E de, 1869 *Rapport sur la situation des musées impériaux pendant le règne de S M Napoléon III (1853–1869)*, Imprimerie nationale, Paris

Ockman, C, 1982 The restoration of the chateau of Dampierre: Ingres, the Duc de Luynes and an unrealized vision of history, unpublished PhD thesis, Yale University

Reinach, S, 1931 l'Encombrement des musées, *Musées*, Cahiers de la République des lettres et des sciences et des arts XIII, Paris, 13–19

Sarmant, T, 1994 *Le Cabinet des médailles de la Bibliothèque nationale, 1661–1848*, École des Chartes, Paris

Schnapp, A, 2004 Eduard Gerhard: Founder of Classical Archaeology, *Modernism/Modernity* 11, January, 173–7

Shedd, M, 1986 Phidias at the Universal Exposition of 1855: the duc de Luynes and the Athena Parthenos, *Gazette des Beaux-Arts* 108, 123–34

Toudouze, G, 1906 Meubles et Bibelots, *Le Musée*, 309–58

Trabaud, P, 1978 (1878) *Esthétique et archéologie*, volume premier, Libraire Renouard, Paris

Watson, J, 1999 *Literature and material culture from Balzac to Proust: The Collection and Consumption of Curiosities*, Cambridge University Press, Cambridge

2

# Introducing Mr Moderna Museet: Pontus Hultén and Sweden's Museum of Modern Art

Stuart Burch

Time: 1:30 pm, Friday 30 May 2008
Place: Moderna Museet, Stockholm

Jean Tinguely's *Fiesta Bar* is lined with liquor bottles. Tasty-looking snacks by Claes Oldenburg are available for visual consumption. People hungry for knowledge can read from an extensive library. The even more inquisitive are able to salve their curiosity by nosing through some postcards sent by On Kawara. Those wishing to exercise their bodies rather than their minds can follow Andy Warhol's handy *Dance Diagram* and foxtrot around the gallery. There is, alas, no musical accompaniment. Indeed, time seems to stand still, like the motionless hands of Ed Kienholz's clock. Suddenly the silence is broken when someone presses an inviting red button, bringing Tinguely's *Fiesta Bar* into life. The metal clanking of this kinetic sculpture harmonises with the click and whirl of a more technologically advanced mechanism. The latter, operated by touchscreen computer, makes it possible for visitors to select a painting from a menu of available works and watch as it glides across the ceiling before slowly coming to rest in the middle of the gallery. Emblazoned on the work I decided to pick were written the familiar words: 'In the future everybody will be world famous for fifteen minutes.'

*

Someone who has been famous for considerably longer than 15 minutes is Pontus Hultén. His renown certainly rivals and arguably even eclipses that of Moderna Museet, the museum he once led. In many respects the late Pontus Hultén *is* Moderna Museet. The entwined lives of the museum and the man make them ideal candidates for discussion in a book entitled *Museums and Biographies*. The case study set out in this particular chapter testifies to the pervasive influence that certain individuals are able to exert over public collections – both during their lifetime and after. The posthumous presence of past protagonists is a timely reminder that museal biographies are processed and renegotiated in the present.

The necessity of scrutinising linkages between the biographies of people, the histories of institutions and the provenance of objects is well illustrated by Sweden's national collection of modern and contemporary art. Its holdings of works by Kawara, Kienholz, Oldenburg, Tinguely, Warhol and many other canonical artists of the 20th century were swelled when, shortly before his death, Pontus Hultén chose to bequeath almost his entire personal collection to his former place of work. The storage and display of this gift will be explored below, as will the ethical dilemmas and interpretive challenges that it raises. Both aspects coalesce around one crucial demand that

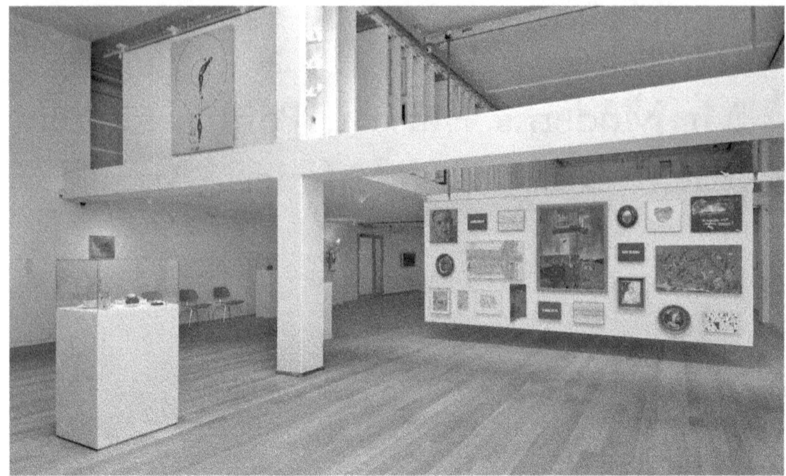

FIG 2.1.
THE PONTUS HULTÉN STUDY GALLERY, MODERNA MUSEET

Hultén made before he felt able to part with his possessions. Yes, Moderna Museet would be given the artworks in perpetuity – but only if measures could be taken guaranteeing that they would remain at all times accessible to the public. Hence the whirling, clicking mechanically powered gallery that was inaugurated at the heart of the museum on 30 May 2008 (Fig 2.1). This technological innovation did more than simply fulfil the stipulation set down by the donor. It succeeded in consolidating Hultén's reputation as a cultural aristocrat. This was a status that he held in life and, thanks to his bequest, now also in death.

There can be no better place to begin a discussion of culture and aristocracy than Pierre Bourdieu's *Distinction: A Social Critique of the Judgement of Taste*, first published in French in 1979 and translated into English five years later. Its opening chapter is entitled 'The Aristocracy of Culture'. In the following section I will give a selective account of this essay before going on to adapt it as a means of 'Introducing Mr Moderna Museet'.

## THE GAME OF DISTINCTION

'Aesthetic stances', Bourdieu (1984, 57) tells us, 'are opportunities to experience or assert one's position in social space, as a rank to be upheld or a distance to be kept'. As such, those in a position to shape any 'system of aesthetic principles' are in receipt of considerable authority. An important marker of cultural competence and pedigree is 'acquisition', the conditions of which 'function like a sort of "trade-mark"' (ibid, 65). The gold standard of legitimacy is 'to possess things from the past', such as 'accumulated, crystallized history' or 'paintings and collections', and pass them on. To achieve this 'is to master time' (ibid, 71).

With this in mind, '[e]very group tends to set up the means of perpetuating itself beyond the finite individuals in whom it is incarnated' (ibid, 72). This is achieved by establishing 'a whole set of mechanisms, such as delegation, representation and symbolization, which confer ubiquity and eternity' (ibid). Portraits, statues, monuments and memorials are all mechanisms that strive to immortalise a person, define their image and secure their legacy. Periodic ceremonies and commemorative anniversaries enable the living to pay homage to the dead and, in so doing, ensure that the dead attain that most coveted of goals: 'eternal life' (ibid). This 'magic stronger than death' (Hultén and Tinguely 1987) also benefits the living by cementing their particular succession claims. This bodes well not only for the likelihood of their own individual perpetuation but also the continuance of the group with which they identify and the shared values it espouses.

Bourdieu (1984, 76) is therefore surely correct to argue that '[e]very material inheritance is, strictly speaking, also a cultural inheritance'. The value of the former is self-evident to the inheritors because it is they who '[possess] the cultural competence, that is, the code, into which it is encoded' (ibid, 2). Those that fit within this structure have both the legitimacy and the competence to assert their rightful lineage and thereby shape 'taste'.

This is why the meaning of an artwork is neither inherent nor self-contained. It is instead determined by 'the system of objects in which it is placed' (ibid, 88), and that system is dynastic, hierarchical and based on material and cultural inheritance. It follows, therefore, that works of art 'always owe part of their value to the value of the chooser … [and] the manner of the choosing' (ibid, 91).

All this, however, raises an imponderable question:

> The paradox of the imposition of legitimacy is that it makes it impossible ever to determine whether the dominant feature appears as distinguished or noble because it is dominant – ie because it has the privilege of defining, by its very existence, what is noble or distinguished as being exactly what itself is … – or whether it is only because it is dominant that it appears as endowed with these qualities and uniquely entitled to define them. (ibid, 92)

Yet we should not be unduly troubled by this uncertainty. It is, after all, simply part of that 'game of distinction' that Bourdieu (ibid, 57) charts so brilliantly. Those with an interest in this 'game' – be they spectators or participants – make regular pilgrimages to that most refined of sporting arenas: the museum. For it is the 'social space' of the museum where 'competence is produced and … given its price' (ibid, 88). Moderna Museet is just such a 'social space'. Its claims to 'strong inherited cultural capital' (ibid, 89) have been bolstered considerably thanks to the generosity of its former director. But who was Pontus Hultén? What prompted him to transfer his art collection to a museum rather than bequeath it to his son and grandson? And what does any of this have to do with Pierre Bourdieu's *Distinction*?

## Sandberg, Stedelijk and Succession

Karl Gunnar 'Pontus' Hultén was 82 years old and in ill health when he eventually died on 25 October 2006. In the preceding year he had decided to gift the vast majority of his art collection to Sweden's museum of modern and contemporary art, Moderna Museet. This amounted to approximately 700 paintings, sculptures, films and posters together with an extensive library, all of which he had built up over the course of a long and very distinguished career as both curator and director of some of the world's most prestigious art institutions, including Centre Pompidou in Paris, Los Angeles Museum of Contemporary Art, Palazzo Grassi in Venice, Bonn's Kunst- und Ausstellungshalle der Bundesrepublik Deutschland and the Jean Tinguely Museum in Basle.

The exhibitions that Hultén had helped devise at these and other institutions forged his reputation as a dynamic innovator who sought continually to break down barriers in pursuit of 'open' museums, accessible to all (Centre Pompidou 2004). His name became synonymous with notions of 'art in motion'. Indeed, *Movement in Art – Rörelse i Konsten* was the title of a pivotal show that can, for the purposes of this chapter, serve as a succinct means of introducing Hultén's museological biography.

*Movement in Art* dates from 1961, two years before the 34-year-old Hultén would be formally appointed director of Moderna Museet. Featuring well over 200 works by artists from 19 countries, it was an early example of Hultén's 'legacy [of] complex, thematic exhibitions' (Muchnic 2006). It was split into two halves: one a historical survey spanning the years from the turn of the 20th century until the 1930s, the other focused on contemporary artists whose work dealt in some way with movement – artists such as Jean Tinguely (1925–91), whose kinetic sculpture *Fiesta Bar* was mentioned at the start of this chapter. Some pieces were made specifically for the show. One such was a 'happening' by Allan Kaprow (1927–2006). This consisted of a specially constructed room in which visitors were invited to paint on cardboard boxes hanging from the ceiling. The idea was to study the results to discern if there were any marked national differences between the museum-going public of Holland, Sweden and Denmark (Granath and Nieckels 1983, 80, 144, 148).

These locations were chosen because *Movement in Art* actually opened not in Stockholm but at the Stedelijk Museum in Amsterdam, where it was given the title *Bewogen Beweging*. Only then did it travel to Moderna Museet before coming to a close at the Louisiana Museum of Modern Art outside Copenhagen. Hultén later explained that this rather unusual decision was made in the belief that the 'unprepared' (*oförberedda*) Swedish public would be more receptive to such an overtly ambitious exhibition if it were first legitimised by 'what was probably the world's best museum for modern art' (Granath and Nieckels 1983, 36). For whereas Moderna Museet had been formally instituted only in May 1958 with the comparatively untried Hultén as its provisional leader, the Stedelijk had been a prominent feature of the Dutch capital since 1895 and was led by the far older and well-established Willem Sandberg (1897–1984). He had taken charge after World War II and remained its director until his retirement in 1963. Shortly before his departure, a host of artists with whom Sandberg had had dealings presented him with artworks. Sandberg in turn gifted 70 of these 'tokens of friendship and esteem' to the Stedelijk (Daniels n.d.; Stedelijk n.d.).

A further token of friendship and esteem can be discerned from the events of 1961. The year began with Moderna Museet entering the Stedelijk in the form of *Movement in Art*. The compliment was returned in December 1961 when the Stedelijk Museum 'visited' Moderna Museet through a loan exhibition of works by a variety of modern and contemporary artists from the Dutch museum's impressive collection (Hultén 1961). It was accompanied by a slender catalogue introduced by Willem Sandberg. His single page of highly polemical prose poetry provided in effect a road map that Hultén was to follow for the rest of his career and beyond.

In that text Sandberg argued forcefully that all so-called 'museums of modern art' fall into two camps: static/dead or moving/living. The former, he claimed, are led by people of rigid, conservative tastes. Suspicious of the avant-garde, they see the art museum as a means to 'escape into the past' by facilitating the 'peaceful contemplation' of an unchanging canon of art that is to be 'worshipped', not questioned. In stark contrast to these staid temples are 'museums … in which there is movement'. More than a simple building for containing art, these institutions are akin to cinemas, concert halls, schools and libraries – as well as being places of leisure and of consumption. Whereas children would shatter the silence of the static museum, 'guests by the

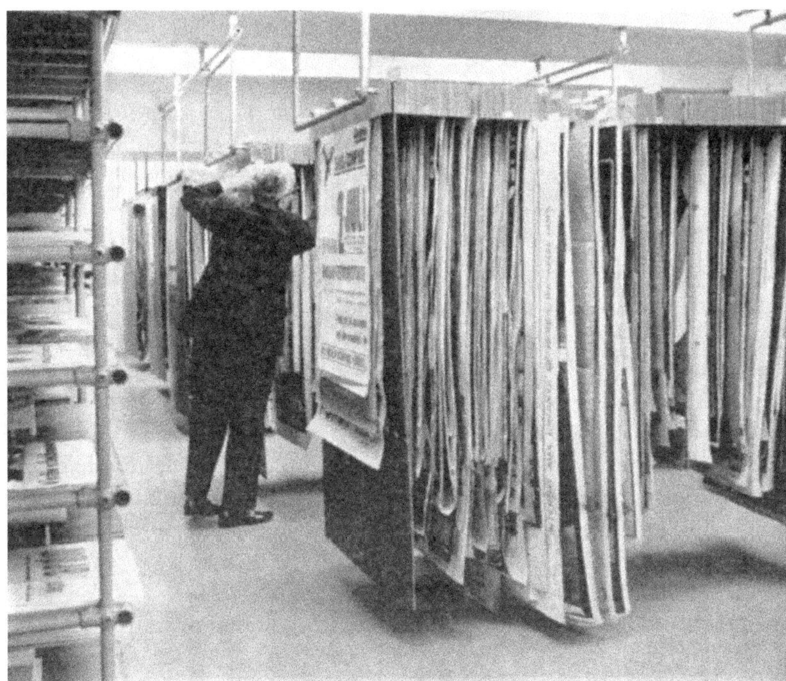

FIG 2.2. 'STUDIEMAGASINET' STEDELIJK MUSEUM

thousand including the young' flock to visit the 'museum which moves a lot'. Movement also extends to the collection, the 'true value' of which is constantly being reassessed in line with the needs of the eternally changing present. Not afraid of creating 'conflicts and occasionally scandals', the 'living' museum is prepared to relegate the work of 'admired heroes ... to the museum store' if they are deemed to have fallen 'silent', replacing them in turn 'with others, which the museum doesn't own – yet' (Sandberg 1961).

Immediately following Sandberg's piece is an article in which Hultén makes clear his admiration for the man who, in his opinion, was single-handedly responsible for transforming the Stedelijk into 'a new type of museum, an active and dynamic affair where the art collection constitutes the core around which the events revolve'. The moveable walls and 'elastic' use of the exhibition spaces mirrored a wider 'democratisation' of the museum that Hultén considered to be accessible to all, irrespective of class, education or age (Hultén 1961, 5–6, 8).

Illustrating Hultén's text are photographs depicting both the façade and interior of the Stedelijk Museum. The latter focus as much on its café and shop as they do its exhibition spaces. In addition, there is an image showing a facility named as the study gallery or store (*studiemagasinet*) (Fig 2.2). A caption describes this as 'a very large, easily accessible poster collection' (Hultén 1961, 7). These artefacts are laid out on racking shelves or hang from a series of suspended units. This can be seen as a precursor to the gallery that, nearly 50 years hence, would be built to house Pontus Hultén's bequest to Moderna Museet.

## PONTUS HULTÉN'S STUDIOLO

In 1998, Sweden's national museum of architecture (*Arkitekturmuseet*) took over the building originally occupied by Moderna Museet, with the latter moving to an adjoining structure designed by Rafael Moneo. A decade later a double-height space was found 'at the very centre of the building' to accommodate Hultén's bequest (Tellgren 2008, 148). It fulfilled the only stipulation attached to this act of generosity, namely that 'any works not shown in the permanent hanging exhibition be made available to the public in a user-friendly warehouse' (cited in Burch 2007, 63).

This rather mundane-sounding facility was constructed by the Swedish National Property Board and White arkitekter AB at a cost of about 10 million Swedish kronor. A sizeable chunk of that money was used to enlist the support of Overhead Conveyor Systems (OCS), a Swedish firm specialising in the sort of mechanical equipment normally to be found on a factory production line. In the unfamiliar surroundings of a museum it provides the means of moving a series of 30 panels that hang suspended from the ceiling. Mounted on these screens are paintings. These are chosen via a touchscreen computer operated by a gallery assistant. Once a selection has been made the panel in question slides across the ceiling and down into an empty space near the centre of the room. Behind this, to the rear of the gallery, is a long table running parallel to wall shelves containing books and other publications. The remainder of the floor space is dotted with three-dimensional works also bequeathed by Hultén.

This ensemble can be understood as a technologically innovative solution to some very long-standing desires. This was alluded to by the man who designed it: Hultén's long-time friend and colleague, Renzo Piano. It was Piano who, together with Richard Rogers, designed Centre Pompidou which Hultén led to great acclaim in the 1970s following his departure from Moderna Museet.

During a seminar organised to mark the inauguration of the Hultén bequest, Piano revealed that he had sought inspiration in the Renaissance-era *studiolo* or 'study'. It has elsewhere been argued that these 'princely collections' served 'to recreate the world in miniature around the central figure of the prince who thus claimed dominion over the world symbolically as he did in reality' (Hooper-Greenhill cited in Bennett 1995, 95). One such example was completed in Urbino in the 1470s for Federico da Montefeltro (1422–1482). Formed with the intention of promoting his 'taste, aspirations and interests', the *studiolo* juxtaposed art and literature with scientific instruments and a suit of armour in such a way as to demonstrate a judicious balance of contemplation and action on the part of its patron (Cheles 1986, 23, 92; Burke 1987, 505–6). The modest dimensions of the space were cleverly mitigated by the inclusion of illusionistic depictions of cupboards and even glimpses of another imaginary *studiolo*. This inventive assemblage, as well as being a place of study, 'must also have been shown to illustrious visitors, thus fulfilling a propaganda function' (Cheles 1986, 23).

It is instructive to bear this in mind when considering Piano's original sketch for the Hultén bequest (Fig 2.3). It depicts the donor sat at the heart of the collection surrounded by 'the world in miniature' – that is, his universe of accumulated artworks and literature. He is the star at the centre of this constellation, watching as it orbits around him, rather like Federico da Montefeltro, five centuries earlier. This connection is reinforced by the name given to this 21st-century *studiolo*: 'The Pontus Hultén Study Gallery'. Intended to store Hultén's donated library as well as his art collection for the purposes of both study and display, it underscores how Hultén, like Federico da Montefeltro, wished to be known as 'a doer and a facilitator', a man of action

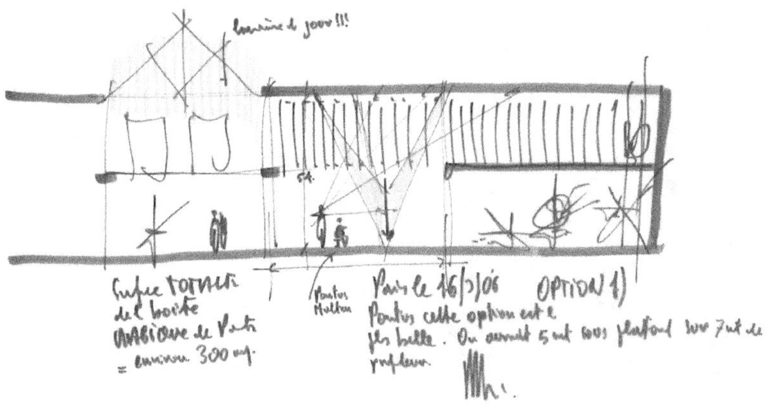


Fig 2.3.
Renzo Piano's initial sketch for the Hultén bequest

and a lover of spectacle (Birnbaum *et al* 2007, 62; cf Granath and Nieckels 1983, 146). This helps explain the need for a dynamic environment, a milieu that might otherwise seem rather perplexing given its intended function as a place of quiet learning.

The Pontus Hultén Study Gallery functions as a forum to flaunt Hultén's taste as a discerning collector and a socially successful individual. The technologically innovative mechanism is also a very conscious nod to the legacy of *Movement in Art* (Widenheim 2008). This link was made in media accounts of the gallery's inauguration, a flavour of which I have tried to convey in my opening paragraph. These reports recalled Hultén's desire for the public to be active and stressed his interest in 'kinetic or moving [*rörlig*] art' (Wadman 2008). The mechanised gallery equates to a pacified version of Allan Kaprow's room of cardboard boxes in *Movement in Art*. In both cases the entire space forms an artistic whole. Kaprow would surely have approved of the sense in which a 'nonart' phenomenon like a factory production line has become 'conscripted' as a 'Kinetic Environment', an impression that is further emphasised by the very deliberate placing of Tinguely's *Fiesta Bar* (Kaprow 2003, 98).

Machines are closely associated with Hultén not only because of *Movement in Art*, but also due to a 1968 exhibition that he curated at the Museum of Modern Art in New York entitled *The Machine as Seen at the End of the Mechanical Age*. It occurred in the same year that Hultén put together the first major showing of Andy Warhol in Europe in an exhibition hosted by both Moderna Museet and the Stedelijk. This link with Warhol was emphasised during the inauguration of the Pontus Hultén Study Gallery through the prominence given to *Dance Diagram (Foxtrot)* (1961). This entered Moderna Museet as a result of *New York Collection for Stockholm* of 1973. This exhibition secured for the museum a stellar array of works by leading artists active on the 1960s New York scene. It proved to be Hultén's audacious swansong as director of Moderna Museet before he left to take charge of the Centre Pompidou.

In 2008, Moderna Museet and the Stedelijk marked the 40th anniversary of 1968 by mounting a new Warhol show. Coinciding with the opening of the Pontus Hultén Study Gallery, this temporary exhibition was as much a heralding of Hultén as it was of Warhol, even to the extent that the museum director was credited with coining that most famous of aphorisms: 'In the future everybody will be world famous for fifteen minutes' (Granath 2008). Another of Warhol's maxims features in his bequest to Moderna Museet: 'Machines have fewer problems. I'd like to

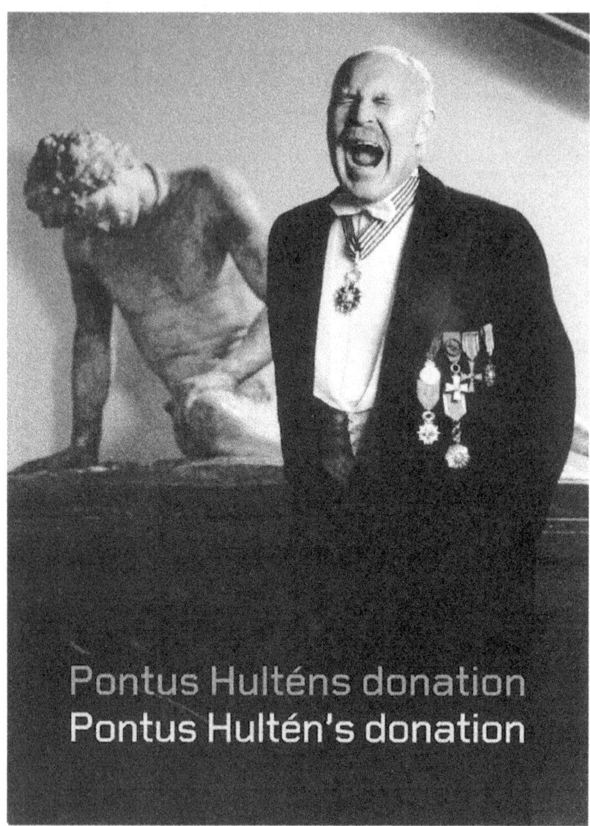


FIG 2.4.
BROCHURE ABOUT THE HULTÉN BEQUEST SHOWING HANS HAMMARSKIÖLD'S PHOTOGRAPH *PONTUS HULTÉN, MUSEUM CURATOR* (1984, STATENS PORTRÄTTSAMLING, NMGRH 4602)

be a machine, wouldn't you?' It is fitting, therefore, that Hultén is now, in a sense, a machine. Or, rather, the Pontus Hultén Study Gallery is the mechanism for his longevity.

This was particularly apparent in the inaugural 'hang' of the gallery. The decision to place Tom Shannon's sculpture *Slumber* (1986) at its entrance was especially evocative. This diminutive work consists of a rectangular block that is kept perpetually afloat with the help of concealed magnets. Thanks to Bourdieu we know that the 'meaning' of such an artwork is determined by 'the system of objects in which it is placed'. In its present 'system', *Slumber* is transposed into something approaching a representation of the undying Hultén. He has passed away, but he is not dead.

This unearthly quality has a miraculous effect on the bequest. The gallery invigilator operating the touchscreen monitor is in reality an acolyte assisting at the altar of high art. Meanwhile the 'food sculptures' by Claes Oldenburg, the drinks on Tinguely's *Fiesta Bar* and On Kawara's postcard series evocatively titled *I Am Still Alive, 1974–1981* are transformed into votive offerings. Such deposits constitute 'an act of giving directed at another-worldly power', in this case the transcending power of art (Osborne 2004). What characterises them is 'exchangeability'. In return for their donation the giver is rewarded with esteem, remembrance and even life after death. Customary divisions between the sacred and the profane are effectively blurred by this pursuit of 'prestige and rank', revealing that 'some gifts to the gods are "manifestly a vehicle for relations between men"' (Gregory cited in Osborne 2004, 2; Braudy 1997, 9).

Notions of prestige, rank and human power relations are in ample supply in an explanatory brochure distributed at the Study Gallery. On its cover is an iconic portrait of Hultén by the Swedish photographer, Hans Hammarskiöld (Fig 2.4). It is, on one level, a very formal representation. Hultén stands before a classical sculpture in a dress suit which is festooned with medals. This contrasts with his mien: his eyes are tightly shut and his mouth forced open as wide as it will go. A clue to this otherwise baffling expression is to be found in another version of the same scene. This time Hultén, mouth closed, stands in front of a different sculpture: a plaster cast copy of a late-16th-century lion by Flaminio Vacca. However, in the far better-known image, the king of the beasts is absent. It is Hultén who roars.

The impression this depiction creates is of a man who has mastered the game of distinction. The photograph was taken shortly after Hultén's brief and rather abortive stint at Los Angeles Museum of Contemporary Art (MOCA) had come to a premature end. It matches a description of him made in 1984, the same year as Hammarskiöld's photograph: 'A huge man, barrel-chested, athletic looking, with shaven head, he possessed great charm, was renowned for his humour, had a reputation for being an artists' museum man, and was known and respected by collectors the world over' (Berelowitz 1994, 273).

This characterisation allied with Hammarskiöld's image and Hultén's appointment at MOCA confirms just how far he had come since those early days when he needed to rely on Willem Sandberg's credentials to help realise his ambitions. Now it was Hultén who took top billing. He was, in the words of the artist Robert Irwin: 'Mr Magic ... a real superstar ... Royalty!' (cited in Berelowitz 1994, 272–3). From being Sandberg's self-appointed heir, Hultén had become a king in his lifetime and an immortal god after his death.

## The Pontus Hultén Collection... Moderna Museet

Fame in the modern sense of the word is frequently understood 'as a way of defining oneself, making oneself known, beyond the limitations of class and family' (Braudy 1997, 14). This has given rise to a plethora of 'familiar strangers': celebrities we feel we 'know' but have never met (Gitlin cited in Turner 2004, 3). One of the means by which Pontus Hultén achieved this status was via a large book he devised to complement his art collection. It was published in conjunction with its initial, temporary display at Moderna Museet in 2004, from where it toured to museums in Finland, Italy and Germany before coming to rest again in Stockholm, this time for good.

Entitled *The Pontus Hultén Collection...* this weighty tome illustrates perfectly Bourdieu's point about the legitimising effect of 'accumulated, crystallized history'. Through its pages Hultén and his relatives have indeed become 'familiar strangers' in the 'extended family' of the art-loving public (Turner 2004, 113ff). Dedicated to the daughter who predeceased him, it catalogues by surname those artists featured in his collection. Interposed amongst the artists beginning with the letter 'H' is Hultén himself. His presence takes the form of family snapshots, commencing with photographs of Hultén's grandfather and parents and going on to include images of Pontus at every stage of life: from infant, toddler, schoolboy and university student, to his professional flowering and physical decline. The montage shows two sides of this modern-day Federico da Montefeltro. On the one hand there is Pontus Hultén, the anarchic man of action, attired in a fantastic antique costume and jousting playfully beside a Venetian canal. This is counterpoised by the dignified, authoritative Hultén, leading the Swedish royal family on a museum tour. Straddling the two persona is Hultén the hands-on deviser of pioneering exhibitions and confidante of artists. We see him chatting casually with Andy Warhol on a visit to Moderna Museet in 1968 or standing proudly alongside Marcel Duchamp amidst the kinetic artworks of *Movement in Art*.

This fusion of the personal and the private corroborates Hultén's own claim that the book, like the collection as a whole, is 'a story of friendships' (Hultén 2004, 176). This raises a host of important but rarely voiced ethical concerns (an important exception is Veier 2007, 53). Hultén was both a buyer of art and a recipient of gifts from artists he promoted and, very often, counted as friends. Today this would be considered to be a conflict of interests. Already in 1986 the ICOM Code of Professional Ethics stated that museum professionals should refrain from 'dealing … in objects similar or related to the objects collected by the employing museum' (§8.3) and that 'no member of the museum profession should compete with their institution either in the acquisition of objects or in any personal collecting activity' (§6.8).

This helps explain Hultén's insistence that his collection came together by 'sheer coincidence' and that 'it would be pointless to look for a plan or a method' (Hultén 2004, 6). This has a number of consequences. First and foremost it snuffs out any potentially awkward ethical questions. Secondly it disguises the fact that the temperamental Hultén had Machiavellian tendencies and 'would ruthlessly exploit every personal connection to make his artistic visions reality' (Lavier cited in Birnbaum *et al* 2007, 65). Thirdly it serves as a mark of distinction, aligning Hultén with Bourdieu's notion of the 'legitimate choice' – one that is 'so sure of itself that it convinces by the sheer manner of the performance, like a successful bluff' (Bourdieu 1984, 92).

Hultén was aided and abetted by Lars Nittve, the director of Moderna Museet at the time of the bequest. In his introduction to *The Pontus Hultén Collection…* Nittve recalled travelling to France to visit Hultén and see for himself 'the selection of works that had found their way to his house' (Nittve cited in Hultén 2004, 7). In other words, Hultén's distinction was so pronounced and irresistible that art itself sought him out. With this fantasy established it became possible for Nittve to make light of the 'resonance' between 'the private walls' of Hultén's home and 'the heart of the Moderna Museet collection'. This was just another one of those cheerful 'coincidences' that Hultén had himself acknowledged.

It is a pity that Nittve chose not to have instead used this happy happenstance to explore 'the paradox of the imposition of legitimacy' identified by Bourdieu. Hultén is habitually lauded because he 'understood what was good art long before others did and thus was way ahead of his time' (Malmberg cited in Burch 2007, 61). But is the art he advocated the 'dominant feature' of Moderna Museet because it is objectively 'good', or is it because it is dominant that it appears to be endowed with these qualities? And is Moderna Museet not obliged to validate Hultén's aesthetic sensibility in order to safeguard not only its material inheritance but also its cultural inheritance – and legitimacy – as well? Hultén's status is symbiotic with that of Moderna Museet in much the same way that it was mutually dependent on the artists he promoted. As Lee Braudy (1997, 490) noted, a personality such as Hultén 'is the artist's fulfilling double, who presents him [sic] to the world'. Hultén's collection is rife with examples of this. Take Ed Kienholz, the hands of whose clock stand still in Hultén's collection. Moderna Museet's acquisition of Kienholz's *The State Hospital* (1966) has been described as 'only a small part of Hultén's contribution to the artist's career'. The subsequent exhibition *11 + 11 Tableaux* (Moderna Museet 1970) 'established Kienholz as one of the major American artists in Europe' (cf Pincus 1990, 45, 105). Hultén was therefore not just a prescient purveyor of art. He helped shape the very criteria – Bourdieu's 'system of aesthetic principles' – by which 'good art' is judged.

With the donation of Hultén's collection to Moderna Museet, 'the paradox of the imposition of legitimacy' becomes even harder to unravel. This is actually visualised in the opening pages of Hultén's catalogue to his collection. Three of the first 11 pages feature the following text:

The Pontus Hultén
Collection...

MODERNA MUSEET, STOCKHOLM

The trio of dots in the title amalgamates the two, giving the private collection precedence: The Pontus Hultén Collection *is* Moderna Museet. Or, more accurately, the museum is the mirror image of Hultén's collection. That much is suggested by the spine of the book, which features the title in both regular and reverse script. Lars Nittve has done his utmost to ensure the maintenance of this state of affairs. Hultén 'laid down the agenda for the future' (Nittve cited in Hultén 2004, 7) declared Nittve, shortly before placing the immortal Hultén into 'the very centre of the building' through the positioning of the Pontus Hultén Study Gallery.

But this is not to say that there is universal agreement over the wisdom of this unquestioning adulation. The Hultén inheritance, whilst desirable for obvious reasons, is not entirely celebrated. Indeed, the timing of the bequest coincided with signs of an interesting reassessment of Hultén. Denigrations of him first voiced in the early 1970s resurfaced (Tellgren 2008, 337). More serious was the revelation that the late Hultén had traded in a set of Warhol's Brillo boxes of decidedly dubious provenance (Ölander *et al* 2007). In addition, Hultén's legacy has been indirectly questioned through criticisms levelled at Lars Nittve's 'infatuation' (*besatthet*) with 'American macho-cultural Pop Art'. That obsession, it is claimed, has been to the detriment of present-day artists: 'Few in the young art scene feel that Moderna [Museet] is a place for them and that Moderna has something important to say about art's role in society and its potential development' (Ravini 2010).

One of Nittve's last actions as director was to help establish the satellite institution, Moderna Museet Malmö. Its long-term inaugural exhibition drew on the museum's rich collection of 1960s Pop Art. There were two routes into the show. In one direction lay Robert Rauschenberg's *Monogram* – a stuffed-goat 'Combine' so boldly acquired for the museum by Hultén in 1964 and which (to recall Bourdieu) 'functions like a sort of "trade-mark"' for his cultural competence and pedigree. The other route led to Carl Fredrik Reuterswärd's *Mascot for Movement in Art* (1960), a bronze figure ironically enough tied to a chair. The statue's bound arms meant that he was unable to reach out to eat an appetising piece of *Gruyère* cheese – another one of those delicious snacks by Claes Oldenburg that Pontus Hultén donated, along with hundreds of other works, to Moderna Museet in Stockholm. Thanks to the theme of its first exhibition, this influence has also been implanted at the very inception of Moderna Museet in Malmö as well. Even when breaking new ground it seems to be impossible for the museum to evade the everlasting Pontus Hultén.

## Distinction After Death

As we have seen, Bourdieu was cognisant of the performative aspects of distinction, whereby choices are legitimised 'by the sheer manner of the performance'. He shows too that this is equally true of the flipside of acquisition, namely how best to divest oneself of prestigious material possessions. One way of doing this and of achieving longevity is through donation. But this has two potentially undesirable consequences. On the one hand, monolithic 'donor memorials' tend to 'create a tomb-like atmosphere' (Duncan 1995, 89). Alternatively, individual works, integrated into other collections and isolated as objects of aesthetic devotion, risk being stripped of their 'real world' associations as they come under the 'pure gaze' of the art gallery. This is what Bourdieu refers to as the 'museum effect' (Bourdieu and Haacke 1995, 91).

Pontus Hultén's bequest to Moderna Museet skilfully avoids both these fates. The decontextualising impact of the art museum was averted through the naming and siting of the Pontus Hultén Study Gallery. The biographical link with the donor was further sustained by the aforementioned book *The Pontus Hultén Collection...* plus two freely available handouts, one featuring Renzo Piano's initial sketch, the other Hammarskiöld's photograph of the lionised Hultén. In addition to these printed documents are video monitors inside and outside the gallery which broadcast *A Magic Box Becomes Real*. The striking title of this specially-made film confirms that 'Mr Magic' really does evince a 'magic stronger than death'. It allows us to see the artworks enter the museum: a liminal moment when they shift from being private possessions to public property. This is memorably illustrated by the case of an untitled sculpture by Niki de Saint Phalle (1930–2002). She, like her husband Jean Tinguely, was a person who Hultén cherished as a friend and promoted as an artist. Her colourful sculpture is shown prior to being restored. We watch as a conservator points out the areas of missing paint and explains how this was a consequence of the many years it spent standing next to Pontus Hultén's bath. This conjures up a vivid image of a wet towel being draped over this artistic masterpiece as its owner emerged from his ablutions. The paint has now been retouched so that it can accept the 'pure gaze' of the museum. Yet it retains its 'living' connection thanks to the accompanying film. The nature of his bequest thus makes it possible for Hultén to have his cake (or cheese slice) and eat it.

*A Magic Box Becomes Real* is described as a 'collage of interviews' (Lundqvist and Wrenfelt 2008). The most significant protagonists, aside from Hultén and Renzo Piano, are Nittve and his then colleague, Cecilia Widenheim. They take the important role of 'gatekeeper critics' of a 'gatekeeper institution'. Together they serve as 'societal guardians of long-term renown ... guard[ing] entrance into canons and pantheons of achievement' (Cowen 2000, 72). Hultén has been well-served in this regard. Olle Granath, his immediate successor as director of Moderna Museet, has been described as 'picking up Hultén's mantle' throughout the 1980s until 'an apostolic succession of sorts' saw the appointment of Hultén's former assistant, Björn Springfeldt (Tellgren 2008, 341). To date the only exception to this rule has been David Elliott, the one foreigner to have held the post. Upon arrival he found himself 'faced with domestic ghosts' and developed an antipathy for 'the mist in people's eyes when they talk[ed] about the old days' (cited in Tellgren 2008, 341). That nostalgia can be summed up in two words: Pontus Hultén.

Lars Nittve, who took over from Elliott, had no such qualms as he drew Hultén into the bosom of the museum. He stepped down in November 2010 and was replaced by Daniel Birnbaum. The latter is clearly aware that, as a 'bulldozer of a director', Hultén is not exactly an ideal role model. Nevertheless, Birnbaum still looks upon him as 'arguably the most influential European museum professional of the twentieth century ... [who] tested the limits of the contemporary art museum from within' (Birnbaum *et al* 2007, 61–2).

Hultén continues to be seen as a hero for influential curators, museum directors and artists such as Hans-Ulrich Obrist, Ann Goldstein and Daniel Buren (ibid; Obrist 1997). Their attitude towards Hultén shows how famous people function as a standard by which to measure others and mark them out for promotion (Braudy 1997, 15). Ann Goldstein, who once assisted Hultén during his time at MOCA, went on to become its senior curator and was recently appointed general artistic director of the Stedelijk Museum. She lauded the 'visionary' Hultén for his 'brilliantly unmanageable ideas' (cited in Birnbaum *et al* 2007, 62, 65). In making such pronouncements, Goldstein captures 'a share of [Hultén's] renown' (Cowen 2000, 88). This demonstrates how the 'fame of others, [especially] their distinguishing marks, becomes a common coin of human exchange' (Braudy 1997, 4).

Hultén made brilliant use of this 'human exchange', as we have seen in his shrewd association with Sandberg's Stedelijk at the start of his career. But this posed a dilemma for the elderly Hultén. How could he secure his posthumous legacy without succumbing to the lure of the moribund 'static' museum so despised by Sandberg? And how could he safeguard the art he collected from future generations who might 'wish to relegate … [them] to the museum store because they no longer have anything to say'? His inspired solution was to subvert this by putting them into store from the outset. And then, in a further stroke of genius, moving that store into the gallery. The Pontus Hultén Study Gallery is therefore a strategically brilliant 'mechanism'. It enforces the visibility of Hultén's collection and disguises this under the logic of a dynamic and audience-focused 'museum which moves a lot'. It achieves the seemingly impossible by being both static/dead *and* moving/living.

What is more, the dot-dot-dot of *The Pontus Hultén Collection…* not only successfully insinuates itself in Moderna Museet's regular collection, but also implies that it is still growing. And with the right 'gatekeepers' who share Hultén's 'code' this will indeed be the case, ensuring that Hultén will continue to 'influence the museum's direction for a good part of the foreseeable future' (Tellgren 2008, 344). The multiple screens of the gallery under Hultén's name can be continually replenished and reconfigured, charging it with 'constantly renewed meaning' (Braudy 1997, 15). This bodes well for Hultén's prospects of enduring fame because the repackaging of celebrity products is absolutely crucial to the fame industry.

Thus it is that Hultén has become a 'vehicle of cultural memory and cohesion … stand[ing] as [an] example for the future' (ibid). This matches his idea of art as 'a guiding element in life. It speaks without speaking. It reveals. It foreshadows. It points the way. It can allow us to see where we are going' (Hultén 2004, 178). This makes his mechanised bequest a sort of oracle; a sacred place where one both pays respects and seeks guidance. Hultén articulates ('speaks') there. Dead as a body, he is undying as a machine (cf Braudy 1997, 6). The Pontus Hultén Study Gallery strives and achieves a *nunc stans* – an eternal now (cf Glennie and McGarry 2007). *When you see it, Hultén will be alive* (cf Alechinsky in Atkins 1986, 11).

This is all the more remarkable because this solitary gallery is in truth quite a modest legacy. Hultén had far grander plans. An entire museum he hoped to build with Renzo Piano in southern Sweden was not realised in his lifetime (Hultén 2004, 430; Eriksson 2005). It is this contingency that led to the Moderna Museet bequest. However, as with any indelicate ethical questions, this is rarely alluded to. This silence lends the bequest a sense of inevitability and properness and enables Moderna Museet to 'remain in the radiance of its former leader' (Tellgren 2008, 334). And yet Hultén more than anyone else was aware of the dangers inherent in all this. An 'institution shouldn't be completely identified with its director', he cautioned, 'it's not good for the museum … When it breaks down, it breaks down completely' (Hultén cited in Obrist 1997, 77).

This raises a key question: why did Hultén ignore his own advice? The mundane answer is that, with his health failing and his plans stalling, he was forced to scale back his ambitions. This would mean that the Moderna Museet option was a necessary compromise, despite his own misgivings. Hultén was surely keen to resolve matters to his own satisfaction while he was still alive rather than run the risk of having his wishes interpreted by others. The undesirable consequences of posthumous legal wrangles is clear from the long-running row over the authenticity of certain works by Andy Warhol.

And it is this that provides a more satisfactory response to Hultén's paradoxical behaviour and an insight into his complex psyche. As this chapter was nearing completion, media stories resurfaced about Hultén's involvement in the Brillo box scandal mentioned briefly above. It would now appear beyond doubt that Hultén oversaw the manufacture of over one hundred wooden boxes long after Warhol's death and that he went on to sell them as genuine works at immense personal profit. Many of these – including six examples at Moderna Museet – have since been downgraded to 'copies' by the Andy Warhol Art Authentication board, which condemned Hultén for having 'misrepresented these works and falsified their history' (cited in Bomsdorf and Gerlis 2010). This means that those collectors, dealers, institutions and the visiting public who put their faith in Hultén have lost out in terms of money, reputation and trust.

One explanation for Hultén's behaviour is that he was at heart 'a sneaky old bastard'. This was the opinion of the former London art dealer, Brian Balfour-Oatts, who had bought several wooden Brillo boxes on the strength of Hultén's credentials (Levy and Scott-Clark 2010). Others interpret Hultén's duping of people like Balfour-Oatts as a conscious 'lampooning' of the art market (Thomas Anderberg cited in ibid). It should be remembered, of course, that if Hultén could claim to be the author of one of Warhol's most famous aphorisms, then he might well have had few scruples about manufacturing a batch of brand-new Brillo boxes.

With the accused dead, one could consider making a pilgrimage to Hultén's mechanised oracle at Moderna Museet in search of answers. However, we would probably be better advised to put this tawdry affair down as a particularly dramatic twist in 'the paradox of the imposition of legitimacy'. The lesson it teaches us is the paramount necessity of maintaining a critical eye on museums and the people and organisations that shape them. It also confirms that Hultén was absolutely correct to highlight the risks that ensue when institutional and individual biographies become entangled. This was something I reflected upon in an earlier version of this paper (Burch 2008). Citing Hultén's warning about the dangers of museums becoming 'completely identified' with their directors, I noted rather facetiously that, when it came to the Pontus Hultén Study Gallery, only severe mechanical failure threatened to jeopardise Hultén's continuing presence at the museum. Ironically enough, since its opening it has indeed been beset by technical problems caused by the limited load-bearing capacity of the screens (Noring 2010). A fitting metaphor not to pile too much onto one individual, perhaps? But then again, the huge, barrel-chested Pontus Hultén did have particularly broad shoulders ...

## BIBLIOGRAPHY AND REFERENCES

Atkins, G, 1986 *Asger Jorn: Supplement to the Oeuvre Catalogue of his Paintings from 1930 to 1973*, Lund Humphries, London

Bennett, T, 1995 *The Birth of the Museum*, Routledge, London

Berelowitz, J-A, 1994 The Museum of Contemporary Art, Los Angeles: An Account of the Collaboration between Artists, Trustees and an Architect, in *Art Apart: Art Institutions and Ideology Across England and North America* (ed M Pointon), Manchester University Press, Manchester and New York, 267–84

Birnbaum, D, Goldstein, A, and Buren, D, 2007 Director of Intelligence: Daniel Birnbaum, Ann Goldstein and Daniel Buren on Pontus Hultén, *Artforum International* 45 (6), 61–6

Bomsdorf, C, and Gerlis, M, 2010 Warhol Brillo boxes downgraded to 'copies', *The Art Newspaper*, October, 20 (217), 1 and 4

Bourdieu, P, 1984 *Distinction: A Social Critique of the Judgement of Taste* (trans R Nice), Routledge and Kegan Paul, London

Bourdieu, P, and Haacke, H, 1995 *Free Exchange*, Polity, Cambridge

Braudy, L, 1997 *The Frenzy of Renown: Fame and Its History*, Vintage, New York

Burch, S, 2007 Museum Landscapes: Zoning in on a Complex Cultural Field, *NaMu I: Setting the Frames*, Linköping University Electronic Press, Linköping, 49–67 [online], available from: http://www.ep.liu.se/ecp/022/005 [23 May 2010]

— 2008 Sliding Doors, *Museum Practice* 43, 18–23

Burke, P, 1987 Book Review: The Studiolo of Urbino, *European History Quarterly* 17 (4), 505–6

Centre Pompidou, 2004 *Pontus Hultén – un esprit libre*, press release [online], available from: http://www.centrepompidou.fr/Pompidou/Manifs.nsf/AllExpositions/E6E13AF10A1B7272C1256ED90050C303 [23 May 2010]

Cheles, L, 1986 *The Studiolo of Urbino: An Iconographic Investigation*, Pennsylvania State University Press, Pennsylvania

Cowen, T, 2000 *What Price Fame?* Harvard University Press, London and Cambridge, MA

Daniels, M, n.d. Sandberg, Willem Jacob Henri Berend, Jonkheer, in *Dictionary of Art Historians* (ed L Sorensen), available from: http://www.dictionaryofarthistorians.org/sandbergw.htm [23 May 2010]

Duncan, C, 1995 *Civilizing Rituals: Inside Public Art Museums*, Routledge, London

Eriksson, T, 2005 35 museimiljoner räckte till en kur, *Dagens Nyheter* [online], 26 March, available from: http://www.dn.se/DNet/road/Classic/article/0/jsp/print.jsp?&a=395432 [26 March 2005]

Glennie, S, and McGarry, E (eds), 2007 *The Eternal Now: Warhol and the Factory '63-'68*, Model Arts and Niland Gallery/Lewis Glucksman Gallery, University of Cork, Sligo

Granath, O, and Nieckels, M (eds), 1983 *Moderna Museet 1958–1983*, Moderna Museet, Stockholm

Granath, O, 2008 *With Andy Warhol 1968* [online], available from: http://www.modernamuseet.se/en/Stockholm/Exhibitions/2008/Andy-Warhol---Other-Voices-Other-Rooms/With-Andy-Warhol-1968-text-Ol/ [4 July 2011]

Hultén, K G, and Tinguely, J, 1987 *A Magic Stronger Than Death*, Thames and Hudson, London

Hultén, P (ed), 1961 *Stedelijk Museum, Amsterdam besöker Moderna Museet, Stockholm*, Moderna Museet, Stockholm

— 2004 *The Pontus Hultén Collection…*, Moderna Museet, Stockholm

Kaprow, A, 2003 *Essays on the Blurring of Art and Life* (ed J Kelley), University of California Press, Berkeley

Levy, A, and Scott-Clark, C, 2010 Warhol's Box of Tricks, *The Guardian* (Weekend section), 21 August, 24

Lundqvist, C (director), and Wrenfelt, S (ed), 2008 *A Magic Box Becomes Real*, press release, Moderna Museet

Muchnic, S, 2006 Obituaries: Pontus Hultén, *LA Times* [online], 31 October, available from: http://articles.latimes.com/2006/oct/31/local/me-hulten31 [23 May 2010]

Noring, A-S, 2010 Personal communication (email exchange with the author), 16 March

Obrist, H-U, 1997 The Hang of It: Hans-Ulrich Obrist Talks with Pontus Hultén, *Artforum International* 36 (8), 74–9, 113–14

Ölander, M, Lagercrantz, L, and Holmén, C, 2007 Warhol-mysteriet med svenska miljonboxar, *Expressen* [online], 30 May, available from: http://www.expressen.se/nyheter/1.701023/warhol-mysteriet-med-svenska-miljonboxar [30 May 2007]

Osborne, R, 2004 Hoards, Votives, Offerings: The Archaeology of the Dedicated Object, *World Archaeology* 36 (1), 1–10

Pincus, R L, 1990 *On a Scale that Competes with the World: The Art of Edward and Nancy Reddin Kienholz*, University of California Press, California

Ravini, S, 2010 Post-Nittve på Moderna, *Göteborgs-Posten* [online], 21 January, available from: http://www.gp.se/kulturnoje/1.293869-sinziana-ravini-post-nittve-pa-moderna [21 January 2010]

Sandberg, W, 1961 STEDELIJK är sextiosex år gammalt, in *Stedelijk Museum, Amsterdam besöker Moderna Museet, Stockholm* (ed P Hultén), Moderna Museet, Stockholm, 3

Stedelijk, n.d. *Stedelijk Museum Collection*, available from: http://www.stedelijk.nl/oc2/page.asp?PageID=148 [30 May 2007]

Tellgren, A (ed), 2008 *The History Book: On Moderna Museet 1958–2008*, Steidl, Göttingen

Turner, G, 2004 *Understanding Celebrity*, Sage, London

Veier, T, 2007 Pontus Hultén's Collection, *Prisma* 2, 53–8

Wadman, A, 2008 Jukebox för konst, *Dagens Nyheter*, 5 June, Kultur, 6

Widenheim, C, 2008 *The Pontus Hultén Study Gallery at Moderna Museet, Stockholm*, press release, Moderna Museet

# 3

# Sydney Pavière and the Harris Museum and Art Gallery, Preston

Laura Gray

After 33 years of service, Sydney Pavière, white-haired and three years beyond the usual retirement age, stood before the Art Gallery Committee. He was there to announce his retirement from his post of art director and curator at the Harris Museum and Art Gallery. Addressing the committee, and speaking with obvious affection and sincerity, he said: 'Gentlemen we have built a monument here. Please see that nothing is done to despoil it' (Rushton 1959, 33).

It sometimes happens that the character, as well as the actions, of a particular curator casts a long shadow within a museum or gallery. In the second quarter of the 20th century, a number of curators brought foresight, good judgement and individualism to their work. Lawrence Haward, appointed director of Manchester Art Gallery in 1914; Vincent Galloway, appointed curator at the Ferens Art Gallery in Hull in 1929; and Peter Floud, who joined the V&A's circulation department in 1935, emerged to establish unique and strong identities for their museums and collections.[1] It is possible to identify an emergence of curators in national and provincial museums, working in the interwar and immediate post-war period, who had a breadth of vision for the collections in their care. Pioneering young creative museum and gallery curators, sometimes with an artistic background (both Galloway and Pavière were painters), were playing an important role not only within their institutions but also in the continuing development of the museum profession, a factor for those curators wishing to exercise within their role a significant degree of individual agency. Sydney Pavière (1891–1971), art director and curator at the Harris Museum and Art Gallery from 1926 until his retirement in 1959, illustrates the importance of individual biography to developing a fuller and more nuanced view of museum history. An examination of Pavière's career at the Harris also explores the question of why this one man in particular appears to have been able to act with a greater degree of individual agency than previous or subsequent curators. Pavière can be seen as an instance of the new professionalism that was emerging in museums during the first half of the 20th century. His work as a curator is important not only because of the collections that took shape during his tenure but because of the principles and ideas that he brought to bear on the museum. Pavière's focus throughout his time as curator was the rehabilitation and development of the Harris. He wished the Harris to again take part in the cultural life of Lancashire, and for the museum to earn a reputation for quality (Rushton 1959, 32). Pavière's collecting did not envisage the museum as a dry repository of acceptable facts and approved knowledge. Instead he worked in areas that were fresh, new and

1 Lawrence Haward worked at Manchester Art Gallery 1914–1945; Vincent Galloway remained at the Ferens Art Gallery in Hull from 1929 to 1960; and Peter Floud worked in the V&A's circulation department between 1935 and 1939 and from 1947 until his death in 1960.

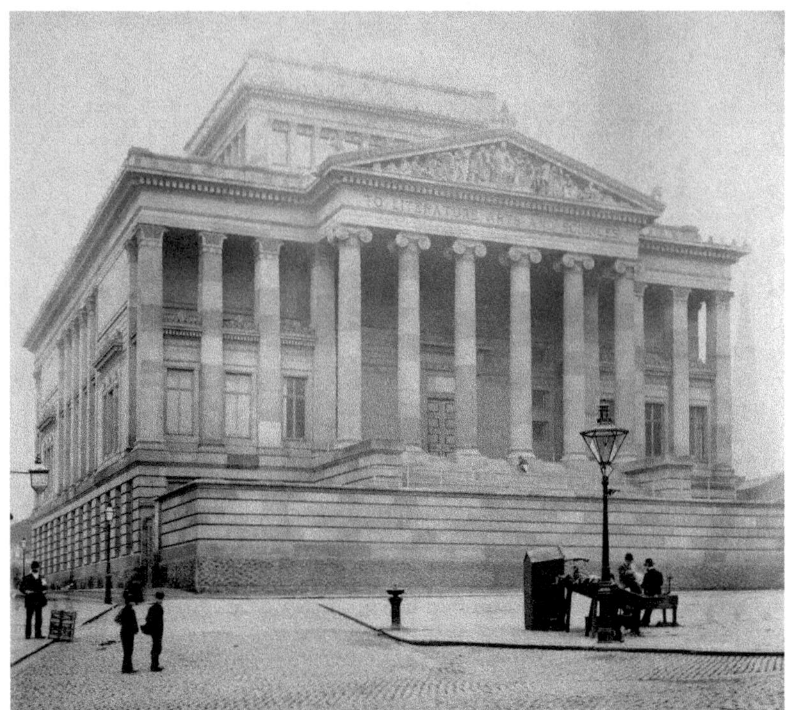

FIG 3.1. EXTERIOR OF THE HARRIS MUSEUM & ART GALLERY, CIRCA 1900

innovative for the museum, particularly in his development of the museum's decorative art collection. Pavière can be considered as part of the second generation of museum reformers, as identified by Noordegraaf, who had by the 1930s made the visitor the central focus of the museum (Noordegraaf 2004, 143). In Pavière's case this is demonstrated by a commitment to evening and bank holiday opening, tours for school groups and public lectures. Noordegraaf claims that what was truly innovative was that reformers of the early 20th century used the layout, architecture and arrangement of the museum as a means to guide the imagined visitor during their visit. With his large-scale rearrangement of the museum and art gallery, which took 25 years to complete, it appears that Pavière was behaving true to this type (Fig 3.1).

From 1922, Pavière had been in the employ of Lord Leverhulme, spending a year as an assistant curator at the Lady Lever Art Gallery in Port Sunlight. In 1923 he became curator of Lord Leverhulme's private collection until Leverhulme's death. Pavière recalled that it was a perfectly timed telegram which eventually brought him to Preston. While he was considering his next move after the death of Lord Leverhulme, the telegram arrived from a friend telling him that Preston needed a curator for its Art Gallery (Anon 1971; Rushton 1959). The museum and art gallery that Pavière took over in 1926 was, by his own account, forlorn and neglected. The force and dynamism of the neo-classical exterior of the building was not matched by the collections and displays within.[2] One strong focus of the museum when Pavière arrived was natural

2 The Harris Free Library, Museum and Art Gallery was funded by a bequest from the Preston lawyer Robert Edmund Harris and designed by James Hibbert, a local architect and Alderman of Preston.

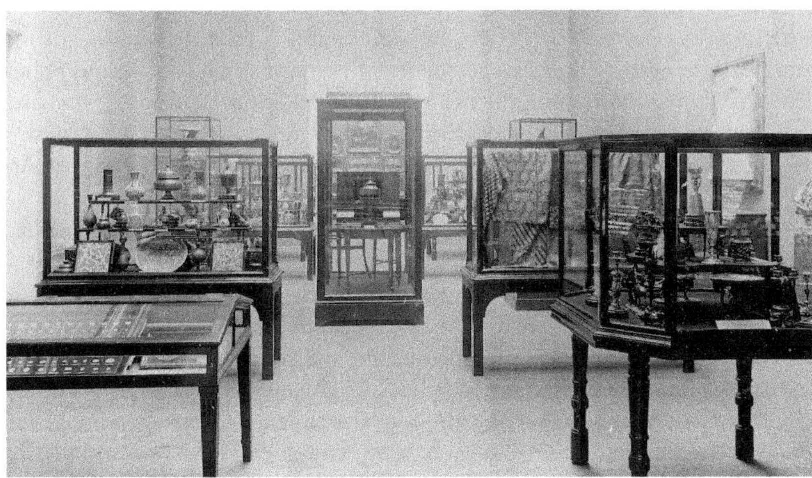

Fig 3.2. Interior of the Harris Museum & Art Gallery, circa 1900

history. Speaking to *Lancashire Life* on the occasion of his retirement, Pavière recalled 'cases of butterflies, moths and other insects [which] had faded to a biscuit colour with age' that greeted him on his arrival at the museum.[3] But there is the possibility that in describing the museum thus, Pavière, on the occasion of his retirement, succumbed to the temptation to mythologise his own past. In view of his intention to continue with curatorial work after leaving the Harris (he had been appointed curator of Rufford Old Hall and the Philip Ashcroft Folk Museum, near Ormskirk in Lancashire), it was expedient for Pavière to shape this view of his legacy, encouraging the acceptance of the view that he had single-handedly rebuilt the Harris from a state of great neglect. In fact, the Harris, though perhaps suffering from a period of weak curatorial leadership, had been founded with strong and clear aims that encompassed both the exterior of the building and the contents within. James Hibbert, the architect and chairman of the Free Library Committee, as well as planning the exterior decoration of the building, also had 'a well-informed personal vision' for what was to go into the museum (Snape 2010, 31). Amongst the first purchases for the museum was a replica of Ghiberti's *Gates of Paradise* and a reproduction of Michelangelo's *David* which would, 'in Hibbert's view, provide an opportunity for everyone to know the masterpieces of sculpture' (Snape 2010, 27) (Fig 3.2). Before Pavière's arrival there had also been a significant bequest of paintings. The fine art collection had been founded in 1883 (the year after the building of the Harris commenced) with Richard Newsham's bequest of his collection of Victorian academic art. The collection numbered 62 oil paintings and 45 watercolours by 19th-century British artists. Newsham, a Preston lawyer, regularly commissioned works and made purchases from the Royal Academy. In fact, Newsham never failed to visit the Royal Academy each year from 1820 to 1870 (Pavière 1949, 3). When Pavière arrived, the art collection was hung in what is known as the Royal Academy or salon style, floor to ceiling, and to his mind, 'needed attention badly' (Rushton 1959, 32). In order to win public attention and

The building of this impressive neo-classical library, art gallery and museum began in 1882 and was completed in 1893.

3 Although, over the years, the museum received a number of important bequests and regularly received work from the Contemporary Fine Art Society from 1910 onwards.

create a profile for the museum and gallery, Pavière embarked on a large-scale redisplay of the collections and initiated what appears to have been a deliberately controversial acquisitions policy for the fine art collection. Though continuing in the Newsham tradition of making purchases at the Royal Academy, he bought paintings that challenged ideas about respectability, Preston's position in the art world and received notions of correct taste amongst the members of the Art Gallery Committee.

The first artwork bought for the gallery on Pavière's recommendation was George Spencer Watson's painting entitled *Nude*. This painting was purchased from the Royal Academy in 1927 and caused an outbreak of letter-writing in the local newspapers when the vote on the purchase of the painting at the committee meeting was reported in the *Manchester Guardian*. Alderman Worden expressed his concern that the picture would contribute to 'the loss of moral grit' (Anon 1927b). Alderman Darham wondered whether they were bound to retain the name of the painting, believing that the title 'drew attention just in the same way as a kinema advertisement labelled "For adults only"'. Councillor Firth said he would not like to think that his sister had sat for the picture while Councillor Morris said he would be proud if his sister had been the sitter. The purchase of the picture was eventually confirmed by 28 votes to 8 (Anon 1927b). This was not the first time that the issue of nudity in art and the question of public decency had arisen at the Harris. In 1894 the *Manchester Guardian* reported on the removal of the plaster reproduction of Michelangelo's *David*: 'The Preston authorities apparently hesitated no longer when they found that "doctors and clergymen" – who are well known to be the best art critics – demanded the removal of the obnoxious work … it is a great pity that an important English town should have made itself so ridiculous' (Anon 1894). Three years after the purchase of *Nude*, Pavière's views on the issue of the nude figure in art, in relation to banned prints at a photography exhibition held by Preston Scientific Society, were reported in the *Manchester Guardian*. He said, 'If we can break down the prejudice of looking at the nude as something disgusting we shall be breaking down a very important barrier' (Anon 1930). The purchase of *Nude* had a number of effects. Firstly, it brought the gallery to public notice; secondly, it engaged the Committee in lively debate about the gallery; and finally, it challenged small town prejudices on the respectability or otherwise of the female nude in art. Pavière also established himself as an artist-connoisseur whose judgement was not to be influenced by the provincial sensibilities of the Preston Aldermen. Even so, parties being shown around the gallery often requested that they 'should not be taken into the room where the naked woman is' (Rushton 1959, 33). Pavière, on asking an organiser who had taken children on a tour of the art gallery what the children had thought of Spencer Watson's *Nude*, was told that 'the children look on the nude as disgusting'. Pavière replied that he was sorry to hear that, and was out to alter that point of view (Anon 1930). This episode in 1927, which had involved clashing with the Committee in the first year of his appointment, must have been at the least uncomfortable for Pavière. At this time it must have seemed that his vision for the Harris as a home of artistic excellence was going to be a struggle to achieve. Perhaps it was for this reason that in 1929 he applied for the post of curator at the Ferens Art Gallery in Hull, a post that was in the end secured by a young Yorkshire painter, Vincent Galloway. Unsuccessful in his application to the Ferens, Pavière remained committed to the development and improvement of the Harris for the rest of his working life.

Resolute in his vision for the Harris, Pavière was keen to increase local interest in art, encourage artists and promote the idea of an artistic heritage in Preston. One of his methods was to instigate an annual open exhibition of contemporary local artists. The open exhibition, which is still an annual event at the Harris, proved hugely popular, attracting entries from all over the county. Pavière's method of fostering the sense of a strong artistic heritage in Preston also led to some astute purchases. Some years before World War II, he decided to form a collection of works by the Devis family of painters, who had originated in Preston in the 18th century. On the second floor of the Harris, Pavière created the Devis room, which contained paintings and other items relating to the family. The Devis collection was conceived as a foundation on which the Harris could continue to build, and as a way in which public interest in art could be re-awakened (Rushton 1959, 32). Vincent Galloway at the Ferens in Hull identified a similar need to connect the local population with the works inside their local art gallery by ensuring it represented the Hull School of marine painting, which until that time had been largely neglected (Hull City Council 2008).

During his time as curator and art director at the Harris, Pavière used the fine art collection in particular to raise the profile of the museum both regionally and nationally. He sought to move the Harris away from being a provincial gallery with limited aspirations to a gallery that housed collections of national importance. When Pavière arrived at the Harris, Preston had not bought in the art market since 1914. This was not due to a lack of funds; instead it was a lack of confidence on the part of the Free Library committee and perhaps the timidity of the previous curator, William Barton, who had been the art master at the local technical college. When the controversial *Nude* was purchased, the councillors who had accompanied Pavière to the Royal Academy paid tribute to his unwavering insistence that that was the right painting for the Harris. Pavière said that he had decided it was that painting or nothing for Preston (Anon 1927a).

The increased confidence and determination that Pavière brought to the museum's acquisition policy culminated in the purchase of *Pauline in the Yellow Dress* by Sir James Gunn. The purchase of this painting, the most expensive at the 1944 Royal Academy, was a considerable statement for a provincial gallery to make. The painting cost £1000, but despite the huge price tag, there was no wavering. Pavière bought it on the opening night of the exhibition and the painting attracted over 100,000 visitors to Preston during the first three months after its arrival from the Academy. *Pauline in the Yellow Dress* has been on continuous display since 1944, and it was the painting that Pavière considered to be the greatest acquisition he made for Preston (Rushton 1959, 33).

It was not only the fine art collections that Pavière used in his drive to revitalise the museum. His desire to attract a wide audience to the Harris is demonstrated by the new collecting areas that he identified and developed. Collections of greetings cards, dolls, cigarette cards and fashion plates were formed. The nascent costume and textiles collection, which contained only a small number of items, was also expanded. Pavière was not the only curator concerned with the decorative arts at work in the North West during this period. In Manchester, Lawrence Haward matched Pavière's drive to develop decorative art collections, but took a different approach. Some of Manchester Art Gallery's earliest acquisitions were decorative art and, although there was an active decorative art exhibitions programme, there was no coherent policy in terms of collecting and display until Lawrence Haward was appointed the first director of the Art Gallery in 1914. Haward was keen to develop a contemporary craft and design collection, which he set up and named the Industrial Art Collection. The IAC at Manchester was formed between 1930 and 1939 in response to the growing public debate over national design standards (Fraser and Paul 1998, 43). It was intended to demonstrate the principles of good design in everyday mass-produced objects. The museum as a proponent of good design connected with the related idea of museums as benchmarks of good taste, and with the further notion of curators such as Haward and Pavière as men able to bring an 'educated eye' to their selection of objects. These well-chosen works would then result in the museum and gallery collection as a site for educating designers, artisans and general visitors. Or as Lord Derby, speaking at the opening of the Harris in 1893, put it, 'The artist and designer would have access to forms of beauty, classical designs, studies of the great masters, and so forth, by which they might correct their taste and improve their fancy' (Anon 1893). Pavière certainly retained some of the didactic spirit expressed by Lord Derby. He often spoke of the need for better art education: 'let us foster a love of the beautiful ... there are thousands crying out for guidance and knowledge' (Pavière 1924). In fact, Pavière seems to have been happy to upset notions of taste in his selection of works for the gallery – the purchase of *Nude* being a good example. But it was in establishing himself as a man who had an educated eye for art that he seems to have gained ascendancy amongst the Art Gallery Committee and to have won the freedom to develop the collections in his own style.

Through his collecting Pavière wished the Harris to look back to the time when Preston had been at its greatest and interpret and reflect this time through a historic decorative arts collection. Pavière wished to develop a collection 'representative of those great years' (Anon 1943a). Lawrence Haward, on the other hand, looked to the present day. In having an overarching vision and a policy of active acquisition in one area, Haward built a collection in Manchester that had coherence and unity of purpose. Nor, in the manner of many private collectors, did the Industrial Art Collection compulsively gather one particular type of object. As a result, the collection comprises examples of ceramics, glass, textiles and printing (Fraser and Paul 1998, 45). Haward also attracted a number of significant gifts and bequests which formed a solid historic foundation for the decorative art collection.[4] Haward stated that: 'Art, like charity, should begin at home' (Fraser and Paul 1998, 43). Although the two men may have felt differently about the merits of developing contemporary and historic collections, Pavière subscribed to Howard's view that art began in the home and began to shape the Harris' decorative art collections accordingly. Despite sharing this starting point, their curatorial approach differed considerably. Haward believed that only by assiduously sifting and exhibiting contemporary work could museums hope to make the general public understand that 'art is living energy and not merely so many obituary notices' (Fraser and Paul 1998, 43). Pavière took an historical approach instead, and tried to use the decorative arts to mark the period when Preston was at her most powerful. Pavière collected pattern books relating to Preston's textile trade because he was concerned with trying to engage the public with the importance of saving recent history, which once lost, would be gone forever.

Despite this historicist approach to the decorative art collections, Pavière asked, 'What of nylon and the future?' (Anon 1943b) at the opening of a textiles exhibition held in December 1943 at the Harris. Referred to in the local press as a historic textiles exhibition, there were in fact contemporary fashions on display. Norman Hartnell's latest fabric designs printed on rayon were displayed alongside 18th-century chintzes, 19th-century crinolines and cashmere shawls. Costume and textiles exhibitions had a mixed reception during the 1940s. The *Preston Guardian* ran concurrent stories about the exhibition under the headlines, 'Rubbish That May Be Valuable, Textiles That Make History' and 'Rare Fabrics in Preston Textile Exhibition' (Anon 1943a;

4 For instance, in 1920 Thomas Greg bequeathed his exceptional collection of English pottery, recording the development of English ceramics from the Roman period to the early 19th century, and in 1934 Mary Greg gave her extensive and eclectic collection of domestic objects, handicrafts, toys and dolls' houses.

1943b). The exhibition, which was on loan from the V&A and the Cotton Board, was installed in one of the main suites of galleries. In this location it was given the same prominent location that was also afforded to exhibitions of fine art. Pavière was happy to spend money in bringing short-term exhibitions to the Harris if he considered that they would 'bring Preston people … back to an appreciation of art' (Rushton 1959, 32). This exhibition, which included examples of contemporary fashion, is a direct descendant of the mid-Victorian approach to the decorative or applied arts – typified by the Great Exhibition of 1851 and subsequently the South Kensington Museum – in which objects were exhibited as useful models for contemporary manufacturers. Although the textile trade in Preston was in decline by the 1940s, the great majority of visitors to the museum would have been employed locally in textile manufacturing. The 1943 exhibition can also be viewed as not only bringing Preston people to an appreciation of art but aiming to improve and broaden the knowledge and educate the eye of those involved in the textiles industry.

In his remarks at the opening of the exhibition, Pavière stated that 'an important part of the exhibition from the trade point of view is the collection of designs which illustrate how some of the most beautiful materials of the early days were embellished … Some day the story of the whole range of the industrial art of the nineteenth century will have to be written' (Anon 1943b). Pavière had the foresight to realise that, in the future, collections and exhibitions of costume and textiles would be taken seriously by the public and by academics. The importance attached to this 1943 exhibition by Pavière (indicated by the large photographs in the local newspaper, the reception for council dignitaries and the use of the large galleries), demonstrates that his interest in decorative art was not limited to an appreciation of style, but was linked to the Victorian idea of the importance of the decorative arts to manufacturing. This view is supported by his attempt, ultimately unsuccessfully, to secure the post-war touring exhibition *Britain Can Make It* for the Harris.[5] Pavière was also attempting to increase the profile of the decorative arts in a museum hitherto given to focusing on fine art and natural history.

However, Pavière did not restrict himself to collecting only textiles that were directly related to Preston's industrial past. He was interested in a wide range of material culture of the Victorian era, saying, 'Preston's prosperity rested at one time upon the cotton industry. Let us have a collection representative of those great years' (Anon 1943a). The comprehensive dress collection that he formed is probably his greatest achievement in representing the Victorian era through the decorative arts, particularly as the value of dress collections in museums has undergone a reassessment since Pavière's day (Taylor 1998). Pavière began collecting examples of Victorian clothing in the 1930s, but met with resistance. In a letter to *The Times* Pavière wrote of the difficulties of building this type of collection: 'Our efforts have met with little success owing to the wholesale and wanton destruction in the past of valuable specimens, the apathy of some manufacturers, and the avarice of many private owners who would neither give nor sell at a reasonable price' (Pavière 1955). And there was still conflict 25 years later when Pavière wrote in a letter to *The Times* that 'many of our more intelligent and educated visitors most strongly object to our collecting costumes … and consider it a waste of space' (ibid). Nevertheless, in a letter written in 1941 to the distinguished scholar Dr Joan Evans, Pavière describes how popular the costume displays are

5 Pavière's request for the exhibition, written to S C Leslie, the director of the Council of Industrial Design in 1947, is in the Harris Museum and Art Gallery archives.

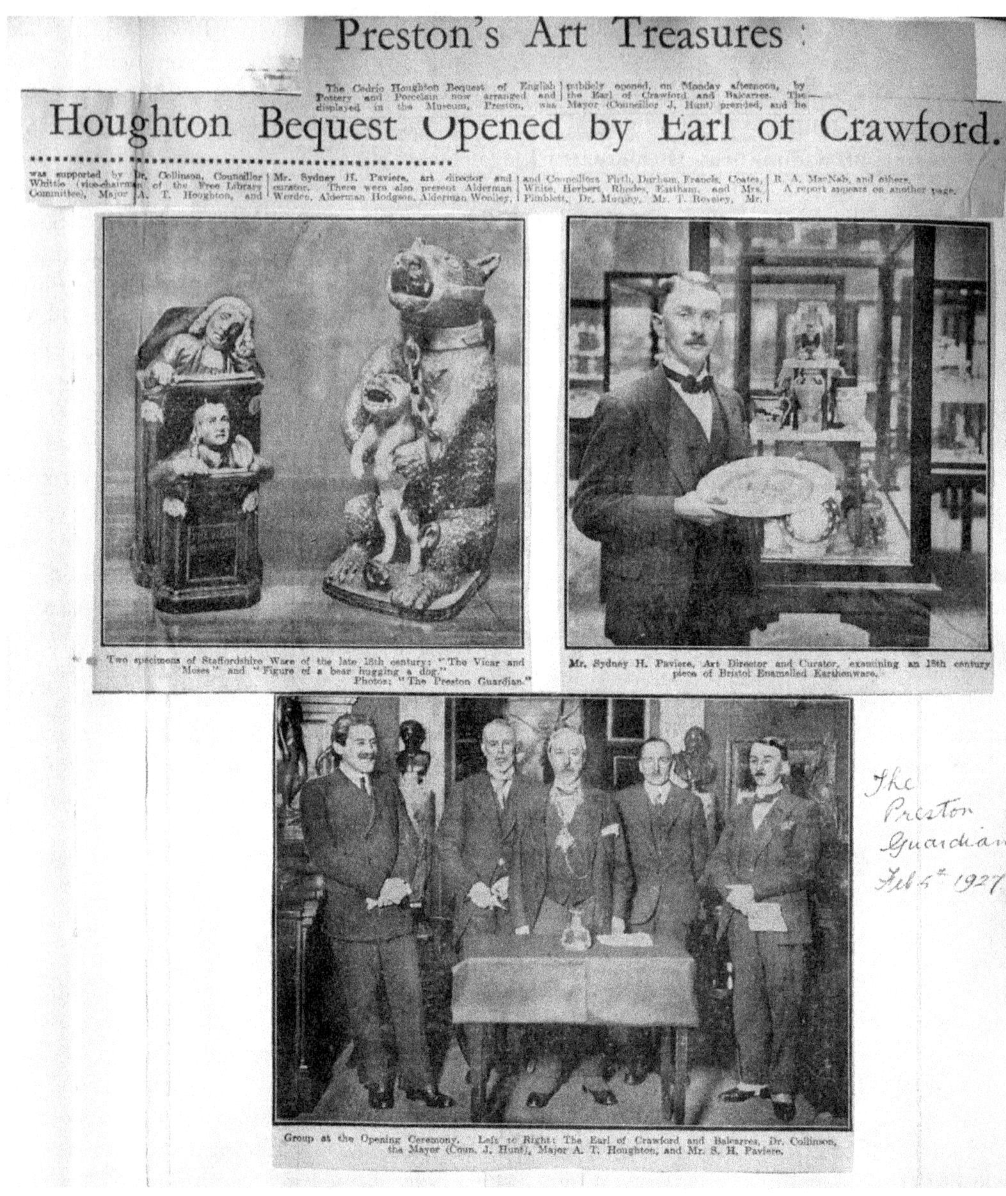

Preston's Art Treasures:

Houghton Bequest Opened by Earl of Crawford.

The Cedric Houghton Bequest of English Pottery and Porcelain now arranged and displayed in the Museum, Preston, was publicly opened, on Monday afternoon, by the Earl of Crawford and Balcarres. The Mayor (Councillor J. Hunt) presided, and he was supported by Dr. Collinson, Councillor Whittle (vice-chairman of the Free Library Committee), Major A. T. Houghton, and Mr. Sydney H. Paviere, art director and curator. There were also present Alderman Werden, Alderman Hodgson, Alderman Woolley, and Councillors Firth, Durham, Francis, Coates, White, Herbert, Rhodes, Eastham, and Mrs. Pimblett, Dr. Murphy, Mr. T. Reveley, Mr. R. A. MacNab, and others.

A report appears on another page.

Two specimens of Staffordshire Ware of the late 18th century: "The Vicar and Moses" and "Figure of a bear hugging a dog."

Photos: "The Preston Guardian."

Mr. Sydney H. Paviere, Art Director and Curator, examining an 18th century piece of Bristol Enamelled Earthenware.

Group at the Opening Ceremony. Left to Right: The Earl of Crawford and Balcarres, Dr. Collinson, the Mayor (Coun. J. Hunt), Major A. T. Houghton, and Mr. S. H. Paviere.

The Preston Guardian Feb 5th 1927

FIG 3.3.
NEWSPAPER CUTTING: SYDNEY PAVIÈRE AND THE HOUGHTON BEQUEST, 1927

with most visitors. Much of Pavière's collecting for the costume and textiles collection, which laid a strong foundation for the development of the collection after his retirement in 1959, took place during the war years and into the 1950s when there were superb opportunities for collecting decorative art for public museums as the prices for many types of objects were depressed and many country house sales were taking place.

The dress historian Lou Taylor claims that it was not until the 1950s that attitudes towards the display of costume began to change, and that this was because professional female curators began to be appointed (Taylor 1998, 342). Yet Pavière was actively collecting fashionable dress two decades before. His approach to collecting and displaying dress shows that he fully understood how museums could contribute to public attitudes to art. While his fine art purchases received more attention, Pavière's more interesting curatorial work can be found in the decorative art collection. The lack of attention previously paid to collecting the decorative arts at the Harris meant that when Pavière joined, he started with what was virtually a blank canvas. He could develop interesting collecting areas and so shape the collection according to his own partiality. Because of this the decorative art collection that he built demonstrates richness and individuality. What Pavière created at the Harris was an appealing and relevant collection that was responsive to the idea that the visitor's interests might range further than oil paintings.

Pavière used the fine art collection to build the prestige of the Harris, but a bequest made to the museum 16 years before he arrived gave him the opportunity to do something similar using ceramics. Early in 1927, only a year after his appointment and the same year that *Nude* was purchased, Pavière brought the Cedric Houghton collection of pottery and porcelain out of the stores and put it on public display. The collection had been languishing out of sight since 1910, but Pavière was quick to recognise its potential importance to the museum. A former workroom was converted into a ceramics gallery and the Earl of Crawford opened the new displays in January 1927. The Earl was an art historian and politician; he had been chancellor of Manchester University and a trustee of the National Gallery and the British Museum, so it was of some import that the museum had attracted such an eminent figure to open the new displays (Fig 3.3). Pavière made a success of bringing a hidden collection into public view in a manner that reflected well on the museum. In turn, he also brought prestige and value to the Houghton collection by making a new space available for its display and having a figure prominent in the world of museums and galleries give the new displays his seal of approval.

As a curator committed to using the collection to build a reputation for quality for the museum, as well as shifting how the Harris was perceived as an institution, Pavière addressed himself simultaneously to two different audiences. He was speaking both to the educated aficionado who had perhaps travelled from Manchester or the surrounding areas to visit the collections, and at the same time to the local population, the majority of whom would have been involved in the cotton trade and worked at the Preston-based Horrockses mill. While the new ceramics gallery appealed to a distinctly connoisseurial audience, Pavière would eventually come to balance this with his collections of costume and his purchase of sensational paintings. The newspaper photographs of servicemen and their girlfriends crowding round the newly delivered portrait of *Pauline in the Yellow Dress* in 1944 is a distinct contrast to the photograph of local dignitaries at the opening of the ceramics gallery, with its genteel atmosphere. In fact, press coverage was vital for Pavière to communicate with both of the publics that he wished to engage. National coverage helped his ambitious aim to position the Harris as having the best decorative art collection in the UK after the V&A.

Meanwhile, local press coverage encouraged local people through the doors. The Harris had never been an exclusive space and the audience for the museum and art gallery had always been broadened by the presence of the Free Library on the ground floor of the building. In the mid-19th century, when Preston's museum was located on Cross Street, the town experienced a succession of traumatic events, beginning with the cotton depression and the shooting of five strikers in Lune Street.[6] With these events came social unrest, culminating in the great lockout, when a third of the population of the town were made idle because workers were demanding pay increases and, as a result, were locked out of the mills by the masters (King 1981, 26–31; Lewis 2001). The great lockout received international attention. Only 30 years later the foundation stone for the Harris building was laid. For James Hibbert, the Harris' architect and a local alderman, an art gallery's primary role was education and improvement. This suggests that the building and collections within were not conceived for the enjoyment of dilettante but for the sometimes-restive people of Preston. Pavière continued in this tradition of education and improvement, attested by the numerous lectures and tours he gave of the museum. James Moore argues that despite its public function and importance to all the people of Preston, the Harris was not built as a collective endeavour, but an expression of one man, Hibbert's, classical cultural and political outlook (Moore 2003). Pavière, as the sole curator, continued in this tradition to a degree. He was an active agent for change, making decisions about collecting and areas and accepting gifts. Yet whether he wanted to or not, he could not achieve autocracy. This was because in order to make purchases he had to convince members of the Free Library Committee, who held the purse strings, to endorse his acquisitions. But endorse they did, and acquisitions such as *Nude* and *Pauline in the Yellow Dress* gave the Harris a profile outside Preston and helped to build Pavière's reputation as an effective and successful curator.

Pavière's place at the heart of the museum, with the opportunity and the imagination to form new collections, reflected the new wave of museum curators who were moving gradually further away from the incomplete state of professionalisation identified by Teather as existing in the late 19th- and early 20th-century museum profession (Teather 1990, 26). Pavière's engagement with the notion of increased professionalisation is demonstrated by his attendance at Museums Association conferences and his election as secretary-treasurer at the first annual conference of the Federation of Lancashire and Cheshire Museums (Anon 1929). Though the collections at the Harris continued to be enhanced by generous gifts and bequests, there had been a shift in power, from wealthy local art collectors such as Newsham leaving their personal collections to galleries to curators such as Pavière following their own curatorial agendas (MacLeod 2007, 85). The strength of Pavière's influence and his ability to drive the Harris in the direction he felt it should go can be attributed not only to his status as art director, but to the confidence he inspired in his good judgement in relation to collecting art. Pavière was clearly a compelling and self-assured individual who brought confidence and even swagger to what had been, when he took up the post in 1926, a neglected provincial museum. And such was his success in transforming

6 The memorial statue that was erected in 1992 to mark the 150th anniversary of the Lune Street protest is inscribed with a description of the circumstances that led to the violence: 'In the 1840s there was a national depression and poverty was widespread in Preston. The mill owners reduced wages by 10 per cent. On 13 August 1842 a large group of cotton workers marched through the town centre in protest. In Lune Street they were met by armed soldiers who attempted to break up the crowd. The soldiers opened fire killing five men.'

the museum that by 1939 he was able to say of the Harris, 'what is not good enough for London is not good enough for us' (Pavière 1939).

Considering Pavière's actions as curator at the Harris Museum and Art Gallery, examining in detail an example of the professional practice of an individual curator is to begin to map the professional history of the museum and consider the importance of the individual to such a history. Pavière was able to act with individual agency, and so his imprint on the museum and collections remains strong. He influenced the direction of collecting at the Harris, shaped the view of the decorative arts being communicated to museum visitors and established strong identities for the collections at the Harris. Pavière was a strong leader who had a well-defined vision for the museum and the collections. In his new post he immediately began to re-imagine and redisplay neglected objects and direct the development of new collecting areas. Although trained as an artist, he was highly engaged with his profession as curator and worked consistently to encourage all the people of Preston into the museum. Pavière's 33-year tenure at the Harris Museum and Art Gallery must be considered as curatorially the most significant period in the museum's history, occurring as it did at a time when power was shifting away from council museum committees towards increasingly professionalised museum staff. Pavière strove to foster an impression of his time at the Harris as a period of renaissance after a dark age of plaster replicas and displays of faded butterflies. Yet at this time other curators were experiencing the same transitions of power but remain anonymous, and for this reason we should not fail to account for the significance of Pavière's intention to write his own history. His career at the Harris is neatly bookended by two newspapers articles that reinforce this view of a man very careful of his public image. Both the first, 'A Pen and Ink Sketch' in *The Herald* describing Pavière's professional career to date, and the last, his interview with *Lancashire Life* in 1959, demonstrate an inclination to self-mythologise. *The Herald*, introducing the appointed curator, reported, 'Mr Pavière, who is of Hugenot descent, comes from an artistic family. His great-uncle was the first Curator of the University Galleries at Oxford … he is a gentleman highly qualified to direct the town in art matters … Mr Pavière is modest but he knows that he is a connoisseur in art' (Anon c. 1928). This article, whose detailed and favourable appraisal of Pavière's career in the art world must have come from Pavière himself, reveals one method Pavière used in his endeavour to position himself as an authority on art in the early years of his employment at the gallery.

So why was this period, from the 1920s until the 1960s, so significant for an individual curator such as Pavière? Perhaps because it was a time when the individual agency of the curator was increasing partly as a result of the continuing move towards professionalisation and the resulting ability to claim authority, combined with an erosion of power of the council-run museum committees. For Pavière, it would seem that the ability to act with individual agency was to some extent a result of his ability to claim a level of professional status not accorded to Barton, the previous curator, but also as a result of his personal confidence. But there is a problem in the use of individual biography in constructing museum history, which is demonstrated by Pavière's example. It was Pavière who started a comprehensive and maintained press cuttings archive at the Harris, material which has been extensively quoted here; he often spoke to the press and published his viewers in letters to *The Times* and as a result our impression of him, received through these sources, is lasting and distinct. His work as a self-publicist as well as a curator has contributed to the development of the myth of the individual that left little or no room for the acknowledgment of the contribution of other museum staff, most notably his assistant and successor Helena Gibbon. In 1928, a local newspaper wrote of Pavière 'In the short period he has been with us, art has had a very practical and remarkable renaissance in Preston … It is all due to him, and I might add, ourselves – the Press' (Anon c. 1928). Although Pavière may have used the press to augment his own reputation alongside that of the museum, the fundamental role that he as an individual had in the development of the Harris between 1926 and 1959 must nevertheless be acknowledged.

## Bibliography and References


Anon, 1893 A New Library and Museum at Preston, *The Times*, 27 October, 4

Anon, 1894 *Manchester Guardian*, 3 July [newspaper cutting], Harris Museum and Art Gallery Archives

Anon, 1927a *Lancashire Daily Post*, August [newspaper cutting], Harris Museum and Art Gallery Archives

Anon, 1927b Object to Purchase for Public Gallery, *Manchester Guardian*, 28 May [newspaper cutting], Harris Museum and Art Gallery Archives

Anon, c. 1928 Pen and Ink Sketch/ Mr Sydney H Pavière, Art Curator, *The Herald* [undated newspaper cutting, c. 1928], Harris Museum and Art Gallery Archives

Anon, 1929 *Manchester Guardian*, 31 July [newspaper cutting], Harris Museum and Art Gallery Archives

Anon, 1930 Banned Prints for an Exhibition, Preston Art Curator's Comment, *Manchester Guardian*, 3 February, 10 [newspaper cutting], Harris Museum and Art Gallery Archives

Anon, 1943a *Preston Herald*, 17 December [newspaper cutting], Harris Museum and Art Gallery Archives

Anon, 1943b *Preston Guardian*, 18 December [newspaper cutting], Harris Museum and Art Gallery Archives

Anon, 1959 *Manchester Guardian*, 28 May [newspaper cutting], Harris Museum and Art Gallery Archives

Anon, 1971 *Lancashire Evening Post*, 12 January [newspaper cutting], Harris Museum and Art Gallery Archives

Draper, A, 2009 Thinking Big: Collecting at the Harris Museum & Art Gallery and the Role of the Contemporary Art Society, in *At The Edge: British Art 1950–2000* (eds S Whittle and D Winch), Gallery Oldham, Oldham, 32–8

Fraser, J, and Paul, L, 1998 Art, Industry and Everyday Things: Manchester City Art Gallery and Industrial Art between the Wars, *Journal of the Decorative Arts Society* 22, 42–57

Hull County Council, 2008 *Purchasing for the People!* [online], available from: http://www.hullcc.gov.uk/museumcollections/collections/ [12 October 2010]

King, J E, 1981 *Richard Marsden and the Preston Chartists 1837–1848*, Lancaster, Centre for North-West Regional Studies, University of Lancaster

Lewis, B, 2001 *The Middlemost and the Milltowns: Bourgeois Culture and Politics in Early Industrial England*, Stanford University Press, California

MacLeod, S, 2007 Occupying the Architecture of the Gallery: spatial, social and professional change at the Walker Art Gallery, Liverpool, 1877–1933, in *Museum Revolutions: museums and change* (eds S Knell, S MacLeod, and S Watson), Routledge, London, 72–86

Moore, J, 2003 Periclean Preston: Public Art and the Classical Tradition in Late-Nineteenth-Century Lancashire, *Northern History* 40, 229–323

Noordegraaf, J, 2004 *Strategies of Display: museum presentation in nineteenth- and twentieth-century visual culture*, NAi Publishers, Rotterdam

Pavière, S, 1924 Art and the Nation, *The Times*, 9 July, 10

— 1939 Letter to the Editor, *The Times*, 13 April [newspaper cutting], Harris Museum and Art Gallery Archives

— 1941 Letter to Dr Joan Evans, 27 September, Harris Museum and Art Gallery Archives

— 1947 Letter to S C Leslie, director of the Council of Industrial Design, 10 January, Harris Museum and Art Gallery Archives

— 1949 Masterpieces in our Public Galleries: The Harris Art Gallery, Preston, *Art Bulletin* 29, Summer, 3

— 1955 Historic Textiles, *The Times*, 6 December, 9

Rushton, J, 1959 He Rebuilt an Art Gallery, *Lancashire Life*, June, 32

Snape, R, 2010 Objects of Utility: cultural responses to industrial collections in municipal museums 1845–1914, *Museum and Society* 8 (1), 18–36

Teather, J, 1990 The Museum Keepers: The Museums Association and the Growth of Museum Professionalism, *Museum Management and Curatorship* 9 (1), 25–41

Taylor, L, 1998 *Establishing Dress History*, Manchester University Press, Manchester

# Problematising Individuals' Biographies

# 4

# 'His Best Successor': Lady Eastlake and the National Gallery

JULIE SHELDON

In 1875, Lady Eastlake, the widow of the first Director of the National Gallery, confided to a cousin that she believed herself to have been the best person to have succeeded her husband in the management of the Gallery:

> I had such an exceptional education in connoisseurship at my beloved One's side – & there is scarcely a creature with whom I can share it. I feel that *I* shld have been his best successor in the direction of the Nat: Gallery. Boxall was unimpugnable, but hated the employmt, the present man is totally unfit for it, & has introduced most inferior things. Without vanity I know I shd have been the right person, tho' the world wd be astonished at such an idea.
>
> (Sheldon 2009a, 407)

Those connected to the National Gallery in the years following Sir Charles Eastlake's death would not perhaps be astonished by the idea. The widowed Lady Eastlake, having spent ten years as the loyal and companionable helpmeet of the first Director, became a relentless campaigner in the preservation of her husband's legacy. 'His best successor' continued to offer intercessory – and not always welcome – advice to Eastlake's official successors, including what to purchase and whom to appoint, and earning herself a reputation for interference.[1] Institutional biographies are often enriched by their association with colourful characters and Lady Eastlake has been a persistent and vivid presence in histories of the National Gallery.

A number of well-placed commentators have observed that Charles Eastlake's career benefited from his wife's knowledge and expertise. Historians of the National Gallery have treated Lady Eastlake kindly, arguing that Eastlake's successful tenure as Director was very much the result of their partnership. Charles Holmes and C H Collins Baker, in their 1924 history, credit the difference between the 'gentle and studious' Eastlake who had resigned as Keeper in 1847 and the 'masterly' Eastlake who took on the Directorship in 1855 entirely to his wife: 'The single external cause to which we can assign a share in this development was Eastlake's marriage. Lady Eastlake was one of the most remarkable women of her time … and the extraordinary improvement in the quality of Eastlake's purchases can hardly fail to have been assisted by her companionship' (Holmes and Collins Baker 1924, 32–3). In 1950 John Steegman wrote: '"Eastlake" really means

1 I recall the first occasion, around ten years ago, that I saw Lady Eastlake's letters to Boxall in the Archive; among several annotations penciled in the catalogue I read the remark 'advise [sic] almost to interfering point'.

"them", a perfect and wonderfully fruitful partnership' or 'rather a joint personality' (Steegman 1966, 364). In 1967 Winslow Ames jointly credited the couple with the fortunate purchases at the National Gallery: 'he and his wife, with their remarkable *expertise*, mobility, and knowledge of private sources, worked as one to build up what was already an important gallery' (Ames 1967, 126). In 1985 Denys Sutton described Elizabeth as making a 'major contribution to Eastlake's assured position in the London art world' (Sutton 1985, 92). In 1992 Adele Ernstrom wrote on the working and married lives of the Eastlakes, arguing cogently in favour of 'their professional as well as personal solidarity' (Ernstrom 1992, 482). Recent publications on the Gallery's history continue to incorporate Lady Eastlake into their narratives: Jonathan Conlin's history of 'the nation's mantelpiece' points out that her knowledge of the history of art was 'at least as great as her husband' (Conlin 2006, 280); Charles Saumarez Smith's history of the Gallery notes Lady Eastlake as 'a formidable scholar', quoting her correspondence to give colour to the otherwise routine details of Eastlake's picture transactions in Italy (Saumarez Smith 2009, 69); and Alan Crookham's illustrated history of the Gallery arranges photographs of Lady Eastlake by the side of her husband's, but underneath a picture of Ralph Nicholas Wornum, to form an uneasy trinity of Director, Keeper and Director's Wife (Crookham 2009, 32).

In contravention of the normal revisionist impulses of women's history, my task is to reassess the generous received view of Lady Eastlake's importance at the National Gallery during her husband's tenure and examine her privileged place in the biography of the institution. I do this in two ways. I consider how Lady Eastlake has come to occupy such an insistent position in the gallery's history. For example, her husband was President of the Royal Academy for longer than he was Director at the National Gallery and yet, until the recent publication of James Fenton's *School of Genius*, she has barely featured in histories of the Royal Academy. Second, I test the assertions of successive writers on the history of the National Gallery that Lady Eastlake exerted a considerable leverage over her husband's professional activities. What follows attempts to disentangle the documentary evidence from institutional persiflage in order to examine the extent of her putative influence over Eastlake and the National Gallery.

First I want to consider why Lady Eastlake has come to be a consistent and, sometimes, looming presence in histories of the National Gallery, frequently represented as the agent of Eastlake's transformation from the 'gentle and studious' or 'vacillating' Keeper into a competent and confident Director – 'masterly' in the view of Holmes and Baker or 'assured' in Sutton's estimation. As the bachelor Keeper of the National Gallery between 1843 and 1847, Eastlake had seemed to lurch from one crisis to the next, with his failures more prominent in the press than his many successes. First, there was the purchase in 1845 of a 'bad' Holbein, then the purchase of old masters perceived to be at inflated prices, followed by the controversial cleaning of paintings in 1846. Each generated a hostile press, most virulently in the pages of *The Times* and in a series of pamphlets, where the connoisseur John Morris Moore combined his censure of each controversy, taunting Eastlake over the 'bad Holbein', accusing him of 'flunkeyism' and of being 'a silly vacillating dupe', writing 'I have long considered him *utterly incompetent to fill any public office*' (Verax 1847, 29, 87). In spite of the support of Sir Robert Peel and the Trustees, Eastlake resigned as Keeper in November 1847. Three years later, when Eastlake was elected President of the Royal Academy, he resumed his association with the National Gallery as a Trustee and became an expert witness to the Government Select Committee of 1853 that reviewed the provisions and operations of the Gallery. On 2 July 1855, Eastlake became the first Director of the National Gallery. The Treasury's appointment of a competent administrator and managerial peace-keeper was not unanimously supported but Eastlake proved his worth over the ten years of his directorship in the purchase of some of the finest acquisitions in the Gallery's history.

Did, as several commentators want to imagine, Lady Eastlake influence Eastlake in his deliberations over the eligibility of purchases for the National Gallery? Certainly Holmes and Baker suggest that her 'companionship' improved the quality of Eastlake's purchases and Winslow Ames also suggests that her expertise was a contributing factor in the acquisition policy of the period. An online Dictionary of Art Historians supposes that Lady Eastlake was 'involved with purchase decisions for the Gallery'. John Steegman, in reviewing Eastlake's career on the centenary of his death, remarked: 'She [Lady Eastlake] had as good a nose for a bargain as he had, though without his meticulous connoisseurship; and she was quite as skilful as he at dealing with impoverished Italian noblemen who might consider selling some of the family works of art' (Steegman 1966, 364). This view of Lady Eastlake as a coadjutor seems to stem, in part, from a misreading of the posthumously published *Journals and Correspondence of Lady Eastlake*, two volumes of letters and a portion of an early journal judiciously edited by her nephew. For example, Steegman probably developed his view of Lady Eastlake's 'nose for bargains' from reading here:

> Our wonder is that the dealers do not come and carry off these treasures, which might command any prices in England, where old masters are now so much sought for. Dealers could make a fortune out of the pictures which we saw, but they are too ignorant, and also can't speak the language … (Smith 1895, vol 2, 20)

The Eastlakes' combined wonder at the lack of interest in 'treasures' suggests shared experiences and a regular exchange of views. The use of the first-person plural pronoun 'we' in the *Journals and Correspondence of Lady Eastlake* would lead readers to think that she co-experienced all of her husband's activities. Rather exceptionally, she did share in a number of Eastlake's professional experiences. In March 1850, she and Eastlake met with Robert Peel in advance of a Parliamentary debate, writing: 'These National Gallery and picture-cleaning questions are to be mooted in the House, and Sir Robert promises his clear voice and able elucidation in our favour' (Smith 1895, vol 1, 243). Lady Eastlake was with her husband when he was offered the directorship, first informally by the Prime Minister, Lord Aberdeen, in the summer of 1854 and again at Downing Street in 1855 when she recorded the prevarications of the appointment (Smith 1895, vol 2, 3233). It may be unusual for a wife to directly witness her husband's professional appointments in the period; however, it is in her accounts of their travels that she, perhaps innocently, plants the idea of her auxiliary importance into the posthumous document, the *Journals and Correspondence of Lady Eastlake*. In 1855 she went on her first visit to Florence with the newly-appointed Director, writing: 'I am fairly bitten with all the true pre-Raphaelites … and I shall be truly proud if we succeed both in rescuing some examples, and introducing them into England, where already there are a chosen few who adore them' (Smith 1895, vol 2, 76). In her consistent use of the plural pronoun 'we' (rather than the magisterial we) as a means of dispatching their joint views, Lady Eastlake appears to have a co-agency in the selection of works for purchase by the nation.

In his formulation of a 'joint personality', Steegman's view, like those of other historians of the Gallery, was informed by the *Journals and Correspondence of Lady Eastlake*. Since Eastlake left no corresponding record of his thoughts and ideas, Lady Eastlake's often strident and colourful accounts of their excursions in Italy may well have led historians to imagine Lady Eastlake's strong and assertive personality periodically galvanising her prevaricating husband into action. However, the *Journals and Correspondence of Lady Eastlake* is an uneven documentary source. Lady Eastlake had ceased to keep a journal in 1848, so the majority of the *Journals and Correspondence* does not hold, as so often is erroneously supposed, the status of a diary. The reportage from the 1850s and 1860s representing her years beside her husband is in fact edited from letters to Lady Eastlake's mother. The Eastlakes' reported joint adjudication on aesthetic matters is therefore not a matter of public record but rather a consequence of a family postcard. Charles Eastlake's concurrent version of their travels, a set of travel notebooks documenting his encounters with art works on the continent, fails to endorse his wife's version; the only time he ever mentions Lady Eastlake is in reference to the drawings that she was independently making, as I shall discuss below, as an *aide-mémoire* for his own research.

The presumption of Lady Eastlake's adjutancy is not simply the result of a post hoc reading of the *Journals and Correspondence of Lady Eastlake*, since the contemporary view of Lady Eastlake as an auxiliary is startlingly illustrated in 1853 when she accompanied her husband to Oxford so that he might be conferred with the degree of DCL. The University's Public Orator described Eastlake as an artist of rare gifts and virtues and, he added, as fortunate in his 'conjugem clarissimam', most distinguished spouse. In the citation the orator noted 'he has a most distinguished wife as the partner in his fame and his work, who is herself as distinguished in letters as he is in art'. According to Lady Eastlake her husband 'liked it', but she objected 'to people's fancying that he has not fully sufficient merits on his own account, without dragging me in' (Smith 1895, vol 1, 308–12). In considering Eastlake's concurrent Presidency of the Royal Academy, there is some evidence that his contemporaries suspected the machinations of a 'conjugem clarissimam'. Isobel Violet Hunt's account of Mrs Rossetti imputed the President and his wife with undermining Pre-Raphaelitism: 'Disliking the morbidity inherent in mediaevalism, the Professor [Ruskin] fought it and its supposed concomitant, sensuality, in Rossetti, just as Eastlake was fighting it in the Royal Academy, while his wife did the same in the Press' (Hunt 1932, 107). This statement is untrue. Lady Eastlake never wrote about the Pre-Raphaelites in the press. She did, however, and ironically in the context of Isobel Hunt's suspicions, anonymously review Ruskin's *Modern Painters for the Quarterly* in 1856. Her article was as much an attack on Ruskin – by this time an implacable enemy to both Eastlakes – as it was on *Modern Painters* and, although it was widely known to be by Lady Eastlake, some thought it was collaboratively produced. For instance, Henry Crabb Robinson enjoyed reading it but concluded that it was written by both Eastlakes: 'for it has all the vituperation which distinguishes the lady's writing and enough of the theory to give the President credit for having written it' (Morley 1938, vol 2, 759).[2]

Such expressions of doubt about Eastlake's independent merits suggest that it is Eastlake's biography that is in some sense lacking. Is he such a vapid presence in his own history that his wife has to assume enough personality for the both of them? If one examines the collective chatter of memoirs, reminiscences, letters and diaries from the period, then a monochrome picture of Eastlake emerges, sketched in recurring grisailles phrases such as 'insipid', 'uninspired',

2 Ruskin certainly came to know that Lady Eastlake had written the article, evidenced by a letter to Pauline Trevelyan in 1861: 'The National Gallery people are fraternizing at last … Overtures – through Mr Wornum, even from Sir C E – declaring Lady Eastlake never wrote the Quarterly Review. I behave in as conciliatory a way as I can. It don't do anybody good to quarrel – and if Sir C wants me in future to look at him as an opaque instead of a transparent body – I will, only I won't say he can paint' (Trevelyan 1978, 129).

'methodical', 'studious', and 'guarded'. Students at the Royal Academy remembered 'only his grave, courtly manner and pale melancholy face' (Marks 1894, vol 1, 236–7). *The Encylopaedia Britannica* recorded his 'unassuming and rather courtier-like bearing; [being] reluctant to oppose or offend, but with a strong sense of official duty' (Encyclopedia Britannica 1877). Otto Mündler, the agent employed by Eastlake to scout for pictures on the continent and one of his closest allies, recalled that 'at first sight there was something dry and monotonous about him, and he was therefore reputed to be unfriendly and curt by those who knew him only from a fleeting meeting' (Mündler 1869, 99ff). By comparison his wife is an animated presence in corresponding literature – intellectually self-assured and not afraid to oppose or to offend. Eastlake's obituary, written by Lady Eastlake's cousin Francis Turner Palgrave, ventured the opinion that Lady Eastlake had compensated for some of her husband's social deficiencies and helped him overcome his reluctance to 'express an unqualified opinion' (Palgrave 1866, 63). Eastlake's reputation for prevarication counterbalanced by his wife's more self-confident nature may well be the consequence of Palgrave's first-hand experience of the couple, but popular notions of their uxorious coupling seem to have stemmed from a physical disparity between Sir Charles and Lady Eastlake that lent credence to the idea that she was the dominant partner. Madame Belloc remembered that 'she was an unusually tall, fine-looking woman, and her distinguished husband … looked extremely small and frail by her side' (Belloc 1897, 11). Several irresistibly comic sketches of the Eastlakes survived their union so that, years later, in 1886 Beatrix Potter reported the gossip that Lady Eastlake 'used to be able to lift up her husband under her arm' (Potter 1966, 55).

Popular views of the dynamics of the Eastlake marriage aside, the prominence of Lady Eastlake in Eastlake's professional life, or indeed lives, may be more securely attributed to the unusually sociable aspects of his career. The institutions that Eastlake governed were in turn governed by the London season. The Royal Academy annual exhibitions were held from the first Monday in May, which incidentally marked the opening of the London season, to the first Monday in August. The presence of a wife to host dinners for Academicians and attend soirees was apparently a successful arrangement under Eastlake's presidency. Every summer the pair was 'dissipated' by the exhibitions season and every August the Eastlakes commenced their excursion in Europe, just before the National Gallery closed for six weeks from the middle of September to the end of October. Eastlake went on all his foreign trips with his wife, except in 1853 and 1856, a situation which was apparently of great mutual satisfaction (Sheldon 2009a, 178). Given that Eastlake's post was unprecedented and that his immediate successors as Director – William Boxall and Frederick Burton – were both bachelors, it is impossible to say whether or not the arrangement was irregular.

In the documentation representing the circumstances of Eastlake's transactions and activities as Director there are disappointingly few instances of Lady Eastlake's arbitration. The contents of the National Gallery Archive fail to corroborate the view that Lady Eastlake wielded any significant influence at the Gallery and there are only instances of Lady Eastlake writing letters for the Gallery to Eastlake's dictation. The picture that has presented itself to me in the editing of her letters, distributed among many archives, is one where the practicalities of their partnership were devolved along private and professional lines. Lady Eastlake writes many letters on behalf of Eastlake – sending replies to dinner invitations, allocating tickets, and writing letters of introduction to private art collections. She also communicated her husband's wishes to friends, such as Layard, whom she instructed on Eastlake's behalf. For example, in a letter to Layard she told him that 'Sir Chas wishes you very much to examine these same noble heads (tho' not all of equal attraction) & then to do as we did & visit all the other specimens of Melozzi in Rome, as follows – in a chapel of the SS Apostoli at Rome' (Sheldon 2009a, 186).

In addition to communicating her husband's instructions, Lady Eastlake also appears to have acted without his sanction to support his professional reputation. As a public servant, Eastlake's actions were open to scrutiny in the pages of *The Times*. On one occasion, she noted: 'Sir Chas is pretty well, and I try and make him bravely indifferent to the nonsense – malicious and ignorant – which goes, and will infallibly go the round of the papers at the acquisition of every new picture in the N: Gallery' (Sheldon 2009a, 181). She pugnaciously supported her husband's professional reputation in a relentless barrage of letters to individuals who, in her eyes, had misjudged Eastlake. For example, in one letter to Austen Henry Layard, she pulls him up for an article in *The Times* questioning the progress of the decoration of the Houses of Parliament, overseen by Eastlake's Fine Art Commission, owning that she was 'much more likely to be the obstinate adversary' (Sheldon 2009a, 197–9); in a set of letters to John Blackwood she beleaguers the publisher into printing a retraction of a remark in his magazine about Sir Charles' policy of glazing pictures (Sheldon 2009a, 131–5); and she 'venture[d], in [her] own name' to seek Sir William Stirling Maxwell's help in assisting her husband in the Commons following the publication of 'two notices by Mr Coningham directed against Sir Charles in the Times of today' (Sheldon 2009a, 191).

The germane question of partnership, however, is that of her influence over his professional activities. Was Lady Eastlake's influence merely one of providing secretarial support and campaigning for her husband among her acquaintances or can it be traced in the actions of Sir Charles Eastlake as the Director of the National Gallery? Historians of the National Gallery have asserted or hinted that Lady Eastlake exercised some influence over her husband's purchases – what Steegman termed her 'nose for bargains'. Again the letters of Lady Eastlake yield disappointingly few examples of this conjectured influence. There are, however, a couple of intriguing – if inconclusive – instances of Lady Eastlake's possible agency in the acquisition of paintings. In a letter of 6 April 1861, she suggests to Austen Henry Layard that she will accompany Eastlake on his inspection of Piero della Francesca's *Baptism* at the Uzielli sale:

> Sir Chas is anxious that you shd kindly inspect the Uzielli P della Francesca on view at Christies on Monday – with a view to giving him your opinion as to the policy of endeavouring to secure it for the N: G: He is irresolute – considering its injured condition – & the silence of Vasari, & the criticism of Passavant. He will also examine it afresh on Monday but has not empowered me to say whether fore or afternoon. I shall probably accompany him, & what influence I have will probably be executed in favour of trying to obtain it. (Sheldon 2009a, 208)

There are two uses of the word 'probably' in this claim so it is by no means an unequivocal declaration of intent. What it seems to show is that Lady Eastlake was an occasional advocate whenever Eastlake was deliberating the eligibility of a purchase. Recalling in Palgrave's obituary that Eastlake had a reputation for erring on the side of caution, it may be that Lady Eastlake's opinion was solicited. It may of course also be a piece of conjugal swagger on Lady Eastlake's part that animates the banter that passed between the couple for the information of their mutual friend, Layard. In another letter to Layard, dated 19 April 1863, Lady Eastlake remarked: 'am also glad that you see beauty in the odd, idyllic Cosimo Roselli – the dear Procris and Satyr – for which I am always a champion with Sir Charles …' (Sheldon 2009a, 219). Just what her championship meant in this context is uncertain. Does 'with' mean alongside and in accordance with her husband or does 'with' mean that she has petitioned for the painting in the light of Eastlake's vacillation? Either way, her partiality for the painting was redundant in April 1863 since Eastlake had already purchased it.[3]

Eastlake had, at one point in the negotiations for Piero's *Baptism*, considered purchasing the painting for himself; so it might be more plausible to ask if Lady Eastlake was consulted over the purchase of works for Eastlake's own collection. Eastlake was able to buy several fine quattrocento paintings, including work by Botticelli, Bellini, Mantegna and Ghirlandaio. However, there is no instance recorded in the correspondence to suggest that her opinion was sought over works that were to return to their London home in Fitzroy Square. While it is evident that Lady Eastlake shared her husband's taste for early Italian art, it also seems that it was an acquired one. As a young girl, Lady Eastlake may well have been primed in her tastes by her visits to an uncle, the antiquarian Dawson Turner, who had a collection that included early Italian art. She would also have formed a secondary knowledge of early Italian art in British art collections by translating the guides of J D Passavant (1836) and Gustav Waagen (1853); and her translation of Kugler's handbook of Italian art would also have given her an overview of her husband's interests (Eastlake 1851). However, any taste for early Italian art was slow and incrementally formed since, on her first tour of Europe with her husband in 1852, Lady Eastlake reported:

> I feel that the early Italian pictures in the Berlin Gallery have spoilt my eye for the late masters; their forte was expression, every element beautiful as contributing to that, but none claiming attention for itself. I had no idea that the Pre-Raphaelites could have given me such intense pleasure. (Smith 1895, vol 1, 285–6)

Any evidence, then, that her interest in so-called Primitives of either the Italian or Early Netherlandish schools predates her husband's is diminished by this statement: at best, the 1852 tour aroused a dormant interest. Furthermore, she continued to learn much from her husband in relation to the designated 'Schools of Painting' by which the old masters were categorised into historical and geographical groupings. To give one example, Lady Eastlake admitted that her own knowledge of art history increased on the 1854 tour: 'Certainly the appetite for seeing pictures *vient en voyant*, and the knowledge too. The different schools of painters, which clustered in the North of Italy – Milanese, Bergamese, Brescian, Paduan, and Venetian – are now getting disentangled in my mind, and I begin to know their differences and affinities' (Smith 1895, vol 2, 24–5).

Lady Eastlake's tastes, however, were resolutely in favour of the Tuscan school of painters. On one occasion she advised a friend visiting Florence 'to try and fill your heart especially with the grandeur and earnestness of the great four – Sandro Botticelli, Dom Ghirlandajo, Fra Filippo Lippi, and his son Filippino Lippi' (Smith 1895, vol 2, 89). Above the 'great four' she placed Raphael: 'It is always a pleasure to find yourself preferring the best. Raphael I always come back to', and in another she wrote that in Raphael there is 'enough of everything, and something of all' (Smith 1895, vol 1, 150, 191). Lady Eastlake shared her husband's dislike for Michelangelo's art.

3 Eastlake's travel notebook, NG22/31, in National Gallery Archive dates his first offer for the painting to 30 September 1862.

Otto Mündler recalled that Michelangelo was 'repugnant to Eastlake's mild and measured being' (Mündler 1869, 99ff). Given Eastlake's longstanding antipathy towards Michelangelo, his wife's may be a codependent response. In 1858 on their way to Rome, the Eastlakes, with Cavalcaselle, stopped at Michelangelo's villa at Settignano and saw a chalk drawing of a satyr on the staircase, Lady Eastlake recording: 'I don't care for his Etruscan extravagance of muscle and action, and never feel the humanity of his works, still less their divinity' (Smith 1895, vol 2, 105). Arriving at Rome and visiting St Peter's, Lady Eastlake remained unimpressed with Michelangelo:

> it does not look like a church at all, but like a club-house, with balconies and entresols, and every kind of mixed ornament, which the worst upholstery and taste could invent ... Art is at its lowest vulgarity, when the artist can only invent things bigger and odder than those before him ... Nor was the Sistine Chapel sufficient to put us in good humour with him [Michelangelo]. The ceiling has that grandeur which will ever distinguish it, though coarse and ungraceful; but the 'Last Judgement' is a daub.

The visit to the Sistine Chapel was redeemed by lowering their gaze to the frescoes beneath the famous ceiling: to cycles by Perugino, Ghirlandaio and Botticelli. One of the Botticellis 'we pronounced to contain every element of art, grace, action, grandeur, splendid colour, and fine landscape, that constitutes the maturity of art' (Smith 1895, vol 2, 108–9).

The Eastlakes' tastes for paintings clearly converged on their Italian tours, perhaps contributing to views, such as those of Steegman, of their 'joint personality'. However, the mutuality of the Eastlakes' experiences abroad, so insistent in Lady Eastlake's letters, is uncorroborated by Eastlake, whose travel notebooks fail to mention his wife except in reference to her drawings of paintings. Eastlake's notes are often accompanied by small drawings (almost one thousand in all) which serve to record details of the subject, or some aspect of technique, or information relating to provenance.[4] He occasionally and parenthetically refers to sketches made by his wife ('see sketch by E'). Lady Eastlake had been drawing portraits and making topographical views since the 1820s. The new sights in Italy combined with opportunities for seeing new paintings and she wrote to her mother of her determination 'to see everything of interest, to sketch at almost every place, and to take copious notes of pictures' (Smith 1895, vol 1, 280). Before her marriage, Lady Eastlake's habitual sketching had not included copying from paintings. Many women artists were copyists but this seems to have been a more recently-formed habit and she certainly made particular efforts to secure opportunities for copying paintings. In 1855, on a visit to the Certosa of Pavia, she was, she noted, restricted from going into the chapels or into the choir on the grounds of her sex and had to peer at the 'forbidden ground' through the grilles of the lady's corner (Smith 1895, vol 2, 63). On the 1858 tour she was at the Uffizi in Florence and recorded enthusiastically:

> I am so in love with some of the early pictures in the Uffizi, that I could draw there all day long. Still, I have not done much, as these early masters are so correct and elaborate in drawing, that one must try to be the same when imitating them. Nor is the light enough – that is, in copying

4 I am extremely grateful to Susanna Avery-Quash for making her transcriptions of Eastlake's notebooks available to me ahead of their publication in 2011.

> a figure from a large picture, which hangs fully high, and can't be unhung: a small picture they take down and put on an easel for me. (Smith 1895, vol 2, 102)

Eastlake's parenthetical references to his wife's drawings in his notebooks indicate an active dimension to the Eastlake partnership. Was Lady Eastlake assisting her husband by making drawings that he was too busy to supply or was she following an independent commission and the pair simply had overlapping areas of interest?

Lady Eastlake had her own commissions and projects when she went abroad. In the early 1850s she wrote articles for the periodical press on Michelangelo, Christian art, photography, and the Louvre; she translated four volumes of Gustav Waagen's *Treasures of Art in Great Britain* and Kugler's *Handbook of Painting in Italy*.[5] In 1860, Lady Eastlake agreed to complete the late Anna Jameson's unfinished outline for the *History of Our Lord*, reorganising her friend's material into chronological order and preparing 300 drawings of old master paintings for the engravers to illustrate the work. Lady Eastlake was using their tours of Italy as a way of collecting and verifying the material she had inherited. Interestingly, the drawings that Eastlake refers to as his wife's (which included images of the Virgin and Child by Leonardo, Boltraffio and Luini in the Litta Collection, Milan[6]) are not reproduced in her *History of Our Lord*, or indeed in any other publication. More interesting in the context of Lady Eastlake as her husband's 'best successor' is her chronological arrangement of the *History of Our Lord*. This did not have the full approval of Mrs Jameson's family, who viewed it as a marked departure from Anna Jameson's typological plan for the work. The chronological structure was, however, matched by Eastlake's curatorial preferences at the National Gallery, where a nascent sequential arrangement of art history was outlined in the re-hang of 1861. The question of Eastlake's influence on his wife's work requires more examination and the details are beyond the scope of this discussion.[7] However, since chronological displays were relatively new in British exhibitions then, Lady Eastlake's ordering of the *History of Our Lord* appears to have been influenced by her husband. Moreover, Eastlake acted as his wife's research assistant during the project. In 1867 she told Augustus Hare:

> it was beautifully ordered … that my 'History of Our Lord' was finished first [ie before Eastlake's death]: I could not have done it now. My darling was like a boy jumping up and down to find the references I wanted, and, if possible, through the book I learnt to know him better. (Hare 1896–1900, vol 3, 155)

Before her marriage, Lady Eastlake's writing consisted in translating texts or in reviewing published material, and by instinct and fashion she had tended to write discursively. Accompanying Eastlake, Lady Eastlake learned how to assign artists to their proper school, how to assign a work to a particular master and, most importantly, she learned the basics of European connoisseurship that would be independently exercised after Eastlake's death.

5 During her marriage, Lady Eastlake's publications included, in addition to Eastlake 1851, translations of the work of Gustav Waagen in 1853 and 1857. She wrote articles on physiognomy, photography, the late Prince Consort, and the Louvre galleries, among others.

6 Re: Beltraffio, see NG22.8.13r, NG22.26.2r; re: Leonardo, see NG22.8.13r; re: Luini, see NG22.14.12v.

7 The suggestion is explored in Avery-Quash and Sheldon 2011.

Some of the journeys that Eastlake undertook were off the beaten track and he gallantly thought to spare his strapping younger wife the arduous coach journeys to which he subjected his own spare and sickly body. Frequently Lady Eastlake was left to socialise with expatriates or sketch topographical views chaperoned by the redoubtable Tucker – Eastlake's manservant. For example, in 1858 she was left alone in Dresden:

> I have had many things to see for Sir Chas in his absence & it is very delightful to have time also to mature one's impressions of certain masters. I have many new loves among the painters, & fortunately in the art world it is not necessary to be off with the old before you are on with the new. I have all Vasari too with me, & pore over him of evengs … (Sheldon 2009a, 184)

Her evidently new reading of Vasari is perhaps a consequence of her improved Italian language skills (Vasari had not yet been translated into English) and possibly a task she had elected in connection to her husband's work. The phrase 'I have many things to see for Sir Chas' is another intriguing, if imprecise, suggestion. Did Eastlake leave his wife to 'see things' in his absence as a proxy and, if so, what kinds of information was she tasked with obtaining? At home in London in 1861 she somewhat mischievously boasted that she had a role to play in adding her thoughts to those of her husband:

> Sir Chas took cold abroad, where it was colder than here, but is quite well now, rather overwhelmed with business, with Christie's rooms perpetually full of pictures of some sort. I am now going to look at a few there, & give him my ideas! (Sheldon 2009a, 210)

In the same way that remarks in letters to Layard are rather playful in their expression of her active opinions, the use of the exclamation mark here renders her suggestion an arch one and implies that Eastlake may not always welcome her ideas or that it is a presumption on her part to offer them in the first place.

If Lady Eastlake's ideas and opinions were ever deployed on behalf of the National Gallery, then they ceased to be of service when Eastlake died in 1865. Her husband's successor, William Boxall, was appointed on 9 February 1866 and Layard became a Trustee of the Gallery on 13 February. With the appointment of Eastlake's two close friends into key positions at the Gallery, Lady Eastlake looked forward to a continuance of her husband's vision, writing to Layard as soon as she received the intelligence:

> This is the first sense of pleasure I have known for long. How thankful I am to you for it! For I am quite sure that good Boxall owes the appointment to you. Now indeed with you as Trustee, my Dear One's plans and views will be reverentially carried out – I shall so gladly make over all he has left into such good and kind hands. (Sheldon 2009a, 246)

Somewhat tactlessly referring to the institution as 'his [Eastlake's] Gallery' in letters to Boxall, Lady Eastlake, in another letter to Layard, tells how she is regularly meeting Boxall to educate him in her husband's methods:

> It has been a great consolation to me to see Boxall several times and to begin to make him acquainted with the methods of work and the materials of information which *he* has left.

> The latter so far exceed my expectations – are so clear and full, and embrace so much that is generally as well as specially interesting that I am lost in sorrowful admiration.
>
> (Sheldon 2009a, 246)

She had inherited the travel notebooks that Eastlake had compiled on their tours of Europe, and only Boxall and Layard were obliged with a sight of them on the occasions when they wished to test the veracity of an attribution. She continued to think of the works in the Gallery that her husband had purchased as 'dear old friends' (Sheldon 2009a, 277) and grumbled when they were re-hung by Boxall's successor Burton:

> I was at the Nat Gal: to day with Boxall. It is truly a splendid collection & dear old friends look some of them to great advantage. Still, the arrangement leaves much to be desired. As to Mr Burton I hope you are not prepared to insist that he is a properly qualified man as Director. If you are, we shall differ, for once! (Sheldon 2009a, 422)

These are just short extracts from numerous letters to Boxall and Layard in which Lady Eastlake seeks to maintain her special covenant with the National Gallery; exercising what influence remained to her in supporting her husband's posthumous reputation. She loyally did this elsewhere in a number of articles that promoted her husband's partisan connoisseurship (Eastlake 1872; 1891). In the ten years following Eastlake's death she undertook work commensurate to her grief. Her first publication as a widow was a volume on mourning entitled *Fellowship*. Next she prepared Eastlake's work for publication as new editions of his books were commissioned, appending a memoir of her husband to *Contributions to the Literature of the Fine Arts* and providing the preface to his *Materials for a History of Oil Painting*. She simultaneously obliged Eastlake's good friend, the recently deceased sculptor John Gibson, by editing his *Life* and wrote Mündler's obituary in the same year (Eastlake C 1869; 1870; Eastlake E 1870a and 1870b). She also began to write articles about artists that would later be collected into two volumes entitled *Five Great Painters*. In the preface to the book she wrote: 'the writer founds her claims to the indulgence of the reader on no study or thought of her own, but solely on the advantages enjoyed by her for long years at the side of the late Sir Charles L Eastlake'.

In Lady Eastlake's attempts to ensure Eastlake's scholarly legacy in the press she was largely unsuccessful and his writing was regarded as rather outdated by the end of Lady Eastlake's life.[8] However, in her efforts to keep Eastlake's flame burning at the National Gallery, she earned herself a reputation for interference that lingers in the oral histories of the Gallery. In addition to sending successive Directors and Trustees letters outlining her thoughts on the running of the Gallery, she also resorted to flagrant nepotism when she tried to advance the career of the Eastlakes' nephew, Charles Locke Eastlake, who became the Gallery's Keeper in 1878. In 1893 she wrote to W E Gladstone to suggest that her nephew would be the best candidate to replace Burton as Director. In an attempt to scupper the possibility of the Directorship going to anyone

8 The publisher, Charles Kegan Paul, recalled Lady Eastlake's 'most touching devotion' to her husband's work which 'was curious to those of a generation which had been formed rather by Ruskin than by Sir Charles Eastlake' (Kegan Paul 1899, 345).

else, she also suggested that the post of Director might be abolished altogether and that the Gallery could be maintained by a Keeper alone.[9]

However, in addition to loyally promoting the name of her husband and his eponymous nephew, 'his best successor' had, during the years of her widowhood, assumed the proportions of an expert, a connoisseur in her own right. There is an example of a conflict of interests arising from this change of status in the years following Eastlake's death. Before her marriage, everything Lady Eastlake had written had been anonymous. As a spinster, she had published her work anonymously or under the epithet 'by a lady', a literary convention that protected her from the crude association of writing for money, but simultaneously vexed any desire she might have for literary fame.[10] Marriage removed her from the suspicion of mercenary writing and she began to add her name to her publications in 1853. In the 1870s she began to consult Eastlake's notebooks for herself in the preparation of the new edition of Kugler's *Handbook of the Italian Schools of Painting* (Eastlake had been the editor of three previous editions) for the publisher John Murray. Murray commissioned Lady Eastlake to painstakingly edit and amend Kugler's material in the light of new attributions of paintings given by Crowe and Cavalcaselle in their volume on Italian art. Lady Eastlake was of course privy to the findings deposited in Eastlake's travel notebooks, perhaps in Murray's mind making her an intercessory in the project rather than an expert in her own right. By the time the new edition of Kugler appeared in 1874 she clearly imagined that her dowager expertise eclipsed that of her husband and she moved for his name to be removed altogether. Murray, anxious to have the authority of the work underwritten by Sir Charles Eastlake's name, insisted on retaining the original attribution and her labour was diminished, as she felt, in the title page to the afterthought: *Revised and Remodelled from the latest researches, by Lady Eastlake*. This tussle over the agency of the Eastlake name seems to me to be permanently visible at the National Gallery. Lady Eastlake donated two paintings to the Gallery: Bellini's *Death of St Peter Martyr* in 1870 and Pisanello's *Virgin and Child with Saints Anthony and George* in 1867. The label for the former records that the painting was 'presented by Lady Eastlake', while the latter has a label that reads 'Presented to the Nation by Lady Eastlake in Memory of her Husband'. It is impossible to read this without wondering which Eastlake is to be remembered.

## BIBLIOGRAPHY AND REFERENCES

Ames, W, 1967 *Prince Albert and Victorian Taste*, Chapman and Hall, London

Avery-Quash, S, 2011 The Travel Notebooks of Charles Eastlake, 1830–65, *The Walpole Society*, 74

Avery-Quash, S, and Sheldon, J, 2011 *Art for the Nation: The Eastlakes and the Victorian Art World*, National Gallery, London

Belloc, B R, 1897 *A Passing World*, Ward and Downey, London

Conlin, J, 2006 *The Nation's Mantelpiece: a history of the National Gallery*, Pallas Athene, London

Crookham, A, 2009 *Illustrated History of the National Gallery*, National Gallery, London

9 Charles Locke Eastlake's career at the National Gallery is explored in Avery-Quash and Sheldon 2011.

10 For a fuller discussion of her literary anonymity see Sheldon 2009b, 839–51.

Eastlake, C, 1847 *Materials for a History of Oil Painting*, Longman, Brown, Green and Longman, London

— 1869 *Materials for a History of Oil Painting*, 2 edn, Murray, London

— 1870 *Contributions to the Literature of the Fine Arts by Sir C L Eastlake: with a memoir by Lady Eastlake*, Murray, London

Eastlake, C (ed), 1851 *Kugler's Handbook of Painting in Italy, Part I: Italian Schools, Translated by a Lady. Edited with notes, by Sir Charles L Eastlake*, 2 vols, 2 edn, Murray, London

— 1864 *The History of Our Lord, commenced by the late Mrs. Jameson, continued and completed by Lady Eastlake*, Spottiswoode, London

— 1868 *Fellowship: Letters Addressed to My Sister Mourners*, Macmillan, London

— 1870a *Life of John Gibson, R A, Sculptor*, Spottiswoode, London

— 1870b Otto Mündler, *The Times*, 21 April

— 1872 Crowe and Cavalcaselle on the history of painting, *Edinburgh Review* 135, 122–49

— 1874 *Kugler's Handbook of Painting. The Italian Schools … Edited, with notes, by Sir Charles L Eastlake … Revised and Remodelled from the latest researches, by Lady Eastlake*, 2 vols, 4 edn, Murray, London

— 1883 *Five Great Painters: Essays Reprinted from the Edinburgh and Quarterly Review*, 2 vols, Longmans, Green & Co, London

— 1891 Giovanni Morelli: The Patriot and Critic, *Quarterly Review* 173, July, 235–52

Encyclopedia Britannica, 1877 Charles Eastlake, *Encyclopaedia Britannica*, 9 edn, Adam and Charles Black, Edinburgh, vol 7, 615–16

Ernstrom, A M, 1992 'Equally Lenders and Borrowers in Turn': The Working and Married Lives of the Eastlakes, *Art History* 15 (4), 470–85

Fenton, J, 2006 *School of Genius, A History of the Royal Academy of Arts, Royal Academy of Arts*, Royal Academy of Arts, London

Hare, A J C, 1896–1900 *The Story of My Life*, 6 vols, Allen, London

Holmes, C J, and Collins Baker, C H, 1924 *The Making of the National Gallery, 1824–1924*, National Gallery, London

Hunt, V, 1932 *The Wife of Rossetti: Her Life and Death*, E P Dutton, London

Kegan Paul, C, 1899 *Memories*, Kegan Paul, Trench, Trübner, London

Levey, M, 1957 *A Brief History of the National Gallery*, Pitkin, London

Marks, H S, 1894 *Pen and Pencil Sketches*, 2 vols, London

Morley, E J (ed), 1938 *Henry Crabb Robinson on Books and Their Writers*, 3 vols, Dent, London

Mündler, O, 1869 Charles Lock Eastlake, *Zeitschrift für Bildenden Kunst* 4, 99ff

Passavant, J D, 1836 *Tour of a German Artist in England*, 2 vols, trans E Rigby [Eastlake], Saunders and Otley, London

Palgrave, F T, 1866 Eastlake Obituary, *Fine Art Quarterly*, 63

Potter, B, 1966 *The Journals of Beatrix Potter from 1881–97*, trans and ed L Linder, Warne, London

Saumarez Smith, C, 2009 *The National Gallery: A Short History*, National Gallery, London

Sheldon, J (ed), 2009a *The Letters of Elizabeth Rigby, Lady Eastlake*, Liverpool University Press, Liverpool

— 2009b 'In her own metier': the Quarterly Review of Jane Eyre, *Women's History Review* 18 (5), 839–51

Smith, C E (ed), 1895 *The Journals and Correspondence of Lady Eastlake*, 2 vols, Murray, London

Sorenson, L (ed), 2000 Rigby [Eastlake], Elizabeth; Lady Eastlake (from 1850), *Dictionary of Art Historians* [online], available from: http://www.dictionaryofarthistorians.org/rigbye.htm [8 May 2010]

Steegman, J, 1966 Sir Charles Eastlake: 1793–1865, *Architectural Review*, 364

Sutton, D, 1985 Aspects of British Collecting Part IV, *Apollo* 123, 84–129

Trevelyan, R, 1978 *A Pre-Raphaelite Circle*, Chatto and Windus, London

Verax [pseud Morris Moore], 1847 *The Abuses of the National Gallery: with the Letters of 'A.G.' of 'The Oxford Graduate' [John Ruskin] the defence of Mr Eastlake in the 'Daily News', etc etc and Remarks upon them by Verax. To which are added Observations on the Minutes of the Trustees of the National Gallery, including Mr Eastlake's Report*, William Pickering, London

# 5

# Women, Museums and the Problem of Biography

ANNE WHITELAW

In the opening pages of *Biography: A Very Short Introduction*, Hermione Lee describes the genre of biography through the striking metaphors of the autopsy and the portrait. A biography is like an autopsy because it literally opens up the individual to 'investigate, understand, describe, and explain what may have seemed obscure, strange, or inexplicable' (Lee 2009, 1). Conversely, the metaphor of the portrait suggests that biographies can capture the character of a subject, bringing a person to life through 'attention to detail and skill in representation' (Lee 2009, 2). Taken together, these metaphors underscore both the analytical and representational operations of biography: a genre that has the ability to look back on a life for the purposes of analysis and assessment at the same time as it seeks to render the subject as a singular entity whose life can be seized as a totality. The tension between the temporality of 'looking back' to chart the unfolding of a past and the seeming fixity of a life captured is another intriguing aspect of Lee's twin metaphors insofar as it highlights the narratological character of biographical writing for the purposes of constructing a unified subject. As Sharon O'Brien notes, biography is conventionally understood as 'a linear, chronological, unified narrative [that] can present us with an essential self' (O'Brien 1991, 126) and as such lends itself fairly easily to uncritical accounts of individual travails and accomplishments. While such narratives have proven useful for scholars wishing to provide a space for the voices of peoples historically overlooked in mainstream accounts of the past, biography's tendency towards what Liz Stanley has described as a 'spotlight focus on the individual' (Stanley 1990, 64) most frequently results in a discourse of exceptionalism wherein the singular story glosses the complexities and contradictions of lived lives and prevents an active engagement with historical facts and the manner in which they were produced.

While much biographical writing addresses the life-stories of individuals, the linking of museum and biography in this volume's title suggests that the principal tenets of the genre can be extended to institutions. And yet when we talk about the biography of an institution such as a museum or an art gallery, what are we talking about? Is the narrative that of the individuals who lead the museum's central activities: the directors, the curators, or the 'starchitects' who design new and much-discussed buildings? Is it an unpeopled account of the institution itself: its building(s), collections and exhibitions? Further, what is the purpose of such biographies: to chronicle the evolution of major museums, to celebrate the achievements of individual figures in those museums, to assert a smaller institution's place on the cultural map of a given society? Writing on museums and art galleries has taken all of the above forms, with a particular emphasis on developments in museum architecture and often-celebratory histories of single institutions or of path-breaking directors.[1] Like traditional biographies, these accounts tend to structure their

1 See, for example, the extensive writings on Alfred Barr, Director of the Museum of Modern Art, New York.

narratives as linear accounts of progress and accomplishment, often arranging an institution's history as a chronological development from humble beginnings to present successes, or focusing on a select figure in the institution's history whose foresight, collecting acumen, or philanthropic generosity made a significant contribution to the institution's fortunes.

In my own research on the history of the Art Gallery of Alberta – a medium-sized art museum located in Edmonton, Alberta, Canada – biography has often presented itself as a potential mode of analysis. Despite being a relatively marginal institution in the Canadian (let alone the international) art world, the Art Gallery of Alberta has a rich past as one of a handful of art museums in western Canada. Its founding in 1924 by a woman keen to bring culture to a young prairie town; the businessmen and art collectors who have sat on its Board of Trustees; its mercurial director in the 1970s and 1980s whose acquisitions were sometimes controversial; its recent move to a spectacular new building designed by a renowned architect: all present instances where a biographical approach to the history of the institution seems appropriate. Yet I hesitate to employ this approach because of what I perceive as the limitations of the genre: the emphasis on a single exceptional figure, the reliance on linear chronologies, the creation of a unified subject. In the specific case of the museum, biography's focus on individuals risks isolating particular figures from the larger institutional structures that shape their activities, and the linear character of its narrative does not account for the complexity of the institution itself, particularly as it pertains to the relations between individuals and the roles they inhabit. The limitations of biography appear particularly evident when examining the roles that women have played in museums. Women have been central to the founding and maintenance of museums and art galleries for the past 150 years, yet, as I will argue, a biographical approach to telling the stories of these figures ultimately valorises those women who have occupied recognisable leadership positions (as directors and curators, for example) and ignores the anonymous labour of predominantly female voluntary groups that have made the museum's existence possible. In what follows I will examine the role of women in the formation of the Art Gallery of Alberta, and in the delivery of its programmes. Through this account I will examine the strengths and limitations of biography as a mode of analysis, not only of women's activities in art museums but also of relations between institutional roles and the individuals who occupy them.

## Maud Bowman and the Formation of the Edmonton Museum of Arts

The story of the Art Gallery of Alberta largely mirrors the development of many similar-sized institutions in North America whose establishment and growth occurred throughout the 20th century. At its opening in 1924, what was then known as the Edmonton Museum of Arts aimed to 'promote the knowledge and enjoyment of, and cultivation of the fine arts and to preserve historical relics',[2] a mandate that highlighted the generalist pedagogical aims of a cultural institution in what was still considered the outer regions of the nation. The effects of the Depression and World War II slowed the expansion of the collection but an active programme of art education classes and loan exhibitions obtained from the National Gallery in Ottawa ensured that the museum remained an active presence in Edmonton and its surroundings. By 1956,

2 Edmonton Museum of Arts, Act of Incorporation, 6 November 1923, Edmonton Art Gallery fonds. Box 14, book 1, Edmonton City Archives.

the museum's standing in Canadian art circles had grown – along with its permanent collection – and, recognising that the majority of its collecting and exhibiting activities were in the area of the fine arts, its name was changed to the Edmonton Art Gallery.[3] During the 1970s and 1980s the Edmonton Art Gallery achieved an international reputation through its collection of American and Canadian modernist painting and sculpture, and forged important connections with artists and critics in Britain and the United States.[4] Most recently the gallery moved into a new building, having rebranded itself as the Art Gallery of Alberta in recognition of its status as the largest art gallery in the province.

The Art Gallery's founder, Maud Bowman, was a middle-class woman with no apparent training in the fine arts and no affiliation with either the Edmonton Art Club or the Edmonton Art Association – the two fine art groups then in existence in the city. She had been a member of the Edmonton chapter of the National Council of Women (itself associated with the International Council of Women founded by Lady Ishbel of Aberdeen, wife of Canada's seventh Governor General), first as a member of the local branch of the Women's Art Association of Canada[5] and then as a member of the executive of the Edmonton Women's Musical Club.[6] In founding the Edmonton Museum of Arts, Bowman enlisted the support of both the Edmonton Art Club and several of the city's financial and political leaders, but it was she who initiated the endeavour, presided over the inaugural meetings, and organised the museum's first exhibitions. While there have always been women artists and women working in museums, their place has often been erased from historical accounts, rendering their efforts largely invisible in the present. The task of rectifying the absence of research on women artists has produced an ever-growing number of monographs, anthologies and exhibitions devoted to 'expanding the discourse' (Broude and Garrard 1992), but the contribution of women in the formation and maintenance of art galleries has received much less attention. As both Kathleen McCarthy (1991) and Dianne Sachko Macleod (2008) have chronicled, women have played leading roles in the establishment of many of North America's best-known fine arts museums: the list includes the Museum of Modern Art New York (Abby Rockefeller), the Whitney Museum of American Art (Gertrude Vanderbilt Whitney – alongside Director Juliana Force), and of course, Isabella Stewart Gardner, whose eponymous museum opened in 1903. In most of the case studies discussed by McCarthy and Macleod, the contribution of women to the founding of these art museums has been given little attention in official histories, a practice that began soon after the institutions became established and as the mostly male boards of trustees and professional direc-

3 This change in collecting focus was also related to the promise of a new provincial museum being established to house historical objects as well as natural specimens; this was the Provincial Museum of Alberta (now the Royal Alberta Museum) that opened in 1967.

4 This was accomplished under the leadership of director Terry Fenton, whose friendship with American art critic Clement Greenberg had a powerful impact not only on the Art Gallery's collection but on the character of Edmonton's art scene (see Whitelaw 2008).

5 The Women's Art Association of Canada (WAAC) was founded in Toronto in 1886 and quickly became affiliated with the National Council of Women. The Edmonton branch of the WAAC was established in 1911 and was operational until 1919 (see McLeod 1999).

6 Bowman was President of the Edmonton Women's Musical Club (also affiliated with the Edmonton Branch of the National Council of Women) from 1912 to 1914 and again from 1919 to 1922. Edmonton Women's Musical Club Fonds, MS 654, Edmonton City Archives.

tors and curators began to determine the public faces of the galleries their wives, mothers and sisters had worked so hard to set up.

Bowman's story is a little different from those of the well-connected and wealthy women listed above. She did not have the economic capital or the social status to be an 'art matron' in the way of Abby Rockefeller or Isabella Stewart Gardner, but she had the powerful reputation of what were often dismissively referred to as 'do-gooders' to support her in founding the Edmonton Museum of Arts. Indeed, Bowman relied on the network of volunteer women that populated the voluntary clubs affiliated with the Edmonton Council of Women to summon the social and political clout necessary to establish one of the first cultural institutions in the province of Alberta. Rather than being purely financial, Bowman's contribution ranged across all aspects of the museum's day-to-day management: from soliciting exhibitions from the National Gallery of Canada in Ottawa and national artists' associations to setting up art classes for children, giving lectures on art in schools and to smaller communities outside of Edmonton, and travelling throughout the United States and Canada to meet with heads of other museums and learn as much as she could about proper museum techniques. In this work she was no different from other director/curators of public museums in the 1930s, a period when work in museums was being increasingly professionalised (McTavish 2012). Museum manuals and reports from the period on the appropriate training of museum professionals frequently comment on the importance of education and strong leadership skills in the 'museum man' of the future. Women, meanwhile, were considered to have certain abilities in the areas of interpretation and education, but were not seen as potential directors of institutions of any size or influence. Indeed, as Kathleen McCarthy has shown, with the beginning of museum professionalisation, women who had been working to catalogue, research, collect and display objects for museums (often without pay) found themselves being pushed out of positions entirely, or passed over as potential candidates when positions became salaried (McCarthy 1991, 111–45).

Maud Bowman received little money for the work she did as Director of the Edmonton Museum of Arts. Initially, because of her status as a married woman, there was no thought of her receiving a salary for work that was still aligned with the good deeds of a voluntary clubwoman. But, with her husband's death, money became more of an issue and Bowman wrote many letters to the Assistant Director of the National Gallery of Canada, H O McCurry, asking for financial assistance for her work in the museum.[7] Members of the Board of Trustees of the Edmonton Museum of Arts were surprisingly reluctant to find funds to pay for Bowman's work as Director and de facto head of the museum's art classes. Despite being composed of some of the wealthiest men in the city – many of whom were developing their own extensive art collections – the Board was loath to pay Bowman a salary when she had the assistance of her three unmarried daughters – all of whom, they carefully noted, were gainfully employed.[8] The Depression and

7 Due to its status as the *national* art museum, the National Gallery of Canada was the conduit for a number of programmes designed to distribute funds and services to art galleries and other organisations across the country. One outstanding example is the Canadian Museums Committee, established in 1933 to distribute funds from the Carnegie Foundation of New York for art education classes in Canadian art museums (including the Edmonton Museum of Arts). This programme was discontinued in 1937 as the Carnegie Foundation shifted its assistance to museums in the Southern Dominions (see Brison 2005, 121–47).

8 Harold Orr to H O McCurry, 4 November 1936. Carnegie Corporation, Alberta. Edmonton Museum of Arts volume 2. Box 291, file 7, National Gallery of Canada Archives.

limitations of wartime resulted in continued financial difficulties for the Edmonton Museum of Arts, yet Bowman continued to organise art exhibitions, most of them obtained on loan from the National Gallery in Ottawa, to solicit donations of art for the permanent collection, to develop the art education programme, and generally to build the institution's status both locally and nationally as a centre for the fine arts in western Canada. In 1943, ill health forced Bowman to resign as Director of the Edmonton Museum of Arts and she died the following year.

## Writing Women into the Museum

The title of this essay belies the fairly conventional biography I have just presented of Maud Bowman, the Edmonton Museum of Art's Founding President and first Director. In my account I may have left out some standard biographical details, such as place of birth, education and professional experience prior to marriage, but this is because I have little information on any of these parts of her life. Writing on Bowman is virtually non-existent: she appeared in a book about Alberta women published to coincide with the province's centenary in 2005 (Anon 1999); she is mentioned briefly in the few histories of Alberta art written over the past 10 years or so (Townshend 2005); and most recently, a statue with a plaque was unveiled on Victoria Promenade near the city centre as part of an effort to celebrate some of Edmonton's important but less well-known citizens. Archival sources are few beyond those of the gallery itself; there are no photographs of Bowman in the Edmonton City Archives (although there are two of her successor Robert Hedley); and the room that was dedicated to her in the old Art Gallery of Alberta has disappeared in the new building. In my research I have not found this lack of information particularly problematic. Bowman's presence in the archive ends up being constructed entirely out of records of her activities, resulting in a history that prioritises her work as a museum director over explicit links between her life and the museum. Unlike much current writing on women and museums which privileges those women whose class, economic status and cultural affiliations ensure that their lives are known and well-recorded, any discussion of Maud Bowman cannot take place outside of her connection to and work with the Edmonton Museum of Arts. As the Director of the Museum for more than 20 years, however, her life-story remains narratable within the dominant conventions of biographical form.

The two main publications that explore the formative contribution of women to the establishment of museums are Kathleen McCarthy's *Women's Culture*, published in 1991, and Dianne Sachko Macleod's *Enchanted Lives, Enchanted Objects* from 2008. Both are invaluable texts that shed a tremendous amount of light on women's roles in American museums from the middle of the 19th century to the 1930s and 1940s. In writing the first such history, McCarthy employs both a thematic and a biographical approach, mapping out broader trends in female involvement in museums by organising her book into sections that situate women's motivations to become involved in art and museums. Linking this involvement to strategies adopted by women in the quest for political emancipation, McCarthy maps women's work in and with museums as a chronological movement from separatism to assimilationism to individualism. Within these sections, chapters on key individuals (such as Candace Wheeler, Louisine Havemeyer and Abby Rockefeller) are employed as case studies exemplifying the larger theme. Written some 15 years later, Macleod's *Enchanted Lives, Enchanted Objects* convincingly links women's interest in the decorative arts and their arrangement of their domestic spaces with the active role many of them played in promoting the fine arts (including the establishment of art galleries) in the United

States. Through an examination of the decorative and fine arts collections of a number of American women between 1800 and 1940, Macleod argues that women's engagement with 'enchanted objects' cannot be dismissed as merely personal interest or a desire for the beautiful, but rather must be analysed for what they can tell us about the sphere of women's influence – in the arts as in public life – during a period of rapid political and social change. My point of contention with these volumes is neither with the thoroughness of their research, which has been invaluable for my own and others' writing on museums, nor with their argument that women have been overlooked as collectors and museum builders. Rather, I question whether a reliance on finding and exploring the work of a selection of 'exceptional women' does not reproduce the narrative of individual progress that feminist historians have critiqued, thereby preventing us from fully appreciating women's overall contributions to museums and galleries. In other words, McCarthy and Macleod's use of biography to explore the contributions of women to the founding of museums and art galleries in the United States results in a privileging of individuals occupying recognisable leadership roles (as collectors, curators, founders) at the expense of uncovering the anonymous, often collective labour of other women working in museums.

Much of my interest in questioning biography as a strategy for writing about women in museums comes from the number of times I came across other women in the archives of the Art Gallery of Alberta. Unlike Maud Bowman, whose name continued to appear in annual reports and Board minutes decades after her death, the members of the Women's Society of the Edmonton Museum of Arts (and later of the Edmonton Art Gallery) were little more than ghostly presences in much of the institution's records. The Women's Society was formed in 1944 following the suggestion of Bowman's successor that 'a Ladies' Auxiliary can do more than any other body to further the general interest in the museum'.[9] In this move, the Edmonton Museum of Arts was following a broader trend in North American museums to establish women's auxiliary organisations to take care of social events, membership drives and fundraising. A strictly volunteer group, all-female until 1988, the members of the Women's Society of the Edmonton Museum of Arts (and at similar museums) were indefatigable workers whose activities not only raised the profile of the institution but also yielded significant amounts of money through a combination of bake and rummage sales, fancy-dress balls, art sales and rental initiatives and more. Yet while these activities were gratefully acknowledged at the time, they have received little attention in subsequent writing on women and museums.[10]

As I have argued elsewhere (Whitelaw 2012), the lack of visibility accorded to the work of women's societies in museums can be attributed to limited public records of their activities, the socially conservative and domestic character of many of their endeavours, and the perception that they played little more than a supporting role to the main activities of the museum's Director, curators and even members of the Board of Trustrees. Of all these factors, it is the socially conservative and domestic character of many of the activities initiated by women's groups that has deterred serious scholarly analysis of women's voluntary organisations in museums. In Edmonton, the Women's Society was initially tasked with increasing the museum's public visibility in order to increase membership. As a result, monthly teas and businessmen's lunches

9 Annual General Meeting, 2 November 1943. Board of Directors Minutes 1942–47. Edmonton Art Gallery Fonds, Box 14, volume 3. Edmonton City Archives.

10 One exception, outside of my own research, is Gregory Nosan's exploration of the activities of the women's auxiliary of the Art Institute of Chicago (Nosan 2003).

were organised to bring both women and men into the gallery; bake and craft sales were also regular events designed to both raise funds and forge connections with city residents. While some fundraising events, such as the annual fancy-dress ball, were geared towards the members of Edmonton's social elite, other activities, such as the gallery's gift shop and the art rental and sales gallery, were intended to bring middle-class men and women into the Edmonton Art Gallery by creating opportunities for the purchase of artworks on a more affordable basis. These and other initiatives, such as the organisation of docent services, were the mainstays of many museums' public programming from the 1940s into the 1980s, and all were started by volunteer women's committees intent on increasing public awareness of the institution and raising funds for its acquisitions programming. Indeed, the Women's Society of the Edmonton Art Gallery raised over a million dollars for the purchase of artworks for the museum's permanent collection, all through proceeds from teas, gala balls and the gift shop. Despite an increasing interest among scholars in women's practices of consumption as sites of empowerment and resistance (Rappaport 2000; Friedberg 2002), the kinds of traditional activities that formed the core of the Women's Society's fundraising have not garnered much interest from researchers.

In addition to the ideological difficulties scholars have with the nature of the Women's Societies' main activities, the collective nature of volunteer organisations and their fluctuating membership also make them difficult subjects for analysis. Although there are central figures associated with the Edmonton Art Gallery's Women's Society, it is the activities of the organisation rather than of individual presidents or committee chairs that are recorded. In addition, the members of the society identified themselves with the group and regularly cited the contribution of all Women's Society members to the success of specific events. There is a degree of effacement that occurs in the annual reports of the Women's Society that further reinforces the collective nature of their work – an effacement that is also found in the acknowledgments and thanks given to the Women's Society by the gallery's Board of Trustees in its own Annual Reports. Viewed in relation to the existing literature on women in the museum, the collective nature of voluntary societies complicates contemporary scholarship's attempts to address them as important contributors to the history of the institution. This is in contrast to the treatment of a figure such as Maud Bowman, who, despite scant biographical information, can still be written about. Much of this is due to the continued bias in historiography toward narratives of individual accomplishments, often told in biographical form. Such a reliance on exceptional narratives of particular women, however, undermines the work of ordinary women, without whose labour such institutions would not have remained open. In this, scholars are replicating the kind of oversight practised by those 19th- and early 20th-century men who swept aside the contributions of their wives, mothers and sisters to establish what they considered to be more professional – and therefore serious or legitimate – institutions.

## Women, Museums and the Problem of Biography

Of all the critical writing on biography, feminist approaches have been the most diligent about giving serious consideration to both its form and its methods. On one hand, biography is a useful tool for 'rescuing' women from historical obscurity: accounts of the lives of the suffragette Susan B Anthony, the artist Frieda Kahlo, or the scientist Margaret Sanger provide insights into the struggles and successes of women whose accomplishments have been recognised and made part of the historical record. Meanwhile, biographical accounts of lesser-known women such as the artist-naturalist Maria Sibylla Merian and the midwife Nina Gellant expand our understanding of women's experiences throughout history by bringing the ordinariness of daily life into focus. As Paula Backscheider has noted, one of the effects of feminism on biography 'is to assure that biographers will think about the significance and amount of space "ordinary" aspects of life merit and that the importance of the private, domestic, or intimate sphere will be given attention' (Backscheider 1999, 153). Indeed, the attribution of a primarily domestic or intimate character to women's lives has been one means by which women's history has been ignored, given its lack of fit with the model of public achievement and measurable success that has shaped the 'chaps and maps' approach of traditional historiography. Since the early 1980s, however, historians of gender have forcefully argued that an attention to the domestic and to the private sphere not only permits an expansion of the sphere of history writing to include women but also deepens our understanding of the experiences of men across both the private and the public spheres (Scott 1999; 1992).

On the other hand, feminist writers on biography have cautioned that simply adding women to the list of figures suitable for biographical treatment will not overcome the limitations of the genre. Rather, they argue that it is crucial for biographic treatments of any subject to remain critical of the conservative assumptions of biographical writing: the tendency to construct a unified subject; seeking objective truths based on documentary facts gleaned from the subject's personal papers; the assumption that the biographer's access to this material provides direct insight into the subject's life. In addition to these criticisms, feminist scholars caution biographers of women against relying on experience as evidence: in other words, finding in the life-stories of their subjects connections with what are assumed to be commonalities of experience among all women rather than seeing how dominant constructions of women's experience or difference function to shape the life-narrative itself. For critics such as Devoney Looser, this reliance on experience results in the tendency of many biographers of women to cast their subjects in the form of a feminist hero who can serve as a model for future generations of women, an approach that relies on exceptionalism rather than on the examination of a life as shaped by complex ideological practices (Looser 1993).

Within the literature on the fine arts, the question of biography is intimately tied to constructions of the artist as a singular genius. In her study of biography as the dominant genre of art history writing, Catherine Soussloff (1997) maps the narrative construction of the artist's life as a linear journey from birth to death – or more precisely, from pre-birth portents to the post-death fate of the artist's works. Soussloff argues that such constructions have become so entrenched in the way artists are written about because their status as 'geniuses' (as figures singled out for their aesthetic vision) depends on their conformity to a set of rhetorical tropes. For artists who are women – as feminist scholarship has uncovered – 'genius' is a historically unreachable goal (Battersby 1989). Yet neither is it entirely desired. Writing about her book on Elizabeth Vigée-Lebrun, art historian Mary Sheriff describes her unwillingness to conform to a standard monographic treatment of the artist. She writes:

> I viewed my book [...] not as a self-contained monument to a single artist, but as a chapter in a different story of art, as well as my contribution to another history – the history of how women talked back to those discourses determined to configure them as incapable of reason or cultural production. In other words, I saw my monograph as part of a collective enterprise. (Sheriff 2003, 52)

Similarly, in her introduction to the collection *Singular Women: Writing the Artist*, Kristen Frederickson notes: 'The risk in describing each artist as a singular case is to make these women seem anomalies, aberrations, rather than examples, case studies of a larger phenomenon. But there is also a risk if we do not acknowledge that the circumstance of women artists differ' (Frederickson 2003, 8).

As Sherriff's and Frederickson's comments make clear, identifying and celebrating the accomplishments of particular women is an important first step in uncovering women's work whether as artists or in the museum; however, it risks participating in a discourse of exceptionalism where only the very few are acknowledged. In this view, the work of Maud Bowman finds an easy place among other early 20th-century female museum directors who struggled against expectations of their inability, as women, to lead significant cultural institutions, while the members of the Women's Society as well as their contributions to the museum are largely invisible. A group with frequently changing presidents and a fluctuating membership whose work was largely anonymous, the Women's Society does not lend itself well to traditional biographical treatment. There are certainly measurable accomplishments in the work of the Women's Society over their 50-year existence at the Edmonton Art Gallery: the significant amount of money raised; the creation of the art sales and rental gallery; the social events that brought the gallery into the public eye. In the minutes of the Society and in the various *Annual Reports*, certain presidents come across as potentially more 'interesting' or as being more active than others, but their identity is subsumed by the office they inhabit and it becomes difficult to write about them as individuals or to see them as necessarily representative of the Women's Society as a whole. In addition, as I argued above, the nature of the Women's Society's contributions – the bake sales, fancy-dress balls and luncheon receptions – do not carry the kind of cultural capital that is considered worthy of serious consideration by art historians, nor do these activities fulfil feminist expectations of agential and resistant female subjects. Indeed, it is difficult to fashion a feminist heroine out of the activities and socially conservative figures that make up the Women's Society. Yet they were central contributors to the success of the Edmonton Art Gallery – and to most museums and art galleries across North America and Europe – and, despite their achievements, they have largely been forgotten. Where such groups still exist they have been transformed into co-ed volunteer groups, managed by a paid volunteer coordinator on the museum's staff, and have little input on the direction of any of the services they provide. Many of the services now seen as integral parts of the museum – the gift shop, docent services and art rental – that were started by women's societies are now managed by professional staff who assign their volunteer workers a limited set of specific tasks. Many of these volunteers were once active members of the Women's Society and some comment on their change in status and the lack of input they feel they have on the activities of the Gallery, yet they continue to support the institution.

Taking seriously feminist biographers' calls for biographical treatments that assert the complexity of their subjects' lives and their imbrication within social networks, that refuse to spotlight the individual, and that recognise the ideological character of experience, is it possible to write an account of the Women's Society that acknowledges their accomplishments and their contribution to the formation and maintenance of museums and art galleries? As my questioning of the genre of biography would suggest, I think writing such an account as a biography would be misplaced: an attempt to bestow feminist agency after the fact to a group that would likely have rejected such an association, or a desire to impart a measure of legitimacy to a site of analysis whose conservative and conformist character required an infusion of feminist intellectual capital.

Instead, serious enquiry into the history of the Women's Society of the Edmonton Art Gallery provides a counterpoint to any tendency to write a conventional biography of Maud Bowman as representative of women's work in the museum. In this view, my ability to cast Bowman as an early 20th-century heroine of either the Edmonton Art Gallery or of Canadian museums writ large is deflected by the Women's Society's regular appearance as background figures, whose anonymity and peripheral status within the records of the art museum belie the significance of their contribution. For every measurable accomplishment of a figure such as Bowman, there are several intangible contributions by the Women's Society that resist narration, at least within the generic logic of biography.

To return to my querying of the articulation of museum and biography that forms the title of this volume, what can this examination of women in museums teach us about the potential pitfalls of biographical form in writing the history of institutions? As I have argued, biography's emphasis on the unified and singular subject emphasises the accomplishment of individuals in identifiable leadership roles. As a result, directors, curators and significant donors are natural objects of biographical analysis, their struggles and successes often standing in for those of the institution itself. Such an emphasis on the singular ignores the workings of the museum as an institution – in other words, the tension between the roles of director and curator and the individuals who inhabit them – at the same time as it overlooks the large number of workers without whose contributions the museum would not function. Within the latter category, the absent history of the Women's Society of the Edmonton Art Gallery is a key example of the ease with which such labour is neglected; but we could also include other figures such as the preparators, exhibition designers and educators whose work enables the more conventionally 'authored' contributions of curators, directors and so on. Such an oversight ends up privileging the work of individual directors and curators as sui generis: as the creative output of individuals more akin to traditional conceptions of authorship than to figures who occupy particular roles within the larger institution.[11] Rethinking such a view – in other words, seeing the work of a director or curator of an art museum as a product of both individual agency and as shaped by the ideological and aesthetic beliefs of the institution itself – would result in a more complex understanding of the art museum and its programming, moving away from the valorisation of individual accomplishment and finding ways of tracing institutional discourses that recognise the effect of the museum on individual practices. In the case of Maud Bowman, such a refocus would result in an analysis that frames her curatorial work within, for example, the ideological goals of the National Gallery of Canada, whose loans of artworks were predicated on the broader aim of bringing a particular kind of Canadian art to smaller institutions across the country. Changing cultural policy at the national level, as well as local shifts in sources of funding, could also be examined for their impact on what Bowman as the Director of the Edmonton Museum of Arts could accomplish, rather than seeing her exhibitions and acquisition programme as the creative products of a sole figure.

In this chapter I examined the different kinds of work undertaken by women in art museums through the very particular example of the Art Gallery of Alberta. Through the exploration of the work of both Maud Bowman and the members of the gallery's Women's Society, I argued that

[11] This questioning is indebted to the interrogation of the increasingly powerful role of contemporary art curators over the past 20 years (see for example Heinich and Pollak 1996).

biography as an approach to writing the history of the institution was limited in its ability to adequately address the complexity of the contributions of these women. Supported by feminist scholarship on biography that questioned the genre's reliance on the construction of a unified subject and on the production of a linear chronological narrative, I argued that biographical writing on women in museums relies on a discourse of exceptionalism that privileges women in leadership positions at the expense of the vast majority of women in museums whose anonymous and voluntary labour does not easily fit into the conventional categories of recognisable accomplishment. This tension between individual and collective activity underscores the larger limitations of biography in its ability to address the relationship between individuals – whether male or female – and the roles they occupy within museums. As central mechanisms in the construction and dissemination of knowledge, the histories of museums are ripe for critical examination. Given the complexity of the institution and the imbrication of its practices with the people – both known and unknown – who contribute to their realisation, biography is inadequate to the task.

## BIBLIOGRAPHY AND REFERENCES


Anon, 1999 *200 Remarkable Alberta Women*, Famous Five Foundation, Calgary

Backscheider, P R, 1999 *Reflections on Biography*, Oxford University Press, Oxford

Battersby, C, 1989 *Gender and Genius: Towards a Feminist Aesthetics*, Women's Press, London

Brison, J D, 2005 *Rockefeller, Carnegie and Canada: American Philanthropy and the Arts and Letters in Canada*, McGill-Queen's University Press, Montreal and Kingston

Broude, N, and Garrard, M (eds), 1992 *The Expanding Discourse: Feminism and Art History*, Icon Editions, New York

Frederickson, K, 2003 Introduction: Histories, Silences, and Stories, in *Singular Women: Writing the Artist* (eds K Frederickson and S E Webb), University of California Press, Berkeley, 1–19

Friedberg, A, 2002 '… therefore I am': the Shopper-Spectator and Transubstantiation through Purchase, in *Shopping: A Century of Art and Consumer Culture* (eds C Grunenberg and M Hollein), Hatje Cantz, Ostfildern-Ruit, 62–8

Heinich, N, and Pollak, M, 1996 From Museum Curator to Exhibition Auteur: Inventing a Singular Position, in *Thinking About Exhibitions* (eds R Greenberg, B W Ferguson, and S Nairne), Routledge, New York, 231–50

Lee, H, 2009 *Biography: A Very Short Introduction*, Oxford University Press, Oxford

Looser, D, 1993 Heroine of the Peripheral? Biography, Feminism, and Sylvia Plath, *a/b: Auto/Biography Studies* 8 (2), 179–97

Macleod, D S, 2008 *Enchanted Lives, Enchanted Objects: American Women Collectors and the Making of Culture*, University of California Press, Berkeley

McLeod, E E, 1999 *In Good Hands: The Women of the Canadian Handicrafts Guild*, McGill-Queen's University Press, Montreal and Kingston

McCarthy, K D, 1991 *Women's Culture: American Philanthropy in Art, 1830–1930*, University of Chicago Press, Chicago

McTavish, L, 2012 *Defining the Modern Museum: A Case Study in the Challenges of Exchange*, University of Toronto Press, Toronto

Nosan, G, 2003 Women in the Galleries: Prestige, Education, and Volunteerism at Mid-Century, *Art Institute of Chicago Museum Studies* 29 (1), 46–71 and 92–5

O'Brien, S, 1991 Feminist Theory and Literary Biography, in *Contesting the Subject: Essays in the Postmodern Theory and Practice of Biography and Biographical Criticism* (ed W H Epstein), Purdue University Press, West Lafayette, 123–33

Rappaport, E D, 2000 'A New Era of Shopping': The Promotion of Women's Pleasure in London's West End, 1909–1914, in *The Gender and Consumer Culture Reader* (ed J Scanlon), New York University Press, New York, 30–48

Scott, J W, 1999 (1988) *Gender and the Politics of History* (rev edn), Columbia University Press, New York

— 1992 Experience, in *Feminists Theorize the Political* (eds J Butler and J W Scott), Routledge, New York, 22–40

Sheriff, M D, 2003 'So What Are You Working On?' Categorizing The Exceptional Woman, in *Singular Women: Writing the Artist* (eds K Frederickson and S E Webb), University of California Press, Berkeley, 48–65

Soussloff, C M, 1997 *The Absolute Artist: The Historiography of a Concept*, University of Minnesota Press, Minneapolis

Stanley, L, 1990 Moments of Writing: Is There a Feminist Auto/biography? *Gender and History* 2 (1), 58–67

Townshend, N, 2005 *A History of Art in Alberta 1905–1970*, Bayeux Arts Inc, Calgary

Whitelaw, A, 2012 Professional/Volunteer: Women at the Edmonton Art Gallery 1923–1970, in *Rethinking Professionalism: Essays on Women and Art in Canada 1850–1970* (eds K Huneault and J Anderson), McGill-Queen's University Press, Montreal and Kingston, 357–79

Whitelaw, A, 2008 *Seeing Through Modernism: Edmonton 1970–1985*, Art Gallery of Alberta, Edmonton

6

# A Curatocracy: Who and What is a V&A Curator?

LINDA SANDINO

## INTRODUCTION[1]

On 5 July 1989, at the opening of the Design Museum in London, the then Prime Minister, Margaret Thatcher, displayed an attitude to museum culture that was to revolutionise the future of such institutions in the United Kingdom. 'I call it an Exhibition Centre and not a museum – a museum is something that is really rather dead' (Thatcher 1989). Some months previously, the Victoria & Albert Museum (the V&A) had experienced a management revolution which became the focus for polarised debates about its meaning and the role of curators: as one curator expressed it in his oral history recording: 'By separating knowledge, care of what the objects were from physical care of the objects, they were in effect planning to destroy the curatorial profession as I understand it' (Curator 2-T19/09).[2]

In recent times the term 'curator' has come to be adopted as a synonym for any activity that involves a selective form of organising, including not just objects but people, or even activities. For instance, the 2009 Deloitte 'Ignite' festival at the Royal Opera House was promoted as having been 'curated' by *Time Out*. Publicly funded museum curators, however, have a distinctive professional identity and expertise that this chapter explores by drawing on V&A curators' oral life history recordings.[3] My neologism 'curatocracy' points to two aspects of their identity: their status as professionals in a museum which proclaims on its website to be 'the world's greatest museum of art and design, with collections unrivalled in their scope and diversity'; and the origin of their role as government civil servants. As such they are subject to certain protocols and assumptions that continued despite the Museum's 'arms-length' status when in 1983 the *National Heritage Act* devolved the V&A from the Department of Education and placed it under the direction of a Board of Trustees.

1 I would like to thank Sir Mark Jones, Liz Miller, Deputy Head of the V&A Research Department, and Anthony Burton for their helpful comments on the first draft of this paper. I am also indebted to the curators who have participated in the project and granted permission to quote from their interviews.

2 In accordance with the Consent and Deposit agreements, all interviewees for this paper remain anonymous. The reference in brackets refers to the track number and the year of the recording. On completion of the oral history project, all material will be deposited in the V&A Archive. The sample of interviewees for this chapter range from one who entered the profession in 1949 to one who joined more recently but with extensive curatorial experience in another national museum.

3 The project is jointly funded by the Camberwell, Chelsea and Wimbledon Graduate School of the University of the Arts London and the V&A Research Department. The author is the principal investigator. Dr Matthew Partington, UWE/V&A Senior Research Fellow and Anthony Burton, V&A Emeritus Senior Research Fellow, are also involved in recording interviews with curators and other retired members of staff.

The chapter begins with a brief outline of the rationale for using life histories to explore curatorial identity and how this might be framed when oral histories form the basis of the research. Individual life history research does not seek to privilege autonomous individualism and agency, but instead demonstrates how selves are entangled in a variety of discourses and fields of action. Arising from a dialogue between two people, oral history produces and demonstrates how selves are created relationally. Museum biographies are shaped by a network of social, political, cultural and historical forces and by 'listening in stereo' we are able to explore how such forces shape the individual and how the institution, as the product of these forces, in turn shapes its personnel. Life history narratives provide the occasion and means to reflect on and create a narrative of the self over time that encompasses change at both personal and institutional levels. I draw, therefore, on the philosopher Paul Ricoeur's concept of *narrative identity*, a dialectic between continuity ('sameness') and change, to map curatorial identity. The chapter examines stories about cataloguing the permanent collection as emblematic of curatorial expertise and how Civil Service protocol, in the form of the *Official Secrets Act*, sustained an object-based connoisseurship.

## CURATORIAL IDENTITY

The chapter draws on seven narrators, called here Curator 1 to Curator 7, to explore the curator-as-official and the temporal conditions of their identity. The interviewees represent both an older, retired generation as well as those currently in-post, though all have been in the profession since the early 1970s. Oral history provides the opportunity to understand what a V&A curator is through the narratives of *who* they are: 'What is a curator?' can be answered by understanding 'Who is a curator?' As Ricoeur proposes: 'To answer the question "Who?" [...] is to tell the story of a life. The story told tells the action of the "who". And the identity of this "who" therefore itself must be a narrative identity' (Ricoeur 1988, 246). As a research methodology, oral life histories are especially suited to understanding how identities are constructed, sustained and deployed, enabling us 'to see how particular categories of person have been formed or made up in specific contexts, at a particular time and through certain practical means' (Du Gay 2007, 25).

One of the themes to recur in the recordings is the commitment to public duty:

> The public function of museums, for me, has always been a very strong motive in my work. (Curator 1-T07/10)

> I don't think museums should be ivory towers where people are paid a lot of money to sit for forty years and do what they feel like. I mean the point of a museum is, is that it is trying to connect with its public. I mean the public are paying for it. (Curator 5-T15/09)

Contrary, therefore, to the contemporary emphasis on curators as international 'superstars', established museum curators continue to work within the tradition of the public service ethos laid down with the establishment of the Civil Service in 1854. As well as loyalty, political neutrality and permanence, civil servants offered 'impartial and courageous advice, *devoted to the public interest*' (Vandenabeele and Horton 2005, 6). How were these qualities inculcated in the museum service?

In questioning curators about their first days at work, I was surprised to hear that they were required to sign the *Official Secrets Act*, a practice that seems to have continued into the 1990s beyond the Museum's devolution from the Department of Education in 1984 to Trustee status. Signing the Act has come to occupy an important place in my research on curatorial identity as a public 'office' and as a signifier of the continuity of a bureaucratic ethos. What did it mean to individuals to sign the Act? How did it affect the 'what' and 'who' of curatorial identity? The constraints imposed by Civil Service protocols promoted a continuity of character, a Ricoeurian identity-sameness that surfaces again and again in curators' accounts in passages relating to the concept of duty and the roles of their office. Consequently, the attempt to reconfigure curatorial identity in 1989 with the separation of scholarship from management of the collections was seen by some as almost an assault, precipitated by a government that made a virtue of its radical attempts to destroy traditional values, install a free-market economy and privatise public services: ie Thatcherism.

The 1989 management revolution at the V&A[4] was not an isolated event and the debates it raised about the role of museums had already been aired within the museum profession.[5] Although the 1989 restructuring figures in the interviews and can be extracted to tell its story, life histories provide a perspective on a curator's selfhood that accounts for the historical specificity of change. It was significant, for instance, that in the extract cited above, the interviewee maintained the consistency of what it meant to be a curator 'as I understand it', not 'as I understood it'. Why was constancy such an important element in this life history? Was it only the effect of a resistance to change, or were there other factors that sustained a coherent persona? Ricoeur's proposal of a dialectic of sameness and self-constancy (Ricoeur 1992, 115–24) is helpful in exploring the curatorial persona, the latter term used here to indicate the public character of this profession. Curators' life histories, like all life histories, are a synthesis of heterogeneous elements that attempt to explain and make sense of their careers within a particular institution (the V&A Museum) and a particular profession (curator). Their accounts, therefore, function as descriptions of 'the ways in which individuals have acquired definite capacities and attributes for distinctive forms of existence as particular sorts of persons' with the 'capacity to conduct themselves' as such (Du Gay 2007, 22). Sociologist Paul Du Gay's study of the bureaucrat is used here to illuminate how the commitment to public service and duty continues to adhere to the persona of long-term curators.

4 The event was widely reported. See, for example, D Sutton, 1989 Drama at the V&A is good enough for fiction, *Financial Times*, 25 February; Gutless Trustees, 1989 *Evening Standard*, 21 March; D Lister, 1989 V&A redundancy terms accepted under protest, *The Independent*, 18 February; M Kemp, 1989 The Crisis at the V&A, *The Burlington Magazine*, vol cxxx, no 1034, May (Kemp resigned his Trusteeship); N Penny, 1989 Diary, *London Review of Books*, vol 11, no 9, 4 May. It was also the subject of a lengthy debate in the House of Lords on 22 March 1989, vol 505, cc 765–810, available from: http://hansard.millbanksystems.com/lords/1989/mar/22/victoria-and-albert-museum [accessed September 2009].

5 In 1983 the ICOM Training Committee had outlined the key issues for new entrants 'regardless of their background or status in the museum's hierarchy', including:

1. Museums – why do we have them and what is their function in society?
2. Collections – how do we get them, how do we study them and care for them, and what do we do with them?
3. Museum organisation – who does what in the museum and how do they do it?
4. The museum and its public services – why do we provide them, how do we organise them, and how are they used?
5. Physical facilities – how do we provide maximum access to museum facilities while safeguarding the collections? (Boylan 2006, 429).

Devolvement from the Civil Service under the *National Heritage Act* (1983) highlighted the distinction between the Museum's curatorial, scholarly activity and its administration, which was no longer carried out by the Department of Education and Science (DES) but had to be done in-house. Previously, a structure had been in place whereby seconded civil servants dealt with administrative matters such as finances and building works, and it was they who dealt with the appropriate ministerial department.[6] The distinction between scholarship and administration was therefore clear, though less evident was the amount of management and administration involved in running the Museum. As one interviewee noted:

> When I became Assistant to the Director, it became clear to me for the first time, which I hadn't realised, how much of the administration of the Museum in those days was done in the Ministry of Education, or it became the Department of Education and Science,[7] and how relatively little was done within the Museum. That is – my memory is vague but there was of course a Finance Officer in the V and A, and extremely good people they were, but they worked in terms of the civil service, at a fairly junior level and the main sort of financial management, I don't mean the detail but the overall financial management was done from the Ministry. I think that was a big change, I'm talking about the period before the Trusteeship and so on which was twenty years later, 1984 (Curator 7-T01/09).

Curators were able, therefore, to concentrate on their duties, aware that the running of the institution was in the hands of the Director and the senior administrative officer, the Museum Superintendent, seconded from the Ministry.

While the V&A restructuring was heatedly debated in the media in 1989–90, discussions over the function or duties of curators, as well as how they should be trained, continued into the 1990s. Defending the 1989 structural divisions into 'documentation' and 'care and access', a senior V&A curator writing in 1992 stated unequivocally:

> One of the most important facts about museums, which we should take every opportunity to stress ... is that sound collections management, defined on the two areas of responsibility [*documentation* and *care and access*], is the key to success. It is this activity, carried out by curators who are scholars but who are also alert to the changing range of skills required to deal with very large numbers of old, fragile and valuable objects, which lies at the heart of our business and constitutes the main challenge for the future. (Murdoch 1994, 144)

Another writer pinpointed the new spirit by welcoming 'the inclusive nature of the concept of the *museum professional*', a descriptor that she saw as being 'more useful and productive than

6 Building works were dealt with by the Property Services Agency (1972–1993), an off-shoot of the Department of the Environment. Previously the Ministry of Works (1943–1962), subsequently the Ministry of Public Buildings and Works oversaw the V&A's buildings.

7 The Ministries responsible for the Museum were the Department of Science and Art (1853–1901/2), the Board of Education (1902–1944), the Ministry of Education (1944–1964). Following devolution in 1983, the related government departments were the Department of Education and Science (1964–1992), the Department of National Heritage (1992–1997), and, to date, the Department of Culture, Media and Sport.

the narrower and exclusive concept of the museum curator [...] *in the long run*' [my italics] (Kavanagh 1994, 7). This expanded definition accepts the challenge and condition of change but nevertheless seeks to encompass some enduring characteristics of what it means to be a curator: specialist knowledge, commitment to the 'ideals of museums provision', and public duty – the last two tellingly reinforced by the proposition that entrants to the profession 'do not come into the museum work because of the salary, but because they hold passionate beliefs about communicating their subject and working with both collections and the public' (Kavanagh 1994, 8). To be a curator is, therefore, a vocation, a mission (although the remark about disdain for a decent salary masks the habitus which makes up most of the profession). The new 'museum professional' is part of a 'museum workforce', *all* of whom share 'the basic tenets of *faith* in collections' [my italics] (Kavanagh 1994, 128). Written in the aftermath of the museum revolutions of 1989, the publications have the tone of manifestos establishing the new vision and order.

## Continuity and Change

Although the 1989 restructuring seems to pivot on a rupture in curatorial identity, nevertheless, as the writers in the 1990s demonstrated, commitment to the concept of public service remained consistent. It is clear, however, that in the case of the V&A, the building itself performs an important continuity function quite apart from the archival character of museums as repositories of the past for the future. For V&A curators the Museum is both a *milieu* as well as a *lieu de mémoire* as defined by Pierre Nora, who contrasted a supposedly 'organic' community of memory with the constructed 'histories' of modernity (Nora 1989). I will take up the latter assertion below but in the case of museums such as the V&A the distinction is blurred since long-serving staff constitute a community that bears comparison with any village made up of a mixture of personalities, competencies, gossip, surveillance, alliances and disagreements but bound by a commitment to a particular sense of place.

In terms of constructing histories, the V&A continues to draw on its 19th-century legacy and mission, 'all sort of starting from (first Director) Henry Cole's idea', as curator Barbara Morris (1918–2009) stated in her interview (Morris -T07/09); or, as another stated: 'The V&A was founded as a public museum with a remit really to reach out as far as possible to everyone' (Curator 1-T08/10). As an institution that emerged during the ascendancy of 19th-century British imperialism and manufacturing, this legacy is both sustained and reinterpreted within the Museum and is the context within which curators situate themselves and their memories. The building is both an architectural site and historical archive which holds not only objects but individuals and their memories. Although prioritising its collections and architectural heritage, curators themselves form an important and active repository of memories. In expanding on the work of Maurice Halbwachs, the historian Susan Crane argues that although recollection takes place within social contexts and sites, collective memory is located within individuals, that is to say 'people thinking historically' (Crane 1997, 1381). In accordance with their role, curators are oriented to 'think historically', not just about the past but also towards the future, embodying and sustaining the collective memory that binds them to their *lieu de mémoire*. Consequently, despite the management revolution, curators' narratives are evidence of the enduring power of their *milieu* but embedded in the structural hierarchy and ideology of exemplary art and design set in place in the mid-19th century. Object traces left by the past, are, for the museum curator (and museum visitors) a direct link to history. Museums signify continuity and engender historical consciousness: 'Part of the value of what museums do … is precisely to give you that kind of [pause] almost uncanny sense, if you really think about it, of close connection to things, which are extremely distant' (Curator 1-T04/09).

Architecture and objects, as well as aspects of their professional role, support a condition of continuity and the museum provides 'some kind of immanent relation' (Curator 1-T04/09) to the past. The challenge to continuity came from the discourse of 'change', a term widely current in Thatcherite Conservative discourse (Du Gay 2007) as well as in the museum profession during the early 1990s, but especially throughout the V&A restructuring. As one curator explained it, on the one hand, the V&A 'desperately needed change [...] We didn't want the curatorial voice to be represented as being against change in the V&A. Change was that most loaded word at the time [used] much too much [giving] a bad name to change' (Curator 4-T07/09). Change, as Du Gay demonstrates, became used in a discourse of organisational change to mobilise support for the 're-invention' or 'modernization' of public administration (Du Gay 2007, 137–8).

## NARRATIVE IDENTITY

The philosopher Paul Ricoeur's concept of 'sameness' provides a conceptual tool for considering continuity and change in the identity of the curatorial persona. While 'sameness' denotes recognition and re-identification, temporality challenges this permanence through, for instance, institutional changes such as the move to Trusteeship. Although Ricoeur is not concerned with actual jobs or professions, his question: 'Is there a form of permanence in time which can be connected to the question of "who?" that is a reply to the question "Who am I?"' (Ricoeur 1992, 117–18) helps unravel the historicity of curatorial identity as expressed in life history accounts. It works also on the level of the individual narrator and how s/he accomplishes identity shifts, but it is also relevant in documenting how the individuals who make up a particular community accomplish professional changes. Ricoeur's concept of *narrative identity* grasps the dialectic of sameness and change implicit in 'the temporal dimension of the [curatorial] self' (Ricoeur 1992, 113) able to encompass a form of continuity that is also, nevertheless, subject to change.

So far I have used the term curatorial 'persona' because it indicated the sense of an adopted, internalised role. However, Ricoeur's concept of *character* is really more useful because it combines reference to the creative construction of the protagonist of a story who we recognise by their personal traits and acquired habits that 'give[s] a history to character' (Ricoeur 1992, 121). Curatorial routines, museum protocols and procedures would account for what we might term a curator's habits and identifications acquired over time. As Ricoeur proposes: 'To a large extent, in fact, the identity of a person or a community is made up of these identifications with values, norms, ideals, models, heroes, *in* which the person or a community recognizes itself. Recognizing oneself *in* contributes to recognizing oneself *by*' (Ricoeur 1992, 121). So, although for some 1989 meant that the 'chain of responsibility and of loyalty was snapped' (Curator 2-T18/09), curators continued to be subjects of the normative public service ethos of the Civil Service as well as those instituted by the Museums Association, the former much stronger than the latter in the national museum context. The public museum curatorial 'character' is one that draws on the discourse of ethical, public responsibility and duty. For instance, the term 'keeper' is now a title restricted to those who oversee large, combined departments at the V&A, but it resonates with another aspect of the dialectic of constancy and change. Implicit in the term is the commitment to maintenance and care.

The traditions of the Civil Service fostered a strong sense of duty, public service, impartiality, integrity and loyalty. As its servants, the staff was obliged to sign the *Official Secrets Act* (1920). The document members of staff were asked to sign lists in detail extracts from the Act that was initially drawn up in 1911, amended in 1920 and signed by staff until the early 1990s. I quote in full the first page of the declaration as set out in the form:

> I understand that the sections of the Official Secrets Acts set out on the back of this document cover material published in a speech, lecture, or radio, or television broadcast, or in the Press or in book form. I am aware that I should not divulge information gained by me as a result of my appointment to any unauthorized person, either orally or in writing, without previous official sanction in writing of the Department appointing me, to which written application should be made and two copies of the proposed publication to be forwarded. I understand also that I am liable to be prosecuted if I publish without official sanction any information I may acquire in the course of my tenure of an official appointment (unless it has already officially been made public) or retain without official sanction any sketch, plan, model, article, note or official documents which are no longer needed for my official duties, and that these provisions apply not only during the period of my appointment but also after my appointment has ceased.

The document inhibits free communication and reinforces bureaucratic hierarchies (though it must be borne in mind that all government civil servants in all departments would have signed it). In addition, publication guidelines of 1952 specifically recommended caution, the avoidance of publicity, and the requirement to 'tell your department about [the publication] and ask permission before going ahead with it' (Chapman 2004, 211).

Commenting on having to sign the Act in the late 1970s, one curator noted that 'the basic thrust was not to say anything that was about sensitive areas of work outside and that one would be bound by that' (Curator 3-T01/09). Signing the Act struck me as an anachronistic anomaly, the legacy of a 19th-century Civil Service, which had remained largely unchanged until the late 1960s.[8] If museums were seen as ivory towers for the cultivation of finer feelings, then the Act reinforced these characteristics and sustained a culture of deference and continuity. For instance, one department delayed in adapting to the use of first names, 'a necessary change which I had never dared to launch in [former Keeper's] time because [he] was my Keeper. He came from a different era and I felt it was my job to back him up' (Curator 2-T09/09).

## Cataloguing: the 'serious stuff'

The architectural layout of the building compounded the sense of introspection of each department, which was 'a world of its own' (Curator 6-T03/09), or 'worlds unto themselves' (Curator 3-T06/09) that fostered a particularly focused approach to the museum's intellectual capital. As one curator put it: 'A lot of curators don't have an intellectual vision, they just have an intellectual

8 The Labour Government under Harold Wilson undertook a full-scale review of the Civil Service in 1966–8, published under the name of its chairman Lord Fulton. The Conservative Government under Margaret Thatcher continued in a more radical manner to disestablish the power of the Civil Service which, in the case of the V&A, led to the managerial reforms of 1989. See Theakston (1995) and Pilkington (1999), both of whom provide histories and assessments of the British Civil Service.

field that they're interested in and they want to be allowed to get on with it' (Curator 5-T15/09). Writing a permanent collection catalogue was 'the ideal of museum intellectual activity' (Curator 5-T02/09) which was inculcated in staff at whatever level they entered the Museum. Beginning his career in the 1970s, the quote below demonstrates the constancy/change dialect in the dedication to scholarship and the shift to incorporating other museum-related activities:

> I think I always thought that cataloguing was the more 'real'; that this was the serious stuff, and that the other was just sort of, you know, on the periphery ... it's a view that I've changed now. You know, that one knows that all of it is important. But then and for a long time I thought that, yes, the academic stuff was more important. (Curator 3-T01/09)

Cataloguing requires detailed, accurate description, focused on individualising each object:

> The key thing was a description of the object which should be succinct and sufficiently detailed so that you knew it was that object and not another object even if it was quite similar. So you had to differentiate that particular object in the description. So if it was a plate that was almost identical to another plate, you had to differentiate it even by saying 'There's a slight nick on the edge'. So if you read it, you would be able to tell it was that object. (Curator 3-T05/09)

Describing how material was accessioned 'systematically and chronologically', another account about an earlier era (1949) shows how such bureaucratic procedures led to the accumulation of curatorial expertise and knowledge of the collections:

> I had to be instructed to make sure I knew the difference between an etching, an engraving, a mezzotint, a lithograph and so, and so on through the various categories of graphic art which wasn't very time-consuming and easily learned. And then we just set to: we were given bundles to get on with it which involved identifying the artist; describing the material; describing what it contained that is, like a German poster for Bavarian bock of circa 1900 which was a colour lithograph and so on, right down to Rembrandt etchings and material of that high quality... [The record] was put in the big Register volumes which was kept by the clerk to the department and she would write in the basic entry saying: Posters ten by so and so, you know, and allocate numbers to them. So there'd be ten numbers allocated to ten posters. And then there would be slips made out afterwards but they would be expanded into proper catalogue entries: Artist's name, title, lettering, medium, colour lithograph, mezzotint or whatever, and, and the registered number. We had registered numbers starting at 1 for each calendar year, that is to say from E one to E whatever it was at the end of the calendar year when material had been accessed. (Curator 7-T01/09)

Systematic, cumulative knowledge linked to the permanent nature of curators' employment under the terms of the Civil Service provided a training ground that cultivated a particular research ethos and expertise. So, although documenting the collection was also described by another as 'the most boring job' (Curator 1-T02/09), he was adamant that:

> actually, the key thing is to get people to know as much as possible about the collections for which they're responsible, and the area in which they're supposed to be expert and you get

> an awful lot out of documenting collections, perhaps that's from my own experience – you know, if you have to go through and describe things, you know, even weigh them and measure them, explain what they are, at the end of all that you'll have a very good visual and, you know, wider memory of the collections that will serve you enormously well as a curator. If you devolve the function of documentation to one person and do the kind of scholarship and interpretation somewhere else, that just never works because people might think that they know the collections because they've looked at it but they won't know it in the way that you know it because you've had to work with it all the time. (Curator 1-T05/09)

The above extract highlights the significance of cataloguing as part of curatorial expertise: its specificity to a defined field, and the development of a 'very good' visual memory of the collection instilled through constant proximity with the objects in the curator's care.

## 'Zap!' The Embodied Eye

The practice of close observation was particularly important in cultivating 'the eye of the connoisseur, which went: Zap! That's quality!' (Curator 2-T05/09). This term marks a specific distinction, even an opposition to current museum practice, which embraces a more diverse set of qualities aimed specifically at increasing and extending audiences, drawing on historical and social contexts as one element of the strategic campaign to attract a non-specialist audience. Previously:

> The old V and A was very much the style, the period, the high aesthetics, the object as a piece of art, not the use of the object, and the historical and social context [...] up to that point you would see a label which just talked about aesthetics and didn't attempt to give any context and [...] laid the V and A open to the charges of elitism. (Curator 3-T05/09)

The restricted conventions of cataloguing and label entries reinforced the inaccessibility of specialist knowledge, which only certain informed visitors could share. Visual identification and comparison, however, was deemed to be the most accessible form of information, providing visitors with at least some currency of cultural capital, however limited. In the Study Collections visitors had the opportunity to view and research the objects arranged according to material type. Here, as one former senior curator explained:

> If you wanted to find out anything you could walk from one end of the galleries to the other and be almost sure of *matching* whatever it was that granny had left you and finding something very similar to it so at least you'd know *its date and place of manufacture.* [my italics]
> (Curator 2-T05/09)

'Study' therefore, conformed to understanding the provenance, place and date of manufacture of a particular object, alongside visual, aesthetic comparisons: understanding an object *visually*.

The meta-narrative of object-based curatorial expertise of V&A curators, where 'you got people who could spend their whole career working with a particular material, a series of techniques, and the history of that' (Curator 2-T17/09), arose, however, within the context of a bureaucracy as outlined above, that specifically discouraged engagement with socio-political context, the danger being that it might, most possibly would, lead to critical perspectives on social class, political power and ideology. By focusing on material, methods of manufacture and provenance, visual identification and authentication, any overtly politically problematic issues were avoided. However, it also reinforced the autonomy of the decorative object grasped via the aesthetics of 'quality', assessed by the cultivated curator's connoisseurial 'eye'. As revealed in their narratives, however, this eye is more than the elitism of a particular habitus. Curators' daily working lives are spent in *physical* proximity with their objects, so their eye is not simply the display of a disinterested Kantian aesthetic, nor is it solely the manifestation of acquired or learnt visual codes as argued by Bourdieu, the 'privilege of those who have access to the economic and social conditions which allow the "pure and disinterested" disposition to be durably established' (Bourdieu 1996, 314). It is rather a specifically *embodied* eye as, for instance, elaborated by the late Barbara Morris, cited above, in her discussion about plastic objects in the collection:

> It was something that had to be *handled* because a lot of the early plastics were all dyed black with logwood and if you just showed a slide of them, they look exactly the same. But if *you could actually see* them, you saw the difference. (Morris-T09/10)

Embodiment was also implicit in the description of a director at Sotheby's in the 1950s, for whom another interviewee had worked before joining the V&A; he commented: 'He had I think an amazing eye for works of art although his eyesight was beginning to go, and he always said young eyesight, I was too old at 25 or whatever I was, I was really too old' (Curator 2-T02/09).

This observation reinforces vision as an embodied experience (Crary 1992). In identifying faked Staffordshire figurines, the Sotheby's director was said to have exclaimed: 'Suddenly the scales fell from my eyes'. The explanation continues: 'On the whole if you have long sight you should study frescos, and if you are short-sighted ceramic often works very well because ... you see with immense sharpness close to, the actual grain of the thing, and without even a magnifying glass' (Curator 2-T02/09).

The point is stressed by making explicit the association with the importance of handling objects: 'It was a very good training in quick appraisal of what an object is. And you always had to handle it. No nonsense with photographs. You could do that afterwards and find comparisons' (Curator 2-T02/09). The development of the embodied curatorial eye was an important skill that curators acquired either through their years of service in the Museum or in an auction house or gallery.

Apart from the financial implications, the identification of fakes provided a challenge to the connoisseur's eye: 'It's not easy to tell a fake. Someone will always catch you in the end' (Curator 2-T02/08). However, rather than embracing the visual/tactile test posed by fakes, another interviewee focused on their ability to provide an insight into historical tastes and aesthetic values, demonstrating the continuity of visual appreciation but through the contemporary register of contextual knowledge:

> I remain interested in principle in the fascinating ability of fakes to allow us *to understand* more about how people *saw* objects in the past and what they valued in them. So, a fake of an Italian sculpture produced in say the 1860s does enable us *to understand* very clearly what it was that people, the market particularly in the 1860s, valued in Italian sculpture of the kind that was being copied or faked, because obviously in responding to the market, you bring out

> those features which are most in demand. And sometimes that means fakes *look* very much like the things they copy but often it *looks* very different and that helps you *to understand* that people do *see* things very differently in different periods. So it's a kind of – a fake can be a sort of time machine that enables you *to step into the shoes*, or you know, *to see through the eyes*, perhaps more accurately, of people who lived at the time that the fakes were produced [my italics]. (Curator 1-T04/09)

In the above passage, we see a shift from the dialectic of hand and eye as a means to identification and provenance to that of seeing as understanding, foregrounding how curators and by implication visitors can 'think historically', as Crane has suggested, by 'seeing historically'. This is not to say that the connoisseur's eye is no longer a valued skill in the museum profession; curators continue to document, work in close proximity to their objects, mount exhibitions and engage in collections-related scholarship. Their visual expertise, therefore, continues to be a professional 'habit', but, as the last extract demonstrated, it is reconfigured to express a changing attitude to how this knowledge is made meaningful to current curators' sense of the functions of their profession and expertise.

## Conclusion

My exploration has focused on the professional identity of curators working at the V&A from the post-war period onwards in which major restructuring was seen by many to have greatly altered the meaning and definition of their roles. Further research will explore other critical moments in the Museum's late 20th-century history. The 1989 proposal to separate scholarship from care and management of the collections threatened to split what had been conceived of as an integrated function and responsibility, a specific type of professional scholar involved in 'developing a type of scholarship [...] people outside such a museum as the V&A had no opportunity of developing' (Curator 2-T17/09). The conception of a coherent, unified identity called 'the curator' was shown, like all identities, to be subject to historical contingency. Ricoeur's concept of identity as a dialectic of permanence and change provided a framework for reconceptualising the curatorial 'character' as created within narratives that nevertheless allowed for continuity of qualities as well as the adoption of new traits and habits, the former reinforced and sustained by the V&A as both *lieu* and *milieu de mémoire.* Curatorial identity needs to be grasped within the contexts of its formation and conditions of possibility for, as Du Gay has suggested: 'It is important not to divorce forms of personhood from the empirical settings within which they are formed' (Du Gay 2007, 26). The 'curator', therefore, can be seen to be constructed *by* as well as being instrumental *in* shaping their own [auto]biographies and that of their museums.

Consequently, rather than dismissing the traditional forms of museum scholarship as narrow elitism, the narratives have been used to understand the expertise of the curator-connoisseur's 'eye' as an embodied faculty formed within and sustained by the conventions and protocols of the Civil Service. The narratives of this group of interviewees brought to light the origin of the museum curator as a public sector profession that has increasingly broadened access to its cultural capital, revealed, for instance, in the conceptual shift that accompanied the meaning and status of fakes, or the role of documentation as only one aspect of curatorial responsibility. Oral history provides access to understanding how curators conceive of their professional (and personal) lives as part of the meanings and values they ascribe to their roles. As Ricoeur succinctly remarked: 'It is the identity of the story that makes the identity of the character' (Ricoeur 1992, 147).

## BIBLIOGRAPHY AND REFERENCES

Bourdieu, P, 1996 *The Rules of Art: Genesis and Structure of the Literary Field*, Polity Press, Cambridge

Boylan, P J, 2006 The Museum Profession, in *Companion to Museum Studies* (ed S A MacDonald), Blackwell, Oxford

Burton, A, 1999 *Vision and Accident: The Story of the Victoria & Albert Museum*, V&A Publications, London

Chapman, R A, 2004 *The Civil Service Commission, 1855–1991: A Bureau Biography*, Routledge, New York and London

Crane, S, 1997 Writing the Individual Back into Collective Memory, *American Historical Review* 102 (4), December, 1372–85

Crary, J, 1992 *Techniques of the Observer: On Vision and Modernity in the Nineteenth Century*, MIT Press, Cambridge, MA

Du Gay, P, 2007 *Organizing Identity: Persons and Organizations After Theory*, Sage, London and Thousand Oaks, CA

Evans, E J, 2004 *Thatcher and Thatcherism*, 2 edn, Routledge, London

John, P, and Johnson, M, 2008 Is There Still A Public Service Ethos? in *British Social Attitudes: The 24th Report* (eds A Park, J Curtice, K Thomson, M Phillips, M Johnson and E Clery), Sage, London

Kavanagh, G (ed), 1994 *Museum Provision and Professionalism*, Routledge, London and New York

MacDonald, S, 2002 *Behind the Scenes at the Science Museum*, Berg, Oxford

Murdoch, J, 1994 Defining Curation, in *Museum Provision and Professionalism* (ed G Kavanagh), Routledge, London and New York

Nora, P, 1989 Between Memory and History: *Les lieux de mémoire, Representations* 26, 7–24

Official Secrets Act 1920 [online], available from: http://www.opsi.gov.uk/acts/acts1920/pdf/ukpga_19200075_en.pdf [December 2009]

Pilkington, C, 1999 *The Civil Service in Britain Today*, Manchester University Press, Manchester

Ricoeur, P, 1988 *Time and Narrative*, vol 3 (trans K Blamey and D Pellauer), University of Chicago Press, Chicago

— 1991 *A Ricoeur Reader: Reflection and Imagination* (ed M J Valdés), Harvester Wheatsheaf, Hemel Hempstead

— 1992 *Oneself As Another* (trans K Blamey), University of Chicago Press, Chicago

Sandino, L, 2009 News From the Past: Oral History at the V&A, *V&A Online Journal* 2, available from: http://www.vam.ac.uk/res_cons/research/online_journal/journal-2-index/sandino-oral-history/index.html [December 2009]

Thatcher, M, 1989 Speech opening Design Museum [online], available from: http://www.margaretthatcher.org/speeches/displaydocument.asp?docid=107722 [September 2009]

Theakston, K, 1995 *The Civil Service Since 1945*, Blackwell, Oxford

Tipton, G, n.d. *How to work with curators* [online], available from: http://www.creative-choices.co.uk/knowledge/quick-guides/how-to-work-with-curators [May 2010]

Vandenabeele, W, and Horton, S, 2005 The Evolution of the British Public Service Ethos: A Historical Institutional Approach in Explaining Change, Joint EGPA-ASPA conference: *Ethics and Integrity of Governance – The First Transatlantic Dialogue*, Leuven, 2–5 June, available from: http://soc.kuleuven.be/io/ethics/paper/Paper%20WS2_pdf/Vandenabeele&Horton.pdf [December 2009]

# Institutional Biographies

7

# Significant Lives: Telling Stories of Museum Architecture

Suzanne MacLeod

## Introduction

This paper explores the potential of biography as a strategy for generating histories of museum buildings and provides a rationale for why this would be an important addition to the architectural history of museums and galleries and museum studies more broadly. Drawing on recent academic research in museum studies, architectural history and theory, as well as biography, autobiography and life writing, the chapter explores aspects of the subjects, methods and outcomes of architectural history. It asks questions about what such an approach might tell us about architecture and what histories it might reveal of museums, galleries and the people who have made them. The chapter argues that we need to develop subtle and nuanced approaches to the architectural history of museums and galleries, approaches which move beyond the lives of museum architects and linear histories of stylistic progress that continue to dominate the literature. Such histories produce a 'smoothed out'[1] version of museum building of little use to the museums field and are complicit in the assertion that architecture is quite simply the activity and aesthetic outcome – the object – of the architect. When combined with recent critical thinking around the nature and production of architecture, a biographical approach can unearth detailed histories of architectural change and development (in relation to the physical structure) and provide glimpses of tangled stories of occupation and use, often revealing social and professional relationships and the politics and tensions behind architectural development. Most specifically, biography offers the promise of moving us towards some sense of the ordinary lives, the human bodily experiences that have made and remade the architecture of the museum throughout its 'life'. What we might broadly describe as a biographical approach to museum history can help us to understand how museum buildings have been built and the ways in which architecture is as much a product of its use and the stories and meanings generated around it as it is of a more formal design process or museum development project. All of these histories have the potential to demystify the architectural process and support a contemporary desire, voiced in some parts of the museum profession, for a more consensual, dialogic, participatory design process (see, for example, papers in MacLeod 2005). Far from an academic trend, biographical histories emerge as routes towards meaningful histories of change which have the potential to tell new stories of

1 Drawing on Henry James' comment that death 'smoothes the folds' of the person one loved and building on the work of David Ellis, Hermione Lee has acknowledged the inevitable smoothing out of the biographical process. 'Alternatives, missed chances, roads not taken, accidents and hesitations, the whole "swarm of possibilities" that hums around our everyday experience, too often disappears in the smoothing biographical process' (Lee 2008, 2–3).

museum architecture necessary for the ongoing development and, potentially, radical remaking of the physical stuff of museums and galleries.

The paper begins by briefly revisiting some of the perceived problems of museum architecture and the complicity of architectural history in the production of this *status quo* (see also MacLeod 2005). It then moves on to consider some of the uses of biography in *retelling* the architecture of one particular museum, the Walker Art Gallery in Liverpool. Finally, the conclusion considers the implications of such a biographical approach for our understanding of capital development processes and of museum architecture more broadly.

## SOME 'PROBLEMS' OF MUSEUM ARCHITECTURE

There is no question that museum architecture and design is now recognised as an important strand in museum studies. However, the field is new and continues to raise challenges for the researcher. As the dust settles on so many capital development projects internationally and as concrete continues to be poured into some of the largest museum projects in the world, museum professionals, academics and an engaged segment of the architectural design profession are raising more and more questions about the drive to build and the choices we are making. There is, however under-researched, an emerging consensus within the museums profession that there is a need to engage with the ethics of museum building and articulate, as a profession, what we want from museum buildings in the future (MacLeod 2011). Questions are now being asked about what we have learned from the recent phase of museum development. Why have some capital projects been deemed unsatisfactory and others not? Where does good practice lie and how might it be improved even further? Do we understand what it means to build an economically or an environmentally sustainable building? And, in the new museums constructed, have we even come close to conceptualising the physical characteristics of a socially sustainable museum? Finally, what can we take from the hard-hitting criticisms of building projects and processes voiced by a number of influential museum theorists? If the answers to such questions are not straightforward, what is very clear is that there is a paucity of research and evaluation in this area; museum architecture and design continues to be under-theorised and essentially remains un-evaluated.

Perhaps the most vocal and most convincing critic of the drive to build has been Robert Janes. In *Museums in a Troubled World*, Janes bemoans the relentless desire to build in the cultural sector. He writes:

> Although often likened to a renaissance, this architectural boom doesn't merit this praise, lacking as it commonly does any vigorous intellectual or creative resurgence within the museum itself. In fact, the opposite prevails, as the 'If you build it, he will come' syndrome readily diverts attention away from a consideration of purpose, values and the requirements for long-term sustainability. (Janes 2009, 108)

In a similar vein, James Bradburne has described the 'overbuilt' nature of museums as a 'poison pill', condemning museums to increased staffing bills and increasingly stretched revenue budgets, the challenges of which will potentially distract from the mission of the organisation (Bradburne 1998). Like others, Bradburne cites the inherent unprofitability of any mission-led organisation as a salutary reminder to museum directors who see capital development as a route to growth and sustainability that the economics of this are far from straightforward. Janes summarises the argument: 'There is no doubt that bold and creative buildings attract visitors and can provide meaningful visitor experiences, but these inducements are increasingly irrelevant, perhaps malevolent, in a world beset by … social and environmental pressures' (Janes 2009, 111).

Janes, quite rightly, demands an alternative to capital development and questions what he describes as myopia, a seeming reluctance to engage with these issues within the profession (Janes 2009, 111). He is not alone. Others have also raised questions about the decision to build and suggested reuse of existing spaces such as shop fronts as offering one route forward for museum development.[2] Further research in this direction is clearly necessary. However, capital development always has been and always will be a part of the museum. Throughout their modern history museums have been shaped and reshaped as ideas about their roles and purposes have changed. Museums deal in the physical and the tangible, and to turn our backs on museum building, at a point where we have a very real chance of extracting some of the learning from recent experience, would seem to be a wasted opportunity. Putting aside our dismay at the sometimes obscene consumerist drama of new museum buildings, we need to ask what we have learned from this unprecedented phase of museum development.

One of the key problems of museum architecture is its opacity. The image of the object is so strong that it masks from view the complex of relationships, interactions and negotiations that produced the physical building in the first place (Borden and Rendell 2000, 3–23). Often, the word architecture is used as a replacement for (or interchangeably with) building, once again masking from view the politics of building and the complex of processes through which certain professional practices produce 'architecture', as opposed to a mere building (see Forty 2000, 13). This opacity makes it difficult to engage critically with architecture. Recent work in architectural history and theory, by thinkers such as Adrian Forty, Jonathan Hill and Jeremy Till, opens up this view of architecture as driven by individuals and social groups who operate in specific ways for a variety of reasons (Forty 1980; 2000; Hill 1998; 2003; Till 1998). From this perspective, architecture is acknowledged as a process of social and cultural production and the built environment is recognised as an embodiment of social values and mores. More than this, the production of a building is only part of the story and it is the peopling of space and the social relationships that are possible and encouraged within the space that will continue to make and remake the built environment. In this sense, architecture is also about power and identity; it is about people, their occupation of space and the way they build their identities in and through space.

2 At a recent panel discussion on the ethics of museum architecture at the University of Leicester, a group comprising a museum architect/designer, a museum policy maker, a sustainability consultant, a display case manufacturer and a project manager from the heritage construction industry discussed the challenges for museums of building economically, environmentally and socially sustainable buildings. The panel was part of *Narrative Space*, an international conference organised by the School of Museum Studies at the University of Leicester and the School of the Built Environment at the University of Nottingham, April 2010. The panel members were: Suzanne MacLeod, University of Leicester; Maurice Davis, Museum Association; Rachel Madan, Greener Museums; Dominic Sore, Patton Heritage; Clive McCready, Click-Netherfield; and Peter Higgins, Land Design Studio. One of the conclusions of the discussion, which was fuelled by a number of perceptive questions and comments from the audience, was that we need to explore something that Peter Higgins referred to as 'the distributed museum': the idea that new capital development be replaced by a better use of existing space and use of other, existing public spaces.

Like the buildings themselves, the majority of architectural histories close off any possibility of such a deep and meaningful reading of the physical stuff of museums and galleries. Here, stories of stylistic development and lives of architects continue to dominate, stories which smooth over the messy, dirty and sometimes bloody view of museum buildings opened up by theorists like Forty, Hill and Till. There are some exceptions, of course. A small number of recent histories have focused on single buildings and have linked specific forms of knowledge to their production (see Noordegraaf 2004; Yanni 1999). This approach certainly helps us to see that individual museum buildings have changed over time and to understand a link between knowledge and space, but there is clearly more at stake. As Forty (1980, 61) noted of the modern hospital:

> The customary explanation [for change] is that their development resulted from advances in medical and scientific knowledge, but this seems inadequate for several reasons. In the first place, it ignores the question of why scientific knowledge develops at all. Moreover, there is no reason why scientific knowledge should be applied to buildings, or to anything else, unless it is in someone's interest to do so.

The same thinking can of course be applied to the modern museum.

At the present time, existing architectural histories of the museum provide little in the way of support to museum professionals in understanding or highlighting architecture as a complex social production. They provide little or no sense of architectural planning processes and work to reinforce problematic notions of the museum as static and unchanging through a focus on the building as object. Where process is considered, it tends to be the process of the architect, obscuring from view the range of stakeholders active in the production of museum space and any possibility of a more dialogic development process that might in turn lead to a rethinking of what we want from the physical structure of the museum or gallery. The sole focus on the architect and architectural style neglects any consideration of the needs of multiple users of the museum and promotes the desire amongst patrons and funders for a signature building by a named architect. Even very recently produced architectural histories of the museum can seem to passively reproduce biographies of architects and architectural styles – repeating received wisdom rather than providing critical and useful readings of museums' architectural pasts. In the process, as Till states, there is no room for the quotidian, for the mess and tangled chaos of lived experience (Till 2000, 291). This is a difficulty if we aim to build museums where life can be lived and where viewing exhibition content is just one dimension, as it always has been, of the museum experience.

## BIOGRAPHY AND STORYTELLING: SIGNIFICANT LIVES

Biography is often described as being in opposition to history. Writers of and on biography and autobiography conceptualise this in different ways. Laura Marcus has described the ways in which some writers see biography as a servant to history or as an historical sub-genre. For others, biography is a separate and distinct field of work defined by its close focus on a 'life' and the presence of internal justifications for the writing of that life – such as the genius or uniqueness of the biographee. For Sidney Lee, biography is akin to chemistry, with its focus on the particular and its attempt to resolve and understand substances. History, on the other hand, is described by Lee as more akin to mechanics, 'the science which determines the power of bodies in the mass' (Marcus 1994, 61). Here, history is defined as dealing with the crowd, the mass, the larger forces at play in society, whereas biography is concerned with the character, the individual and the particular. Of course social history and particularly oral history have challenged such sweeping generalisations.

Regardless of where one places disciplinary boundaries, if at all, between biography and history, as a writer of museum history I find the field of auto/biography and life writing fascinating. Literary theorists, critics and writers of biographies are consciously engaged with issues that resonate for the historian, such as the availability or unavailability (and often intentional destruction) of sources or the representation of conflicting versions of events within and between sources. Many biographers are all too aware of their own presence in the text; there are multiple stories of biographers stepping into the shoes of their subject and identifying to the point of adopting some of the perceived characteristics of the biographee. Of course, this is also a part of the myth of biography.

Similar to the experience of the historian, a whole range of methods are open to the biographer from disciplines as varied as politics and social history, sociology, psychology and fiction (Marcus 1994, 3). The difficulty of pinning biography down within disciplinary boundaries has led to discussion of its transgressive character: an ability to cross boundaries and challenge conventions in a way that could, in the language of Raymond Williams, 'appear either as a dangerous double agent ... or as a magical instrument of reconciliation' (Marcus 1994, 7). Auto/biography has certainly undergone radical reassessment in recent years as a direct result of feminist critiques. Most fundamental has been the shift in understanding of what qualifies as a 'significant life'. Feminist writers have worked to write women into the field, a process which has also resulted in a loosening of definitions of autobiography and the growth of interest in life writing; a valuing of diaries, journals and so on not simply as sources but as literary texts in their own right (Marcus 1994, 1). The parallels are not difficult to draw with architectural history. Approaching a building like the Walker Art Gallery is a specific decision to write a large regional art gallery into the history of museum architecture. But such a process inevitably demands a rethinking of where the evidence for that history will be drawn from and how the narrative will be constructed.

The notion of biography – of a life – has appealed to a range of museum historians because it is a mechanism for placing limits on a historical study and, importantly, for narrowing the focus of a piece of historical research, enabling a deeper engagement with a micro history. Regardless of whether it is different from or similar to certain kinds of historical studies, it enables a focus on the detailed and the particular that is required if historians are to move beyond 'smoothed out' histories of museum development. It chimes with Jeremy Till's comments on the quotidian and Hermione Lee's comments on the desire for a 'warts and all' approach to biography which might provide 'a vivid sense of the person' (Lee 2008, 3). Of course, the historian could aim for this focus without the identification of an arbitrary 'life', but just as biographers now recognise the connections between lives – that biography is always about more than one life – so architectural projects which focus on a single building have the potential to delve into the complex of lives lived around and through the building in order to understand more about the reality out of which the building and the architecture have emerged time and again.

So what might such a history look like? The tangle of lives and the messy reality behind the initial building of the Walker Art Gallery is certainly not obvious at first sight. Indeed, the civic celebrations on the day of the opening of Liverpool's new gallery of art were precisely intended to mask the complex social and political contexts and events through which it emerged. On the morning of 6 September 1877, 8000 working men organised in their Trades Associations and Friendly Societies marched six abreast through the streets of the city, symbolically united through the wearing of white Library, Museum and Art Committee rosettes. The procession passed by the Town Hall, where the Mayor of Liverpool and donor of the Walker Art Gallery, Andrew Barclay Walker, his wife and the Earl of Derby looked on and waved gaily at the city's working men. As the procession made its way from the Town Hall towards the Lime Street area of town, the streets were crowded with onlookers and decorated with flags and bunting. Once the procession passed by the Town Hall, eight carriages containing Liverpool's leading men as well as a host of invited dignitaries joined the procession and on arrival at the gallery, where the city's Volunteers had entertained the waiting crowd, thousands of people crowded onto St George's Plateau and up the steps of St George's Hall, vying to gain a vantage point from which to view the opening ceremony. Once the city's leading men had made their way onto the specially constructed platform in front of the gallery, Andrew Barclay Walker was presented with a silver gilt casket representing the new building, after which he handed a gold key to the Earl of Derby, symbolic of the handing over of the new gallery to the Corporation.

The image of the great and the good of Liverpool, from across the political spectrum, celebrating the gallery and its donor must have been an impressive sight. Such an impression of unity, however, belied the series of events that led to the building of a gallery of art in the city. For many years a number of prominent Liberal councillors had attempted to establish a public gallery in Liverpool. From the 1850s, various possibilities for a gallery had been explored and in 1868, under the stewardship of James Picton, this had gone as far as the drawing up of architect's plans. From 1871, following the failure of Picton and his colleagues to muster enough support for the project, Picton, along with Edward Samuelson and Philip Rathbone, established the annual art exhibition held in the William Brown Museum. However, in 1873, the idea of a gallery of art took on a new urgency (Anon 1877a; Morris 1994; 1999; 1996). Driven once again by James Picton and the Library, Museum and Art Committee, a proposal was prepared to erect a gallery of art at the cost to the public purse of £18,000. Picton's proposal was based upon the redistribution of the penny rate, the rate from which the museums and libraries were funded, and included a reduction of £300 to the library provision.

The proposal generated a strong response from the local taxpayers and specifically from the Vigilance Committee, a self-formed group of ratepayers of Lime Street, 'the object of which is to watch the corporate expenditure in the interests of the ratepayers, with the view of checking extravagance and preventing unnecessary additions to the present rates' (Anon 1873a). For this group of lower-middle-class shop owners and businessmen, art was the pastime of the wealthy upper middle classes and merchant princes and it was regarded as something of a scandal that it might be funded from the public purse (Moore 2004). In the context of the 1870s and the tightening of Corporation purse-strings following the vast public expenditure over the preceding two decades, the idea of a gallery of art would receive short shrift from many in Liverpool.

On the morning of 6 August 1873, the day that the Library, Museum and Art Committee was scheduled to formally present the proposals to the council, the Vigilance Committee prepared a delegation to the Mayor at the Town Hall to put forward their case against the development. The Mayor, Mr W B Forwood, then took the Vigilance Committee's view to the council meeting where the proposal was also opposed by a Mr J A Forrester, councillor for Lime Street ward who, like the Vigilance Committee, focused on the potential additional costs of the build and fit out as well as the cost of the land. The proposals were then, according to the *Liverpool Leader*, 'demolished' by Alderman Weightman, Chair of the Finance Committee, who caused some comment by launching into a 50-minute lecture against the project at 1 pm, completely ignoring lunch (Anon 1873b). Drawing attention to the running costs of a new building in addition to the capital development costs, Weightman used his financial expertise to illustrate that the cost of the gallery could not be contained within the penny Library and Museum rate and described the estimated annual costs of £250 for maintenance of the building as 'absurdly inadequate' (Anon 1873b). The gallery had become a divisive issue before an agreement to build it had even been reached. In late August the Vigilance Committee were still holding meetings and sending delegations to the Mayor, by then Edward Samuelson, to protest against the proposed plans, and by the end of August 1873 *The Daily Courier* could describe the proposal as 'shelved' (Anon 1873c).

As the gallery was picked up as a political issue and recognised by a number of Conservative councillors as an opportunity to generate a public perception of the Liberal minority as easy with public money, Picton's grasp on the situation slipped further away. At a protest meeting against rising civic expenditure in late August, Picton was placed under pressure by his Conservative colleagues and specifically R R Minton, a Conservative and a 'grog' man,[3] to withdraw his plans for a publicly funded gallery. James Moore has documented these events where, 'in a clear move to outflank his opponents, [Picton] offered to fund an art gallery for the town providing that his main Conservative opponent, Councillor Richard Minton, would provide a lending library' (Moore 2004). Minton then forced Picton's hand by stating that he would finance a lending library so long as Picton funded a picture gallery. Picton promptly denied any suggestion that he would fund a gallery in its entirety, stating instead that he would put £1000 towards the gallery if a further 19 benefactors would come forward and do the same. Picton was then joined by four others, but at this point momentum dwindled and no further pledges were forthcoming.

In an unprecedented move to salvage the situation, Samuelson called a meeting at the end of September in the Town Hall to open a public subscription. The subscription failed to raise any broader interest in the scheme, a situation debated and lamented in the local press. In a city which suffered from immense social problems and poverty, the building of a gallery of art with public funds – or even, it would seem, with the usual mix of public or private where in some form it would certainly 'come upon the rates' – was highly problematic. Suspicions were very real that however much such a project was articulated as serving the entire city, the reality was that a gallery of art would serve the few, rather than the many. The project was dead in the water and no-one could have predicted, at what must have been a particularly low point for James Picton, that Andrew Barclay Walker, local brewer, publican and Conservative, would offer to cover the entire cost of the new gallery on the occasion of his becoming mayor. Nonetheless, this is exactly what happened on 9 November 1873 (Borough of Liverpool 1874).

Almost as soon as the question of funding was resolved, attention turned to the physical site and structure of the new gallery. Clearly a man of action, Walker got straight to work on the project. He immediately instructed Cornelius Sherlock, the architect of his private residence, to prepare designs for the new gallery. Detailed scrutiny of the minutes of the Library, Museum and Art Committee and the Finance Committee between 1873 and 1877 make it very clear that the design and construction of the building took place outside of the committee room, the building

3 'Grog man' was a term used to describe businessmen involved in the drinks trade either as a brewer or a publican. In Liverpool there was a distinct correlation between business interests in alcohol and Conservative politics.

effectively being built as a private project. Walker and Sherlock, along with H H Vale,[4] who had been drafted in to aid Sherlock with the design, presented their plans for the building to the Town Council in April 1874 and they were immediately approved. The presentation of this design to the council would be the only occasion where the design was considered within the committee system, a situation which must have proved incredibly frustrating for Picton, Rathbone and Samuelson. Walker used the building as a mechanism to score a political point and, by excluding Picton and his colleagues from the entire building process, effectively managed to disempower the group and appropriate their pet project.

This brief story begins to expose some of the political tensions and individual agendas that led to the building of a Gallery of Art in Liverpool and to illustrate some of the amazing similarities to contemporary struggles over museum development projects. The Walker Art Gallery has in fact been reshaped many times and wherever the historian/biographer dips in there are multiple stories of museum-making to tell. Here, the traditional sources of architectural plans, drawings and photographs need to be supplemented with committee minutes, correspondence, newspaper editorials and other such sources which offer up glimpses of the people actively involved in the production of the building. The challenges of this wealth of data are many; stories need to be communicated and the process of writing them down into a recognisable narrative and within a given word limit inevitably means that selections need to be made from the 'swarm of possibilities' of everyday life, each time smoothing the folds of the past.

So far, none of this is particularly groundbreaking: it seems rather obvious that a biographical approach could enable a focus on a single building and a rewriting of the agendas of architectural history in the process. But there is also a creativity and a warmth to some work on life writing which I can relate to as someone who has undertaken work into the life of one specific building, a project which inevitably results in the writing of multiple human lives, however brief each appearance might be. Beyond the key issues of methods and sources, many biographers talk about the aim of getting close to their subject, a subject who is more often than not dead. The idea of the generous biographer, attempting to understand their biographee and the desire to find sources or texts that reveal the 'likeness' of the person, has been explored by a number of literary theorists. Richard Holmes has reflected on his method of 'footstepping', living aspects of his subject's life in order to feel some of the sensations that the person may have felt in order to add a 'physical layer' into the writing process (Wroe 2008). This is perhaps where the biographical approach can add most value to the historical approach. Architectural histories have until very recently (and with some much-admired exceptions such as Borden *et al* 1995) been drawn to the surface of things. What is both touching and exciting about biography is the desire to locate the lived reality – the body – of the subject. In architectural history, understanding architecture through the lives lived in and around and through the building would seem to offer a mechanism for understanding more about how architecture gets made. But getting close to the real bodily experiences of those people in that place is incredibly challenging.

4 Vale committed suicide during the building project and his name then disappears from any documentation of the project. The building design is certainly initially accredited to both architects but following Vale's death, Sherlock states publicly that the design was always his. Perhaps unsurprisingly in view of the scandal surrounding suicide, Vale is not mentioned in the long speeches and thanks that were given at the opening, the banquet and in the press. For an early reference to Vale see Anon 1874.

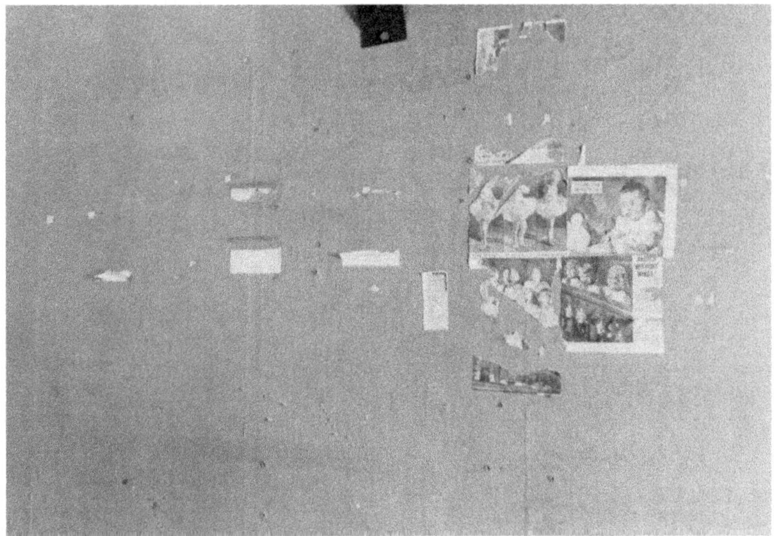

Fig 7.1.
Fragments stuck to the gallery wall photographed as part of the Engineering Department survey of the Walker Art Gallery in 1948 following removal of the Ministry of Food

Hermione Lee (2008) has traced literary biographers' fascinations with particular, intimate moments in writers' lives. She has explored, for example, the ways in which a particular moment in the life of Jane Austen – a moment where she faints as a result of being told that her family was moving from Steventon to Bath – has been dealt with by Austen's various biographers. The interpretations vary, as one might expect, but the analysis reveals the fascination of biographers with such moments of intimacy, however small or unsubstantiated, as they reveal or offer up the potential of a closeness to a moment of lived, bodily experience. Locating, identifying and getting close to past users of museum buildings is nigh on impossible from the scraps of paper and photographs that comprise museum archives and the range of other primary sources that the architectural historian of the museum might use. Here too, and without the mass of anecdote, myth and legend passed on in a variety of forms around a writer like Jane Austen, there is a very obvious temptation to make more of and fetishise certain tantalising, but often opaque, sources.

In my history of the Walker Art Gallery this is the case with an image: a photograph of what look like scraps from a newspaper stuck to the gallery wall (Fig 7.1). I am fascinated by this image, which was taken as part of an architectural survey of the gallery in 1948 upon the removal of the Ministry of Food which had occupied the Walker for a full ten years during and after World War II. During that time, hundreds of Liverpool women occupied the building and carried out the administration of war time rationing as well as finding numerous social uses for the building to fill the long, dark evenings. Beyond what amounts to one or two photographs and a large amount of written material on the occupation, use and disputes over the building at this time, I have to date located very little visual 'evidence' of this period. The usual tropes of

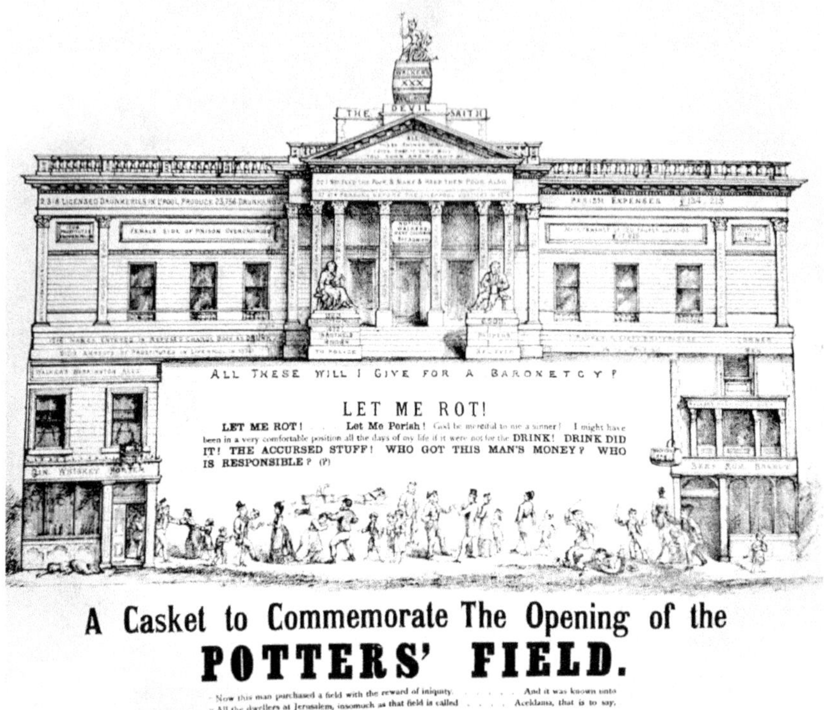


FIG 7.2.
A CARICATURE ILLUSTRATING THE WALKER ART GALLERY. THE REFERENCE TO THE 'CASKET' RELATES TO THE SILVER-GILT CASKET REPRESENTING THE BUILDING PRESENTED TO WALKER AND THE WALLS ARE SCRAWLED WITH GRAFFITI DOCUMENTING THE ABUSES OF ALCOHOL AND THE RESULTING CRIME IN LIVERPOOL. ABOVE THE DOOR IT READS 'WALKER'S BESY CUSTOMERS NOT ADMITTED'

the historian/biographer, such as the use of supplementary or comparative sources,[5] can be used to fill these gaps, but this image is, to me, like Jane Austen's faint: a glimpse of what I read as something intimate, a user of the building at that time pinning personally meaningful cuttings to the gallery wall. The image provides a mechanism for getting beyond the mass, beyond the crowd, to an individual person in a living body occupying and using the space. This trace of human contact suggests something of the occupation and use that left the building in a semi-derelict state in 1948. Despite Lee's warning of descending too far into fiction when filling the gaps between already slippery sources, such an interpretation of the image gets us somewhere

5 For example, publications from the Ministry of Food offer a glimpse of how canteens were added in public buildings like the Walker. Similarly, the oral testimony of a librarian from the Picton Library on the habits of the Ministry workers stationed there offers a glimpse of the use of these buildings at that time.

close to the presence of these Liverpool women as well as illustrating how buildings are changed and adapted in piecemeal ways through use, sometimes to quite startling effect.

Other traces or fragments that can be attached to the hand of an occupant or a character who operated within or around the building – whose life the building played some role in and who has played some role in the production of the building – are equally powerful. One such fragment is a caricature located in Liverpool Records Office which has never previously been published in any history of the Walker (Fig 7.2). From archival research, it seems highly likely that this is the caricature cited in a scandalous episode that took place in Liverpool in 1877, the year of the opening of the gallery. Walker's position of power within Liverpool at this time was evident and there are repeated discussions in the press and in the minutes of the various council committees to suggest that this was a cause of great irritation and discomfort to many. Temperance was an absorbing issue and the source of Walker's wealth placed many in an uncomfortable position of being genuinely grateful to a man for such a generous gift to the city when his business was so clearly linked to the social problems and negative aspects of Liverpool life. For a minority of teetotallers, members of the temperance movement who preached abstinence rather than moderation, the situation was simply too much to bear. Ronald McDougall, Liberal councillor for St Anne's ward, undertaker, owner of a number of non-alcoholic refreshment houses in the city and a prominent temperance reformer, fell firmly within this camp.

In December 1876, a cartoon comprising 23 sketches arrived on the tables of every member of the Town Council, the magistracy and the Earl of Derby, as well as a number of other Liverpool gentlemen and members of the British Government. The cartoon, entitled 'The Pilgrim's Progress', showed a series of scenes depicting a figure, clearly identified as Walker, leaving Scotland and arriving in Liverpool with the intention of creating his fortune. Reports in the press describing the series of sketches make clear the sequence of events depicted, including under-the-table deals with magistrates to secure licences and other suggestions that Walker abused his public role for financial gain. The libellous nature of the cartoon and the direct assault on Walker's character, as well as the character of others depicted, sent ripples of shock through the Town Council and ensured that its appearance and circulation did not go unremarked. John Hughes, Deputy Chairman of the Watch Committee and a solicitor, was called in to investigate the matter and through a testimony from the printing house was able to trace the cartoon back to Ronald McDougall, who was reported to have commissioned 3000 copies, 100 of which had been circulated (Anon 1877b).

The matter was raised at the monthly meeting of the Town Council on 3 January 1877, where McDougall was subjected to an interrogation and the available evidence was laid before the members. In what was clearly a well-prepared presentation, Hughes set the scene for McDougall's 'diabolical' act and proceeded to share the information he had uncovered during his investigations to cries of 'Hiss' and 'Oh' from the council members (Anon 1877c). Amongst the sketches described, sketch number 21 represented the exterior of the Walker Art Gallery with the text 'Art Gallery Exterior', written underneath. Sketch 22 was described as representing 'a drinking bar', with the text 'Art Gallery interior' written underneath. Hughes' presentation was detailed and long and ensured that every detail of McDougall's underhand plan was laid bare before the Council. During this 'extraordinary scene', McDougall was accused of having produced a second cartoon, 'of a more discreditable character', for circulation during the opening of the Walker Art Gallery (Anon 1877c). A copy of the cartoon was put before McDougall, who denied any knowledge of it. Following these exceptional scenes, the councillor for St Anne's ward was given a few minutes to prepare a response, after which an abject apology was delivered to the council and the press.[6] Even though the *Liverpool Mercury* would report that following the apology the matter had been drawn to a close, the issue of the outstanding cartoon was left unresolved. It would, however, resurface on the day of the opening, when it was reported that 200,000 copies of the offending cartoon were distributed.

The suggestion that the caricature was commissioned by McDougall makes it all the more potent. It reveals the emotions that McDougall felt about Walker and about the monument he was building. Most importantly, the caricature is revealing of some of the stories that circulated around the building in 1877, beyond the official stories of its building and opening. Once again – and here there exists a cavernous gap between the caricature and the press reports – such an interpretation gets us a little closer in the biographical sense, to the mind of, on this occasion, a critic of the project. On a broader level, it illustrates the ways in which architecture can be as much a product of the representations that are made of it and the stories that are told about it as it is a product of design or direct physical use (see Hill 2003).

In relation to both of these particular historical fragments of architectural production – the photograph and the caricature – the aim of building a version of the past that seems credible and is supported by a range of sources demands interpretation. In biography, the 'art' of storytelling is a key component of constructing a 'life'; the art of the biographer lies somewhere between fact and fiction. The biographer's role is to explore, investigate, judge, recount, empathise with the 'life' with which they are concerned and to do so in a way which reveals the 'likeness' of the subject in a format that enthrals the reader; what Alun Munslow (2003, 2) refers to as the 'narratively constituted nature' of biography. As Richard Holmes put it, 'I found in that most English of forms, the biography, everything I wanted from writing. I could combine the scholarly and critical elements of finding things out and getting them right with more writerly and storytelling skills. If you are only a scholar, your story will be dead, but if you are only a storyteller then it will be ludicrous' (Wroe 2008). This complex approach to writing and the awareness of the need to tell a story, to construct a narrative through the tropes and structuring devices of fiction, is characteristic of biography and could also have potential for architectural history. Architecture has always been produced through the stories we tell about it and so consciously harnessing the power of storytelling to these ends offers, I would argue, a route towards revealing complex histories of occupation and use.

## CONCLUSION

This chapter has explored the idea of biography as a strategy for developing critically engaged and targeted architectural histories of museums and galleries. Recent experiences of involvement in capital development projects in museums and galleries have exposed the complexity of museum architecture and placed a spotlight on architectural development processes. So often perceived as unsatisfactory at some level, there is a desire within the museums profession to understand more

6 The apology read: 'I acknowledge that I have done wrong in issuing the cartoon reflecting on the mayor, magistrates and members of the council. I deeply regret this, and humbly beg to apologise and express my sorrow and regret for so doing, and authorise this acknowledgement to be made public' (Anon 1877b).

about how museums and galleries get made. At the most basic of levels, such an understanding demands a broader conception of architecture which can be drawn out from cutting-edge architectural history and theory and which identifies architecture as a system of practices and power relations and rethinks architecture as a product of use as much as it is a product of design. Once this rethinking is accepted, a recognisable story of architecture and of the architectural process is opened to view, a story which has the capacity to challenge outdated approaches to constructing the architectural history of museums and galleries. It is here that a biographical approach can point the historian towards a micro museum history and offer routes into the messy reality of museum-making as well as, importantly, the bodily occupation of museum space.

A biographical approach to museum history is nothing new; early histories of museums often focused on the 'life' of the donor or the collector and more recently numerous historians, including myself, have explored the lives of museum objects and collections.[7] In terms of architecture, however, recent thinking on auto/biography and life writing which prioritises the connections between lives and the physical, bodily reality of lived experience has the potential to open up routes into meaningful histories of architectural production and use. Such histories – and we need more of them – are fascinating for what they can tell us about the ways in which museum buildings have been made, occupied and understood. If we can acknowledge the lives lived in and through the physical stuff of museums and galleries in the past as 'significant', perhaps we can move towards a deeper engagement with contemporary capital development processes as complex social productions. Such an approach might reduce the myopia observed by Janes and enable a loosening of the hold of the architectural object towards a radical re-visioning of the economically, environmentally and socially sustainable museum building.

## Bibliography and References


Anon, 1873a Opposition to the Proposed Gallery of Art, *The Daily Courier*, Thursday 7 August (Document 2b in *Documents Relating to the Opening of the Walker Art Gallery, 1877*, Liverpool Records Office, H. F708.5 DOC.)

Anon, 1873b *The Liverpool Leader*, Saturday 9 August (Document 3c in *Documents Relating to the Opening of the Walker Art Gallery, 1877*, Liverpool Records Office, H. F708.5 DOC.)

Anon, 1873c The Art Gallery Scheme, *The Daily Courier*, Saturday 9 August, n.p. (Cutting in *Documents Relating to the Opening of the Walker Art Gallery, 1877*, Liverpool Records Office, H. F708.5 DOC.)

Anon, 1874 The Walker Art Gallery, *Liverpool Mercury*, Thursday 2 April, Issue 8175

Anon, 1877a Art in Liverpool, *The Daily Albion*, Thursday 6 September

Anon, 1877b An Apology, *Liverpool Mercury*, Thursday 4 January, Issue 9039

Anon, 1877c Libelling the Mayor, Magistrates, and Town Council; Extraordinary Scene – Censures Upon a Councillor, *Liverpool Mercury*, Thursday January 4, Issue 9039


7 Such histories are always more interesting for what they might tell us about the institution or the people who utilised the objects in some way in writing their own life, rather than for what they might reveal about the objects themselves.

Borden, I, Kerr, J, Pivaro, A, and Rendell, J (eds), 1995 *Strangely Familiar: Narratives of Architecture in the City*, Routledge, London

Borden, I, and Rendell, J, 2000 From Chamber to Transformer: epistemological challenges and tendencies in the intersection of architectural histories and critical theories, in *InterSections: Architectural Histories and Critical Theories* (eds I Borden and J Rendell), Routledge, London and New York, 3–23

Borough of Liverpool, 1874, *Proceedings of the Council 1873–74*, p 4 (Liverpool Records Office, H352 COU.)

Bradburne, J M, 1998, *The museum time bomb: overbuilt, overtraded, overdrawn* [online], available from: http://www.bradburne.org/downloads/museums/InstitutioninCrisisWEB.pdf [28 June 2010]

Forty, A, 1980 The modern hospital in England and France: the social and medical uses of architecture, in *Buildings and Society, essays on the social development of the built environment* (ed A D King), Routledge and Kegan Paul, London, 61–93

— 2000 *Words and Buildings: A Vocabulary of Modern Architecture*, Thames and Hudson, New York

Hill, J (ed), 1998 *Occupying Architecture: Between The Architect and the User*, Routledge, London and New York

Hill, J, 2003 *Actions of Architecture: Architects and Creative Users*, Routledge, London

Janes, R, 2009 *Museums in a Troubled World: Renewal, Irrelevance or Collapse?* Routledge, London

Lee, H, 2008 *Body Parts: Essays on Life Writing*, Pimlico, London

MacLeod, S, 2005 Rethinking Museum Architecture: towards a site-specific history of production and use, in *Reshaping Museum Space: Architecture, Design, Exhibitions* (ed S MacLeod), Routledge, London, 9–25

— 2011 Towards an Ethics of Museum Architecture, in *The Routledge Companion to Museum Ethics: Redefining Ethics for the Twenty-First Century Museum* (ed J Marstine), Routledge, London

Marcus, L, 1994 *Auto/biographical Discourses: Theory, Criticism, Practice*, Manchester University Press, Manchester and New York

Moore, J, 2004 The Art of Philanthropy? The formation and development of the Walker Art Gallery in Liverpool, *Museum and Society*, July, 68–83 [online], available from: http://www.le.ac.uk/ms/m&s/Issue%205/moore.pdf [28 June 2010]

Morris, E (ed), 1994 *The Walker Art Gallery*, Scala Books/National Museums and Galleries on Merseyside, London

Morris, E, 1996 *Victorian and Edwardian Paintings in the Walker Art Gallery and at Sudley House*, HMSO, London

— 1999 The Liverpool Academy and other art exhibitions in Liverpool 1774–1867, in *The Liverpool Academy and Other Exhibitions of Contemporary Art in Liverpool 1774–1867* (ed E Morris and E Roberts), Liverpool University Press and National Museums and Galleries on Merseyside, Liverpool

Munslow, A, 2003 History and Biography: An Editorial Comment, *Rethinking History* 7 (1), 1–11

Noordegraaf, J, 2004 *Strategies of Display: museum presentation in nineteenth- and twentieth-century visual culture*, Museum Boijmans Van Beuningen, Rotterdam

Till, J, 1998 Architecture of the impure community, in *Occupying Architecture: Between The Architect and the User* (ed J Hill), Routledge, London and New York, 62–75

— 2000 Thick time: architecture and the traces of time, in *InterSections: Architectural Histories and Critical Theories* (ed I Borden and J Rendell), Routledge, London and New York, 283–95

Wroe, N, 2008 Following his Footsteps, *The Guardian* [online], available from: www.guardian.co.uk/books/2008/sep/27/biography1 [22 June 2010]

Yanni, C, 1999 *Nature's Museums: Victorian science and the architecture of display*, Athlone Press, London

# 8

# Schinkel's Museums: Collecting and Displaying Architecture in Berlin, 1844–1933

WALLIS MILLER

The story of architecture museums in Berlin is, in one sense, a short one.[1] Although Berlin's collection of archives dedicated to architecture is quite deep, it was only in 2007, when the Technical University renamed its archive and exhibition space after its historic Architekturmuseum, that the architecture museum as a type of institution re-established itself in the city's cultural landscape.[2] Before this, the last time there was an architecture museum in Berlin was from 1931 to 1933. It was called the Schinkel Museum, and its short lifespan is surprising, given that Karl Friedrich Schinkel (1781–1841) was – and still is – recognised as Prussia's most famous architect. As the head of the Prussian Oberbaudeputation (the State architectural administration), Schinkel built an extraordinary number of public projects in addition to his private commissions, namely villas and commercial buildings. But he was most notable for 'giving Berlin a face' after the Napoleonic Wars, transforming it from a military garrison into a capital city. His urban design for the area around Unter den Linden unified the boulevard and added urban spaces from which people could behold several of his masterpieces: the Neue Wache (1816–18); the Schauspielhaus (1819–21); the Altes Museum (1823–30); and the Bauakademie (1832–36).

Of course, the short and complex story of architecture museums does not end here. First of all, it is not clear whether the Schinkel Museum can (or could have been) considered as an architecture museum at all because it was not an independent institution but part of the National Gallery. Secondly, there was another, earlier incarnation of the museum. This one, which can be considered an architecture museum, was the second public museum in Berlin and the first dedicated to a single person; it opened in 1844 and closed in 1924. But its 80-year existence was largely in name: for its first 30 years (1844–72) it was a small public museum located in Schinkel's apartment in the Bauakademie or the 'Building Academy', a building of his design. In the 1870s the director of the Bauakademie put the collection into storage because the school was running out of space and interest in Schinkel. The name 'Schinkel Museum' resurfaced in 1884, after the Bauakademie became a part of the newly-established Technische Hochschule (Polytechnic). But this version of the museum was only of interest to a few students when school was not in session. As a result, the Schinkel Museum was so neglected that, in 1924, Berlin's National

1 Sigrid Achenbach's article 'Die Schinkel-Sammlung im Berliner Kupferstichkabinett' was an inspiration for this project (Achenbach 2002). Its tracing of the rich history of the collection sparked my interest in architecture collections generally and motivated me to pursue the quandaries associated with placing architecture in museums discussed here.

2 For more information on the Technical University's Architekturmuseum and its history, see Architekturmuseum TU Berlin (2010).

Gallery was able to acquire the collection and, seven years later, open its own Schinkel Museum. That museum, the first mentioned above, was only open for the better part of two years: once the National Socialists assumed power in 1933 the collection landed in storage and did not re-emerge until after the war (Rave 1968, 115–16). Eventually, the National Gallery consolidated the collection in an archive, now located in its Kupferstichkabinett [Prints and Drawings Collection] (Achenbach 2002, 93–100; Klause 1997, 84–8). There had also been a more general Architecture Museum at the Technische Hochschule for several decades (1888–1930); its study collection and public exhibition space was the source and inspiration for the recently reopened 'Architekturmuseum'. But from the beginning, it suffered alternately from the lack of a substantial collection and the absence of an interested audience. And, although architects at the time investigated it as a potential building type, the 1905 Schinkel-Competition for the design of an architecture museum, sponsored by Berlin's Society of Architects and Engineers [Architekten- und Ingenieur Verein zu Berlin], was but a flash in the pan. Scholars and curators attribute the complex institutional histories of architecture museums in Berlin to personalities, politics and the fractured landscape of cultural institutions in this city. I would like to add another explanation: the architecture museum's complex history is also a result of the ambivalence associated with the definition of architecture and the ambiguity inherent in the word 'museum'. Both, I would argue, contributed to the transformations of the Schinkel Museum over the course of the 19th and early 20th centuries.

The Schinkel Museum's complex history likewise attests to the architect's significance. In this case, the institutional biography of the museum is as important as that of Schinkel himself. Against the timeless portrait of his work offered by every iteration of the museum – more monograph than biography – the life-story of the museum unfolds as a sequence of shifting configurations and affiliations mirroring the changing reception of his architecture. Rather than indicating the tenuousness of Schinkel's role as an historic figure, I would argue that the instability was a consequence of his continued influence on the landscape and relevance to discussions of professional identity. Schinkel was always a force to be reckoned with. Seen within an expanded field, the chequered history of the Schinkel Museum reveals as much about an architecture museum as any success of the institution would have done on its own.

When it emerged as a public institution in the 19th century, the museum found itself caught between its commitments to scholarship and civic symbolism. In Berlin, this conflict manifested itself in the controversy over the inscription on the Royal Museum (known today as the 'Altes Museum') designed by Schinkel in 1822–30. The inscription, which reads 'Friedrich Wilhelm III founded this museum for the study of antique objects of every kind and the liberal arts', was composed in Latin by Alois Hirt, a professor at the Academy of Fine Arts, and installed before academy members had a chance to discuss it (Bergdoll 1994, 84). Indeed, many of Hirt's contemporaries, including Schinkel, registered their discontent as soon as the inscription saw the light of day (Süvern 1827, 272; Crimp 1987, 262). They believed that the inscription's definition of the museum as an academy was anachronistic, even though they did not reject the use of the building as a place of study or ignore the royal patronage of the collection. Instead, they applied Greek and Roman precedents for the housing of public art collections to their own situation: the recovery of the Prussian, not royal, cultural treasures after Napoleon's defeat. Still using the term 'museum', Hirt's opponents insisted that the Royal Museum should serve as a public treasury of sculpture and painting or a temple to peace (Tieck n.d., 274–5). Their goal was to transform the museum's function without changing its name.

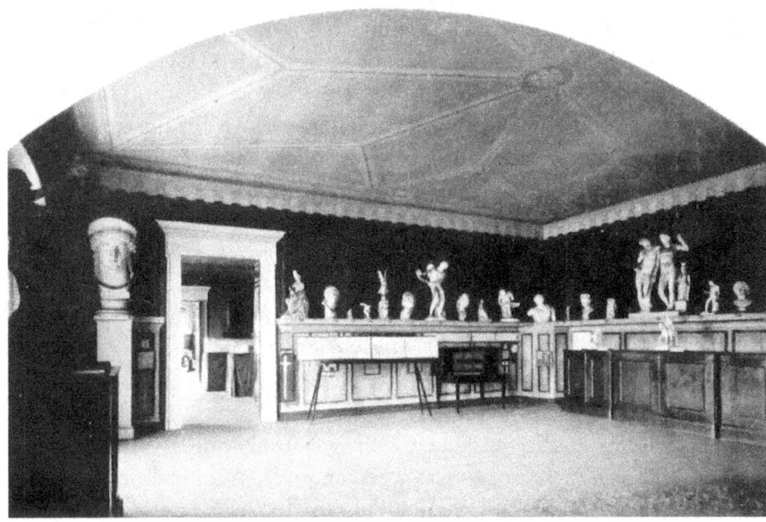

Fig 8.1. Schinkel Museum in the Bauakademie, c. 1875. This is most likely the only extant image of the museum

The Schinkel Museum embraced the ambiguities now suggested by the term 'museum': it was established as a Prussian treasury with royal patronage and as an academy. Less than a month after the architect's death in 1841, King Friedrich Wilhelm IV called for the collection of Schinkel's paintings and drawings 'to ensure that they would be safeguarded in a worthy manner' (Rave 1935, 236). The King's plan to secure Schinkel's reputation was supported by Schinkel's family's desire to secure their financial situation by selling his drawings. Although the King initiated the idea and provided the means to create the Schinkel Museum, he conceived of it as a public monument, fulfilling to some extent the earlier expectations for the Royal Museum. Peter Beuth, Schinkel's friend and colleague in the movement to reform the applied arts, was in charge of assembling the collection. According to Beuth, the Schinkel Museum 'would preserve a spiritual treasure of one of its greatest men for the benefit of the Prussian state and its further artistic development' (ibid, 237).

The museum did not simply confirm the architect's greatness, it constructed it. The King had suggested that the Schinkel collection be displayed in several rooms within the architect's apartment in the Bauakademie (Fig 8.1). As a result, when visitors entered the museum – Tuesdays and Fridays, 11 am–12 pm – they probably thought that they had entered into the very context in which Schinkel produced his designs (Beuth 1844).[3] The museum, which had opened to the public in November 1844, was located in just the rooms that visitors would have seen had Schinkel himself extended the invitation: in his studio and two public rooms, which contained displays of his collection of plaster casts and a series of his own paintings and drawings. The rooms also contained a long worktable – allegedly seven or eight metres long – which Schinkel had designed so that he could view the large portfolios of his work more easily. This was exactly how it was used in the museum for a collection of portfolios that was larger than life (Waagen 1841; Rave 1935, 240). When Schinkel died, there were 22 of these portfolios and 11 sketchbooks in the apartment, along with the plaster casts and the work on the wall. But, in preparation for

3 Three years later, the hours were extended to 11 am–1 pm (Salzenberg 1847).

the museum's opening, bookbinders had to prepare 66 additional portfolios to contain all the work that Beuth had collected in the three intervening years (Zusammenstellung 1844, 85r; Rave 1935, 240). What had been scattered across Schinkel's 60-year lifetime and among his clients, friends and colleagues now converged in the studio and public rooms in his apartment. The collection realised the 'rich whole' called for by the art historian Franz Kugler, who had already completed a monograph on Schinkel in the first year after the architect died (Kugler 1842, 152).

In terms of their sizes, the various collections of work assembled while Schinkel was alive seemed insignificant compared to what Beuth amassed in the museum after Schinkel's death, according to the inventory taken in the 1860s by Schinkel's son-in-law, Alfred Freiherr von Wolzogen. For example, Schinkel's *Sammlung Architektonischer Entwürfe* [Collection of Architectural Designs] had been published in its entirety before Schinkel died, but its 174 plates appeared inconsequential in the face of the quantity of the material held by the museum.[4] And the *Architektonisches Lehrbuch*, his incomplete theoretical work, existed as a series of notes and sketches in only 9 of the 88 portfolios in the museum (Wolzogen 1862 vol 2).[5] As Véronique Samuel-Gohin has argued, the unfinished *Lehrbuch* was a testimony to Schinkel's capacity for constant invention, which caused his theory to be repeatedly superseded by his practice (Samuel-Gohin 1995, 52).[6] But the case of the *Lehrbuch* also shows that Schinkel generally viewed his career as progressive, in no small part due to his attention to what was new: materials, construction technologies and function. The unity presented in the museum, which gave his projects equal value, was therefore at odds with Schinkel's approach to architecture in which new work supplanted previous designs and theory. The museum gave its visitors access to an enormous body of work, something that Schinkel did not have as he developed his theory and practice in the very same rooms (Waagen 1841, 48).[7]

It was evident that, given the quantity of work, the Schinkel Museum could not put the 'rich whole' on exhibit in order to communicate the architect's greatness to the public. In modern terms, the museum had to become both an archive and an exhibition and conceived of its audience in a similarly hybrid way: as generating as well as gaining an understanding of Schinkel. While there were framed drawings and paintings on display and plaster casts on the shelf where Schinkel had left them, most of the drawings, especially the architectural drawings, were in portfolios stored in cabinets made especially for the museum (Wolzogen 1863 vol 3, 400).[8] In order to begin to see this unity, visitors had to request specific portfolios and use the museum as an archive, similar to the way scholars used the ancient museum. In fact, the museum's curators had expected that this is how most visitors would experience the museum, and, from the start, they restricted the number of visitors according to the number of portfolios they ordered, conscious of the amount of space the open portfolio would occupy (Rave 1935, 240). The experience of the first few years proved the curators right: during that time they received requests for over

4 There were 28 installments of the *Sammlung Architektonische Enwürfe* altogether. The first appeared in 1820, the last in 1840 (Wolzogen 1862 vol 2, 350; Pundt 1989, 5–26).

5 Portfolios 40a–c, 41a–e, 42 contained 463 drawings.

6 '[T]his incapacity of Schinkel to finalize his treatise, the theory having been constantly superseded by practice, is without a doubt the clearest proof of the constant renewal of his creative force and his capacity for invention.'

7 Schinkel moved to this apartment from a crowded one on Unter den Linden in order to have easier access to his work, although, as was shown, his collection was not at all comprehensive.

8 They also had 'a number of sketchbooks from his hand from different times'.

1000 portfolios (ibid, 241). But the curators did not assume that all of the visitors had a scholarly interest in the work. They distinguished between those to whom they would issue tickets for a single visit and 'the architects who would get tickets for a longer period of time for study purposes' (ibid). This they advertised in several of the local newspapers (Salzenberg 1847). For the visitors who were not scholars, the museum offered Schinkel's display of paintings, framed drawings and plaster casts. But it did not leave them with just that. The paintings, drawings and casts were in the very same rooms as the portfolios and the scholars busily studying them. Rather than separate the archive from the exhibit, the curators' planning resulted in displaying the archives and the scholars working in it – that is, the academy in the ancient sense – to its new public audience.

The Schinkel Museum's confrontation with convention extended beyond the definition of the museum to the hierarchies established by the art academy, echoing the situation faced by architecture more generally. The art academy placed great value on authorship as a way to guarantee an artwork's authenticity. It identified authorship with craftsmanship, with objects rather than content, and regarded painting as first among the arts. In contrast to painting, architecture confounded the academy's standards. In the exhibitions at the Prussian Academy of the Arts, depictions of new buildings were scattered throughout the academy exhibitions, appearing in sections devoted to engraving, modelling, drawing and even painting. Many of Schinkel's architectural designs appeared in the engraving section displaying the talent of the engraver. Models were shown similarly, exhibiting the talent of the cabinetmaker, for example. Architectural drawings posed a special problem because someone other than the architect often made them, although this fact did not threaten the architect's claim to authorship because, as design tools, the drawings' content was more important than their role as objects. Clearly, the academy did not agree because it only exhibited drawings made by the architects so it could display them as 'independent artistic creations' [*freie Kunstschöpfungen*] and preserve the status of object-based authorship (Börsch-Supan 1971, 16). To reinforce that the architectural drawings were important in their own right rather than as tools to create buildings, the academy restricted their content to unbuilt projects. Indeed, after 1820 it was hard to find any of Berlin's new buildings, including Schinkel's, in the architecture section; they were more likely to turn up as the subject matter of someone else's *Vedute* in the painting section (ibid). At the Prussian Academy exhibitions, a building compromised the identity of a work of architecture – that is, the identity of a drawing – as a work of art.

Wolzogen's inventories of the collection, and his record of the museum installation, demonstrate the extent to which the Schinkel Museum reinforced the distinctions important to the art academy. Specifically, the museum reinforced the hierarchy of the arts but challenged the importance of object-based authorship and the exclusion of buildings. Schinkel's oil paintings were in the first room and his architectural drawings in the last. The inventory of the entire collection separated drawings by Schinkel from drawings made by others of his designs, and the colour-coded labels in the museum exhibition followed its example: yellow labels indicated works by Schinkel, red indicated works by others. According to Wolzogen's record, all the drawings on exhibit had yellow labels, indicating that they were 'in Schinkel's hand'; only his collection of plaster casts and the two lone building models (a cork model of the Friedrichwerdersche Church and a wood model of Schloß Kurnik) were by others and, so, labelled in red (Wolzogen 1864 vol 4, 600–16). Schinkel seldom, if ever, made models for his own use. In the context of a respect for authorship, the men who made the models were listed in the catalogue. The cork model of the church was by Kallenbach, the creator of the series of cork models of ancient ruins that would later be associated with the Schinkel Museum under Kallenbach's name, once both collections had landed at the Technische Hochschule. Not only did the standards of the art academy place Schinkel's artistic accomplishments before his architectural ones, but they also weakened his exclusive claim to authorship of the architectural objects in the museum's collection.

The architectural objects on display reciprocated by challenging the art academy's standards. If Schinkel was to be honoured as an architect as well as an artist, the content depicted by the drawings and models had to be viewed as being as important as their physical attributes. This challenge to object-based authenticity valued by the art museum was not only made in the form of architectural drawings, engravings and models. On one of the portfolio storage cabinets in the middle of the room were three albums of photographs depicting Schinkel's studies of the frescos for the Royal Museum, his set designs, his travel and landscape sketches and his drawings of buildings, furniture and objects. In 1858, an 'enterprising woman' named Frau Laura Bette had proposed to take photographs of the drawings in the collection for use by architecture students and architects (Rave 1935, 248). After some negotiation with the Minister of Trade she was authorised to make six prints of each negative (Bette 1858).[9] She issued five series of 30 photographs each, which she had bound into three albums. According to Wolzogen's record, these photographs of drawings of buildings lay in the middle of the Schinkel Museum, allowing visitors access to the archive without actually disrupting it. Laura Bette's albums provided the site for the archive to meet the public exhibition and for architecture to doubly confront the art academy's high regard for authenticity. The photographs were neither unique works of art nor important because of the reputation of the artist who made them. They were in the museum to give the public a view of Schinkel's work that was not present (or accessible) in its original form.

The consequences of the introduction of photographs of drawings into the museum were complicated. On the one hand, the presence of photographic reproductions signalled architecture's participation in an initial transformation of existing conventions. On the other, it reinforced the centrality of drawing to a definition of architecture as art. But this apparently conventional move had unexpected consequences: the centrality of drawing reasserted the architects' conception of architecture, which linked drawing to building. Although members of the Academy of Arts ultimately may have excluded drawings of buildings because they viewed them as derivative, architects and builders at the Bauakademie and the Oberbaudeputation viewed drawings as primary; drawings were the language in which they spoke about building. For them, drawings adhered to the standard of *Akkuratesse*, a high degree of formal precision that assimilated making the drawing to making the building (Sukale 2000, 76). Students at the Bauakademie spent an enormous amount of time in drawing classes. In the first years after the Bauakademie opened in 1799, students spent ten hours each week in classes for freehand drawing and 21 hours in architectural and machine drawing but only three or four hours in other classes such as construction, statics or trigonometry. They only studied design as they prepared for their second State examination to qualify as *Bauinspektoren* (building inspectors), a step to becoming a State architect. For Schinkel, as for other architects since the late 18th century, saying that drawing was a new

9 In a letter of 4 March, Bette asks the Trade Minister, von der Heydt, for permission to take the photographs. By 16 September 1864, a letter from the Curatorium of the Beuth-Schinkel Museum indicates that she had completed the project and sent the required photographs to the Schinkel Museum (Bette 1858).

language for a new way of life may have been the equivalent to what 20th-century architects later said about building (Strecke 2000, 141).

Beginning in the 1870s, the Schinkel Museum's fate revealed the divergence of architectural and cultural interests in Berlin. Specifically, its fate was linked to changing institutional affiliations and shifts in architectural preferences. In 1879 the Bauakademie merged with the Gewerbeakademie (Academy of Applied Arts), founded by Schinkel's colleague Beuth, to create the Technische Hochschule, located in Charlottenburg, just outside of Berlin. As a result of the move, the Schinkel Museum joined the library and the instructional collections (the cork models and, after 1888, the Architecture Museum) on the second floor of the Technische Hochschule's main building. However, the Beuth-Schinkel Museum (as it had been called since the merger of the two collections after Beuth's death in 1853) attracted few visitors during the semester (Rave 1931, 13). Its lack of popularity marked some significant cultural and architectural changes. First, the institutional change had compromised architecture's cultural relevance. The architecture department had moved from the Bauakademie, a prominently-located institution dedicated to architecture, to the Technische Hochschule, an educational institution with a broader mission, located on what was then Berlin's periphery. Architecture as an institution was no longer a visible part of Prussia's cultural centre. Secondly, the faculty had decided not to integrate the Beuth-Schinkel Museum into the curriculum, suggesting that Schinkel's work was of little consequence to contemporary architecture. Nonetheless, the museum's historic relevance as a precursor to the merger that formed the Technische Hochschule is what probably allowed it to survive, although just barely, the museum falling into a steady decline for several decades.

Just after World War I, the faculty of the Technische Hochschule seemed to have a change of heart. At a meeting in 1918, the faculty declared it necessary to wake the museum out of its 'sleeping beauty slumber'. Looking beyond the museum's significance to Prussian culture, they emphasised that it established connections to their own architectural culture, which they did not want to break. But they were still reluctant to integrate it into the curriculum and restore it to its former role as a study collection because they felt that its exact relevance was not yet clear. The material required scholarly research 'in order to make it useful' (Zimmerman 1918). The faculty's ambivalence ultimately had practical consequences: by 1924, they had all but lost the museum because the Minister of Science, Art, and General Education had decreed that the Beuth-Schinkel Museum had to move. Although it would remain at the university, he stipulated that it had to move out of the main building and that the National Gallery would assume responsibility for it (Krencker 1930).[10] The Ministry decision was telling: the architecture faculty's argument about the influence of the collection on future architectural designs was overwhelmed by the collection's importance to Prussian culture.

The faculty of the Technische Hochschule was complicit in the decision that ultimately resulted in their loss of the Beuth-Schinkel Museum. In order to build a new library, it approved, in 1928, the destruction of the building that was to house the museum. But that was not the end of the story. When, in response, the National Gallery proposed to move the museum to the centre of Berlin – to the Prinzessinnen-Palais (the Princesses' Palace) on Unter den Linden

10 The Beuth-Schinkel Museum was supposed to share its new location with a museum dedicated to the work of sculptor Christian Daniel Rauch, also maintained by the National Gallery. The decision to relocate the three collections to this new building was in the works since 1913 (Klause 1997, 73–5).

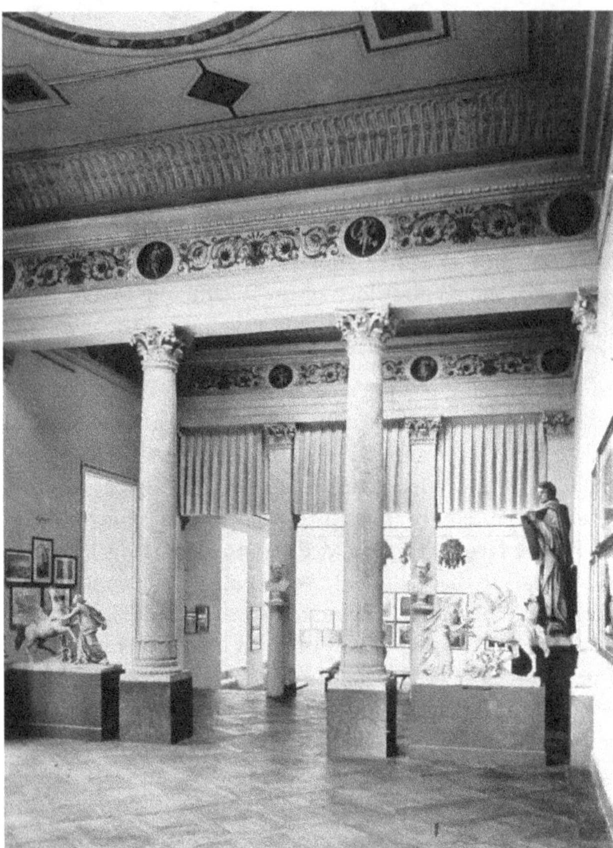

FIG 8.2.
SCHINKEL MUSEUM IN THE NATIONAL GALLERY, 1931. ENTRANCE

– the faculty protested.[11] They argued that the Schinkel collection was crucial to building an archive of Prussian Architecture, which would aid architects, not the public, in constructing a Prussian architectural tradition (Krencker 1929). Notable is their choice of an archive rather than a museum, which reflected their earlier insistence on the need for research due to their uncertainty about Schinkel's significance. The faculty's position, favouring a professional rather than a public audience, caused the Technische Hochschule to lose the collection once and for all and allowed Ludwig Justi, the director of the National Gallery, to acquire it. Unlike the faculty, Justi was certain about Schinkel's cultural significance and dismissed the central importance of Schinkel's architectural accomplishments in order to argue that his collection belonged in a museum. '[Schinkel] was not a professional architect', he claimed, 'but an artist with a wide range of interests and accomplishments' (Justi 1929). Insisting on the importance of culture over architecture made it easier for Justi to claim Schinkel as a significant artist, a claim confirmed by the fact that several of Schinkel's paintings were a part of the Wagener collection, the basis for

11 The National Gallery had already decided to split the collection and planned to move the objects in the Rauch Museum to the Orangerie in Schloß Charlottenburg (Rave 1931, 13–14; Klause 1997, 76–7).

establishing the National Gallery. Agreeing with Justi, the Minister of Science, Art and General Education decided to award the collection to the National Gallery because 'of its general value to a museum and not only because of its architectural significance' (Becker 1929).

Given Justi's lack of interest in Schinkel the architect, it should be no surprise to hear that he was generally not very enthusiastic about holding architecture exhibitions in the National Gallery. He perceived them as professional events with little attraction for a broader audience. They had no place within his programme for museum reform. This had as much to do with the kinds of objects on display as with their content. Calling Schinkel an artist was not only a tribute to the high aesthetic quality of his work but to the legibility and resonance of what would be on display. Justi's worry, for example, about a proposed exhibition called 'Classical Architecture from the Schinkel Period', sponsored by the Association of German Architects and Engineers (which would coincide with the opening of the Schinkel Museum), was that it would consist largely of plans, sections and construction drawings 'which are incredibly important and interesting for architects but less charming for a broader public that is more interested in the concrete side of art' (Thormaelen 1930). Following the principles of the museum reform movement (where he had significant influence, although was not the most progressive reformer and was criticised for it), Justi wanted to transform the museum from an archive serving professionals into a cultural symbol serving as a centre for public education. Architectural drawings, being neither authentic objects of art nor particularly legible, disrupted Justi's plans.

When the Schinkel Museum opened as a part of the National Gallery on 13 March 1931, the 150th anniversary of Schinkel's birth, it asserted the significance of Schinkel as an artist rather than an architect (Fig 8.2). The galleries exhibiting the Schinkel collection were located on the *piano nobile* of the Prinzessinnen-Palais. A bridge leading to the neighbouring Kronprinzen-Palais (the Crown Prince's Palace) provided a direct connection to the National Gallery's collection of contemporary art. Known again by its original name, the 'Schinkel Museum' still contained the 'Beuth art collections' but, as the name suggests, they were secondary. Furthermore, the Beuth collections and the archives were on the ground floor, directly below the Schinkel galleries, reinforcing the fact that the museum's function as a professional resource was not as important as its commitment to the public.

Justi's commitment to legibility and art was reflected in the exhibition's clear organisational structure. He and curator Paul Ortwin Rave segregated works of art from those of architecture and used different rooms to distinguish medium and subject matter. Design drawings, travel drawings and oil paintings were generally kept separate, as were 'Buildings for Berlin', 'Interiors of Royal Palaces', 'Palaces of Foreign Rulers', furniture and set designs (Fig 8.3). Justi and Rave's apparent adaptation of the idea of artistic genre not only helped to classify the various objects on display but also structured the entire sequence of the museum. Visitors did not trace the progress of Schinkel's career chronologically but moved between various oppositions that characterised Schinkel's body of work. They walked from a room of art (paintings and drawings of things he observed) to one of architecture (design sketches and drawings); between various types of built and unbuilt projects; and from art with a specific location in a work of architecture to unbuilt architecture with no other location than inside a frame. The organisation of the first Schinkel Museum in the Bauakademie had similarly abandoned chronology. But, after separating paintings from drawings, it freely combined diverse subject matter and, so, hinted at the 'greater whole' that defined Schinkel's work. Resting on finer genre distinctions beyond that of painting, drawing and architecture, the National Gallery's organisation articulated Schinkel's work as a set

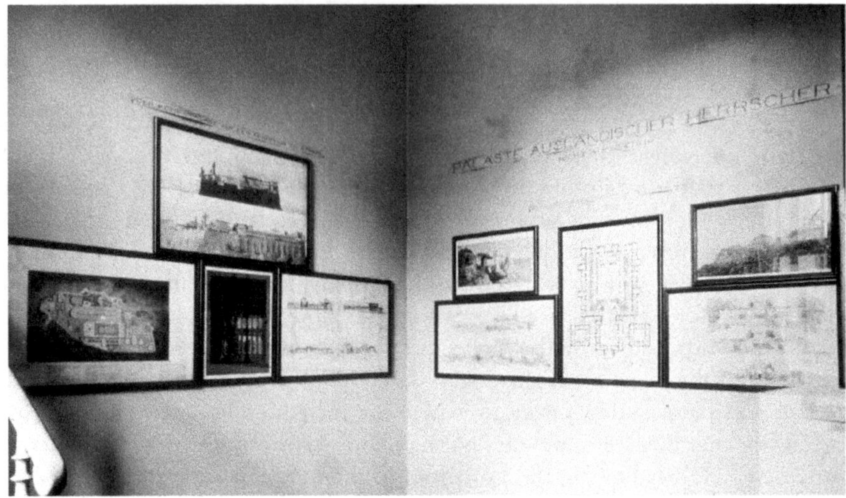

FIG 8.3.
SCHINKEL MUSEUM IN THE NATIONAL GALLERY, 1931. PALACES OF FOREIGN RULERS

of discrete facets that, considered together, created a complete portrait of him. As Rave put it, 'the different rooms and alcoves each reveal a special side of the many sided artist' (Rave 1931, 15).

Like the museum's organisation, Rave's guidebook texts rendered Schinkel's work as fine art. The new book contained descriptions of individual projects on exhibit rather than the inventory lists of the 1860s, certainly a result of the existence of the archive and its contributions to the understanding of Schinkel in the intervening years. Rave's texts described Schinkel's artistic works as central, explaining that this gave Schinkel's architectural designs their ultimate significance. To describe the 'Unbuilt Projects' in the section on 'Great Ideas for Buildings', Rave wrote:

> [t]he more that one is led by the artistic instead of by the purely objective [*Sachlich*], the richer the work will be … The way in which he [Schinkel] conceived of urban spaces or great individual buildings – a cathedral, an aristocratic estate, a monument, those are utterances of a will to art, which does not know the measure of someone who is 'only an architect' anymore. (Ibid, 79)

Under such conditions, was there any space left for architecture to assert itself in the Schinkel Museum? Perhaps in the installation, where some aspects suggest that a new form of exhibition had entered the galleries. In the room dedicated to Schinkel's Berlin projects, the drawings were placed so that when the viewer looked at one of them he or she would also be looking towards the site of the project (whether or not the building ever stood there and whether or not it still did) (ibid, 43). While this may have been legible only to those visitors who read the guide book, the curators' intention was to shift the viewing context from the gallery to the city in order to simulate the experience of looking through the drawings to the buildings. The Berlin installation shifted the viewers' attention away from the objects on display: the drawings, which were of central value to an art exhibition, and led it to their subject matter: the buildings on the street. In this way, the installation used buildings to radicalise the relationship of architecture to the

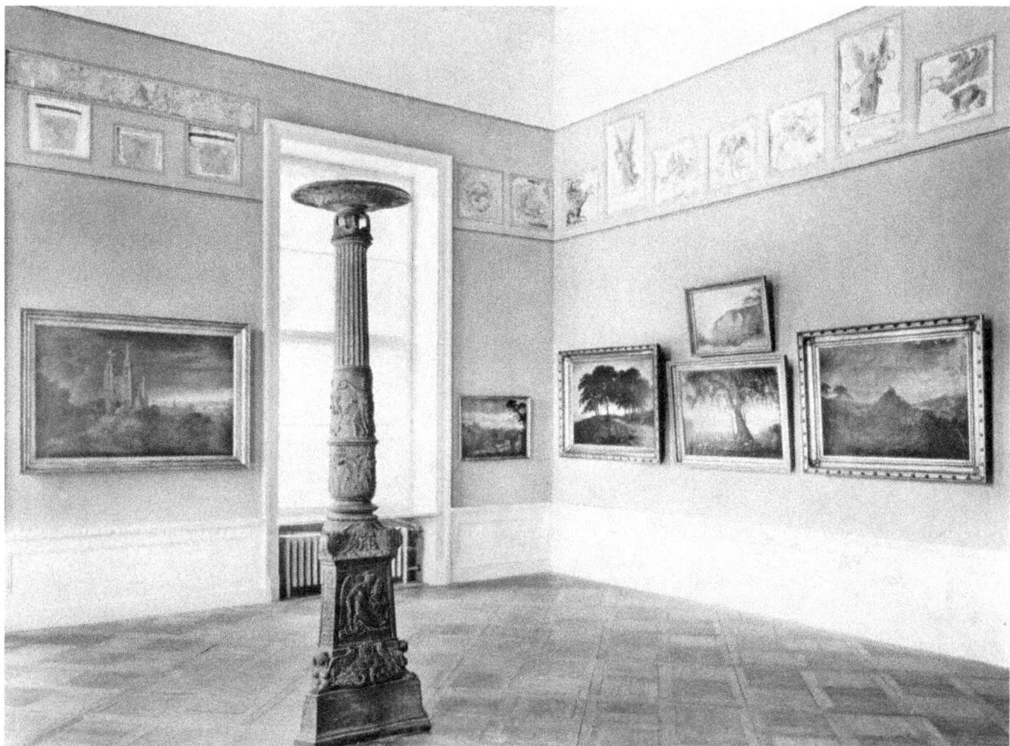

Fig 8.4.
Schinkel Museum in the National Gallery, 1931. Murals and Landscapes. The wall paintings are from the Palais Redern (right) and the Bauakademie (left). The candelabra is from the Palais Redern

museum: buildings would have been seen both as a challenge to the authenticity of the museum's collection and as a part of it.

The museum also contained an authentic work of architecture that took the form of a series of fragments: wall paintings mounted on panels. These had been recovered from the staircase in the Bauakademie leading to Schinkel's apartment and from the Palais Redern on Pariser Platz, a building razed in 1906 to make way for the Hotel Adlon (Fig 8.4). The panels were installed high on the walls and over the doors, simulating their placement in the original buildings. At once, they resurrected and mourned the missing buildings as did the wallpaper from the Palais Redern, which was exhibited with a series of photographs of Schinkel's buildings in the stairwell connecting the exhibition to the archive below. Likewise, the placement of several drawings of the Palais Redern reinforced the building's absence because they were located by a window looking out to its radically transformed site. In this case of putting the building – or at least its parts – on display, the museum's exhibit could not help but assert that authenticity could only lend architecture artistic legitimacy for the price of a functioning building.

The Schinkel Museum's existence and its significance as an architecture museum owe much to its namesake. The museum's embrace of oppositions – archives and exhibits, scholars and the

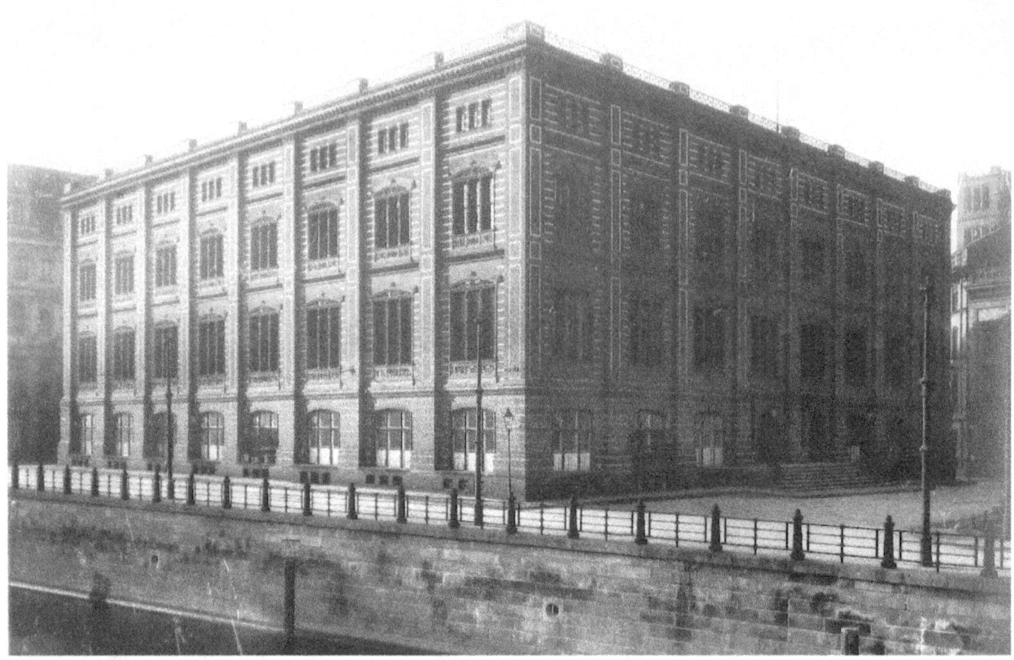

FIG 8.5.
WALDEMAR TITZENTHALER, BAUAKADEMIE AM SCHINKELPLATZ, 1905

public, and authentic objects and their representations – signal that, like Schinkel, the architecture museum was a new type defined by its struggle with convention. Its long history echoes the conflicts generally experienced by architects as they tried to assert their professional identity in a rapidly modernising context. How fitting that these histories converge in the only well-known Schinkel building that repeatedly escaped a conventional form of exhibition: the Bauakademie. This was the site of the newly-developed curriculum for the training of architects, the first location of the museum and Schinkel's own rise to fame (Fig 8.5). The Bauakademie was never exhibited with original drawings. In the case of the first Schinkel Museum, the Bauakademie building was on display because it housed the museum. It was also exhibited there as a drawing reproduced in one of Frau Bette's photographs; in the last, it was shown with artefacts from the building. By not putting actual drawings on display, both museums exhibited the Bauakademie in a way that was as revolutionary as its design and its reputation as an educational institution. The photographic reproduction of one of its drawings avoided the conventional reliance on originality while its presence at full-scale (as a complete building and in parts) staged a daring challenge to authenticity and value in the fine arts. Beneath these concerns lay an even larger issue: the nature of architectural objects. Museums are characterised by objects but architecture museums are characterised by confrontations with objects, confrontations that have ontological significance. Such is the life-story of the Schinkel Museum. Although its inconsistency is at odds with the reputation of an architect whose importance has remained generally undisputed since his death, the museum's story is nonetheless exemplary, like Schinkel himself, because it raises essential issues about architecture and points to the importance of a material culture of architecture seldom acknowledged elsewhere.

## Bibliography and References


Achenbach, S, 2002 Die Schinkel-Sammlung im Berliner Kupferstichkabinett, in *Die Hand des Architekten. Zeichnungen aus Berliner Sammlungen* (ed Bauakademie Berlin), Verlag der Buchhandlung Walther König, Cologne, 82–101

Architekturmuseum TU Berlin, 2010 *Wilkommen im Architekturmuseum* [online], available from: http://architekturmuseum.ub.tu-berlin.de [May 2010]

Becker, C H, 1929 Letter: Prussian Minister for Science, Art and General Education [Becker] to Director of the National Gallery [Ludwig Justi] and Director of the Architecture Museum [Daniel Krencker], 2 July, Zentralarchiv der Staatlichen Museen zu Berlin, [hereafter ZA SMB], Akte 'National-Galerie, Prinzessinnen-Palais, Schinkel-Beuth-Museum, Kunstsachen, 1929–1932, Specialia 57, Band 1'

Bergdoll, B, 1994 *Karl Friedrich Schinkel. An Architecture for Prussia*, Rizzoli, New York

Bette, L, 1858 Letter to Trade Minister von der Heydt, 4 March, Geheimes Staatsarchiv Preußischer Kulturbesitz [hereafter GStPK], HAI Rep 76Vb Sekt 4 Tit.X Nr.11 Bd.III/Beuth-Schinkel Museum 1858–1876

Beuth, P, 1844 Letter to Bremiker, GStaPK, 26 October, HAI Rep 76Vb Sekt 4 Tit.X Nr.11 Bd.I/Schinkel Museum 1844–45, 94r

Börsch-Supan, H, 1971 Introduction, in *Die Kataloge der Berliner Akademie Ausstellungen 1786–1850*, 2 vols and index, Hessling, Berlin, 8–23

Crimp, D, 1987 The End of Art and the Origin of the Museum, *Art Journal* 46 (4), 261–6

Justi, L, 1929 Report by the Director of the National Gallery [Justi] to the Minister for Science, Art and General Education, 12 April, ZA SMB, Akte 'National-Galerie, Prinzessinnen-Palais, Schinkel-Beuth-Museum, Kunstsachen, 1929–1932, Specialia 57, Band 1'

Klause, N, 1997 Die Geschichte des Schinkel-Museums in Berlin, *Der Bär von Berlin* 46, 63–92

Krencker, D, 1929 Statement by Director of the Architecture Museum [Professor Krencker], Meeting Minutes from Negotiations over the location of the exhibition of the Schinkel collection, 1 March, ZA SMB, Akte 'National-Galerie, Prinzessinnen-Palais, Schinkel-Beuth-Museum, Kunstsachen, 1929–1932, Specialia 57, Band 1'

— 1930 Letter: Director of the Architecture Museum [Professor Krencker] to the Rector of the Technische Hochschule, 29 April, ZA SMB, Akte 'National-Galerie, Prinzessinnen-Palais, Schinkel-Beuth-Museum, Kunstsachen, 1929–1932, Specialia 57, Band 1'

Kugler, F, 1842 *Karl Friedrich Schinkel. Eine Charakteristik seiner künstlerischen Wirksamkeit*, Verlag von Georg Gropius, Berlin

Pundt, H, 1989 A Tribute to Karl Friedrich Schinkel, Architect, in *Collection of Architectural Designs by Karl Friedrich Schinkel* (eds K Hazlett, S O'Malley, and C Rudolph), Princeton Architectural Press, New York, 5–26

Rave, P O, 1931 *Das Schinkel-Museum und die Kunst-Sammlungen Beuths*, Ernst Rathenau, Berlin

— 1935 Urkunden zur Gründung und Geschichte des Schinkel-Museums, *Jahrbuch der Preußischen Kunstsammlungen* 56, 234–49

— 1968 *Die Geschichte der Nationalgalerie Berlin*, Nationalgalerie der Staatlichen Museen Preussischer Kulturbesitz, Berlin

Salzenberg, W, 1847 Bekanntmachung, 11 July, GSTPK, HAI Rep 76Vb Sekt 4 Tit.X Nr.11 Bd.II/Beuth-Schinkel Museum 1847–1857

Samuel-Gohin, V, 1995 La création d'un mythe: Karl Friedrich Schinkel dans les discours de Carl Boetticher, *Histoire de l'art* 29/30 (May), 45–54

Strecke, R, 2000 *Anfänge und Innovation der Preußischen Bauverwaltung*, Böhlau, Cologne

Sukale, R, 2000 Die Bauakademie nach Schinkel und die sogenannte 'Berliner Schule', in *1799–1999. Von der Bauakademie zur T.U. Berlin. Geschichte und Zukunft* (ed Karl Schwarz), Ernst und Sohn, Berlin, 75–7

Süvern, 1827 Gutachten des Staatsraths Süvern über die Inschrift am Museum vom 15. Oktober 1827. Aufgesetzt für den Geheimen Kabinetsrath Albrecht, cited in Wolzogen 1863 (3), 272–4

Thormaelen, L, 1930 Letter: Curator of National Gallery [Thormaelen] to President of the Architekten und Ingenieur-Verein [Kühn], 30 December, ZA SMB, Archtekten- und Ingenieur-Verein, Akten der Ausstellung Klassischer Baukunst

Tieck, L, n.d. Gutachten Ludwig Tieck's über die Inschrift, cited in Wolzogen 1863 (3), 274–5

Waagen, G F, 1841 Karl Friedrich Schinkel als Mensch und als Künstler, *Berliner Kalender* (reprint Werner, Düsseldorf 1980), cited in Zadow 1980, 48

Wolzogen, A F von (ed), 1862–1864, *Aus Schinkels Nachlaß. Reisetagebücher, Briefe und Aphorismen*, 4 vols, Verlag der Könlglichen Geheimen Ober-Hofbuchdruckerei (R v Decker), Berlin

Zadow, M, 1980 *Karl Friedrich Schinkel*, Rembrandt, Berlin

Zimmerman, M G, 1918 Letter: Director of Architecture Museum, Technische Hochschule (Professor Zimmerman) to Minister for Religious and Educational Affairs, 6 January, GStaPK, HAI Rep 76Vb Sekt 4 Tit.X Nr.11 Bd.IV/Beuth-Schinkel Museum 1877–1925

Zusammenstellung der Einrichtungs-Kosten für das Schinkelschen Museum, 1844 GStaPK, HAI Rep 76Vb Sekt 4 Tit.X Nr.11 Bd.I/Schinkel Museum 1844–45, 85r

9

# Personifying the Museum: Incorporation and Biography in American Museum History

Jeffrey Abt

The subtitle of Bayle St John's 1855 book *The Louvre, or, Biography of a Museum*, telegraphed the Englishman's humanisation of the museum's history and collections so that it would be 'interesting even to readers who have never seen it'. Although he did not intend to treat the Louvre as a 'personified institution', St John hoped a biographical approach might prove more attractive to a potential readership (St John 1885, v–vi, 2). St John's use of 'biography' to characterise his approach was novel and followed by just a year the earliest deployment of the word for writings about subjects other than persons.[1] By casting his discussion of the museum as though it were a biography, St John not only humanised his topic for potential readers but also made it easier to write about the Louvre as though its building wings, collections and curators were in fact an indivisible, living entity.

While St John's biographical approach was largely a rhetorical stratagem, his analogy resonated with an increasingly common phenomenon in England and America: the designation of enterprises composed of many people as 'corporate', that is, legally entitled to function as though single individuals. By the 19th century these 'artificial persons', formed to serve religious, educational, charitable, civil, or commercial purposes, were recognised with growing frequency through royal charters or legislative acts. In America, incorporation was the most common method for creating museums because the still comparatively young country, unlike those of Europe, had no history of royal or aristocratic collections that might be transformed – whether through revolution, as with the Louvre, or by donation, as with the Ashmolean – into public entities. Instead, America's museums were created out of whole cloth by locally organised groups of individuals who pooled their wealth and political connections to establish institutions. Although they were inspired by the great national museums of Europe, American museums typically began with legal submissions rather than large collections. By the late 19th century a number of new municipal museums arose, established as private non-profit corporations, each with a self-governing board of directors that aspired to obtain collections, buildings and financial assets that would endure in perpetuity. American law bestowed upon these museum corporations 'most of the legal rights of a human being, without the attendant disadvantages of biology: they are not condemned to die of old age' (Micklethwait and Wooldridge 2003, xv). In articulating the conditions by which museums might be brought to life, the American legal system also influenced public and scholarly perceptions of these beings as they matured into mainstays of the nation's cultural family. This chapter explores the idea of incorporation, its crucial role in the formation of America's governmental

1 *Oxford English Dictionary*, 1989, 2 edn, s.v. 'biography'.

and cultural institutions, and its impact on American public perceptions and scholarly studies of the nation's museums today.[2]

## HISTORICAL BACKGROUND

The idea of 'incorporation', of uniting a group of individuals and collectively-held assets into a body 'corporate', is quite old. Scholars attribute to ancient Rome the underlying concepts of corporate law, especially the notion that 'an association of people could have a collective identity that was separate from its human components' (Micklethwait and Wooldridge 2003, 4). Traces of that heritage are evident in the etymologies of 'corporation', 'incorporate', and related words which entered English usage via the Latin *corporatus* or *corporare* meaning 'to make into a body'. The classes of Roman groups thus designated included governing agencies, not unlike municipalities; religious societies; administrative cadres, such as scribes employed by the empire; and trade societies. These categories were mirrored in English law via distinctions rendered among municipal, ecclesiastical, educational and charitable institutions.[3]

The earliest manifestations of the corporate idea in English society appeared in the 15th century as a means of organising town governments. By the 16th century it was extended to the establishment of professional and religious sodalities, including guilds and charities, and in the 17th century it was applied to commercial entities. But the evolution of English corporate law was anything but orderly and was mostly driven by royal fiat, typically in response to local contingencies. A prominent and ambitious lawyer of the time, Sir Edward Coke (1552–1634), was among the first to compile and publish English common law rulings, including those that adumbrated a 'conception of corporations' (Davis 1905 vol 2, 210). It was Sir William Blackstone (1723–1780), however, who was the first to glean and systematise the underlying principles dispersed through Coke's work; and Blackstone's writings deeply influenced American jurisprudence (Blackstone 1765–69; Bailey 1997).

Although his predecessors contributed to the language of personification in discussing corporations, Blackstone raised it to a literary art. Explaining that all the individuals associated with a corporation, from its foundation to future generations, are 'but one person in law, a person that never dies', Blackstone suggested that this 'artificial person' is 'in the like manner as the river Thames is still the same river, though the parts which comprise it are changing every instant'. The given name of a corporation is 'a proper name, or name of baptism' which, when bestowed by a 'private founder …, [is done] as godfather'. While the 'general duties' of a corporation

2 The importance of incorporation in creating American museums first came to my attention when I began studying art museums established there in the late 19th century (Abt 2001, 32–3). The evolution of the public-museum concept, from its origins in Europe to its particular articulation in America, plays an important role in my topic. Space limitations prohibit a discussion of this insufficiently studied matter. For two different but complementary introductions, see Abt 2006 and McClellan 2008.

3 One can obtain a good sense of the many ways the concept worked its way into English society by reading the etymologies of key terms: *Oxford English Dictionary*, 2 edn, s.v., 'corporate', 'incorporate', 'corporation', and 'incorporation'. The most common terms used in ancient Rome to describe comparable entities were *collegium* and *universitas*. On the parallels between Roman and English legal classifications for corporate entities, see *Encyclopaedia Britannica*, 11 edn, s.v., 'corporation'. An oft-cited definition of corporations is in Boone 1887, 1. Boone's *Manual* provides a relatively concise and readable compendium of corporate law and legal precedents in England and America in the late 19th century as well.

'may, like those of natural persons, be reduced to this single one; that of acting up to the end or design' for which it was created, it cannot 'be excommunicated; for it has no soul'. However, this 'body politic' can be 'dissolved in several ways; which dissolution is [its] civil death'. Among those ways is the return of its founding charter 'into the hands of the king, which is a kind of suicide' (Blackstone 2005, 283, 286–9, 291–2).

The concepts and practices of English corporate law were transmitted to America through the chartering of colonial enterprises. The corporate charter was a convenient tool because it allowed the English government to 'secure the development of colonies, a public purpose, through the stimulation of private interest by grants of political and commercial privileges'. Bestowing political rights was crucial because 'wherever an English colony was planted ... English subjects [were] to be governed' (Davis 1905 vol 2, 157–8, 184–5). By and large, the interests of England and the colonists were identical: colonisation of the 'new world', pursuit of commerce, expansion of the crown's dominion, propagation of Christianity and provision of fresh economic opportunities to impoverished members of English society. There was a subset of colonists whose expectations diverged from the mainstream, however, those fleeing political or religious oppression in England. Even though there were plenty of colonists who were or who became disloyal to the crown, they nonetheless quickly embraced the principles of English corporate law and adapted them to create new political and social institutions in North America.

When, in 1606, James I granted a charter to the London Company to colonise the Virginia territory, he established a Council of Virginia to preserve the crown's *political* power over the region even as he delegated *commercial* autonomy to the company. However, the separation of political and commercial powers made solving the many problems of colonial life too cumbersome and James conceded more political powers to the company, opening the door to its 'substantial independence'. When one of the colony's earliest governors was removed for incompetence his successor attempted to improve conditions by convening an 'assembly' in 1619. It was the 'first representative legislature in America' and led to the creation of an 'Ordinance and Constitution' for the colony's self-governance in 1621 (Davis 1905 vol 2, 158–9, 163–4, 166–70).

These developments were echoed in New England where the Plymouth Company was chartered, also in 1606, but with some significant differences. After a less-than-successful beginning, it was granted a new charter that expanded political incentives in the hope of stimulating economic development. These extended to colonists 'all the rights of British subjects' and authorised the company to subcontract colonisation through land grants to other entities. One grant, in 1628 to the Massachusetts Bay Company, 'was so predominantly political in character that its economic organization had almost no influence' on its development. Qualifications to serve on the company's governing council were not, as was the case in the London Company, based on economics and instead relied on a broader conception of 'social fitness ... narrowed somewhat by ... membership in colonial churches'. Over time the charters and governance of Virginia and Massachusetts Bay became models for other colonies (Davis 1905 vol 2, 169–72, 174–5).

The loosening of self-governance restrictions in corporate charters was not intended to be a political concession, but rather an acknowledgment of the particular circumstances under which colonisation had to be accomplished. Efficient organisation of the population was necessary if colonisation was to succeed and if that could not be accomplished by remote control from London, it had to be delegated to agencies in America. When, as was the case in Virginia, 'nothing short of participation by the colonists in the government of their affairs promised permanent relief', the response was increasingly to set up independent governors, councils that evolved into local legislatures, and the 'principle of representation' when appointing or electing legislators. In form, if not in fact, the 'colonies had become states whose sovereignty and independence' were limited only by occasional English interventions in their electoral and deliberative processes (Davis 1905 vol 2, 196–7).

The notion of 'corporate autonomy' spread so quickly and became so deeply entrenched among the colonies that they began to drift out of England's imperial grasp. Yet, when the colonies declared their independence, they 'reproduced in their State constitutions' features of self-governance that were learned during the colonies' experiences with charters. Further, they utilised much of the legal framework erected during their growth from colonies into states when drafting the Articles of Confederation and Constitution that formed the United States of America. Thus the charters and related legal principles employed by colonial trading companies are echoed in the country's state and federal constitutions.[4]

## VOLUNTARISM, INCORPORATION, AND INDEPENDENCE

America's social transition from colonial rule to independence was brought about by voluntary associations. Alexis de Tocqueville noted this phenomenon in *Democracy in America*, his observations of early 19th-century politics and life in the new nation. In his chapter on 'The Use Which the Americans Make of Public Associations in Civic Life', de Tocqueville drew a distinction between those which were formed for political reasons, specifically the American Revolution, and those for a host of other purposes. 'Americans of all ages, all conditions, and all dispositions constantly form associations', he famously remarked. 'They have not only commercial and manufacturing companies, in which all take part, but associations of a thousand other kinds, religious, moral, serious, futile, general or restricted, enormous or diminutive'. De Tocqueville believed the Americans had 'carried to the highest perfection the art of pursuing in common the object of their common desires and have applied this new science to the greatest number of purposes', one of which would include the creation of museums. Yet, de Tocqueville wondered, was 'this the result of accident, or is there in reality any necessary connection between the principle of association and that of equality?' (de Tocqueville 1840 vol 2, 114–18). It remains an unsettled question.

The 'theory of voluntary association' adumbrated by de Tocqueville is, as one scholar noted, 'identical, when applied to the state, with the theory of the "social contract"' upon which America is based. The social-contract idea was derived from the experience of the corporation 'created by the state, a higher power, before which it is strong because it may rely on it for the protection of its exceptional rights and weak because it depends on the higher power for its existence. Its strength and its weakness both demand a strict definition of its rights and duties; it must therefore have a charter.' When the colonies threw off English rule, they also dissolved the bonds of political stability and imperial security written into the charters that established

4 Davis 1905, 199–201. After the American Revolution, the structures of political organisation contained in former colonial charters such as those for Connecticut and Rhode Island were found to be a 'developed form' and were not modified until they were replaced by state constitutions in 1818 and 1842 respectively. Indeed, 'so clearly was the charter organization recognized as a fit structure for the government of a commonwealth that when the formation of state constitutions was recommended by the Colonial Congress in 1776, it was merely enacted in Connecticut' (Davis 1905, 182).

them *and* guided the colonists' lives. Nonetheless, the 'perpetual recourse to charters taught the Americans ... to value' written constitutions as a means for transforming the colonies into states and their confederation into the United States of America. As a result, 'the system of public law developed in the United States' suggests that the nation's founders 'simply created corporations of themselves and construe[d] their rights and duties accordingly' (Davis 1905 vol 2, 206–7).

When the new republic was founded, the states reserved for themselves – rather than the federal government – the power to confer corporate status; and that remains the law of the land to this day (Hamill 1999, 83). From the beginning, states were amazingly active in establishing corporations, the vast majority 'bodies politic' such as towns, counties, or similar units of local government, or other entities ostensibly serving the 'public interest' including religious and educational institutions, cemeteries and charitable organisations. Massachusetts, perhaps because of its experiences beginning with the Massachusetts Bay Colony in the 1600s, led the way in helping define what the 'public interest' might mean and in the 1780s chartered the Massachusetts Historical Society and the Massachusetts Medical Society. The act of incorporation conferred on such entities the rights to self-government, to function under law 'as a single person', to retain material and financial holdings in perpetuity, and thus to protect their assets 'after the lifetimes of their founding members' (Maier 1993, 52–4, 56).

While there were similarities in the types of institutions upon which the original 13 states conferred corporate charters, the policies and acts by which states did so remained quite varied and *ad hoc*. It was not until the first few decades of the 19th century that states began to enact general statutes to guide incorporation approvals. The process was begun by New York in 1811; but it was the laws established by Pennsylvania and Connecticut in 1836 and 1837 respectively that launched a trend which, by the end of the Civil War in 1865, included over 80 per cent of all states and territories in the embattled union (Hamill 1999, 92, 101–4). In systematising their policies for granting charters, legislatures hoped to 'encourage private efforts to improve or develop their states'. As a result there was a great 'proliferation of corporations' that suggested to some 'an extension of American federalism down into the day-to-day, local associational relationships, so that "the whole political system" was made up of a "concatenation of various corporations, political, civil, religious, social and economical" in which the nation itself was a "great corporation, comprehending all others"'. Indeed, the very concept of statehood in America was likened to a 'plurality of corporations' (Maier 1993, 55, 82–3).

Over the course of the 19th century, however, this teeming progeny of incorporation began to be sorted out by state legislatures as they distinguished between commercial and non-profit entities. Sometimes these taxonomies were driven by the imposition of taxes and regulatory reforms that required, in turn, exemptions for certain kinds of institutions; and sometimes they were driven by differences in the extent to which they served the 'public good'. In tandem with this effort was one defining private corporations as possessing different rights than public corporations. Together these actions let to the emergence of a particularly privileged legal category – private non-profit corporations – that was especially important in the development of American museums (Hansman 1988–89, 809–10).

Although corporations in the new republic possessed many of the legal rights of persons, their freedoms remained an open question. The US Constitution limited governmental power over, and guaranteed certain rights to, each person; and it set out legal protections for every individual regardless of the state or municipality in which that person lived. But such was not the case for corporations whose 'lives' were governed entirely by the states in which they were chartered. During the 19th century, however, the powers of the states over corporations began to be contested. Although Americans at the time 'viewed charitable, religious, and educational institutions as public enterprises', they were legally private corporations and the question of who best represented the 'public interest' was not at all clear. Were the state legislatures that chartered corporations best suited for this responsibility? Or were the governing boards of the corporations better equipped for the task?

Implicit in the debate was a question of whether or not private non-profit corporations could prevent states from meddling in their 'private' affairs and a series of legal cases over the autonomy and self-governance of higher-education institutions ensued. One was a lawsuit over Dartmouth College, chartered by the crown in 1769, whose independence was challenged in the early 1800s by the State of New Hampshire. When the college's governing board took the state to court, New Hampshire's chief justice sided with the state, arguing that 'if Dartmouth College was a public corporation and a public trust, the powers of the legislature over its affairs was unquestionable'. The issue was appealed to the US Supreme Court which ruled in favour of Dartmouth's board based primarily on a single issue: the purposes of the corporation. The court found that the character of institutions is determined by 'how and why they are formed, not by their incorporation'. Thus the mere fact that Dartmouth was incorporated in the State of New Hampshire did not entitle the state legislature to impose its will on the college unless the college violated the terms of its founding charter. Because the decision turned on Dartmouth's existence through private donations, the Supreme Court's decision 'did more than protect corporations from legislative interference: It advanced the notion that the will of the public could be expressed by other than electoral and governmental means. In doing this, it legitimated the idea of private associational initiative in the public interest' (Hall 1997, 7–9).

The Supreme Court thus established a fundamental precedent on an issue residing at the heart of the corporation's 'personality' – the relation of the corporation to the power of the state. When, in English history, the monarch initially permitted and later in effect created corporations, the sovereign's act of chartering was 'universally said in so many words [to] "incorporate": that is, [it] … created the legal person' of the corporation (Raymond 1906, 363–4). Yet, under English common law, the sovereign and eventually the parliament retained far more power over 'corporate persons' than over 'natural persons' (Hall 1997, 9). Because the US Constitution did not address the rights of corporations *per se* and could only address them as they might surface in American jurisprudence as 'persons', for example in relation to free-speech rights, the Supreme Court had to find another approach to the legal relations between corporate 'persons' and the states which created them. It now did so by taking into consideration the property and purposes of the corporations, drawing a distinction between those that are public, such as municipalities, and those that are private, such as colleges and museums. '[T]he division of corporations into the two categories of public and private, with radically different legal relationships to the state, was a dichotomy which American judges did not find ready-made for them in English law but fashioned for themselves' (Dodd 1954, 17). Yet, in carving out a sphere of independence for private corporations, the Supreme Court inadvertently limited the extent to which a broader public interest might be brought to bear on corporations who strayed from serving the 'public good'.

## Enterprise and Accountability

The laws by which states authorised corporations also required these entities to establish self-governance structures that included elected boards of directors and written bye-laws. The independence implied in those bye-laws was virtually unlimited so long as they were not 'contrary to the law of the land' (Blackstone 2005, 287). Similar to the debate over Dartmouth College's autonomy, however, was another over the selection of governing board members among private institutions, especially institutions of higher learning. A battle over the board membership of Yale University in the 1860s and 1870s turned on differences between an old hierarchy of clergy and their associates on one hand, and alumni and faculty sympathisers on the other. The latter, viewed as 'laity' by the clergy who founded and guided the university for generations, sought reforms to bring it into line with the changing mores of an industrialising and modernising American society. The alumni eventually prevailed, marking a trend toward lay control that by the late 1800s spread beyond universities to other types of private institutions too. 'More centrally', as one scholar commented, 'this effort signaled the replacement of professional self-government with decision making by "disinterested" businessmen and their allies' (Hall 1997, 12–14). Crucially, many in that era identified 'business as a model of efficiency' that ought to be replicated in the self-governance and administration of educational, cultural and charitable corporations (Trachtenberg 2007, 164).

This trend coincided with a sharp growth in the business world's influence on American life, as well as the evolution of a distinctly 'modern corporate form of ownership' that was based on 'minority ownership – that is, on the legally established authority of a small group of directors and managers to act in the name of a larger, amorphous body of otherwise unrelated' stakeholders. While this new form was largely a refinement of colonial and early American corporate precedents, its concentration of power in a small group of directors provided capitalists a 'flexible and far-reaching instrument' for pursuing profits; and it provided philanthropists an equally effective tool for pursuing non-profit purposes (Trachtenberg 2007, 4).

These developments occurred during the late 1880s, a period of great industrial growth and relative prosperity in America, leading in turn to rapid urban expansion and the creation of enormous wealth in the country's municipal centres.

> Advocates and guardians of culture performed a major role in these years, setting in place what remain … key official institutions: large private universities, municipal museums and concert halls, immense central public libraries. In a mere decade, an entire apparatus appeared, an infrastructure which monumentalized the presence of culture, of high art and learning, within the society. (Trachtenberg 2007, 144)

It was during this period that many of America's major art museums were established: the Metropolitan Museum of Art and Boston Museum of Fine Arts in 1870, the predecessor to the Philadelphia Museum of Art in 1876, the Art Institute of Chicago in 1879, and the Detroit Institute of Arts in 1885 (Howe 1913–46; Whitehill 1970; Zolberg 1974; Abt 2001; Fox 1995).

This convergence of legal, economic and cultural developments meant that 'by the turn of the century, businessmen dominated the boards of most' private institutions of higher learning and museums; and 'through the establishment of grantmaking foundations, had created powerful instruments for shaping the priorities and policies of a wide range of cultural institutions' (Hall

1997, 14). Museums in particular 'seemed to their advocates and supporters democratic enterprises, serving to diffuse knowledge, taste, and refinement. What they in fact diffused, however, was a set of corollaries to the idea of culture'. Because they were organised by an 'urban elite' and filled with masterpieces of European and American art donated by wealthy collectors, 'the museums ... associated art with wealth, and the power to donate and administer with social station'. As a result, no matter how well intended, the efforts of these institutions' founders inadvertently appeared to be 'privileged culture distributed and administered with condescension from above' (Trachtenberg 2007, 144, 158). The utilisation of the corporate form to establish museums imitated practices among American voluntary associations that were fairly common by the end of the 19th century. But the timing, coming as it did during a period in which colleges and universities had attempted to 'create a new kind of public accountability', resulted in 'accountability not to the public as represented by government or by professional authority, but to the public as represented by the most economically successful' (Hall 1997, 14).[5]

## PRIVILEGE AND THE PUBLIC INTEREST

When these museums were being established, their founders often sought special privileges in the form of municipal or state support, land grants and tax exemptions. The preservation of legal authority to grant corporate charters at the state rather than the federal level worked to the advantage of leaders who drew on their political connections with local legislators to assure states' laws accommodated the creation of museums. Accordingly nearly all of America's largest and most prominent museums are municipal or state, rather than national institutions. Indeed, were it not for the generosity of an Englishman, James Smithson, there would be hardly any national museums on the Mall in Washington, DC (Oehser 1983).

State legislators provided special legal accommodations for museums by amending corporate charter statutes with a definition that distinguished museums and comparable institutions from their commercial brethren: the absence of a profit motive. If a group wishing to establish a museum could prove it met that criterion, it was granted special exceptions, most notably classification as tax-exempt, which eliminated the institution's obligation to pay property, sales and income taxes. Thus was born the expression 'non-profit corporation' as a catch-all phrase for the host of institutions and agencies accorded this special status. In exchange for the privilege, however, it was assumed that while all American corporations served 'purposes clearly in the public interest', private non-profit corporations were expected to adhere to especially high standards of public trust and service (Trachtenberg 2007, 6).

To some Americans, the notion of permitting a handful of citizens to create a private non-profit organisation, like a museum, and conferring upon it special legal and tax privileges was

5 Concepts of American museums' efficiency and efficacy evolved over the course of the 20th century in ways that had relatively little to do with business-world standards and practices. The most notable changes were stimulated by funding agencies that began demanding, in exchange for operating-expense grants, evidence of museums' effectiveness, specifically with reference to public service and educational outreach. As Stephen Weil noted, these demands and responses might best be understood as conforming to an emerging 'social enterprise' model (Weil 1999, 239–40; see also Dees 1994; 1996). Significantly, social enterprise agencies, like museums, have developed differently in the US and Europe (Kerlin 2006).

un-egalitarian.[6] That scepticism has its origins in the nation's founding and 18th century debates about America's political institutions and the roles of voluntary associations and private organisations claiming to act in the 'public interest'. Opponents of such entities felt they 'threatened democracy by permitting small groups of citizens, particularly the wealthy, to exercise power disproportionate to their numbers'. Did it make sense, they argued, to leave 'such essential public concerns as culture, education, health, and social welfare to the discretion – or to the neglect – of the few wealthy enough to concern themselves' with these vital functions? Was it not as 'dangerous to democracy as leaving the banking, transportation, and communication systems unregulated?' Non-profit advocates countered that 'democracy attains its fullest institutional expression ... through government encouragement of private action, including grants of incorporation, tax exemptions, [and] tax regulations providing incentives to individuals who make donations to nonprofit organisations, and the ability to set property aside in perpetuity for charitable and educational purposes' (Hall 1992, 15).

Most concluded that 'while nonprofit organizations yielded particular benefits for their creators, they were no less effective in providing crucially important services for the general public'. And in reality the founders of many non-profits included the less well-to-do who devoted themselves to 'schools, colleges, hospitals, medical societies, orphanages, asylums, and other charitable enterprises that offered essential services that few governments or private groups were willing to undertake'. Moreover, the early successes of museums 'lent credibility to their [founders'] claims for political leadership – which were based on a rhetoric of public stewardship – and legitimated their accumulation of wealth – which, as their charitable actions showed, they held as stewards' (Hall 1992, 35). The corporate form had become an indispensable tool for individuals building America's cultural infrastructure; and it had become an impregnable shield for those individuals when critics assailed their actions.

## Personifying the Museum

To think historically about a museum's development, or critically about its effectiveness, requires a conceptual step that, like the act of incorporation, binds together its collections, building, staff and governance into an indivisible whole that can be understood within, but separate from, its environment. The legal basis of the American museum, as a private non-profit corporation, facilitates that step by implying the museum's internal cohesion while at that same time obscuring its relationship, as a public trust, with the immediate community in which it was incorporated. As one observer remarked, 'the persons who constitute [a] corporation are not necessarily coincident with two other classes of persons who are directly associated with it ...: (a) Those persons through whom the corporation acts [its staff] (b) those persons in whose interests the corporation exists [the public]' (Brown 1905, 366).

6 There are several discussions of this problem. In addition to the following, see also Trachtenberg 2007, 179–80. Curiously, de Tocqueville felt that a democratic society like America would not be as conducive to the interests of small circles of 'aristocrats' seeking to exert power collectively as, for example, would be less-democratic societies like England, because America's associations were composed of larger groups of citizens with fewer economic interests to protect. Had de Tocqueville travelled through America four or five decades later, he might have come to a very different conclusion (de Tocqueville 1840, 114–16).

Certainly the inclination to think of museum boards of directors or trustees, their staffs and audiences as though they *are* 'coincident' derives from the age-old 'germ of the corporate idea' that 'lies ... in a mode of thought; in thinking of several as a group, as one'. A 'group', so the thinking goes, might be defined as 'such a collection of individuals as may be represented by a word of the singular number', some examples being: crowd, crew, team, regiment, army, flock, herd, or congregation. An important characteristic of the 'group idea' might be 'an identity of interest' (Raymond 1906, 350–1, 354–5). Thus even a crowd of individuals who happened to cluster on a street corner while waiting for a traffic signal to change share an 'identity of interest': eagerness for the signal to change. While, from a legal standpoint, the American museum is an 'artificial person', whole and integrated, practically speaking it is often more like a confederation of several groups – board, staff, volunteer corps, audience – each of which possesses interests that are 'not necessarily coincident'.

Writings about individual American museums are rarely, if ever, described as biographies, although most *have* been in the sense that they treated their topics as though they were born, struggled to overcome life's impediments, matured and reached great success in old age. To a significant extent this approach can also be attributed to the museum-history genre as practised during the last century or more. Many museum biographies were self-published by their subjects, written by current or former employees, and intended to celebrate institutional milestones like major anniversaries or new building or addition openings. They thus emphasise life-cycle events like the donations of major collections, the acquisition of notable masterpieces and the tenures of prominent directors or curators. These 'auto'-biographies written to mark special occasions do not lend themselves to probing self explorations because the texts are not designed to expose internal disputes among leaders, staff members and their publics. To the contrary, they wish to avoid conveying a sense of institutional dis-ease and mortality because they were sponsored to celebrate institutional accomplishments.

Neither do such biographies invite considerations of the social or cultural contexts of museums' development. This is a particularly important oversight because the American museum's incorporation not only binds its founders, adherents and resources into a single entity before the law, it also confers a variety of privileges predicated on assumptions of public service that entwine the institution with the locality in which it was established. Incorporation ought to invite an ecological treatment of the American museum because it is, after all, a product of its environment and its evolution is profoundly shaped by its immediate setting far more than is generally appreciated (Abt 2001, 15–19).

Whether viewed from the perspective of historical scholarship or social policy, the utilisation of corporate non-profit law to create the American museum inadvertently conferred upon the institution an impression of internal and external coherence, a sense of being that smoothes over very real differences among its constituent parts, as well as its relations with its immediate socio-cultural context. Over a hundred years ago, one legal scholar expressed discomfort with the personification analogy in corporate law because, even then, it was clear that the legal 'conception of an institution found in a prevailing system of law is not always identical with a sociological conception of it'. The legal system is not only slow to comprehend 'new social relations', it tends to preserve structures designed for older situations long after they changed. When this happens, the legislative and judicial processes will turn to 'fictions – intentional assumptions of things as facts that are in truth not facts'. A perfect example of how a fiction is created 'to bring new social relations into harmony with established law' is the legal view of the corporation as an 'artificial person' (Davis 1905, 209–10).

Although seemingly an old and long-settled issue in American law, the extent to which the legal and social concepts of the corporation remains a live concern is evident in a 2010 US Supreme Court ruling that Congress could not limit campaign spending by corporations. The court found in part that because corporations are in effect citizens, just like the natural kind, they are entitled to the same free-speech protections enshrined in the US Constitution (Supreme Court 2010). The subsequent public furore over the notion of allowing corporations, especially business corporations, to participate in American election campaigns because they are – before the law – like natural persons, reveals the extent to which this legal analogy fails the common-sense test for most Americans.[7]

When Bayle St John subtitled his book on the Louvre a 'biography', he was adopting an analogy to humanise what might otherwise have appeared to be a dry institutional history. Analogies, metaphors and similes are powerful conceptual forms. They breathe life into otherwise dull texts and throw into sharp relief otherwise flat descriptions. When misapplied, however, they can also mask significant errors and contradictions. It is not hard to understand why St John, or more recent generations of museum history scholars and critics, write about museums as though they are single persons or isolated actors. Yet there is much to learn about the inter-animations of museums and the societies that created them. In focusing on the origins of the American museum, I have attempted to flesh out a fundamental aspect of its history that has been overlooked by scholars and that, I believe, not only helps illuminate that history but – I hope – will invite further consideration of the many ways individual museum histories have been essentialised or rendered into stereotypes. Further, I am well aware that there are many parallels between treatments of American museum histories and those of their European forebears. In focusing on the legal origins of American museums and their intimate relations with the legal and social foundations of American society, I hope to establish a basis for their comparison with European precursors and to stimulate fresh research on the beginnings of these 'fictive persons'.

## Bibliography and References

Abt, J, 2001 *A Museum on the Verge: A Socioeconomic History of the Detroit Institute of Arts, 1882–2000*, Wayne State University Press, Detroit

— 2006 The Origins of the Public Museum, in *A Companion to Museum Studies* (ed S Macdonald), Blackwell Publishing, Oxford, 114–34

Bailey, G, 1997 Blackstone in America, *Early America Review* 1 (4) [online], available from: http://www.earlyamerica.com/review/spring97/blackstone.html [28 April 2010]

Blackstone, W, 1765–69 *Commentaries on the Laws of England*, 2 vols, Clarendon Press, Oxford

— 2005 (1765) *Commentaries on the Laws of England, Book the First*, electronic transcription and edn, Lonang Institute, Novi, Michigan

Boone, C T, 1887 *A Manual of the Law Applicable to Corporations*, Bancroft-Whitney Co, San Francisco, California

7 The relevant part of the First Amendment, passed in 1791, reads 'Congress shall make no law … abridging the freedom of speech, or of the press…'.

Brown, W J, 1905 The Personality of the Corporation and the State, *Law Quarterly Review* 21 (4), 365–79

Davis, J P, 1905 *Corporations: A Study of the Origin and Development of Great Business Combinations and Their Relation to the Authority of the State*, 2 vols, G P Putnams and Sons, New York

de Tocqueville, A, 1840 (1835) *Democracy in America*, trans H Reeve, 2 vols, J & H G Langley, New York

Dees, J G, 1994 Social Enterprise: Private Initiatives for the Common Good, *Harvard Business School Notes* 9-395-116, 1–13

— 1996 The Social Enterprise Spectrum: Philanthropy to Commerce, *Harvard Business School Notes* 9-396-343, 1–7

Dodd, E M, 1954 *American Business Corporations Until 1860, with Special Reference to Massachusetts*, Harvard University Press, Cambridge

Fox, D M, 1995 *Engines of Culture: Philanthropy and Art Museums*, Transaction Publishers, New Brunswick, New Jersey

Hall, P D, 1992 Inventing the Nonprofit Sector, in *Inventing the Nonprofit Sector and Other Essays*, Johns Hopkins University Press, Baltimore, 13–83

— 1997 *A History of Nonprofit Boards in the United States*, National Center for Nonprofit Boards, Washington, DC

Hamill, S P, 1999 From Special Privilege to General Utility: A Continuation of Willard Hurst's Study of Corporations, *American University Law Review* 49, October, 82–180

Hansmann, H, 1988–89 The Evolving Law of Non-Profit Organizations: Do Current Trends Make Good Policy? *Case Western Reserve Law Review* 39 (3), 807–27

Howe, W E, 1913–46 *A History of the Metropolitan Museum of Art*, 2 vols, Metropolitan Museum of Art, New York

Kerlin, J A, 2006 Social Enterprise in the United State and Europe: Understanding and Learning from the Differences, *Voluntas* 17, 247–63

Maier, P, 1993 The Revolutionary Origins of the American Corporation, *William and Mary Quarterly* Third Series 50 (1), 51–84

McClellan, A, 2008 The Public, in *The Art Museum from Boullée to Bilbao*, University of California Press, Berkeley, 155–92

Micklethwait, J, and Wooldridge, A, 2003 *The Company: A Short History of a Revolutionary Idea*, Modern Library, New York

Oehser, P H, 1983 *The Smithsonian Institution*, Westview Press, Boulder, Colorado

Raymond, R L, 1906 The Genesis of the Corporation, *Harvard Law Review* 19 (5), 350–65

St John, B, 1885 *The Louvre or, Biography of a Museum*, Chapman and Hall, London

Supreme Court of the United States, 2010 *Citizens United v Federal Election Commission*, 558/2 US 08-205

Trachtenberg, A, 2007 (1982) *The Incorporation of America: Culture and Society in the Gilded Age*, 2 edn, Hill and Wang, New York

Weil, S E, 1999 From Being *About* Something to Being *For* Somebody: The Ongoing Transformation of the American Museum, *Daedalus* 128 (3), 229–58

Whitehill, W M, 1970 *Museum of Fine Arts, Boston: A Centennial History*, 2 vols, Belknap Press, Harvard University, Cambridge

Zolberg, V L, 1974 The Art Institute of Chicago: The Sociology of a Cultural Organization, unpublished PhD thesis, University of Chicago

10

# Making an Exhibition of Ourselves

Helen Rees Leahy

In recent years, museums have staged a number of 'exhibitions of exhibitions'. These experiments in institutional, curatorial and artistic revivalism have ranged from allusions to, and quotations from, past installations to full-scale re-enactments and reconstructions (Greenberg 2009). Some have reproduced assemblages that were first exhibited two centuries ago, while others have remounted exhibitions from the recent past. The motivations of the curators and artists responsible for these diverse projects have included the desire to mark famous anniversaries, to recuperate long-forgotten shows, to examine the effects of different modes of display and spectatorship, and to construct an archive of the immaterial through retrospective and performance practices. To give a flavour of the trend, examples of 're-dos' have included historical reconstructions, notably 'Art on the Line' (2001), curated by David Solkin at the Courtauld Institute, a composite reconstruction of Royal Academy exhibitions staged in the Great Room at Somerset House between 1780 and 1836. The year 2009 saw two experiments in revisiting the avant-garde of the 1950s onwards: the transposition of Robert Morris' famous 1971 exhibition 'Bodyspacemotionthings' at the (then) Tate Gallery to Tate Modern; and 'Vides', a retrospective of exhibitions of empty rooms organised by the Centre Pompidou. Past exhibitions have formed the subject of new ones, such as: 'Art Treasures in Manchester: 150 Years On' (2007) at the Manchester Art Gallery, which celebrated the 150th anniversary of the Manchester Art Treasures Exhibition; and 'William Blake 1809' at Tate Britain, a fragmentary evocation of Blake's unsuccessful one-man show mounted in rooms above his brother's hosiery shop in Soho, London.

These brief examples indicate the diversity of recent re-display projects and hint at the many issues that they raise. While the history of exhibitions has become an established field of enquiry within the wider field of museum history (Altshuler 1994; 2008; Haskell 2000), the fashion for 're-dos' points to an emerging interest in institutional historiography – or even autobiography, as the theme of this volume suggests. Museums have conventionally disavowed their own temporalities, but by turning back to past exhibitions, whether in a spirit of celebration or reflection, they are now acknowledging histories of curatorial, as well as art, practice. The referencing of past exhibitions in the contemporary museum reminds us that exhibitions have critical careers that extend from the time before, during and after the duration of their initial exposure. When is the significance of an exhibition first recognised – at the moment of its original opening when it is feted (or not) by the press and visited enthusiastically (or not) by the public? Or it is some time later, when its influence on artists' reputations and on subsequent exhibitions can be discerned? What kinds of evidence enable us to know how an exhibition looked and was experienced long after the doors closed and the last work was taken down? These questions are both prompted and also addressed by exhibitions of exhibitions, which inevitably consecrate the original exhibition as a significant ancestor through a process of curatorial resurrection.

Before going any further, I want to make a distinction between temporary exhibitions that remount past modes of presentation and spectatorship, and the fashion for historicism in collections displays (Barker 1999; Saumarez Smith 2007). For example, the re-hangs devised by Timothy Clifford at Manchester City Art Gallery and the National Gallery of Scotland, in the 1970s and 1980s respectively, were prescriptive rather than experimental. The same is true of the Enlightenment Gallery in the British Museum, which opened in 2003. The reference point for these projects is not a specific, durational exhibition, but a much looser assemblage of historical display coordinates. Thus, the integration of paintings, sculpture and furniture in Clifford's 'heritage hang' constitutes an argument as to how old master paintings should be viewed and understood by present-day audiences: namely, within an ensemble of fine and decorative arts that is designed to evoke the appearance of an aristocratic picture gallery (Clifford 1982). The impetus here is to mount an argument about the cultural value of art collecting. The same is true of the Enlightenment Gallery, which provides an aesthetically intriguing (if historically disingenuous) account of the origins of the British Museum and, by extension, a justification of its present-day claims to universality (Lord 2005; O'Neill 2004).

By contrast, temporary reconstructions offer different challenges to, and possibilities for, historical research and curatorial reflexivity. Turning first to issues of production, how does the reproduction of a past exhibition compare with, say, the performance of a piece of music or a play? Is there an exhibition equivalent of a musical score or a dramatic script? What kind of interpretative practices are involved in the selection and re-presentation of past exhibitions? Clearly, much depends on the exhibitionary archive, by which I mean the disparate documentation that may (or may not) survive from a show, including: exhibit lists; designs and floor plans; organisational files and correspondence; images of the installation; texts and labels; publicity and ephemera such as tickets and invitations; catalogues and publications; contemporary criticism; visitors' records. But even when a historical exhibition is extremely well documented, as is the case with the Manchester Art Treasures Exhibition of 1857, its reconstruction may be impracticable, as Manchester Art Gallery discovered during the organisation of its commemorative exhibition 'Art Treasures in Manchester: 150 Years On' (Rees Leahy 2009a).

Historical reconstructions depend on both the survival and availability of the original exhibits. Many of the works first shown in the 1857 Art Treasures Exhibition have since been exported, some have been destroyed, and the location of others cannot be traced. Even so, thousands remain in Britain and could, in theory, have been reunited once more. However, in 1857, a loan request was something of a novelty and many owners agreed to have their fragile paintings transported by rail to Manchester. No longer: in 2007, risk-averse museums effectively precluded the reassembly of the famous 'Ancient Masters' section of the Art Treasures Exhibition, which had consisted almost entirely of paintings on unstable wooden panels that are rarely lent today. Similarly insurmountable was the issue of scale. The Art Treasures Palace was large enough to accommodate some 16,000 exhibits and, thankfully, Manchester Art Gallery is not. Although the design of the anniversary exhibition 'Art Treasures in Manchester' was intended to evoke the interior style of the Art Treasures Palace, actual reconstruction was ruled out; the sheer scale of the 1857 exhibition vastly exceeded the spatial and organisational resources of Manchester Art Gallery, and its re-presentation in 2007 was therefore avowedly partial and fragmentary.

If the problem for Manchester was one of historical superfluity, a commemorative exhibition at Tate Britain was equally constrained by a paucity of evidence and the absence of nearly half the original exhibits. The basis for the Tate show 'William Blake 1809' was primarily Blake's self-published catalogue for his exhibition of 'Poetical and Historical Inventions', which was almost entirely ignored by his contemporaries and resulted in none of the sales that he had hoped for (Myrone 2009). This 66-page pamphlet amounted to a manifesto of Blake's artistic beliefs and, together with the history of the exhibition itself, provided the curatorial spur to recall Blake's enterprise on its bicentenary. However, six of the 16 works shown in 1809 no longer exist or are untraced, including Blake's largest and most ambitious painting, 'The Ancient Britons'. The absent canvas was represented on the gallery wall by a blank, white rectangle of the same dimensions: it was a poignant commentary on the histories of survival, and as a display device it neatly disrupted the museum's conventional resistance to acknowledging the contingencies of presence and absence.

The spectatorship invoked by both 'Art Treasures in Manchester' and 'William Blake 1809' was located firmly in the present: neither departed from a horizontal axis of display whereby pictures are viewed serially along a wall, each accompanied by a small text label and separated from its neighbour by a respectful gap. 'Art on the Line' at the Courtauld Institute was a more ambitious reconstruction in terms both of presentation and also conditions of reception. Key to its rationale and impact was the opportunity to mount the exhibition in the same room as its historical referents – namely the former Great Room of the Royal Academy in Somerset House – complete with the construction of angled walls to increase the visibility of 'skied' pictures, as had been done in the past. Contemporary prints of the 'Exhibition' provided the curators with accurate visual accounts of the combined spectacle of pictures and viewers, added to which lists of exhibits and numerous commentaries constituted a rich archival record (Fig 10.1). As a result, 'Art on the Line' not only replicated a typical Academy hang of the early 19th century, but also its modes of spectatorship (Fig 10.2).

However, the opportunity to reuse the site of an earlier exhibition is rare. The history of the empty room as an exhibitionary gesture was recalled in 'Vides': nine whitewashed rooms were exhibited on the fourth floor of the Centre Pompidou (which usually houses part of the permanent collection), each instantiating a project by nine different artists from Yves Klein to Laurie Parsons. There was no attempt to replicate the dimensions or character of each of the original spaces whose emptiness had, for the duration of the artist's project, constituted an aesthetic and curatorial statement. The starting point was Klein's empty room shown at the Galerie Iris Clert in 1958, and 'Vides' traced how, after Klein's intervention, 'the empty space as an object of exhibition … became a kind of classic of the radical mode, and was to be replayed in other contexts …' (Copeland *et al* 2009, 29), culminating, of course, in 'Vides' itself. The retrospective therefore gathered together a succession of immaterial exhibitions that were already connected via artists' dialogue, revision and critique. The memories of these transient gestures were now accumulated in a further museological experiment that functioned as both inventory and evaluation; the temporary re-collection of empty spaces was itself a conceptual, rather than an archaeological, endeavour.

'Vides' was first shown at the Centre Pompidou and then at the Kunsthalle Bern. No exhibits were transported from one venue to the other; the only thing that travelled was the concept of the exhibition itself. In principle, 'Vides' could be reinstalled *ad infinitum* (and also simultaneously), but that would miss the point. The impermanence of 'Vides' was as essential to its polemical capacity within the official museum cultures of France and Switzerland as it had been to the artists' original gestures. Rejecting the inclusion of archival or documentary displays, the curators declared that their idea was 'truly to face empty exhibitions' (Copeland 2009, 29). What

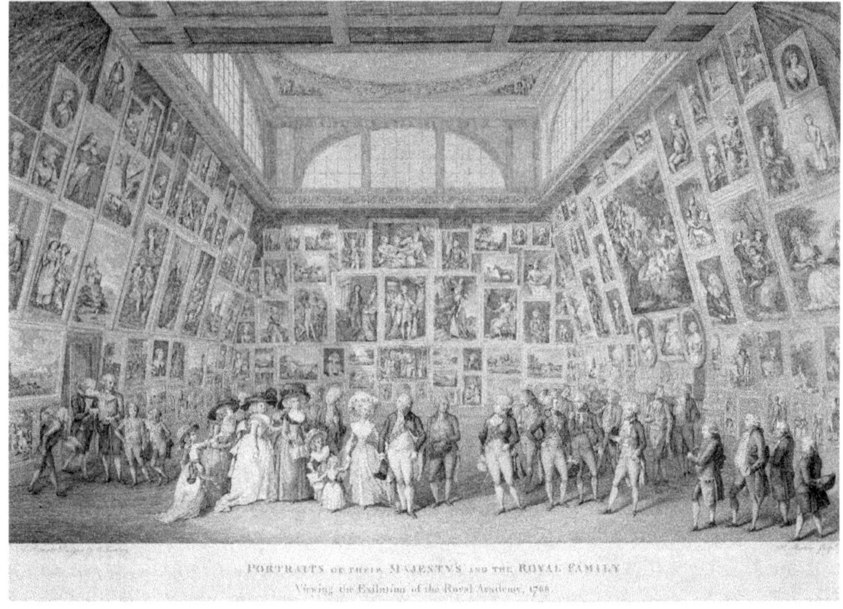


FIG 10.1.
PIETRO ANTONIO MARTINI (AFTER JOHANN HEINRICH RAMBERG), THE ROYAL FAMILY AT THE ROYAL ACADEMY, LONDON, 1788

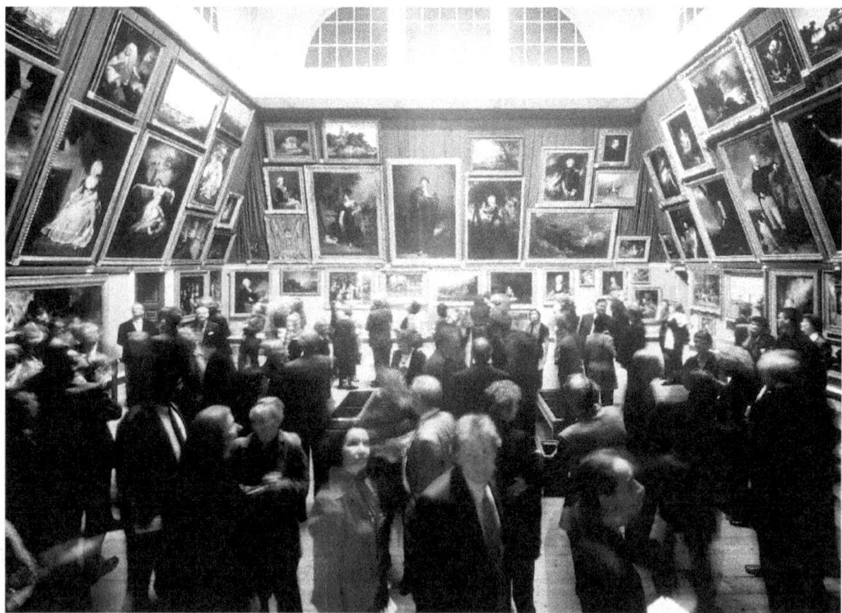

FIG 10.2.
ART ON THE LINE, THE COURTAULD GALLERY, LONDON, 2001

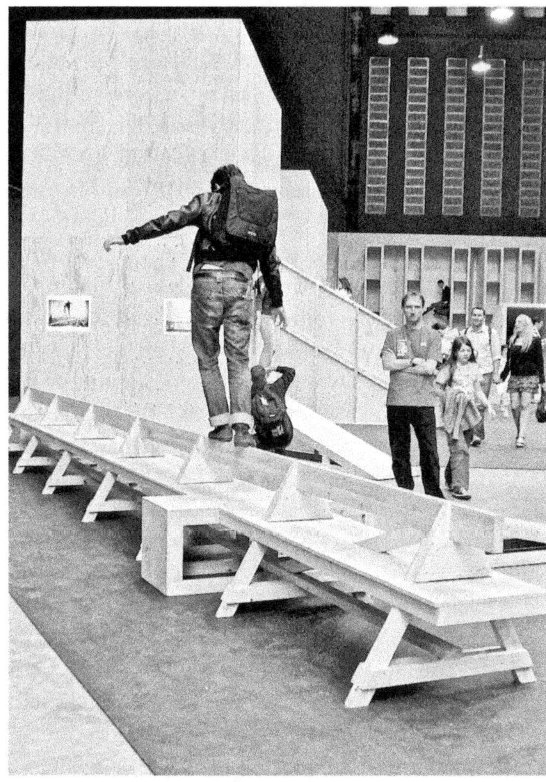

FIG 10.3.
BODYSPACEMOTIONTHINGS, TATE MODERN, LONDON, 2009

had by now become a cliché of conceptual art was re-presented in a format that now subverted the practice of that museum staple: the retrospective.

'Vides' showed that distinct issues in relation to authenticity and artistic intention are raised by re-presentations of immaterial practices, such as conceptual and performance art. Marina Abramovic has used recent projects, notably '7 Easy Pieces' (2005) at the Guggenheim Museum and 'The Artist is Present' (2010) at the Museum of Modern Art (both New York), explicitly to stage re-performance as an archival endeavour. As her own trajectory of practice becomes increasingly museological and concerned with the history of her and others' work, Abramovic has argued that the only way to document the history of performance is through re-performance (Spector 2007). During '7 Easy Pieces' she re-enacted five performances of artists from the 1960s and 1970s, plus two of her own earlier works. On her re-performance of Joseph Beuys' 'How to Explain Pictures to a Dead Hare' (1965), Abramovic explained that she did not pretend that she was Beuys; rather, she interpreted the record of his work as if it were a musical score.

What is the effect of re-collecting such experimental and experiential projects within the museum? Arguably, their unpredictability is inevitably erased and their cutting edge blunted by the passage of time and their legitimisation reinforced through revival. This was certainly the effect of restaging Robert Morris' 1971 exhibition in the Turbine Hall at Tate Modern (Fig 10.3). The example of 'Bodyspacemotionthings' clearly demonstrates how the reinstallation of an exhibition 28 years after its original incarnation cannot guarantee the recovery of its radical impact. This was partly due to the effects of present-day health and safety policies on the 2009 reconstruction and the regulation of visitor access to Morris' interactive sculptures. In 1971, Morris' exhibition was closed after just six days due to a number of injuries suffered by members of the public and also damage to some of the exhibits resulting from the 'exuberant and excited' response of some visitors to the radical possibilities of the museum as a space of play (Bird 1999, 102ff). In an attempt to avoid a repeat of the apparent chaos of the original show, in 2009 exhibits were modified and made from less hazardous materials in order to reduce the risk of injury, and visitors were carefully supervised by gallery staff who watched over every piece. Far from creating the 'bedlam in which all rules of decorum had been abandoned' (Banham quoted in Bird 1999, 104), the show now resembled an extremely well-mannered playground. Had the exhibition been reinstalled in the neo-classical Duveen Gallery at Tate Britain (where it was originally staged), the disjunction between Morris' invitation to roll, climb and wobble and the etiquette of the traditional art gallery might have been maintained. Transposed to Tate Modern, 'Bodyspacemotionthings' became just another jolly exercise in relational aesthetics within the well-established art playground of the Turbine Hall. After sunbathing in Olafur Elliasson's 'Weather Project', hurtling down Carsten Holler's slides and falling into Doris Salcedo's 'crack', the Tate Modern crowd was already over-familiar with the rules of the game that Morris was in the process of inventing in the early 1970s (Rees Leahy 2009b).

In each of these examples, the question of reflexivity is prompted by the production of an exhibition of an exhibition: to what extent is an institutional capacity for self-awareness and a capacity for critique activated by such projects? The concept of the 'fourth wall' in theatre may provide a useful analogy here. Arguably, this engagement with the exhibition itself as medium is the curatorial equivalent of the actor turning to the audience and talking to the audience directly through the invisible fourth wall beneath the proscenium arch. However, the critical edge of some 're-dos' is rather blunter than others. 'Bodyspacemotionthings' at Tate Modern restaged Morris' radical challenge to the museum as family entertainment: the risk of the original was erased, not only with deference to contemporary practices of health and safety, but also because interactive art has now become commonplace. Arguably, a blank space delineated on the gallery wall to mark the absence of a lost masterpiece in 'William Blake 1809' was more unsettling: the quiet, reflective gesture has greater resonance in today's museum than the noisy playground. Why is this? The next part of this chapter explores these questions through two critical lenses which, I believe, can enable us to theorise the meanings and effects of exhibition revivals: namely, Michael Baxandall's notion of the 'period eye' as a way of historicising the experience of the exhibition viewer, and Andre Gide's idea of *mise en abyme* as a reflexive device.

First, Baxandall's 'period eye' (1972) is based on the premise that the skills involved in apprehending works of art are historically and culturally acquired and that, in turn, the artist responds to the en-skilled (or attuned) viewer. As Randolph observes, the period eye 'emphasizes the cultural-constructedness of vision, characterizes a set of viewing norms, and charts the manner in which artists responded to those norms in their works' (2004, 538). Taking the example of Piero della Francesco's *Annunciation*, Baxandall suggests that a 15th-century Chinese man, entirely unfamiliar with the conventions of perspectival painting and the biblical story depicted, might suppose that the figures whom we recognise as the Virgin Mary and the Archangel Gabriel were paying homage to the column in the centre of the picture. Can we extend this idea to the operation of visuality within an exhibition? Carrier suggests that we can: 'Because we are accustomed to the ways in which visual artworks are displayed in modern galleries and museums, it is easy to forget how recently these ways of presenting art have been created and how they influence our judgment of artworks' (1987, 83). If this is so, do exhibitions of exhibitions have the capacity to disrupt our viewing practices and thereby reveal our taken-for-granted habits of looking as historically grounded?

Bourdieu takes up Baxandall's thesis in an essay entitled 'The Social Genesis of the Eye' (1996), in which he addresses the problem of comprehending historical works or practices in the present. The paradox identified by Bourdieu arises from the fact that whereas a historical spectator would have immediately grasped the artist's (or curator's) intention, the modern viewer must reconstruct the code within which the work is embedded whilst also realising that no such effort of construction and translation was required in the original context of reception. According to Bourdieu, what is called for is not an act of mimicry, but rather a willingness to comprehend in a 'somewhat vicarious mode' (1996, 315). In the case of exhibition reconstructions, this means putting ourselves in the position of past viewers.

Merleau-Ponty describes how, in an art gallery, we place ourselves in relation to the paintings or sculptures on display so as to achieve the optimum 'balance between the inner and outer horizon' (1962, 302). In other words, practised gallery-visitors know how and where to position themselves in relation to the object so that 'it vouchsafes most of itself' (ibid). The viewing body of the visitor is attuned to the requirements of the object on display; each stands before the other in a relationship of dynamic symbiosis with each other, and also with the space that they occupy and with the bodies of other spectators (Rees Leahy 2009b). Our incorporated responses reveal a degree of 'habit acquisition' (in this instance, familiarity with the operation of the museum) that provides us with a repertoire of potential, appropriate and situated actions (Merleau-Ponty 1962, 142). Constrained by questions of scale and access to original works, many exhibitions of exhibitions (such as 'Art Treasures in Manchester' and 'William Blake 1809') have reconstructed historical assemblages without substantially disrupting the museum's paradigm of display; viewers did not need to invoke a 'period eye' to realign their looking. For example, while many visitors to the 1857 Art Treasures Exhibition complained about the overwhelming density of display, as well as the difficulty of seeing certain works that were awkwardly placed, no such challenges confronted visitors to 'Art Treasures in Manchester' (Rees Leahy 2009a).

By contrast, 'Art on the Line' deliberately repositioned contemporary viewers in the same physical and visual relation to the paintings on display as their 19th-century predecessors at the Royal Academy. A different (and for many, surprisingly pleasurable) technique of looking was invoked by the densely packed display of pictures wall to wall, and floor to ceiling. Viewing pictures in these conditions also enabled an appreciation of the visual tricks deployed by artists to ensure that their works stood out from the crowd, a point which is lost when the same paintings are hung at eye level and separated from other works against a plain background. Accustomed to viewing works placed sequentially along a wall, with the optimal viewing position squarely in front of the individuated work of art (in obedience to the laws of perspective long since abandoned by many artists), the 'gaudy chaos' (quoted in Solkin 2002, 4) that greeted visitors to 'Art on the Line' required a process of visual and physical retuning. Put another way, the installation required an activation of the 'period eye' in order both to decode the visual effects of the exhibition and also to relocate oneself in the position of historical spectators at the Royal Academy. Instead of being guided along a sequence of paintings on the wall (as if reading like a line of text), the viewer's eye was free to roam the crowded wall, making one's own connections and following one's fancy (Solkin 2002, 3). Freed from the need to stand in the 'proper place', everyone in the exhibition saw the pictures from a slightly different vantage point, both physically and metaphorically. It is this social aspect of viewing the 19th-century exhibition that Solkin was keen to emphasise and that, as curator of 'Art on the Line', he sought to recreate on the basis that, 'instead of being just one, there are many equally proper "points of sight", that these will necessarily give rise to a variety of opinions, and that pleasure will arise from their expression and exchange' (2002, 4). The experience of viewing that was mounted by 'Art on the Line' was a reminder that the eye of the spectator is also attached to a physical body: within the exhibition, visuality is always structured through comportment and movement and in this sense, the period eye cannot be separated from the 'museum body' that responds to its spatio-visual coordinates.

Turning to the *mise en abyme*, Gide first discussed the idea of a story within a story, or an image within an image, in a diary entry from 1893: 'In a work of art I rather like to find transposed, on the scale of the characters, the very subject of that work. Nothing throws a clearer light upon it or more surely establishes the proportions of the whole' (Gide 1967, 30). According to Gide, the critical function of the *mise en abyme* is that the embedded image or narrative within a larger whole also resembles the thing that contains it, and that this resemblance illuminates the form or meaning of the whole. For example, in *Hamlet* the Prince has the players perform *The Murder of Gonzago*. Not only is this a play within the play, but crucially, the plot of *The Murder of Gonzago* resembles the story of Hamlet himself, who stages it in order to 'prick the conscience of the King' and so provoke the latter into revealing his guilt (Gide 1967; Ron 1987). A similarly famous visual example of *mise en abyme* is contained within the *Arnolfini Portrait* by Jan Van Eyck (National Gallery, London). The little mirror hanging on the far wall reflects both the backs of Arnolfini and his new wife, and also the wedding guests whom they are facing and who would otherwise be 'outside' of the picture. On the basis of the inscription within the painting, we assume that one of the guests is Van Eyck himself; in other words, the self-aware artist has painted himself into the picture, and the reflection in the painted mirror has become a reflexive device that illuminates how and why the artist made the picture. Dällenbach describes the *mise en abyme* as a modality of reflection and as an organ of the work turning upon itself (1989, 16). How, then, do exhibitions of exhibitions employ *mise en abyme* in order to reveal their structuration and to display their own making?

The use of a large-scale image of the 1857 Art Treasures Palace within 'Art Treasures in Manchester' threw both the 1857 and 2007 exhibitions into relief, inviting the viewer to reflect on each in relation to the other. Similarly, 'Pop Life: Art in a Material World' at Tate Modern (2009) included exhibits of past sites where the currency of art had been traded in ways that deliberately subverted the authority of the dealer and curator in controlling gallery space (Bankowsky *et al* 2009). These included a section in the exhibition devoted to 'The Shop' (London, 1993) where Tracey Emin and Sarah Lucas parodied conventional gallery space by selling art in a space that was more bric-a-brac than white cube, and also a reconstruction of Keith Haring's 'Pop Shop' (New York, 1986) where the artist had sold his trademark products (badges, posters, t-shirts) directly to the public. The Haring-branded reconstructed shop also included a counter where exhibition-visitors could re-enact the core performance of the original 'Pop Shop': namely, buying stuff. The insertion of a shop within (rather than at the exit from) the exhibition was double-coded: it not only functioned as an actual commercial outlet and source of revenue, but also as a wry commentary on the relationship between art and money within, as well as beyond, the museum.

If the scale of the embedded image within the whole is a crucial aspect of the *mise en abyme*, is total replication always less reflexive? Not necessarily: I have argued that 'Art on the Line', which was a scale replica of its source exhibitions, succeeded in revealing its structuration through its invocation of the period eye. Solkin's hang defied a familiar mode of viewing that could otherwise overlook the constructedness of the exhibition itself. However, the project included a further element that stood outside of the narrative space of the Great Room. In an adjoining gallery, a small screen showed continuous closed circuit television footage of the audience next door in the main exhibition. Visitors could thus watch each other as they looked, talked, walked and sat. It was a device that closed the loop, as spectators became the spectacle – just as they were depicted in the historic prints of the Royal Academy that provided the visual template for 'Art on the Line'. The video screen also constituted a disruptive, non-diegetic element within the exhibition: standing outside of, and looking into, its internal world. Watching other people performing the double-act of 21st-century visitors experiencing an early 19th-century exhibition, the invisible hand of the curator became doubly apparent. The visual equivalent of a voiceover narration in a film, the video provided a silent commentary on the action within the exhibition.

Robert Morris' 1971 exhibition at the Tate Gallery had included a similarly non-diagetic element: a number of black and white photographs and films showed people (in fact, Tate staff) interacting with his sculptures, whose inclusion in the exhibition functioned as a kind of 'how to' guide for the public. However, given the energetic and unruly response of many visitors to the show, presumably these images were largely ignored. Their reappearance in the 2009 version of 'Bodyspacemotionthings' was equally redundant in terms of visitor instruction, but now they additionally acted as both referents to, and quotations from, the earlier show. As an instance of the *mise en abyme*, they incorporated a fragment of the 1971 exhibition within its 2009 re-do, and worked not as a demonstration of appropriate behaviour but as a reminder of the radical origins of the project.

In conclusion, the interest in staging exhibitions about exhibitions signals a maturation of the field of exhibition history, as well as an 'institutional turn' within curatorial practice. Projects like these offer a practical methodology for researching exhibition histories; of course, they are problematic, but their shortcomings are also a resource for the development of understanding and critique. This chapter shows that not all reconstructions are equally reflexive in intention and effect, but they are each a reminder that every exhibition gallery is a kind of palimpsest of past shows. Sometimes the museum is haunted by previous exhibitions, and only their public re-evaluation will exorcise the spectre. One final example illustrates the point. 'The Fake Vermeers of Van Meegeren' (2010) at the Museum Boijmans van Beuningen was a display of ten famous forgeries by Han van Meegeren in the styles of Johannes Vermeer, Frans Hals, Pieter de Hooch and Gerard ter Borch. The exhibition explored Van Meegeren's technique, his masterpieces and his downfall. The exhibition spectre now laid to rest was an exhibition held at the Boijmans Museum in 1938 called 'Masterpieces from Four Centuries' in which a new and celebrated acquisition by the museum occupied pride of place: what was then believed to be a recently rediscovered work by Vermeer, *The Supper at Emmaus*. The subsequent revelation of Van Meegeren's deception consigned the painting to the storeroom, from which it emerged for the Fakes exhibition as an eloquent object lesson in institutional hubris.

## BIBLIOGRAPHY AND REFERENCES


Altshuler, B, 1994 *The Avant-Garde in Exhibition: New Art in the Twentieth Century*, Harry N Abrams, New York

— 2008 *Salon to Biennial: 1863–1959 vol 1: Exhibitions That Made Art History*, Phaidon, London

Bankowsky, J, Gingeras, A, and Wood, C (eds), 2009 *Pop Life: Art in a Material World*, Tate Publishing, London

Barker, E (ed), 1999 *Contemporary Cultures of Display*, Yale University Press, London and New Haven

Baxandall, M, 1972 *Painting and Experience in Fifteenth-Century Italy*, Oxford University Press, Oxford

Bird, J, 1999 Minding the Body: Robert Morris's 1971 Tate Gallery Retrospective, in *Rewriting Conceptual Art* (eds M Newman and J Bird), Reaktion Books, London, 88–106

Bourdieu, P, 1996 The Social Genesis of the Eye, in *The Rules of Art: Genesis and Structure of the Literary Field*, Stanford University Press, Stanford, CA, 313–21

Carrier, D, 1987 The Display of Art: An Historical Perspective, *Leonardo* 20 (1), 83–6

Copeland, M, Armleder, J, Le Bon, L, Metzger, G, Perret, M, Phillpot, C, and Pirotte, P (eds), 2009 *Voids/ Vides: A Retrospective*, JRP|Ringier, Zurich

Clifford, T, 1982 The Historical Approach to the Display of Paintings, *The International Journal of Museum Management and Curatorship* I, 93–106

Dällenbach, L, 1989 *The Mirror in the Text* (trans J Whitely with E Hughes), University of Chicago Press, Chicago

Gide, A, 1967 *Journals 1889–1949*, Penguin, Harmondsworth

Greenberg, R, 2009 'Remembering Exhibitions': From Point to Line to Web, *Tate Papers* Issue 12 [online], available from: http://www.tate.org.uk/research/tateresearch/tatepapers/09autumn/greenberg.shtm [March 2010]

Haskell, F, 2000 *The Ephemeral Museum: Old Master Paintings and the Rise of the Art Exhibition*, Yale University Press, London and New Haven

Lord, B, 2005 Representing Enlightenment Space, in *Reshaping Museum Space* (ed S MacLeod), Routledge, London, 146–5

Merleau-Ponty, M, 1962 (1945) *Phenomenology of Perception* (trans C Smith), Routledge, London

Myrone, M, 2009 *'Seen in My Visions': A Descriptive Catalogue of Pictures by William Blake*, Tate Publishing, London

O'Neill, M, 2004 Enlightenment museums: universal or merely global?, *Museum and Society* 2 (3) [online], available from: http://www.le.ac.uk/ms/m&s/Issue%206/ONeill.pdf [March 2010]

Randolph, A W B, 2004 Gendering the Period Eye: Deschi da Parto and Renaissance Visual Culture, *Art History* 27 (4), 538–62

Rees Leahy, H (ed), 2009a Art, City Spectacle, *Special Issue of the Bulletin of the John Rylands University Library*

— 2009b Watch your step: Embodiment and Encounter at Tate Modern, in *Museum Materialities* (ed S Dudley), Routledge, London, 162–74

Ron, M, 1987 The Restricted Abyss: Nine Problems in the Theory of Mise en Abyme, *Poetics Today* 8 (2), 417–38

Saumarez Smith, C, 2007 Narratives of Display at the National Gallery, London, *Art History* 30 (4), 137–53

Solkin, D (ed), 2001 *Art on the Line. The Royal Academy Exhibitions at Somerset House 1780–1836*, Yale University Press, London and New Haven

Spector, N, Fischer-Lichte, E, and Umathum, S, 2007 *Marina Abramovic: Seven Easy Pieces*, Edizione Charta, Milan

11

# Institutional Autobiography and the Architecture of the Art Museum: Restoration and Remembering at the National Gallery in the 1980s

CHRISTOPHER WHITEHEAD

This chapter explores some of the ways in which art museums speak with and about their own pasts through focusing historically on events at the National Gallery in the 1980s and 1990s. The ongoing revalorisation of Victorian interiors within museums which commenced in those decades has led to a spate of restoration projects. These ostensibly reverse the modernist project of stripping away (or, more accurately, overlaying) Victorian features. Such restorations re-inscribe a heritage of Victorian museology into the modern-day art museum as a building and as an institution. What emerges is a special kind of institutional autobiography in which the art museum's relationship to its own past is literally fabricated, negotiating tense connections and effecting considered disconnections between shifting values, ideals and social and intellectual projects over the different chapters of institutional and cultural life. After all, as Tim Barringer has noted, museums like the National Gallery in London 'stand in complex and sometimes tormented relation to the Victorian epistemologies which produced them' (2006, 133). The 'restoration' of the late 19th-century Barry Rooms at the National Gallery in the 1980s provides a case study of the politics involved in such projects, in which the balance between the preservation and the construction of the gallery's physical past is delicate. The project also involved encounters with complex issues relating to the concept of authenticity and to decisions about which period of the building's architectural history should be privileged and which should be literally hidden from view or excised, presenting questions about the veracity of the institutional history written not in text but, as it were, on the walls, in ceilings and in décor.

Meanwhile, contemporary architects involved in developing extensions to Victorian museum buildings play key roles in the perpetuation or transformation of museum identities, by referencing or rejecting the Victorian past. The restoration and extension of Victorian museum buildings turn out to be interrelated, in that both tell us things about the ways in which museums work with, work against, or simply construct their own physical histories. And the physical architecture of the Victorian museum, as has been explored at length (MacLeod 2005; Giebelhausen 2003; Whitehead 2005), is both expression and embodiment of political action, in its historicist grandiosity, its civic and historiographical emblematism, its role (along with the display of material culture) in its spatialisation of history and its radical implication for the visitor experience. Put bluntly (and this is a very basic point), museum buildings represent attitudes to knowledge specific to the cultures which give rise to them.

This chapter considers the complex political meanings of this in terms of postmodern attitudes to museums, to visiting and to museum identities and histories. It therefore addresses a series of interrelated questions: in what ways do art museums 'come to terms' with the history (or histories) of their buildings? What art histories and what museum histories are generated through the survival, reconstruction or rejection of the Victorian in art displays? How do they interlock? In what ways might visitors survey or engage with these histories?

The main project upon which I will focus is that of the Barry Rooms in the north-east wing of the National Gallery, but if there were space one could equally look at other important projects, such as the works at the National Gallery in Edinburgh in the late 1980s; the V&A Ceramic Gallery, which was reinvented as the Silver Gallery in 1996; those at Manchester City Art Gallery completed in 2002; or most recently of all, the central hall, again at the National Gallery in London. Well before popular DIY television programmes and manuals suggested that one could remove old-fashioned door panels from sight by boarding over them, at the National Gallery and elsewhere the Victorian or Edwardian decorative features of many of the interiors were overlaid or boxed in, while the traditional rich red and green wallpapers were very often substituted with beige fabrics. Of course, this was not just a simple reaction against old-fashioned architecture and interior decor, but a reaction against old-fashioned ways of looking at, understanding and experiencing art. In these modernised spaces works of art were isolated in space and their context – the physical frame of the museum interior – was rendered as discreet (or 'neutral') as possible in an attempt to liberate the contemplative and sometimes epiphanous experience of viewing from all possible distractions, in the name of an idealised aesthetic encounter rooted in a kind of spiritualised formalism. Andrew McLellan quotes a source from as early as 1937 which describes this tendency:

> The modern sensibility, no longer seeking in a work of art an historical witness but an individual aesthetic phenomenon, has led museums to efface themselves behind the masterpieces they display. Walls stripped of décor are nothing more than an abstract background against which objects may be seen; those objects are well-spaced in order that the visitor may examine each one without distraction, all in keeping with the demands of the modern aesthetic. (2003, 25)

And in his 1967 book *The Museum Age*, the former chief curator of paintings at the Louvre, Germain Bazin, reported that 'The museum must no longer be a palace … but a clinic for masterpieces':

> In the last half century, the public aesthetic has been profoundly modified. Statues must be isolated in space, paintings hung far apart, a glittering jewel placed against a field of black velvet and spotlighted; in principle, only one object at a time should appear in the field of vision. Iconographic meaning and overall harmony no longer interest the contemporary museum goer, who is obsessed with form and workmanship; the eye must be able to scan slowly the surface of a painting. The act of looking becomes a trance uniting spectator and masterpiece.
> (Bazin 1967, 265)

In the 1980s and 1990s there was a significant about-face, and important and costly restoration programmes were developed. They were part of a shift in attitudes towards the Victorian past which had begun in the late 1950s with the establishment of the Victorian Society in 1958; in the early 1960s listing criteria for Victorian buildings were redesigned to be more inclusive and this new sympathy was galvanised by high-profile cases such as the demolition in 1962 of both the London Coal Exchange and the Euston Arch. Simultaneously there was a certain frustration amongst some at the inconsiderate character of much modernist building and town planning, while the new UK government agency English Heritage was established in 1983 with an administrative purview including historic buildings (Delafons 1997, 82–94, 132–41). This was accompanied by the burgeoning of museum historiography (some of which was primarily focused on buildings, such as John Physick's 1982 monograph on the V&A), and new developments in museum studies and art history: in the former the idea that museum space could ever be 'neutral' and rendered free from ideology was rejected as an impossibility; in art history (and 'new' art history) ideas about the social histories of objects were accompanied by re-evaluations of the importance of histories of display. Here, for example, Carol Duncan and Alan Wallach's theory-informed and generalising work on the 'Universal Survey Museum' in 1980 arguably helped to move the physical history of museums from the margins of disciplinary enquiry to the centre.

While these might be seen as more or less progressive factors, there were also atavistic attitudes which contextualised the restorations. In the context of the restoration of the National Gallery's Barry Rooms, the Keeper Michael Wilson noted that:

> Until recently the view that great paintings could best be seen in neutral settings, isolated from the distraction of historic decorations or furnishings had powerful support in and out of the Gallery. Only recently has it once again become accepted that a splendid setting can enhance the spectator's enjoyment of the art within it. (National Gallery Archive[1])

Complementary voices, interested in contesting the 'effortless superiority of Modernist museum practice' (Barringer 2006, 134), catalogued crimes against the fabric of Victorian museums. Gervase Jackson-Stops noted that 'time and time again the staff of our national museums astonish us by the lack of sensitivity shown to the buildings in their care', pointing to the Tate's lamentable 'addiction to battleship grey', the 'fashionable tangerine' of the V&A cast courts and other 'bilious' colour experiments at that museum. The National Gallery's 'potentially noble rooms', meanwhile, had hitherto been disfigured by 'drab colours, blacked-out skylights, ugly raised platforms and walkways, and plasterboard partitions' (1986, 1966). The architectural critic Gavin Stamp joined in, noting that the contemporary aesthetic of displaying works in isolation had led to 'but one painting hung on a bare, colourless wall, ignoring the complementary power of fine architecture and rich colour': 'The result has been that so many of our museum interiors have been neutralised with dropped ceilings, hessian walls, incongruous display stands and gallons and gallons of white paint ....' He went on to note that it had been the National Gallery which had 'triumphantly exemplified the worst aspects of the architectural blindness of our modern museum culture' (1986, n.p.).

The Barry Rooms are eight in number; they were designed by Edward Middleton Barry, one of the sons of Charles Barry. They were completed in 1876 as an extension to the north-east of the original Wilkins building, which had opened in 1838. Fig 11.1 shows the rooms, based around a Greek-cross shape, at the back of the older building. The plan is organised around a

1 The National Gallery archive documents referred to can be found in file S4499. I am grateful to Alan Crookham for facilitating my access to them.

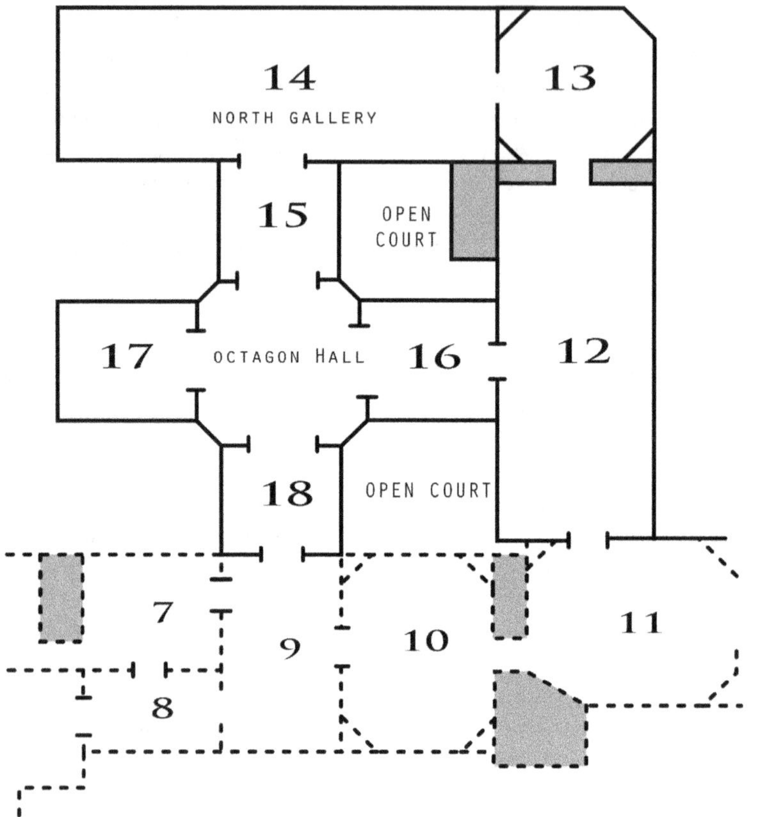


FIG 11.1. NATIONAL GALLERY: GROUNDPLAN OF THE EAST WING, 1878

highly ornamental Octagon Hall with four vestibules; two of these lead to longer galleries which are almost identical (there is a slight difference in dimensions) and whose main feature was the inclusion of ornate painted lunettes: one of the rooms (the larger of the two) was intended for Italian paintings and the other for British paintings, although it was actually used for German and Dutch-Flemish works, in contrast to the canon of British artists whose names appeared in the lunettes. This represents a much more usual binary in 19th-century art historiography: Gustav Friedrich Waagen, for example, talked of Italian and northern renaissance productions as exhibiting 'ideal' and 'realistic' tendencies respectively (Waagen 1853, 103), while the unusual Italian–British binary arrangement might have been intended to aggrandise the British School of painting by analogy. There is no documentation known to me of the circumstances of the decision to go against the historiographical scheme suggested by the interior decoration in the display itself (and hardly any documentation indicating that there was much dialogue between the architect and gallery officers regarding such matters). But it is characteristic of the ways in which architectural/intellectual projects were regulated in the 19th-century National Gallery –

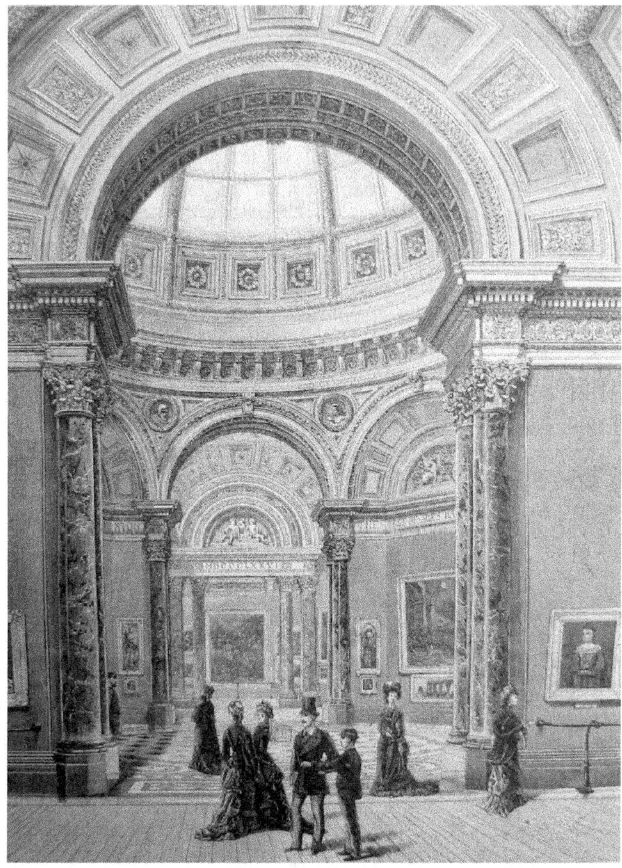

Fig 11.2.
National Gallery: E M Barry's Dome Room

an area to which this chapter will return. In the Octagon Hall and vestibules (Fig 11.2) there was and is also much sculptural decoration, including gilded busts of artists and sculpted reliefs showing important scenes from the history of art, such as Michelangelo presenting a model of St Peter's to the Pope.

Over the course of the 20th century the interiors underwent some modification. The laylights were removed and substituted with concrete and steel clerestory lights. In one of the main rooms the ornate decorative coving was entirely removed; in another it was covered with light grey paint, while general whitewashing appears to have taken place in 1948 (Getty Trustees, n.d.); an arched doorway between two of the galleries was altered in the 1960s to a square-headed opening; floor and, sometimes, wall carpet predominated in place of the original wooden floors and colour scheme, and at one point the 'total remodelling of the rooms and the obliteration of the ceilings was contemplated' (National Gallery, n.d.). The 1984–6 project, managed by the Property Services Agency (PSA),[2] was called both a 'restoration' and a 'refurbishment', both of

2 The UK government's Property Services Agency was a successor to the Ministry of Works which had overseen the extension of the National Gallery in the 1870s. The PSA existed from 1872 to 1993 to

which are politically loaded terms: the first suggests a return to something like an original state, and more complex connotations of this for architecture will be explored shortly; the second is a little vaguer. (I will use 'restoration' precisely in order to highlight the tensions which the concept evokes.) The project was heavily publicised and externally funded and was the subject of a number of publications (eg Jackson-Stops 1986; Taunton 1987; Robinson 1989; Sunter 1995). The work was in two phases: the 22-month restoration of the Octagon Hall and its four vestibules, begun in December 1984 (which is the main focus of this chapter), and the refurbishment of Room 34 (now the Sackler Gallery, so named because its transformation was funded by the Sackler Foundation) in the early 1990s. It was costly and painstaking work, using documentary sources such as designs, newspaper reports, contemporary visual evidence and paint layer analysis. The work also involved the replacement of the ceiling lights, the installation of state-of-the-art artificial lighting and environmental control systems.

The Barry Rooms themselves have a complex history in that their development replaced a much larger project, which entailed the complete rebuilding – and potential re-siting and reconceptualisation – of the National Gallery. The 19th-century rebuilding project was situated within a vast debate about the purposes of museums, of collecting and display, of art and so on which dragged on for decades through innumerable select committees and other fora (Whitehead 2005; 2009). The demise of the rebuilding project was related to circumstance, economics, party politics and personal antagonisms, and not really to coherent museological and cultural strategies, or indeed to any desire to preserve William Wilkins' National Gallery building, which was almost universally disparaged. This complicated story makes the rooms important in terms of the gallery's history, as they encapsulate so many decades of debate, theorising and thinking about what the National Gallery should be, but also so much failure and compromise – in other words, they encapsulate something of what the National Gallery might have been. The rooms were also seen to be, to quote the National Gallery's own press release announcing the renovation, 'architecturally the most distinguished in the Gallery'. Other reasons for taking on the project included the need to replace leaking ceilings and the discovery of drawings in the Public Record Office by Barry for the decorative and colour scheme. At the same time, it is also possible to think about the instrumental and political use of refurbishment projects by institutions: it might be argued that the refurbishment balanced out the mid-1980s publicity surrounding the debacle over the National Gallery's new wing (upon which this chapter will touch later), as though, in times of controversial expansion, it were politic also to exhibit some conservative tendencies.

In a short text of 1986 on the restored Octagon Hall and vestibules (the first phase of the restoration project), the then deputy keeper Michael Wilson quoted a review printed in *The Times* upon the opening of the Barry Rooms in 1876, which stated that their decorations were 'more prominent than is conducive to the repose which is so desirable an element in the enjoyment of fine pictures'. Wilson then went on to make a revealing parallel, noting that this comment was made when 'extravagant decoration was prevalent and to be viewed with a critical and perhaps jaded eye'; but that in the 1980s visitors' 'palates' would be 'jaded with a diet of modernism in architecture and design' which the 'unfamiliar note of splendour' of the Barry Rooms would refresh. In other words, just as the late Victorians were weary of profusion, 1980s

'provide, manage, maintain, and furnish the property used by the government, including defence establishments, offices, courts, research laboratories, training centres and land' (Property Services Agency (1988). *Annual report 1987–88*).

visitors would be weary of modernist blankness. But, noted Wilson, fortunately the modernists had not succeeded in inflicting any 'lasting damage' and the 'tide of taste' had turned: the interiors could, 'after years of neglect', be 'respected and duly restored' (Wilson 1986).

Can one 'respect' an interior? Perhaps one can 'respect' its integrity, or the intentions of its creator. Indeed, press releases and publications made much of the notion that the interiors now appeared 'as Barry intended' and much play was made of the vexed notion of restoring the interiors to an authentic state (although not, it should be noted, to an 'original' state – a distinction which repeatedly exercises conservation professionals (see Bridgwood and Lennie 2009, 288)). As the sometime Director of the International Centre for the Study of the Preservation and Restoration of Cultural Property, Paul Philippot, emphasised some time before the National Gallery restoration works:

> It is an illusion to believe that an object can be brought back to its original state by stripping it of all later additions. The original state is a mythical, unhistorical idea, apt to sacrifice works of art to an abstract concept and present them in a state that never existed.
>
> (1976, 32, also cited and contextualised in Jokilehto 1999, 239)

These issues of authenticity, integrity and intention are interesting for a couple of reasons: firstly, the Barry Rooms were an accretion to a building designed by a different architect (William Wilkins), whose intentions were not considered in the 1980s restoration project; secondly, many (if not most) of the ideas introduced by Barry himself were eliminated or modified either during the design process, for example by Office of Works staff, or afterwards, by Gallery trustees. So, in terms of bestowing respect in the late 20th century, whose intentions are paramount, and what notion – whose idea – of integrity should be privileged within the architectural autobiography of the museum?

An interesting episode in this context is the choice of a colour scheme for the restoration. Paint layer analysis initially provided confusing results, but it appeared that the first layer of paint did not respect Barry's intentions as evidenced in his designs, which had employed a 'raspberry red' colour presumed different from the crimson described by critics upon the opening of the rooms (Jackson-Stops 1986, 1967). It was supposed that the Trustees in 1876 had intervened and had gone against Barry's wishes in this. Indeed, some areas appeared to have been overpainted sooner than others and, as Geoffrey Taunton of the PSA noted, 'it was reasonable to speculate that some areas had been repainted during the initial decoration works' (Taunton 1987, 136). Consequently, two colour schemes were trialled for the refurbishment: one based upon the evidence of paint samples and of a contemporary painting by Giuseppe Gabrielli showing the interiors,[3] and another based on Barry's designs. As noted in a press release:

> The National Gallery Scientific Department took numerous minute core samples throughout the galleries, which revealed a bewilderingly complex sequence of paint layers. However, what became clear was that the earliest decoration did not conform to Barry's instructions, and that at some point, possibly after the decorations had been begun, the decision had been

3 There are in fact two known paintings of the interiors: one, *Room 32 in the National Gallery* in the Government Art Collection and viewable at: http://www.gac.culture.gov.uk/search/Object.asp?object_key=22891 [17 May 2010] and another in a private collection in Italy.

> taken to adopt a less bold colour scheme in which green predominated. Consequently samples both of Barry's scheme and of the one actually executed were prepared for comparison. In the event Barry's proposal were [sic] felt by The Trustees and the PSA to be better suited to the architecture and it was decided to proceed with a scheme based as closely as possible on his drawings. (National Gallery, n.d.)

In a letter to Michael Wilson reflecting on the colouristic aspect of the restoration project, the external colour-specialist consultant Alan Dodd asked: 'Dare we hope Barry would have approved?' (Dodd, n.d.). Likewise, Taunton noted that the 'appearance of the finished rooms would seem to demonstrate that Barry would have been justified in overriding the Craces and insisting that his own designs be executed'. He went on to conclude that it was 'gratifying that, 110 years later, his better, if unexpressed, judgement has been allowed to prevail' (1987, 140). In fact, not even Barry's intentions with regard to wall colour were fully realised, for the colour employed was 'slightly more pink than the original', because the rooms were now to house British paintings which were thought to need 'a less robust background' than the Italian Renaissance paintings which hung there in the late 19th century (PSA, n.d.).

The issue, of course, is that the restoration embodies a culturally located, selective reading of the complex histories of the gallery building – in this case it did not 'restore' the building to a pre-existing physical state but rather to something close to a pre-existing conceptual state of design. But it is also worth pointing to two interrelated discourses: one concerning the primacy of the architect and his intentions, even where they were not realised; another about the halting of the destructive advance of modernism and its disrespectful or insensitive protagonists. The former ignores the multiplicity of agents and agencies involved in the production and development of a building, and the second is no less teleological or absolute in its terms than was the rhetoric of modernism itself. One may consider Cesare Brandi's 1963 dictum that artworks can be restored only through an 'aesthetic' approach involving the re-establishment [of the] 'potential unity' of the work of art (2000, 13). But is this achievable where the work of art in question is a gallery building with so complex a history? One could say that the potential unity of the rooms was compromised when Barry's plan for an entirely new building, in which the existing rooms were only a small part, was shelved in 1876. Barry's intention was to see the Wilkins building demolished and to rebuild the entirety of the National Gallery, and while this would have been too much to respect, there is no significant intellectual difference between the choice to employ a (modified) wall colour which was never used and to build a building that was never built. One could also see the notion of 'unity' as an object of restoration as a characteristically modernist one, which is insensitive to the nature of the building as a longstanding event; in other words, buildings have histories and are arguably never finished, and restoration often struggles with this by working synchronically to reflect one single moment of the physical history of galleries, or even one single *imagined* moment of potential unity which is somehow more 'true' or 'right' than others which are kept from view.

To exemplify this again, we can instance the inscription originally underneath the cornice of the Octagon Room's Dome, which read 'THE WORKS OF THOSE WHO HAVE STOOD THE TEST OF AGES HAVE A CLAIM TO THAT VENERATION TO WHICH NO MODERN CAN PRETEND'. This was a quotation from Joshua Reynolds which was not well received by the Trustees upon the opening of the rooms in 1876, and they lobbied government to have it removed. Interestingly, in the 1980s restoration the inscription was not reinstated, contrary to much of the rhetoric about respecting

Barry's design intentions. Gervase Jackson-Stops, writing in *Country Life*, stated that the decision not to reinstate the inscription was a 'distinct sense-of-humour failure on the gallery's part' (1986, 1967). What is at stake here is an ethics of museum conservation: not an ethics concerned with inequalities visited upon living people but an ethics concerned with the unequal representation of different pasts, and the surgical reconstruction of an institution's own history to excise no-longer-desired features.

Even pitched against international codes of practice, the ethics of the restoration are questionable. Article 11 of the 1966 Venice *Charter for the Conservation of Monuments and Sites* reads:

> The valid contributions of all periods to the building of a monument must be respected, since unity of style is not the aim of a restoration. When a building includes the superimposed work of different periods, the revealing of the underlying state can only be justified in exceptional circumstances.

Here, however, a critical area of discretion emerges, for one can also strip away features when: 'what is removed is of little interest and the material which is brought to light is of great historical, archaeological or aesthetic value ...' (ICOMOS (Venice)).

And while there is provision that this is not a decision to be taken by one person alone, of course it is essentially culturally negotiated and promotes hierarchical thinking about the past in terms of greater or lesser 'value', just as David Hume's 'standard of taste' was to be culturally and socially negotiated. A quote from a different but comparable context can be brought into play here. This is Timothy Clifford, a sometime director of the National Gallery of Scotland, discussing its refurbishment in 1988: 'The purist approach would have been to destroy all that was not Playfair [the Gallery's architect], but this has not been followed; rather, there has been an attempt to retain a palimpsest of *all that has been good* subsequently ...' (1988, 54, emphasis added).

While this is obviously not the synchronic history presented in the refurbishment of the Barry Rooms, and nor does it privilege the architect above all else and all others, the decision about what to save or reinstate, and what to exclude, is once again a matter for personal taste. At the National Gallery, the 'restoration' was an act of creative remembering (in both senses of the term), which, given warrant by archival research and the investigations into Barry's designs for the interior decoration, managed nevertheless to adhere to the terms of the Venice Charter's definition of restoration. The 'aim [of restoration] is to preserve and reveal the aesthetic and historic value of the monument and is based on respect for original material and authentic documents. It must stop at the point where conjecture begins ...' (ICOMOS).

Like any charter or doctrine depending on the notion of *value*, individual and collective subjectivities and relative cultural politics are at play. This, indeed, is acknowledged in one of the principles of the 2003 International Council on Monuments and Sites' *Charter for the Analysis, Conservation and Structural Restoration of Architectural Heritage*, where it is stated that 'value and authenticity of architectural heritage cannot be based on fixed criteria' (ICOMOS).

As I hope I have shown so far, restoration of the kind attempted at the National Gallery is beset by a number of philosophical and practical problems. From a philosophical point of view we must note that these restorations have effectively privileged Victorian displays at the expense of those which replaced them. This may signify an *in toto* rejection of the recent modernist past; in this sense those involved in decision-making processes relating to restorations were as reactionary as those who removed or covered what they saw as 'Victorian excesses' in the early 20th century, and modernist attitudes to art and its display are being carefully cut out of history, notwithstanding their importance and intellectual legacy. Otherwise, the privileging of the Victorian may relate to the idea of restoration as the excavation and literal 'discovery' of the 'original' and 'authentic' aspect of a given building, where all else is just superfluous accretion. But with what authority does one decide that modifications made in the 1950s, 1960s or 1970s are, to use the words of the Venice Charter, 'of little interest'?

Similarly, if authenticity is an aim of some kind then one may question the limits of this in the 1980s or indeed now at the time of writing, when cultures and practices of curatorship and visiting differ enormously from those of the late 1870s. Is the reinstatement of Victorian architecture expected to posit again all that came with it, such as the imposition of 19th-century taxonomies, ideologies, ways of seeing and thinking and the instrumental uses of museums and their collections? One would imagine not, although it is not difficult to identify precedents for 21st-century concerns, such as the idea that the intrinsic benefits of museums in alleviating social exclusion can be traced to the 19th-century project of moral improvement (Mason 2004). Indeed, the Victorian architecture of the museum is a difficult presence: it can be, and has been, seen as a deterrent to the visitor who may see its grandeur and pomp as exclusive (Fleming 2005, 54); this in turn endangers some of the contemporary museological agendas that were beginning to emerge in the 1980s, such as the need to facilitate attitudinal access. The idea quoted earlier, 'that a splendid setting can enhance the spectator's enjoyment of the art within it', would now, in museological circles, tend to be qualified by noting that the visitors whose experience will be enhanced are only those with sufficient and appropriate cultural capital, and are not necessarily typical.

The point is that there is a careful compromise to negotiate in the restoration of Victorian museum interiors. There is also a certain fallacy of authenticity at play: visitors simply do not see displays as they would have been in the 19th century, for we usually subject our paintings to artificial light and surround them with modern museal apparatus; and of course, visitors cannot possibly respond to displays with the kinds of behaviour which would have been expected in the Victorian museum for the obvious reason that social, intellectual and political contexts are different. Another factor which complicates the representation of Victorian museum interiors and the experience of visiting them is architectural historicism – which I define, in the spirit of Pevsner, as the purposeful reconstruction of previous architectural contexts. Restoration historicises the architecture of the 19th-century museum, which itself often involved historicist decoration alluding to architectures of the past – the Italian palace, the Egyptian temple, and so on. The art museum was already exploring and imagining its own architectural ancestry and heritage even upon its initial construction in the 19th century. This means that the visitor is left to survey and traverse a number of different pasts within his or her visit (not just those embedded in the architecture but also those embedded in the works of art), which may make for a dizzying experience if any attention is paid to the complexity of temporal references. At what point does the museum begin explicitly to exhibit not only its objects, but also itself? In what ways perceptible to visitors can these two histories harmonise or intertwine (for want of better words)? Or, as one curator recently suggested to me, should historically reflexive practices in the museum – museum autobiography – simply be eschewed as so much indulgent 'navel gazing'?

Meanwhile, contemporary architects involved in developing extensions to Victorian museum buildings play key roles in the perpetuation or transformation of museum identities, by referencing or rejecting the Victorian past. The Sainsbury Wing at the National Gallery, for example, can be seen as a careful assimilation and simulation of trends in Victorian museology and museum building and therefore appears to propose a perpetuation of some Victorian values and a (fictitious) continuum between past and present. The politics of the commission were important in this respect, when Prince Charles famously brought about the demise of the design by Ahrends, Burton and Koralek, and of any other modernist design for an extension, in a speech made before the RIBA:

> Instead of designing an extension to the elegant facade of the National Gallery, that complements it and continues the concept of columns and domes, it looks as though we may be presented with a kind of vast municipal fire station, complete with the sort of tower that contains the siren. [...] Apart from anything else, it defeats me why anyone wishing to display the early Renaissance pictures belonging to the Gallery should do so in a new gallery so manifestly at odds with the whole spirit of that age of astonishing proportions. (in Amery 1991, 49)

This is a very clear attempt to carry certain Victorian values into the present, both in terms of architectural language and in terms of display, for example in the idea that there should be congruence between the works on display and the architecture surrounding them – this in particular was later built into the architects' brief to Venturi, Scott Brown and Associates, and accounts for the references to Florentine renaissance architecture in the Sainsbury Wing, such as the use of the grey *pietra serena*. However, the building also references the *Victorian* past, in its monumental staircase, the artists' names carved in the frieze, the enfilade of rooms and the construction of vistas. Indeed, it is interesting that Barry had intended to include a monumental staircase in the 1868 design for a new National Gallery which was superseded by the commission for the much smaller north-east wing. Some were annoyed by the Sainsbury Wing's historicising and judged the building as 'pompously Victorian in spite of its modern look' (Millard 1991, 32). Others have also perceived numerous postmodern ironies, noting that the building's historicism and use of quotations are subversive and emblematically heterotopic. It has also been said, however, that such subtle allusions 'emerge only from specialist literature and to the learned gaze' (Farelly 1987, 32–7).

The Sainsbury Wing, however, is a relatively unusual extension project in seeking to harmonise with the original Wilkins façade of the National Gallery. Further west, the V&A Spiral extension designed by Daniel Libeskind (and abandoned in 2004) post-modernised the museum in a different way by more explicitly deconstructing its traditional structures of architecture and display, creating an institution with multiple and in some ways clearly conflicting identities. Libeskind's impulse here was thwarted and the extension was never built, although he realised a similarly disjunctive design in the form of the angular, glass and aluminium 'Crystal' extension to the early 20th-century neo-Romanesque building of the Royal Ontario Museum in Toronto between 2002 and 2007 (Fig 11.3). This kind of architectural practice points to a confusion of museum identities – museums present themselves on the one hand as historical institutions which prize their own history (or aspects of it) and, on the other, as constant reinventors of themselves, whose dynamism is manifest in the periodical emergence of new and fascinating encrustations, in the form of extensions which may communicate subversively or not at all with the historical museum. The museum is like an individual sustained by the lives of many people, over many generations, some of whom have been animated by the desire to characterise

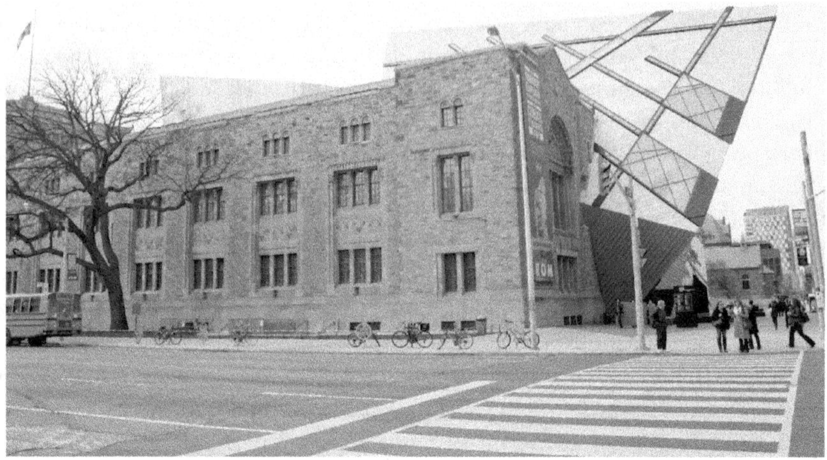

FIG 11.3.
THE EXTERIOR OF THE ROYAL ONTARIO MUSEUM, SHOWING THE MICHAEL LEE-CHIN CRYSTAL EXTENSION DESIGNED BY DANIEL LIBESKIND AND OPENED IN 2007

the museum anew and/or to speak autobiographically for the museum. Telling the story of the institutional self – whether the narrative looks forwards, backwards or both – is a complex desire involving the incomplete honouring of the distant past (the impossibility of remaking buildings and displays as they were, and the architectural play of respect for, or dialogue with, the pre-extant in new extensions), set in inevitable tension against the exigencies of the present. The joint imperatives of conservation and innovation relate to complex and potentially conflicting needs on the part of museums: to situate themselves within historic and contemporary city-scapes, within emerging historical narratives and understandings, within the spectacular spaces and cultural politics of modern leisure, within the tourist economy, and within the consciousness of politicians and funders.

It would be absurd to conclude that we should not restore or that we should not extend historic museum buildings, or that we should only extend them in a certain fashion. I have been sketching out some impossible dilemmas which cannot be extricated from questions of value judgement, subjectivity, personal taste or from the problem that by doing one thing we are inevitably undoing something else. I think, however, that we need to do three interrelated things. One is to broaden ideas of museological heritage beyond the Victorian or the idea of the 'authentic'. The second is to recognise – and recognise publicly – that the choices we make about building and preserving museum architecture are historiographical and political and as crucial as any autobiographical impulse in refracting the desire to remember, to forget, to connect and to curate the histories of the institutional self. The third is to provide visitors with the information they need to interpret as coherently as possible both the historical identities of museums and their buildings and how they relate to historical and contemporary ways of displaying, seeing and visiting.

## Bibliography and References


Amery, C, 1991 *A Celebration of Art and Architecture: the National Gallery Sainsbury Wing*, National Gallery, London

Barringer, T, 2006 Victorian Culture and the Museum: Before and After the White Cube, *Journal of Victorian Culture* 11 (1), 133–45

Bazin, G, 1967 *The Museum Age*, Universe Books, New York

Brandi, C, 2000 (1977) *Teoria del Restauro*, 2 edn, Einaudi, Turin

Bridgwood, B, and Lennie, L, 2009 *History, Performance and Conservation*, Taylor and Francis, Abingdon

Clifford, T, 1988 A Guide to the Present Redecoration and Display, in *The National Gallery of Scotland: an architectural and decorative history* (eds T Clifford and I Gow), Trustees of the National Gallery of Scotland, Edinburgh, 54–61

Delafons, J, 1997 *Politics and Preservation: a Policy History of the Built Heritage, 1882–1996*, Chapman and Hall, London

Dodd, A, n.d. Letter from Alan Dodd to Michael Wilson, NG archive

Duncan, C, and Wallach, C, 1980 The Universal Survey Museum, *Art History* 5 (4), 448–69

Farrelly, E M, 1987 The Venturi effect; Contumacy and Contravention in Architecture, *Architectural Review* 181 (1084), 32–7

Fleming, D, 2005 Creative Space, in *Reshaping Museum Space: Architecture, Design, Exhibitions* (ed S MacLeod), Routledge, London and New York

Getty Trustees, n.d. Letter from Getty Trustees to American Friends of the National Gallery of England, NG archive

Giebelhausen, M, 2003 *The Architecture of the Museum: Symbolic Structures, Urban Contexts*, Manchester University Press, Manchester

ICOMOS Charters [online], available from: http://www.international.icomos.org/charters.htm [17 May 2010]

Jackson-Stops, G, 1986 Return to Splendour: the Restored Barry Rooms at the National Gallery, *Country Life*, December, 1966–8

Jokilehto, J, 1999 *A History of Architectural Conservation*, Butterworth-Heinemann, Oxford

MacLeod, S (ed), 2005 *Reshaping Museum Space: Architecture, Design, Exhibitions*, Routledge, London and New York

Mason, R, 2004 Conflict and Complement: An Exploration of the Discourses Informing the Concept of the Socially Inclusive Museum in Contemporary Britain, *International Journal of Heritage Studies* 10 (1), 49–73

McLellan, A, 2003 *Art and Its Publics: Museum Studies at the Milennium*, Whiley-Blackwell, London

Millard, J, 1991 On a Higher Plane, *Museums Journal*, October, 31–4

National Gallery, n.d. Draft press release, NG archive

Philippot, P, 1976 Historic Preservation: Philosophy, Criteria, Guidelines, in *Preservation and Conservation: Principles and Practices* (ed S Timmons), The Preservation Press, Washington DC, 367–82

Physick, J, 1982 *The Victoria and Albert Museum: a History of Its Building*, Phaidon, London

PSA, n.d. Press Release, National Gallery archive

Robinson, J M, 1989 Reviving the splendour of the National Gallery, *Apollo* 129 (323), January, 48–52

Sunter, N, 1995 Creating the Sackler Room, *Museum Development*, Jan–Feb, 33–9

Stamp, G, 1986 The Artless Treatment of Our National Gallery, *The Daily Telegraph*, 3 November

Taunton, G, 1987 The Refurbishment of E.M. Barry's Rooms in the National Gallery, London, *The International Journal of Museum Management and Curatorship* 6, 121–41

Waagen, G F, 1853 Thoughts on the New Building to be Erected for the National Gallery of England, and on the Arrangement, Preservation, and Enlargement of the Collection, *The Art Journal*, 101–3 and 121–5

Whitehead, C, 2005 *The Public Art Museum in Nineteenth-Century Britain: the Development of the National Gallery*, Ashgate, Aldershot

— 2009 *Museums and the Construction of Disciplines: Art and Archaeology in the Nineteenth-Century Britain*, Duckworth, London

Wilson, M, 1986 The restored Octagon Hall and vestibules, unpublished document, NG archive

# Object Biographies

12

# Classifying China: Shifting Interpretations of Buddhist Bronzes in Liverpool Museum, 1867–1997[1]

Louise Tythacott

## Introduction: The Lives of Objects

This chapter examines the lives of a set of five Chinese Buddhist deity figures in Liverpool Museum, from 1867 to 1997.[2] The largest figure, an almost-life-size bronze statue of the Goddess of Compassion, Guanyin (see Fig 12.1), probably dates from the early 15th century. The other four – Wenshu, Puxian, Weituo and Guangong – are early 17th-century creations. All five belonged to a temple on Putuo Island, off the east coast of China. For over a thousand years this was one of the most important Buddhist pilgrimage sites in the country, devoted to the worship of Guanyin. The statues were taken from their temple in the 1840s by a British soldier just after the First Opium War (1839–42). Once transported to England, they appeared at the Great Exhibition in 1851 and the Manchester Art Treasures Exhibition of 1857, and were auctioned at Sotheby's two years later. After passing through the hands of antiquarian collectors, the Chinese statues were accessioned into Liverpool Museum in 1867, where they remain to this day (Tythacott 2009, 90–97).

This chapter draws upon Igor Kopytoff's essay, 'The cultural biography of things: commoditization as process' (1986), in order to examine the biographies of these figures at Liverpool Museum. Kopytoff was the first to suggest that objects, like people, have 'social lives'. Just as we may analyse the biography of a person, he argued, so too it is possible to examine the lives of objects and ask of them similar questions:

> What, sociologically, are the biographical possibilities inherent in its 'status' and in the period and culture, and how are these possibilities realized? Where does the thing come from and who made it? What has been its career so far, and what do people consider to be an ideal career for such things? What are the recognised 'ages' or periods in the thing's 'life', and what are the cultural markers for them? How does the thing's use change with its age, and what happens to it when it reaches the end of its usefulness? (Kopytoff 1986, 66–7)

1 I am grateful to Professor Sian Jones at the University of Manchester for her insightful comments on this subject. I also thank Professor Piotr Bienkowski, former Curator of Antiquities at National Museums Liverpool; Dr Rob Philpott, Head of the Field Archaeology Unit at National Museums Liverpool; and Dr Eldon Worrall, Research Associate at the National Museums Liverpool, for supplying valuable information.

2 The chapter is based on research for a book, *The Lives of Chinese Objects: Buddhism, Imperialism and Display* (Tythacott 2011).

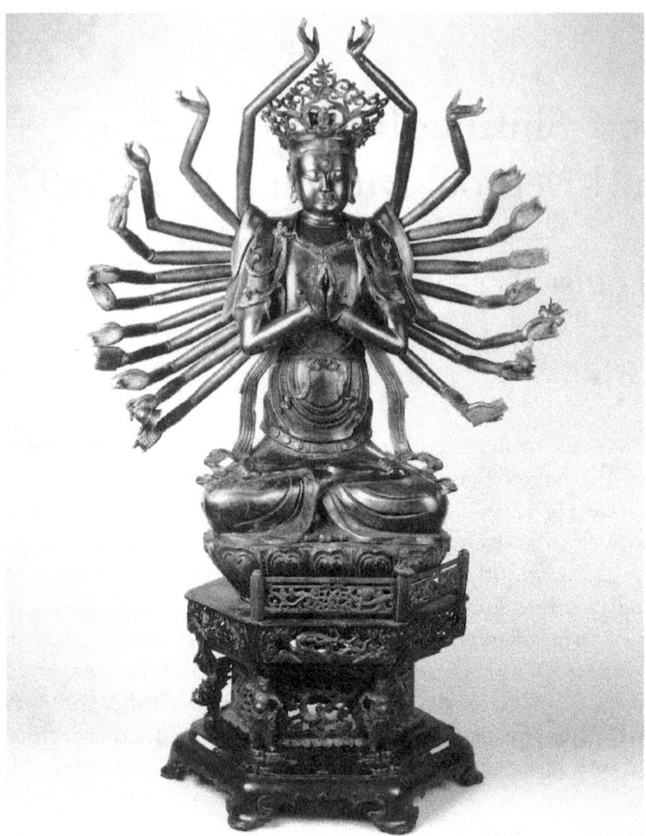

Fig 12.1.
Statue of multiple-armed Guanyin. Putuo island, China. Probably early 15th century, Ming dynasty (1368–1644). Cast bronze. H: 1130mm, L: 1050mm, W: 400mm

This approach holds that it is not possible to fully understand an object by focusing on one particular moment or aspect of its lifecycle. Rather, it is accumulated experience that gives things their identities (Gosden and Marshall 1999, 170).

It will be argued in this chapter that the succession of identities experienced by the bronzes reflected the changing ideologies and circumstances of Liverpool Museum. The Buddhist images were perceived initially as objects of ethnology, and later in the 20th century as 'specimens' of the 'Mongolian' race. By the 1930s they had been reconceptualised as Oriental art by a new curator of ethnology inspired by modernist aesthetics. Despite being confined to boxes for almost 60 years (1939–97), they remained conceptually active, moving in and out of a range of classifications: 'ethnology', 'archaeology', 'antiquity', 'Oriental antiquity' and 'Asian collections'. The paper contends that the placement of these objects was more complex than for many other artefacts at Liverpool Museum in whose classificatory group they initially found themselves. Collections from Africa, the Americas and the Pacific remained within one department: ethnology. Chinese and other Asian collections, by contrast, received very different treatment.

As well as documenting the biographies of the five bronzes, I shall be concerned with the ways in which Chinese objects have been classified in museums. Fundamentally museums operate to codify knowledge, to organise material culture and place it in taxonomies. The moment an object arrives at such an institution it is assigned a category: accession numbers, registers, lists, catalogues and labels, as well as departments and curatorial expertise, function to sort, locate and separate objects into groups, imposing order and meaning (Sherman and Rogoff 1994, x–xi). Yet while categorisation is often seen as a neutral activity, predicated upon science, it is the perceived objectivity of classificatory regimes that makes them so powerful. As Hill reminds us: 'any category referred to (in a museum) is not an absolute division corresponding to a "real" group in the material world, but rather an imposition on that world created by structures of knowledge' (Hill 2005, 73).

## Objects of 'ethnology': 1867–1896

After the arrival of the Buddhist statues at Liverpool Museum in 1867, the first Keeper, Ecroyd Smith, worked quickly to impose order onto the collections. By December 1871, however, he had resigned (West 1981, 2). Charles Gatty succeeded him in 1872–3, and continued with his work (Burman 1988, 201). Ecroyd Smith had established four- and five-digit museum accession numbers in 15 different categories. For example, 1–5131 was Medieval, ivories, pottery and miniatures; 10,000–10,999 was Greek and Roman; 12,400 to 12,999 was Egypt and Miscellaneous. The accession number given to the bronzes – 12,908 – indicated allocation in this last block. The next set, running from 13,000 to 13,499, was ethnographical. As other Chinese objects were listed at the beginning of the latter, one wonders whether Gatty intended to classify the Buddhist deity figures as part of 'ethnography', but, running out of numbers, simply used space in the previous category instead. By at least 1873, a paper slip had been made out for each artefact, which was then stored by department (West 1981, 2). The blue slip for the images can still be found today. It reads: 'Chinese Buddhist figures (5), see ethnographical cat'.

It is unlikely that the five were on display when they first arrived at the museum. Of the many newspaper reports that describe the opening of the new museum in 1867, none refer to the bronzes specifically, nor to any other Chinese objects. In 1880, the importance of the ethnology collection was recognised by a temporary exhibition of 'Prehistoric Antiquities and Ethnography' staged at the Walker Art Gallery next door – though only 15 Asian objects were included in this display, from places such as Afghanistan, Malaya and Burma. According to Gatty, this was due to the fact that: 'the large majority of Asiatic civilizations are too cultivated to be of much interest to the ethnographical student' (Gatty 1880, 47). In 1882, the deity figures were exhibited, in an annexe at the back of the Walker Art Gallery, in a geographically organised display. In his accompanying catalogue, Gatty penned over a thousand words in praise of these statues, focusing on their iconographies and religious meanings. Yet here once again he questioned the inclusion of 'Oriental' objects in a classification reserved largely for 'primitive' culture:

> As most of the Asiatic races from whom these objects come, are, or have been, in a highly cultivated state, it has not been considered necessary to be so particular – with regard to the arrangement and description of these specimens, as has been the case with those from more primitive tribes. Indeed many of the Asiatic pieces can hardly be said to fall strictly within the limits of an ethnographical collection. (Gatty 1882, 86)

Gatty thus distinguished Asia's 'highly cultivated' races, that were not part of 'ethnology', from the 'aboriginal races' that were – a perception of Asian cultures that was characteristic of the time.

Distinctions between the material culture of 'civilised' and 'primitive' peoples were embedded within the organisational schema of many Western museums; objects from China often straddled disciplinary boundaries, being classified as either 'ethnography' or 'decorative art'. Everyday Chinese objects tended to be placed in ethnographic museums. By contrast, porcelain, jade, metalwork, ivory, furniture, glass, cloisonné and textiles, which testified to sophisticated technology and craftsmanship, were deemed suitable for admission into decorative arts collections.

As far back as 1850, Masson's guide to the British Museum noted that the antiquities of China, India and Japan should be separated from the material culture of more 'primitive' peoples (Clunas 1998, 45). In the 20th century, the divisions continued. In the layout of the Ethnology gallery at Manchester Museum in 1958, for example, there were two separate exhibitionary spaces – one for 'Asia: Civilizations' (China, Japan, 'Ceylon', 'Siam', Burma and India) and one for 'Asia: Tribes' ('The Naga' and Indonesia) (Willet 1958, n.p.). In the University of Manchester museums in the 21st century, Chinese material culture is still divided, with the bulk of ethnographic artefacts located at the Manchester Museum, while textiles are placed separately at the Whitworth Art Gallery.

Even in Liverpool, the home of the bronzes for the past 150 years, Chinese objects have been distributed between ethnology in Liverpool Museum and decorative arts at the Lady Lever Art Gallery. Until 2005, Asian material culture at the British Museum too was placed in different departments – ethnography and Oriental antiquities. Further afield, in places such as Paris, these divisions remain unchanged. At the Musée du Quai Branly, the ethnographic museum of France which opened in 2006, only certain elements of Asian material culture are displayed – textiles and puppets mainly from Southeast Asia, the kinds of objects that Gatty had classed as 'ethnographic' in the 1880s. It is necessary to visit the Musée Guimet for the art – Buddhist and Hindu stone-carving, Chinese porcelain, cloisonné and lacquer.

How, then, might Gatty have positioned the five deity figures in the early 1880s? Somewhere between 'ethnology' and 'antiquities' perhaps, but not as 'decorative art' and certainly not as 'fine art'. The incorporation of the material culture of China into the Western canon of aesthetics came only in the 20th century. Though certain Chinese creations had been labelled 'works of art' in the 19th century, almost none made their way across the disciplinary boundaries into public fine art galleries. There was nothing from China in London's National Gallery, for example, despite the culture's refined scholarly tradition of painting and calligraphy (Vainker 2000, 9; Clunas 1997, 9).

## OBJECTS OF THE 'MONGOLIAN' RACE: 1896–1929

In 1896, the *Annual Reports* at Liverpool Museum initiated the listing of humanities accessions according to racial type. The director, Henry Ogg Forbes, itemised three: 'Melanian', 'Mongolian' and 'Caucasian'. The 'Melanian' objects included accessions from Africa and the Pacific. 'Caucasian' comprised predominantly European things. The 'Mongolian', or 'yellow' race, consisted of a diversity of peoples from the Americas and Asia. The Chinese figures were clearly placed in this last category, designated a position somewhere between the 'civilised' white and the 'uncivilised' black races of the world.

The positioning of Chinese people in relation to a hierarchy of race had been articulated over previous decades by a number of scholars. Well-known figures – Thomas Huxley, Pitt Rivers and Edward Burnett Tylor – in their differing ways characterised the Chinese as part of a 'racial stock' that was conservative as well as technically and culturally backward. Yet the exact positioning of China was not always clear. We have already seen a sense of ambiguity in the placement of the material culture from this country in Western museums, and this is evident too with the positioning of Chinese peoples in anthropological discourses. In 1865, for example, Huxley had discussed the 'two great stocks' of the Xanthrocoi (mainly the Chinese) and the Melanochroi (mainly the Western Europeans) who have 'originated everything that is highest in science, in art, in law, in politics, and in mechanical inventions' (Bennett 2004, 58). Tylor, too, ranked societies in a descending order below Europeans and North Americans, for example Italian, Chinese, Aztec, Tahitian, Australian (Gosden and Marshall 1999, 165). Despite the diversity of approaches, the Chinese were consistently placed above African and Oceanic peoples, yet below Europeans.

By the early 20th century the categories that were initially articulated in the accession lists of the *Annual Reports* became the overall organisational classification for the galleries at Liverpool Museum (Tythacott 2001, 161–2). The Melanian objects were in the basement; the Caucasian antiquities were placed on the ground floor, while the Mongolian objects were moved to the top floor. And it was here that the Chinese deities would have been placed on public display.[3]

What might this have meant for these Buddhist figures? Their incorporation into a gallery devoted to the 'Mongolian' race, along with the products of other 'yellow' races, conceptually signified a subordinate position to 'white' races within the evolutionary ladder. In this display realm, the statues were intended to demonstrate not the efficacy of sacred imagery, or the high level of technological sophistication of bronze casters, but the fact that China was considered to be less civilised than the West. The five performed here as 'utterances' within a wider Eurocentric discourse of race.

## Objects of 'Art': 1930–1940

Chinese objects had been collected in Europe for centuries, and ornately decorated porcelain had been a feature of much Victorian praise. With the looting by British and French regiments of the Summer Palace in Beijing in 1860, many imperial pieces also found their way to Europe. But it was only in the early decades of the 20th century that new kinds of Chinese objects started to appear – archaeological material uncovered during the construction of China's railways (Green 2002, 64–6).

As the availability of excavated wares and tomb figures increased, so the perception of the range of China's material culture, and of the sense of its history, expanded. By 1915, Hercules Read of the British Museum wrote that it was 'hard to recall so fundamental a revolution in the opinions of the world of art as the marked change of attitude towards Chinese art among the leaders of artistic thought' (Read 1915, ix). By the early 1920s, a coterie of dedicated collectors and connoisseurs had coalesced, who wrote articles, organised exhibitions and, in 1921, formed the influential Oriental Ceramic Society (OCS). Collectors associated with this society, in particular, went on to dominate the taste in Chinese art in Britain over the following decades (Pierson 2003, 2).

Only certain things, however, qualified for this new category of art. There was a preference for 'early' objects, initially those of the Ming (1368–1644), later on the Song (960–1279), Tang

3 Though it has not been possible to identify object lists for the Mongolian gallery, the Chinese deities were included in an inventory in 1929, where they were located on the top floor alongside objects from Asia and the Americas.

(618–907) and Han (206 BCE–220 CE) dynasties. Collectors sought out things that fitted their pre-existing ideas of 'primitivist' aesthetics – the formal and chromatic simplicity of Song dynasty stoneware, modelled pottery figures from the Han and Tang dynasties, and ancient Buddhist sculpture.

By the early 1930s, the institutionalisation and professionalisation of Chinese art in Britain was also taking place. In 1930, for example, a lectureship in Chinese art and archaeology was created at the University of London at a time when Western art history was not even on offer. Two years later the post was transferred to the Courtauld Institute of Art, where a chair in the subject was established (Clunas 1998, 49).

This epistemological shift was accompanied by changes to the visual and spatial organisation of Chinese material culture in the museum. By the mid-century, a number of museums displayed connoisseurs' collections of ceramics, jades, bronzes, cloisonné and lacquer.[4] Oriental objects were being exhibited in ways that emphasised their formal as well as historical qualities.

The reorientation of Liverpool Museum's Asian collection in relation to these broader changes was explicit by the early 1930s. In the news section of the *Museums Journal* in 1931, a paragraph on 'Liverpool Museum: Oriental Ethnology' noted: 'while London is discussing some future Asiatic Museum, Liverpool is setting to work. The Introductory Room at the Liverpool Museum is to become a museum of Oriental Ethnology in five sections: China, Japan, Burma, India and Malaya' (*Museums Journal* 1931, 213).

The arrival of a new curator of ethnology at Liverpool Museum in 1931 precipitated the change of focus. Trevor Thomas was a modernist and moderniser who immediately turned his attention to the Asian collections, developing an Oriental gallery on the top floor between 1934 and 1935. Thomas' views on non-Western art were set out in articles in the *Museums Journal* between 1933 and 1939 – and these give a strong sense of the new interpretative world the bronzes entered in the years immediately before World War II.[5] For Thomas, the 'function' of the museum was 'an arbiter of aesthetic taste'. Asian collections, he argued, were eminently suited for a formalist approach: 'One of the latest developments of this policy has been the reorganization of the Oriental Gallery … this section with its objects of intrinsic beauty would lend itself admirably to modern settings' (Thomas 1934, 221).

Terms such as 'formalised' and 'individual' were also used by the director, Douglas Allan, when referring to the Oriental objects. Indeed, Allan chose to illustrate a 1937 text with cases depicting Chinese porcelain figures of Guanyin. Another small sculpture of this Chinese goddess was used three years earlier in a sketch of one of Thomas' cases (Thomas 1934, 223). Here was an object type eminently suitable to demonstrate the modernist approach.

Thomas was concerned to elevate objects, and so a series of interchangeable 'blocks for staging' was constructed, which he referred to as 'cubic units'. His formalist approach intended to focus attention on individual things. The museological devices used to perpetuate this are immediately

4 For example, the Percival David Foundation, the British Museum and Fitzwilliam Museum, Cambridge. Glasgow received the Burrell collection in 1944 and started building a museum at Pollocks Country Park in 1967. The Oriental Museum in Durham, comprising ceramics and jades, was built in 1960; the Barlow collection of ancient Chinese bronzes and ceramics was given to the University of Sussex in 1974.

5 While it is not known for sure if the five Chinese deity figures were on display, whether or not Thomas chose to include them, as curator, his interests inevitably became attached to these things.

recognisable – the plinth, the frame, the spotlight – tools employed in many museums to influence the way visitors relate to collections.

Colour schemes were also important. Thomas insisted that each object should be placed against a 'clear background, an uninterrupted field against which to express its character' (Thomas 1939, 10). Neutral backgrounds were intended to highlight the Asian collections. As the director wrote in 1937: 'The general scheme of the gallery is a cool series of greys to act as a foil for the striking character of some of the exhibits' (Allan 1937, 20). It is certainly the case that light colours are used as the marker of the aesthetic in the vocabulary of museum display; pure white being the signifier of modern or contemporary art. Oriental material culture, even today, is usually displayed within spaces that have a slight shade – grey, salmon, magnolia, lavender.

Such displays were worlds apart from the visual realm of the Buddhist temple, where the Chinese deities would have been surrounded by a darkened atmosphere and colours that had symbolic meaning within the religious system. Deep and dark reds were probably used on columns to suggest happiness; ceilings may have been painted in a palette of gold or red to represent power and glory (Lip 1986, 12). The insipid pastel shades of Thomas' 1930s designs would have been highly inappropriate – white, above all, being inauspicious, associated in China with death and mourning. In this new display space in Liverpool Museum, the bronzes may well have travelled up a Western hierarchy, for objects of 'art' have a higher status than objects of 'ethnography', yet this interpretation, nevertheless, contravened the original world the deity figures were created to inhabit.

With the new focus on aesthetics and the new display techniques, the conditions of viewing also changed – aesthetic modernism, after all, is an interpretation that tries to regulate a particular mode of looking. Buddhist sources, by contrast, rarely apply aesthetic criteria to deity figures. Kieschnick observes that Buddhist images were hardly ever 'purely decorative' (Kieschnick 2003, 56, 79). In their original abodes the five were not intended to be seen as individual artistic entities but belonged within a complex system of signification. Their symmetry and design was constituted so that they were to be addressed from the front and below, not the sides, the back, or at eye level. The idea of being able to walk around such images, to be able to go up close and inspect them as three-dimensional sculpture, transgressed the scopic regime they were created to exist within.

Thomas left Liverpool in July 1940 to take up the directorship of Leicester Museums. The previous year, after the outbreak of war, the five statues had been moved hurriedly into storage and they were to languish in this state for almost 60 years. Upheaval in a time of crisis resulted in records of their lives being lost: Guanyin and Wenshu (at least) were dismantled and the five were kept in appalling conditions for a great many years.

## Objects of 'archaeology': 1940–1966

It was just after World War II that Elaine Tankard (1901–1969) began to extend her curatorial remit to the Ethnology Department, focusing on the Oriental material. Tankard had arrived at the museum in 1931 and later, in 1935, became keeper of archaeology and ceramics (West 1981, 10). Thomas' post was not filled after the war, so it was Tankard who became the guardian of the Chinese deity figures – and with her background in archaeology she engaged with them in a very different way.

It is certain that the five magnificent bronze statues, the largest and most prominent Buddhist objects from China, would not have escaped Tankard's attention. Her curatorial specialism was in the ancient, the archaeological and the religious, and, under such custodianship, the statues took on interpretations different from those of the modernist aesthete, Thomas. As these objects moved into the orbit of this curator so the epistemological framework that surrounded them changed: in Tankard's regime, the five were designated 'archaeological', valued for their testament to traditions of Buddhist belief and bronze-casting in ancient China.

While no records exist of Tankard's particular perceptions of these images, some of them were clearly being looked at in the stores, for the tail of the lion upon which Wenshu sat was relabelled under her documentation programme in 1955.[6] The fact that only one fragment had a new number suggests it had already been separated from the rest of its body.

Yet it is evident that Tankard was fascinated by Buddhism, particularly Tibetan Buddhism, and expended much energy obtaining Himalayan material from renowned political officers and collectors, such as Charles Bell and Francis Younghusband. In 1953 she mounted the ground-breaking *Tibet* exhibition at the Walker Art Gallery. She also saw China as an essential focus. Soon after her arrival she set to work on the Oriental ivories (West 1981, 9), and later, in 1956, wrote a note on the loan and display of the Sassoon collection of Chinese ivories for the *Museums Journal* (Tankard 1956, 287–8). That year she penned a handbook to the Chinese pottery collection to accompany a small exhibition, demonstrating her knowledge of ancient wares. Tankard had much richer information to draw on than previous curators, for Chinese exhibitions were becoming more specialised by this time. In 1955, the Oriental Ceramic Society (OCS) organised an exhibition of Tang (618–907 CE) material at the Arts Council, their first exhibition focusing on a single period. The same year, the British Museum mounted 'Art under the Mongol dynasties', to be followed by other key OCS exhibitions: 'The arts of the Ming dynasty' (1957) and 'The arts of the Sung dynasty' (1960). Pierson argues that these types of exhibition represented a new period in the development and understanding of Chinese art in Britain (Pierson 2003, 231).

In 1960 the position of keeper of ethnology at Liverpool Museum was re-established. Yet, in the absence of a specialist custodian, Tankard had extended her curatorial remit to aspects of the collections which interested her. Despite the new post, a large section of the Asian collections remained in archaeology. Tankard released certain things to the new incumbent – objects from Indonesia, Malaysia, the Philippines, Thailand and parts of India. Not all Southeast Asian material was transferred. Items considered in some way to qualify for 'decorative arts' (in that they demonstrated skilled craftsmanship or used high-quality materials), or that could be seen as 'antiquities', stayed with her – silverware, lacquer ware and an imperial ivory throne from Burma, as well as Hindu and Buddhist stone sculpture from Thailand and Java. The newly formed collections from Tibet, as well as those from India, Japan and China, remained in archaeology. This dismemberment of the Asian collections seems to have been predicated not only upon the proclivities of the curatorial regime but in relation to a more deeply rooted separation that we have encountered before. We saw Gatty's division of Asia in his catalogue of 1882. Eighty years later, Asian material culture was still being sorted into things deriving from 'civilisations' considered to have 'history' and 'art', and those that did not. It is noteworthy, however, that the

6 It was given a separate accession number – 55.8.5 – indicating that it was renumbered in 1955, probably by Miss Tankard, or someone working under her guidance. No other information was included.

Chinese figures had now crossed a boundary: this was the first time since their arrival at Liverpool Museum that they were no longer classified as 'ethnology'.

The personal interests of Tankard apart, the transformation of the epistemological framework that surrounded ancient Chinese material culture must have been another factor in the ability of the bronzes to become 'archaeology'. Archaeology had emerged in the Chinese context as a discipline in the 1920s with the first tentative excavations. By the 1930s, the Guomindang government had put in place its Academica Sinica, under which archaeological work was formalised. After the founding of the People's Republic of China in 1949, serious archaeological research began, and over the following decades one spectacular discovery after another was revealed to the outside world – the result being the transformation of the study of Chinese archaeology in the West. In 1955, the Chinese art course at the School of Oriental and African Studies at the University of London was placed within Archaeology and it was now possible to study an Academic Diploma in Chinese Archaeology or an MA in Chinese Art and Archaeology (Pierson 2003, 71). As the archaeology of China became institutionalised and professionalised in both the East and West, a new period in the understanding of Chinese objects began. By the 1950s, the possibility of conceptualising the Chinese Buddhist statues in archaeological terms thus existed as never before.

## OBJECTS OF 'ANTIQUITY' AND CHINESE METALWORK: 1966–1997

In 1966, the bronzes were transported to an old dockside warehouse near the centre of the city. Dorothy Downes described the way that everything was crammed in here when she arrived in the 1960s to take up the post of keeper of antiquity after Elaine Tankard retired. The statues were initially placed on the stone stairwell, not the most respectful of places, she notes, 'but at least they were safe' (Downes 2007).

The position assumed by Dr Downes in 1966 had transmuted from keeper of archaeology to keeper of antiquities – though it is not clear why this occurred. As archaeology is a discipline and a process, it might not have been suitable as a collective name for ancient objects in a museum. By the 1970s, antiquities would also have been used to distinguish this section from the Field Archaeology Unit at Liverpool Museum.[7] In a museum guide in 1993, these differences were put into print. Antiquities were described as 'everyday items or artistic treasures from ancient civilisations'; ethnology was the 'study of peoples and cultures from around the world, and specifically Africa, the Pacific Islands and the Americas' (Liverpool Museum 1993, 29). Antiquities emphasised 'items' and 'artistic treasures'; ethnology was concerned with 'people'. While antiquities had an historical dimension, ethnology, it seems, did not. Terms such as 'civilisation', 'art', 'treasure' and 'Asia' were excluded from ethnology, a discipline of relevance, in this context, to Africa, the Americas and the Pacific. The five Chinese deity figures, now consigned to antiquities, thus qualified as 'artistic treasures' from an 'ancient civilisation'.

By this time the separation between the two departments was manifested in the organisation of stored material culture, with antiquities on the first floor and ethnology on the second floor of the stores. This represented more or less a geographical divide: Europe, the Middle East and Asia were on one level; Africa (excluding Egypt), the Americas and the Pacific were above.

7 The Merseyside Archaeological Survey (forerunner of Field Archaeology) was established in 1977.

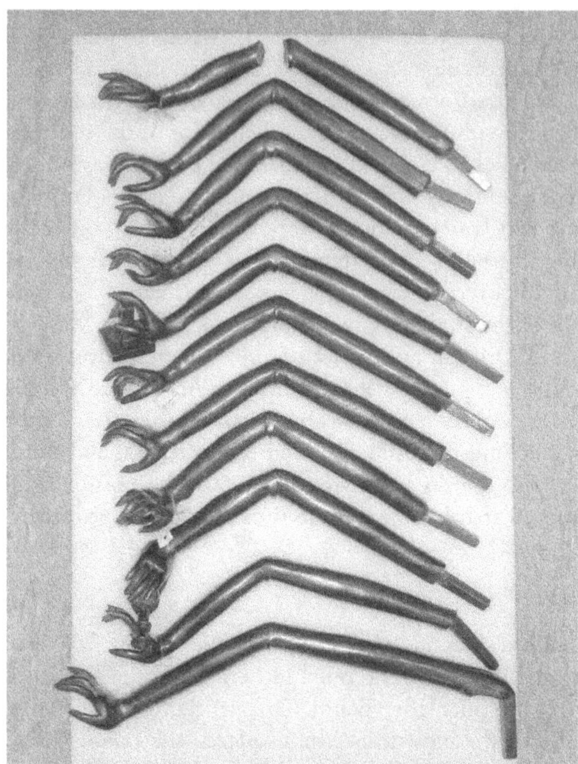

FIG 12.2.
ARMS OF THE GUANYIN STATUE.
CAST BRONZE

By the late 1970s, the bronzes found themselves subjected to yet another regime of interpretation. Eldon Worrall, a local Liverpool antiquarian undertaking research on the Oriental metalwork collection, came across bits of Guanyin crammed into a wooden crate. It took him almost a decade to locate the separate pieces of the statue and reconstruct it from parts scattered around the stores.

Worrall became interested in identifying the metallurgical origins of Chinese objects in the collections, and so the deities became absorbed into his research on the material and the technology of construction. Analytical techniques were applied and samples were taken to determine exact chemical structure. In the 1980s, minute scratchings were removed from interconnecting parts of Guanyin (such as the arms), which were sent to a metallurgical specialist at the University of Liverpool in an attempt to identify the composition of the alloy (Worrall 2008).[8]

This period also coincided with the exposure of the bronzes to a range of specialists. In 1977, Worrall had worked with the highly renowned scholar Margaret Medley, Curator of the Percival David Foundation at London University, to research the Liverpool Museum's collection. Worrall recalls Medley's remark when shown Guanyin: 'fantastically important' (Worrall 2008). In the late 1980s, Worrall also arranged for Rose Kerr, the key expert on Chinese metalwork at the Victoria and Albert Museum, to comment on this statue.

8 Worrall arranged for metallurgical examination with the University of Liverpool. However, I have not been able to locate the paperwork associated with this test.

In examining the five bronzes from the perspective of metallurgy, each component merited study, sometimes in microscopic detail. An extension, and embodiment, of the interest in physical manufacture was a set of photographs commissioned by Worrall for a metalwork catalogue. These depict the bronzes in fragments. Rows of Guanyin's arms are laid out (see Fig 12.2). Fragments from the crown are singled out and placed in front of the camera for documentation, each individually framed, photographs which remain a vivid record of the state of dismemberment of once pristine figures.

In 1996, when I arrived at Liverpool Museum to take up the position of curator of ethnology, I discovered these statues in a thoroughly dismembered state. I had been surprised to find the bulk of the collections from Asia residing in 'antiquities', with only a fraction of the objects from this continent classified as 'ethnology'. The year after I arrived I was asked to incorporate 'Oriental Antiquities' into my orbit of responsibility. The collections – including the five Chinese deities – were moved (conceptually, not physically) to ethnology and renamed 'Asian collections'.

## Conclusion

This chapter has explored how the interpretations of the Buddhist statues were refracted through changing regimes of ethnology, art history and archaeology between 1867 and 1997. Their careers at Liverpool Museum can be used to illustrate the complex ways in which Chinese objects have been classified in the West. We have seen, too, how the bronzes gained new 'social lives' and how their biographies became ever more complex during their time at Liverpool Museum.

As well as analysing the shifting meanings attributed to objects, this paper has explored the relationships between people and things – a key element of the biographical approach (Alberti 2005, 561; Gosden and Knowles 2001, 22–3; Steiner 2001, 210–11). Indeed, the significance of the bronzes waxed and waned according to the personal interests of their guardians: they were sometimes given a prominent place and, at other times, were marginalised from regimes of interpretation. It is evident, of course, that all museum professionals transmit specific interpretations in their dealings with objects, which inevitably carry ideological messages. Curators are products of their time and in their professional practice reflect contemporary perspectives and scholarship. The museum staff in whose care the statues resided placed quite differing interpretations on them: Gatty, with his evolutionary perspective; Forbes, with his theories of race; Thomas and his aesthetic modernism; Tankard and her passion for Buddhism; Worrall and his focus on metallurgy. Their personal biographies thus intersected and overlapped with the biographies of the five Buddhist deities.

## Bibliography and References

Alberti, S J M M, 2005 Objects and the Museum, *ISIS* 96 (4), 559–71

Allan, D, 1937 *The collections of Liverpool Public Museums*, Liverpool Museums, Liverpool

Bennett, T, 2004 *Pasts beyond memory: evolution, museums, colonialism*, Routledge, London and New York

Burman, L, 1988 Joseph Mayer's Wedgwood Collection, in *Joseph Mayer of Liverpool 1803–1886* (ed M Gibson and S Wright), Society of Antiquaries of London, London, 195–211

Clunas, C, 1997 *The Barlow collection of Chinese ceramics, bronzes and jades: an introduction*, University of Sussex, Brighton

— 1998 China in Britain: the imperial collections, in *Colonialism and the object: empire, material culture and the museum* (ed T Barringer and T Flynn), Routledge, London and New York, 41–51

Downes, D, 2007 Personal communication (letter), 20 December

Gatty, C, 1880 *Catalogue of the loan exhibition of prehistoric antiquities and ethnography held at the Walker Art Gallery, Liverpool*, London

— 1882 *Catalogue of the Mayer Museum II: prehistoric Antiquities and Ethnography*, London

Gosden, C, and Knowles, C, 2001 *Collecting Colonialism: Material Culture and Colonial Change*, Berg, Oxford and New York

Gosden, C, and Marshall, Y, 1999 The cultural biography of objects, *World Archaeology* 31 (2), 169–78

Green, J, 2002 Britain's Chinese collections, 1842–1943: private collecting and the invention of Chinese art, unpublished DPhil thesis, Brighton University

Hill, K, 2005 *Culture and class in English public museums, 1850–1914*, Ashgate, Aldershot

Kieschnick, J, 2003 *The impact of Buddhism on Chinese material culture*, Princeton University Press, Princeton and Oxford

Kopytoff, I, 1986 The cultural biography of things: commoditisation as process, in *The Social Life of Things: Commodities in Cultural Perspective* (ed A Appadurai), Cambridge University Press, Cambridge, 66–7

Lip, E, 1986 *Chinese temples and deities*, Times Books International, Singapore

Liverpool Museum, 1993 *Guide*, Liverpool

*Museums Journal*, 1931 August, 213

Pierson, S, 2003 Private collecting, teaching and institutionalisation: the Percival David Foundation and the field of Chinese art in Britain, 1920–1964, unpublished PhD thesis, University of Brighton

Read, C H, 1915 Introduction, *Catalogue of a collection of objects of Chinese art*, Burlington Fine Arts Club, London

Sherman, D, and Rogoff, I (eds), 1994 *Museum Culture: histories, discourses, spectacles*, Routledge, London and New York

Steiner, C, 2001 Rights of Passage: On the Liminal Identity of Art in the Border Zone, in *The Empire of Things: Regimes of Value and Material Culture* (ed F Myers), Santa Fe: School of American Research Press and James Currey, Santa Fe and Oxford, 207–31

Tankard, E, 1956 News and Notices, *Museums Journal*, February, 287–8

Thomas, T, 1934 Modernism in Display, *Museums Journal*, 221–5

— 1939 Penny Plain, two pence coloured: the aesthetics of museum display, *Museums Journal*, 1–12

Tythacott, L, 2001 From the fetish to the specimen: the Ridyard African collection at the Liverpool Museum 1895–1916, in *Collectors: expressions of self and other* (ed A Shelton), Horniman Museum and Gardens, London, 157–79

— 2009 Sacred island deities, *Apollo*, CLXIX (563), March, 90–97

— 2011 *The Lives of Chinese Objects: Buddhism, Imperialism and Display*, Berghahn Books, Oxford

Vainker, S, 2000 *Chinese paintings in the Ashmolean Museum, Oxford*, Ashmolean Museum, Oxford

West, A, 1981 Notes on the history of the ethnology department, unpublished manuscript, National Museums Liverpool Archive

Willet, F, 1958 Manchester Museum's Ethnology, in *Manchester Museum Handbook*, Manchester Museum, Manchester

Worrall, E, 2008 Personal communication (interview), 12 July

# 13

# 'Dressed like an Amazon': The Transatlantic Trajectory of a Red Feather Coat[1]

Mariana Françozo

## Introduction

In 2000, the Brazilian Ministry of Culture prepared and organised an exhibition commemorating the 500th anniversary of the arrival of Europeans on the South American continent. Located at the Ibirapuera Park in the city of São Paulo, the exhibition was called 'Mostra do Redescobrimento' ('Rediscovery Exhibit') and aimed at showcasing a wide variety of examples of Brazilian art, including Portuguese–Brazilian, African–Brazilian, Amerindian, Baroque and Popular Art.[2] For this occasion, the Danish National Museum agreed to lend a particularly rare artefact that was produced during the first century of colonial contacts: a 1.2m-long, 60cm-wide red feather coat, most likely made by the Tupinambá Indigenous group of coastal Brazil. This object had been housed at the Danish Museum for about 350 years, and was therefore making its first appearance in Brazil since its departure almost four centuries previously.

The coat made an immediate and powerful impact on the audience of its original country. The feather cape was displayed in a way that granted it an aura of aristocracy and sacredness: it stood alone, dimly lit in a glass window, at the end of a white, empty, 30m-long corridor, which visitors would reach only after having passed through a number of other rooms dedicated to Amerindian Art. The cloak was soon considered one of the most important pieces of the exhibition. In fact, it was considered one of the two 'historical relics' of the exhibit, alongside the notorious letter written by Pero Vaz de Caminha (1450–1500) which announced to Portuguese king Dom Manuel (1469–1521) the discovery of the lands later called Portuguese America (Caversan 2000, E1).

Apart from the rather predictable spellbound reaction of the public to the object's unique display, an unexpected event was set in motion by the very physical presence of the red feather

1 This chapter presents part of the results of my PhD dissertation 'From Olinda to Olanda: Johan Maurits van Nassau and the circulation of objects and knowledge in the Dutch Atlantic', defended in November 2009 at Unicamp, Brazil. I would like to thank the Coimbra Group for providing me with the 'Scholarship for Young Latin American Researchers' at the University of Aarhus, Denmark. An earlier version of this paper was presented at the 'The Public Lives of Things' Seventh Annual Symposium on Material Culture at the Winterthur Museum, Delaware. I wish to thank the participants of the symposium for their comments and suggestions. I would also like to thank Dr Peter Bjerregaard and Dr Peter J Yoder for their invaluable help.

2 The exhibition received a total of 1.8 million visitors in a 120-day period. It was (and still remains) the largest art exhibition ever to be held in Brazil, totalling 60,000 square metres divided into four buildings.

coat in Brazil. A group of Tupinambá Amerindians, now living in the State of Bahia, claimed that the cloak was part of their ancestral heritage and therefore belonged to them. The feathered cloak was considered a piece of their material cultural heritage and, as such, should be seen as an inalienable item. Although there was some media coverage of this dispute, it remained a national debate while never culminating in legal action. When the exhibition came to an end, the Brazilian State returned the cloak without seeking to reclaim the artefact. As the years passed, the subject was eventually dropped by the Tupinambá community.

What is there to be learned from this event? The aim of this chapter is to show that ethnographic artefacts can be used by museums not only to instruct visitors on topics such as the costumes and cultures of foreign societies – the obvious usage of ethnographic pieces – but also to contribute to controversial contemporary debates on cultural identity and heritage rights. The underlying argument is that by drawing attention to an object's (social) trajectory, museums can present artefacts in a much richer, dynamic way and therefore stimulate their visitors to think critically about the aforementioned political issues.

The theoretical framework of this chapter derives from Arjun Appadurai's book *The Social Life of Things*. In his now classic introductory essay, Appadurai points out that 'even though from a *theoretical* point of view human actors encode things with significance, from a *methodological* point of view it is the things-in-motion that illuminate their human and social context' (Appadurai 1986, 5). This methodology applies particularly well to an object whose history spans more than 350 years and two continents: it has passed through various hands, it has been used for diverse purposes, it has been seen by different audiences. Therefore, its meanings have been constantly shifting – and will continue to do so, as it continues to be exhibited in museums.

Drawing on 17th-century visual and textual sources, in this chapter I will try to reconstruct the trajectory of a group of feather capes from the place where they were originally made to the National Museum in Copenhagen, which houses them today. By following the traces of these artefacts – that is, by reconstructing these objects' biographies – I will also explore symbolic and political aspects of the colonial relationships between subjects of different empires and political regimes in the early modern Atlantic World.

## From Ritualistic Dress to Collectible Item

The existence and the importance of feathered ornaments in South American Indigenous societies has been widely documented and acknowledged, both in the colonial period and in the daily life of contemporary Amerindian groups. The chroniclers of 16th-century Portuguese America described their encounters with the Tupi groups, particularly with the Tupinambá, and mentioned featherwork as a key element of their material culture and their spiritual life.[3] Hans

3 The term 'Tupi' encompasses all groups of Amerindians living on the coast of Brazil around 1500. The Tupi is a linguistic and ethnic family which incorporates many sub-groups, such as the Tupinambá, the Tupiniquim and the Tobajara. They shared linguistic and cultural affinities but did not form a political unity. In the second century of contact, when the European colonisers started to penetrate the backlands of Brazil, they met numerous other Indian groups, speaking different languages and belonging to different ethnic groups. The Tupi called all non-Tupi Indians 'Tapuia', and that is how all of these non-coastal groups came to be known in contemporary sources. For the purposes of this chapter I will mostly use the terms Tupi and Tapuia as general descriptions of coastal and non-coastal groups, even though this differentiation has been largely discussed by Brazilian Ethnology (see Monteiro 1999).

Staden (c. 1525–c. 1576), the German mercenary who was captured and imprisoned by the Tupinambá around 1554, mentions throughout his account that these Indians adorned themselves with birds' feathers. In his chapter about the Tupinambá's possessions, he firmly states that 'They do not know anything of money … Their treasures are the feathers of birds' (Staden 2008, 123). André Thevet (1502–1590), a French Franciscan priest, also mentioned the importance of bird feathers to the Tupi groups and relates that these groups usually traded coloured feathers amongst themselves as well as with the interior Tapuia groups (Thevet 1557, 90–91). This statement evidences the circulation of feathers and feathered products as well as supporting the idea that inter-Amerindian trade existed since pre-Columbian times. The French Protestant pastor Jean de Léry (1534–1611) informed his readers that the Tupi liked to coat their bodies with coloured feathers and feather necklaces and bracelets when going to war or when killing a prisoner (Léry 1578, 116). Beginning with the aforementioned letter by Pero Vaz de Caminha, Portuguese explorers who left accounts of their encounters with Indigenous groups also stressed the presence and the use of birds' feathers amongst the Tupi.

Thus, it is clear that feathers and featherwork were an important element of the material culture of Tupi societies. They 'attached a significance to the feathers … that far exceeds the aesthetical one' (Due 1979/80, 260). Twentieth-century ethnologists have analysed pre-Columbian Tupinambá society based on 16th- and 17th-century travel accounts, and have linked the use and meaning of feathered ornaments to religious and warfare practices. French ethnologist Alfred Métraux, author of one of the first and most important detailed studies of Tupi material culture (Métraux 1928), argues that the Tupinambá believed the ornaments embodied magical powers and that those individuals who wore the ornaments would acquire such powers. Specifically, enemy prisoners wore the feather cloak at a particular point in the legendary Tupinambá anthropophagic ritual (Métraux 1979, 120). Brazilian ethnologist and sociologist Florestan Fernandes furthered Métraux's arguments and demonstrated that feathered ornaments embodied the values and powers of the male Tupinambá warriors and were an important element of Indigenous war equipment. They were the symbol through which personal power and charisma were publically exhibited and recognised (Fernandes 1970, 36).

If in pre-contact times feather adornments were used in religious and war rituals, after 1500 the use and trajectory of these pieces underwent a meaningful change. It is clear that from the very first decades of the colonial encounter, feathered ornaments became a highly valued object for European travellers and colonisers, and the Tupi populations started to manufacture this item in order to exchange it with Europeans. It is in this context that one can understand, for example, the sophisticated process of *tapirage*, through which the Tupi dyed the feathers of chickens and other birds in order to obtain feathers of different colours for their ornaments (Due 1979/80, 257; Buono 2007, 111). In this new context, the feather capes were no longer used as war or religious ritual items but rather became representations of South American exotic new peoples. Whoever owned one of these artefacts would be unequivocally linked to the New World and its inhabitants. Similarly, from the Indigenous groups' perspectives, feathered ornaments were now powerful items to be used in commercial and political negotiations.

There is no precise estimate as to the number of feathered adornments made in the first century after European contact. However, specialists claim that there were hundreds of feather cloaks circulating in Europe in the 16th and 17th centuries (Buono 2007, 286). These capes were often placed in *kunstkammers* – that is, collections of curiosities – owned either by the nobility or by members of the highly educated and enriched bourgeoisie (Feest 1993; Mason 1994). Today, research indicates that there are only eleven such feather cloaks left in European museums.[4] Their presence in museums is material evidence of the role that these feathered Tupi cloaks played in the early modern world; their continued exhibition a sign of the continued interest of contemporary museum visitors.

Although the Portuguese Crown increasingly controlled most of the commercial activities in the lands of present-day Brazil, French navigators actively engaged in the trade with the Tupi populations from the beginning of the 16th century. Through these contacts – through French hands – feather ornaments made their way to Europe. Franciscan André Thevet mentioned that he owned a hat made of toucan feathers which he took with him back to France in 1556 (Thevet 1557, 109). According to Métraux, Thevet also owned a feather cloak, which he gave as a gift to Jean Bertrand, future cardinal of Sens, and Bertrand in turn gave it to King Henri II (1519–1559) (Métraux cited in Mason 1994, 3). Léry claims that he took a large number of feathers and feathered ornaments with him to France, but while in Paris a member of the king's court insisted he give these items to him (Léry 1578, 171).

In addition to French commercial activity on South American shores, Dutch merchants also established and maintained regular commercial contact with Amerindians from the end of the 16th and well into the 17th century. In doing so, they also had access to a variety of ethnographic items and to natural species sold or given to them by the Tupi. These items were highly prized in the Dutch Republic, even more so – or on a larger scale – than in France. In the Low Countries, from the end of the 16th century it became more and more fashionable to own a collection of curiosities. Members of the nobility and, in increasing numbers, intellectuals and the high bourgeoisie searched tirelessly for *exotica* from distant lands (Bergvelt and Kistemaker 1992). Items from Portuguese America soon made their way into Dutch collections. For instance, Bernard Paludanus (1550–1633), doctor in Enkhuizen, possessed the greatest and perhaps most famous *kunstkammer* in early modern Holland. The collection included Amerindian items such as clubs, music instruments, and, not surprisingly, feathers and feather ornaments, as recent studies have shown (Schepelern 1985; Gelder 1998). It is precisely this Dutch connection that will help us trace the biography of the feather cape now in Denmark.

## MARY STUART AS AMAZON

In 1637, German count Johan Maurits van Nassau-Siegen (1604–1679) was appointed by the Dutch West Indian Company (hereafter, WIC) as Governor General to the Dutch Colony in Northeastern Brazil.[5] During his eight-year tenure, he assembled one of the most interesting

4 There are five cloaks (of different sizes and shapes) at the National Museum of Denmark, in Copenhagen; one at the Museum der Kulturen in Basel, Switzerland; one at the Musée Royale d'Art et d'Histoire in Brussels, Belgium; two at the Museo di Storia Naturale in Florence, Italy; one at the Musée du Quai Branly, in Paris; and finally one at the Museo Settala dell'Ambrosiana in Milan, Italy.

5 After an unsuccessful attempt to conquer Brazil in 1624 through the invasion of its capital, São Salvador da Bahia, six years later the Dutch finally managed to conquer and occupy Pernambuco, the most lucrative sugar-producing province in all of Portuguese America. The first five to six years were spent fighting the Portuguese–Brazilian army and guerrillas throughout the region, but in 1636 the West Indian Company appointed Johan Maurits Governor-General to the Dutch Colony of New Holland. As is widely acclaimed, he was responsible for the expansion of the Dutch territory in Brazil and for eight years of what has been called a prosper administration. For the history of the Dutch in Brazil, see

collections of curiosities of the early modern period. It was comprised of Brazilian and African plants, animals and artefacts, as well as studies of natural history, portraits and landscapes by scientists and artists in Johan Maurits' private entourage.[6] After returning to the Netherlands in 1644, he exhibited his collection to scientists, humanists and members of the high Dutch and English nobility in The Hague. There, he had just finished the building of his very own palace, the Mauritshuis, where he lived for a few years. By presenting his collection to powerful members of the Dutch political scene, Johan Maurits made sure that his name and the memory of his successful and powerful experience in Brazil would not go unnoticed.

Two written accounts of visits to the Mauritshuis offer a valuable view of the contents of this collection. In a letter dated 12 December 1644, natural historian and professor Adolph Vorstius (1597–1663) mentions paintings of fish, quadrupeds, birds, insects and plants from America, rare woods, ivory, animal fur, and colourful feathers. Furthermore, the host offered Vorstius a spicy, unpleasant drink, which he considered 'a gift not worthy of such name' (Vorstius 1979, 240). The second description of the Mauritshuis was written by a certain Jacob de Hennin (1629–c. 1688), who presented a full description of the house in a small book about human beings' five senses. De Hennin observed tapestries with Brazilian motifs, wall paintings depicting pagan peoples such as Hottentots, Tupi Indians, Tapuia Indians and 'other savages', stuffed animals, Amerindian weapons and musical instruments, precious minerals and beautiful wood furniture (Hennin 1681, 118–21). While both texts testify to the abundance of Johan Maurits' collection, Vorstius' letter is the first piece of evidence that Johan Maurits possessed feathered adornments in his *kunstkammer*.

Four portraits of Mary Stuart I (1631–1660) comprise a second, more compelling source of evidence. Dutch court painter Adriaen Hanneman (c. 1604–1671) composed these paintings of the wife of Prince Willem II of Orange-Nassau (1626–1650). After having worked in London beside Anthony van Dyck (1599–1641), by the second half of the 17th century Hanneman had established himself as a prominent portraitist in The Hague. In the 1650s and 1660s, Hanneman was one of the most solicited portraitists of both the Dutch court and the English court in exile. It was therefore only natural that Willem III van Oranje (1650–1702), future king of England, would choose Hanneman to paint a posthumous portrait in 1664 in honour of his deceased mother (Kuile 1976, 113).

Today preserved by and exhibited at the Dutch National Portrait Gallery in The Hague – which, not coincidently, is located at the Mauritshuis building – Hanneman's *Posthumous portrait of Mary I Stuart with a servant* (c. 1664) shows Mary I wearing an Amerindian cloak of coloured feathers over a white satin gown, as well as a headdress made of red ostrich feathers (Fig 13.1). A young black servant helps Mary get dressed by tying a pearl bracelet around her wrist. He is clothed in a beautiful golden fabric, and a pearl adorns his ear. The half-opened curtain before which Mary and her servant stand reveals a background setting from classic antiquity. The rather unconventional costume worn by Mary Stuart suggests that this portrait was made on the occasion of a costume ball, or masquerade. However, while the image of noble ladies dressed up for

Boxer 1957. For the most complete analysis of Johan Maurits' accomplishments in Brazil and in Europe, see Boogaart 1979.

6 This group of artists included the painters Albert Eckhout (c. 1610–1666) and Frans Post (1612–1680), and the naturalists Willem Piso (1610–1678) and George Marcgraf (1610–1644). See Whitehead and Boeseman 1989.

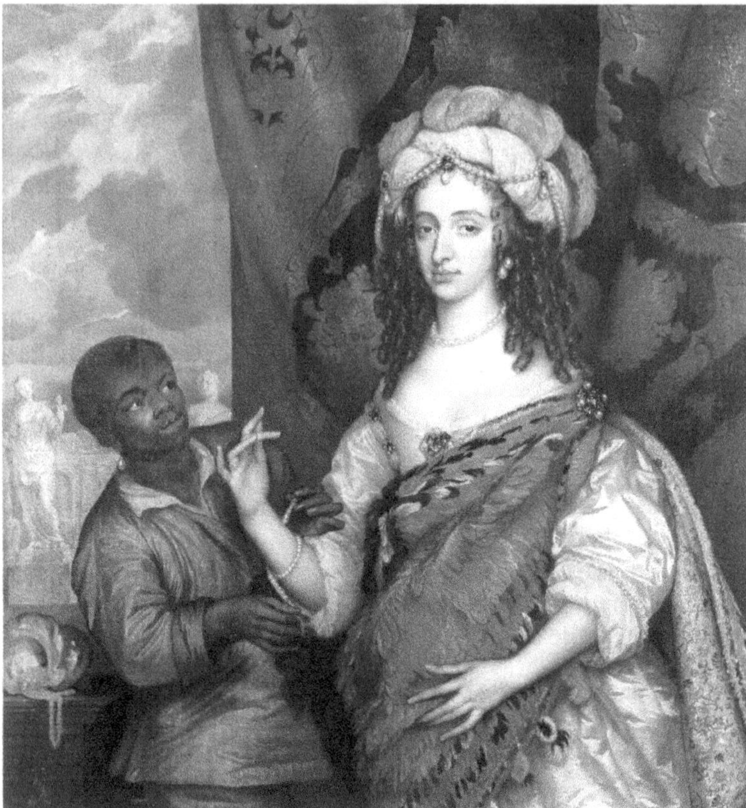

FIG 13.1. ADRIAEN HANNEMAN, *POSTHUMOUS PORTRAIT OF MARY I STUART WITH SERVANT*, C. 1664

costume parties was not an uncommon subject matter for portraits in the early modern period, the feathered ornaments, an unconventional choice of dress for a Dutch painting, highlights the uniqueness of this portrait.

At St James's Palace, in England, another portrait attributed to Hanneman presents Mary Stuart wearing a red feather cloak, presumably the same that appears in the Mauritshuis painting: *Portrait of Mary Stuart* (c. 1656). According to specialists, the painting is of poor quality. Toynbee argues that it might be a copy of a lost work by Hanneman (Toynbee 1950, 74); Millar states that it is so worn out and painted over that one cannot tell whether it is an original or a contemporary copy (Millar 1963, 115). In any case, it is not unlikely that this is the first portrait of Mary Stuart dressed as an Amerindian, from which three others were copied. Besides the Mauritshuis painting, there were once portraits of Mary Stuart with a red feather cape in the Zuilenstein Castle in the Netherlands (destroyed during World War II) and at Lord Dillon's collection at Ditchley (Millar 1963, 116). The existence of at least four different versions of this painting, as well as the prominent collections to which they belonged, attest to the importance of the subject matter.

A letter written by Elizabeth of Bohemia (1596–1662) to her nephew Charles II (1630–1685) reveals the event that motivated the painting of these specific portraits: a masquerade that occurred in January 1655 in The Hague. On that occasion, a few selected noble gentlemen danced a ballet especially written for the ball – the *Ballet de la Carmesse*. The venue where this festivity took place is not known, but the political importance of the ball cannot be underestimated. Organised by Elizabeth herself, the masquerade brought together the Dutch court of Amalia van Solms (1602–1675) and its rival counterpart, the English court in exile, as well as royal princess Mary Stuart's own court (Akkerman and Sellin 2004, 209). In a period of uncertain allegiances and political instability for both royal houses, the masquerade reaffirmed 'the extravagance of Anglo-Dutch social life at The Hague' and its success echoed in the international press (Jardine 2008, 190). As to the events of the festivity, in her letter to Mary's brother Charles II, Elizabeth recounts that 'Your sister was very well dressed like an Amazon', the Princess of Tarente like a shepherdess, the Madamoiselle d'Orange (the stadholder's daughter) like a nymph (Elizabeth of Bohemia 1742, 675). The choice of costumes was not unusual, for English masquerades commonly included characters from Greek mythology, European folklore and suchlike. However, the inclusion of the Amerindian character indicates that a new element had been incorporated into the traditional court festivity structure – namely, New World Indians.[7]

Mary Stuart's choice of costume can only be explained by Johan Maurits' presence in The Hague in the mid-1650s. There was no other collector at that time in the capital of the Dutch Republic who would not only possess, but more importantly, be in a position to willingly lend such a feather cape to be worn at a festive occasion – more often than not, *kunstkammer* items remained in the *kunstkammers*. In this sense, it is important to remember that Johan Maurits returned to Europe in disagreement with the directors of the West Indian Company. He did not hold an official position either in the political arena or in the Dutch army. For this reason, it was critical that he secure his alliances with the high nobility in The Hague. Therefore, in the 1650s he was eager to establish a good and profitable relationship with the English court in exile. By offering a red feathered cape from his collection to the royal princess, he not only pleased Mary Stuart – and thereby strengthened his relationship with the Stuart and Orange dynasties – but also made sure that his name and his deeds in Brazil would be mentioned and noticed during the festivity, even if he did not attend it. In fact, after Johan Maurits' return to The Hague, the Amerindian subject became a common theme among Dutch court festivities and events (Oudesluijs 1999, 362).

## Gift-giving and the circulation of objects

In the *Ballet de La Carmesse*, the red feather cape worn by Mary Stuart symbolised Johan Maurits' connection to the Dutch and English Royal families; likewise, it indicated that the New World and its exotic inhabitants were now an integral part of the European imaginary and symbolic political language. However, the means through which Johan Maurits obtained feathered artefacts, as well as the fate of these objects once in Europe, also demonstrate the extent to which a single ethnographic object, or a group of objects, can shed light on wider political and colonial processes – a topic which, in turn, should be explored by museums when such objects are displayed.

7 In fact, there were even some occasions when Amerindians themselves were part of court festivities. For instance, in 1644 Johan Maurits van Nassau held a reception at the Mauritshuis where he had some Tapuia Indians dance half-naked in front of his rather shocked visitors (Bots 1979, 104).

Once Johan Maurits arrived in Brazil in 1637, he immediately started to both expand the boundaries of Dutch Brazil and to establish political alliances with communities that were strategically important to his governorship. In his first military expedition to the province of Rio Grande in 1638, a group of Tapuia Indians came to meet him close to the Fortress 'Reis Magos', which the Dutch had recently conquered and renamed Fort Ceulen. The Amerindian group offered the new governor a gift containing 'beautiful and colourful bird feathers' as well as bows and arrows (Barleus 1974, 76). Although there is no record of the exact contents of this gift, it is not inaccurate to assume that at least one feather cloak was part of it. In order to show his appreciation and to reinforce the alliance with the Tapuia, Johan Maurits also rewarded them with linen, women's clothes, knives and fishhooks.

The fact that the Amerindians quickly sought to make contact with the Dutch, even before the colonisers started to develop their own alliance tactics, is worthy of attention. This indicates that the Tapuia were well aware not only of the presence and movements of the new governor but also of the strategic political alliance they could make with the Dutch against the Portuguese. In other words, the Tapuia had their own agenda and acted as political agents in the colonial world. Giving Governor Johan Maurits a set of feathered items was a tactful way of beginning an opportune political association with the then ruling power in Northeastern Brazil.

In fact, in the early modern period, gift-giving was one of the most useful and effective ways to begin, maintain or enhance political alliances. In the Dutch 17th-century Atlantic, this practice was by no means an exception. The contents of a gift were always carefully chosen. They would include materials and artefacts such as beaver fur from the colonies in North America, textiles such as silk from the East Indies, Japanese lacquer work and all sorts of strange and peculiar animals from all over the world (Brook 2008). For instance, the South American parrot was one of the most wanted commodities in the colonial period, but larger animals such as Indian elephants and rhinoceros were also given to European rulers (Bedini 1998). In this chain of cultural interactions, South American Indigenous groups provided Europeans with all sorts of multi-coloured bird feathers, as well as artefacts made of them. The German count received many other such gifts from Amerindians.

Just as the feather cloaks and other feathered items entered Johan Maurits' collection as gifts from Indigenous allies, it was also through gift-giving that some of these items were removed from the collection. In 1654, the German count gave his cousin Frederik III (1609–1670), king of Denmark, a most valuable present. This would not be the first time that elements from Johan Maurits' *kunstkammer* would be sent away as gifts; in 1652, just two years earlier, he had given Friedrich Wilhelm, Great Elector of Brandenburg (1620–1688), Brazilian wooden furniture, ivory and more than a thousand natural history drawings (Lemmens 1979; Bencard 2008). The gift to the Elector signalled and sealed the political alliance between these two nobles, which would be the most profitable and useful of Johan Maurits' political relationships in the decades to come.[8] The gift for the Danish king followed the same logic of creating and maintaining political alliances. While in Brazil, Johan Maurits met Admiral Christoff Lindenov (c. 1612–1679), a Dane who was working for the Dutch West Indian Company in South America. As a high-ranking officer, Lindenov had access to the Danish royal family. Once he returned to Europe in 1644,

8 The Elector of Brandenburg helped Johan Maurits be appointed Prince of the Holy Roman-German Empire in 1653. On Johan Maurits' relationship to Brandenburg, see Opgenoorth 1979 as well as the recent collection of essays edited by Brunn and Neutsch 2008.

he worked as an intermediary between the Danish crown and the Dutch nobility. As such, he indicated to Johan Maurits that Frederik III was interested in adding Brazilian ethnographica to his own *kunstkammer* (Bencard 2008, 166). In 1649, Frederik III granted Johan Maurits and his brother Hendrik van Nassau Siegen (1611–1652) membership of the Danish Order of the Elephant, the most important noble Order in Denmark. Five years later, the German count decided to offer nothing less than the 26 portraits and still-lifes which Albert Eckhout had painted for him in Brazil. A letter dated 1654 attests that these paintings were sent via Lindenov (Thomsen 1938, 11–12). Furthermore, this document also suggests that other ethnographic items accompanied the paintings.

There has been much scholarly discussion as to whether or not Johan Maurits gave Frederik III ethnographic material for his royal museum. In a recent study, the Danish Museum's curator Berete Due analysed the provenance of a number of artefacts related to Johan Maurits and concluded, with some reluctance, that the feather items may have been given by him (Due 2002, 190).[9] In fact, a detailed comparison of the collection's inventories dated 1617, 1674, 1696, 1737 and 1743 shows that there were three sources of Brazilian ethnographic items: Bernard Paludanus' collection, acquired via the incorporation by royal decree of the Duke of Gottorp's *kunstkammer* in 1742; the collection of naturalist Ole Worm (1588–1654), bought by the Danish king in 1654, which included South American items given to Worm by Dutch scholar and WIC director Johannes de Laet (1581–1649) (Schepelern 1971, 72); and finally Johan Maurits' gift. It is remarkable that, in all three cases, the South American elements arrived in Denmark through Dutch hands. It is even more remarkable that in the two latter cases, the German count was directly responsible for collecting and bringing the items to Europe, since Johannes de Laet never visited the New World and had obtained his objects from the former governor of Dutch Brazil.

Johan Maurits possessed a large quantity of Brazilian and some African material, and he repeatedly gifted portions to a number of beneficiaries: the Botanical Garden of Leiden University; Amalia van Solms, the Great Elector of Brandenburg; and finally French king Louis XIV (1638–1715). It is therefore likely that several of the 16th- and 17th-century Brazilian items currently housed in the Danish museum were given to Frederik III by Count Johan Maurits. These garments and crafts once belonged to South American Indigenous groups; through the hands of the Tapuia, they found their way into Johan Maurits' *kunstkammer*; and after being showcased to the high Dutch and English nobility, they became symbols of Johan Maurits' allegiance to the Danish royal house. In Copenhagen the feathered ornaments found their last home and thus ended a long circuit of symbolic and material exchanges that had started in the backlands of Portuguese America and ended in European courts.

## Conclusion

The Tupi feather cloak now housed in Denmark is a remarkable artefact for multiple reasons. First, and most obviously, it is one of the few feather ornaments from the colonial epoch that still exist today, and as such it is worthy of careful preservation, attention and study. However, this object's biography makes it truly extraordinary. Its trajectory is the key to uncovering connec-

9 The first scholar to suggest that Johan Maurits' gift included ethnographic items was Thomsen 1938. For recent discussions, see Brienen 2006 and Buono 2007.

tions, conflicts and social processes that took shape while this artefact was being given, worn and displayed. The feather cape is a significant example of how meaning and value are not inherent properties of an artefact but rather social and historical constructs.

Though one cannot be completely sure about their use in pre-Columbian times, it is very likely that feather cloaks were used by warriors and shamans in ritualistic performances. After 1500, these objects started to be manufactured by the Tupi with the purpose of being exchanged for goods with European travellers and explorers. In the particular case of the feather cloak that made Mary Stuart look like an Amazon in the eyes of the audience in the Hague festivity of 1655, it was possibly part of a larger gift given by Tapuias to Johan Maurits van Nassau. In this context, the feather cape was no longer a ritualistic dress but rather a materialisation of that Indigenous group's alliance with the Dutch conquerors. It had, therefore, a political meaning that surpassed its original purpose. When Count Johan Maurits took his feathered artefacts back to the Netherlands and exhibited them to the Dutch nobility, they acquired yet another meaning also embedded in political relations: they symbolised Johan Maurits' governorship in Brazil, his deeds and successes in maintaining order in a colony that by then was already at risk of being lost. In other words, Johan Maurits' whole collection, including the feathered ornaments, represented the richness and prosperity of Dutch Brazil while in the hands of its most ingenious leader. During the *Ballet de La Carmesse*, the fact that a feather cape was worn by the royal princess pointed to two important facts: on the one hand, the place of the New World and its exotic inhabitants in European imaginary alongside elements from the ancient world; on the other hand, it personified Johan Maurits' alliance with the English court in exile. A few years later, by giving ethnographic artefacts – and Eckhout's ethnographic portraits – to the king of Denmark, Johan Maurits secured his position as an ally of the Northern European Protestant dynasties. At the same time, by having at least one of his feathered capes enter into one of Europe's greatest *kunstkammers* of its time, Johan Maurits made sure his name would be unequivocally and forever linked to his presence and accomplishments in the New World.

Nowadays, visitors can see a red feather cape (the same that was exhibited in Brazil in 2000) in a rather small room dedicated to South American peoples at the 'Peoples of the World' exhibition in the Danish National Museum. It is placed inside a glass cabinet with other ethnographic material, such as a Brazilian club and arrows. Five Eckhout portraits of native Brazilians line the wall in front of the cloak. In this room some of the surviving pieces of Johan Maurits' gift to Frederik III are kept together. By simply looking at these items, one is confronted with the complexities of the colonial encounter that took place between Brazil and the Netherlands in the mid-17th century. However, through closer examination, these artefacts help to shed light on the detailed, deep interconnections that engaged representatives of the Dutch West Indian Company, the Dutch nobility and Amerindian groups, whose agency is much too often under-appreciated by traditional historiography.

Ultimately, the cloak's appearance in the Brazilian Rediscovery Exhibit added yet another layer of significance to the biography of this much-coveted object, insofar as it allowed present-day Tupinambá Indians to draw attention to their continuing struggle for the recognition of their heritage and their rights. As a result of the political concern raised by this struggle, the Brazilian 2000 exhibition of the feather cloak became itself also part of this object's biography, proving once more that it is the object's movement – not merely the object itself – that gives it meaning. As Mary Bouquet has suggested, the public of an exhibition is not passive but rather becomes active in the shaping of an object's meaning (Bouquet 2000, 221). The value of (museum) objects lies in their circulation, their movement – including their production, their consumption, their shifting usages and, last but not least, their movement from one collection or exhibition to another. Hopefully, future exhibitions of this feathered artefact will take its biography into account and give visitors the chance not only to admire its peculiar trajectory but also to reflect on the complex nature of colonial history, which is particularly well represented by the coat's very biography.

## Bibliography and References


Akkerman, N, and Sellin, P, 2004 A Stuart Masque in Holland. Ballet de La Carmesse de La Haya (1655), *Ben Jonson Journal* 11, 207–58

Appadurai, A, 1986 Introduction: Commodities and the Politics of Value, in *The Social Life of Things: Commodities in Cultural Perspective* (ed A Appadurai), Cambridge University Press, Cambridge, 3–63

Barleus, C, 1974 (1647) *História dos Feitos Recentemente Praticados Durante Oito Anos no Brasil*, Edusp and Itatiaia, São Paulo and Belo Horizonte

Bedini, S, 1998 *The Pope's Elephant*, J S Sanders & Company, Nashville

Bencard, M, 2008 Fürstliche Geschenke, in *Sein Feld war die Welt. Johann Moritz von Nassau-Siegen (1604–1679) Von Siegen über die Niederlande und Brasilien nach Brandenburg* (eds G Brunn and C Neutsch), Waxmann Verlag, Münster, 159–77

Bergvelt, E, and Kistemaker, R (eds), 1992 *De Wereld binnen Handbereik. Nederlandse kunst- en rariteiten-verzamelingen, 1585–1735*, Waanders, Zwolle

Boogaart, E (ed), 1979 *Johan Maurits van Nassau-Siegen 1604–1679. Essays on the Occasion of the Tercentenary of his Death*, The Johan Maurits van Nassau Stichting, The Hague

Bots, H, 1979 Johann Moritz und seine Beziehungen zu Constantijn Huygens, in *Soweit der Erdkreis Reicht. Johann Moritz von Nassau-Siegen, 1604–1679* (ed G Werd), Stadt Kleve, Kleve, 101–106

Bouquet, M, 2000 Thinking and Doing Otherwise: Anthropological Theory in Exhibitionary Practice, *Ethnos* 65 (2), 217–36

Boxer, C, 1957 *The Dutch in Brazil 1624–1654*, Clarendon Press, Oxford

Brienen, R, 2006 *Visions of Savage Paradise. Albert Eckhout, Court Painter in Colonial Dutch Brazil*, Amsterdam University Press, Amsterdam

Brook, T, 2008 *Vermeer's Hat. The Seventeenth Century and the Dawn of the Global World*, Bloomsbury Press, New York

Brunn, G, and Neutsch, C (eds), 2008 *Sein Feld war die Welt. Johann Moritz von Nassau-Siegen (1604–1679). Von Siegen über die Niederlande und Brasilien nach Brandenburg*, Waxmann Verlag, Münster

Buono, A, 2007 Feathered Identities and Plumed Performances: Tupinambá Interculture in early modern Brazil and Europe, unpublished PhD thesis, California University at Santa Barbara

Caversan, L, 2000 Carta de Caminha e manto são preferidos no Redescobrimento, *Folha de São Paulo*, 11 May, E1

Due, B, 1979/80 A Shaman's Cloak?, *Folk* 21/22, 257–62

— 2002 Brazilian Artifacts in the Royal Kunstkammer, in *Albert Eckhout Returns to Brazil, 1644–2002*, Nationalmuseet, Copenhagen, 187–99

Elizabeth of Bohemia, 1742 Letter to Charles II, 17 January 1655, in *A Collection of the State Papers of John Thurloe, volume 1: 1638–1653* (ed T Birch), Thomas Woodward, London, 675

Feest, C, 1993 European Collecting of American Indian Artefacts and Art, *Journal of the History of Collections* 3 (1), 1–11

Fernandes, F, 1970 *A Função Social da Guerra na Sociedade Tupinambá*, Editora Nacional, São Paulo

Gelder, R, 1998 Paradijsvogels in Enkhuizen. De relatie tussen Van Linschoten en Bernardus Paludanus, in *Souffrir pour Parvenir. De Wereld van Jan Huygen van Linschoten* (eds R Gelder, J Parmentier, and V Roeper), Arcadia, Haarlem, 30–50

Hennin, J, 1681 *De Zinrijke Gedachten toegepast op de Vijf Sinnen van's Menschen Verstand*, Jan Claasen ten Hoorn, Amsterdam

Jardine, L, 2008 *Going Dutch. How England Plundered Holland's Glory*, Harper Colllins, New York

Kuile, O, 1976 *Adriaen Hanneman, 1604–1671. Een Haags Portretschilder*, Vis-

Druk, Alphen aan den Rijn

Lemmens, G, 1979 Die Schenkung an Ludwig XIV und die Auflösung der Brasilianischen Sammlung des Johann Moritz 1652–1679, in *Soweit der Erdkreis Reicht. Johann Moritz von Nassau-Siegen, 1604–1679* (ed G Werd), Stadt Kleve, Kleve, 265–93

Léry, J, 1578 *Histoire d'un voyage fait en la terre du Brésil, autrement dite Amérique*, Antonie Chuppin, La Rochelle

Mason, P, 1994 From Presentation to Representation: Americana in Europe, *Journal of the History of Collections* 6 (1), 1–20

Métraux, A, 1928 *La Civilisation Matérielle des Tribus Tupi-Guarani*, Libraire Orientaliste P. Geuthner, Paris

— 1979 (1928) *A Religião dos Tupinambá*, 2 edn, Editora Nacional, São Paulo

Millar, O, 1963 *The Tudor-Stuart and Early Georgian Pictures in the Collection of Her Majesty the Queen*, Phaidon Press, London

Monteiro, J, 1999 The crises and transformations of invaded societies: coastal Brazil in the sixteenth century, in *The Cambridge History of the Native Peoples of the Americas*, volume III, part 1 (eds F Solomon and S Schwartz), Cambridge University Press, Cambridge, 973–1023

Opgenoorth, E, 1979 Johan Maurits as Stadholder of Cleves under the Elector of Brandenburg, in *Johan Maurits van Nassau-Siegen 1604–1679. Essays on the occasion of the tercentenary of his death* (ed E Boogaart), The Johan Maurits van Nassau Stichting, The Hague, 39–53

Oudesluijs, D, 1999 Albertine-Agnes van Oranje-Nassau, vorstin van Nassau-Dietz, in *Onder den Oranje boom. Nederlandse kunst en cultuur aan Duitse vorstenhoven in de zeventiende en achttiende eeuw* (ed M Schacht), Hirmer Verlag, München, 357–68

Schepelern, H, 1971 *Museum Wormianum, dets forudsaetninger og tilblivelse*, Wormianum, Odense

— 1985 Natural Philosophers and Princely Collectors: Worm, Paludanus, and the Gottorp and Copenhagen Collections, in *The Origins of Museums. The Cabinet of Curiosities in Sixteenth- and Seventeenth-Century Europe* (eds O Impey and A MacGregor), Clarendon Press, Oxford, 121–27

Staden, H, 2008 (1557) *Hans Staden's True History. An Account of Cannibal Captivity in Brazil* (eds N Whitehead and M Harbsmeier), Duke University Press, Durham and London

Thevet, A, 1557 *Les Singularitez de la France Antarctique, Autrement Nommée Amerique & de Plusieurs Terres & Isles Decouvertes de nostre Temps*, Heritiers de Maurice de la Porte, Paris

Thomsen, T, 1938 *Albert Eckhout. Ein niderländischer Maler und sein Gönner Moritz der Brasilianer. Ein Kulturbild aus dem 17. Jahrhundert*, Munksgaard, Copenhagen

Toynbee, M, 1950 Adriaen Hanneman and the English Court in Exile, *The Burlington Magazine* 92 (564), 73–80

Vorstius, A, 1979 letter to Constantijn Huygens, 12 December 1644, in *Zo Wijd de Wereld Strekt*, Mauritshuis, The Hague, 239–41

Whitehead, P, and Boeseman, M, 1989 *A Portrait of Dutch 17th century Brazil. Animals, plants and people by the artists of Johan Maurits of Nassau*, North-Holland Publishing, Amsterdam

14

# Individual, Collective and Institutional Biographies: The Beasley Collection of Pacific Artefacts

Lucie Carreau

Ethnographic collections housed in museums are, in theory, no different from any other collections of arts or crafts. They are made of objects assembled by a collector with a particular motive, in a particular historical and cultural context. In practice, however, ethnographic collections tell a very different story.

From the outset, collecting from the Pacific was the by-product of a scientific project of discovery and encounters. Although some ethnographic objects had been displayed in *wunderkammer* and cabinets of curiosities in the Renaissance period, it was James Cook's three voyages of exploration (1768–71, 1772–75 and 1776–79) that revealed the Pacific to Britain. It was not until the middle of the 19th century, however, that these 'artificial curiosities' (Kaeppler 1978; Thomas 1994) became objects of scientific enquiry. The development of ethnology, ethnography and anthropology in the late 19th century placed 'exotic' material at the centre of a broader field of scientific enquiry aimed at unlocking the mysteries and diversity of mankind. This shift in the perception of ethnographic objects triggered a new attitude within academia and museums. Because each new piece of material culture could contribute to a better understanding of foreign lands and peoples – and by extension, of our lands and peoples – collecting artefacts from the cultures of Oceania, Africa or North America became a scientific priority (Gowland 1904, 13–14).

The fact that ethnographic material culture and knowledge became entangled with science had a strong impact on collection-making. On the one hand, collections made by scientists in the field (regardless of their area of expertise) were considered rational and systematic and held great potential to contribute to the advancement of science. On the other, collections made by 'amateurs' gathering objects on the British market (auction houses, dealers, etc) were considered of little scientific significance. For over a century, the professional biographies of those who formed collections were determinant in assessing the quality and potential of those collections to contribute to scientific and museum discourses. In the last 30 years, however, some publications have attempted to challenge this view and revealed non-professional collections as complex constructions informing a wider colonial context (see Stanley 1989; Corbey 2000; O'Hanlon and Welsch 2001).

Interestingly, as I began my doctoral research on private collector Harry Geoffrey Beasley (1882–1939) in 2004 (Carreau 2009), I met with an array of warnings. Several academics and museum professionals explained that although Beasley's collection of Pacific material contained many interesting pieces, the collection as a whole was more an accumulation of objects made by a money-maker and passionate amateur than a careful and rationalised scientific assemblage. Simultaneously, contemporary private collectors warned me that, in their view, Beasley did not have 'a good eye' and his collection was of low quality. In short, Beasley's approach to collecting

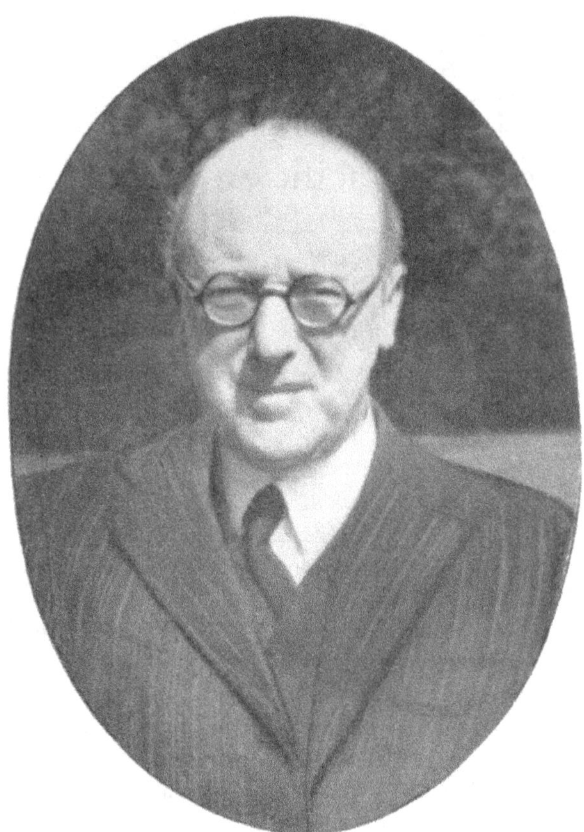

FIG 14.1.
PHOTOGRAPH OF HARRY BEASLEY, 1939

and, as we shall see, his biography were not considered scientific enough to make his collection fit within the broad disciplines of anthropology and ethnology, nor were they aesthetically stimulating enough to position him as a precursor-collector in the field of primitive art.

Beasley was a director of the North Kent Brewery, a family business based in Plumstead, near London (Fig 14.1). Very little is known about his professional life and his involvement in the brewery. Similarly, little remains to inform us about his private life and personal interests, and there is no statement about what he set out to achieve with his ethnographic collection. What remains, however, is a collection of over 10,000 objects scattered in public and private collections throughout the world, four ledgers in which the collector recorded his acquisitions between 1904 and 1939, two ledgers in which he recorded his visits to museums in and outside Britain,[1] and some correspondence between Beasley and a few museum professionals.

If Beasley's biography is little more than fragmentary, the few elements that are known place him in the less distinguished 'amateur' and 'unprofessional' category of collectors. Nick Stanley, in his examination of missionary collections, has observed that, in a museum context, collections

1 The four acquisition ledgers and two ledgers (entitled 'Home' and 'Abroad') recording Beasley's visits to museums are housed in the Centre for Anthropology, British Museum, London.

are often considered 'contaminated by those who make them' (1989, 107). Collections made by amateurs (ie individuals located outside a museum or academic framework) thus appear unsuited to a museum discourse built around notions of science and education and based on *systematic* and *rationalised* collecting practices.

There is little doubt that individual personalities and specific interests in aspects of material culture are often visible through the examination of these non-professional collections. However, this is by no means limited to individuals outside the professional fields. Recent publications have illustrated how individual input and personal interest also occurred within professional institutions (Gosden and Knowles 2001; Gosden and Larson 2008). Collections are always 'contaminated' (to use Stanley's term) by the people who make them. The contaminant, however, varies and determines the appropriateness and suitability of a collection to fit a particular museum's discourse.

This chapter demonstrates how the limits of Beasley's biography can be challenged by a closer examination of individual objects' biographies and that of the collection. The very act of selecting objects and articulating them within a developing collection informs the collector's attempts at creating an order reflecting his knowledge and position within a large network of individuals and institutions preoccupied with ethnographic material culture. On a smaller scale, individual objects' biographies reveal that objects were not always collected for their materiality but sometimes for the potential they held to weave relationships between Beasley and other individuals and institutions, in Beasley's past and present.

By highlighting the entanglement of object, individual and institutional biographies (see Thomas 1991), this paper advocates the necessity to engage with collections following a plurivocal and pluri-biographical model. The collection is here divided into distinctive biographical trends to demonstrate the continuity, plurality and concomitance of biographical elements within and beyond a given collection of artefacts. Four distinctive biographical 'aspects' are here under scrutiny: the collector, the private museum, the objects and collection, and Beasley's collection after the collector's death.

Beasley's private collection (1893/5–1928) marks the emergence of the collection and the development of Beasley's network and persona. The transformation of the private collection into a private museum, the Cranmore Ethnographical Museum (Chislehurst, Kent), in 1928 marks the beginning of the second biographical aspect of the collection, lasting until Beasley's death in 1939. The shift from personal to institutional voice had a significant impact not only on the collection but also on its perception and resonance in the ethnographical world within and outside Britain. The third section examines how the biographies of the collection and of individual objects impacted on the collector's discourse and his own biography. Lastly, the dispersal of Beasley's collection and its subsequent (and ongoing) absorption into British public museums questions the abilities of museums to retain, interpret and make visible the complex, multiple and combined aspects of a collection and collector's biographies when a collection has become fragmented.

## Emergence and Development of a Private Collection: 1893/5–1928

As mentioned above, little is known about Beasley. As a director of his family business, he had the financial means to engage in what was to become the central activity of his life: the collection of ethnographic material. His collection was one of the most extensive in early 20th-century Britain, numbering over 10,000 artefacts from Oceania, Africa, the Americas, Asia and northern Europe. The largest sub-collection was that of the Pacific, on which this essay will draw, numbering over 6000 objects.

Beasley never travelled to the Pacific. His knowledge of the antipodes derived from the publications and objects he had access to and gathered. Although he collected his first object in the late 19th century while still a schoolboy,[2] it was not until the beginning of the 20th century that he started developing his collection on a large scale. Beasley's ledgers are invaluable sources of information, for their qualitative and quantitative examination reflects the various transformations of the collection.

The ledgers reveal that during the first years of the century most of his acquisitions were through dealers (such as W D Webster and W O Oldman), sales rooms (such as Stevens and Glendinning's Auction Rooms) and junk shops or curio shops in and around London. Such sources by no means isolated the collector within a non-scientific community. Dealers' shops and auction rooms were not only populated by the handful of private collectors and dealers interested in ethnographic material at the time but were also buzzing with a number of curators from the British Museum, Pitt Rivers Museum and Cambridge Museum of Archaeology and Anthropology, all eager to acquire objects to complement their existing collections. While anthropology was starting to advocate methods of collection based on ethnographic fieldwork *in situ* (ie in Oceania), museums were continuing to acquire through non-professional sources.

Throughout the early years of the century, the collection grew slowly but steadily, with an average of 30 artefacts a year (Beasley 1904–39). In the 1910s, Beasley's yearly acquisitions tripled (ibid). While this change of pace in the collection was partly due to the developing market in ethnographic material (Corbey 2000), it was also the result of Beasley's pro-active search for artefacts and his abilities to generate the opportunities leading to the development of the collection. To begin with, Beasley's acquisition ledgers reveal that he extended his collecting territory to continental Europe, where he became acquainted with dealers and private collectors in France and Germany, gaining access to objects originating from French and German colonies in the Pacific. Missions (in particular the Melanesian Mission and the London Missionary Society) and their associated missionaries also became great sources of artefacts during this period (O'Hanlon and Welsch 2001).

Another element that impacted greatly on Beasley's persona and collection was his election as a fellow of the Royal Anthropological Institute in 1914. Only a handful of collectors had been accepted within the circle of the Institute at the time. Beasley's interest and involvement in the Institute's activities is reflected by the various positions he held, being elected to the Council for the first time in 1920 and the Executive Committee in 1931, and being Vice-President in 1932 (Waterfield 2006, 79). Through the RAI, Beasley not only gained access to knowledge about the geographical areas he collected from and awareness about the current debates. Being a Fellow allowed him to publish (he contributed 25 short articles to the Journal of the *Royal Anthropological Institute* and *Man* between 1914 and 1938, in which he usually showcased some of his new acquisitions) and to gain access to objects. Indeed, the Institute's fellows also counted many individuals involved in colonial activities (missionaries, traders, colonial administrators),

2 Some sources state that Beasley bought a Melanesian lime spatula in 1893 (Palmeira Auction Rooms catalogue 1975, 3), others affirm that his collecting started in 1895 with the purchase of a few weapons from the Pacific (Miles 1939, 3; West 1982, 1).

who would contribute papers to the Institutes' ordinary meetings. These individuals became a valuable source of objects and information about who had come back from the Pacific (and thus, where objects could be found).

Although joining the RAI marked a profound turn in Beasley's networking and collecting strategies, his activities were not impermeable to political and economic disruptions. World War I greatly impacted on the activities of the collector. From 1915, Beasley was involved in wireless telegraphy in the Flying Corps, a full-time activity that would keep him away from home and away from his collection.[3] Acquisitions decreased significantly and it was not until 1920 that Beasley was able to resume the development of his collection (Acquisition Ledger, vol II).

While Beasley's objects and ledgers do not provide enough information to reconstruct the collector's endeavour with accuracy, they are valuable elements through which to engage with his transforming collecting practices, developing network and growing expertise. Beasley's collection was private in that it was personal, kept away from public view and made visible to only a *chosen* few. This notion of choice is crucial to understanding the first phase of the collection. From selection to labelling, from publication to networking, Beasley appears to be the central and possibly sole figure dictating the direction in which his collection was to develop. But was he? From the 1910s, Beasley started looking back on material he had acquired earlier, resulting sometimes in the exclusion of artefacts from his collection and their sale or exchange with other individuals or institutions (Acquisition ledgers, vols I–IV). This reflective approach may be seen as demonstrating a better expertise, but can the development of his expertise be detached from the expansion of his network of relationships, his wider access to knowledge through the RAI and his museum acquaintances? Can the transformation of his private collection into a private museum be isolated from the contemporaneous change in Britain's ethnographic museums and his familiarity with these museums' collections and personnel? While there is no doubt that Beasley was in control of his collection, it is essential to highlight how other institutional and individual biographies have determined, consciously or unconsciously, the path taken by the collector and his collection.

## From Individual to Institutional Voice: The Creation of the Cranmore Ethnographical Museum

In 1927, Beasley, his family and his collection moved to a house called 'Cranmore', in Walden Road, Chislehurst, Kent. The collection was given a specific space in a separate building, fitted out with state-of-the-art cases from Sage & Co, electric ceiling lights and under-floor heating.

The Cranmore Ethnographical Museum opened in early 1928 and was developed several times between 1928 and 1937 (Miles 1939, 3). Up until 1934, the museum was formed of a large room exhibiting artefacts from all continents (Fig 14.2). In 1934, an annex was added to display the Benin and Tibetan collections. In 1937, a third gallery exhibiting his Northwest Coast and Inuit collections opened, leaving Oceania as the main focus of the original and much larger gallery.

With the transformation of the collection into an institution, Beasley became its Director and recruited a team. His first private secretary and curator was Arthur Madan, who, during his

3 Honolulu, Bernice Pauahi Bishop Museum archives, MS SC Brigham 1.5, letter from Beasley to Brigham (director of the Bishop Museum), 1 November 1917.

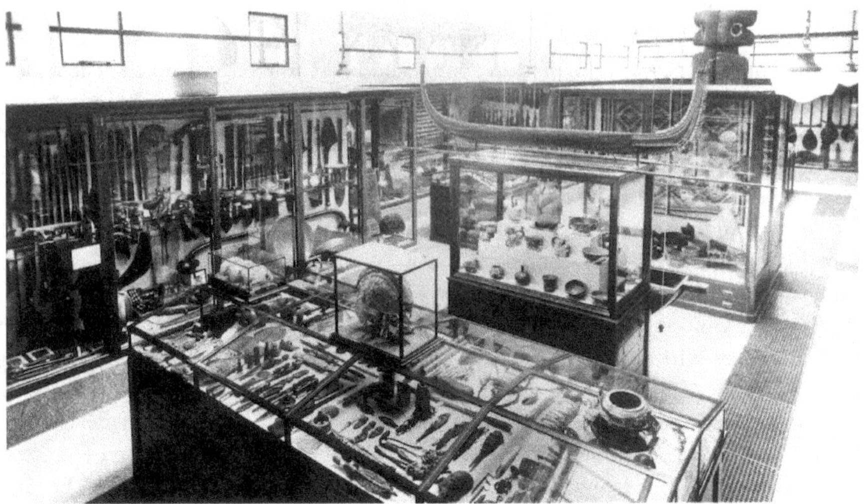

FIG 14.2.
POSTCARD OF THE CRANMORE ETHNOGRAPHICAL MUSEUM, 1933

tenure, became a fellow of the Museums Association (1929) and the RAI (1930). Through the former institution he undertook one of the first exams conferring museum qualifications to individuals and left the Cranmore Museum for a curatorial position at the Torquay Museum in 1933 (Chandler 2007). Gerald Miles replaced him at Cranmore in 1934, also joining the Museums Association and the RAI (1935). He was seconded by Miss Joyce Gillett, assistant curator.

The adjunction of the team transformed the collection. While Beasley remained in charge of deciding what was to be acquired, the curatorial team helped locate new sources of artefacts, answered and initiated correspondence and processed newly-acquired objects by inscribing them in the ledgers and labelling them. Beasley's private collection was a single-headed and single-handed enterprise. The Museum, however, while remaining single-headed, became multi-handed. Objects could be processed quicker and in larger numbers: an average of 400 objects were added each year (Acquisition Ledgers, vol III–IV).

This shift from personal to institutional was crucial. Despite Beasley's connection to the RAI and many museum professionals in Britain and abroad, his status remained that of a private collector with extensive financial means but no professionally recognised status and position. Establishing the Cranmore Museum gave him the credentials to position himself closer to the museum and academic realm and gain recognition as a professional. As a consequence, it helped him weave new relationships with other professionals worldwide who had not been keen on including private collectors within their networks. The Bernice Pauahi Bishop Museum in Honolulu had been the only museum exchanging artefacts with Beasley prior to the establishment of the Cranmore Museum (Acquisition Ledger vol I). The institutionalisation of Beasley's collection marked a great shift in acquisition practices. Many museums in Britain (Bristol, Cardiff, Dover, Edinburgh, Kelso, Salisbury, York), France (La Rochelle), Germany (Hamburg), New Zealand (Dunedin), Sweden (Gothenburg), The Netherlands (Amsterdam, Leiden) and the USA (Chicago, Salem) now considered the Cranmore Museum trustworthy enough to sell or exchange parts of their collections (Acquisition Ledgers, vol II–III).

To further his institutional claim, Beasley attempted to legitimise his institution and present it as a credible and professional exchange partner. Between 1928 and 1938, he published monthly the following advertisement in the *Museums Journal*:

> The curator of the CRANMORE ETHNOGRAPHICAL MUSEUM, Chislehurst, Kent, founded in 1895, would be glad to enter into correspondence for the acquisition, either by purchase, or exchange, of ETHNOLOGICAL SPECIMENS. The principal interests of the Museum are; – The South Seas, New Zealand, North and South America, Benin, and the Esquimaux peoples. (Beasley 1931, front matter)

In this advertisement, Beasley makes no mention of the private status of the Museum. To add to the legitimacy of the institution, he also invented a date of foundation, 1895, the date when he, as a 'private collector', bought his first object (aged 13). There was a clear effort to create a history of the museum, to make it look as public as possible and to give it an air of respectability and permanence through age.

This new identity brought a new dimension to the collection. As a 'museum', Cranmore aimed at displaying ethnographic material culture in a rationalised and museographical way. Its internal ordering – geographical and typological within each geographical area – was inspired by the displays of many contemporaneous collections in Britain and abroad ('Home' and 'Abroad' ledgers). Objects were labelled and, sometimes, contextualised by small text panels or drawings. In this new setting, Beasley attempted to remove domesticity and personality from his display, moving toward rationalism and professionalism. The Cranmore museum was a museum, not a home, a study-room or an office, the only visible sign of Beasley's presence being the few ashtrays scattered around the galleries. Transformed into museum phenomena, Beasley collection objects evoked social, cultural and historical contexts prior to their acquisition by the British collector, while the context of their 'museumification' (ie the set of relationships and influences that led Beasley to *select* these artefacts) remained invisible. Following Roberta Bonetti, 'the [museum] artefact does not appear for what it is – that is, a process set in motion by the encounter between people and institutions within a social milieu, its *habitus* – but as something with a univocal, universal status' (2007, 169).

Despite its obvious connection to other displays in Britain and abroad, the Cranmore Museum was not a replica. Beasley had been visiting museums and private collections across Europe and in the United States throughout his collecting career. His impressions (and lists of objects he was eager to acquire!) were recorded in two ledgers entitled 'Home' and 'Abroad'. Short comments about the casing, lighting, labelling and general arranging of collections visited demonstrate that Beasley's interests reached beyond the act of collecting. Such interest in museography[4] materialised in an article Beasley published in the *Museums Journal* in 1933. 'New Suggestions on Museum Lay-Out' engaged with the technical side of museum-making (cases, lights, dust, etc). The article was not specifically directed to the display of ethnographic material, nor did it even mention the Cranmore Museum. The concept of a museum was at the core of the paper, not the content of a museum.

4 At the beginning of the 20th century, the term encompassed a narrower range of ideas than today – concerned with issues of space and display that would confront the director or curator of a museum (Gob and Drouet 2003, 11), not the public.

His interest in museography is further highlighted by his acquaintance with French academic George Henri Rivière. Rivière, who contributed to 70 exhibitions at the Musée du Trocadéro between 1928 and 1937, had conducted extensive museological research in Europe (in particular, Scandinavia). He was considered the father of a new museology which he developed at the Musée des Arts et Traditions Populaires, Paris, in 1937 (Rivière 1993). Rivière visited the Cranmore Museum several times – it was included in one of his research tours to museums in Northern Europe – and corresponded with Beasley regularly. It is thus likely that his thoughts and museological experiments inspired the British collector.

But the Cranmore Museum was also much more than a gallery. Throughout the years, Beasley created structures and devices in which the wide range of material he gathered could be duplicated (through casting or photography), preserved and interpreted (Miles 1939). The Museum included a workshop and a large reference library relating to the various geographical areas from which he collected. Beasley also created a journal, *Ethnologia Cranmorensis*.[5] Each issue was made available to ethnological museums, free of charge. While Beasley and his curator, Miles, contributed several articles, the journal also published papers from a number of established scholars and curators discussing topics related to ethnological matters. Most of the articles drew on material culture, incorporating many artefacts from Beasley's collection.

Examining the development and functioning of the Cranmore Ethnographical Museum reveals a hitherto unknown but significant aspect of Beasley's project. Following Beasley's death in 1939, the collection has mainly been engaged with as a private and personal endeavour, as an assemblage of objects that reflected Beasley's expertise (or lack thereof). In the 70 years since it was divided, the collection has never been considered as a whole that would reflect a museological or research experiment. It has never been considered a 'proper' museum collection. Beasley's freedom to experiment was, however, dependent on the private status of the collection. None of the museum professionals operating in public institutions at the time were given such freedom to explore and engage with their collections in novel ways. None of the institutions displaying ethnographic material had the financial resources to attempt such experiments.

In many ways, Beasley's very fragmentary personal biography has eclipsed the rich institutional biography of the Museum he created. The collection's resonance today could, however, be greatly enhanced by a wider recognition of the entanglement between personal and institutional biographies. Moreover, it seems essential to acknowledge that both personal and institutional biographies feed from and inform the biography of the collection as a whole and that of individual objects in the collection. In Beasley's case and, I would argue, in the majority of cases, personal, institutional, collection and object biographies are elements that need to be examined *together* in order to illuminate the complexity of the collection and of the collector's endeavour.

## COLLECTION AND OBJECTS' BIOGRAPHIES

A number of individual objects illustrate Beasley's personal interest and life. Although very little is known about Beasley's family, glimpses of relationships and interactions are visible by examining the collection and the acquisition ledgers. His aunt, Mrs George Beasley, gave him a Maori

5 Only four issues of *Ethnologia Cranmorensis* were published: one in 1937, two in 1938 and one in 1939.

flax basket (*kete muka*) in 1925.[6] Another relative, Mary Ann Beasley, bequeathed three Maori artefacts in 1914. It was his wife, Irene, however, who made the most significant family contribution to the collection. There is no evidence that the couple discussed potential acquisitions, nor do we know whether Irene was involved in the labelling or displaying of the collection within their home. But her input to the collection was certainly more than incidental.

Fifteen objects were acquired by Irene and presented to her husband on various occasions (such as Christmas). Up until the 1930s, she bought her presents from dealers whom her husband frequently visited, such as Oldman and Fenton in London and Heymann in Paris (Acquisition Ledgers, vol I–II). These dealers would have known which type of artefacts appealed to the collector (based on his previous purchases) and would have thus been able to advise Irene on what to buy. From the 1930s, however, Irene stopped visiting dealers and started acquiring from private sources, auction rooms and the Caledonian Market in London (Acquisition Ledgers, vol III–IV). This suggests that by the end of the 1920s Irene had not only become familiar with auction rooms but could also navigate networks of individuals who could provide her with artefacts. The presents mentioned above were particularly dear to her. When organising the partition of the collection after her husband's death, she took great care in excluding these objects from her donations to museums and kept most of them until her own death.

Despite the lack of archival evidence, Irene may have been an important figure in the development of the Beasley collection. In 1928, Harry published his first monograph: *Pacific Island Records: Fish Hooks*. The book was dedicated to 'I M B [Irene Marguerite Beasley] whose fertile mind, ever keen, has lightened my task' (1928, v). To what extent Irene participated in the intellectual or practical development of the monograph is unknown, but she may have been more than a patient observer.

As illustrated by the monograph, fishhooks were of great interest to Beasley. No doubt their portability, variety, wide distribution across the Pacific, price and easiness to display would have appealed to the collector. Beasley's obsession was such that over 40 years he compiled one of the largest and most comprehensive collections of such objects: over 800 numbered and labelled fishhooks (representing almost 15 per cent of the whole Pacific collection) and many more un-numbered ones that may have been considered better suited to study than exhibition. His monograph reflects 15 years of thorough research and was considered by Henry Balfour, curator of the Pitt Rivers Museum, as a 'praiseworthy and welcome addition to ethnological literature' (1929, 91), while Henry Skinner, curator at the Otago Museum (Dunedin, New Zealand), remarked that 'Beasley's book marks a further great advance in our knowledge and will be indispensable in museums which collect Pacific material' (1930, 309). Beasley's interest in fishhooks did not cease after the publication of his monograph, as his acquisition ledgers demonstrate that he continued to collect many specimens in the 1930s.

Combs or, rather, hair ornaments also fascinated Beasley. Shortly after the publication of *Pacific Island Records*, Beasley started conducting preliminary research in the arts and techniques of dressing and embellishing hair – a concern that he would not have personally faced, for he himself had little to dress or embellish. This new and rather sudden interest led him to acquire large quantities of them in a limited time, an enterprise facilitated by a new acquaintance, Arthur Henry Voyce (a Methodist missionary based in the Solomon Islands), who sent several

6 World Museum, Liverpool (1954.160.85).

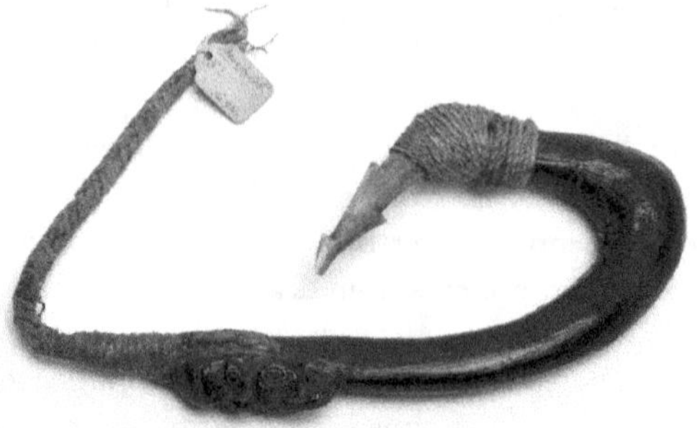

Fig 14.3.
Shark hook. New Zealand. Collected by Erskine. Wood, vegetable fibre, flax, bone. 18.5cm long. Cambridge, Museum of Archaeology and Anthropology (1977.818)

hundred of them to Cranmore along with Indigenous names of patterns and precise collection information. By 1939, Beasley had acquired over 650 combs, representing almost 12 per cent of his whole collection. The manuscript for the comb monograph was never completed due to Beasley's sudden death.[7]

Whilst individual artefacts make specific interests or relationships visible, examining the combination of objects within the collection helps interpret Beasley's project. Following its partition in several dispersed entities, the collection has often been engaged with as eclectic, and thus, made to reflect the activities of an undiscerning collector, a hoarder. In reality, the collection was conceived as an overview of Pacific material culture, across time and space.

Within Beasley's collection cohabited many voices from the past and the present, from the far and the near, and from the professional and the amateur. Beasley was always attracted to historical Pacific artefacts connected to well-known figures involved in the exploration of the Pacific. He owned a number of pieces collected by James Cook as well as Otto von Kotzebue and John Elphinstone Erskine (Fig 14.3).[8] Recent research has suggested that an object's genealogy – or 'pedigree' – is considered inscribed in it, through visible or invisible marks that previous owners have left on its surface (Derlon and Jeudy-Balliny 2008, 196). The potential to see (or feel) these marks is determined by the 'quality' of the object's new owner, and his potential to create a connection between previous collectors and himself. In other words, objects become containers of past events and individuals that have interacted with them. Inheriting a prestigious biographical heritage and inscribing his name at the end of a list of important collectors must have generated enough motivation to justify the time and money spent in the search and acquisition of these artefacts. In many ways, by collecting artefacts, Beasley was also collecting people. But besides their connections to important historical figures, these objects were also important for they originated from a time when interactions between Europe and the Pacific had not been intense enough to transform Indigenous material culture. To many amateurs and professionals of the beginning of the 20th century, 'old' often equalled 'authentic'.

In contrast to these ancient and pristine artefacts, Beasley also collected contemporary objects that had sometimes never even been used in an Indigenous context. This is an important aspect of Beasley's collection. From the early 20th century, private collectors and museum professionals

7 Fragments of the manuscripts are housed in the Centre for Anthropology, British Museum, London.
8 Russian navigator Kotzebue conducted two voyages to the Pacific (1815–18; 1823–26). Erskine conducted a survey of the southwest Pacific on *HMS Havannah* (1849–50).

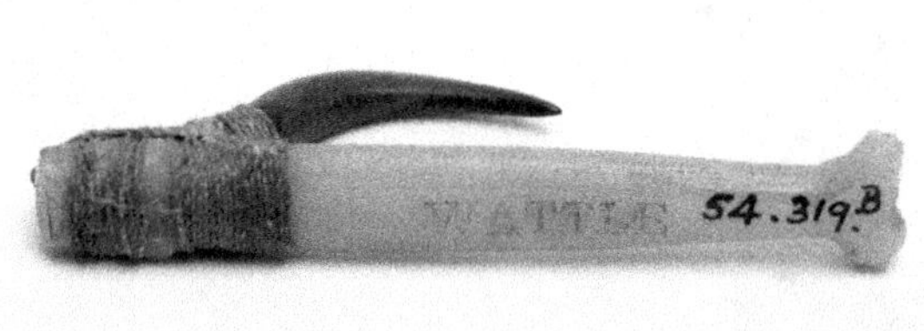


Fig 14.4.
Fishhook made of a green Bakelite toothbrush handle engraved with 'Wattle'. Papua New Guinea, Bougainville Island. Pre-Beasley collection history unknown. Bakelite, turtle shell, wood and coir. 6.7cm long. Cambridge, Museum of Archaeology and Anthropology (1954.319 B)

alike had expressed concerns about the multiplication of inauthentic material (Edge-Partington 1901; Roth 1901). This included objects that had not been used by Indigenous communities, artefacts that had been made to be exchanged with foreigners, and pieces containing non-Indigenous material. Many individuals and institutions were suspicious of contemporaneous material and sometimes even rejected such artefacts. Beasley, however, made the conscious decision to collect them. His collection included, amongst many other such objects, a Christian cross made of shell sculpted in a Solomon Islands style,[9] and a series of fishhooks with shanks sculpted from the Bakelite handles of European toothbrushes (Fig 14.4).[10] By acquiring material from the early contact and colonial periods alike, Beasley created a collection that illustrated continuity, change, discovery and encounters. His collection also reflects the diversity of Oceanic material culture across space (from New Guinea to New Zealand, The Hawaiian Islands and Easter Island) and its colonial ties to Europe (by collecting from colonial countries such as Britain, France or Germany). In addition, the various sources of artefacts inscribed in his acquisition ledgers suggest that Beasley was also collecting across individuals. Museum curators, anthropologists, dealers, auction houses, private collectors, missionaries and traders all contributed objects to the collection, reflecting the various activities and ideologies of the colonial period.

## Cumulative Biographies

What has until recently been understood as an uninformed, accidental and amateur collection may need to be re-examined in a different light. This chapter has shown the limits of interpreting material through the biography of its collector alone. Ethnographic collections, just as much as any other, are not only made of objects brought together by the will and intentions of one individual; they are made of interconnected objects that, individually and collectively, carry with them previous biographies and connections to other objects, institution and individuals scattered in time and space. They are made of fragments of individuals and previous intentions that need to be woven together with Beasley's own intentions and interests to make a coherent story that is, at once, singular and multiple. Such weaving, however, has been made difficult by further fragmentation.

9 London, British Museum (Oc1944,02.1782).

10 London, British Museum (Oc1944,02.484, Oc1944,02.487, Oc1944,02.515). Cambridge, Museum of Archaeology and Anthropology (1954.319 B).

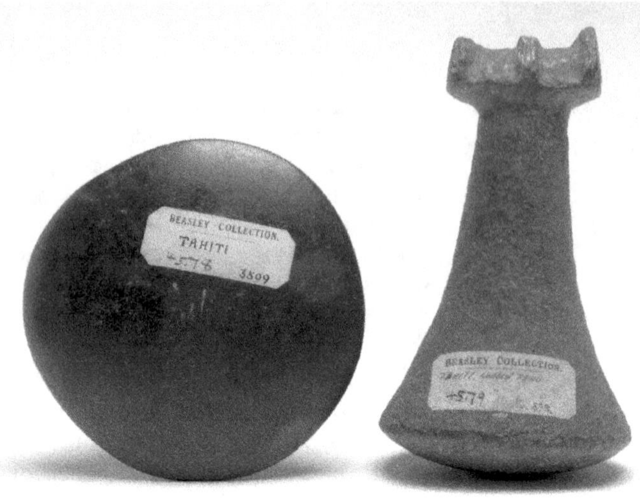


Fig 14.5.
Beasley label pasted on two stone pounders. Society Islands. 17.5cm and 16.5cm high. Cambridge, Museum of Archaeology and Anthropology (1945.78 & 1945.79)

Beasley died in 1939, leaving behind him a fully functioning museum. In 1940, World War II and its constant threat of air raids forced Irene Beasley to close the museum. It was bombed in November 1940. By this time, Irene had safely packed away a large part of the collection. A number of objects were, however, destroyed, and the museum suffered irreparable damage. Unable to continue caring for the collection, Irene presented it to four public institutions in a particular order, following her husband's wishes: British Museum (London), Pitt Rivers Museum (Oxford), Museum of Archaeology and Anthropology (Cambridge) and National Museums of Scotland (Edinburgh). To this list, she added two institutions: the World Museum (Liverpool), which had lost most of its Oceanic collections in the Blitz, and the Red House Museum (Christchurch), which had expressed interest in developing an ethnographic collection. The British Museum made a first selection in 1941 (Braunholtz 1941). It took 15 years for the remains of the collection to be divided and transferred to their new homes. In the meantime, the collection was stored in the basement of the British Museum, awaiting curators to visit, make selections and arrange transportation of objects. This dividing exercise was made difficult by the lack of information available. Deprived of their Cranmore Museum context and separated from the acquisition ledgers that informed their biographies, objects from the collections turned into an incoherent gathering. All they displayed were their small rectangular cream labels with cut corners stating their Beasley number, geographical origin, date of acquisition and, when prestigious or historically significant, their previous collector (Fig 14.5).

What each institution selected was not a representative portion of Beasley's collection. Objects were chosen for their potential to complement these Museums' collections, fill in some of their gaps and, when known, for their history *prior* to their acquisition by Beasley. In many ways, these Museums did what individuals and institutions had always done: selecting material that best suited their own collection development policies, not accommodating within their galleries and stores a differently articulated product. It was not the narrative of the collection or the relationship that Beasley entertained with particular artefacts or group of objects that interested them.

Returning to Stanley's 'contaminated collections', it is undeniable that Beasley's collection is contaminated. In fact, it is even more contaminated than previously thought. Beasley was not just an amateur private collector. He was the founder and director of a museum. He was an experimental museologist. He was an active member of the Royal Anthropological Institute. He was the author of a valuable monograph. These aspects, too, need to be considered as 'contaminating' and, thus, should contribute to the interpretation of his collection. Further, each object of the collection also came with its own biographical background, connecting it to multiple individuals and places and contaminating the collector and the collection as it was being formed. I argue that this process of contamination is intimately linked to the biographical baggage of people and things: far from being a problem, it is productive of a clearer picture of the history of collections and their journeys into and out of museums.

## BIBLIOGRAPHY AND REFERENCES


Balfour, H, 1929 Review: Pacific Island Records: Fish Hooks, *Man* 29, 90–91

Beasley, H G, 1904–39 Acquisition Ledgers, Vol I–IV, unpublished, Centre for Anthropology, British Museum, London

— 1928 *Pacific Island Records: Fish Hooks*, Sealey, Service & Co, London

— 1931 Cranmore Museum advertisement, *Museums Journal* 31 (5), front matter

— 1933 New Suggestions on Museum Lay-Out, *Museums Journal* 32, 421–5

Bonetti, R, 2007 The Museum as an Inhabited Object, *RES* 52, 169–80

Braunholtz, H J, 1941 Letter to W Fagg, 2 January, 95/11/1, unpublished, Archives of the Royal Anthropological Institute, London

Carreau, L, 2009 Collecting the Collector: Being an Exploration of Harry Geoffrey Beasley's Collection of Pacific Artefacts Made in the Years 1895–1939, unpublished PhD thesis, Sainsbury Research Unit, University of East Anglia

Chandler, B, 2007 The Fijian collections at Torquay Museum, *Journal of Museum Ethnography* 19, 77–89

Corbey, R, 2000 *Tribal Art Traffic: A Chronicle of Taste, Trade and Desire in Colonial and Post-Colonial Times*, Royal Tropical Institute, Amsterdam

Derlon, B, and Jeudy-Balliny, M, 2008 *La Passion de l'Art Primitif: Enquête sur les Collectionneurs*, Gallimard, Paris

Edge-Partington, E, 1901 Note on Forged Ethnographical Specimens from the Pacific Islands, *Man* 1, 68–9

Gob, A, and Drouet, N, 2003 *La Muséologie: Histoire, Développements, Enjeux Actuels*, Armand Colin, Paris

Gosden, C, and Knowles, C, 2001 *Collecting Colonialism: Material Culture and Colonial Change*, Berg, Oxford and New York

Gosden, C, and Larson, F, 2008 *Knowing Things: Exploring the Collections at the Pitt Rivers Museum, 1884–1945*, Oxford University Press, Oxford

Gowland, W, 1904 The relationship of museums to the study of anthropology, *JRAI* 34, 10–19

Kaeppler, A L, 1978 *Artificial Curiosities*, Bishop Museum Press, Honolulu

Miles, G P L, 1939 Harry G Beasley: An Appreciation, *Ethnologia Cranmorensis* 4, 2–5

O'Hanlon, M, and Welsch, R L (eds), 2001 *Hunting the Gatherers: Ethnographic Collectors, Agents and Agency in Melanesia, 1870s–1930s*, Berghahn, Oxford

Palmeira Auction Rooms Catalogue, 1975 *Ethnographic & Tibetan Art, Monday 3rd March, 1975*, Graves Sons & Pilcher, Hove

Rivière, G H, 1993 *La Muséologie selon Georges Henri Rivière*, Dunod, Paris

Roth, H L, 1901 Note on the Occurrence of Forgeries in the Pacific, *Man* 1, 116–17

Skinner, H D, 1930 Review. Pacific Island Records: Fish Hooks, *American Anthropologist* 32, 309–12

Stanley, N, 1989 The Unstable Object: Reviewing the Status of Ethnographic Artefacts, *Journal of Design History* 2 (2/3), 107–22

Thomas, N, 1991 *Entangled Objects: Exchange, Material Culture and Colonialism in the Pacific*, Harvard University Press, Cambridge and London

— 1994 Licensed Curiosity: Cook's Pacific Voyages, in *The Cultures of Collecting* (eds J Elsner and R Cardinal), Reaktion, London, 116–36

Waterfield, H, 2006 Harry Geoffrey Beasley, in *Provenance: Twelve Collectors of Ethnographic Art in England, 1760–1990* (eds H Waterfield and J C H King), Somogy, Paris, 64–77

West, A, 1982 H G Beasley and his collection. Notes, Unpublished letters, Centre for Anthropology, British Museum, London

15

# Sculptural Biographies in an Anthropological Collection: Mrs Milward's Indian 'Types'

Mark J Elliott

In 1947, the year India gained its independence from Britain, an English sculptor named Marguerite Milward wrote to her friend, the Cambridge archaeologist John Henry Hutton, offering to donate to the Cambridge Museum of Archaeology and Ethnology her entire collection of portrait sculptures of native 'types' from the Indian subcontinent.[1] The collection was the product of three years of expeditions throughout India's Deccan Peninsula and up into the Himalayas, and constituted over 100 representations of men and women, mainly from *Adivasi* or 'tribal' communities. Her offer was eagerly accepted by Hutton, himself a former administrator in north-east India and a prominent authority in physical anthropology. He considered the heads to be a great 'service' to anthropology, describing them later as 'the most accurate representations of tribesmen from the Himalayas to Cape Cormorin' that he had ever seen (Hutton 1949).

The portraits were accessioned into the Museum's collections in two stages: a first series of 100 plaster casts in 1948 and a smaller consignment of bronzes in 1951, two years before the artist's death.[2] Following the initial eagerness with which the heads were received, however, it seems that their significance and usefulness to the Museum, and to anthropology, was swiftly re-evaluated. There is no living or institutional memory of the heads ever having been exhibited following their donation and they were soon removed to a behind-the-scenes corridor of the Museum, where they would eventually be rediscovered in the 1980s.

Some time around 1985, amid preparations to redisplay the anthropology gallery of what was now known as the Cambridge University Museum of Archaeology and Anthropology, several museum staff were tasked with emptying an old display case. Its contents had been masked by a display of Indian textiles and when its doors were prised open, they revealed row upon row of pale plaster heads staring down at the unsuspecting museum employees. The discovery came as something of a shock, and the reactions of those who came to see what had been found ranged from surprise through to discomfort and even disgust. Indeed one senior member of staff is reported to have asked whether or not the things were accessioned, because if they weren't, they could be easily thrown away.[3]

It was soon determined that the heads had been both accessioned and catalogued, and were identified as the donation of an unknown artist named Mrs Milward. Rather than being disposed

1 Letter from M Milward to J H Hutton, 16 November 1947. MAA archives W07/1/9.
2 The first gift is given special mention in the *Annual Report of the Faculty Board of Archaeology and Anthropology of the Museum of Archaeology and of Ethnology*, 1947–48, 10 November 1948, 3.
3 I am grateful to several current and former members of staff at the Museum of Archaeology and Anthropology for providing fragments of this story, in particular Anita Herle and Thomas Cadbury.

of, therefore, they were transplanted to a new storage location and effectively forgotten once more.

My aim in this chapter is to delve into the multiple biographies of the Milward collection, to both make sense of its marginalised position within the Museum in the past, and to explore its potential role in the present and the future. The kinds of biographies with which I engage here are those which chart the transformations that the heads have undergone in the course of their career as museum objects, in terms of their value, significance and exhibitability: from highly prized visualisations of anthropological data to embarrassing anachronisms and unwanted junk.

What concerns me here is the potential that objects have to make possible different kinds of biographies, and the implications of this potential to the work of museum curators and researchers in the present and future. If the 'cultural biography' approach associated with Kopytoff (1986) demonstrates the value in seeing objects as having biographies in their own right, other authors have paid closer attention to the 'biographical space' that things occupy, within which 'culture is picked up, transformed, and passed on, through a series of life-stages' (Gell 1998, 11). Things are 'cognitively sticky' (ibid, 86) – they accumulate the agency of those who interact with them, taking on and influencing social relations in a way that is 'person-like' (ibid, 96).

Janet Hoskins' *Biographical Objects* (1998) expands the notion of object-biographies to consider how objects can be productive of the life histories of people. Storytelling, she reminds us, is a formative process – the act of narration a fashioning of identity and a construction of self. Narratives are not discovered, she argues, but constructed. Beginning with the observation that during her fieldwork on the Indonesian island of Sumba, people did not 'tell' their life-stories directly to other people, Hoskins suggests that the histories of objects and of people are in fact inseparable. She focuses on how objects can be constructive of, or productive of, biography in a society 'that has not been "psychologised" in a confessional tradition' (Hoskins 1998, 1–2). We might equally transpose this insight into a context where personal histories are lost, or where complex or troubling histories have been (intentionally or unintentionally) left unexplored and undiscovered.

A space is thus cleared in which to consider how biographies are constructed around objects, and the implications this may have upon our understanding of those objects and the different human and non-human actors with whom they engage. The museum collection, of course, offers an ideal environment in which to tackle such questions, and in which to observe these effects. Perhaps just as importantly, however, recalling the necessary fiction and partiality of all narrative construction (ibid, 2) encourages us to reflect upon the role of the curator and the researcher in biography, and to the inherently partial and contested nature of the biographies that we produce.

This chapter therefore explores the biographies of agents which surround the objects and the artist – the associations that they 'pick up' and which cohere around them during the course of their 'social lives'. It sketches a series of biographical fragments which have shaped the collection and the agents which surround it, beginning with a sketch of the biography of the artist-collector Marguerite Milward herself, focusing on the events and encounters that led to the production of her collection. This leads to an examination of her Indian expeditions in the 1930s, with attention to her practices and her engagements with individuals, objects and various disciplinary methodologies and theories. These encounters compose a picture of the collection as an assemblage – of the artist, of her materials, methods and models, and of the people, things and ideas that shaped her and her work. In the process, it offers an explanation as to why the heads were produced, and why they were received in the way that they were, at different times and by different people. Finally, I turn to the recent past and the present, to examine how the heads are once again being reinterpreted. Unravelling the tangle of connections and relationships that compose the collection illustrates the potential of the Milward heads to make possible biographies not only of artists, models and artworks but also of the institutions, disciplines and practices which produced them. These biographical fragments, I argue, point to the transformative effect that collections can have on institutions and disciplines, as well as vice versa. In so doing, they highlight the importance to contemporary museums of engaging with the more awkward or ambiguous aspects of their collections, and their own institutional biographies.

## Marguerite Milward, 1873–1953

Milward's own biography comes to us through a number of sources, from her own written accounts of her expeditions to India (Milward 1948) and the years leading up to it (Milward n.d.) to the reminiscences of friends and acquaintances. From the point of view of the researcher interpreting her collection, her biography is full of mysteries, the most significant being her motivation for beginning her series of Indian 'types' in 1935, which she never cogently explains. She appears to have led a remarkable life, both personally and professionally, living at one time or another in South America and Asia as well as in Paris and London, and forming lasting acquaintances with celebrated artists, thinkers and politicians. Many of these connections are foregrounded in her own writing, emphasising their importance in her autobiographical construction. Others have had to be construed through the researcher's own discoveries of clues in documentary sources and chance encounters.

Marguerite Milward was born Rosa-Marguerite Edge in Harborne, near Birmingham, in 1873. Her family was prosperous and well-known in the region, her father and grandfather, both named Charles Edge, having been well-known architects. Marguerite studied at the Bromsgrove School and Birmingham School of Art, and had apparently set up private practice as a wood-carver before marrying Philip Milward in 1901 (Hutton 1953). The couple travelled to South America, where Philip had business interests, but separated several years later. Marguerite returned to England and soon after, in 1907, moved to Paris to study painting at the Academie Colorossi and the Academie de la Grand Chaumière. She quickly discovered that painting offered little fulfilment and switched to sculpture, becoming one of the first students of the celebrated Emile-Antoine Bourdelle, himself a disciple of Rodin, and whose other students included Alberto Giacometti.

Bourdelle enjoyed an immensely high profile in France and internationally, producing monumental sculptures for the Théâtre des Champs-Élysées and well-known portraits of celebrities of the age. His training was famously inspirational, described as teaching not a style, but rather 'how to see' (Milward n.d.). The intellectual milieu surrounding Bourdelle's studio was lively with debate and discussion, populated by leading artists and scholars as well as celebrities such as Jiddu Krishnamurti – philosopher, peace campaigner and, at the time, championed by the Theosophist movement as the prophesied Maitreya Buddha, the World Teacher (ibid).

By 1911, Milward was beginning to enjoy success as a sculptor, with a well-received exhibition at the Salon des Beaux Arts, where her work was praised by Rodin and others, and her name put forward as an Associate. Her career abruptly stalled, however, when she was reconciled with her estranged husband. Philip was now a planter in Sri Lanka, and in 1912 she sailed to join him there, leaving behind her the success and connections of her life in Paris (Bourdelle-Sevastos 2005, 113–14).

In Sri Lanka, Marguerite immediately felt the lack of a circle of like-minded artists and the inspiration that came from such company. She nevertheless persevered in producing what she described as her 'dream of long years before – a collection of native types' (Milward n.d.). She began drawing, painting and sculpting portraits of local people, from a Tamil rickshaw puller and Sinhalese lace factory workers to an aged Muslim holy-man from the village of Pettah with whom she had become friends. The whereabouts of the resulting sculptures are unknown (ibid).

In 1914 events again conspired to change the course of Milward's life and career. With the outbreak of World War I, Marguerite returned to Europe with her husband, who led the Milward Contingent, a small force of volunteers from the 'British mercantile and planting elite' affiliated to the Ceylon Planters Rifle Corps and the Ceylon Rifle Corps (DeSilva-Ranasinghe 2004). Philip was killed in action in December 1915 and Marguerite spent much of the rest of the war in France. In between periods of service as a nurse at military hospitals in the north and on the Mediterranean coast,[4] she returned to assist Bourdelle in his Paris workshop, as his team of male assistants had been called up to fight in the war. They worked together on the completion of a monumental equestrian sculpture of the Argentine hero General Carlos Maria de Alvear, which now stands in Buenos Aires (Milward n.d.).

It is unclear what first led Milward to travel to India. Perhaps her encounters with Krishnamurti and his circle in Paris, or the time she spent in Sri Lanka, ignited her interest. It is likely, however, that she had some connection to the subcontinent prior to her Indian travels because during her first stay, over four months in 1926, she was the guest of the poet, polymath and nationalist figure Rabindranath Tagore at his newly-established Vishwabharati University in Shantiniketan, West Bengal. Milward invokes her association with Tagore at the start of her autobiographical account of her Indian expeditions (Milward 1948, 1), well before her first mention of Bourdelle (ibid, 6), explicitly situating herself and her work in relation to the world-famous Nobel Laureate and to the progressive intellectual elite in India that he represented.

In 1929 she returned to India, and to Shantiniketan, on the invitation of Tagore and became the first teacher of sculpture at Kala Bhavan, the University's art school. Among her students was Ramkinkar Baij, who would go on to be one of the leading Indian sculptors of the 20th century. During this time she also convinced a reluctant Tagore to exhibit his paintings, which few people had seen, and six months later he appeared in Europe with a portfolio of his works, exhibiting them first in Paris and then in London (Dutta and Robinson 1995, 287). She added to her growing *oeuvre* of portraits of Indian celebrities, including that of the scientist Jagadish Chandra Bose and the politician Kedarnath Chatterjee as well as Tagore himself. This sculpture, which has been described as 'perhaps the best one there is' of the oft-represented Bengali culture hero (Fig 15.1), is now in India House in London (Dutta and Robinson 1995).

Back in Europe, she continued to produce sculptures of the kind that were evidently of the greatest interest to her – studies of the diversity of human features. In a solo exhibition at London's Beaux Arts Gallery in 1933, several of her 'Eastern Types' were displayed alongside 'portrait busts' of notable celebrities such as David Lloyd George.[5]

4 Letter from M Milward to E Bourdelle, August 1916, Musée Bourdelle archives, Paris.

5 *Sculpture by Marguerite Milward*, 2–14 October 1933, Beaux Arts Gallery, London.

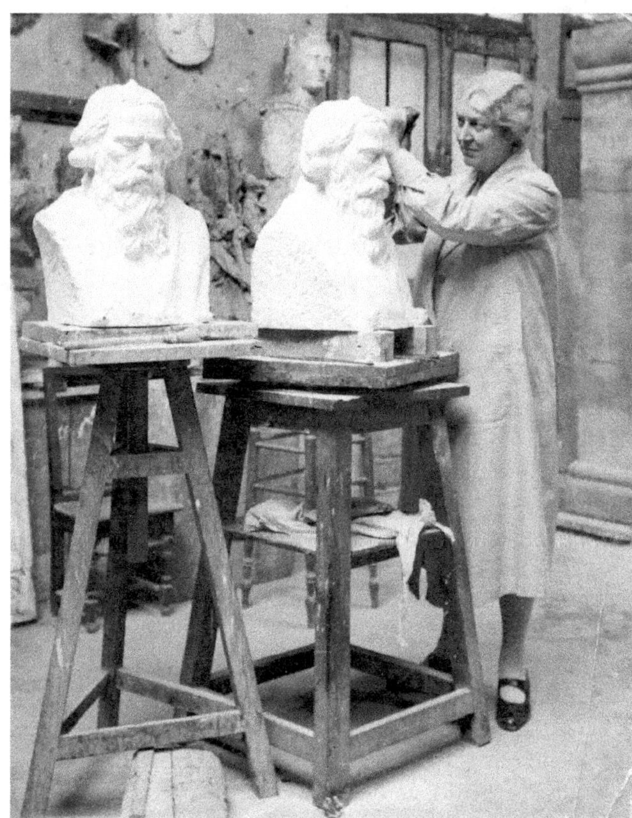

Fig 15.1.
Marguerite Milward carving a bust of Rabindranath Tagore from a marked up plaster maquette in Bourdelle's Paris workshop.
MAA P.87044

By the mid-1930s, then, Milward had established a large number of acquaintances in, and experience of, India as well as a significant body of sculptural studies of ethnic 'types' from Africa and Asia, alongside her more commercial portrait sculptures. However, it seems that despite her experiences to date, and a long-standing interest in 'types of different races', a more ambitious project of the kind she would soon undertake had not been anticipated. Writing of her decision to embark on a sculptural expedition to India in 1935, she describes herself as preparing 'almost without knowing it' for what she would come to think of as her life's work:

> It was during that year in London that I began to long for new inspiration and a fresh aim. The idea that had been born years before of sculpting types of different races returned with insistence. It had been conceived in the days of my girlhood when, during a visit to an Exhibition in Paris, I had been utterly fascinated by a collection of African native heads in bronze. Even then I had felt that this was the kind of work which I would like to do. Why should I not go back again to India and make a collection of the Primitive Tribes to be found there? (Milward 1948, 1)

Having consulted with friends, including the archaeologist Kenneth de Burgh Codrington, Milward sailed to Bombay in November 1935, beginning an expedition during which she would begin work on her 'first collection in sculpture of Primitive and Aboriginal Tribes of India' (ibid).

## AN ARTIST IN 'UNKNOWN' INDIA

Milward arrived in Bombay shortly before Christmas 1935, accompanied by 'coffin-like cases of plaster of Paris' and 'barrels of French clay'. From the outset her project was facilitated by the network of acquaintances in India and in Britain that she had built up over the years. She was met by a 'valuable old bearer' who had been recommended to her by Codrington, and by her friends the Keips, a Dutch couple resident in Bombay. Mr Keip stored her plaster and clay in a warehouse in the city and dispatched it to her wherever she had need of it on her journey, and arranged for the shipping of her completed works back to England (ibid, 2–3).

The series of one hundred sculpted heads of Indian 'types' were completed during two expeditions, one of eight months in the Deccan Peninsula from Bombay to Cochin in 1936 and a second of ten months in 1937 and 1938, when she travelled through central and eastern India up to Nepal. The labour involved was immense, with even the most straightforward portrait taking at least 26 hours to complete (ibid, 224), and numerous sources refer to the hardy constitution of the sexagenarian artist.[6] Each sculpture was completed in an *ad hoc* studio, mostly in the open air and usually surrounded by a significant proportion of the local population. After selecting her model, she would take measurements of her subject before beginning to mould the clay, finishing the sculpture over several sittings. The clay head would then be cast *in situ*, and the plaster moulds packaged and sent back to England. As well as producing the portraits, the artist made drawings and took photographs of many of her models, and collected ethnographic curios such as jewellery, tools and weapons. Significantly for the collection's subsequent career, her work also had an evident anthropological objective. The precision of her measurements and the tools she used may have been motivated by her artistic practice, but she also recorded the genealogies of almost all of her models, armed with a questionnaire she brought with her from England.

Besides the daunting labour involved, her expeditions required extensive planning on her own part, and cooperation from various local fixers and connections back home. At each stop on her itinerary, which had been drawn up by Codrington, but to which she occasionally added as a result of chance encounters, she was assisted by an assortment of missionaries, government servants, anthropologists, artists, plantation managers and royalty. In Hubli, at a labour camp housing 3500 members of different 'Criminal Tribes', she was hosted by the head of the Mission and his sister, whom she had met on the crossing from England, and who assisted her in the selection of representative 'types' from each tribe as models (Milward 1948, 15). In Hyderabad, she was a State Guest of the Nizam, and granted access throughout the Princely State. She spent an extended period with the popular anthropologist Verrier Elwin, for whose book *The Baiga* (1939) she made the drawings, and towards the end of her second trip spent several weeks in Kohima in north-east India, aided by the State in the person of the acting District Officer, Eric Lambert.

The diversity of her connections in India, and in particular her close links to colonial authorities, missionaries and capitalists of various kinds, serve on one hand to entwine Milward and her work into a significant and highly contested period of British and Indian history. Moreover, they add to the ambiguity and ambivalence of the heads as they have been interpreted by postcolonial audiences.

6 In his obituary of Milward in *The Times* (17 February 1953), the ethnomusicologist Arnold Baké refers to her 'splendid physique' which 'stood up to the heavy work of casting and stone work'.

Milward's project, undertaken towards the end of British rule in India, followed decades of State-sponsored scientific investigation of the colony, its resources and its peoples. Generations of European administrators and scholars had struggled to fill the gaps in their all-too-obviously incomplete understanding of the subcontinent's linguistic, cultural and 'racial' diversity. This struggle had been given greater urgency in the wake of the trauma of the Indian rebellion of 1857, when British belief in the relationship with their subject populations had been shaken to its foundations. From 1871, a decennial census counted, ranked and classified Indians on the basis of evolving categories of 'caste', 'tribe' and ethnoreligious 'community' (Bayly 1999, 100).

Intrinsic to the development of these categories was a belief in the interconnectedness of physical characteristics and physiological or mental capacities. Census commissioner and anthropologist Herbert Risley enshrined this relationship in his Law of Caste. Drawing on data gathered from anthropometric measurements, and in particular through an analysis of the 'nasal index' (the ratio between the height and the width of a subject's nose), Risley concluded that there was a clear correlation between the nasal index and the level of civilisation of not only an individual, but of whole groups: 'Everywhere we find high social position associated with a certain physical type and conversely low social position with a markedly different type' (Risley 1891, 259). Or, more specifically, that the 'social status of … a particular group varies in inverse ratio to the mean relative width of their noses' (cited in Bayly 1999, 132).

Such theories were employed throughout the policies of the British Raj. Certain groups, such as the Gurkhas, Sikhs and Jats, were valorised as 'martial races' – innately warlike, brave and loyal, and thus actively recruited into dedicated regiments of the Indian army, many of which still exist. Other groups, such as the Haran Shikaris or Bhats, whom Milward encountered and sculpted in the Hubli Industrial Settlement (see above), were defined by law as hereditary 'Criminal Tribes' and made subject to internment and discrimination that continues to impact on the lives of such groups today.

By the 1930s, when Milward embarked on her first expedition, the relationship between anthropology – in particular racial anthropology, or ethnology – and the State had been consolidated. The Commissioner of the 1931 census in Assam, J H Hutton, and the first Director of the Anthropological Survey of India, B S Guha (both of whom were friends and advisers to Milward), rejected many of Risley's more outlandish and sinister theories. However, they nonetheless attempted to reaffirm the value of race science using anthropometric techniques to create what they saw as a definitive analysis of India's racial construction (Bayly 1999, 143).

Milward was not commissioned or employed by the State. She appears to have funded herself through her own means and her motivation could be perhaps described as that of an amateur or, in her own words, a 'mad artist' (Milward 1948, 82). However, the influence of this tradition of ethnology in and of India is clear both from her own account of her project and in the artefacts and data she left behind. Throughout her expeditions she attempted to follow the methodologies of anthropometric measurement and data-collection. Risley and his successors had cautioned that randomly collected anthropometric data was useless unless it was accompanied by a certainty of the group or family from which the subject came. In addition to searching for 'good' or 'representative' types, therefore (ibid, 134), Milward's recording of genealogies detailing her models' parents, village and clan as well as their age, occupation, spouse etc was thus in part to make the sculptures more useful to students of anthropology.

If this association with anthropology and the colonial enterprise would go on to influence the reception of the heads in museums and the academy, both favourably and unfavourably (see below), it also profoundly influenced the encounter between artist and model in the field. Milward employed technologies of measurement and data-collection such as callipers, photography and interrogation using questionnaires that were so widely used by agents of the State, which clearly impacted on the experiences of the models. The fact that she was frequently accompanied and assisted in procuring subjects by labour managers, civil servants or local police can only have exacerbated this.

In Khandala, the first stop on her 1936 journey after leaving Bombay, Milward selected a Khatodi woman named Suni, who was visibly terrified by the encounter, bringing her entire family with her to her sittings for protection and reassurance (Milward 1948, 9). Again, in Chota Nagpur in eastern India, an Oraon man brought to Milward's *ad hoc* studio by local police was so disturbed by the situation that, just as the artist was about to begin work on his portrait, 'he said to the guard that he had a call of nature, slipped behind a tree and vanished for ever. The police gave chase but we never saw him again' (ibid, 201).

It is the disturbing connotations of colonial oppression, racial prejudice and the objectifications of individuals into representatives of primitive tribes or other anthropological categories that has influenced the ambivalent reception of Milward's sculptures by postcolonial museum curators and academics. For the museum staff who rediscovered them in the 1980s, and for some viewers since then, the heads were reminiscent of the life casts of racial types that can be found in museums throughout the world.[7] These artefacts, and the reams of anthropometric data that flooded into institutions like MAA throughout the first half of the 20th century, evoke an anthropology that has no place in the academic departments or museums of today. MAA is an institution that has placed great emphasis in recent decades on forging new relationships with 'source' communities (Herle 1994; 2003) and whose displays and research highlight the historical connections and relationships that have formed its collection and the institution itself. In such an environment, the Milward heads have been seen as anonymous, dehumanised objectifications (Rycroft 2006, 151), troubling, or at least irrelevant, to the project of the Museum today. They do not represent the kind of anthropology we want to do, or the kind of museum we want to be.

## From 'Type' to 'Portrait'

But for all that the collection has undoubted associations with an obsolete and embarrassing period in the history of the discipline of anthropology, and the institution of the museum, the complex assemblage of people, events, materials and ideas that have participated in its production and reception can, I argue, offer an invaluable tool with which to reengage with these troubling histories. It makes visible a multitude of biographical fragments that can be woven together to create a different, much more nuanced account of cross-cultural encounter and interaction (Fig 15.2).

If Suni and the anonymous Oraon man were clearly traumatised by their encounter with the European sculptor, other models in other places demonstrated a very different reaction. This is exemplified by Milward's account of two portraits from the north-east of India. Milward spent six weeks in May and June 1938 making studies of people of the hills in north-eastern India, in

7 These busts, frequently coloured for more accurate representation and with eyes closed as an index of the casting process, have frequently been similarly marginalised in museum collections. For a discussion of one such collection and its use in a recent exhibition, see Bouquet 2000.

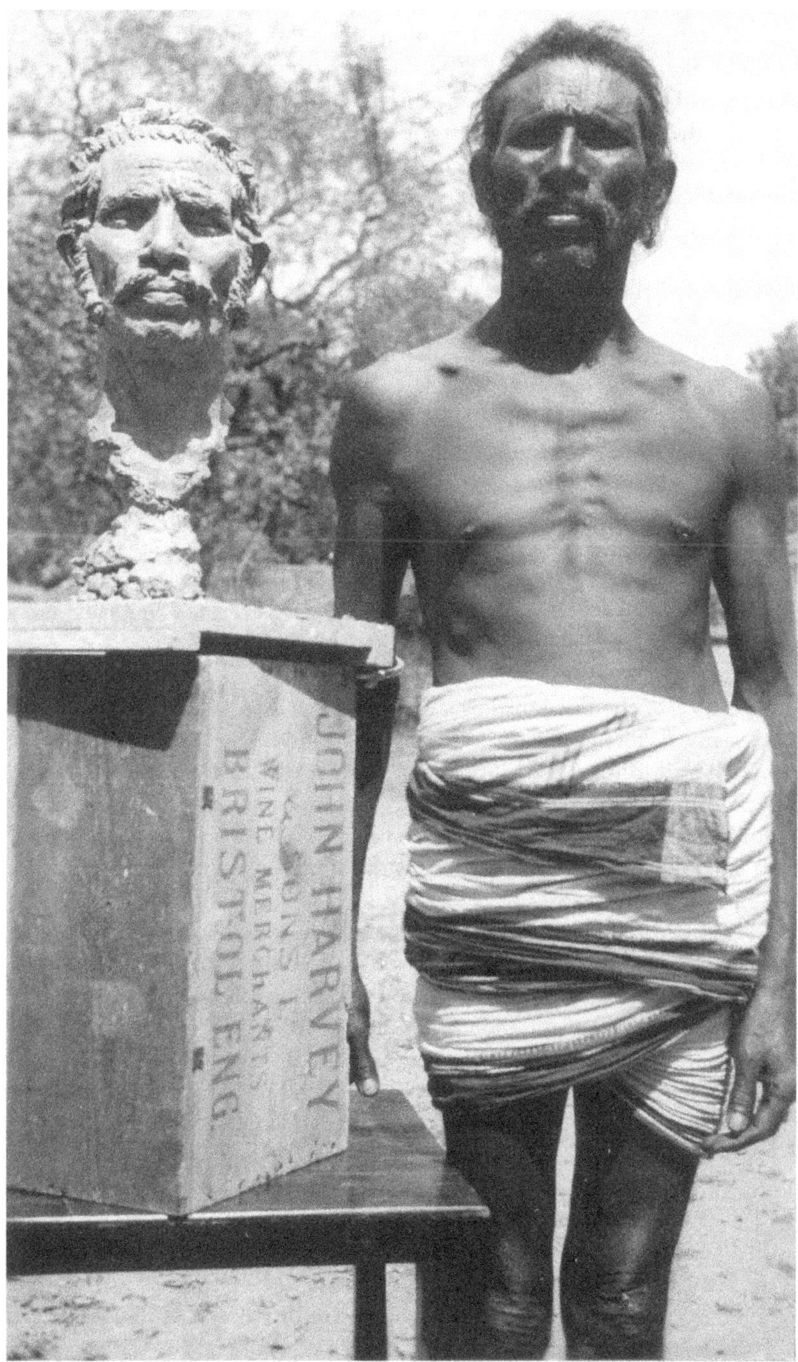


Fig 15.2.
Tandur, a Pardhi man posing with his portrait. Photograph by Marguerite Milward. Hyderabad, India, 1936. MAA P.6333.ACH1

what are today the states of Nagaland and Manipur. She was again assisted by agents of the State, this time in the person of the Irishman Eric Lambert, the District Commissioner in Kohima, and, as well as travelling to remote locations throughout the region herself, several models were brought to her in the provincial headquarters. One such figure was Katun, a member of the chiefly Ang clan of the Konyak Nagas, who travelled with two other men for five days by bus and on foot from their village on the edge of British-Administered territory in order to pose for the visiting artist (Milward 1948, 219–20). Some encounters were clearly much more interactive than the majority of those with models in the plains. The sittings with Koba, a Marring man from Manipur, merited this account by the artist:

> My Marring took far too much interest in what I was doing and was a sore trial to me. He suggested alterations and gave me criticisms which, of course, I could not understand, and by way of demonstration proceeded to smooth the clay on the cheek that I was working at. Probably this tribe is good at sculpture and pottery and he really did know more about it than I did. The boy posed in an idle and slovenly way, sat down and smoked whenever he wished, and one morning proceeded to take down his hair. He combed it from the back over his face with his fingers, tied it with a bit of string holding one end in his teeth, then padded it on the top with a filthy bit of rag … Then he twisted a curl on the top of his head almost over his nose and wound the hair round and round, threading long strings of white and brown beads in it with long sensitive fingers. (ibid, 224)

The radical difference in the relationships she was able to have with her models was doubtless dependent on many factors, from the differing relationship between the State and the local population in each area to the personality of the sitter or the conditions in which the encounter took place. Each encounter, as materialised in the sculpture and described in the account that the artist left behind, can thus be used to construct a narrative that extends far beyond the meeting between artist and model itself, to touch upon the prevailing power dynamics in a particular time, for instance, or the intricacies of professional networks in anthropology.

However, these portraits also make possible rich and intriguing individual biographies of the subjects themselves, constructed from Milward's own accounts and other fragments within the ethnographic archive. These biographies are profoundly transformative: of the artworks themselves and of the biographies of the individuals they represent, as well as of the collection as a whole and the people and institutions that it has touched.

One of the first portraits Milward made in Kohima was of Nihu Agami, a 68-year-old Naga man and retired chief *dobashi* or interpreter (literally 'two languages') to the British administration of the Naga Hills (Fig 15.3). She described him as her best model and 'a grand old man' (Milward 1948, 218), and published his genealogy in an appendix to *Artist in Unknown India* (ibid, 260). This gives the names of his parents, Puletha and Sathu, as well as those of his mother's brother and his current wife (his seventh – he had been widowed six times) and records that he had four children. These few details are supplemented, however, by other published and unpublished sources that not only enrich our knowledge of Nihu's own biography but highlight the extent of the network of relationships in which he participated, as a government servant and a friend and informant to a number of anthropologists. Milward records that he had been a government servant for 20 years (ibid, 218). During this time, around 1917 to 1922, he is mentioned in the tour diaries of the Deputy Commissioner Keith Cantlie, J H Hutton (1921)

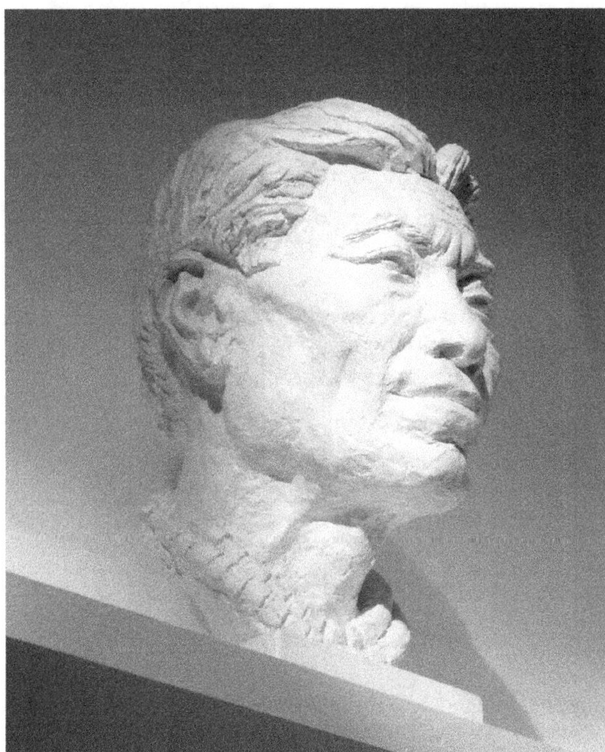

Fig 15.3.
Portrait bust of Nihu Angami, Marguerite Milward, 1938. Plaster of Paris. MAA 1948.139

and the curator of the Pitt Rivers Museum, Henry Balfour (1923). He also appears in Hutton's *The Angami Nagas*, where his genealogy or 'pedigree' is again given (Hutton 1921c, 123) and in *The Sema Nagas* (Hutton 1921c, 205). While the incidents reported in these accounts give little insight into Nihu's character or achievements, we do learn that he was a trusted companion to colonial officers and to travellers in often perilous circumstances, and a respected arbitrator of local disputes (Cantlie n.d.). Although translated as 'interpreter', the position of *dobashi* in fact involved mediation between the British and Nagas on a number of levels, and bore judicial responsibility for customary law. Nihu Angami was therefore an influential figure in Naga society. This translated into influence in politics. In 1919 he joined other Nagas in Government service who had returned from military service in France to establish the Naga Club (Jacobs 1998, 151), an organisation intended to represent the concerns of Naga people to the British, and which has been described as the first stirrings of Naga separatism (Kotwal 2000). In 1929 the Club submitted a memorandum to the Simon Commission, which had been charged with determining the political future of India, demanding that the Naga Hills be kept separate from the rest of India and remain under British rule.

Milward's sculpture of Nihu is thus transformed from a study of an Angami Naga 'type' into the portrait of an influential figure in Naga political history. The implications for the collection as a whole are significant. Milward had hoped that she would find a market for her heads in ethnographic museums and indeed she did sell a consignment of 32 bronzes to the Government of

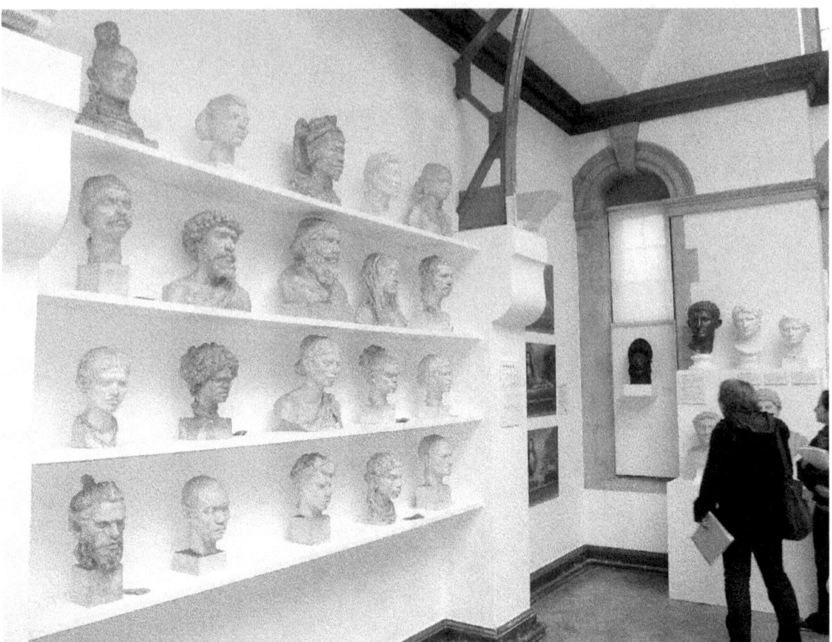

FIG 15.4.
PORTRAITS BY MARGUERITE MILWARD, 1935-1938, ON DISPLAY IN ASSEMBLING BODIES: ART, SCIENCE & IMAGINATION. MUSEUM OF ARCHAEOLOGY AND ANTHROPOLOGY, UNIVERSITY OF CAMBRIDGE, MARCH 2009 – NOVEMBER 2010

India in 1939, for display in the Anthropology gallery of the Indian Museum in Calcutta (Anon 1939). However, with the beginning of World War II and in its aftermath, this market seems to have eventually disappeared, prompting her to donate her entire series to the Cambridge in 1948. Interest in physical types within anthropology soon largely disappeared too and the heads, as discussed at the beginning of this chapter, were consigned to oblivion. But the example of Nihu, and the preceding account of the circumstances in which the heads were produced, recasts the sculptures as portraits of individuals, with real lives and real relationships: sculptural fragments of biographical detail that become invaluable tools for a museum that seeks to bring audiences into dialogue about the complex colonial history of our collections and the shared heritage of communities in Britain and places like India. These fragments also signal the potential of collections to index, or make visible, multiple biographies: multiple histories of institutions like the Museum of Archaeology and Anthropology, of disciplines such as social anthropology, and the practices and theories which so closely embedded them in the colonial project.

It is the capacity of the Milward heads to engage audiences and researchers with these complex histories that has occasioned their exhibition, for the first time in memory, in Cambridge (Fig 15.4). The exhibition *Assembling Bodies: Art, Science and Imagination* (March 2009–November 2010) explored technologies through which human bodies have been produced and made visible across time periods, cultures and disciplines. It thus created a space to reflect upon more difficult and contentious periods in the history of the museum and the discipline of anthropology, alongside a range of scientific and scholarly traditions from archaeology to the history of medicine. It also recast the Museum as a space in which such questions can be engaged with. The Milward heads were mobilised as examples of traditions that saw the human body as something that could be measured and analysed as an assemblage of external signs of an inner nature (Herle *et al* 2009, 32). Yet, juxtaposed alongside 21st-century body maps by South African women and portrait busts of Roman statesmen, the sculpture-as-portrait, as an index of an individual, sits in the same space as the sculpture-as-specimen, an index of an anthropological type. This polysemy of the portraits, which this chapter has attempted to sketch, both corroborates and challenges easy assumptions about colonialism and anthropology, about the individuals depicted and about bodies in general (ibid, 51). They are provocative, and productive: sculptural 'biographies' in the truest sense: constructed, contested, complex and in flux.

## Bibliography and References


Anon, 1939 Chief Racial Types of India, *Current Science* 13 (12), December, 573

Baké, A, 1953 Mrs Marguerite Milward, *The Times*, 17 February

Balfour, H, 1923 Diary of a Tour in the Naga Hills, 1922–1923, unpublished manuscript, Pitt Rivers Museum archive, Oxford

Bayly, S, 1999 *Caste, Society and Politics in India from the eighteenth century to the modern age*, Cambridge University Press, Cambridge

Bouquet, M, 2000 Thinking and Doing Otherwise: Anthropological Theory in Exhibitionary Practice, *Ethnos* 65 (2), 217–36

Bourdelle-Sevastos, C, 2005 *Ma Vie Avec Bourdelle*, Paris Musées/Éditions des Cendres, Paris

Cantlie, K, n.d. Memoir of time in the Naga Hills as a Deputy Commissioner, 1919–1920, unpublished typescript [online], available from: http://bamdemo.lemurconsulting.com/bamdemo [16 March 2009]

DeSilva-Ranasinghe, S, 2004 *Sunday Times*, Colombo, 14 November

Dutta, K, and Robinson, A, 1995 *Rabindranath Tagore, The Myriad-Minded Man*, Bloomsbury, London

Elwin, V, 1939 *The Baiga*, John Murray, London

Gell, A, 1998 *Art and Agency: an anthropological theory*, Routledge, London and New York

Herle, A, 1994 Museums and shamans: a cross-cultural collaboration, *Anthropology Today* 10 (1), 2–5

— 2003 Objects, Agency and Museums: continuing dialogues between the Torres Strait and Cambridge, in *Museums and Source Communities* (eds L Peers and A Brown), Routledge, London

Herle, A, Elliott, M, and Empson, R, 2009 *Assembling Bodies: Art, Science and Imagination*, Cambridge Museum of Archaeology and Anthropology, Cambridge

Hoskins, J, 1998 *Biographical Objects: How things tell the stories of people's lives*, Routledge, London

Hutton, J H, 1921a Tour diaries in the Naga Hills, unpublished typescript, Pitt Rivers Museum archive, Hutton Ms Box 2

— 1921b *The Angami Nagas*, Macmillan, London

— 1921c *The Sema Nagas*, Macmillan, London

— 1949 Mrs Milward's Heads of Indian Tribesmen, *Man* 49, 12

— 1953 Marguerite Milward: 1873–1953, *Man* 53, 40

Jacobs, J, 1998, *The Nagas*, Thames & Hudson, London

Kopytoff, I, 1986 The cultural biography of things: commoditization as process, in *The Social Life of Things: Commodities in Cultural Perspective* (ed A Appadurai), Cambridge University Press, Cambridge

Kotwal, D, 2000 The Naga Insurgency: The Past and the Future, *Strategic Analysis* 24 (4), 751–72

Milward, M, 1948 *Artist in Unknown India*, T Werner Laurie, London

— n.d. Indian Studio, unpublished typescript, MAA archives, Cambridge BA4/2/33

Risley, H, 1891 The Study of Ethnology in India, *Journal of the Royal Anthropological Institute of Great Britain and Ireland* 20, 235–63

Rycroft, D, 2006 Santalism: Reconfiguring 'The Santal' in Indian Art and Politics, *The Indian Historical Review* 33 (1)

# Museums as Biography

16

# Houses and Things: Literary House Museums as Collective Biography

Alison Booth

In 1979, not long after David Parker became curator of the Charles Dickens Museum in London, he addressed one of the first conferences on literary museums, reflecting on the designs and effects of an exhibit in a writer's former home (Barthel and Kunze 1986, 4).[1] He expressed envy of Thomas Carlyle's House, a museum that inherited many original possessions and documentation of the arrangement of the rooms along with a large body of biography about Thomas and Jane Carlyle: 'The rest of us should be so lucky!' (Parker 1986, 2).[2] The museum's trust, first private and then national, had been able to reconstruct the former residence of the Carlyles. Some even more fortunate collections had never been dislodged: houses like 'Kipling's Batemans ..., Shaw's Corner ..., and even Disraeli's Hughenden Manor ... in which the principal rooms, at least, survive ... intact, as they were the day the author died'. In such as-lived-in museums, the challenge for the curator is 'conservation' rather than reconstruction of rooms, with possible 'annexes' for exhibiting 'showcase' objects (Parker 1986, 25). Yet some museums begin with little else than a house associated with the figure who once lived there. Whether and how to recreate a typical period setting or to reproduce the rooms at one phase in the life of the house; to exhibit an archive or to mount thematic displays – the decisions must be made in any house museum. A writer's former residence, according to Parker, has a special mission, to document something intangible, the 'cerebral art' of literature. A literary museum should be 'transparent', allowing 'the visitor to see through the physical objects to the man beyond, and ... to the imagined worlds he created' (Parker 1986, 26–7). Parker commented: 'a lot of people speak about ghosts in writers' houses, about unseen but felt presences'. However embarrassing such talk may be, museum professionals should admit that 'we are not simply in the business of preserving artifacts; we are also in the business of calling up ghosts' (Parker 1986, 27–8).

Like many authors, Dickens lived in a series of houses that retained no domestic traces of him; most of these buildings disappeared before preservation was alerted, and possessions have flown to the winds. The spirit of the famous author pervaded Dickensian London, Rochester, and elsewhere, even in Dickens' lifetime. How to invite it to reside once more in the nondescript house in Doughty Street where he and his family lived for a few early years? The Dickens museum, like others, is a cabinet of curiosities, not a restored home; in-context, not *in situ* (Kirshenblatt-Gimblett 1998, 3). Many persons, including fictional characters, are documented

1 The International Committee for Literary Museums began meeting in 1977.

2 Parker served as curator of the Dickens museum in London from 1978 to 1999. In August 2005, he and I shared a panel on the Dickens House Museum (now renamed Charles Dickens Museum) at the annual conference of the Dickens Universe at the University of California, Santa Cruz.

there in portraits, materials and texts interconnecting them. Anything associated with the great man, his relatives and companions, and his works takes on priceless value. The everyday object, if held to be original or at least a typical antique, is transmuted as heritage. As a case in point, we see on display Dickens' wooden commode – re-contextualised, we could say, so that using it is out of the question. Parker and his collaborators and successors have reconstructed the drawing room in Doughty Street based on correspondence and inventories of other Dickens residences. In other rooms, rare authenticated pieces of furniture from his last home, Gad's Hill, have been placed as if to be used – but again, not by the visitor. On the whole, the Doughty Street museum is about the author and his period rather than his house; the upper floor features rotating exhibitions on such themes as Victorian 'Ignorance and Want' (Booth 2009). A visitor, especially if a crew happens to be filming a period drama in the museum that day, re-emerges from the museum amused, bemused, with souvenirs or impressions to bring along on further literary walks in Bloomsbury.

There may be nothing particularly ghostly in the familiar story of the Charles Dickens Museum and the experiences of its audience and presenters – nothing, at least, more extraordinary than making 'physical objects' reveal the author and 'the imagined worlds he created' (Parker 1986, 27). This is a feat of narrative invention. A museum dedicated to a person can be read as a kind of biography or narrative that uses factual evidence to represent lived experience. As Mieke Bal observes, 'exhibitions produce a narrative for the visitor' shaped 'by the expository agent' (Bal 2010, 14). This expository agent, the museum's curators or presenters in their various roles, resembles a narrator, as the visitor resembles reader or audience; their communication concerns persons, events, objects – standard components of narrative. A house museum in particular exhibits other basic elements of prose narrative, including setting or place and time. Within the material medium of a building with collected objects, the museum makes location its central theme, and description of interior design – usually secondary to plot and characterisation in a realist novel – comes to centre stage. Time, also essential to narrative, is thoroughly inscribed in a memorial house museum, concentrated on chronologies of the building, the inhabitants' lives, the foundation of the institution and the provenance of the artefacts. Like a modern research-based biography, an exhibited house and belongings take responsibility for accurate documentation and reliable inference of actions over time, as in: 'here [he] used to entertain distinguished guests; a walking stick [he] used during a tour of Switzerland in 1852'. In the manner of historical fiction, a display may refer to typical manufactures or period culture, or individual historical events and persons. But, unlike historical fiction, the museum in a person's house sticks to the facts for all the agents and events, not just the 'historic' ones. A decent museum will prefer truth to sensation, even if its 'mission' is mainly to entertain; authenticity should overrule simulation. (When imaginary beings such as the author's characters are invoked, they will be true to some illustration or adaptation of the role. And if the walls were really painted that hideous colour, it will have to do.) The challenges facing David Parker and his peers in creating a memorial house museum, balancing the documented and the imaginary, strike me as similar to the predicament of any biographer trying to instill personality into dead facts, or to reconcile what Virginia Woolf called 'granite' and 'rainbow'. The biographical house museum is a house haunted in a way that echoes the reader's response to written lives in non-fiction as well as fiction. The ghosts in these printed or spatial narratives are familiars of the audience's imagination, welcoming if somewhat uncanny spirits (Freud 1955, 219–52).

While reanimating a home-like space and material objects, a literary house museum immerses us in multiple life narratives. In this brief chapter I consider the literary house museum as a collection of biographical narratives.[3] The auto/biographies of the eponymous author, family, and friends absorb further tributary narratives from the collectors, donors, trustees and curators examined by others in this volume. I write, however, not as a museum professional but as a literary historian, in slightly disreputable territory. Yet, as recently as a century ago, colleagues in literature would have felt at home in the business of raising authors' ghosts. There was little social or conceptual gap between many of the earliest academic experts on modern literatures and the founding members of author societies and museum boards. Even today, when author-worship is an embarrassment in academia, the intersection of critical study and popular reception is tight. The Emily Dickinson Museum is a notable example: a pair of neighbouring houses in Amherst, Massachusetts, united to represent a complex of family biography, owned and sponsored by a prestigious college; here Dickinson scholars rub shoulders with curious visitors, devotees of the poet, volunteers, trustees and staff.[4]

I view literary house museums, along with series and volumes of biographical and topographical essays known as 'homes and haunts', as tools that carved the canons of English and American literature. It is a rich and complex history that has received increasing critical attention (Watson 2006; 2009; Hendrix 2008b). Below I render some historical account of cultural tourism as performance of shared, personified memory – or alternatively, as collaboration in topographical biography – in which the non-profit museum in an author's former residence is a relatively recent development. Before I turn to this historical and conceptual review and offer some examples centring on Washington Irving as well as Dickens and Thomas and Jane Carlyle, it will help to examine further the ways that house museums may be read as biographical collections both concrete and imaginary, literal and haunting.

This inquiry, as part of a longer study, unites with ongoing exploration of everyday practices of memory, narrative and representation. I consider houses and things as *lieux de mémoires* and nodes of narrative that guide collective memory in modern, mobile society. Following Walter Benjamin, Michel de Certeau, Pierre Nora and others, many have perceived museums and exhibits as texts, and the itineraries of everyday life as narratives or performative readings. Mieke Bal compares exhibitions of art to poems, narratives, theatre, and film (2010, 10). The analogies to genres seem more than figures of speech when we examine the practices of presentation and audience response in the narrative model I outlined above. The kinetic performance of textual interpretation is all the more dramatic in the case of museums representing a writer and the scene of writing, prominently the desk, chair, pen and study. Literary house museums may be considered as stage sets with props and script, the participants having learned different parts and improvising to some extent. An even better analogy for the house museum is the genre of biography. Although the building inscribed with the person's proper name resembles the cover of a book as well as a grave marker, the museum never has a single subject or author but is assembled as if by committee, starting with the author-subject and associates, passing through

3 The Winston Churchill Museum curiously claims to be 'the first *personality museum* across the UK', its target audience the British educated class, age 35–54 (Sillignakis 2007, 3–7).

4 The public interface (online or in print) of a literary house museum narrates the biography of the place. Amherst College bought Emily Dickinson's house, The Homestead, in 1965 and in 2003 united it with her brother's house, The Evergreens; see Emily Dickinson Museum 2010. For an autobiographical and biographical response to the house, see Cotter 2010.

contemporary and posthumous visitors to the house, supplemented by many texts narrating visits or representing the place; the anthology or collection 'published' when the museum opens is under constant revision by the museum's personnel.

Studies of museums have begun to speak of the life histories or biographies of museums. Inanimate objects, too, have life-histories; museums collect 'biographies of the objects in their collections', according to Samuel Alberti (Gosden and Marshall 1999; Alberti 2005). This recognition of narrative in material form coincides with widespread adoption of a narrative approach in many disciplines. Yet too often the approach is narrowly applied within one discipline. Within literary studies, narrative theory needs to attend more to non-fiction, spatial practices and material culture. In the interrelated disciplines of art history, museology, heritage or tourism studies, and social sciences, the terms of biography or narrative are often applied as rather dead metaphors without regard for literary and publishing history or the specific form and rhetoric of the narratives inscribed in the institutions and practices under study.

If it is worthwhile to attend to the tangible and spatial forms of biographical narrative in house museum collections, it is likewise illuminating to acknowledge the mortality within these dead figures of speech. Tourism, while obviously a leisure activity, has deep roots in religious pilgrimage and leans toward 'common places' at which groups may imagine spirits of the past (Rigney 2008, 75). Many a beaten track since the Grand Tour has led to cemeteries, battlefields, ruins and monuments, and today's so-called dark tourism or thanatourism to sites of genocide or disaster merely heightens a longstanding heritage theme of death. Public museums, flourishing after tourism was established, may seem comparatively clean, well-lighted, rational spaces, but they share a strange impulse to reanimate surviving objects. Students and critics of such institutions have viewed them as mausoleums or cemeteries, as repositories of obsolete objects (Rovee 2008; Orlando 2006). Alternatively, museums are said to serve 'as shrines where civil religious rituals are enacted' (Robson 2010, 122) in a kind of State religion that forms 'the new liberal subject' (Kriegel 2006, 682–3). These associations of cultural tourism and museums with community, identity, heritage and the afterlife are promising, in my view, for an interpretation of the particular case of the literary house museum as collective biography. Such institutions commemorate the original occupants and preserve the collection and the building – a reliquary writ large – within a heritage that constructs the literate traveller as a kind of lateral descendant or heir. The most devout will sense the aura of cultural heroes at the mere sight of a handkerchief or top hat in its reverential, referential context.

As sites of cultural tourism and as museums, then, literary houses suggest a haunting of materiality akin not only to biography but also to traditions of the Gothic. The museum dedicated to a writer gains effect if it inhabits a house, so resonant a setting for a narrative of family fate in literature from Atreus to Usher. Of course the significance of a house is over-determined, as in Gaston Bachelard's influential psychoanalytic model of the house as correlative to the body, to psychological origin (family romance), to the unconscious and memory (Bachelard 1957). Another key to the effect of the house is Freud's concept of the uncanny or *unheimlich*. Uncanny effects may result from crossing thresholds between the animate or inanimate, or from transgressive desire to inspect private scenes. The ghosts we speak of in authors' houses not only come from the reader's experience of the personified author or poet in reading the works. They arise too from our intrusive scopophilia. Like biographies, house museums allow us to snoop into daily habits and sleeping arrangements, to imagine a kind of virtual reality from the author's focal position. The visitor might be the child prying into the aftermath of some primal scene

– or at least like the heroine of a gothic novel probing a cabinet or secret room. But of course the museum ensures that we remain unharmed. As in printed biography, we turn our backs on decay and bodily function. There may be a very clean chamber pot, but some rooms and scenes in the house are always concealed, and some are used today as private offices or residence. It is sanitised, symbolised materiality that rouses no horror.

I suggest the thematic and historical associations of house museums with Gothic and cultural pilgrimage, but of course modern curators like modern biographers adhere to documented credibility and an objective stance. Susan Stewart notes that the modern museum controls the visitor's sensory experience. While labels connect the visitor to 'collective memory', the displays serve a 'deictic, or presentational function' to 'show forth' to the sense of sight; presenters perform 'a series of gestures and actions' that elicit a series of responses from the viewer, premised on 'an elaborately ritualized practice of refraining from touch' (Stewart 1999, 28–30). On an everyday, crowded heritage tour, a visitor who has no passion for the dead writer quite sensibly skims through the house museum as if it were a model of a domestic interior from a Victorian novel.[5] There may be aspects of the tour that also resemble auctions of antiques and real estate.

Yet much as museums and houses are haunted spaces, things in general seem uncannily alive.[6] The simple facts of an object's history, its contact with the dead person or its wanderings before recapture in the display, may be stirring indeed. The death of an author, like a bankruptcy in a Victorian novel, threatens such demotion of possessions to junk (Trotter 2008, 13, 15). An estate sale or heirs often did disperse the writer's things without proper name and narrative attached. But if the author continued to be sufficiently renowned in the era when preservation began in earnest, circa 1890s, the living would reassemble and reassess the materials according to the former owner's estimated worth. Virginia Woolf, whose father Leslie Stephen chaired the committee that established the museum in Carlyle's house, wrote with some frequency and ambivalence about literary pilgrimage, but she affirmed the special value ascribed to literary remains: 'writers stamp themselves upon their possessions more indelibly than other people … They seem to possess … a faculty for housing themselves appropriately, for making the table, the chair, the curtain, the carpet into their own image' (Woolf 1932, 23). A visitor attuned to the mutual portraiture of authors and possessions may also sense the uncanny effect of a prohibited wish to touch the things the author handled, to feel the death mask or other bodily relic, to sit where the author sat.

Artefacts have a way of moving around from hand to hand, from heir to collector to donor to curator, and from room to room when no-one is really looking. A museum's narratives of mobile, personified matter follow the precedents of the relics of saints in medieval Europe, as suggested in the corresponding practices of cultural pilgrimage.[7] Other precedents appear in the 18th-century

5 A vast literature on the home, domesticity, interiority and gender comes to mind here; for example Fuss 2004; Neiswander 2008.

6 Literary studies have seen a surge in interest in so-called thing culture or thing theory, drawing on Marxian theories of the commodity in relation to industrialism, colonialism, realism. See, for example, Freedgood 2006; Brown 2003; Wall 2006.

7 The local rites inaugurating relics of Catholic saints required a repeated tale of provenance along with reiteration of the saint's life (Geary 1986). Others in this volume also point to this important collection of essays edited by Arjun Appadurai, *The Cultural Biography of Things* (1986), 64–91, notably Igor Kopytoff's influential contribution.

English novels known as 'it narratives'.[8] Museums do not parade the relic through the streets or produce entire novels of its life history; the label usually resembles a very short biography of the object, its use in life and its posthumous journey to the exhibit. At the same time, objects in the memorial museum share in the uncanny transformations of the commodity according to Marxist theory. In 'Paris, Capital of the Nineteenth Century', Walter Benjamin writes, 'World exhibitions are places of pilgrimage to the commodity fetish'; they 'glorify the exchange value of the commodity. They create a framework in which its use value becomes secondary' (243). In modern times, documented creative beginnings and shrines to cultural heroes have been written about (in homes and haunts literature) and displayed (in house museums) as if participating in exhibits of manufactures or ethnic habitats at a World's Fair. Memorial house museums began to be established in significant numbers in England some four decades after the Great Exhibition, and they glorify neither use nor exchange value but the transferable quality of being possessed: they commemorate the idea of unique dead genius as something that stamps matter with meaning. Accordingly, Bill Brown writes of 'talking things', or matter infused with 'genius' or spirit (112–14),[9] souvenirs of the aura of the work of art. This perceptible animation originates in the residents' arrangement of the home, but largely it is the succession of presenters and audience who rehearse and perform the animating acts, filling in the gaps as narrative theorists say, to tell tales of provenance and authenticity, of sentimental value and personal associations.

If house museums are collections of biographical narratives and if they serve to reanimate places, buildings and objects that support rites of national and personal identity, they may usefully be read in terms of prosopography or collective biographical history as I have conceived it (Booth 2004). Suffice it to say here that prosopography entails tropes of personification or prosopopoeia – the rhetoric of elegy – and that it takes the form of collections of portraits and narratives or other representations of individuals in groups, much like the house museum. In prosopography as in museum collections there is always a sense of loss, decontextualisation, or omission because the re-collection is imperfect. In a house museum, the restoration of rooms and the exhibited collection appear as complete as possible. But the very premise of the museum is the death of the subject; the author must be gone for this private space to become a public museum. The frames and labels, the displays and explanatory text, velvet ropes and closed doors, the redundant images of the missing subject have an elegiac purpose, a funereal air. These prosopographies in word, image, multiple dimensions and media commemorate an international imagined community seeking a rooted past and a sense of literary affiliation.

In the haunted houses of authors and the spirited things collected in literary museums, we may interpret many different categories and versions of biographical narrative as prosopography. All kinds of object or artwork, manuscript or book may be displayed or hidden in various narrative contexts or frames. Some of the subgenres of these implicit object-narratives include: useful former possessions, especially those handled or worn (clothing, canes, eyeglasses) or closely associated with the body (chairs, washstands, commodes); gifts given to the famous subject by other famous associates, from manuscripts to locks of hair; books, keepsakes, *objets d'art* or other correlates of the inhabitants' education, taste, and personality; portraits or other representations

8 'It narratives' are novels that tell the life-story of a guinea, a bible, a lapdog, a sedan chair (Lupton 2006).

9 Peter Pels goes further than Arjun Appadurai in discovering potency in the strange social life of things in motion; for Pels, 'the fetish presents a *generic* singularity … apart from *both* the everyday use and exchange *and* the individualization and personalization of objects' (1998, 98).

or parts of the subject such as death masks or hair; display cases, signs and other materials that signal museum space, cheek by jowl with materials and designs typical of a period household; not least, the goods in the gift shop, including images of the house or study.

One of the most important categories of items in authors' houses represents the act of writing: the study, the desk and chair, the pen (or typewriter or computer). Just as the interview of the author perennially asks 'How, when, and where do you do your writing?', the literary museum and its printed or online literature relentlessly pursue the autobiographical act of creating a site of creativity. A case in point is Charles Dickens' desk and chair in engravings of the study at Gad's Hill, as if inviting us into the scene. Many paintings and engravings repeat that chair, featured in the painting *The Empty Chair* and its many popular appropriations once Dickens had died. Dickens had set up a small Swiss chalet as a detached summer study at Gad's Hill; it is now to be seen in the garden of the Rochester civic museum, Eastman House. Such metonymy of a literary house – the detachable study – has its own tradition, with examples in a scale model of Henry James' Garden Room at Lamb House or the still-standing summer writing house at Virginia Woolf's Monk's House in Rodmell (a National Trust site). As in life writing of many designs, we – the audience – want contact with explanatory icons: images of a site of birth or source of inspiration. We also join in a collective commemoration not unlike the funeral oration or pilgrimage.

In the above sampling of the narrative resources for personifying literary spaces and objects as sites of collective commemoration, I have already sketched some of the historical dimensions of these practices. Without broaching a full history, we can suppose that the concurrent rise of biography, tourism, collecting and museums in general since the 17th century was more than a coincidence. In particular, I note some interdependent developments leading to the later-19th-century institution of literary house museums. Since ancient times, literary associations have imbued landscapes that served as settings for the writer's life or scenes within the works, and in turn the localities have promoted the presence (Petrarch in Provence, Rousseau in Switzerland, Dickens in Kent). As early as the 17th century, travellers began to publish travel memoirs that guide the reader on a pilgrimage to the various places associated with favourite authors. Many early museums were amateur productions in an individual's home, such as Sir John Soane's, gathering concrete perspectives on their own travel and study. Collections and the museums that house them often immortalise their donors or founders, as in the Ashmolean in Oxford or the Smithsonian Institution in Washington DC. By the later 18th century, more cultural figures began to arrange their own homes to be visited in their lifetimes and after. The popular response to renown, acted out in tours to the sites associated with the celebrity, remapped many cities and regions for national heritage and the tourist gaze, as it influenced the ongoing reception of the eminent person. House museums for artists, composers, statesmen, celebrities and others, as well as writers, have been established in many countries (Hendrix 2008a).

Such an apparatus of reception was not confined to the landmarks and the collections within museums, but always concurrently depended on published life narratives. Emerging from a long tradition of travel writing, a new kind of prose 'pilgrimage' became fashionable in the era of illustrated periodicals and rail tours. Books that would later be termed literary geography began to be published around 1850 in Britain and the US. A founding text is William Howitt's *Homes and Haunts of the Most Eminent British Poets* (1847), two volumes of biographical sketches of great poets (some women) and descriptions of any existing site in Britain that held the poets' aura or memory. The Romantic prosopography of British poets, in the hands of the middle-class

Quaker reformer Howitt, provides a national open-air museum for self-education; its topographical prose and illustrations identify portraits and houses as well as haunts and shrines, but specific identification blends into a national ensemble. There is never only one memorial house, as Parker's envious glances at other museums suggest; never only one object, or never the last object, in a collection, but always a hint that it could be more complete. A pilgrimage is a serial journey – and written pilgrimages string incidents along a picaresque route – to be repeated by the faithful. We tend to assume the purpose of biography is to establish the unique individual, but in this context more is to be gained by inclusiveness and even digression.

Homes and haunts books assisted in the rise of literary house museums, often in effect serving as 'guides' to a series of interiors. By the mid-19th century, a growing body of professional writers independent of country-house patronage set up their own hospitable, presentable homes, as necessary to the 19th-century career as the book tour is today. Anticipating the audience for their home settings, authors and their families constructed the entertainment or 'public' spaces of their houses as living museums of literature, with collections of souvenirs, mementos of famous people, displays of their own taste or creative habits. Literati participated in long-standing customs of exchanging portraits, manuscripts and signatures, collecting memorabilia and placing unofficial markers upon hallowed homes or sites. Increasingly after 1830, periodical articles combined biography of the author with short travel memoir, descriptive house tour, interview and illustrations of persons and settings. These texts insert the narrator-reporter, and vicariously the reader, into the sphere of the eminent host and his environment. Such pieces might then be reprinted in a collection that suggests a kind of route for perusing the notable authors of the region or nation. Later in the century, more of the famous authors had died, more homes had been vacated, and survivors published literary memoirs recalling the salons or intimate circles within these much-written-about houses (for example, Hall 1871; Fields 1871 (1900)).

Biographies, whether monographs or collections, were essential to building demand for the collection of materials associated with authors, and eventually to the movement to establish house museums. As Victorian writers died – the Brontës on the early side – the remaining family or subsequent occupants might fend off pilgrims and relic-hounds, as Patrick Brontë, Arthur Bell Nicholls and the later incumbent foiled Brontë fans at Haworth Parsonage. But survivors were often the instigators of the writer's biography, as Charlotte Brontë's father and widower commissioned the successful biography *The Life of Charlotte Brontë* by Elizabeth Gaskell (1857). This in turn brought the tourists and drew out the collectors, and the international readership of the Brontës won out as family and contemporaries died off: every inch of the parsonage and indeed of Haworth has become associated with literary biography. Soon many shorter or longer narratives of biography, homes and haunts memoirs-cum-guidebooks, and pieces on Bronteana published by the Brontë Society (founded in 1893), along with a tourist trade in Haworth itself, reinforced the demand that eventually made it possible to establish a museum in 1928 to gather various private collections for display in the former home.

Biographies, then, go hand in hand with the house museum, but it requires public performance of readerly response to make it possible to develop correlatives of the life in real estate and documentary collection. The development of the Brontë Parsonage Museum is a typical delayed sequence – though the vast majority of professional writers get no museum at all. Before there can be a museum, a series of representations and rites must be performed, from markers and publications of various auto/biographical narratives, to the actions of pilgrimage and collecting. It is important to acknowledge the agency of the audience in establishing what Dean MacCannell calls the attraction (MacCannell 1999, 44). Much of the reception of authors was in the hands of amateurs far and wide. Readers of Shakespeare, Burns, Scott and Wordsworth ensured that literary spirits pervaded the real world and supported literary settings suitable for tourism.

The celebration of Dickens from the beginning until now, in all its forms, is as representative and instructive as that of the Brontës. Both examples reveal all the forms of collaborative prosopography or collective biography that crystallise in the literary house museum. However high the cultural aspirations of a museum, it must be audience-driven. Dickens devotees began flocking to the settings of his fiction before his death in 1870, and began to map out Dickens Country. One guest at the Bull Hotel in Rochester in 1877 wrote a verse in the guest book that confirms that the aura of the author and his characters haunts the historic city; a tourist pamphlet reprinted the testimonial to promote both city and hotel as heritage destinations inviting the amateur of Dickens to 'trace/The scenes where Dickens' characters have stood' and revere the great writer in a 'favourite scene/Which for all time shall keep his memory green' (Harris 1908).

The audience constructs the site by rereading it as inhabited. Readers may occupy spaces in overlaid storyworlds (Herman 2002) of fiction and biography, in companionship with author and characters as well as fellow pilgrims.[10] Arguably, an urban and peripatetic author like Dickens has less need of a museum since his fictions have populated many of the favourite haunts of the British public, beyond the biographical focus of the literary pilgrim. But the wish to contact Dickensian aura seems insatiable, with the creation of the Dickens Fellowship (1902), opening of the Dickens House Museum in 1925, and founding of the Dickens Society in 1970.

The preservation of the author in a museum, as in tours and collections, is a collective undertaking, as I have insisted; it not only supports a canon of national literature but it personifies the spaces of a country's landscape. A new focus for the effort to build a transatlantic Anglophone heritage came in 1895, a high tide of North American tourism in England, when preservation began to encompass landscapes as well as historic buildings. The founding of the National Trust in 1895 aimed at preserving the open spaces of England – particularly the Lake District, saturated with the lives of the poets – as a cultural resource to improve the population; it was almost immediately devoted to catching the country houses before they fell, especially with rising taxes and war in the early 20th century. Also circa 1895, the 'homes and haunt' genre developed into series of model cultural pilgrimages, quite distinct from tour guides, providing advice on food and shelter. Publishers were ready to ensure that such tourists also had a supply of narratives of previous visits to the suitable sites of pilgrimage, as in North American topo-biographies, Elbert Hubbard's *Little Journeys to the Homes of the Great and Good* series beginning in 1895, and Theodore Wolfe's series with such titles as *A Literary Pilgrimage* (1897). These books confirm that the visitor should identify as an amateur antiquarian on a well-trodden ramble, recalling or reading companion narratives as he or she goes. The National Trust was slow to acquire authors' houses, which often were architecturally negligible and held only small collections of things of more sentimental than artistic value (Gaze 1988, 164). Real estate values and impending demolition or sale often dictate the life-story of the museum.

Non-profit groups and staff design spatial prosopographies in these museums as part of a national and international network. Their collections and buildings reassemble the 'circle' of

10 Today in Rochester there are semi-annual festivals with parades of locals in Dickensian costume, reanimating the spirit of the town in a different way than Dickens World in nearby Chatham (Booth 2009).

habitués of the house as these people are virtually or materially documented in correspondence, memoirs and biographies as well as in objects and arrangements by many agents, from the museum's subject to connoisseurs and custodians. Yet I have insisted on the role of audience participation; it is the reader or visitor who activates an exhibit, museum, biography, or other text. This audience is preconditioned by social scripts or rituals as well as texts, perhaps vicariously through reading homes and haunts books, guidebooks, or more recently websites, perhaps by reading the original works of the author or biographies about him or her. This narrative prescription may be fulfilled by a tour, whether of one museum or a whole country, following footsteps or trails over one or more lifetime or landscape.

Such rites are only enlivened by experience, and I conclude with some very brief scenes with Washington Irving and the Carlyles, from opposite ends of the 19th century. Irving participated in every aspect of the culture of literary memorial houses. He wrote an early example of cultural pilgrimage, *The Sketch-Book of Geoffrey Crayon, Gent.* (1819–20), which included descriptions of visits to Shakespeare's birthplace – a humorous rite of author-worship – and to Walter Scott's Abbotsford, where the great novelist hosted him for three days in 1817. But Irving was not content until he had established his own biographical seat. In the 1830s, renowned for having proved that North Americans were eligible to compete for literary immortality, Irving designed his own site on the Hudson with deliberate archaism. He bought an old Dutch farmhouse associated with the van Tassels of 'The Legend of Sleepy Hollow' and transformed it into Sunnyside, a sort of collage of architectural traditions including Arab-Spanish, Dutch bourgeois and Anglo-American cottage gothic, a domestic model of his cultural travels. While Irving was alive, any writer or literary amateur would include a stop at Sunnyside on his or her itinerary. Postcards and engraved prints broadcast the idea of the author's house; in a Currier and Ives image, Irving is seated under trees at the approach to the house, the welcoming spirit of the place. Other images focus on an interior scene of inspiration, Irving's study, which became a national 'shrine' (McClatchy and Lennard 2004, 113). Sunnyside is now a splendid museum (purchased by John D Rockefeller and opened in 1947, a National Historic Landmark since 1966); many of its rooms and its beautiful gardens and parkland appear as they might have in the author's lifetime (Historic Hudson Valley). Labels, barriers, guides, picnic tables in the paved area for school groups, parking lots and marked paths – all the signs of a working museum seem to fade in this experience, as the original furniture and the guide's tales blend a sense of the host, his family and their guests.

What you encounter at the museum is less a ghost of Irving and more a saturation of bygone literary America personified in belongings and representations of Irving and his visitors. In 1863, Christian Schussele painted *Washington Irving and His Literary Friends at Sunnyside* (now in the National Portrait Gallery in Washington, DC) (Fig 16.1), a conversation piece of famous men of letters – Hawthorne, Emerson, Cooper, Longfellow, and eminent though now eclipsed historians or justices (Historic Hudson Valley). Some of these literary friends, like Irving himself, were already dead when the painting was created. A conversation piece personifies a group genius or tradition; it is visual prosopography. Schussele's painting directly 'quotes' a very similar tableau of literary men set at Abbotsford: Thomas Faed's *Sir Walter Scott and His Literary Friends at Abbotsford*, 1849. Many a literary house museum resembles Schussele's or Faed's conversation pieces, name-dropping social networks. Everything must be detailed down to the décor, as if we too were there; these also might be portraits of the personal shrines envisioned by the authors and eventually opened to the admiring traveller to upstate New York or Scotland. Walls of author

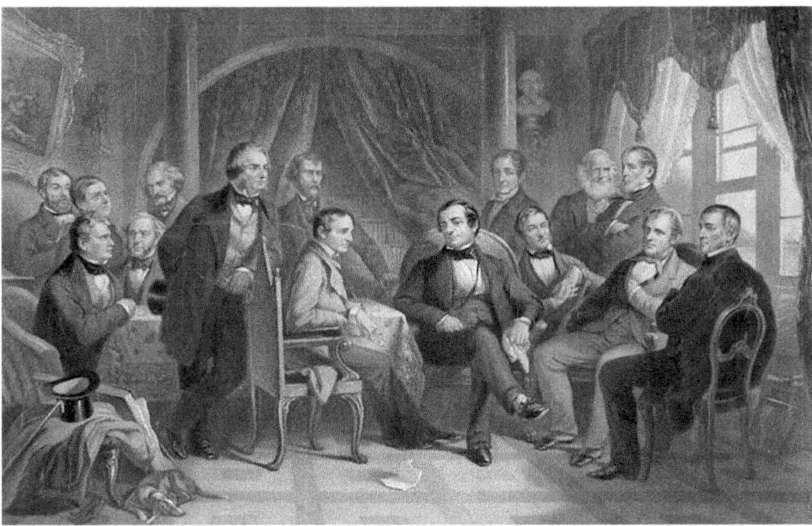

FIG 16.1.
'WASHINGTON IRVING AND HIS LITERARY FRIENDS AT SUNNYSIDE', ENGRAVING BY THOMAS OLDHAM BARLOW, 1864

museums feature portraits (and short biographical information) of the subject's affiliations, as in the all-male series of framed black-and-white sketches that lines one wall of the entrance hall in Henry James' Lamb House in Rye, Sussex, representing the literary figures who visited James there.[11] Such portrait groups capture a series of encounters as if in one moment, and could be seen as visual analogs for the literary home-visits in the 'homes and haunts' genre, which in turn inspire a series of visits to each site.

One of the most famous literary house museums was also one of the earliest founded: the house of Thomas and Jane Carlyle in Cheyne Row in Chelsea. From the moment they moved there in 1834, the Carlyles began curating a collection in a literary landmark, soliciting collaboration from correspondents and visitors, whose written recollections help to flesh out the place to this day. Thomas Carlyle made pilgrimages to famous writers' houses and hung in his own home portraits of great men (and their relatives or homes), including Goethe, Spinoza, Milton and Cromwell. Jane Carlyle's famous folded screen with its lacquered collage (1849) is itself a collection of famous culture representatives as well as animals (National Trust 1998, 27). Books, manuscripts and gifts from various celebrated figures mingled with heirlooms. A circle of Victorians preserved themselves as they tried to arrest time in the house. In 1857, anticipating the sage's immortality, Robert Tait photographed and painted the interior, garden and street as well as the protagonists Jane, Thomas and Nero the dog (Ashton 2002, 1–4). Tait's indelible painting, *A Chelsea Interior*, was exhibited at the Royal Academy in 1858 and now hangs in the room that has been restored to the painting's likeness. After Jane's death, Thomas began the chain of biographical memorials that continued posthumously with James Anthony Froude's volumes

11 James wrote a fond but patronising sketch of Sunnyside in *The American Scene*: a 'temple', 'treasure of mild moralities', epitome of the 'little American literary past' (1907, 482–5).

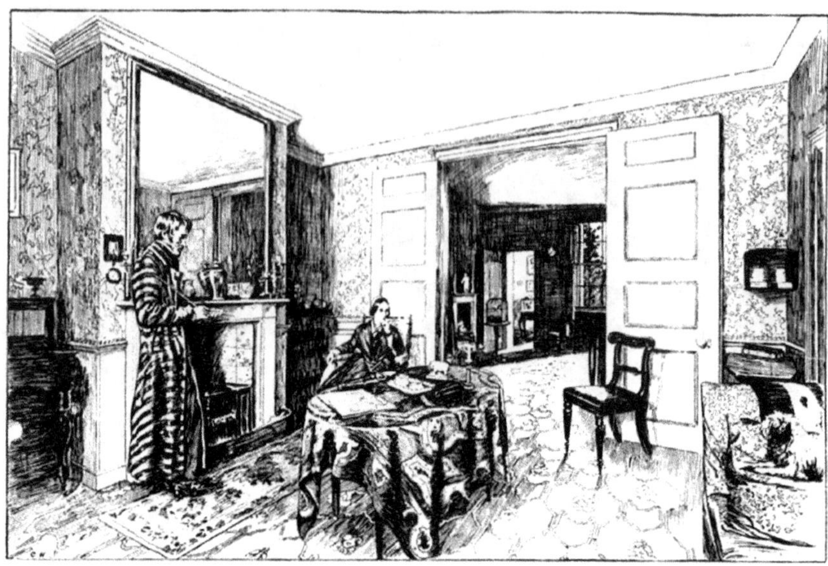

Fig 16.2.
The Carlyles' house, 'The ground floor rooms in 1857', R Blunt 1895. 'Drawn from a photograph' from the painting by Robert Tait, A Chelsea Interior

of biography and the monumental editions of correspondence, keeping alive the personalities in the Queen Anne row house near the river. Near the end of the sage's life, the painter Helen Allingham, widow of Carlyle's friend, the poet William, created a visual inventory of the rooms and the surviving inhabitant, rivalling Tait's images for 'Vandyke fidelity' and 'posthumous fame', in Jane Carlyle's words (Ashton 2002, 2). Those who record the interior in prose, visual art, or donated collections get a piece of the immortality.

Concerned by the scandal surrounding Froude's and Thomas Carlyle's revelations about the difficult marriage, a committee of admirers erected a statue of Carlyle on the embankment and placed a bas-relief of his famous face on the front of the house. Yet only the impending sale of the property spurred an international committee to raise funds to open the museum in 1895, again a key year in preservation (the National Trust took over the house in 1936). Reginald Blunt, whose father was a neighbour of the Carlyles, made a living in part by writing books preserving Old Chelsea, and repeatedly worked up Carlyle reminiscences and associations from material he and other Carlyleans eagerly preserved. He produced a heavily illustrated album, a sort of exhibition catalogue for the new house museum in 1895 (a more modestly illustrated visitor's guidebook, updated in 1907, survived through 1998). Blunt's *The Carlyles' Chelsea Home* includes an engraving of Tait's painting (Blunt 1895, facing 28) (Fig 16.2). This curious memorial volume, with funnel-shaped epigraphs of Carlyle's words in gothic script, is laid out both biographically and spatially, according to episodes in the inhabitants' lives and according to floor plan, with short narratives about activities in the house in the Carlyles' day. The frontispiece of this collection of Carlylean life shows the house as portrait or prosopon, the street as cemetery. The illustrator includes the bas-relief and adds an epigraph or epitaph to the very tree in the street (Fig 16.3). At this date, the museum had little to show inside. It took some time to gather

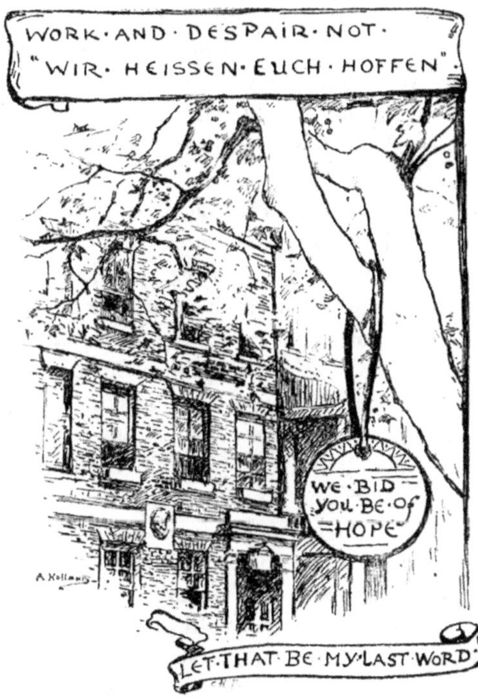


Fig 16.3.
The Carlyles' house, exterior. Ada Holland, 'Frontispiece', R Blunt 1895, *The Carlyles' Chelsea Home*, George Bell, London

back the former possessions. The China Closet in the Carlyles' House, for instance, now displays 'personal relics of the Carlyles, which belonged to their servant, "Little Charlotte" … who lived and worked at Cheyne Row from 1858–1860' (National Trust 1998, 23).

Of course any restoration, no matter how accurate, is never the same. The labels and display cases, the masses of portraiture and the imagery of death give it away: this is a memorial home, signifying the loss of the original. Even in the 1890s some visitors to the house doubted that strangers they encountered at the site actually had read Carlyle or knew why he was famous or important. Other visitors read the house as an indictment of Victorian marriage and lack of plumbing. Websites today encourage tourists to visit Carlyle's House when in London, praising the Queen Anne house in the quiet corner of historic Chelsea in language that resembles real estate ads and home-décor magazines. The National Trust and others, who in various ways write upon the surfaces of the museum today, insist on the legibility of the lives of the Carlyles in this material collection, never doubting the warrant for the museum. At times they do articulate the difficulties of preservation or reconstruction, as David Parker did in 1979.

For instance, do we want the house to be as it was in a certain year of the Carlyles' long occupancy, or in a convenient exhibit? There were different calls as to where to exhibit the desk, considered a key to the great man's work. In Thomas Carlyle's lifetime, the desk, which had belonged to Jane Carlyle's father, had rotated through the house in the author's quest for the *feng shui* of writing. It was willed to Virginia Woolf's uncle James Fitzjames Stephens, and in the 1890s returned to the drawing room that had been used as the study in the last years of Carlyle's life (Krout 1899, 50; *Carlyle's House* 1907, 49). At least by 1968 the soundproof room on the top of the house had become an exhibit of the Victorian author's writing, displaying framed photographs of desk and chair with and without the sage. Now these original pieces of furniture have been placed in the famous solitude project, open for occupation (in the visitor's imagination) and surrounded by portraits of Carlyle and other great men. Yet this was not in fact the arrangement when most of the works were written, in the rooms below.

As any biographer or curator learns, there are infinite narratives to trace about each thing, each date and incident, each itinerary through phases of life. Like other museums, literary house museums guide a visitor to perform certain rites of interpretation. Unlike large, eclectic museums of art, the house museum invites an imagined sense of home as it would have been, accessible to all the senses including taste and touch. A reconstructed house, like descriptive settings in biographies or novels, provides a great deal of material for this mental simulation, with contextual information on the probable scenes once performed there. This imaginative re-enactment echoes the act of literary creation that inspires the pilgrim, the author society or museum foundation in the first place. A single museum honouring an author is itself a prosopography overlaying life narratives of many participants, from historical inhabitants and contemporaries to presenters to audience. Such institutions in a region or country become part of an association, a network for potential tours as well as a genre of communicated conventions, emulating each other's techniques of preservation, exhibition and audience development. The literary heritage of each nation is substantiated and narrated with regard to how it is preserved in other countries, as well as a sense of the hospitality and reception of authors within their own social networks. In all this, a visitor may play an unwitting part, curious, admiring the antiques and soaking in historic atmosphere. Or the literary pilgrim may indeed see ghosts – things with a strange life of their own, voices or spirits of the past. Picturing ourselves in the place of genius, with the genius of the place, we may contribute to international prosopographies of literary history. Our own recollections in pictures or words add to the many life narratives open to access in literary house museums.

## BIBLIOGRAPHY AND REFERENCES


Alberti, S J M M, 2005 Objects and the Museum, *Isis* 96, 559–71

Appadurai, A (ed), 1986 *The Social Life of Things: Commodities in Cultural Perspective*, Cambridge University Press, Cambridge

Ashton, R, 2002 *Thomas and Jane Carlyle: Portrait of a Marriage*, Chatto & Windus, London

Bachelard, G, 1994 (1957) *The Poetics of Space* (trans Maria Jolas), Beacon Press, Boston

Bal, M, 2010 Guest Column: Exhibition Practices, *PMLA* 125 (1), January, 9–23

Barthel, W, and Kunze, M, 1986 Preface, in *Literary Memorial Museums* (eds W Barthel and M Kunze), ICOM National Committee GDR, Frankfurt and Berlin

Benjamin, W, 1999 Paris, Capital of the Nineteenth Century, in *The Arcades Project* (trans H Eiland and K McLaughlin), Harvard University Press, Boston, 14–26 [originally published as 'Paris, Capitale du XIXémesiecle', *Gesammelte Schriften* 5, 60–77, 193]

Blunt, R, 1895 *The Carlyles' Chelsea Home*, Bell, London

Booth, A, 2004 *How to Make It as a Woman: Collective Biographical History from Victoria to the Present*, University of Chicago Press, Chicago

— 2009 Time-Travel in Dickens' World, in *Literary Tourism and Nineteenth-Century Culture* (ed N J Watson), Macmillan, London, 15–63

Brown, B, 2003 *A Sense of Things*, University of Chicago Press, Chicago

*Carlyle's House*, 1907 The Carlyle's House Memorial Trust, London

Cotter, H, 2010 My Hero, the Outlaw of Amherst, Arts and Leisure, *The New York Times*, 16 May, 1, 28

Emily Dickinson Museum, 2010 *History of the Emily Dickinson Museum* [online], available from: http://www.emilydickinsonmuseum.org/history [20 April 2010]

Fields, J T, 1871 *Our Whispering Gallery* (series in *Harper's*), reprinted as 1900, *Yesterdays with Authors*, Houghton Mifflin, Boston

Freedgood, E, 2006 *The Ideas in Things*, University of Chicago Press, Chicago

Freud, S, 1955 The 'Uncanny', *The Standard Edition of the Complete Psychological Works of Sigmund Freud* (ed and trans J Strachey, A Freud, A Strachey, and A Tyson), vol 17, Hogarth, London, 219–52

Fuss, D, 2004 *The Sense of an Interior: Four Writers and the Rooms That Shaped Them*, Routledge, New York

Gaskell, E, 1857 (1997) *The Life of Charlotte Brontë*, Penguin Books Ltd, London

Gaze, J, 1988, *Figures in a Landscape: A History of the National Trust*, Barrie & Jenkins/National Trust, London

Geary, P, 1986 Sacred Commodities: The Circulation of Medieval Relics, in *The Social Life of Things: Commodities in Cultural Perspective* (ed A Appadurai), Cambridge University Press, Cambridge, 169–91

Gosden, C, and Marshall, Y, 1999 The Cultural Biography of Objects, *World Archeology* 31 (2), October, 169–78

Hall, S C, and Hall, A M, 1871 *A Book of Memories of Great Men and Women of the Age*, Virtue, London

Harris, E, 1908 *The 'Bull Hotel', Rochester, and its Dickens Associations (Illustrated)*, Rochester

Hendrix, H, 2008a Writers' Houses as Media of Expression and Remembrance: From Self-Fashioning to Cultural Memory, in *Writers' Houses and the Making of Memory* (ed H Hendrix), Routledge, New York, 1–11

— 2008b (ed), *Writers' Houses and the Making of Memory*, Routledge, New York

Herman, D, 2002 *Story Logic: Problems and Possibilities of Narrative*, University of Nebraska Press, Lincoln

Historic Hudson Valley [online], available from: http://www.hudsonvalley.org [15 September 2009]

Howitt, W, 1847 *Homes and Haunts of the Most Eminent British Poets*, 2 vols, Harper, New York

Hubbard, E, 1896 *Little Journeys to the Homes of Famous People: American Authors*, Putnam's, New York

Irving, W, 1819–1820 (1998) *The Sketch-Book of Geoffrey Crayon, Gent.*, Oxford University Press, New York

James, H, 1993 (1907) The American Scene, in *Collected Travel Writings: Great Britain and America*, Library of America, New York

Kirshenblatt-Gimblett, B, 1998 *Destination Culture: Tourism, Museums, and Heritage*, University of California Press, Berkeley

Kopytoff, I, 1986 The Cultural Biography of Things: Commoditization as Process, in *The Social Life of Things: Commodities in Cultural Perspective* (ed A Appadurai), Cambridge University Press, Cambridge, 64–91

Kriegel, L, 2006 After the Exhibitionary Complex: Museum Histories and the Future of the Victorian Past, *Victorian Studies* 48 (4), Summer, 682–704

Krout, M H, 1899 *A Looker-On in London*, Dodd, Mead, New York [online], available from: http://www.victorianlondon.org/publications2/lookeron.htm [15 September 2009]

Lupton, C, 2006 The Knowing Book: Authors, It-Narratives, and Objectification in the Eighteenth Century, *Novel*, Summer, 402–20

MacCannell, D, 1999 *The Tourist: A New Theory of the Leisure Class*, 2 edn, University of California Press, Berkeley

McClatchy, J D, and Lennard, E, 2004 *American Writers at Home*, Vendome/The Library of America, New York

National Trust, 1998 *Carlyle's House*, National Trust, London

Neiswander, J A, 2008 *The Cosmopolitan Interior*, Yale University Press, New Haven

Orlando, F, 2006 *Obsolete Objects and the Literary Imagination* (trans G Pihas, D Seidel, A Grego), Yale University Press, New Haven

Parker, D, 1986 Literary Museums: Present Opportunities, in *Literary Memorial Museums* (eds W Barthel and M Kunze), ICOM National Committee GDR, Frankfurt and Berlin, 25–9

Pels, P, 1998 The Spirit of Matter: On Fetish, Rarity, Fact, and Fancy, in *Border Fetishisms: Material Objects in Unstable Spaces* (ed P Spyer), Routledge, New York, 91–119

Rigney, A, 2008 Abbotsford: Dislocation and Cultural Remembrance, in *Writers' Houses and the Making of Memory* (ed H Hendrix), Routledge, New York, 75–91

Robson, J, 2010 Faith in Museums: On the Confluence of Museums and Religious Sites in Asia, *PMLA* 125 (1), January, 121–8

Rovee, C, 2008 Trashing Keats, *ELH* 75 (4), Winter, 993–1022

Sillignakis, K, 2007 *Churchill Museum: How should the Cabinet War Rooms generate pre-opening interest in the Churchill Museum*, available from: http://www.sillignakis.com/other_research.html [25 August 2010]

Stewart, S, 1999 From the Museum of Touch, in *Material Memories* (eds M Kwint, C Breward, and J Aynsley), Berg, Oxford, 17–36

Trotter, D, 2008 Household Clearances in Victorian Fiction, *19: Interdisciplinary Studies in the Long Nineteenth Century* 6, 1–19, available from: http://www.19.bbk.ac.uk/index.php/19/issue/view/69 [5 September 2011]

Wall, C, 2006 *The Prose of Things: Transformations of Description in the Eighteenth Century*, University of Chicago, Chicago

Watson, N J, 2006 *The Literary Tourist*, Macmillan, London

— (ed), 2009 *Literary Tourism and Nineteenth-Century Culture*, Macmillan, London

Wolfe, T F, 1897 *A Literary Pilgrimage Among the Haunts of Famous British Authors*, Lippincott, Philadelphia

Woolf, V, 1932 Great Men's Houses, in 'The London Scene', *Good Housekeeping* (1931–32), 23

17

# 'Keepers of the Flame': Biography, Science and Personality in the Museum[1]

SOPHIE FORGAN

## INTRODUCTION

In 1854 Charles Dickens visited Paris, the scene of one of his most famous novels, *A Tale of Two Cities* (1859), and found inspiration in what he termed the museum of 'Second-Hand Sovereigns'. There, in the Louvre, he found a museum of the 'Paraphernalia of the Kings and Emperors of France', and, despite railing against the rottenness of human grandeur, he was carried away by seeing the boots, the hats, the voluminous crimson mantle, the Emperor's writing-table which bore 'oh! such unmistakeable signs of hard work, indomitable perseverance, and iron will! … splashed with ink … punched with penknives … scorched with sealing wax …' Indeed he was 'so saturated with notions of the Empire' as to be veritably transported in time. Hearing a pair of boots creak next door, he almost expected to see Duroc, Bertrand, or Rapp come in and ask '*Que diable?* What am I doing here? And out of the lofty windows the illusion continued, he could 'see on parade' the Imperial Guard, and it only wanted to complete the picture a distant roll of drums, a sharp rattle of arms presented, 'and then, cantering into the square upon a white horse, a little man with a cocked hat and a grey great coat' (Dickens 1855, 511–16).

Dickens' imagination was one which ranged more powerfully and creatively than most and there is a nice tension between the scornful reference to Second-Hand Sovereigns and his actual response to the objects on display. His account confirms that shrines and relics devoted to great historic figures have long been a spur to the imagination and helped to shape our knowledge of that past through their focus upon the individual. Such 'personality museums' are of course only one form of commemoration alongside statues, eulogies, the naming of buildings, anniversary celebrations, and so on. Recent work has shown this to be a fruitful field for understanding the construction of scientific identities, often, indeed, 'heroic' identities, and locating them within more nuanced contexts of place and debate (Jordanova 2000; Fara 2002; Browne 2009). Museums which are focused on a single personality are a popular sub-type of the museum genre, with over 170 in the UK alone, of which the birthplace museum is the best-known type.

1 I would like to thank Shirley Chubb for first interesting me in the personality museum through her project *Thinking Path* at Down House in 2004, and Vanessa Morrell for generously allowing me to use the data she compiled for work done as an MA student at Teesside University. I am especially grateful to Randall Keynes and Janet Browne for their assistance on material relating to Down House. Leonée Ormond clarified the authorship of 'Second-hand Sovereigns' as almost certainly Dickens, rather than his fellow contributor Wilkie Collins. My thanks respectively to the Royal Society Archives for access to the Henry Dale Papers concerning Woolsthorpe, and to the Royal College of Surgeons for files relating to Down House and the Minutes of Council.

Such museums are an international phenomenon, and range from founding fathers (Jefferson at Monticello), influential thinkers (Marx's birthplace in Trier), great inventors and industrialists (at least five museums about Edison in the USA) to numerous literary figures, artists and musicians. In Britain the greatest number are devoted to writers and poets – Shakespeare and Burns each have five museums or heritage sites devoted to them, and Charles Dickens has four. *Genius loci* and the sense of viewing the same landscape that the writer saw daily have always appealed (Marsh 1993, xiv). Next in popularity come artists, and national heroes such as Nelson, Livingstone and Cook. Museums on individual women form a tiny minority, although the homes of writers such as the Brontës and Beatrix Potter are among the most well-visited. Scientists, however, appear only in modest numbers, with a few more than a dozen in total, to which may be added a similar number on engineers and technologists. The majority have been founded since the mid-1970s, which parallels the general growth in museums during the last four decades, and of course the interest and popularity of biography at all levels, from the highly academic to the 'warts and all' popular dissection.

This chapter examines some of the particular problems attending this form of scientific biography and how it reflects attitudes to scientific knowledge and its place in culture. Three examples relating to major scientific figures have been selected: Newton's birthplace at Woolsthorpe, Darwin's home and working laboratory at Down House and Freud's final refuge at 20 Maresfield Gardens, London. I first examine how these sites came to be turned into museums and who was instrumental in keeping 'the flame' alive, before exploring questions relating to biography and personality, and what happens when 'the life' becomes the master-narrative in the case of these notable scientists.

## Woolsthorpe Manor, Lincolnshire

Newton's birthplace at Woolsthorpe has played a central role in the construction of Newton as a surpassing genius. Historians have outlined the creation of the birthplace shrine at Woolsthorpe and its significance in having the 'holy tree marking Newton's inspiration as a young man' (Fara 2002, 241). It was purchased by the Royal Society during World War II, and donated to the National Trust, where what was a fairly ordinary farmhouse has become the distillation of romanticised rural Englishness. Let us, however, re-examine how the purchase by the Royal Society was made. 1942 marked the tercentenary of Newton's birth but was a difficult year. The Royal Society were hopeful 'if the course of the War permitted it' of having some celebration during the year. As a result Sir Henry Dale (1875–1968), President of the Royal Society, got in touch with the historian G M Trevelyan (1876–1962), Master of Trinity College, Cambridge, to see if a joint event could be arranged (Royal Society Archives, HD/6/8/17/12). For Dale, this would be good propaganda, both for science and for England. Trinity, however, decided to postpone any celebration due to the difficulties of getting food as well as the 'unsatisfactory nature of the war news'. In the event Dale turned the autumnal Royal Society anniversary meeting into a Newton celebration, with special lectures by Edward Andrade, Sir James Jeans and Lord Rayleigh on Newton's achievements, and announced the Royal Society purchase of Woolsthorpe.

This was the background against which negotiations with the inheritors of Woolsthorpe, the Turnor family, had been held. Major H Turnor generously agreed to sell the property to the Royal Society for considerably less than its value, and a price of £1000 was agreed for the house and orchard, site of an apple tree, possibly a descendent of the famous tree which had been the young Newton's inspiration (ibid HD/12/42). The Pilgrim Trust contributed to the cost and the Royal Society set out to find a suitable custodian to look after the site. The choice fell upon the National Trust, about the only body at the time with the relevant expertise which could be relied upon to maintain it in the public interest. In 1945 a Woolsthorpe Advisory Committee was set up, with Dale, Jeans, Andrade and Trevelyan; it was decided that the house should not be made into a Newton museum, but let to a suitable tenant who would be prepared to show the public over it at stated times (ibid HD/8/2).

With post-war restrictions on building materials in place, it took time for repairs to be made, and eventually the house was let in 1947 to the headmaster of a school in Grantham. It remained tenanted until the 1970s, when a flat was created on the upper floors for a custodian. In 2000 renovations were undertaken to create a new entrance and construct the adjacent Science Centre which focuses on Newton's key contributions to science. The point about the 'saving' of Woolsthorpe for the nation is that it was due to extremely effective contacts between influential people who had the ability to tap sources of finance. Dale might have been at the later stages of his career, but he was President of the Royal Society, the first Director (1928–42) of the National Institute for Medical Research and chairman of the Wellcome Trust (1936–60), as well as chairing the Government's scientific advisory committee. Dale could make things happen. He also had local links to Grantham, being a Foundation Governor of the King's School, and his son was living there at the time.[2] And George Macaulay Trevelyan was a hugely respected historian, lover of the English countryside and author of the beguiling and nostalgic *English Social History*, first published in 1944 (Cannadine 2004). Besides being Master of Trinity College, Cambridge, Newton's *alma mater*, Trevelyan was extremely active in the National Trust, and chairman of the key Estates Committee, which managed all the properties other than country houses. He argued passionately on behalf of particular properties that he felt the National Trust should accept, and believed that the Trust was the guardian of the nation's spiritual values, arguably never more under threat than in the midst of war (Lees-Milne 1992, 102–3). Furthermore, Trevelyan was very friendly with the first chairman of the Pilgrim Trust, Stanley Baldwin, and with John Buchan, another trustee, which helped to ensure that by 1939 more than £28,000 had been directed towards the National Trust (Jenkins and James 1994, 72). Dale likewise sounded out Lord Macmillan, 1942 chairman of the Pilgrim Trust, about possible support (Royal Society Archives HD/12/42). Macmillan was an eminent lawyer, involved in numerous national bodies, one of which was the National Trust. With such connections, it is not surprising that the purchase of Woolsthorpe was successful.

However, what did the National Trust feel about taking on the birthplace of England's most famous man of science? The working officials were lukewarm, to judge at least from James Lees-Milne's reactions. He recorded visits to the house and clearly felt that it was nothing very special (Lees-Milne 1975, 160, 164). But, as he said, 'The Royal Society regards the little house as of the very highest importance from the historical point of view, the formative years, the vision of the falling apple, etc. To them Newton is what Shakespeare is "to us", as Mrs Montgomery would

2 Dale also suggested to the National Trust that they could enlist the help of the mayor of Grantham, 'a Mr A Roberts, a grocer along North Parade … a decent person and likely to be helpful, if he can' in finding a suitable tenant (RS Archives HD8/3). Mr Roberts was, of course, the father of Margaret Thatcher, who included the figure of Newton in her coat of arms. Fara (2002, fig.1.1), has pointed out this claim to a scientific genealogy, which receives further substantiation here.

say.' With waspish confidence in his own aesthetic superiority, he never bothered to refer in his diaries to anyone at meetings from the Royal Society by name, including even the President. Lees-Milne had mixed feelings too about G M Trevelyan, whom he regarded as having no taste at all, no sense of what was the right period decoration, as being as dry as a stick, uncouth in dress and person, and apt to take out his false teeth and clean them with a handkerchief, but 'on all other counts he was highly respected and indeed venerated by all of us' (Lees-Milne 1992, 35). However, as Macaulay's biographer David Cannadine points out, 'He was devoid of vanity, pretence, or pomposity, he was free from envy or small-mindedness, he was outstandingly public-spirited, and he was a generous benefactor to people and causes in which he believed' (Cannadine 2004). At this time, of course, the National Trust, and Lees-Milne in particular, were in the throes of trying to save as many as possible of Britain's great country houses rather than concerning themselves with modest vernacular buildings, whatever their personal associations. Happily, it was not Lees-Milne's views which swayed the National Trust to accept the property.

## DOWN HOUSE, BROMLEY, KENT

Woolsthorpe may be regarded as a classic example of high-level negotiations which transferred the house from private ownership to the National Trust in a relatively straightforward way. The history of Down House, the second-oldest scientific personality museum, is more complex (the first was the preservation of geologist Hugh Miller's cottage in Cromarty in 1890). After Charles Darwin's wife, Emma, died in 1896 the contents were divided among the family, much furniture was sold, and the house let to a school. By the mid-1920s the house was unoccupied and neglected. Sir Arthur Keith (1866–1955), the palaeoanthropologist and Royal College of Surgeons Hunterian curator, was alerted to its state and used his presidential address on 'Darwin's theory of man's descent as it stands today' to the British Association for the Advancement of Science in 1927 to make an appeal. The appeal, rather to everyone's surprise, was answered by a wealthy surgeon and collector, Sir George Buckston Browne (1850–1945). Browne bought the house, spent £10,000 and more of his own money on repairs and on restoring the main ground floor rooms as a memorial to Darwin, created an endowment of £20,000 and handed the property to the British Association to care for and maintain.[3] All went well until the late 1940s, by which time the endowment had shrunk and the British Association were increasingly anxious to offload their responsibility. The most promising solution was to hand it over, with the remains of the original endowment, to the Royal College of Surgeons, who owned the research station adjoining the property (Royal College of Surgeons, 1954–64). The College were persuaded to take it on in 1953, but were horrified a year later to find that the house was riddled with wet and dry rot, and needed a great deal of money spending on it. They also found that the remaining endowment was some £1200 less than the book value quoted by the British Association. Desperate to find a solution, they recommended that the house be demolished, but found that it had just been scheduled as being of historic interest earlier in that year (1954). In 1956 an appeal was launched in conjunction with the Royal Society. Despite the Royal Society committee being extremely high level, the results were disappointing, raising only a little over

3 The English Heritage (2002 and 2009) guides say that the endowment was £2000, but Hedley Atkins (1974, 114) says £20,000, which relates more nearly to the figures in the Royal College of Surgeons papers.

£7100, rather than the hoped for £20,000 (Royal Society Archives HD/6/2/5). It was, however, sufficient to deal with the immediate crisis and put the house and grounds more or less in order before the 1958/9 centenary celebrations of *The Origin of Species* publication.

By the late 1980s the Royal College of Surgeons took a hard look again at the finances, which had been kept afloat by selling one of the pictures, a Stubbs, which had belonged to Buckston Browne. This coincided with the College's decision to close their research station in the village of Downe and ensure that in future their commitments would never again materially exceed their income (Royal College of Surgeons 1988; 1989a). The situation was back to that of the early 1950s: the house in a deteriorating state and the College keen to shed what it saw as a burden. The Museum of Natural History looked as though it might come to the rescue; a lease was negotiated, but sufficient funding was not found (Royal College of Surgeons 1989b). Rescue was nevertheless achieved in 1996, with grants from the Wellcome Trust and the Heritage Lottery Fund, together with those monies raised by the Natural History Museum. The property was passed to English Heritage, to restore and open to the public in a manner 'worthy of Charles Darwin', as the joint press release said (Royal College of Surgeons 1996). English Heritage undertook an extensive and thoroughly researched restoration and in 1998 it opened once again to the public.

A key point to emphasise about Down House is its fragility – a physical fragility which undermined the efforts of successive keepers. In the 1920s the house was empty and deteriorating. In the 1950s demolition was seriously suggested. Rescue in the early 1990s was far from certain and the contents of the house were actually valued for sale by an auction house. Physical condition alone can determine survival. And Down was more than just a house. It had a garden, an estate, it was Darwin's laboratory, his thinking path, set in a still remarkably unspoilt landscape. Everything about the house and its surroundings spoke of their relationship to Darwin's work, providing an ecology in miniature of *The Origin of Species*.

But beyond the institutions which took over responsibility for the house and estate, Down had an influential keeper of the flame during a key period of its history. Buckston Browne is properly acknowledged as rescuing Down in 1928, but it was Sir Arthur Keith who set everything in motion (Power 1953, 116–19). Keith, an influential populariser of scientific work, first visited Down in 1921, when it made a deep impression on him (Keith 1955, 285–6). His own work, of course, rested on Darwin's theories of the ancestry of man. It was Keith who presided over the opening of the house in 1929, and whose speech formed the major part of the first guide book issued by the British Association in the same year (Royal College of Surgeons Archives 1929). It was Keith who suggested to Buckston Browne in 1931 that it would be an excellent idea for there to be a country retreat for young surgeons of the College. Buckston Browne acted on the suggestion and bought the 13 acres adjoining Down House for what became known as the Buckston Browne Research Farm. This created a physical link between Downe and the Royal College of Surgeons, without which they would have had *no* interest in acquiring the house in the 1950s. Keith also rented one of the cottages on the estate from 1930 until his death in 1955, when he was buried in the churchyard at Downe. He did not boast of his role, and seems to have been content to move quietly behind the scenes. For who was on the Royal College of Surgeons committee which discussed the acquisition of Down House in 1953 but Sir Arthur Keith? It might be too much to accuse Keith of helping to sell the College a pretty duff deal, but no doubt he rehearsed the arguments in favour – its historic importance, a valuable addition to the Buckston Browne farm, the dangers of having a hostile owner next door, especially since animal experiments were being conducted on the farm (work involving animals tended to raise the spectre of vivisection and there had been complaints about dogs barking). To be fair, Keith does not seem to have known about the dry rot and in his final book, *Darwin Revalued*, he added an impassioned postscript appealing to all who cherished Darwin's memory (Keith 1955, 290).

## 20 Maresfield Gardens, London (Berggasse 19, Vienna)

In contrast to the iconic Down House site, 20 Maresfield Gardens in West Hampstead, London, is a handsome middle-class residence built in the 1920s in the then fashionable 'Queen Anne' style of Hampstead Garden Suburb. It was here that Sigmund Freud lived after his departure from Vienna in 1938, during the year before his death in 1939. The downstairs is left very much as it was in Freud's day, especially the library and study, with the upstairs turned into exhibition space and a room devoted to his daughter Anna Freud (Freud Museum 1998). The house, however, represents powerfully two aspects of Freud's life which reflect intensely the concerns of the keepers of his flame.

First, it was Freud's refuge from the Nazi regime, a place where he could, already gravely ill, die in liberty with the knowledge that his immediate family were safe. The story of Freud's arrival has often been told – the difficulties of exiting from Vienna, the increasing threats, the indefatigable efforts of Princess Marie Bonaparte and others to extract not only Freud himself, but also his library, letters and his art collection. The story has all the drama of an eleventh-hour escape, to a refuge not enjoyed for long. The house survived because Anna Freud continued to live there after her parents died, and maintained his study-consulting room as an untouched shrine, while continuing to practise and develop her own work in psychotherapy. Before she died, she sold the house in 1980 to a trust, and on her death left the contents to become a museum dedicated to her father. The museum opened in 1986, drawing heavily on funding from the US, above all from the psychology profession, as it still does. It acts now as a memorial to Freud, a meeting centre for Freudian psychoanalysts, and supports education and artwork inspired by his ideas.[4] It is therefore a site still involved in scientific work and to some degree carries the flag for the Freudian school of psychoanalysis worldwide.

Second, in certain major respects it is the mirror image of that other home, the apartment on Berggasse 19, where Freud lived for so many years (1891–1938), and where he had written most of the works which formed the basis of a new discipline, the study and treatment of the psyche. Because Freud was able to take his possessions with him, his family took care to reproduce in London something which was as close as possible to the arrangements of the rooms that he had left in Vienna. There was the same furniture as in Vienna, the famous couch and chair, and Freud's desk with the same arrangement of objects on it (Fig 17.1). Added to this, there is the extraordinary richness of his collection, the overt and implicit meanings of the statuettes, masks, vases and amulets, many relating to death, childhood and totemic beliefs. Thus everything in the house, and particularly in the study, evokes 'Freud's absent presence', and the sense of 'privileged access to a secret place' in a private house, where many of the objects are not labelled, but juxtaposed with cards which cite a passage from a dream or another piece from Freud's writings

4 In 2006 the Sigmund Freud Archives Charity became the Freud Museum Trust and extended its purposes by naming Anna as well as her father among its objectives. It has, however, struggled to maintain its relevance as a museum at a time when Freud's theories are less widely accepted, as shown all too clearly in the BBC4 programme *Behind the Scenes at the Museum: the Freud Museum*, 20 May 2010.

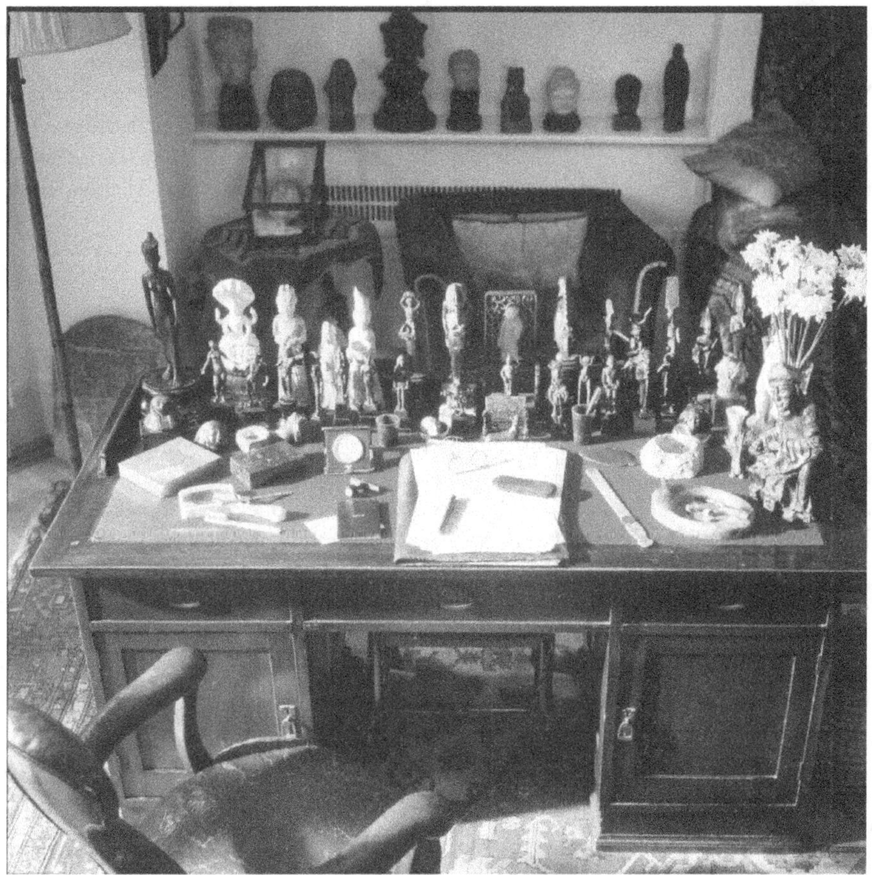

Fig 17.1.

Freud's desk. This assemblage bears eloquent testimony to its erstwhile owner's presence – the writing paper, spectacles, ashtray, and row of mysterious antique statuettes facing the writer as though lined up for interrogation. Against the wall opposite is Freud's chair, placed at right angles to the couch on which patients lay so that he could not be seen. The room conveys a rich sense of personality, of learned and abstruse knowledge, as well as indicating to the student of psychology the separation between theory (the desk) and therapy (the couch)

(Freud Museum 1998, 50). Using dream-passage labels was one result of an exhibition in 2000 marking the centenary of the publication of Freud's key work, *The Interpretation of Dreams*. It is, as Marina Warner writes, a 'cult site, a place of mythic memory, a shrine, a monument, a haunted house' (ibid, ix). A dream-saturated place, it evokes the feeling that dreams are a little uncomfortable and all too revealing of the self. At the same time, the interior constantly evokes the other, Berggasse 19, the place left, the loaded atmosphere of pre-war Vienna, from which temporarily the name of Freud was expunged.[5]

## KEEPERS AND BIOGRAPHY

Some general comments may first be made about keepers of the flame. The three houses examined here have no particular architectural distinction, and their intrinsic value and lasting appeal therefore depend on their personal associations with these giants of scientific thought. All have passed into the care of institutions or charities responsible for maintaining their heritage. However, as emphasised earlier, the role of individuals in their survival was crucial and it is noteworthy that many of those discussed (Dale, Trevelyan, Keith, Buckston Browne) were Victorian in birth and intellectual formation. Public service was certainly an important factor, but keepers of the flame found something more compelling in these relatively modest sites. Sir Arthur Keith provides good evidence. Whatever other factors may also have been present, it was arguably his imaginative response to Down when he first visited in 1920 that formed the basis of his emotional commitment to the site. Just like Dickens in the Palace of Second-Hand Sovereigns, Keith was transported. As he wrote, 'Henceforth Darwin became a real man for me; I saw him as he moved about from day to day' and formed 'a mental picture in which the living Darwin, moved, experimented, thought and suffered' (Keith 1955, 285–6). As he argued in his revealingly entitled address 'Science and Sentiment' at the opening of Down House in 1929, Keith believed that place was inseparable from personality: 'It is because there is here enshrined the personality of a great man' (Royal College of Surgeons Archives MS0018/3/3/2). To see the site, the space, the objects, was to meet the subject with the mind's eye, to bring the photographic image off the surface of the page to life and to provide a particular insight into his work. The majority of personality museums in this country have been founded by individuals passionate about their subject – a testament to their belief in their subject's importance and genius, their intimate knowledge of the life in question, as well as their own drive and energy. In this respect there is little difference between sites devoted to literary or to scientific geniuses.

Families are frequently important keepers of the flame, not always to the benefit of balanced interpretation as the temptation to edit out less complimentary features could prove irresistible (Hamilton 1992, ch 14; Brown 2005, 235–6). The Darwin family have been consistent and exemplary supporters over the years of efforts to preserve the home of their illustrious forebear, giving both money and material, treating Down as a source of family pride and scientific interest. Anna Freud was the keeper of her father's work and achievement. She kept his study and library more or less exactly how they were and, even had she wished to, it might have been difficult for her to alter those spaces much. Already in Freud's lifetime people made pilgrimages to see the

5 Berggasse 19 was neglected in the post-war years, but it too is now a museum (opened c. 1971) and also lays claim to be the founding site of one of Europe's great intellectual movements. Freud's birthplace in Pribor (Freiberg), in Moravia, the Czech Republic, opened as a museum in 2006.

couch and workplace of the famous psychoanalyst, both in Vienna and London. Freud, indeed, continued his practice in London until a few months before his death, so the couch was still in use.[6]

There are, of course, other keepers. Some museums are managed by local authorities and contribute to ideas of local identity. The Alexander Fleming laboratory museum in St Mary's Hospital, Paddington, was founded at a time of reorganisation in the National Health Service, when the hospital was keen to maintain a sense of its own identity and community pride (Brown 2005, 241). The National Trust is the custodian of many notable literary shrines, as well as Newton's birthplace at Woolsthorpe. However, the Trust's approach and overall branding tends to present sites in terms of their architectural, landscape or cultural heritage, rather than exploring the personality, though at Woolsthorpe the literature does emphasise the location of the 'eureka moment' there. Finally, it should be noted that the State in Britain is not a founder of such museums, although Down has now moved to semi-detached national treasure status under the custodianship of English Heritage. Elsewhere, personality museums have been used as an instrument of State: in the former Deutsche Demokratische Republik, important historic individuals were co-opted as forerunners to the contemporary Communist utopia, such as Goethe or Frederick the Great. Many examples may be found in the former Soviet Union, which had (and still has) numerous Lenin museums, including those in Moscow, St Petersburg, Krasnoyarsk, Kiev, and Baku (now the national carpet museum), as well as one founded by the Finnish–Russian Friendship Society in Tampere, Finland, in 1946. That is not to say that in Britain political arguments were not pressed into use when necessary – both Darwin's and Newton's essential Englishness were emphasised, especially during wartime, and served as a useful means of bolstering scientific authority at times of uncertainty. It was an effective argument which had been used by scientists in the interwar years, when they were competing for moral and intellectual authority in a society which was often critical of modern, scientific civilisation (Mayer 2000). At the same time, claims to universality were reinforced, as Dale remarked in his letter to *The Times* of March 1942: 'Though we are proud to think of Newton as an Englishman, his achievement in science, one of the greatest ever attained by the human mind, is the heritage of all men'. Keith expressed similar sentiments about Darwin and, likewise, the Freud Museum emphasises Freud as one of the essential thinkers of the 20th century, and thus significant worldwide.

Turning now to the problem of biography within the museum, much has been written about the general development of biography which need not be rehearsed again, from the 'Victorian enthusiasm for personality' as the expression of the individual's ability to shape his or her life and destiny to the current popularity of biography at almost every level of writing, including both spill-the-beans celebrity biographies and the most elevated of academic writing (Matthew 1993; Collini 2008; Soderqvist 2007). There has, indeed, been a parallel growth in both biog-

6 It might be argued that Anna's preservation of the Freud shrine could be questioned in psychoanalytic terms, given her sometimes troubled but very close relationship with her father. However, the space was used after Freud's death as an analytic space on occasion by Dorothy Burlington, Anna's co-worker in child psychology, and Anna took forward her career in the particular field of child psychoanalysis. The Freud Museum today covers Anna's life, which in turn helps to portray an aspect of Freud's family life, but regards her intellectual achievement as being commemorated in the Anna Freud Centre rather than the Museum, despite their amended Articles of Association, 2006. That may, of course, change as efforts are made to broaden the Museum's appeal.

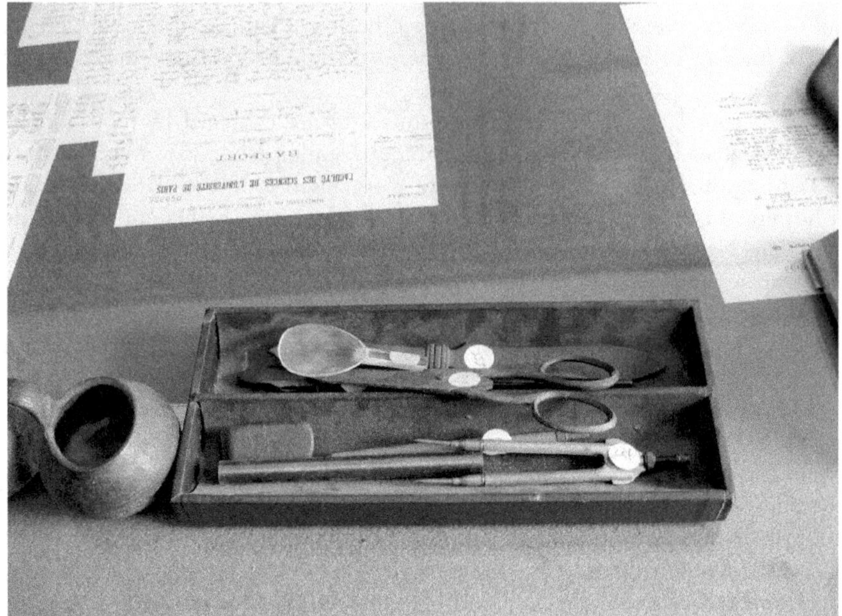

Fig 17.2.
Desk used by Marie Curie, and later by Irène Joliot-Curie. The Marie Curie Museum occupies the space used by Marie Curie, and later by her daughter Irène Joliot-Curie, in the Radium Institute of the University of Paris. The office and adjoining chemical laboratory were preserved unaltered from 1956 when Frédéric Joliot died. The report and correspondence on the table testify to the scientific work, but the scissors, compasses, letter-opener and writing implements stand as relics linked to the family which won five Nobel prizes, their banality transmuted by the addition of museum identification labels

raphy and in the formation of personality museums in recent decades, but the two are essentially different genres with different disciplinary histories. The development of more probing analysis and contextualisation of the subject, a key feature of academic biography, has been perhaps less marked in the museum. This is in large measure because biography in the museum presents particular problems, due to the nature of the available material, the visual conventions of the time, and the limitations on what can be said or conveyed in any single display. Sometimes the lack of authentic material relating the subject to the site in question may be a problem. For example, birthplace museums often lack original artefacts, as most of the interesting things in the person's life happened elsewhere (Lotz 2009, 32–5). On the other hand, the Freud Museum in London has the vast majority of Freud's personal possessions, papers and collections, while the Vienna Museum in Berggasse 19, where he spent most of his life, has few personal relics. To surmount the problem, the walls of Freud's consulting room are lined with photographs taken in 1938, photos which deliberately recorded an 'historic laboratory' threatened with destruction

(Engelmann 1976, 15). While there are reflections of biographical trends in the museum, they are largely separate.

In Freud's case, he was no lover of biography. He tried to control the use of his letters (for example, his correspondence with Wilhelm Fliess), as indeed did many writers who tried to control their legacy (Gay 2006, 612–14; Hamilton 1992, 219). The presentation of Freud highlights a central tension: does it illuminate the understanding of our own psyches, or that of Freud? What is the balance between the discipline and the man? As the character and psyche of Freud remains today problematic in the practice of psychoanalysis, it is not surprising that there is no clear answer. What is clear, however, is that in the contemporary museum, presentation has to focus on the man (or woman) first and foremost, and the site, the house, its contents are seen as the key to unlocking personality. The purpose is threefold: to humanise the subject and create a sense of the person; to allow key objects to stand in for a long and complex 'whole life', and finally to provide models for inspiration and emulation. Let us examine how this is done.

The life becomes the master-narrative, and objects are used to give meaning to the life (Arnold 2006, 91–2). One does not need to resort to semiotics to recognise how objects act as 'bridging devices' to carry a story across time and space. Intimate personal belongings carry a freight of emotional meaning. Indeed, no object is too humble or trivial to be excluded, if reliably provenanced to the great man or woman: the hat still hanging on the peg, the chipped teacup, the worn study chair. The Marie Curie Museum laboratory in Paris displays broken pens and pencils on Curie's desk, each with a museum identification label attached (Fig 17.2). The humbler the object, the greater indeed seems to be its aura (Workman 2007). This acts to provide both an essential humanising effect and authentication of the site's former resident. This is particularly important in the case of scientific men, since scientific writing from the 19th century asserted that objectivity was the key characteristic of science, that scientists were, above all, 'truth-seekers' (Shortland and Yeo 1996, intro). In consequence, any detail of the personal life of scientific men was generally excluded in order to focus solely upon the professional achievements. This has changed in more recent biographical studies of scientists, however, where visual images are studied to excellent effect (Secord 2009, 538–9). The museum, like the best biography, has to attempt to re-integrate the personal and the scientific life, but in a very different genre. Darwin is revealed at Down as a devoted family man, whose essential honesty and lovable qualities thus provide an underpinning integrity to his groundbreaking theory. Newton is more difficult, in part because of the greater distance of time and the absence of personal memorabilia. The current publicity leaflet characterises Woolsthorpe as the 'Birthplace and family home' of Newton, which at least provides Newton with a familial context, and a portrait of Newton in old age without a wig by Sir James Thornhill does give some sense of personality (Woolsthorpe Manor 2006, 10). There is graffiti on the walls of the house, probably of a later date, but there is little sense of Newton's character or indeed of 'his somewhat quarrelsome disposition' in the clean and sparsely furnished rooms (Woolsthorpe Manor 1979, 12). On the other hand, Freud, regarded as austere and forbidding by many, is shown as someone who liked jokes, kept dogs, watched home movies – in other words, as a real person (Ward 2000, 98–112). Anna Freud wrote a doggy poem as if from the current pet chow and presented it to her father every year on his birthday. Freud is also presented as a collector, with a tactile love of art objects, all of which had meaning for his thought as revealed in the statuettes marshalled on his desk (Molnar 2006; Forrester 1997). The effect is to provoke respect, but also ambiguity and uncertainty about a very different sort of groundbreaking work.

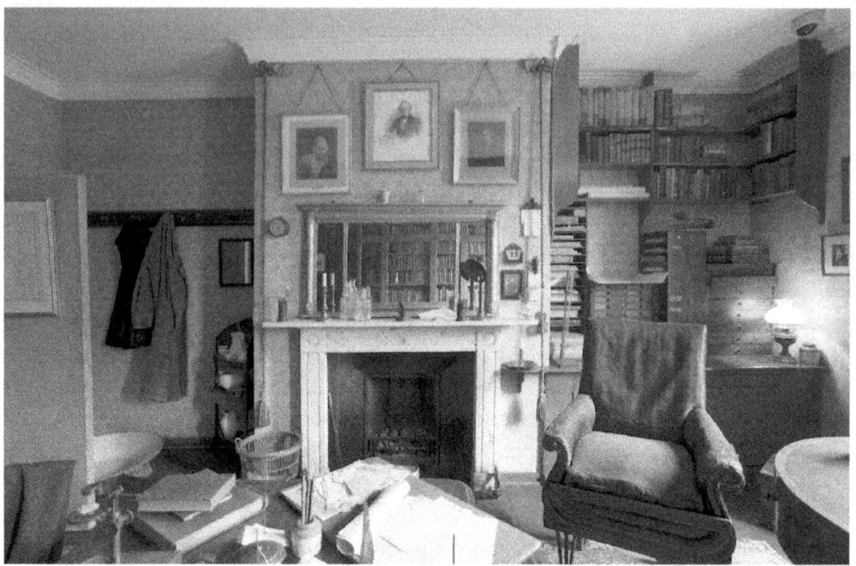

Fig 17.3.
Charles Darwin's Study at Down House. This room was not only the site where Darwin thought, wrote and experimented, but shows the semi-screened area to the left with bowl, water, towels and dressing gown. This allowed Darwin, who was frequently ill, not to have to leave the room. The clutter, the worn armchair and personal privy not only exemplify the 'lived-in' look, but serve to emphasise Darwin's poor health and contrast it with the magnitude of his achievement

The museum has in most cases to provide a narrative of the whole life, wherever it was actually lived. Brevity of occupancy is no obstacle, as Maresfield Gardens shows. Sites rarely survive unchanged, and all are to a greater or lesser degree constructions, however thorough the underlying research, and are well categorised by Julius Bryant as 'authentic fakes' (Bryant 2002). Sometimes, indeed, custodians are quite open about the constructed nature of the site.[7] Rooms, after all, are unlikely to remain completely unchanged, particularly laboratories, as in the case of Fleming, where the laboratory is in the same room but has been cut in half in order to allow the public to view it. Down House has had extensive alterations, and the current interpretation seeks to restore the ground floor as closely as possible to its appearance towards the end of Darwin's life, 1876–77 (Bryant 1998, 4). There was good reason to choose this date as there were a number of documentary sources available, including a set of contemporary photographs. However, as

7 An excellent example is the Maison de Victor Hugo in the Place des Vosges, Paris. This includes the Chinese drawing room Hugo designed for his muse, Juliette Drouet, for the house in which he installed her in Guernsey, a few doors away from his own during his period of exile there. Nevertheless the museum gives a real sense of Hugo's tastes and his sense of the didactic mission that furnishings should perform, as well as giving a sense of direct connection with the writer himself through the writing table, desk, bed and so forth (Charles 2003).

English Heritage agreed, even a photograph is not necessarily 'typical', but represents a tidied-up view composed for the photographer. Display trends change, and the 'lived-in look' is very much the current orthodoxy with curators (Fig 17.3).

However, objects and personal settings do not simply connect the visitor with some mythic past; they shape the type of personality presented and provide examples for emulation. Certain features are particularly noticeable in scientific personalities. First and foremost, the view that scientists are 'truth-seekers' persists, and the personality, however human, rarely includes weaknesses, quarrels, or ways in which the data might have been trimmed or selectively deployed. Darwin 'permitted the bare unbusked truth to speak for itself', as Keith declared with Shakespearean fervour, and, indeed, the wealth of material laid out for the visitor's inspection serves as visual confirmation. There is a Smilesian emphasis on our hero's industriousness, his continuous labour in his chosen field. But more than simple industry, the favoured trope is that of 'ceaseless thought'. As the 1973 Goethehaus guide put it, 'always there is evidence of the active Goethe!' (Jericke 1973, 34). The description of Darwin's routine at Down House serves to show him as incredibly productive and detailed in all his investigations. The same may be said of Freud, working until incapacitated by pain and approaching death. Newton at Woolsthorpe is stereotypically presented as absent-minded, forgetting to eat meals set in front of him, a characteristic often attributed to the creative mind. The 'ceaseless thought', the 'restless mind' which challenged conventional ideas, the single-minded pursuit of evidence to support a new theory, all help to create a picture that while these might be mere men, their minds operated on quite a different plane. Naturally, therefore, they serve as fit models for reverence, admiration and inspiration, but at the same time fit neatly into the professional stereotypes that we expect. As so powerfully in Darwin's case, his numerous images continue to resonate today, 'with his great beard and deep, sad eyes, [he] helped to sharpen stereotypes of the scientific genius as sage and seer' (Secord 2009, 538) (Fig 17.4).

In conclusion, personality museums work by using sites and artefacts to collapse imaginatively the distance of time and space. As Virginia Woolf wrote about great men's houses, 'it would seem to be a fact that writers stamp themselves upon their possessions more indelibly than other people. Of artistic taste they may have none; but … a faculty for housing themselves appropriately, for making the table, the chair, the curtain, the carpet into their own image' (Woolf 1932/1982, 37–8). To her, Carlyle's house spoke audibly 'of the sound of pumping and the swish of scrubbing', as Jane Carlyle and her successive maids laboured to surmount London's dirt and noise, providing a haven for the great man's labours. Responses obviously operate at different levels and in different registers, reflecting the conventions of the period. As Keith himself admitted, in his passion for Down he was not that different to all those who 'besiege the homes and invade the lives' of famous people and seek personal details of celebrities. We should remember, however, that this has been the case since the 18th century, and the case of the 'celebrity intellectual' is a thoroughly 19th- and 20th-century phenomenon. However, many would argue that the authority and public presence once enjoyed by intellectuals is now being displaced 'by the glitzy superficiality of celebrity culture' (Collini 2006, 473).

The way, too, that such sites are used today has changed beyond all recognition. The democratisation of culture may mean some loss of aura as the heroes of the past are joined by those with perhaps less groundbreaking intellectual achievements. Personality museums have the problem of maintaining that indefinable quality called 'atmosphere', whilst at the same time attempting to diversify the visitor experience, whether by means of spectacle or by child-directed interactives

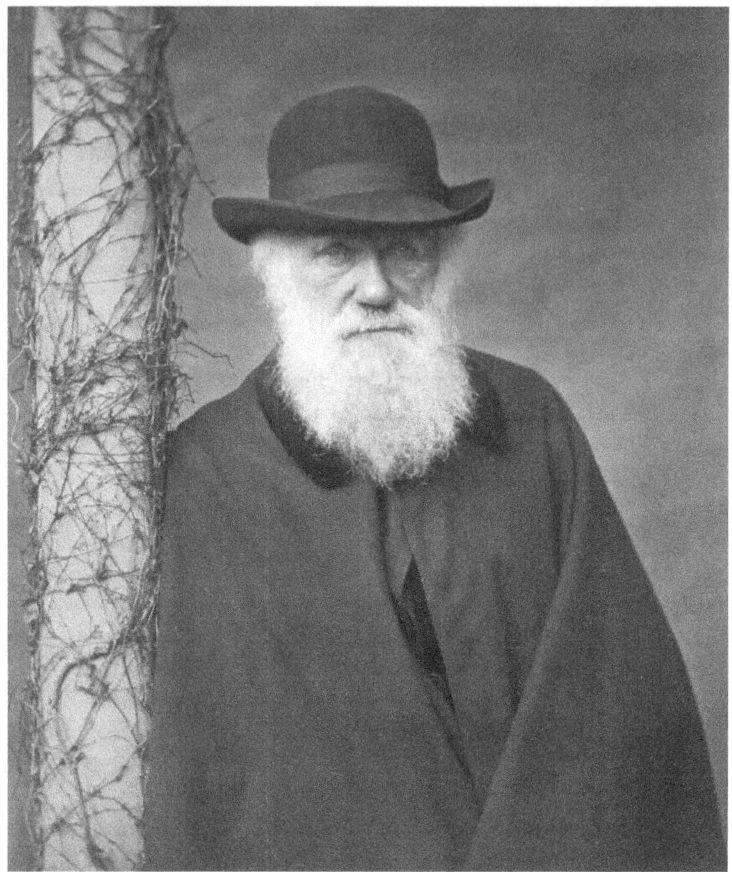

FIG 17.4.
CHARLES DARWIN ON THE VERANDAH OF DOWN HOUSE, C. 1881. ONE OF THE MOST PHOTOGRAPHED AND CARICATURED MEN IN HIS DAY AND SINCE, NO PHOTOGRAPH BETTER CHARACTERISES THE CONTINUING IMAGE OF DARWIN AS SAGE AND SEER. WITH HIS CLOAK AND SOFT BLACK HAT, SNOWY BEARD AND STEADFAST GAZE, HE GAZES AT POSTERITY WITH EXTRAORDINARY IMMEDIACY, BRIDGING THE DISTANCE BETWEEN PAST AND PRESENT. THE PHOTOGRAPH SERVES AS FRONTISPIECE TO THE CURRENT DOWN HOUSE GUIDEBOOK

and actors in costume. Digital photography means that visitors may record sites and then use them in any way they like. Hence it is not uncommon for people to photograph themselves in Darwin's study or in the grounds of Down House, taking possession of the spaces and inserting themselves into the great man's actual creative scientific environment. They then put their photos on the web, write blogs, address Darwin as if he were still alive, rate the site for other tourists, and enjoy it in quite non-traditional ways. Historic personalities in this context become infinitely malleable and sites endlessly re-usable, a sort of individualised consumption by the tourist made manifest for the world on the web to see, along with a picture of the beer at the local pub. The keepers of the flame become the global fan club as much as the devoted keeper or professional curator.

Finally, as museums have moved from private cabinets to the public sphere, so there has been a similar movement for the private to become public. Every detail of the private life may be exposed, and every quirk of personality deployed for public interpretation. Nevertheless, personalities are constructed, with greater or less knowledge, according to prevailing social and intellectual preoccupations of the time. Thus we have moved from tombstone-like memorialisation of great men to a variety of more 'human' presentations of the unique, if still stereotypical, talents of our heroes. A mixture of aesthetic and intellectual delight, personality museums are houses of mirrors. They act as mirrors, both to long gone individuals, to their creative endeavours and towering intellects, and also to ourselves – to our changing values, tastes and desires.

## Bibliography and References


Arnold, K, 2006 *Cabinets for the Curious*, Ashgate, Aldershot

Atkins, H (Sir), 1974 *Down: the Home of the Darwins: the story of a house and the people who lived there*, Royal College of Surgeons, London

British Association for the Advancement of Science, 1929 *Down House: Here Darwin Thought and Worked for Forty Years and Died, 1882*, BAAS, London

Brown, K, 2005 *Penicillin Man: Alexander Fleming and the Antibiotic Revolution*, Sutton Publishing, Stroud

Browne, J, 2002 *Charles Darwin: The Power of Place*, Jonathan Cape, London

— 2009 Looking at Darwin: Portraits and the Making of an Icon, *Isis* 100, 542–70

Bryant, J, 1998 Darwin at Home: The Down House Collection and Interior Restoration, internal report for English Heritage

— 2002 Homes for Heroes: the Rise of the Personality Museum in Britain, 1840–2002, in *Historic House Museums as Witnesses of National and Local Identities* (ed R Pavoni), Acts of Third Annual DEMHIST Conference, 51–7

Cannadine, D, 1995 The First Hundred Years, in *The National Trust: the Next Hundred Years* (ed H Newby), The National Trust, London

— 2004 'Trevelyan, George Macaulay (1876–1962)', *Oxford Dictionary of National Biography*, Oxford University Press, Oxford [online edn, Jan 2011], available from: http://www.oxforddnb.com/view/article/36554 [3 March 2011]

Charles, C, 2003 *Victor Hugo: interior visions: from furniture to decoration*, Paris-Musées, Paris

Collini, S, 2006 *Absent Minds: Intellectuals in Britain*, Oxford University Press, Oxford

— 2008 Well Connected: Biography and Intellectual Elites, in *Common Reading: Critics, Historians, Publics*, Oxford University Press, Oxford, 283–98

Dale, H (Sir), 1942, letter to *The Times*, 16 March, Royal Society Archives, HD/12/14

Dickens, C, 1855 Second-hand Sovereigns, *Household Words* 251, 13 January, 511–16

Down House, 1981 *The Charles Darwin Memorial at Down House, Downe, Kent* (guidebook, rev P Titheradge), Beric Tempest & Co Ltd, St Ives, Cornwall

Engelman, E, 1976 *Berggasse 19: Sigmund Freud's Home and Office, Vienna: The Photography of Edmund Engelmann* (introduction P Gay), Basic Books, New York

English Heritage, 2002 *Down House: The Home of Charles Darwin* (guidebook, text by S Morris and L Wilson; contributions to 'garden' section by L McRobie and N Biddle), English Heritage, London

— 2009 *Down House: The Home of Charles Darwin* (guidebook, text by T Reeve), English Heritage, London

Fara, P, 2002 *Newton: The Making of Genius*, Columbia University Press, New York

Forrester, J, 1997 *Mille e tre:* Freud and Collecting, in *The Cultures of Collecting* (eds J Elsner and R Cardinal), Reaktion Books, London, 224–51

Freud Museum, 1998 *20 Maresfield Gardens: A Guide to the Freud Museum*, Serpent's Tale, London

Gay, P, 2006 *Freud: A Life for our Time*, Max/Little Books, London

Hamilton, I, 1992 *Keepers of the Flame: Literary Estates and the Rise of Biography*, Hutchinson, London

Jenkins, J, and James, P, 1994 *From Acorn to Oak Tree: the Growth of the National Trust 1894–1995*, Macmillan, London

Jericke, A, 1973 *Goethe's House*, National Research and Memorial Places of Classical German Literature, Weimar

Jordanova, L, 2000 Remembrance of science past, *British Journal for the History of Science* 33, 387–406

Keith, A (Sir), 1955 *Darwin Revalued*, Watts, London

Lees-Milne, J, 1975 *Ancestral Voices*, Chatto & Windus, London

— 1992 *People and Places: Country House Donors and the National Trust*, Murray, London

Lotz, C, 2009 Home Truths, *Museums Journal*, November, 32–5

Marsh, K, 1993 *Writers and Their Houses: A Guide to the Writers' Houses of England, Scotland, Wales and Ireland: Essays by Modern Writers* (foreword by Melvyn Bragg), Hamish Hamilton, London

Matthew, C, 1993 Introduction to *Victorian Biography: A Checklist of Contemporary Biographies*, P Bell, Edinburgh

Mayer, A-K, 2000 'A combative sense of duty': Englishness and the Scientists, in *Regenerating England: Science, Medicine and Culture in Inter-War Britain* (eds C Lawrence and A-K Mayer), Rodopi, Amsterdam, 67–106

Molnar, M, 2006 *Freud's Sculpture*, Henry Moore Institute, Leeds, exhibition catalogue

Power, D'Arcy (Sir), 1953 Sir George Buckston Browne, in *Lives of the Royal College of Surgeons 1930–1951*, Royal College of Surgeons, London, 116–19

Royal College of Surgeons Archives, 1929 File MS0018/3/3/1–2

— 1954–64 Down House finances files, BA/1952

Royal College of Surgeons, 1988 Minutes of Council, 8 December 1988

— 1989a Minutes of Council, 9 March 1989

— 1989b Minutes of Council, 8 June 1989

— 1996 Minutes of Council, 9 May 1996

Royal Society Archives, files HD/6/8/17/12; HD/12/42; HD/8/2–3, HD/6/2/5

Secord, J A, 2009 Introduction: Darwin as a Cultural Icon, *Isis* 100 (3), 537–41

Shortland, M, and Yeo, R (eds), 1996 *Telling Lives in Science: Essays on Scientific Biography*, Cambridge University Press, Cambridge

Soderqvist, T (ed), 2007 *The History and Poetics of Scientific Biography*, Ashgate, Aldershot

Ward, I, 2000 Presenting Freud at the Freud Museum, *Free Associations* 7.4, 98–112

Woolf, V, 1982 (1932) Great Men's Houses, originally published in *Good Housekeeping* 1932, reprinted in *The London Scene*, Snowbooks, London, 37–47

*Woolsthorpe Manor* [D Howarth], 1979/rev 1984 guidebook, National Trust

— [S Haddelsey and S Haimes], 2006 guidebook, National Trust

Workman, L, 2007 *Dr Johnson's Doorknob and other significant parts of Great Men's Houses*, Rizzioli, New York

Young-Bruehl, E, 1994 A History of Freud Biographies, in *Discovering the History of Psychiatry* (eds M S Micale and R Porter), Oxford University Press, Oxford

18

# National History as Biography: Alexandre Lenoir's Museum of French Monuments

Alexandra Stara

Alexandre Lenoir's Museum of French Monuments in Paris (1795–1816) began life as a temporary depot during the French Revolution, sheltering artefacts salvaged from nationalised church, royal and aristocratic property. Following Lenoir's dogged pursuit of his cause, the depot was eventually turned into a public museum that fused emerging ideas about art, history and personality, enhanced with the flair of Lenoir's creative curation, to produce a unique representation of France. Unlike the model of the great museums, which was developing nearby in the high-profile Louvre and was to become the norm in the 19th century, the Museum of Monuments presented an alternative way of engaging with art and history, investing in imagination, allegory and empathy rather than abstracted rational principles. In that sense, despite its provenance and nationalist rhetoric, Lenoir's project has greater affinity with the idiosyncratic personal collections of the 18th and 19th centuries, rather than the public institutions that came to define the modern museum (Fig 18.1).

The largest of the Revolutionary depots in Paris was the convent of the Petits-Augustins on the left bank, whose keeper, appointed in 1791, was Alexandre Lenoir, a former student of the painter Doyen. Lenoir immediately embraced his task as guardian of the depot with zeal beyond the requirements of his job, which involved mainly the recording and labelling of objects. He would accompany the Commission of Monuments on its daily surveys of churches and attempt to exert some influence in order to steer pieces that interested him to the Petits-Augustins. Back at the depot, he occupied himself extensively with the restoration and arrangement of the pieces, betraying a vision of the collection that clearly transcended its anonymous and transitory present state.

During the first three years of his guardianship, Lenoir's intention for a permanent public display flew in the face of policy towards the collected objects, which were mostly seen as disposable products of the corrupt *ancien régime* – destined either for the foundry to retrieve their precious metals, or for the fires of the 'expiatory festivals' of the Revolution. The exception to this rule – objects recognised as legitimate works of art – were instantly claimed by 'the Museum' (the Louvre), the Revolution's cultural showpiece. However, the debate about 'national patrimony' and 'historic monuments' was ongoing from the earliest years of the Revolution, and although there was great divergence over the nature of the issues at stake, let alone the measures that needed to be taken, a sense of the urgency these new categories carried for the future of the nation was prevalent. This context eventually worked in Lenoir's favour and, after extensive correspondence with the authorities, he was finally granted permission to open his exhibition to the public, temporarily in 1793 and permanently in 1795. The depot of the Petits-Augustins was thus transformed into the Museum of French Monuments.

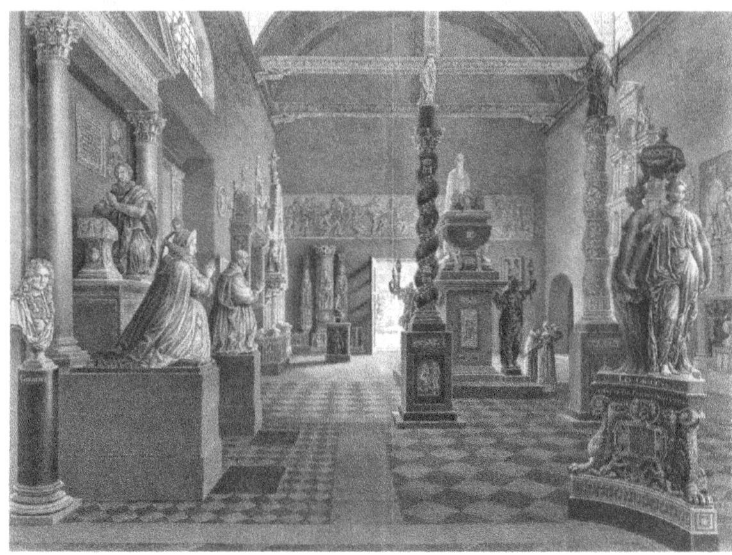

FIG 18.1. MUSEUM OF FRENCH MONUMENTS: THE INTRODUCTORY HALL, 1816

The idea of making art collections – almost invariably royal – available for public viewing and instruction had been developing across Europe since the middle of the 18th century. Notable examples include the Luxembourg Gallery (1750), the first public art museum in France, showing painting arranging according to Schools, and the Imperial Gallery in Vienna (1784), which was the first art collection to be arranged chronologically. Proposals for transforming parts of the Louvre palace into a public museum were already ongoing for a decade before the Revolution, when the project was finally realised, highlighting the importance the public display of art was acquiring as a manifestation of enlightened rule and cultural achievement (McClellan 1994, 1–12). All of these projects involved objects belonging to the recognised category of 'art', where ideological issues related to the works' provenance or content were, generally, overcome by what was seen as their aesthetic accomplishment.

Unlike established masterpieces such as classical sculptures and Renaissance paintings, however, the objects in the Museum of Monuments were not yet accepted in the canon of art. They consisted of sculptural and architectural fragments never previously seen detached from their settings, nor conceived of as separate from their royalist and religious affiliations until very recently. The possibility that such objects, as well as their settings, might be ideologically transformed into testimonies of historical development and national heritage to be preserved for public instruction, rather than corrupt *ancien régime* leftovers to be destroyed, was put forward as a proposition by a few pioneering individuals in the first years of the Revolution. Figures like Puthod de Maisonrouge, the count de Kersaint, and the eminent academic de Bréquigny, as well as the painter Doyen, who played an important role in the eventual appointment of Lenoir to the depot, had all proposed some form of conservation project for those contested monuments in 1790–91 (Poulot 1996). But none of these projects were realised and the proposals did not consist of sufficient detail to allow for a concrete image to emerge. This is not surprising due to the considerable uncertainty surrounding such objects and the novelty of their potential as museum exhibits.

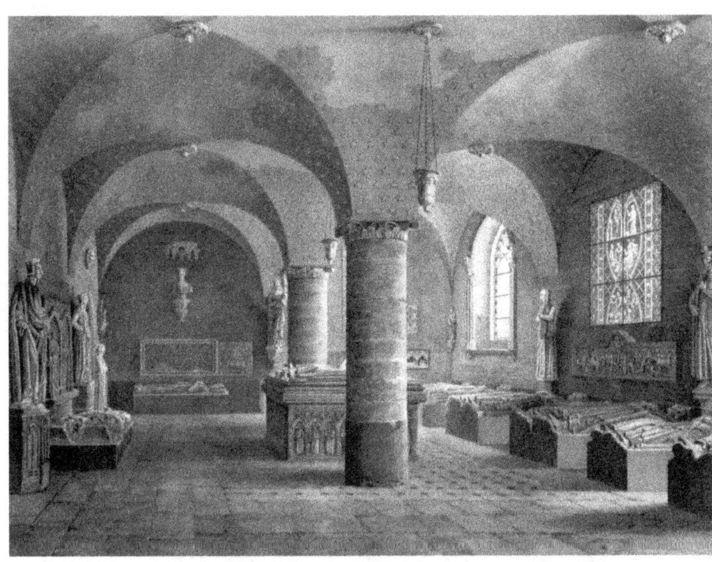

Fig 18.2. Museum of French Monuments: The Thirteenth-Century Hall, 1816

Although Lenoir would have known of these proposals, the pioneering element of his own project lies in the execution of what was just a roughly sketched, theoretical possibility voiced by a few contemporary thinkers; an execution, to boot, which persisted during the most difficult Revolutionary years with the harshest policy towards all things *ancien régime*. Furthermore, Lenoir's museum couched this scheme in an original combination of rigorous chronological sequence and sentiment, investing in historical monuments as both examples of a period and evocative representations of the personalities they commemorated.

The most obvious aim of the Museum of Monuments was to present a panorama of the development of French sculpture from its origins to the present. For this purpose, the collection was arranged chronologically – a novel and hotly debated principle at the time. Each hall around the cloister of the former monastery was dedicated to a century, from the 13th to the 17th, with a projected hall for the 18th century that was never executed. The 13th-century hall was the most sepulchral and moody in order to convey the origins of the nation in the Dark Ages (Fig 18.2). It featured architectural fragments and funerary statues of kings and nobles from the 4th to the 14th century. Chronological consistency was clearly not the issue here, but rather the ideological coherence of a particularly vague yet significant era – the sprawling field of the Middle Ages, where the roots of the nation and all things French lay. The 14th-century hall was particularly opulent in its decoration; as Lenoir explained in the catalogue, during this century, the artists who had travelled to Asia with the crusading Louis IX brought back to France 'a new style of decoration in the Arabic taste'. The centrepiece was the mausoleum of Charles V and Jeanne de Bourbon, one of Lenoir's famous *fabriques*, discussed later in this chapter. As the 15th century was considered the most dramatic for the progress of French art, manifesting the shift from the earlier styles to the height of later accomplishment, so the whole decoration of this hall was an elaboration on the style of Louis XII and Anne de Bretagne's tomb, which was representative of the era and, again, a piece 'embellished' by Lenoir's additions to make it more descriptive. Two other important pieces in the 15th-century hall were also the product of creative restora-

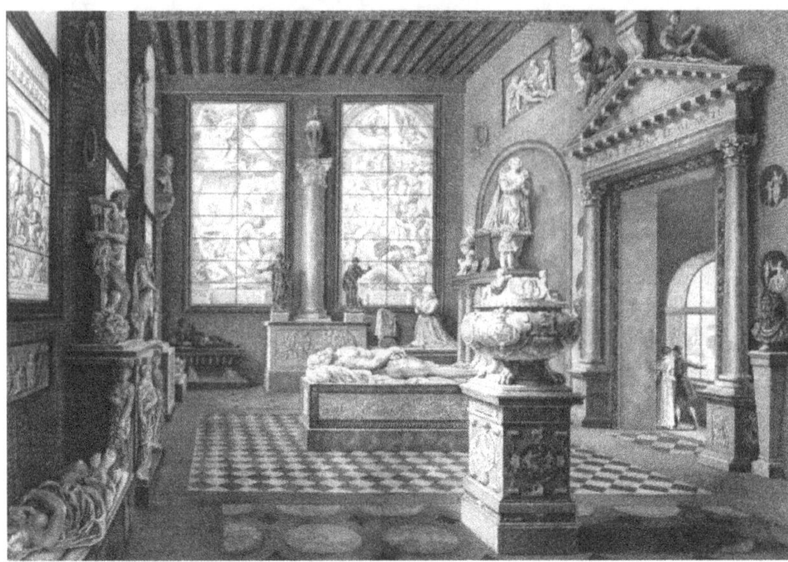

FIG 18.3. MUSEUM OF FRENCH MONUMENTS: THE SIXTEENTH-CENTURY HALL, 1816

tions – the mausoleum of brothers Philippe and Charles d'Orléans and the mausoleum of Renée d'Orléans Longeville. The 16th-century hall accentuated the celebratory character of the display, in view of the height of achievement in French art. Several of the key artists of the century, like Germain Pilon, Jean Goujon, Jean Cousin, Pierre Bontemps and Barthélemy Prieur, had individual memorials erected to them by Lenoir, usually consisting of funerary stele adorned with reliefs of their portraits and casts of some of their work. Prominent personalities of the century commemorated through sculptures were the admiral Chabot, Catherine de Medici, Henri II and the century's central figure, King François I. The 17th-century hall was the least decorative and most personality-orientated, where almost exclusively commemorative monuments found their place, either as representative of the figure they depicted or of the artist who created them. Artists singled out were Anguier, Coysevox, Le Sueur, Poussin, Puget and Sarrazin, celebrating them both through their work and their marble busts, commissioned for the purpose. Personalities like Henry IV, France's most popular king and symbolic of the nation's triumphs, were also commemorated in this hall (Lenoir year X) (Figs 18.3 and 18.4).

The museum also included an introductory hall in the monastery's church, which was the first space to be encountered in chronological circuit; and a sculpture garden, named the Elysium, which opened beyond the cloister in the north-west edge of the former monastery's grounds, and was meant to be seen last in the museum visit. Both these spaces flaunted chronological order and invested more openly in the aesthetic and emotive effects that guided Lenoir throughout his project. Despite this irregularity, which would appear to mar the clarity of the chronological principle seen in the rest of the exhibition, those spaces were central to Lenoir's project, as is evident from the importance placed on them throughout his writings. This is a strong indication that the entire museum can be read as being less about chronological rigour and the idea of progress in the arts – much advertised as they were – and more about a looser understanding of history as common ground and source of shared identity. In this scheme, individual personality played a central role. The chronological panorama of the museum was not an end in itself but a vehicle

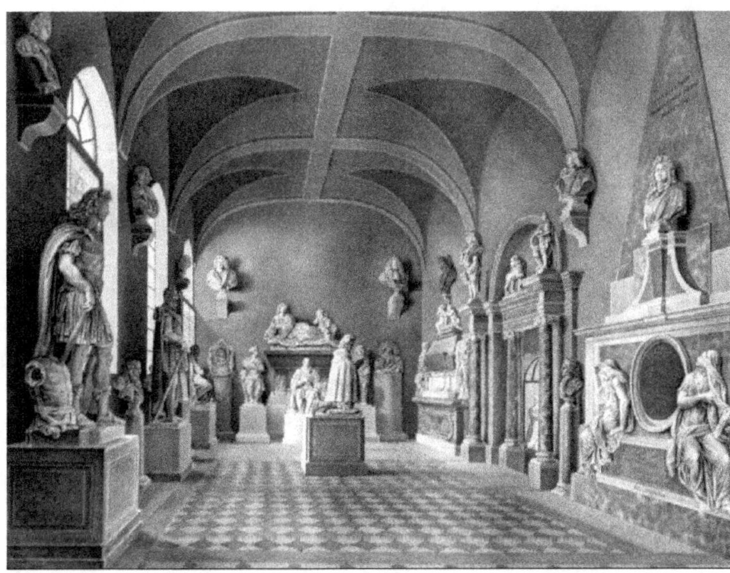

Fig 18.4. Museum of French Monuments: The Seventeenth-Century Hall, 1816

for carrying several other possible readings and experiences for the visitor, key among which was the remembrance of prominent personalities from France's past, and the opportunity for visitors to empathise with aspects of their lives and character, rather than merely gather information.

As soon as the museum was made official, Lenoir was authorised to seek the pieces that would complete his collection (Courajod vol 1, 163–4). Quite what that meant, however, was at best vague, not only because the Louvre remained the priority as the 'national museum' and had first say on all acquisitions but also because no final goal was ever set by Lenoir for his collection. It is apparent, however, that one of the key principles defining the quest for exhibits was the commemorative agenda of individuals.

Lenoir acquired monuments for his museum in a number of ways. He made forays to sites across Paris and beyond, looking for pieces of potential interest. Rarely were the monuments he brought back intact and often he would only find fragments, in all cases proceeding to imaginatively restore or outright compose new constructs for his purposes – his famous *fabriques*. He would also occasionally commission new pieces that he felt were needed for the narrative coherence of his collection. All his commissions and *fabriques* were exclusively monuments to prominent historical figures and important artists and men of letters of France. He also encouraged donations to the museum, which were usually private commemorative monuments of famous, or just noteworthy, individuals, given by the family of the deceased for display in the Elysium (Fig 18.4). In 1793, when the Petits-Augustins was still a depot and acquisitions were largely beyond Lenoir's control, the pieces commemorating a personality were about half of the total collection – the rest being non-representational objects of worship, ornaments and architectural fragments. By 1799, four years into the life of the museum, commemorative pieces formed nearly three-quarters of the collection (Lenoir 1793 and year VIII).

In the first years of the museum, the majority of new acquisitions were triggered by reports to Lenoir from individuals who wanted to sell monuments, or fragments thereof, which they themselves had bought in the massive sales of nationalised property in earlier years. However, as the museum grew and Lenoir's ambitions with it, the enterprising curator would increasingly attempt to bring items to his collection that were actually removed from their original location for the purpose. This flew in the face of the nominal *raison d'être* of the museum, especially with the shift of power towards the end of the century and the restitution of the church. Nevertheless, the confusion within the political scene, which was reflected in an amplified manner in cultural policy, and the intellectual grey area encompassing Lenoir's monuments served him well and allowed for considerable, if controversial, additions to his collection. For example, in 1798 the Directoire had sent the bodies of Turenne, Molière and La Fontaine to the Museum of Monuments, thus putting an end to the continuing embarrassment surrounding their fate under the Revolution (AMMF vol I, 141). Lenoir also managed to transport the remains of the philosopher and poet Boileau from the Sainte-Chapelle, arguing that he was a friend of Molière and La Fontaine – completely by-passing the fact that the church had been recently returned to Christian worship, and therefore there was no conceivable danger to it, or any of its contents. He commissioned monuments for all of these famous remains, which were placed in the Elysium (AMMF vol II, 427).

Perhaps the most telling phenomenon regarding Lenoir's pursuit of historical personalities for his museum is that of exchanges he would initiate, with pieces already in the collection that he considered 'useless' for the museum. In 1801, the mayor of Magny consented to the transportation of the Villeroy tombs to the Petits-Augustins, in exchange for a statue of the Virgin and two columns of black marble, to decorate the altar of a local church. Lenoir was granted the Minister's approval for this transaction, having stated that the sculptures in question were not contributing in any way to the museum (AMMF vol I, 251–2). Another of the many examples was the portico from the château of Anet, purchased from its current owner (having been privately sold after nationalisation) in exchange for 'twelve statues of marble and other fragments of this nature, all of them objects of devotion' and 'of no use to the museum' (AMMF vol I, 153). Lanzac de Laborie recounts that when the parish priest of the Petits-Pères requested the return of the statues of a Virgin and a St Augustin to his church (in line with Napoleon's recent policy of Church appeasement), Lenoir responded 'with perfect *sang froid*' that the two statues were of no use to the arts, and had thus been exchanged for a Diane de Poitiers (Lanzac de Laborie 1913, 347–8). Vanuxem also lists a considerable number of pieces which were either sold or exchanged by Lenoir between 1795 and 1800, all of them mere 'objects of devotion', with no relevance to the museum's increasing investment in personal histories (Vanuxem 1914).

The museum's extensive catalogue was a quintessential companion to the visit, providing the supplementary material required for the interpretation of the project as Lenoir intended. Lenoir published a total of 12 editions during the institution's life, under varying titles. Although the overarching narrative of the collection would have been legible without the catalogue, the details provided for each piece, as well as various supplements and appendices, were crucial for the full experience of the collection. With a wealth of biographical detail for almost all of his commemorative pieces, the catalogue was particularly important for understanding the central role of personality in the Museum of Monuments. As would have been expected, this practice really flourished after the Revolutionary decade, when it was no longer dangerous to address the royal associations of the historical figures. Nevertheless, in the first edition of the catalogue Lenoir had already begun personalising the figures, through the inclusion of such material for some of the more innocuous of the personalities – such as the young painter Drouais, recently deceased, for whom Lenoir composed a lengthy epitaph to accompany the monument he had constructed for him (Lenoir year V, 355). The catalogues also contributed to the personalisation of the museum more indirectly, through a list of all artists featured in the museum, to the extent that they were known.

Throughout the life of the museum there were dramatic changes of regime, from Revolution to Directoire and Empire, and then to the restitution of Monarchy twice, via the period of Napoleon's Hundred-Day resurrection. Lenoir was extremely keen to show his project as perpetually topical, so he made adjustments to the various editions of his catalogue to suit the current regime. It is true that, on a certain level, these modifications were political opportunism, to ensure his museum remained open. But, arguably, a more significant intention was also at work, relating to Lenoir's desire to create a representation of France that remained relevant and meaningful for the whole nation and its people throughout history, regardless of contingencies. This is evident from the consistent character the museum itself had, even as a developing project, regardless of the occasionally varying rationalisation Lenoir offered to justify it. Whether calling the Christian faith a superstition or one of nation's unifying traits, or presenting François I as a patron of the arts or glorious monarch, the museum was a project aiming to narrate the story of France through its monuments and the personalities commemorated therein. Lenoir wanted, in other words, to place the emphasis of his project not on political or religious affiliations, but on something more enduring and essential from which would be extracted the ideal of a unified nation, across all vicissitudes.

The importance of the notion of personality and its links to the idea of the nation was developing rapidly during the Revolution, with one of its more prominent manifestations seen in the Pantheon, inaugurated in 1791. The transformation of the church of Sainte Geneviève into a 'temple' to France's great men was quite a modern idea, which celebrated individual attributes, such as bravery and genius, over and above the traditional structure of divinely ordained, hereditary hierarchy. Nevertheless, such an idea of 'great men' was significant in the plural, as a collective that defined the spirit of the nation through best example. As Mona Ozouf has pointed out, death had no place in this representation – the great men were immortal (Ozouf 1984, 151). The Pantheon celebrated not the individual persons as such, but the ideal they all represented, something eternal and unchanging, despite the men themselves having been mortal. The Museum of Monuments, however, invested in its cohort of historic figures in a different way, focusing on showing them each in a personal light, as fellow men and, crucially, women with whom the visitor could identify and empathise. Lenoir went to great lengths in the display and in the catalogues to present them as distinct personalities, through details of their lives outside the abstracting realm of historical and national 'greatness' – as we shall see later in this chapter. Wherever possible, he would attribute to the royals represented in the collection sensitivities, flaws and all manner of interesting incidents, to reveal them as real human beings, beyond their status.

Already from the earliest centuries represented in the museum, the attempt at personalisation was evident. In the 'Medieval Monuments' section of the catalogue, at number 5, is the entry for the stylistically unusual sepulchral monument to Dagobert I, which stood in the Elysium. This king, it appeared, had distinguished himself in the wars against the Gascons and Bretons, but he tarnished his victories through 'terrible cruelties' and a licentious lifestyle involving numerous women (Lenoir year X, 100). In the 13th-century hall, a statue of Louis IX was accompanied by lengthy praise of the man's character. His institution of laws against blasphemy and duels aside, he was truly a virtuous and courageous man, who was 'compassionate for all the world despite his own misery'. In this last phrase Lenoir must have been referring to the tragic death of both of Louis' sons before him, whose mausolea, built by the king, were also in the same hall of the museum (Lenoir year X, 132). In the 15th-century hall, the tomb of Pierre de Navarre provided Lenoir with an opportunity to reminisce about the prince's father, Charles II, also known as Charles le Mauvais, who did not possess a monument in the museum, but in whom Lenoir clearly was more interested because of intriguing anecdotes from his life. It would appear, according to Lenoir, that the king had requested to be wrapped from head to toe in bandages soaked in an alcoholic solution in order to relieve an ailment of his, and a careless servant holding a candle accidentally set him alight (Lenoir year X, 169). Still in the same hall, the monuments of Philippe d'Orléans and Charles VI gave Lenoir the opportunity to recall the former's considerable poetic talents with an entire ballad attributed to the prince quoted in the catalogue, and the latter's fondness for card-games. It appeared that the unfortunate Charles had suffered sunstroke which deprived him of the power of reason, after having been a particularly wise and competent ruler. Nevertheless, he retained his life-long love for cards, which were invented during his rule. This is why, added Lenoir – when he was restoring the statue of the king, which was missing a right hand – he felt justified in replacing it with one holding some playing cards (Lenoir year X, 170–71).

The bust of Charles VIII in the 16th-century hall was an opportunity for Lenoir to recount the extraordinary story of his first wife, Marguerite of Austria. She was the only daughter of Maximilian I, to whom Charles returned her shortly after the wedding, without having consummated the marriage. While Charles went on to marry Marie de Bourgogne, Marguerite's hand was requested by Ferdinand and Isabelle of Spain for their son. On the way to Spain, the boat carrying her nearly sank, so the princess, convinced she was going to die and showing 'a courage uncommon to her sex', composed her own epitaph: 'Here lies Margot, the gentle maiden / Who had two husbands yet died a virgin' (Lenoir year X, 185). A similar story of extraordinary courage in the face of death was associated with the monument to the constable of François I, Anne de Montmorency, placed in the introductory hall. The constable had proven an intrepid warrior in a number of battles, no less than in his last, at Saint Denis. Having received eight grave wounds, wrote Lenoir, this man of 74 years gathered all his might and killed an enemy officer. Finally, a Scottish gentleman dealt him a fatal blow, but not before Montmorency had managed to break two of the Scot's front teeth (Lenoir year X, 203).

One of the key personalities of the 16th century in the museum was undoubtedly Diane de Poitiers, 'a woman famous for her love-life as much as her talent in affairs of government'. In all three pieces directly associated with her in the museum – her cenotaph, the portico of her home at Anet and the fountain representing her as Diana the Huntress – Lenoir took the opportunity to muse on her talents and to recall episodes of her life. Several pages were dedicated to recounting how the nobility and beauty of the young Diane charmed François I when she implored him to spare her captive father's life; how the rumours of the elderly king having demanded her virginity as a price could not be true because 'a noble knight, friend of the sciences and the arts, would not have sullied his life by such an odious act'; and how this 'adorable woman' subsequently seduced Henri II, who became her lover and commissioned the magnificent refurbishment of her residence at Anet, calling to the task the greatest talents of the time such as Goujon, Cousin, Bullant, de l'Orme and Pilon (Lenoir year X, 229–35).

The most striking and popular of all personal stories recounted in the museum was the one attached to the tomb of Héloïse and Abélard, the unfortunate medieval lovers. Lenoir started the catalogue's long section devoted to the piece with a disclaimer, stating that by erecting this monument he was not trying to recount the actual story of the lovers, as Clio (the muse of history) had already done this. Instead, what he wished was for the visitors to read the admirable verses of Pope and Colardeau in order to come and recite them at the feet of this sanctuary. Quite openly, therefore, this monument eschewed history-as-fact in order to invest in an empathetic experience with the past. Mentioning the inscription he placed on the tomb, 'Forever joined', Lenoir continued: 'Within their marble tomb, they love each other forever, these adoring spouses; one seems to hear escaping from the stone that covers them sighs of tenderness and of love.' Lenoir concluded his long, lyrical discussion of the piece in the catalogue by emphasising the indissoluble link between the lovers that this monument firmly established, thus implying a happy conclusion of sorts to the tragic story (Lenoir 1803, 102–4).

The investment in personality and biographical detail at the Museum of Monuments related to the contemporary fascination with theories of physiognomy – most notably those of J K Lavater. Visitors' accounts suggest that they observed with great interest the facial features of the statues, attempting to relate them to character traits, in tune with the represented figure's life and deeds. Lenoir himself encouraged this in a number of ways. He provided the sculptor Deseine with the actual skull of Héloïse in order for her likeness to be captured as closely as possible on her effigies, in the absence of an original image. He also repeatedly referred in the catalogue to the characteristics of various figures in relation to their features – relating them also to their effect on the spectator. He wrote, for example, that 'the eyes of Charles IX are still livid and on his forehead appears, like an aura, all the blood that he has spilled'. Lenoir went on to sympathise with Germain Pilon, the statue's celebrated sculptor, for having to endure such a face while working on it (Lenoir year X, 10). The 'cortège of assassins' in the 16th-century hall included Birague and Catherine de Médici – the latter disguising her crimes behind the 'seductive smile colouring her lips'. But, thankfully, the visitor then encountered Montaigne, whose features would 'calm one's memories' from the horrors implied in the previous images. A little further, the features of the chancellor Michel de l'Hôpital lying in his tomb were the embodiment of the honour and glory of his century, inviting the visitor's reverence and adoration (Lenoir year X, 12).

The most extreme manifestation of the investment in personality at the Museum of Monuments, however, was the interest in human remains. Far from simply being viewed with morbid fascination, relics of the famous or the merely interesting enjoyed great popularity at the time, and their collection was taken very seriously. The massive exhumations of the royal tombs at Saint-Denis in 1793 fuelled this trend on a grand scale, both in terms of spectacle and actual material. Lenoir, who attended throughout their duration, included a full account of the events and the fate of several of the most notable relics 'salvaged' from the lime pits in a number of his catalogue editions (for example, Lenoir year X, 338–56). For decades to follow, respectable guidebooks in many languages gave details of venues where one might purchase such relics, with a certificate of authenticity (for example, Anon 1814, 27). Louis XVIII himself, apparently, was given the toenail of his more famous predecessor, Louis XIV, as a congratulatory gesture upon his ascension to the throne in 1815. Even more significantly, Vivant-Denon, director of Parisian museums since 1802, was the proud owner of an entire cabinet of relics which included, amongst other items, a bit of Henry IV's moustache, the bones of Molière and La Fontaine, one of Voltaire's teeth and some of Héloïse's ashes. It is no coincidence that Lenoir also held remains of most of these personalities in the Petits-Augustins, linked to the most popular of his exhibits. His own part as an entrepreneur in this trade aside, Lenoir understood the importance of relics to produce a particular effect in his museum and its crucial investment in personality. It is not hard to imagine that a tomb actually containing the remains of the person it commemorated would have elicited a more visceral and immediate response from the visitor than an empty monument. The sudden implication of the physical reality of death in those monuments would have dramatically shifted the character of the visit from the realm of abstractions such as art, history and progress, to something deeply experiential and personal.

There exists considerable documentation of visitors' responses to the Museum of Monuments, which confirms the primacy of the personalities for the experience and underlines the display's emphasis on emotional engagement. Perhaps as to be expected, the most noticed monuments were those Lenoir himself distinguished in his catalogue, bringing them to life through biographical detail and anecdote (Poulot 1996, 420). Ann Plumptre, having lived for three years in France and after repeated visits to both the Louvre and the Petits-Augustins, expressed the general mood most eloquently, in 1810:

> The fabled gods and heroes at the Louvre, while we regard them with the highest admiration as models of perfection in the art of sculpture, yet cannot produce the same effect upon the feelings as is experienced in contemplating these monuments of departed worth and greatness. We admire the beautiful proportions, the exquisite symmetry of the Apollo and the Diana, yet no emotion of sympathy for the original is excited in the bosom; but who can contemplate the tomb of Héloïse and Abélard without a sigh! (Plumptre 1810, 25)

In 1816, William Stevenson wrote that he 'could not, indeed, sufficiently express' his admiration for Lenoir's 'able and learned classification'. But he was equally full of praise for 'these correct and splendid illustrations of human character and of national genius' (Stevenson 1817, 146). As mentioned earlier, visitors would attempt to match what was known of the historical figures' personalities with the facial features and expression on their effigies. An interesting reversal of this process is recorded in A H Niemeyer's comments: after observing the statue of Charles d'Anjou, he wrote 'never would a physiognome detect in the expression [of the statue] the merciless man who had the young Conradin, age sixteen, decapitated in the market of Naples'. And he proceeded to cite parts of the Sicilian Vespers (Poulot 1996, 426). Of the various visitors' commentaries to the Museum of Monuments, particularly significant were those of the great historian Jules Michelet. He wrote repeatedly, describing his emotive experiences there, and claimed that it was his childhood visits to the museum that gave him his first sense of history. The fusion of all the elements that gave Lenoir's project its unique character was masterfully expressed in Michelet's lines:

> I still remember the feeling, always the same and always vivid, which made my heart beat when, as a little boy, I would enter under those sombre vaults to contemplate those pale faces (…) I was not sure whether perhaps they still lived, all those sleepers of marble, laying on their tombs. I could not tell if Chilipéric and Frédégonde were not about to sit up, or if Diane d'Anet, charming and nude, was not just sheltering from heat and resting after her hunt. Wasn't she just about to stand up? (…) [In this museum] France could finally see its own development from century to century, from person to person. (Michelet 1847–53, book XII, chapter VII)

The investment in personality at the Museum of Monuments resonated with a major shift in the awareness of the role of the individual in society and culture at the time. It could be said that the exhibits were personalised even as the public, the visitors, were themselves increasingly understood as distinct individuals. As Richard Sennett has pointed out, by the end of the 18th century the role of the individual in society had taken on a new significance and the cult of personality, one of the founding stones of modernity, was already blossoming. 'As the gods fled', Sennett writes, the idea of personality as that which was innate and unique in each individual rapidly became the way to think about the meaning implicit in human life. This gave added weight to the immediacy of sensation and perception, while phenomena came to seem real in and of themselves as immediate experience (Sennett 1992, 152–3). The Museum of Monuments relied greatly on these ideas, offering an experience that was as much addressed to the soul as it was to the intellect. Beyond the rational principles of chronology and progress, there was a whole world that could only be accessed with imagination and sentiment. The visitor participated in the experience as a distinct individual, through his or her personality and 'inner world', where the communication of history occurred on the level of empathy of one personality for another.

Lenoir's personalities were not 'great men' in the sense of the Pantheon – hence the emphasis on figures like Héloïse and Abélard, Diane de Poitiers and many similar others, who had no claim to conventional greatness. Lenoir wanted to allow for a different kind of order to emerge in his history, one of character and emotions, beyond the established, Pantheon-like definition. Beyond courage, dignity and virtue in battle or in affairs of the state, history was also woven through simpler human tragedy and fortitude, through passion, love, hatred and cruelty. In this scheme, therefore, it was essential that not only were the officially great figures shown to be human, but also that a host of lesser characters were presented, celebrated precisely for their humanity, so that the visitor could experience history by empathising with them. Ultimately, such was the importance of the visitors' emotional participation that Lenoir erected a monument to pure sentiment, in the form of his *fabrique* to Héloïse and Abélard.

The investment in sentiment and empathy as a crucial medium for the experience of history left the museum's audience with a large part of the responsibility for the extraction/construction of meaning. The Museum of Monuments was clearly not a simple case of a didactic institution, but relied instead on active participation for its completion. This was enhanced by the nature of the exhibits and the display as a whole, which addressed their audience largely through allegory and the half-concealed language of monuments, demanding that the visitors themselves complete those sentences, through their own memories and imagination. Furthermore, the museum's experience was one of self-discovery as much as empathy, implying and implicating the visitor in the various layers of its representation and meaning. The truths waiting to be discovered in the museum were to be affirmed through their reflection on and reworking by the people who experienced them – whether they be pride in the shared national identity, the universality of feeling, the frivolity or importance of stylistic preferences, the sublime aversion for the early ages of one's own nation, or the equality of all men in the face of death.

The Museum of French Monuments emerged from the context of the great inventive project of history and the nascent idea of the nation which dominated the period. Between the lines of its advertised 'chronological panorama of the arts', a rational, abstract concept, it proposed a definition of nationhood and its historicity as something more individual and emotive, through an investment in personality. It could be said that the version of national patrimony presented in Lenoir's museum was less about the monuments as 'art' and more about the people and the events they represented, which those material representations were nevertheless essential in communicating. Between allegory, physiognomy, biographical anecdote, decoration and overall atmosphere, the visitors would identify France's personalities with France, and, through sentimental engagement and empathy, they would thus feel themselves part of the same history and the continuity of the nation.

## Bibliography and References


AMMF, 1883–1897 *Inventaire général des richesses d'art de la France*, Archives du Musée des monuments français, 3 vols, Paris

Anon, 1814 *A slight sketch of Paris by a visitor*, London

Courajod, L, 1878–87 *Alexandre Lenoir. Son journal et le Musée des Monuments français*, 3 vols, Paris

Hampson, N, 1968 *A cultural history of the Enlightenment*, Random House, New York

Haskell, F, 1993 *History and its Images: Art and the Interpretation of the Past*, Yale University Press, New Haven and London

Lanzac de Laborie, L, 1913 *Paris sous Napoléon*, vol VIII: Spectacles et Musées, Paris

Lenoir, A, 1793 *Notice succinte des objets de sculpture et architecture réunis au dépôt provisoire national, rue des Petits-Augustins*, Paris

— year IV/1795–6 *Notice historique des monumens des arts réunis au dépôt national, rue des Petits-Augustins*, Paris

— year V/1796–7 *Description historique et chronologique des monumens de sculpture réunis au Musée des monumens français*, 1 edn, Paris

— year VIII/1799–1800 *Description historique et chronologique des monumens de sculpture réunis au Musée des monumens français*, 3 edn, Paris

— year X/1801–02 *Description historique et chronologique des monumens de sculpture réunis au Musée des monumens français*, 4 edn, Paris

— 1803 *Description historique et chronologique des monumens de sculpture réunis au Musée des monumens français*, 5 edn, Paris

McClellan, A, 1994 *Inventing the Louvre: Art, Politics and the Origins of the Modern Museum in Eighteenth-century Paris*, Cambridge University Press, Cambridge and New York

Michelet, J, 1847–53 *Histoire de la Révolution française*, Paris

Ozouf, M, 1984 Le Panthéon: L'École normale des morts, in *Les lieux de mémoir, i.La Republique* (ed P Nora), Gallimard, Paris

Plumptre, A, 1810 *A narrative of three years residence in France*, London

Poulot, D, 1996 'Surveiller et s'instruire': La Révolution française et l'intelligence de l'heritage historique, *Studies on Voltaire and the eighteenth-century*, vol 344, Voltaire Foundation, Oxford

Sennett, R, 1992 *The Fall of Public Man*, Norton & Co, NY and London

Stevenson, W, 1817 *Journal of a tour through part of France, Flandres and Holland ... made in the summer of 1816*, Norwich

Vanuxem, J, 1914 La sculpture religieuse au Musée des monuments français, in Position des thèse de l'Ecole du Louvre, Paris, unpublished PhD thesis

# Museums as Autobiography

# 19

# Autobiographical Museums

Belinda Nemec

By an autobiographical museum I mean a museum of which the principal subject is the story of the life and/or career of the person who established the museum. Many of these museums are well known, but the autobiographical museum as a distinct genre has been given little scholarly attention.

Although it can be argued that all personal collecting is an exercise in self-expression and identity-formation, not all personal collecting is autobiographical. Conversely, some highly personal collections, dwellings or environments arranged for the purpose of permanent public display were not dubbed 'museums' by their creators but can be characterised as autobiographical museums. Other collections include a specifically autobiographical element but go well beyond this in scope and ambition; Henry Ford, for example, began his collecting by re-purchasing his own Quadricycle, acquiring children's readers of the type he had used at school, relocating his family farmhouse and then excavating the site for remnants of his childhood. Later he built a scale replica of his first assembly plant and relocated the mill where he and his father had taken the wool from their farm. Although Ford's Greenfield Village and its associated folk museum eventually grew into something broader in scope and larger in scale, its nostalgic autobiographical origins were significant in defining its character (Kaufman 1989, 36–8).

The various types of autobiographical museum tell, or illustrate, their maker's life-story in different ways, and although 'autobiographical' is a convenient term by which to identify these museums or collections as a genre, the analogy with the typical book-length, chronological, written autobiography is not always a close one. Some of the museums, for example, are similar to a diary or journal, being regularly maintained as the life is being lived; others are more like a memoir, a sequential narrative written towards the end of a life and based on recollection; while others may resemble a scrapbook, with no clear chronology but containing numerous anecdotes or clues which, taken together, reveal much about the creator's life, milieu, tastes and personality. The 'scrapbook' museum may also have characteristics of the reliquary, with relatively insignificant objects being imbued by the collector with a high level of spiritual, almost religious, significance. Many of the museums also include elements of the memorial, for which there is not necessarily a strong literary analogy; the similarity here is more with the biographical records formed by plaques, tombstones and other permanent physical biographical records that society depends upon to preserve historical information. Normally, memorials are created posthumously by a group or an individual who admired the deceased subject; but in autobiographical museums these memorial elements are created, or at least initiated, by the subject himself.

My first example is the Grainger Museum at the University of Melbourne, which preserves the material evidence of the multi-faceted life of its creator, the Melbourne-born composer, pianist, folklorist and educator Percy Aldridge Grainger (1882–1961). Grainger himself conceived the idea of the museum. Although he had already been collecting since his youth, in the early 1930s he proposed to the University of Melbourne (which he had never attended but which was located in his 'birth-town') that he would pay for the construction and upkeep of a 'Grainger Museum' on the campus. The University provided a small piece of land for the purpose. Grainger himself paid for the building, briefed the architect, donated the exhibits, recruited, paid and supervised the curators, and met the running costs during his lifetime. The remarkable breadth and diversity of Grainger's interests are reflected in the size and variety of his collection of letters, scores, books, pictures, garments, ephemera, furnishings, decorative arts, musical instruments and other materials which over his lifetime he accumulated or deliberately acquired, and then documented and preserved. Grainger's Museum represented a significant element in his life-long campaign to leave a legacy which would position him as a major international modernist composer, and as Australia's first great composer.

Grainger originally envisaged the museum as having two distinct halves: the 'Grainger Museum', to be filled by Grainger himself and devoted to Grainger as subject matter, and the 'Music Museum' – possibly to be complemented by a future Music Library (Grainger 1938a) – to be filled by the University and 'to preserve and exhibit things of general musical interest and things connected with the general musical life of Australia' (Grainger 1938b). Due partly to a lack of interest by the University but also to Grainger's own over-riding interest in his own personal story, the Music Museum element rather withered on the vine. The actual museum as realised in Grainger's lifetime was far more personally focused even than its aim as stated by Grainger in 1955: to illuminate the processes of composition (rather than performance) from about 1880 onwards, a period in which Australia had been prominent in music (Grainger 1955).

The catalyst to the establishment of the Grainger Museum was the most tragic loss to occur in Grainger's life: the suicide of his mother Rose in New York in 1922. Percy and Rose's relationship had been unusually close, with Rose directing every aspect of her son's education, career, social life and sexual relationships. Her death was a terrible shock to Percy and led him to feel that he too might die soon. His immediate emotional response was extreme but, rather than dwelling only on his loss, he fixed his eye firmly on the future, taking steps towards confirming his place as Australia's first great composer through the publication of all his works and the establishment of two museums. He wrote a detailed letter to his old friend, composer Henry Balfour Gardiner, setting out precise instructions in case he, Percy, died before he could get home to New York (he was in California when his mother died), together with a blank cheque to use for publishing his music:

> I am all in life that remains of my beloved mother, & I wish to live so as to make her as sweetly remembered as possible [...] You understand the general need of bringing out everything [...] that, together, could place me a[s] Australia's 1st great composer & make Australia *& my mother's name shine bright.* [... Long list of compositions and tasks includes:]
>
> 29 All very intimate letters or notes should be deposited in an Australian Grainger Museum, preferably in birth-town Melbourne
>
> 30 Mother's ashes & mine (both cremated) to be placed beside her mother's in cemetery (which?) in Adelaide South Australia [...]
>
> 31 Could plot of ground (owned by me) next to White Plains home be used for building small *fireproof* Grainger Museum? (Grainger 1994)

Although collecting and preserving objects are well-recognised means of relating to the deceased

(Gibson 2004; Pearce 1995, 238), and the death of a loved one has been a catalyst to many prominent collectors, such as Sigmund Freud, J Pierpont Morgan and le Duc Jean de Berry (Belk 1995, 28, 49; Muensterberger 1994, 169), Grainger took this response to a further extreme. He was concerned not only with preserving memories, but also with preserving truth: 'When remarkable people die (such as my mother [...]) no-one seems able or willing to describe them justly, faithfully [...] There is some conspiracy going on anent the remarkable dead' (Grainger 1949–54, 66). His compositional output declined after Rose's death, but the bereavement triggered autobiography (Perry 2001, 126), a documentary habit which ran parallel to his collecting. Although a prolific correspondent and essayist, Grainger never wrote a formal autobiography, but from 1922 onwards he produced over 500,000 words of rambling memoirs, essays and anecdotes (Gillies *et al* 2006). Characterised as a manifestation of Grainger's long-standing documentary obsession (Perry 2001), their underlying motives were principally to examine Grainger's relationship with his mother, to place himself and his circle in a position of primacy in the history of 20th-century music, and to explain his own sexuality (Gillies and Clunies-Ross 1999). These also figured among the concerns of the Grainger Museum. This alignment between his writing and museum activities demonstrates how Grainger moved seamlessly between collecting, recording, preserving, analysing and promoting; all were integrated in his project of creative memorialising. However, his continuing work on the museum suggests that Grainger did not feel that his written narratives and memoirs, albeit lengthy, were sufficient to communicate the full depth and breadth of his life and work to future generations; the vast quantity of raw data contained in the museum collection was also necessary. Conversely, in recording his memories in such detail, Grainger was acknowledging that the museum was also insufficient in itself, although the very act of writing appears to have been of therapeutic value.

Collecting and preserving were significant in giving meaning to Grainger's life and to defining his sense of personal and artistic identity. To Grainger, 'art & things are unsunderably twined together' (Grainger 1933–34, 65). Grainger's parents had also been collectors. When Rose died, Percy preserved her collection of his childhood memorabilia and other items, not only for their relevance to his own life, but also as part of Rose's legacy. If collecting is indeed 'identity work' (Belk and Wallendorf 1994, 240), then Grainger's incorporation of Rose's collection into his own after her death demonstrates their close relationship, the feminine nature of his upbringing and his strong identification with her; the very identification which, potentially ruptured by her suicide, initiated his Museum project.

## THE GRAINGER MUSEUM AS AUTOBIOGRAPHY

'Let the genius be presented *whole*, as life made & moulded him' (Grainger 1944).

Grainger's museum has characteristics of the archive, library and museum. His collection includes the most trivial, and intimate, items, including those relating to his sado-masochistic flagellantism (Pear 2003). Grainger felt that his sexuality was an integral and significant part of his creative personality and therefore its evidence should be preserved. Here Grainger diverged from the typical museum- and exhibition-makers of his day, who maintained a clear distinction between the 'higher' cultural and intellectual pleasures and 'lower' pleasures such as sexual ones (Greenhalgh 1989, 86). Grainger claimed to be, and perhaps sincerely believed that he was, all-encompassing in what he included in his museum. In 1941, for example, he wrote, 'Most museums, most cultural endeavors, suffer from being subjected to TOO MUCH TASTE, TOO MUCH ELIMINATION, TOO MUCH SELECTION, TOO MUCH SPECIALISATION! What we want (in museums & cultural records) is ALL-SIDEDNESS, side-lights, cross-references' (Grainger 1941). In fact, however, Grainger, like all museum makers, made choices about what to include and exclude, both within the stored collection and presented in the displays.

Even Grainger's idiosyncratic method of cataloguing his correspondence was autobiographical, embodying a hierarchy based on the degree of closeness of the personal relationship between Grainger and the correspondent, or their significance in his eyes. For example, letters from 'Servants to RG [Rose Grainger], PG [Percy Grainger], EG [Ella Grainger]', were grouped together under one catalogue number, as were 'American (not closest) friends to PG, EG' and letters from 'RG to British (not special) friends'; but each correspondent whom Grainger considered important – such as his fellow students from Frankfurt, Rudyard Kipling, and his Museum's curator Richard Fowler – was given his or her own catalogue number.

Grainger was familiar with house museums and memorials to geniuses and believed that, as he too was a genius, he was equally deserving of a museum. He was particularly inspired by visiting the childhood home of one of his favourite authors, Mark Twain, that had recently opened as a museum in Hannibal, Missouri (Grainger 1939). But Grainger wanted autobiography, not posthumous biography. In 1956, he wrote that museums 'should be done while the composers themselves are still alive & able to provide information that outsiders don't know' (Grainger 1956).

## COLLECTORS' HOUSE MUSEUMS

Most collectors' houses, such as that of the Pittsburgh steel magnate Henry Clay Frick, the house and library of J P Morgan in New York, Dr Axel Munthe's Villa San Michele on Capri, or the Isabella Stewart Gardner Museum in Boston, are autobiographical only insofar as all collections reveal *something* of the collector, and all homes reveal *something* of their occupants. Isabella Stewart Gardner (1840–1924), initially with her husband, purchased the 'best' she could afford of the accepted high-art canon, often based on professional advice. In establishing her museum, Gardner was influenced by European house museums, particularly Milan's Museo Poldi-Pezzoli (Coolidge 1989, 4; Goldfarb 1995, 6). I contend that such a museum is less personally revealing, less autobiographical than Percy Grainger's, which centres on his own creative output. Works of 'high' art such as those acquired by Gardner have a ready reception and market, and bring social prestige upon their owners, even if only recently acquired. Much of the material in Grainger's collection would not have been considered museum quality at the time he preserved it. Grainger was operating to a different, much more personal, set of values.

Conny Bogaard argues that intentionally educational collectors' house museums such as the Gardner emerged in western Europe and North America between about 1870 and 1930, alongside wealthy private citizens donating their fortunes or collections to public art museums (Bogaard 2002, 1–4). Other examples include Museo Bagatti Valsecchi in Milan, Museo Sibbert and Museo Horne in Florence, Musée Jacquemart-André in Paris, and Palazzo Primoli in Rome. While they do reveal something of the tastes and lives of their founders, these do not meet my definition of an autobiographical museum. However, one collector's house museum with a strong autobiographical element is that of C H C A Van Sypesteyn (1857–1937), heir to a patrician Dutch family which had lost much of its traditional property. In 1902, Van Sypesteyn established a foundation:

> to gather, keep and maintain and extend the family archives and portraits, coat of arms, valuables and rarities and all other objects related to or proceeded from the Van Sypesteyn Family [...]. The Founder, as the last male descendant of the Van Sypesteyn Family, wishes with this foundation to honour the family's name.
>
> (Van Sypesteyn Foundation Archive, 16 May 1902, quoted in Bogaard 2002, 8)

Thus autobiography here is defined as family heritage rather than personal chronological narrative. I would argue, however, that this is indeed how some people define themselves, and can therefore be legitimately argued to be autobiographical. Between 1911 and 1922, Van Sypesteyn built a museum in the style of a gothic castle, on a site which had once belonged to his family. As Bogaard points out, the result was ahistorical with a highly illusory sense of habitation, the collections (some of which had been gathered by his forebears) simulating 'an atmosphere of generations of domestic life'. Van Sypesteyn was creating an autobiographical/family history museum in a historically based faux-domestic building in which he sought to contextualise his family history within the Dutch national golden age (Bogaard 2002, 8–16). The closest literary analogy for this aspect might be the fictional elaborations or 'improvements' sometimes inserted, either deliberately or subconsciously, by a family into its own historical narrative.

## ARTISTS' HOUSE AND STUDIO MUSEUMS

The display of an art collection can, however, result in an autobiographical statement, when it is displayed by a painter or sculptor, rather than by a connoisseur collector like Frick or Gardner. Closer to Percy Grainger's conception of an autobiographical legacy was the creation of the controversial Australian artist and writer, Norman Lindsay (1879–1969). Late in life, Lindsay facilitated the sale of his home 'Springwood' (where he and his wife Rose had lived since 1912) to the National Trust, modifying it for its posthumous opening as a house-museum-memorial containing artworks, his painting and etching studios, letters, manuscripts, furniture, personal relics and his books comprising 'works of the writers who have meant most to me in prose and poetry' (Norman Lindsay, quoted in Hetherington 1973, 256). His will bequeathed to the National Trust: 16 watercolours; 17 oil paintings; 9 original pen drawings; together with pencil drawings, ship models, sculptures and statuary: plus 'all my paints, painting table and other materials dealing with my craft', and 'all book cases and other pieces of furniture decorated by me, together with all books which may be therein at the date of my death' (National Trust of Australia (New South Wales), n.d.). Such self-memorialising was a Lindsay family trait. Norman's brother, the artist and gallery director Sir Daryl Lindsay (1889–1976) and his wife, the writer Lady (Joan) Lindsay (1896–1984), bequeathed their home 'Mulberry Hill' (containing Daryl's painting studio and Joan's writing room as well as all their more prosaic domestic chattels) as a house museum to the Victorian National Trust, of which they were among the founders (Clark 1996, 11–12, 51, 62). Daryl and Joan's decision might have been prompted by sibling rivalry upon learning of Norman's actions to preserve Springwood, but it also followed Daryl's disappointment in an earlier plan to create a National Trust museum of 'Lisnacrieve', the Lindsay family's original country home (Lindsay 1965, 197–8).

The only woman artist I have come across who independently created a museum entity along these lines was a sculptor and to a lesser extent painter, Adèle d'Affry (1836–1879), the Duchess Castiglione Colonna, known professionally as 'Marcello'. Her most famous work is the bronze sculpture *Phythia* of 1870, installed in the Paris Opéra since 1875. Suffering for some time from tuberculosis, she spent her final years painting rather than sculpting, designing her tombstone (on which the epitaph included a comment to the effect that her works survived her: '*Elle aima le beau et le bien et ses oeuvres lui survivent*'), organising her affairs, and planning the creation of the Musée Marcello, to open posthumously in her Swiss birth-town, Fribourg (Pierre 2003). The eventual result was predominantly memorial in nature: a pair of rooms (within Fribourg's Cantonal museum) displaying her collection of her own works, those of her contemporaries, and her own furniture, tapestries and other possessions, including gifts from artist friends. One of these rooms was set up as an artist's atelier. This museum closed in 1936 (Pierre 2006).[1]

A substantial museum legacy was left by the French symbolist painter Gustave Moreau (1826–1898). The museum he established late in life on the premises of his Paris studio and family home shares some characteristics with the Grainger Museum, as did the two men's lives. Like Grainger, Moreau pondered immortality. At 36, when his father, his teacher and a dear friend all died in the one year, Moreau wrote on a sketch: 'This evening 24 December 1862. I think of my death and of the fate of my poor little works and all these compositions which I have taken pains to keep together. Separated, they perish; taken together, they give some idea of what I was as an artist and of the milieu in which I pleased to dream' (Mathieu 1986, 31, trans B Nemec). Although achieving public acclaim as a painter and continuing to exhibit sporadically, Moreau largely withdrew from the public eye from his early forties. From about 1890 he envisaged a permanent museum in which his life's work and family history could be kept together and displayed, in 1895 commissioning architect Albert Lafon to enlarge and redesign his house to achieve this end (Listri 1997, 76; Mathieu 1986, 31; Lacambre 1999, 90–91). He made detailed plans for the museum, which opened in 1903, some five years after his death (Musée Nationale Gustave Moreau). Ironically, Moreau's painting studio, created for him by his father in 1853, was destroyed as part of these alterations (Lacambre 2006, 6). The crowded, dim, claustrophobic domestic spaces contrast dramatically with the large, airy (although densely hung) galleries on the second and third storeys which he commissioned to display his artworks: mostly large paintings on historical, biblical or mythological subjects, supported by cabinets of preliminary drawings, watercolours and other works. The collection also includes a vast documentary archive. In the rearranged private rooms on the first floor, Moreau created a 'musée sentimental' by displaying possessions of personal value, preserving his parents' belongings, hanging family portraits in his bedroom and furnishing one room as a memorial to his beloved friend Alexandrine Dureux (de Contenson 1998; Lacambre 2006), whose death he also memorialised in the mournful painting *Orpheus at the tomb of Eurydice* (Lacambre 2006, 16). Like Grainger – who was unconcerned with the monetary value of his collection – Moreau valued things for their associations, numen, aura, or souvenir value, rather than for their more widely acknowledged aesthetic qualities which often translate into market value. When a friend commented on Moreau's mediocre furnishings, he replied: 'Do you think I don't know as well as you that the chandelier, the candlesticks and most of the furniture here are valueless? But they suited my parents, and that's enough for me. When I want to see beautiful things, I go to the Louvre' (Paladilhe 1972, 55). Moreau bequeathed all to the State on the condition that it 'retain its character of ensemble in order to bear witness

1 Another larger museum that includes a discrete autobiographical element is the recreation of his Beverley Hills office that Sir Arthur Gilbert insisted be included in the display of his lavish collection of decorative arts at Somerset House in London (Blom 2003).

forever to the sum of the artist's labour and effort during his lifetime' (Gustave Moreau, Will of 1897, quoted in Mathieu 1986, 31, trans B Nemec). His student and friend Henri Rupp brought the master's ideas to fruition, arranging the collection in accordance with his wishes.

Moreau's one-time protégé Edgar Degas (1834–1917) was in the 1890s planning to establish a museum, to display his work not in 'splendid isolation' like Moreau's, but among that of selected (mostly French) predecessors and contemporaries in a context 'both autobiographical and polemical' (Loyrette 1998). He subsequently gave up the idea, due perhaps to his negative response to Moreau's museum which reminded him of a mausoleum and thesaurus or *Gradus ad Parnassum* (Dumas 1997, 25). Other painters and sculptors who established museums dedicated to their own life and work include the English botanical artist Marianne North (1830–1890) at Kew Gardens; the Dutch marine painter Hendrik Willem Mesdag (1831–1915); the French sculptor Auguste Rodin (1840–1917) (said to have been inspired by Moreau's example); the Norwegian–American sculptor Hendrik Christian Andersen (1872–1940); the Basque painter Ignacio Zuloaga y Zabaleta (1870–1945) and the Spanish surrealist Salvador Dalí (1906–1989).

As mentioned earlier, many autobiographical collections and museums also serve as a memorial. Percy Grainger's will provided for his skeleton to be displayed in the Grainger Museum. Although this did not eventuate, some artists or founders have had their physical remains placed in their museums or libraries: Yale University's Trumbull Gallery, the Thorvaldsen Museum in Copenhagen, Antonio Canova's *Tempio* in his home-town of Passagno, the founders of the Folger Shakespeare Library in Washington DC, the Henry E Huntington Library in California and the Dulwich Picture Gallery in London, the last designed by Sir John Soane (1753–1837).

Surprisingly perhaps, Soane's own remarkable autobiographical house museum does not hold its creator's tomb. It does, however, hold the resting place of his wife's dog 'Fanny', scale models of ancient tombs and mausoleums, and Soane's proudest acquisition – the impressive alabaster sarcophagus of Pharaoh Sethi I (Blom 2003, 224–5). Soane combined in one house a family residence, studio, laboratory, teaching facility, classical cabinet and museum (Black 2000, 67–70). He began this project at the turn of the 19th century in his country home, Pitzhanger Manor, where he hoped through his sons to establish an English architectural dynasty (his own father had been but a humble bricklayer). But his sons disappointed him and Soane transferred his efforts to his London townhouse at Lincoln's Inn Fields, which he expanded and transformed from 1811 until his death in 1837. He collected classical antiquities and neo-classical objects both architectural and non-architectural; medieval, Peruvian, Chinese and Indian works, some fossils and minerals, many oil paintings, thousands of architectural drawings and nearly 8000 books (Millenson 1987, 77–8). Described variously as 'an autobiographical creation' (Millenson 1987, foreword) and a *Gesamtkunstwerk* (Blom 2003, 223), the result served, amongst other things, to demonstrate its creator's place in architectural history. Soane used his collection to situate his own architectural creations as the culmination of a tradition stretching back to classical antiquity (Elsner 1994), and in a more nationalistic vein, sought to elevate the status of the architectural profession in England (Feinberg 1984, 225; Black 2000, 69; Elsner 1994, 157–8). In this sense, therefore, his museum serves the typical purpose of the traditional written autobiography of a successful, high-profile professional. His legacy became permanent through his bequest of the house and collection to the State. Although Soane, like Isabella Stewart Gardner, collected material widely prized by contemporary private collectors and museums, the complex project in which he realised some of his own design and technical innovations, and his positioning of his own work in the classical tradition, gave the material from past eras an immediate personal relevance.

There are of course many autobiographical collectors who never think of establishing a museum. It is arguable, for example, that any person who retains his or her archival records – letters, bills, tax records, school reports, testamurs, legal papers, family birth, death and marriage certificates, greeting cards, etc – is creating an autobiographical collection. Some of these individuals, usually if they have achieved some public renown during their lifetime, give or bequeath their papers to an existing institution such as a national archive. But they do not usually go that extra step, to create a stand-alone establishment dedicated exclusively to the subject of themselves. The composer Manuel de Falla (1876–1946), for example, collected autobiographically in great detail (Archivo Manuel de Falla 2010), but the organisation now dedicated to preserving his archive was established posthumously and there is no evidence of his having considered establishing a museum (Garcia de Paredes de Falla 2005).

For some creative people, their autobiographical collecting interacts with their artistic output. Soane used collected architectural fragments, casts and statuary as examples for his own work (Millenson 1987, 6–7). The folk music that Percy Grainger collected served as the source for much of his musical output. Andy Warhol (1928–1987) collected art and artefacts intentionally through purchase, as well as accumulating (and boxing up in 'time capsules' which he then placed into cold storage) the vast quantity of material generated in the course of his daily life (Barclay 2005). Both of Warhol's modes of collecting – active and passive – were relevant to his art practice, being concerned with contemporary consumerism and mass production. The writer Walter Benjamin (1892–1940) extended his book collecting – his 'central passion' – to collecting quotations, which became source material for some of his writings (Arendt 1968, 38–9), and the graphic designer and collage-maker Kurt Schwitters (1887–1948) collected rubbish and ephemera to include in his artworks (Cardinal 1994, 71–6).

Sigmund Freud, although not an artist, formed a collection which interacted with his professional practice. From 1896, shortly after the death of his father, he gradually accumulated a collection of more than 2000 artefacts, mostly archaeological finds, displayed in his study. Janine Burke discusses the interplay between Freud's collection and psychoanalysis: 'The collection offers multiple readings: as the embodiment of Freud's theories; as an investigation and celebration of past cultures; as an exercise in aesthetics; as a quest for excellence; as a memento of real and imagined journeys; as a catalogue of desires; and as a self-portrait' (Burke 2006, 2). The metaphor of an archaeological collection to represent a method of mental analysis built on the gradual, layer-by-layer uncovering and interpretation of childhood memories is easy to see. But again, these individuals did not create a museum (or at least did not intend to: Freud's home in London was turned into a museum by his family after his death; see Forgan, this volume).

## Christian C Sanderson

For another example of an autobiographical collector who was intentionally also a museum maker, I look to a more unpretentious, unknown person than those discussed so far. This was Christian C Sanderson (1882–1966), a rural Pennsylvanian school teacher. Sanderson was an active, well-liked and respected member of his community, a bachelor who lived with his widowed mother, who through lectures, broadcasts and re-enactments also served as an unofficial or vernacular local historian over many decades (Thompson 1973; Barnett 2003, 223–4; Dorst 1989, 192–203).

Sanderson's collection, accumulated over his entire life, is vast but meticulously – if idiosyncratically – labelled. It mostly comprises 'relics': thousands of numinous souvenirs or relics that tell his own life-story, and that of his mother and forebears. Many of these items also link Sanderson's own life with the past and unfolding history of his nation, and to some extent, other world events. Examples include a fragment of the raincoat Sanderson wore at President Eisenhower's second inauguration; the match Sanderson used to light his own 60th birthday candles in 1942; a string from the violin he played at his mother's funeral; Easter eggs dyed by his mother in 1886; melted ice from the South Pole; a fragment of tile from Eva Braun's bathroom; and a piece of the fuel tank of the *Spirit of St Louis* (Barnett 2003, 222; Maines and Glynn 1993, 24–5; Dorst 1989, 195). By acquiring such items, Sanderson forged links between his own life-story and American history. He also collected more overtly 'national' symbols – such as a lock of George Washington's hair and a piece of bandage placed on Abraham Lincoln's final wounds – which he labelled as 'relics'. Teresa Barnett describes Sanderson as:

> a compulsive memorialist – an individual who seemingly felt a need to turn every object he came into contact with to the task of remembering. He preserved his life and he preserved the century's life, and he preserved them with a fervor that seemed undeterred by any generally accepted notion of significance. (Barnett 2003, 222–3)

This is also a collection that resembles a scrapbook, one which Sanderson shared with visitors – that is, the public. From 1906 to 1922 he and his mother lived in a house which had been George Washington's headquarters for two days in the revolutionary war, running what was in effect a house museum and battlefield memorial. They welcomed thousands of visitors, free of charge, to this and their subsequent dwellings (Thompson 2002, 23).

As with Grainger, closely connected with Sanderson's collecting was his assiduous record-keeping. Both these men blurred any possible distinctions between recording, producing and collecting. Sanderson wrote thousands of notes and letters and was a compulsive photographer and diarist, documenting in particular his own participation in, or response to, national events. For example, on Armistice Day he wrote in his songbook:

> I am writing this on Monday morning, Nov 11, 1918. This morning I used this book for singing in the Dilworthtown School which stands on the spot where Lafayette was wounded, Sept 11, 1777. We sang America and the Star Spangled Banner and Marsellaise [sic] from this book. Those singing were Anna Norman, Walt Dilworth, Howard Collins, Lee Parry, William Winston, Russell Kitzleman. Thus celebrating the surrender of Germany to the United States. Christian C Sanderson, Teacher. (Quoted in Thompson 1973, 198)

Thus Sanderson created a link between the American War of Independence, World War I, his own life, and those of his students; the songbook which he happened to be using on the day came to embody this moment of historic convergence.

Sanderson's approach to collecting has parallels with Grainger's. Although Grainger was interested in Australia's evolving *cultural* history while Sanderson focused on military events, political inaugurations, anniversaries and nation-building, both saw themselves as active participants in a living history which was contributing to the forging of their respective nations. Neither discriminated between 'high' and 'low' culture in his collection and each perceived even the most trivial item as integral to the whole.

## MAISON PIERRE LOTI

Another striking example of a domestically focused autobiographical collection and display was the home of the French writer Louis-Marie-Julien Viaud (1850–1923), known as Pierre Loti. Loti's collection reflected, on a personal level, the European imperial project, combined with a compulsion to preserve souvenirs of his past to counter a fear of death, and the creation of an alternative persona, based partly on his own travels as a sea-captain, partly on the adventures of the protagonist of his semi-autobiographical but exotic novels. Although constituted only posthumously as a public museum, the house was a deliberate and strongly personal memorial and showcase, and its creator an artist and life-long collector. I would argue that the result today is in part an autobiographical museum, although one that is presented much more theatrically than Grainger's, which is more literal.

Loti's sometimes autobiographical novels evoked sea voyages and exotic, faraway places, for a readership of largely armchair travellers (Blanch 1983, 12). In a period of accelerating colonisation, he penned tales of distant lands explored or conquered by the West. Loti was also a naval officer, traveller, artist and photographer. The modest middle-class house in which he had been born and raised served as a display case for his childhood memories, treasures gathered during his naval adventures, and his historical fantasies. From 1877 he began creating a series of thematic display rooms: a Turkish room, an Arab room, a Japanese pagoda, a Renaissance hall, a mosque, a Chinese room and a monk's room. By appropriating the trappings of exotic or colonised lands visited during his naval career, Loti linked his personal and national stories. Contrasting with these theatrical creations was the more intimate universe of his own personal and family life, as shown in the Red Sitting Room, his bedroom, his father's study and the conventionally bourgeois dining room (Scaon 2001, 49, 55; Pavoni 2002, 1–2). He also purchased the two houses adjacent to his own, gradually adding more display rooms, although leaving the exterior intact, giving no hint of this fantastic interior (Armbrecht 2003).

Although he did not specify that his house become a public museum, Loti went to great lengths to ensure that all his treasured objects would be taken care of after his death. He left meticulous instructions on preservation, destruction, or sale, even for the care of his pets and garden. He arranged for future publication of unpublished works, particularly his journals. He specified that he be buried alone in the garden of his mother's ancestral home (Blanch 1983, 313–17). His desire to freeze the passing moment through the creation of elaborate interiors based on the peregrinations of his own life, even if originally intended for his own benefit and that of his friends, shares much with the self-museumising spirit of the Grainger Museum, and the common if unacknowledged motivation of many collectors, including Grainger, to cope with the passing of time, and thus by implication the approach of death, as observed by Jean Baudrillard (Baudrillard 1994, 15–18).

Young Julien created a museum in the attic which he preserved all his life, always kept a journal (Blanch 1983, 31–6), and preserved *memento mori* 'as holy relics' (Blanch 1983, 22–3). Loti's writing may also have reflected his urge to memorialise. Interestingly, Loti was Marcel Proust's favourite author of prose (Armbrecht 2003). As Armbrecht points out, although Loti's writings and his house rooms were wildly fantastic, not realistic – that is, they were utopias – they were still personally revealing: 'Loti's utopias are perfect places in that he recreated only the most personally important features of a culture or time period in his writing and architecture, that is, those that meant something to him' (Armbrecht 2003). And the only link between these rooms, which represent wildly different cultures, places and time periods, is their creator or, more specifically, his memories. They were 'idealized memories of places from his past; in other words, they were utopias in which he took refuge'. 'Loti lived through his literature, not only for his public but also for himself.' His first room creation, the Turkish room, Loti created while simultaneously writing his first novel, *Aziyade*, both begun soon after his return from Turkey in 1877, and named after Loti's actual Turkish mistress, a married woman (although possibly in reality a man) whom he could not bring back to France (Armbrecht 2003). It is important to note that in his novels, Loti's hero/protagonist was called Pierre Loti. Loti was a pseudonym for Julien Viaud but its use for his literary creation shows that his books are a type of invention of self, an autobiography but also fantasy. This literary creation is paralleled by his exotically theatrical domestic creation.

## Gabriele d'Annunzio and *Il Vittoriale degli Italiani*

Another highly artificial, theatrical place that is now in effect an autobiographical museum, although not called a museum by its creator, is *Il Vittoriale degli Italiani*. This was the final home of Gabriele d'Annunzio (1863–1938), a celebrated Italian writer turned flamboyant military hero and right-wing, nationalist political identity (Klopp 1988). It was created by its subject during his own lifetime, with a view to establishing a public memorial to himself and his contribution to his nation's history. The result combines a strongly nationalist narrative with autobiography.

By 1921 D'Annunzio felt dissatisfied, disappointed, uncertain and disoriented, firstly with the outcomes for Italy of World War I and subsequently at the failure of his own audacious Fiume escapade (Bonadeo 1995, 143; Woodhouse 1998, 2, 315–52). Rather than entering the political fray of the Fascist years, he retired to the fashionable holiday resort area of Gardone Riviera, acquiring a substantial 18th-century farmhouse which he gradually transformed and expanded into the extravagantly decadent *Vittoriale*, funded largely by monies extracted from Mussolini's government (Licht 1982). According to his biographer:

> For most of his life D'Annunzio's sole concern was self-gratification and glory [...] to create a work of art from his life and to immortalize it in words. [...] And when inspiration for creative writing ran out, after his expulsion from Fiume in 1921, he spent the next sixteen years in the creation of a vast physical artefact which might reflect his life and achievements: the Vittoriale.
> (Woodhouse 1998, 4–5)

Thus, like Grainger but unlike Loti, D'Annunzio began creating his memorial when he had achieved celebrity but his most artistically fruitful years had ended. In collaboration with architect Gian Carlo Maroni, D'Annunzio transformed the estate into an ostentatious monument to his life and Fascist-leaning political beliefs, and eventually into his mausoleum. He covered the façade of the main house with emblems, coats of arms, statues and bas-reliefs, all recalling incidents from his life, created stiflingly claustrophobic, dimly-lit interiors, filled with objects ranging from casts of famous sculptures to bric-a-brac, relics and personal mementoes, and named the rooms after his personal philosophical and literary preoccupations (Woodhouse 1998, 372–5; Mazza 1987).

In 1923 D'Annunzio declared:

> Everything here has, in fact, been created or transfigured by me. Everything here bears the stamp of my style. My love for Italy, my cult of memory, my striving after heroism, the presentiment of my country as it will come to be, all these things are embodied here, in every search for a line, in the matchings and clashings of colours. (Singley 1996, 1)

He added a war museum displaying the car from his triumphant march into Fiume and the aeroplane from his celebrated wartime propaganda flight over Vienna hanging under a grand cupola. His torpedo boat was exhibited behind the house, while projecting impressively from a hill was the prow of the battleship *Puglia* from his Fiume campaign. In 1930 D'Annunzio donated the Vittoriale to the Italian State, and in the same year commissioned a mausoleum on the site's highest point, inspired by ancient Roman tombs. D'Annunzio was eventually interred there, surrounded by the remains of ten of his comrades-in-arms from Fiume and his architect Maroni[2] (Mazza 1987, 84–5). Many of the Vittoriale's rooms are like theatrical tableaux; in this it is similar to the Maison Pierre Loti, and it is perhaps no coincidence that two writers should turn to elaborate visual display to complement or expand upon their mostly literary careers.

## CONCLUSION

It can be argued that all collecting is autobiographical to some degree, in that it tells us something of the collector's tastes and personality. Thus the countless public collections which were originally private collections have an autobiographical element. Many art collectors have gone to great lengths to present their collections as an expression of their intellectual and artistic pursuits or social status, often for the benefit of visitors to their homes. Some are now open to the public as house museums, whether due to the express wishes of the collector or through the efforts of other individuals after the collector's death. Some collections embody information on the facts of the collector's life. But relatively few collections can be described as autobiographical in the sense that they were deliberately created in order to communicate the detailed narrative of the collector's life. Of those collections that do convey such a narrative, rare examples such as Percy Grainger's, Gustave Moreau's and Gabriele d'Annunzio's were presented with the intention of permanence and public accessibility – a museum, even if not always called by this name. Of these, the Grainger Museum is unusual in two ways: it was never a house – indeed it is the only example I have come across that is in a building that was conceived and created deliberately and solely as an autobiographical museum – and it was created over a long period while the life being documented was actually being lived, rather than towards the end of the life or career. Examples of the latter – museum-based retrospectives or memoirs – include the museums of Gustave Moreau and 'Marcello'. John Soane's house-museum was created over a long period of time but is less literally autobiographical than Grainger's. Christian Sanderson's collection is intimately autobiographical although not organised or presented according to any clear narrative.

I would argue, therefore, that no other museum shares the singularly personal detail, focus or intimacy of Grainger's museum, its long period of gestation, and its attempt to describe its creator's familial, artistic and social milieu. Only in Grainger have I been able to find the combination of a lifelong and consistent collector and retainer of *explicitly, primarily and self-consciously*

2 D'Annunzio's body was relocated in 1963 to the Tempietto on the Vittoriale site (Mazza 1987, 85).

autobiographical material with an urge to create a dedicated, permanent, physical display space. The Grainger Museum can therefore be seen at one end of a spectrum of 'autobiographicalness' of museums, with other museums and collections showing this trait to varying extents and in varying ways.

## Bibliography and References

Archivo Manuel De Falla, 2010 Official Website of Manuel De Falla [online], available from: www.manueldefalla.com [2 April 2010]

Arendt, H, 1968 Introduction, in *Illuminations* (ed W Benjamin), Schocken Books, New York, 38–9

Armbrecht, T J D, 2003 The Nostalgia of Nowhere: Pierre Loti's Utopian Spaces, *Mosaic (Winnipeg)* 36 (4), 81ff

Barclay, A, 2005 *Andy Warhol's Time Capsules*, National Gallery of Victoria, Melbourne

Barnett, T, 2003 Tradition and the Individual Memory: The Case of Christian C Sanderson, in *Acts of Possession: Collecting in America* (ed L Dilworth), Rutgers University Press, New Brunswick, 221–35

Baudrillard, J, 1994 The System of Collecting, in *The Cultures of Collecting* (eds J Elsner and R Cardinal), Melbourne University Press, Melbourne

Belk, R W, 1995 *Collecting in a Consumer Society*, Routledge, London & New York

Belk, R W, and Wallendorf, M, 1994 Of Mice and Men: Gender Identity in Collecting, in *Interpreting Objects and Collections* (ed S M Pearce), Routledge, London & New York

Black, B J, 2000 *On Exhibit: Victorians and Their Museums*, University Press of Virginia, Charlottesville

Blanch, L, 1983 *Pierre Loti: Portrait of an Escapist*, Collins, London

Blom, P, 2003 *To Have and to Hold: An Intimate History of Collectors and Collecting*, Overlook Press, Woodstock & New York

Bogaard, C, 2002 Sypesteyn Castle: A Special Kind of Collector's House in the Netherlands, *Open Museum Journal* 5, July

Bonadeo, A, 1995 *D'annunzio and the Great War*, Fairleigh Dickinson University Press & Associated University Presses, Madison [NJ], London & Cranbury, NJ

Burke, J, 2006 *The Gods of Freud: Sigmund Freud's Art Collection*, Knopf, Sydney

Cardinal, R, 1994 Collecting and Collage-Making: The Case of Kurt Schwitters, in *The Cultures of Collecting* (eds J Elsner and R Cardinal), Melbourne University Press, Melbourne, 68–96

Clark, M R, 1996 *In Trust: The First Forty Years of the National Trust in Victoria 1956–1996*, National Trust of Australia (Victoria), Melbourne

Coolidge, J, 1989 *Patrons and Architects: Designing Art Museums in the Twentieth Century*, Amon Carter Museum, Fort Worth

De Contenson, M-L, 1998 Le Musée Gustave Moreau: Visite Guidée, *Dossier de l'art: Gustave Moreau* 51, 66–72

Dorst, J D, 1989 *The Written Suburb: An American Site, an Ethnographic Dilemma*, University of Pennsylvania Press, Philadelphia

Dumas, A, 1997 Degas and His Collection, in *The Private Collection of Edgar Degas* (ed A Dumas), Metropolitan Museum of Art, New York

Elsner, J, 1994 A Collector's Model of Desire: The House and Museum of Sir John Soane, in *The Cultures of Collecting* (eds J Elsner and R Cardinal), Melbourne University Press, Melbourne, 155–76

Feinberg, S G, 1984 The Genesis of Sir John Soane's Museum Idea: 1801–1810, *Journal of the Society of Architectural Historians* 43 (3), 225–37

Garcia De Paredes De Falla, E M D-a M D F, 2005 Personal communication (email to Belinda Nemec), 24 June

Gibson, M, 2004 Melancholy Objects, *Mortality* 9 (4), 285–99

Gillies, M, and Clunies-Ross, B (eds), 1999 *Grainger on Music*, Oxford University Press, Oxford & New York

Gillies, M, Pear, D, and Carroll, M (eds), 2006 *Self-Portrait of Percy Grainger*, Oxford University Press, Oxford

Goldfarb, H T, 1995 *The Isabella Stewart Gardner Museum: A Companion Guide and History*, Isabella Stewart Gardner Museum and Yale University Press, Boston and New Haven

Grainger, P, 1933–34 The Aldridge-Grainger-Ström Saga, Manuscript, September 1933–January 1934, Grainger Museum, University of Melbourne

— 1938a Letter to A W Grieg, 6 September, Grainger Museum, University of Melbourne

— 1938b Letter to Sir James Barrett, 24 August, Grainger Museum, University of Melbourne

— 1939 Letter to Clara Aldridge, 25 April, Grainger Museum, University of Melbourne

— 1941 Letter to H Balfour Gardiner, 7 June, Grainger Museum, University of Melbourne

— 1944 Letter to Cyril Scott, 6 June, Grainger Museum, University of Melbourne

— 1949–54 Grainger's Anecdotes, Manuscript, 8 October 1949 – 6 November 1954, Grainger Museum, University of Melbourne

— 1955 The Aims of the Grainger Museum, Museum Legend, October, Grainger Museum, University of Melbourne

— 1956 Letter to Elsie Bristow, 3 April, Grainger Museum, University of Melbourne

— 1994 Letter to H Balfour Gardiner, 3 May 1922, in *The All-Round Man: Selected Letters of Percy Grainger 1914–1961* (eds M Gillies and D Pear), Clarendon Press, Oxford, 55–60

Greenhalgh, P, 1989 Education, Entertainment and Politics: Lessons from the Great International Exhibitions, in *The New Museology* (ed P Vergo), Reaktion Books, London

Hetherington, J, 1973 *Norman Lindsay: The Embattled Olympian*, Oxford University Press, Melbourne

Kaufman, E N, 1989 The Architectural Museum from World's Fair to Restoration Village, *Assemblage* 9, 20–39

Klopp, C, 1988 *Gabriele D'annunzio*, Twayne Publishers, Boston

Lacambre, G, 1999 *Gustave Moreau: Magic and Symbols*, Harry N Abrams, New York

— 2006 *Gustave Moreau Museum: Petit Guide: English*, Editions de la Réunion des musées nationaux, Paris

Licht, F, 1982 The Vittoriale Degli Italiani, *Journal of the Society of Architectural Historians* 41 (4), December, 318–24

Lindsay, D, 1965 *The Leafy Tree: My Family*, Melbourne, Cheshire

Listri, M, 1997 *Where Muses Dwell: Homes of Great Artists and Writers*, Rizzoli, New York

Loyrette, H, 1998 Degas's Collection, *Burlington Magazine* 140 (1145), 556–8

Maines, R P, and Glynn, J J, 1993 Numinous Objects, *Public Historian* 15 (1), 8–25

Mathieu, P-L, 1986 *Le Musée Gustave Moreau*, Editions de la Réunion des Musées Nationaux: Albin Michel, Paris

Mazza, A, 1987 *D'annunzio E Il Vittoriale: Guida Alla Casa Del Poeta*, Edizioni del Vittoriale, Brescia

Millenson, S F, 1987 *Sir John Soane's Museum*, UMI Research Press, Ann Arbor

Muensterberger, W, 1994 *Collecting: An Unruly Passion: Psychological Perspectives*, Princeton University Press, Princeton

Musée Nationale Gustave Moreau Website [online], available from: http://www.musee-moreau.fr/homes/home_id24501_u1i2.htm [4 December 2006]

National Trust of Australia (New South Wales), n.d. The Bequest, Website of the Norman Lindsay Gallery and Museum [online], available from: http://www.normanlindsay.com.au/normanlindsay/bequest.php [4 December 2006]

Paladilhe, J, 1972 *Gustave Moreau: His Life and Work*, Thames & Hudson, London

Pavoni, R, 2002 Visiting a Historic House Museum, *Open Museum Journal* 5

Pear, D, 2003 The Passions of Percy, *Meanjin* 62 (2), 59–66

Pearce, S M (ed), 1995 *On Collecting: An Investigation into Collecting in the European Tradition*, Routledge, London and New York

Perry, S, 2001 Grainger's Autobiographical Writings: New Light on Old Questions, *Australasian Music Research* 5, Percy Grainger Issue, 125–34

Pierre, C Y, 2003 'A New Formula for High Art': The Genesis and Reception of Marcello's Pythia, *Nineteenth-Century Art Worldwide* 2 (3), 1–13

— 2006 The Rise and Fall of the Musée Marcello, *Journal of the History of Collections* 18 (2), 211–23

Scaon, G, 2001 Pierre Loti's House: The Balancing Act between Exhibition and Conservation, *Museum International* 53 (2), 49–55

Singley, P, 1996 Disarming Nike, *Architronic: The Electronic Journal of Architecture* 5 (1), May, available from: http://corbu2.caed.kent.edu/architronic/v5n1/v5n1.05a.html [21 February 2012]

Thompson, T R, 1973 *Chris: A Biography of Christian C Sanderson*, Dorrance & Co, Philadelphia

— 2002 *The Washington's Headquarters Story: The Eventful Years* [The author], USA

Woodhouse, J R, 1998 *Gabriele D'annunzio: Defiant Archangel*, Clarendon Press, Oxford

20

# Who is History? The Use of Autobiographical Accounts in History Museums

Steffi de Jong

## Introduction: We are History![1]

From October 2007 until May 2008, on the occasion of the celebration of the 50th anniversary of the Rome Treaties, the Brussels-based non-profit organisation Museum of Europe showed the exhibition 'It's our history!'.[2] 'It's our history!', which was originally meant as the opening exhibition of a bigger museum of European history,[3] was on display in a slightly altered form under the title 'Europa – To nasza historia' in Wrocław[4] during the summer of 2009. Its subject was the history of European integration from 1945 to 2007 and, as the title – It's our history! – indicates, it was the Museum of Europe's aim to show this history as a history from below; as a history of Europe's citizens.

The exhibition started in the lobby with an introductory 'manifesto' stating that 'the History, with a capital H, of European construction is inextricable from our own personal history, that of each European citizen. It is not the reserve of those who govern us.'[5] This concern for a history of the people found its materialisation in the use of '27 ordinary citizens from the 27 countries of the European Union' (Tempora 2009, 23) who told episodes from their life-stories in video stations distributed throughout the exhibition. Here, the Germans Inge and Klaus Stürmer, for example, related their flight from the GDR in 1962; the Belgian Rita Jeusette told of her participation in the 1966 strike at the National Weapons' factory in Herstal, where women workers fought for equal pay; and the Hungarian Gyula Csics recollected his experience of the Hungarian uprising that he witnessed in 1956 as a 12-year-old. Visitors met the 27 for the first time in the second room of the exhibition, where they saw them form a group picture covering a whole wall. In its educational guide, the Museum of Europe compared this picture to the 'family pictures' taken of the heads of state at EU summits: 'This could have been an official photograph of a European

1 This chapter has been written as part of the research project 'Exhibiting Europe. The development of European narratives in museums, collections and exhibitions'. Exhibiting Europe is financed by the Norwegian Research Council under its programme *Assigning Cultural Values* (KULVER).

2 The exhibition was on show from 26 October 2007 to 12 May 2008 in the Brussels exhibition space Tour et Taxis.

3 For an outline of the history of the Museum of Europe see Charléty 2006 and Mazé 2008.

4 The exhibition was on display in the Hala Stulecia from 1 May 2009 until 5 August 2009. The Polish *To Nasza Historia* is a direct translation of *It's our History.*

5 This is the wording that was used in the Wrocław version of the exhibition. The museum texts were altered considerably for the exhibition in Wrocław. Whenever I cite from the museum texts, I will use these most recent versions.

summit with the EU heads of state and government, but it isn't. These are 27 ordinary European citizens' (Tempora 2007, 2). Thus, at the very beginning of the exhibition, a close relationship between a history of the people and the history of 'those who govern us' was established. The title of the exhibition, 'It's our history!', turned into 'We are history!' and the 27 became representatives of European integration history for the simple reason that, during the time covered by the exhibition, they happened to have lived in a country that, today, is an EU member state. As such, they were, in principle, exchangeable, as another museum text underlined:

> The 27 people you will meet here sum up the history of Europe that, for 50 years, has been broken down into the diversity of individual destinies. Others could no doubt have been chosen who have similar stories to tell. But this only goes to prove that what is true for these 27 is also true for a great many other people. At the end of the day, it is true for everyone. For each of us, the history of Europe is our history.

'It's our history!' was thus based on the double presupposition that History (with a capital H) is the sum total of numerous individual stories and that therefore anyone can act as a valid and competent witness of historical events.

The Museum of Europe is neither the first nor the only history museum to use video recordings in which ordinary people remember historical events. The self-narrated autobiographies of 'people like you and me' have become valuable exhibits in museums on contemporary history. Concentration Camp Memorials and other museums treating World War II and the Holocaust in particular have, for about the last ten years, been integrating videos in which witnesses of historical events remember (parts of) their life-stories into their permanent exhibitions. In this chapter, I aim to delineate the societal prerequisites for this integration of autobiographical videos into museums as well as analysing their museal functions and representations.

According to the most recent definition issued by the International Council of Museums, a museum is 'a non-profit, permanent institution in the service of society and its development, open to the public, which *acquires, conserves, researches, communicates* and *exhibits* the tangible and intangible heritage of humanity and its environment for the purposes of education, study and enjoyment' (ICOM 2007, my italics). Starting with the museum's functions defined here – namely acquiring, conserving, researching, communicating and exhibiting – and basing my analysis on selected examples, I will show how autobiographical accounts have evolved from historical sources and central elements in collective memory and public history to authenticating exhibits in museums.

## ACQUIRING, RESEARCHING, CONSERVING: AUTOBIOGRAPHICAL ACCOUNTS AS HISTORICAL SOURCES AND AS COLLECTION ITEMS

Museums usually acquire items according to internal collection strategies. The questions about what to collect, and under which categories to group the collected items, have changed over time and differ from museum to museum.[6] Whatever the collection criteria may be and what-

6 The literature on museum history is extensive. For an analysis of the relationship between museums' collection and exhibition practices and their socio-cultural environments, see, for example, Habsburg-Lothringen 2007; Bennett 1995; Kirshenblatt-Gimblett 1998; Hooper-Greenhill 1992.

ever the arrangement within the exhibition, the aim behind the act of collecting is to reach the highest possible degree of representativeness and completeness. As research institutions, moreover, museums do often acquire objects that are not directly meant for the permanent exhibition. A considerable number of the collected items end up in the museums' storage spaces and never enter the exhibition galleries.

In many museums, autobiographical interviews were, and are, mostly conducted as part of the museums' research and collection activities. People's autobiographies are here part of the research activities surrounding the acquired material objects (Kavanagh 2000). Especially in city museums or community museums, where the value of an object lies in the story that surrounds it, rather than in the object itself, autobiographical accounts are an indispensable research tool. The results of the interviews, which are conducted with the explicit aim of discovering the history of the object under investigation, might end up as museum text and, very rarely, as audio files in the exhibition space. Thus, the new exhibition at the Museum Neukölln in Berlin presents 99 objects, at first sight rather unspectacular, that, in the digitised museum texts, are linked to personal stories. Here, visitors can even enter their own stories in relation to the objects on show. Conducting autobiographical interviews only in connection to objects does, however, mean treating people's biographies as secondary to the actual objects. One of the first museums to discover autobiographical accounts as primary collection items was the Imperial War Museum. As early as 1972 the museum had already established its Sound Archive. The aim was and is, according to Margaret Brooks, the keeper of the archive, 'to cover all aspects of twentieth and twenty-first century conflict and ensure that we do this before it is too late' (Brooks 2010). To date around 56,000 hours of oral recordings on all possible historical events have been gathered. It would, however, be a long time before the collection items were discovered as exhibition items. Even if some of the recordings have by now become part of the museum's permanent exhibition, the Sound Archive was never primarily meant to provide exhibition material.

In concentration camp memorials, interest in individual life-stories was at first mainly the result of the scarcity of remaining sources. A large number of the documents had been destroyed before the liberation of the camps. Others were, for a long time, kept under restricted accessibility in Eastern European archives. The memory of survivors was often the only available source. Moreover, with the appearance of oral history as a research method during the late 1970s and its focus on a history from below that 'asks after the subjectivity of those whom we had learned to see as the objects of history' (Niethammer 1985, 10), new research interests began to also appear in the historiography of concentration camps. For a long time, research on concentration camps had mainly focused on the political and economical functions of the camps and on the 'resistance fight' of their inmates. With oral history at their disposal, researchers started to 'fathom the prisoner's multilayered "everyday life", the inner structures of the camp society, the conditions for survival and the perspectives of the different prisoner groups' (Garbe 1994a, 35). 'In order to fathom the perspective of those who suffered under the SS regime, we need a different approach. It is exclusively enshrined in the memory of former prisoners', observes, for example, the director of the Neuengamme Memorial, Detlef Garbe, in what concerns the memorial's first major interview project which took place between 1991 and 1993 (Garbe 1994b, 6). In the context of the Holocaust, interviews were, however, never merely historical sources. From the very beginning research interests were coupled with a desire to give their voice back to the victims of national socialist terror and extermination.

Over the years, the range of interviewees and the questions asked during those projects have evolved significantly. During the first projects, which took place when there was still a lack of concrete information on the different prisoner groups, survivors were mainly asked about living conditions in the camps. Now, the focus is also on the survivors' lives before and after the Holocaust. More recently, there have been interview projects with the survivors' children and the people who lived in proximity to the camps. A heightened interest in the workings of personal memory has now also led to questions about the way in which survivors deal with their difficult memories (Garbe 2009; Gring 2009). What is more, the initial research interests have now partly given way to a salvage effort. With the number of Holocaust survivors constantly declining, every survivor who agrees to be interviewed will be interviewed.

Most memorials have by now integrated several hours of this interview material into their permanent exhibition. Compared with the collected material, the number of autobiographical accounts that are exhibited is, however, minute. The Bergen-Belsen Memorial and the Neuengamme Memorial will here serve as illustrations. At the Bergen-Belsen memorial, there were several interview projects with survivors from the early 1990s. The first projects were, however, rather small in scope. Since 1999 the memorial itself has been running its own major video interview project and, by 2005, 340 interviews had been collected. The focus was at first on the different persecuted groups (Gring and Theilen 2007). The project has since started to conduct interviews with witnesses for whom Bergen-Belsen played an important role after 1945, such as a person born in the Displaced Persons Camp Bergen-Belsen, and a graveyard gardener. When in 2000 the decision for a new permanent exhibition was taken, the curators decided to include some of the video interviews in the exhibition. The exhibition conception was now planned in parallel to the interview project – a circumstance which, according to Diana Gring, one of the interviewers, did not, however, have an impact on the interview project as such (Gring 2009).

At the Neuengamme Memorial, the first interview project was carried out with a first permanent exhibition in view. When the staff of the memorial started to interview survivors in 1979, they did so 'at a time when there were still doubts about whether one would find enough material to present the history of the camp' (Garbe 2001, 57). The interviews were also meant to prove the possibility of a museal presentation of the camp's history. Having been completely deserted at the time of its liberation, material sources were to a great extent lacking. Extracts from the first interviews were integrated into the museum texts of the first permanent exhibition 'Arbeit und Vernichtung' (Work and Extermination), which opened in 1981 (Garbe 2009). The memorial worked with audio files and video interviews in all of its subsequent exhibitions and video recordings are a major element of the current permanent exhibition 'Zeitspuren' (Traces of History), which opened in 2005. At the time of the conception of 'Zeitspuren', the curators already had several hundred recordings at their disposal.

The zealous collection effort described here is not merely a museal phenomenon. It is to a certain degree the outcome of a societal change in dealings with the past. From a very early stage, oral history was a favourite of lay historians (Wierling 2003). Since the 1980s, history workshops, schools and other educational institutions have been conducting numerous, more or less professionalised, oral history projects. As early as the mid-1990s, Pierre Nora considered these projects to be the expression of a society obsessed with conserving and archiving relics of the past and wondered: 'whose will to remember do they ultimately reflect, that of the interviewer or that of the interviewee?' (Nora 1996, 10). Many recordings have by now been edited, published partially or in their entirety and used for educational purposes. Nevertheless, considering the enormous number of projects that have been carried out, most interviews are probably in archives and museum storage spaces, still awaiting an encounter with the public. What does it now mean to present autobiographical interviews with witnesses of historical events to a larger public and to make them part of exhibition narratives?

## Communicating: Autobiographical Accounts in the Floating Gap

Referring to Maurice Halbwach's concept of 'collective memory' (Halbwachs 1997 (1950)), Jan and Aleida Assmann have defined two modes for collectively remembering the past: 'communicative memory' and 'cultural memory' (Assmann 1992; 2006; Assmann and Czaplicka 1995). Like Halbwach's collective memory, communicative memory is based exclusively on everyday oral communications. By conversing about the past, the members of a group form a group identity and create their own individual identities as members of this group. Communicative memory is fluctuating and has a limited time horizon, spanning at most four generations. Cultural memory, on the other hand, is 'oriented towards benchmarks in the past' (Assmann 1992, 52). Its subject matter is 'events in an absolute past' (Assmann 1992, 56) which a society remembers through ritual practices and carriers of cultural memory such as 'texts, dances, pictures and rituals' (Assmann 1992, 53), in this way affirming its collective identity. Both mnemotechnic modes are linked by a 'floating gap', a time of transition during which communicative memory is slowly materialised, ritualised and institutionalised.

Since 'the birth of the museum' (Bennett 1995) in the late 18th century, public museums can be regarded as carriers of cultural memory. In public museums a societal elite collects and conserves the material relics of a – generally imagined – common past and exhibits them to the public. In this way, an official narrative about the past is constructed and communicated (Anderson 1983). The selection of objects to collect and to exhibit is crucial for this communication. Just as the interpretation of the past is in constant flux, and just as its museal presentation differs from museum to museum, so too do the ideas of what can serve as a legitimate and appropriate testimonial. The definition of items as museum objects precedes their actual exhibition within the museums' galleries.

Autobiographical videos are among the most recent acquisitions of historical museums. That they have been recognised as adequate means for testifying the past and transmitting knowledge about it is, *inter alia*, a consequence of the fact that the memories of those who have witnessed historical events have, over the last 50 years, gradually been recognised as important carriers and testimonials of historical events within public history and memory cultures.

This has, for one, to do with the popularity of oral history in both professional and – especially – lay circles. With oral history, recorded, spoken memory was included in the canon of historiographically relevant sources. The life-story of the man from the street was suddenly of historiographical interest for many. At the same time, oral historians, by guiding the autobiographical accounts with their questions, recording, archiving and editing them, materialise communicative memory. Oral history transforms communicative memory, or at least selected parts of this memory, into potential carriers of cultural memory. For the first time in history, recording techniques allow the transformation of the very act of remembering, of narrating one's life-story, into a carrier of cultural memory.

However, even before oral history turned into a mass phenomenon, the figure of the Holocaust survivor appeared as a mediatised, socially recognised carrier of a public memory of the

Holocaust. Two events need to be mentioned here: the Eichmann trial in 1961 and the foundation of the Fortunoff Archive for Holocaust Testimonies in 1978. Only very few survivors were called to the witness stand during the Nuremberg trials and their main duty was to attest to the facts that had previously been reconstructed with the help of documents. The witnesses at the Eichmann trial, on the other hand, were put centre-stage. Their role was both testificatory and didactic (Wieviorka 1998; Keilbach 2008). With the trial against Adolf Eichmann, the Prime Minister David Ben-Gurion and the attorney general Gideon Hausner wished to give a history lesson to Israel and the world. 'It was imperative for the stability of our youth that they should learn the full truth of what happened, for only through knowledge could understanding and reconciliation with the past be achieved' (in Wieviorka 2006, 68) observed Gideon Hausner, while David Ben-Gurion underlined: 'we want the nations of the world to know ... and they should be ashamed' (in Arendt 1994, 10). Since Hausner that documents 'failed to touch the hearts of men' (in Wieviorka 2006, 68), he decided to call a large number of survivors to the witness stand. Their role was less that of attesting to Eichmann's guilt than that of reconstructing and authenticating the whole horror of the Holocaust. 'I hope to superimpose on a phantom a dimension of reality', underlined Hausner (in Wieviorka 2006, 70). Together with the commissar Michel Goldman, he viewed the witness accounts deposited at Yad Vashem and chose 111 witnesses for the trial. Hausner and Ben-Gurion's technique, of bringing the whole horror of the Holocaust to life and sentimentalising the audience in the courtroom and viewers and listeners in front of their TV screens and radios at home, worked. While four cameras had been installed in the courtroom, international TV stations soon requested only the recordings of the witnesses, and audience members within the courtroom observed that, over the course of the testimonies, they forgot about 'the man in the glass booth' (Shaw 1967).[7] For the French historian Annette Wieviorka, the trial led to the social recognition of the figure of the survivor as a 'homme-mémoire', a 'memory man' (Wieviorka 1998). Indeed, with the Eichmann trial, the figure of the Holocaust survivor emancipated from communicative memory in order to become a medially transmitted carrier of an official public discourse on history. After the Eichmann trial, the Holocaust was no longer merely the six million who were murdered. The 'endless sessions' (Arendt 1994, 229) of testimonies at the trial made the Holocaust appear as the sum total of individual life-stories.

The Fortunoff Video Archive for Holocaust Testimonies constitutes the first large-scale effort to record on video and archive the testimonies of Holocaust survivors. While at the Eichmann trial the life-stories of survivors had served the secondary purposes of finding evidence against Eichmann and of emotionalising the audience, with the Fortunoff Archive the survivors' life-stories themselves and the way in which they were remembered by them became the focus of attention. For one, the Fortunoff Archive wanted to give survivors a platform from which they could tell their story (Felman and Laub 1992). At the same time, the videos were meant as educational means for present and future generations of potential secondary witnesses. This didactic designation of the videos also explains the choice of recording the interviews on video rather than audio. The founders of the archive thought that the witnesses' faces would add 'immediacy and evidentiality' to the interviews, but also considered that 'audiences now and in the future would surely be audiovisual' (Hartman 1996, 144). Further video interview projects, such as,

7 The journalist and poet Haïm Guri, for example, observed: 'Suddenly I realise that I have not been looking at the glass booth today. Things have taken dimensions that surpass him, even if he is the one who gave them those dimensions' (in Wieviorka 1998, 112).

most famously, Steven Spielberg's Shoah Visual History Foundation, followed the example. As opposed to traditional oral history projects, the aim of those projects right from the beginning was to present the videos themselves, and not merely the transcriptions of interviews, to a large audience. With the Fortunoff Archive, the video interview became established as a genre for the registration of personal memory and as a medium for presenting this memory to the public.

Alongside those interview and archiving projects, extracts from autobiographical videos with witnesses of historical events – not only of the Holocaust – telling their life-stories have, since the 1960s, appeared again and ever more frequently in television documentaries.[8] Examples include, from the beginning of the 1960s, the Dutch documentary *De Bezetting* and the German documentary *Das Dritte Reich*; in 1973 in the United Kingdom *The World at War*; in 1979 the German documentary *Lagerstraße Auschwitz*, and, of course, in 1985, Claude Lanzmann's *Shoah*. Today it seems difficult to imagine a documentary on contemporary history in which witnesses of historical events are not supporting and complementing the main narrative with examples from their own lives. But self-narrated autobiographical accounts do not only play an important role on television. A heightened interest in the memories of everyman can be detected in society in general. Publishers such as the German firm Zeitgut[9] have specialised in the publication of memoirs by ordinary people and websites such as Archiv der Zeitzeugen[10] allow everybody to publish non-fictional texts. There are even specialised associations for people who want to make their life-stories public. The Zeitzeugenbörse in Berlin, for example, prepares people who present their life-stories to a larger audience for their public appearance and manages their appearances on TV, in schools and in museums.

It thus appears as if, during their lifetime, witnesses of historical events have converted from a communicative memory group to bearers of cultural memory. During this process of mediatisation and popularisation, their function has changed as well. 'The mission that has devolved to testimony is no longer to bear witness to inadequately known events, but to keep them before our eyes. Testimony is to be a means of transmission to future generations', observes Annette Wieviorka (1994, 24). Life-stories have become instruments for transmitting historical narratives to the public with individual memory serving as representative of broader historical and societal processes.

The integration of autobiographical videos into historical museums further intensifies this function of witnesses of historical events as transmitters of historical discourses. The very introduction of recorded autobiographical accounts into the exhibition space means that the recorded interviews have to be transformed into an objectified, digestible form. This introduction is preceded by a selection and editing process during which curators are not only deciding whose account to present in their exhibitions and whose to ignore but also selecting the parts of those accounts that are going to be presented. Exhibiting their selection to a large public, they are therefore helping to define exactly which elements of communicative memory are going to become cultural memory.

8 Especially in Germany, in recent years there has been a lot of research on the representation of the 'historical witness' figure in TV documentaries. See, for example, Bösch 2008; Elm 2008; Fischer 2008; Keilbach 2003; Keilbach 2008.

9 Available from: http://www.zeitgut.com [19 February 2010].

10 Available from: http://www.archiv-der-zeitzeugen.de [19 February 2010].

## EXHIBITING: AUTOBIOGRAPHICAL ACCOUNTS AS MUSEUM OBJECTS

Traditionally the objects exhibited in museums are material objects. The ever-more frequent presence of autobiographical videos in the exhibition galleries points towards the fact that, at least in some museums, they are taking up the position, characteristics and functions of those material objects.

The fact that museums are still (mostly) about objects means, first, that the museal communication of a historical narrative is primarily a visual communication. We go to museums in order to *see* – and not only to hear or to read about – relics of the past. Museums are, secondly, based on the concept of preservation, not on that of evolution or change. They are generally meant to be the last station of museum objects and, ideally, the state in which the objects enter the exhibition galleries will be their final state. Museum objects are, thirdly, what Krzysztof Pomian has termed 'semiophores': 'they have got a material and a semiotic aspect'. While their material aspect 'consists as for any other object in the entirety of [their] physical and external characteristics', their semiotic aspect 'consists mainly of [their] visible characteristics in which one can detect a reference to something that is not there at the moment, possibly also to something invisible' (Pomian 1988, 84). Pomian opposes the semiophores to 'things' (*choses*). Unlike semiophores, things 'are useful: they can be means of production and consumer items' (ibid). While not all semiophores are museum objects and some semiophores might even be of use, all museum objects are semiophores. By the time of their entry into the museum collection at the latest, they have lost their use value. In history museums, the invisible something that semiophores refer to and represent is the past that they come from. Objects are staged in such a way as to underline and construct the traces of the circumstances that have made them historical. The semiotic and testimonial aspects of museum objects can, finally, generally not be deduced from the objects themselves. 'Secondary museum objects such as models, replicas, reconstructions and pictorial displays, as well as textual information' (Fayet 2007, 24) are necessary to inform the visitors about what an object serves as testimony to and in which way it should be read in the context of the whole exhibition.

Like traditional museum objects, autobiographical videos are (also) transmitting knowledge visually. The way they differ is in the mode of their visuality. It has been observed that visitors generally do not spend more than 3–5 minutes contemplating one object (von Plato 1992, 223). With traditional museum objects, a glance is usually enough to get at least an idea of what an object looks like and what it might represent. Videos, however, need to be watched in order for their meaning to be revealed. The gaze of the museum visitor is different from that of the cinema-goer: most museum visitors are not willing to spend a long time in front of a screen. The videos are therefore generally adapted to the visitors' viewing habits. The accounts, which are mostly several hours long, are cut into easily digestible bites of 10–20 minutes maximum length. In order to catch the visitors' interest, the most exciting and best-told interview sequences are selected. When the curators at the Imperial War Museum, for example, chose the Holocaust survivors whose autobiographical accounts were going to be presented in the Holocaust Exhibition from the recordings in the Sound Archive, they noted 'those whose stories were especially well told, or who were special for some historical reason' (Bardgett n.d.). The chosen survivors were interviewed again in front of a camera. The interviewer, Annie Dodds, observes that, even while she was interviewing, she tried to produce the most suitable clips for the exhibition: 'What we wanted above all was for [the witnesses] to try and remember what it really felt like then, when they were young [...] and we did try to steer them towards this – away from the purely factual account'. She confesses that her interview technique compromised cohesion, but: 'it did not matter to us, as the editing process would enable us to sort that out, and we were never going to follow one person's story through' (Kushner 2001, 91f). It is rare that, as in the case of the Imperial War Museum, videos are produced for the exhibition itself. Most museums choose the material for the exhibition from pre-existing videos, group them thematically[11] and edit them into short biographical films[12] or loops of short, anecdotic episodes.[13] Whether recorded for the exhibition or selected from an archive, unlike traditional museum objects, that can merely be restored, video interviews allow and even necessitate a production process. At the same time, it is through this very production process that the videos are adapted to museum visitors' viewing habits and become more like traditional museum objects: the most interesting and representative examples are selected from a large sample and staged in such a way as to highlight their most expressive characteristics.

Even more obviously than traditional museum objects, autobiographical videos serve as semiophores, as testimonies and representatives, of past events. However, unlike with traditional museum objects, the testimonial aspect of video interviews is not limited to the mere affirmation of an event. The witnesses in the videos are at once relating what the past has been like, respectively how they experienced it and how they are now remembering it. They can therefore serve as supplements or comments to other museum objects and might even serve to revise the information that is transmitted by the latter. The section 'Hunger Rations' in the Bergen-Belsen Memorial may serve as an example here. The section treats the insufficient provision of food for the Soviet prisoners of war in the camps in the Lüneburg Heath between 1939 and 1945. It is illustrated with pictures taken by German soldiers showing large stockpots, loaves of bread being distributed and prisoners with soup plates. What the pictures do not show is what the section is actually about: namely the lack of food. What hunger might mean is transmitted only through two extracts from written records by prisoners, and especially through the video placed next to the section. Only here do visitors learn that 'people started eating grass', that 'one was even eating belts' and that hunger is 'worse than physical pain', that it is 'absolute hopelessness' (Stiftung niedersächsische Gedenkstätten 2009, 222).

The visual quality of autobiographical videos, the fact that in them we can see witnesses of historical events at the moment in which they are remembering and narrating their life-story, means that, here, the past is not only testified through words, but also through the witnesses' appearance. A lot has been written in recent years on the importance of the body as a carrier of a witness' testimony and on videos as adequate means to transmit non-verbal acts of communication.[14] However, the aged body with its wrinkles and age spots – human patina in other words – serves as a testimony of history in itself. If nothing else, the witnesses in the videos are testifying that the past has existed.

11 This is the case in, for example, the Bergen-Belsen Memorial and in the Neuengamme Memorial.

12 This is the case in, for example, the Bergen-Belsen Memorial, the Neuengamme Memorial, the Mauthausen Memorial, the Museo Diffuso in Turin and the Museum of Europe.

13 This is the case in, for example, the Musée Royal de l'Armée et de l'Histoire Militaire in Brussels.

14 See, for example, Agamben 1998; Hartman 1996; Hirsch and Spitzer 2009; Lanzmann 2000; Laub 2000; Young 1992.

The life-stories in the museums are not only used to testify and represent a mere historical event or period. The narrating witnesses are at the same time representing other people that have experienced this time. Let us return for a moment here to the exhibition 'It's our history!' and the project of the 27 Europeans telling their life-stories. The Museum of Europe commented on its project with the following words: 'Through their unique personal stories, these 27 Europeans represent only themselves. However, in a certain sense, they represent us all because their history is both unique and typical' (Tempora 2009, 24). The specific stands here for the universal. Or at least it seems to. The Museum of Europe had chosen to include exactly 27 citizens into its exhibition – one from each member state. This decision points towards the fact that, in reality, not everybody can immediately serve as a representative for all other members of a society. Societies are simply too complex and divided into too many subgroups. Museums are therefore generally trying to include at least one member from each one of the groups into which *they* have divided the society that they want to represent. For the Museum of Europe this meant one citizen from each member state. For concentration camp memorials and Holocaust museums, it usually means that all national groups of inmates, all reasons for persecution and all prisoner positions in the camp are to be included. This desire to be as representative and as complete as possible often leads to an overburdening mass of interviews within the exhibitions. The second section of the permanent exhibition in the Neuengamme Memorial treats 'The different prisoner groups' and, as far as this was possible, each group is represented by one, and generally more, survivors. All in all, there are around 25 hours of interview material in the exhibition. It is impossible to watch even a fraction of the interviews during an ordinary museum visit in most museums.

In the context of the Holocaust, witnesses have, furthermore, to fulfil the difficult task of testifying in the name of all those who are not represented in the exhibition or who cannot give testimony anymore. 'Very few people had to speak on behalf of the millions who simply disappeared. We had to universalise their experiences while at the same time retaining the intimate and personal', observes Annie Dodds concerning the planning for the Imperial War Museum's Holocaust Exhibition (Kushner 2001, 91). Unlike other museums, the Imperial War Museum decided to produce only thematic stations and no biographical ones. Here the individual person with his or her specific biography disappears almost completely. Only in very few cases is it possible to make out the country of origin, the reason for persecution or other biographical details. Merely the witness' name is shown as a means of identification and even that disappears completely when, in the Auschwitz section of the exhibition, the testimonials are exclusively transmitted over audio stations. It was the curator's idea that, as in the camps, the former inmates would disappear in anonymity. Their stories were merely a means for illustrating and testifying the horror of camp life (Bardgett 2009). A similar effect is produced by the archival footage that has been placed in between the interview sequences. Uncontextualised, they often show places and circumstances that are not mentioned by the survivors themselves. The specific within the individual story is here merely representative of all possible similar stories.

Finally, autobiographical videos also differ from more traditional museum objects in their use and need of secondary museum objects. Of course, the witnesses' names are mostly shown, the videos are given a title and sometimes – though not very frequently – the extracts are embedded into the context of the witnesses' biography. Unlike traditional museum objects, however, autobiographical videos combine verbal and visual means of communication. This means that they are usually not accompanied by explanatory museum texts. There seems to be a consensus among museum professionals that autobiographical accounts have self-explanatory value regarding the reason for their presence in the exhibition and their semiotic aspect. At the same time, videos can be used as secondary museum objects for other museum objects. One of the very few objects in the Bergen-Belsen Memorial is a pair of woollen gloves. Just next to the showcase, the curators have placed a video in which the concentration camp survivor Yvonne Koch relates how she was given these gloves by a Russian woman, who, in the camp, provided her with food and became a kind of substitute mother. We can say that the video and the object stand here in a relationship of mutual authentification. Yvonne Koch's account attests the originality of the gloves, while we might be more apt to believe the truth of what she is telling us because we see the gloves. For the curators of the exhibition, this interrelation has a 'corrective' effect: 'By connecting the object to a concrete history and a concrete person – thus by contextualising it – it evades the risk of "staging" or "superelevation", which would complicate an approximation to the actual events' (Gring and Theilen 2007). It might be that, by embedding it into the context of the witness' biography, the object escapes dissociation from the context of its production and use. At the same time, Yvonne Koch's emotional story, with its almost classical fairytale elements – the orphan looking for food, the adoption through the good foreigner, the metaphorical and concrete donation of warmth – might add to, rather than prevent, an auratification of the gloves.

## Outlook: Whose is History?

Autobiographical videos have thus become authentic and authenticating exhibition objects. Over more or less the last ten years, autobiographical narratives have been integrated into the permanent exhibitions of history museums as testimonials of the past and as transmitters of official historical narratives, and adapted to the viewing habits of museum visitors. With the emergence of oral history and a heightened societal interest in the individual, museums started to get interested in the memories of those who had formerly been regarded as history's objects and to collect and exhibit the autobiographical accounts of ordinary people. To answer the question posed in the title of this article: the ordinary man from the street has become history.

I want to close by reflecting on a related question: namely, the identity of the narrator in this endeavour to make autobiographical accounts carriers of larger historical narratives. *Whose* is history in this process of musealisation of autobiographical videos? The fact that museums have started collecting and exhibiting autobiographical accounts signifies a multiplication of narrative voices. Historical narratives are no longer told only through the means of objects, documents and museum texts penned by a hegemonic curatorial staff. A voice has been given to *the people*. This is commendable. At the same time, it needs to be asked, who exactly has the last word in this endeavour? The interviewing process for the videos has had a major impact on the way witnesses narrate their life-stories. The biographical account that is given during an interview is structured by the questions that are asked and by the relationship between the interviewer and the witness. As has been shown through the example of the Imperial War Museum, questions might even be directed towards the goal of producing the best possible extracts for the exhibition. In addition, the presence of the camera will have an impact on the manner in which the witness is dressed, the way in which he or she acts during the interview and the choice of the episodes of his or her life-story that he or she is willing to reveal and the ones that he or she decides to hide. In museums, only short extracts from those already highly-constructed narratives are shown. They are put in relation to other narratives, exhibition texts and objects. Visitors will therefore receive a witness' life-story, or the parts of it that are exhibited, in connection to a host of secondary impressions.

Moreover, as has been shown, museums do not generally use autobiographical videos in order to tell ordinary people's lives, but in order to advance secondary messages. In the case of the Museum of Europe, this was the message: that the EU has a (positive) impact on the life of its citizens. The ultimate goal here was the construction of a European identity and a European citizenry. In Holocaust museums, witnesses illustrate the horrors of camp life and speak in the name of those victims and survivors who can no longer give testimony. The message here is that that which has happened is never to happen again and that we should never forget the victims. Using autobiographical videos in history museums means adapting them to the semantic structures of these museums. A democratisation of the narrative voice therefore goes hand-in-hand with a devaluation of the individual life-story. When presented in museums, extracts from autobiographical videos become samples. The individual life-story is turned into a semiophore and represents a time, a generation, a community, an event or a course of action. Exactly what events and ideas the life-stories are representing and whose life-stories are chosen to represent those events is therefore determined by a curatorial team that, generally, has not witnessed the events in question. In the present time, when the memory of World War II and the Holocaust occupies a floating gap, the transformation of communicative memory into cultural memory depends on the group of individuals who are willing to give testimony and on the elements of their life-stories that they reveal. It depends even more on the interests of a second or third generation audience that decides both on the stories that it deems important enough for preservation and on the individuals that it considers fit to tell those stories. Further research will be necessary to discover the exact nature of the stories that are selected for display. Who is allowed to act as a witness and which stories are considered worthy of being told?

## BIBLIOGRAPHY AND REFERENCES

Agamben, G, 1998 *Was von Auschwitz bleibt: Das Archiv und der Zeuge*, Suhrkamp, Frankfurt a M

Anderson, B, 1983 *Imagined Communities. Reflections on the Origin and Spread of Nationalism*, Verso, London

Arendt, H, 1994 (1963) *Eichmann in Jerusalem: A Report on the Banality of Evil*, Penguin, New York

Assmann, A, 2006 *Der lange Schatten der Vergangenheit – Erinnerungskultur und Geschichtspolitik*, C H Beck, München

Assmann, J, 1992 *Das kulturelle Gedächtnis: Schrift, Erinnerung und politische Identität in frühen Hochkulturen*, C H Beck, München [translation from German by the author]

Assmann, J, and Czaplicka, J, 1995 Collective Memory and Cultural Identity, *New German Critique* 65, 125–33

Bardgett, S, n.d. *The use of oral history in the Imperial War Museum's Holocaust Exhibition* [Document available from the Imperial War Museum]

— 2009 Personal Communication (interview with the author), 21 July

Bennett, T, 1995 *The Birth of the Museum: History, Theory, Politics*, Routledge, London and New York

Bösch, F, 2008 Geschichte mit Gesicht. Zur Genese des Zeitzeugen in Holocaust-Dokumentationen seit den 1950er Jahren, in *Alles authentisch? Popularisierung der Geschichte im Fernsehen* (eds R Wirtz and T Fischer), Universitätsverlag Konstanz, Konstanz, 51–69

Brooks, M, 2010 Personal communication (email exchange with the author), 4 February

Charléty, V, 2006 Bruxelles: capitale européenne de la culture? L'invention du Musée de l'Europe, *Etudes Européennes* [online], available from: http://www.cees-europe.fr/fr/etudes/revue9/r9a3.pdf [12 February 2010]

Elm, M, 2008 *Zeugenschaft im Film. Eine Erinnerungskulturelle Analyse filmischer Erzählungen des Holocaust*, Metropol Verlag, Berlin

Fayet, R, 2007 Das Vokabular der Dinge, *Österreichische Zeitschrift für Geschichtswissenschaften* 18 (1), 7–31

Felman, S, and Laub, D, 1992 *Testimony – Crisis of Witnessing in Literature, Psychoanalysis, and History*, Routledge, New York and London

Fischer, T, 2008 Erinnern und Erzählen. Zeitzeugen im Geschichts-TV, in *Alles authentisch? Popularisierung der Geschichte im Fernsehen* (eds T Fischer and R Wirtz), Universitätsverlag Konstanz, Konstanz, 33–49

Garbe, D, 1994a Das KZ-Neuengamme, in *Überlebensgeschichten, Gespräche mit Überlebenden des KZ-Neuengamme* (eds U Jureit and K Orth), Dölling und Galitz, Hamburg, 16–43 [translation from German by the author]

— 1994b Vorwort, in *Überlebensgeschichten, Gespräche mit Überlebenden des KZ-Neuengamme* (eds U Jureit and K Orth), Dölling und Galitz, Hamburg, 6–8 [translation from German by the author]

— 2001 'Das Schandmal auslöschen'. Die Gedenkstätte Neuengamme zwischen Gefängnisbau und -rückbau: Geschichte, Ausstellungskonzepte und Perspektiven, *Beiträge zur Geschichte der nationalsozialistischen Verfolgung in Norddeutschland* 6, 51–71

— 2009 Personal communication (interview with the author), 14 December

Gring, D, 2009 Personal communication (interview with the author), 17 December

Gring, D, and Theilen, K, 2007 Fragmente der Erinnerung – Audiovisuelle Medien in der neuen Dauerausstellung der Gedenkstätte Bergen-Belsen, in *AugenZeugen – Fotos, Filme und Zeitzeugenberichte in der neuen Dauerausstellung der Gedenkstätte Bergen-Belsen* (eds R Schulze and W Wiedemann), Stiftung Niedersächsische Gedenkstätten, 153–216

Habsburg-Lothringen, B, 2007 Was dem 'bain des Risen' folgte. Ausstellungswirklichkeiten als Weltbilder, *Österreichische Zeitschrift für Geschichtswissenschaften* 18 (1), 62–90

Halbwachs, M, 1997 (1950) *La memoire collective*, Albin Michel, Paris

Hartman, G H, 1996 *The Longest Shadow. In the Aftermath of the Holocaust*, Indiana University Press, Bloomington and Indianapolis

Hirsch, M, and Spitzer, L, 2009 The witness in the archive: Holocaust Studies/Memory Studies, *Memory Studies* 2 (2), 151–70

Hooper-Greenhill, E, 1992 *Museums and the Shaping of Knowledge*, Routledge, London and New York

International Council of Museums, 2007 *ICOM Definition of a Museum* [online] available from: http://icom.museum/definition.html [12 February 2010]

Kavanagh, G, 2000 *Dream Spaces. Memory and the Museum*, Leicester University Press, London and New York

Keilbach, J, 2003 Zeugen der Vernichtung. Zur Inszenierung von Zeitzeugen in bundesdeutschen Fernsehdokumentationen, in *Die Gegenwart der Vergangenheit. Dokumentarfilm, Fernsehen und Geschichte* (eds E Hohenberger and J Keilbach), Vorwerk 8, Berlin, 155–74

Keilbach, J, 2008 *Geschichtsbilder und Zeitzeugen. Zur Darstellung des Nationalsozialismus im bundesdeutschen Fernsehen*, Lit, Münster

Kirshenblatt-Gimblett, B, 1998 *Destination Culture – Tourism, Museums and Heritage*, University of California Press, Berkley, Los Angeles and London

Kushner, T, 2001 Oral history at the extremes of human experience: Holocaust testimony in a museum setting, *Oral History*, 83–94

Lanzmann, C, 2000 Der Ort und das Wort: Über Shoah, in *'Niemand zeugt für den Zeugen': Erinnerungskultur nach der Shoah* (ed U Baer), Suhrkamp, Frankfurt a M, 101–18

Laub, D, 2000 Zeugnis ablegen oder Die Schwierigkeit des Zuhörens, in *'Niemand zeugt für den Zeugen': Erinnerungskultur nach der Shoah* (ed U Baer), Suhrkamp, Frankfurt a M, 68–81

Mazé, C, 2008 Von Nationalmuseen zu Museen der europäischen Kulturen – Eine sozio-historische und ethnografische Annäherung an den Prozess einer 'Europäisierung' der ethnologischen und historischen Nationalmuseen, *Museumskunde* 73 (1), 110–26

Niethammer, L, 1985 Einführung, in *Lebenserfahrung und kollektives Gedächtnis: Die Praxis der 'Oral History'* (ed L Niethammer), Suhrkamp, Frankfurt a M, 7–33 [translation from German by the author]

Nora, P, 1996 General Introduction: Between Memory and History, in *Realms of Memory – The Construction of the French Past, Vol 1, Conflicts and Divisions* (eds P Nora and L D Kritzman), Columbia University Press, New York, 1–20

Pomian, K, 1986 Pour une histoire des sémiophores. A propos des vases des Médicis, *Le genre humain* 14, 17–36 [translation from French by the author]

— 1988 *Der Ursprung des Museums. Vom Sammeln*, Klaus Wagenbach, Berlin

Shaw, R, 1967 *The man in the glass booth*, Chatto and Windus, London

Stiftung niedersächsische Gedenkstätten, 2009 *Bergen-Belsen. Katalog der Dauerausstellung*, Wallstein, Göttingen

Tempora, 2009 *Europa – To Nasza Historia – Exhibition Catalogue*, n.p.

— 2007 *L'Europe, c'est ton historie. Cahier pédagogique*, np [translation from French by the author], available from: http://www.expo-europe.be/images/pdf/c%5C%27est%20notre%20histoire.pdf [19 September 2011]

von Plato, A, 1992 Lebensgeschichtliche Erinnerungszeugnisse in Museen und Ausstellungen, *BIOS – Zeitschrift für Biographieforschung und Oral History* 2, 213–30

Wierling, A, 2003 Oral History, in *Aufriß der Historischen Wissenschaft. Neue Themen und Methoden der Geschichtswissenschaft*, Vol 7 (ed M Maurer), Reclam, Stuttgart 81–151

Wieviorka, A, 1994 On Testimony, in *Holocaust Remembrance: The Shapes of Memory* (ed G Hartman), Basil Blackwell, Oxford, 23–32

— 1998 *L'ère du témoin*, Hachette, Paris [translation from French by the author]

— 2006 *The era of the witness*, Cornell University Press, New York

Young, J E, 1992 *Beschreiben des Holocaust. Darstellung und Folgen der Interpretation*, Suhrkamp, Frankfurt a M

21

# Community Biographies: Character, Rationale and Significance

ELIZABETH CROOKE

This chapter is an exploration of community projects in which members have been engaged in writing their own histories. In the examples cited, oral history and photographs are used as building blocks to tell community stories and are eventually the basis of community collections, archives or exhibitions. In this chapter these initiatives are interpreted as acts of community autobiography – they are a means for groups to research, construct and disseminate their histories for themselves. The examples discussed in this chapter were developed with the assistance of local museums or other learning bodies, and the analysis is based upon discussions with those involved in the projects, such as the members, museum curators and tutors. Participants have shared with me the nature of the projects, the rationale underpinning their development, and the significance of the projects to their institution or local community. They place immense value on the local experience and the stories of individuals, places and groups, which in many cases are being told for the first time. This self-construction of group narratives is revealed as highly meaningful and purposeful: these histories are shared amongst the group for the purposes of drawing members closer and to achieve a common goal.

## COMMUNITIES WHO WRITE HISTORIES

Oral history projects, archives and exhibitions have become tools for community groups seeking to establish their position. Even a brief search of the internet reveals countless examples of community groups engaged in community history projects offered for public view. These may be grassroots initiatives, entirely based within a community and drawing from expertise available to them within the community. Or they may be projects that harness and develop community capacity by means of history projects. When researched and then written by the members themselves, these examples of history exploration are contributions to community autobiography. Often the initiatives are led by key people, acknowledged as 'the local historian(s)' or the 'local expert(s)'. These people are reference points for local history initiatives, school research projects and museum outreach projects as well as visiting academics, curators or archivists. Often these self-taught experts begin with an interest in family history and, when that is satisfied, their interest spills into research into extended family, local neighbours, schools and the Church. They may compile intricate archives of their areas of interest, used by and shared with like-minded individuals.[1] It is such people that frequently lead community history groups and are the driving

1 This account refers to a cousin of my grandfather, the late Willie Parke, who researched both the Parke and Crooke families as well as the history of his village and the local church. In 1988 he published his autobiography, *A Fermanagh Childhood* (Parke 1988).

force behind eventual community books or exhibitions. In the cases described in this chapter the community members are not only the researchers and authors of their histories, they are also the publishers. Community members conduct interviews, gather photographs and research document sources. They construct the narrative in written or visual forms. The members control both the interpretation and the dissemination of their findings in the forms of exhibitions, books and websites. This form of self-publication enables the community to be both the author and the censor of community stories. Biographical projects bear the hallmarks of the practice of selecting and narrating personal stories. Interpretation is within the community and undertaken by the community. Together they select key events, people and places – often the 'hidden histories' lost to view in the formal archives and usual sources. For many community groups concerned with local histories, the process of exploring that history is just as important as the end product, be that a book, exhibition or archive. Investigation of the history of a group, place or region is for some a cathartic process, one that establishes connections, interprets the past and creates meaning in the present. The biographical process of constructing the history of one's own locality, people and family forges deeper connections with a place and its inhabitants.

Interest in biography comes with a purpose. Only at a certain stage in life, when life-review is useful, do we stop to reflect upon our place and situation. By researching their past a group is often motivated by a desire to take hold of their present, assert their position and enable change for the future. In Northern Ireland, community heritage projects have been presented as an opportunity to articulate goals of community change and social improvement. In 2007 in Derry/Londonderry, five members of the Bogside and Brandywell Women's Group created an exhibition of their family histories. Each woman had a single panel and she displayed her family tree, a selection of photographs of their family (such as weddings), and memorabilia such as a National Registration Identity Card. The women were participating in a personal development programme and the autobiographical exhibition was regarded as a means to enable local women to get a greater sense of the history of their town, community and family. This idea of development also underpinned an exhibition hosted in 2003 by the 'Heritage Committee' of the Linenhall Community Association, Newry, which reflected on the area in the 1950s and 1960s (see Crooke 2007, 115–17). Focusing on the pre-Troubles period, a happier time of music, dancing, sport and people gathering on the streets was conveyed – preferable to the intense Troubles of the 1980s and 1990s from which the area had just emerged. The exhibition was presented as a means to explore 'hopes and aspirations for the future'. This belief in the restorative power of historical review underpins the interest in life history as a means to recover from trauma, as a learning aid and a form of empowerment (see chapters in Perks and Thomson 1998). This is also evident when the heritage project is part of the process, and one of the outcomes, of a community movement; when, for instance, distrust exists of dominant interpretations of history and new explorations are used as a means to collapse existing hegemonies. Community heritage projects in South Africa in the 1980s and 1990s, for example, provided a means for groups to take control of the representation of their history, develop a sense of pride in their past, and strengthen bonds and group identities (Rassool 2006). These examples demonstrate that the construction of community histories is often a response to circumstances – be it awareness that this history has been neglected or belief in the positive social impact of producing such a history.

A successful community group history project will forge a collective or shared story that weaves together people and places and constructs a narrative that is 'dense with interpersonal meaning and evaluation' (Fivush 2010, 89). Key here is how relevance to the people concerned is understood, constructed and communicated. Community history projects are often a reversal of the conventional channels of expertise and authorship of the history of place and people found in established museums, archives and academia. Instead of the traditional concept of histories written externally and offered to the people concerned, the authorship, and later the publication of that history, becomes an internally generated process. The group itself selects what is important to consider, rather than being told by others. For those examples of community heritage projects presented in this chapter that began as collaboration between the group and the 'expert' (the museum or college), this link later became a means to transfer skills to group members to enable them to achieve their goals. In these cases the museum sees the project as an acknowledgment of the skills and enthusiasm amongst communities, and it is keen for that to flourish. This is not necessarily a paternalistic relationship; rather, it is an acknowledgment of one institution's inadequacies (that of the museum and its lack of knowledge of the community) and of the expertise amongst the community, about to be acknowledged and shared. The connection between the two is also a means for the museum to access information otherwise unavailable to them.

The value now placed on contemporary community history projects has been enabled by both epistemological and technological shifts. The expectation of what history is, with whom it is concerned, the sources it draws upon and who should be its author has dramatically changed. At one time, for instance, it was considered innovative for a museum to take an interest in community histories (rather than only national events); now the community members are being invited to write those histories for themselves. The museum is no longer the expert on the local group; instead, the groups are to be their own narrators. This is not only a top-down process; often community groups take the lead in exploration and narration of this history. As well as this shift in what history is considered of value, and change in who is considered best-placed to research, write and disseminate that history, technological change has altered the nature of that process. It is now easier for people to access historical resources online (such as Census Records) and to upload their community stories and photographs once that process is complete. Our attitude to what history is may have been democratised, but so too has the means of dissemination broadened. In the UK at least, many community groups engaged in historical research go beyond the community exhibition or book and make the contents available online. Now, at the touch of a button, images of people and places, once kept private and shared amongst a few, are available online to all those who stumble across them.

In this context, community groups are the acknowledged 'gatekeepers' to a rich source of information that is now highly prized by museums and academia. In the past the majority of historians and many museum curators would not have thought to consider the local or individual experience: it was not documented in the archives, they did not ask those questions and few university-trained historians had the skills (of engagement) to access this history. The people who had the insight to collect oral history in a widespread manner created archives that are now highly valued and extensively used (such as National Folklore Collection, University College Dublin).[2] Times and approaches have since changed: contemporary practice amongst historians encourages value to be placed on the local and the individual, because of the richness and relevance of the stories that are uncovered. In a role reversal, academics and curators of recent history, and those

2 See National Folklore Collection at University College Dublin: http://www.ucd.ie/folklore/en/ [19 September 2011].

interested in issues of identity, for instance, are now indebted to the people on the ground, the 'informants'. The community biography provides rich pickings that enhance museum displays and give depth to academic work. These life-stories are valued by both the insider and the outsider, but for different reasons.

While communities may be spurred to produce 'hidden histories', a certain amount of their story will always be beyond our reach – whether that is because of choices made by the community or external constraints. In every case a narrative is constructed that reflects the values important to the members and, often, aspirations for the future. Auto/biographies will incorporate exclusion. They are as much about concealing as revealing: 'it is clear that biographies are not necessarily anything approaching the whole truth or even part of it' (Evans 1993, 8). A selective editing of life histories means we can eliminate the ordinary, the everyday, or that which may be shameful or dishonourable (unless, of course, that is the attraction of the story) to produce a history we consider worth sharing. Through the creation of the media of communication, maintained by the group, their identity and purpose is asserted through to the final stage of the process. The histories are written for their peers – the authors are fully aware of the social context in which they are constructing the historical narrative and are conscious of their likely impact. Roberts, for instance, recognises that 'the telling and writing of lives presumes an audience' (Roberts 2002, 167). When a history or an experience is written down it immediately becomes a construction, an imitation or an interpretation. Any diarist knows that, even when we write such histories (or thought journals, as they are sometimes known), we are aware of how the construction will appear when we read it back. In autobiography we create the version of our lives we think we have lived. This is what we believe and, if we have a readership, what we want others to believe. In community biography, when this is a collective task, a negotiated history with a social purpose suited to that group will be created.

## THE BUILDING BLOCKS OF COMMUNITY BIOGRAPHIES: ORAL HISTORIES AND COMMUNITY PHOTOGRAPHS

In Northern Ireland, near the north-east coast, a community history group formed in 2010 with the title 'The Shared History Society'. The title is quite deliberate: it is a confirmation of the aspirations of the group in a region that is known for the decades of hurt and tension caused by the Troubles. In a place where history often divides the desire to negotiate that past is valued. The members have agreed on a common purpose and one that is essential for their survival and for a peaceful future. It is a reminder that looking back is frequently necessary to enable people to look forward, and this belief underpins the group. The title is also one of confidence: a group of people who admitted to having known little local history have now asserted themselves as prepared to revise the history of their region to create a shared narrative. It is also a statement of purpose laid bare for their peers and a suggestion of an approach that non-members could also take: replacement of a history that divides with one that a diverse range of people can adopt. This would sound over-simplistic if it were a top-down initiative, but it is more convincing when generated from within the communities concerned. The title also ties in nicely with one of the most significant good relations documents in Northern Ireland of recent years, *A Shared Future* (Office of the First Minister and the Deputy First Minister 2005).

The Shared History Society is a working-class cross-community group (a mixture of Protestants and Catholics) and is comprised of both men and women. There are currently 22 members ranging from 37 to 83 years old (Laverty 2010). The group is the outcome of involvement with the Ulster People's College (UPC), an adult education enterprise based in Belfast (for background see Crooke 2007, 111–15). In 2008 the members participated in the UPC People's History Initiative and, as a result of the programme, researched the history of their area leading to the publication of a number of books and, in 2009, an exhibition in a local community centre. The exhibition, which has since toured 16 venues in the area and continues to be exhibited, uses photographs as the main display material. Almost 500 photographs illustrating the 20th-century history of the area, each with explanatory paragraphs, have been shared with visitors. The group has forged its history and filled gaps in local knowledge. It was an awareness of the lack of teaching of 'their own history' in school that led many of the members to participate in the UPC People's History Initiative (Laverty 2010). In their experience, national or international events, which formed the mainstay of history teaching at school, were not offered with any connection to local experiences. Instead, the members were interested in personal histories, family stories and local incidents and experiences. They felt it was important to value these personal experiences. The group is also drawn to the history of the 'underdog', those stories previously untold and concerned with the people who did not seem to matter in history books and conventional teaching. Topics of interest include social and labour history, particularly when connection could be made with local experiences. For example, they are interested in the local industry, such as the linen mills, but primarily when this history is considered in terms of the experiences, skills and connections of the people who worked in them. There has been particular delight when members of the group have found out for the first time that their parents and grandparents worked alongside the parents and grandparents of other members of the group: people of different religious backgrounds. This is something the people today may not have previously experienced. This factor has been an inspiration for the group. The title 'Shared History Society' is a direct response to the divisions in Northern Ireland and an open aspiration. The cross-community aspect of this particular history group is an attraction for many of the members. People who, because of the political context of Northern Ireland, may not know or understand those from 'the other side', saw the group as a means to acknowledge shared issues, such as anti-social behaviour or a sense of disengagement, and to investigate common and new histories (Laverty 2010).

In these examples, collecting photographs and oral testimonies are the core community history activity. Oral memories give voice to the people engaged in the process; photographs capture moments in these experiences and, on occasion, objects provide a material presence. Currently in Northern Ireland there are a number of initiatives based upon encouraging community groups to gather and record their histories and form either a photographic or an oral archive. It is impossible to generalise about the character of these initiatives and their ambitions. The initiatives range from those developed by public bodies (such as the Public Record Office Northern Ireland[3] or local museum services[4]) to those initiated by community activists (such as Falls Community Council, Belfast or the Bloody Sunday Justice Campaign, Derry) or educational institutions (the Ulster People's College or University of Ulster, for example). The topics also vary. Some of these are related to the Troubles, such as the Prison History Archive based at the University of Ulster,[5]

3 PRONI: http://www.proni.gov.uk/index/your_records/creating_a_community_archive.html [19 September 2011].

4 Northern Ireland Community Archive: http://www.niarchive.org/ [19 September 2011].

5 Northern Ireland Prison Archive: http://www.prisonsmemoryarchive.com/ [19 September 2011].

and others are based upon stories of people and places captured by local history projects across the region.[6] Projects developed by the Ulster People's College or supported by local museums provide examples of the latter (various examples of these are touched upon in Crooke 2007).

The above initiatives are examples of communities creating their histories, and the resulting exhibitions can be interpreted as exercises in community autobiography. Groups are encouraged to research, interpret and construct their own history, and to tell their story in their own way. Unearthed fragments of the history of their area, photographs belonging to different people and individual stories are used to tell a community's history. The process is a means to construct a common history and evoke shared memories. The Northern Ireland Community Archive web portal is one such site. Launched in October 2008, the archive brings together museums, archives and the local communities to share stories, documents, photographs and recordings. Once online, the user can search a database of hundreds of images, uploaded by 'the community', on subjects such as local people, industry, farming and buildings. Although linked to Causeway Museums Service, the essence of the project lies in the principle that 'the material is generated and managed by the community, who has full ownership of the archive'. The website enables communities to upload photographs, memories, audio recordings and film footage to a cross-searchable database. The hope is that communities will then create online exhibitions drawing together a story from material within the database (Northern Ireland Community Archive 2010). Groups are motivated by a desire to preserve historical information before it gets lost. The projects are also regarded as a means to forge interest amongst people, particularly young people, in their local area. It is a process with personal significance that people want to be included in. There is a belief that 'this is our history and we want others to recognise it'. For the museum, strengthening bonds with their local communities enabled access to community knowledge. Now Causeway Museums Service is able to identify more of the people in their photographic collections and record their stories (Weir 2010).

At this stage, the Northern Ireland Community Archive is almost entirely based upon photographs. Participating groups upload photographs of their area and so far the themes have concentrated on familiar topics such as school days, 1950s/1960s, farming, traditional machinery and local families. The Northern Ireland Community Archive is a work in progress, with plans to add further images and additional text to the database. For the moment, viewing the collection as it stands is intriguing – the outsider gets a tantalising glimpse of times gone by. The viewer is provided images of people and places with minimal, and sometimes no, historical or social context provided. The photographic archive represents a collective system that communicates the complex values of those who compile it. The photographs are 'material performances' that engage with ideas of truth, accuracy, inscription and statement, as noted by Edwards, as well as 'an intense awareness of the past and its potential loss' (Edwards 2009, 131). Through the production, circulation and experience of these archives, the viewer is introduced to what Gillian Rose refers to as the 'imagined geographies' of a social group, institution or place (Rose 2000, 555). One viewer may see black and white images of Irish thatched cottages, smiling families in the 1950s or now outdated farming practices as romantic representations of the simplicity of times past. Another viewer may look and see the absence of the people or circumstances that were not photographed or the untold stories associated with the photographs. This may convey

6 See a list provided on the PRONI site mentioned in note 3, above.

a sense of loss and exclusion. An outsider viewing the collection is led by the choices made by the photographer in the first instance and later by those made by the archivist. What each person valued is revealed: excluded people and stories may be strongly felt and the absence of explanation of the images suggests the viewer should be able to make the necessary connections, or they should look elsewhere. As a user, how should the success of online archives, such as this one, be assessed? Even with little supplementary information, the archive may more than satisfy the community group at its core. They have made the selection and, presumably, are satisfied with it. In this case, the purpose always was for the group to maintain their site, so if they choose to include little information, or particular images, that is their choice. As an outsider looking in at the community, it seems churlish to review it according to any other criteria. However, we should consider that once a community archive is put online it stops being only about the membership who constructed it in the first place. Leaving the private space of home albums and collections, the online archive has entered the public space. Its responsibility and impact has altered with this change in environment and the consequences of inclusion and exclusion are greater.

These recent projects in Northern Ireland share some characteristics with more established initiatives found elsewhere. The Eastside Community Heritage (ECH) project in London, established in 1993, presents itself as seeking to 'build, service and enable' partnerships with people and groups, in order to record, document and preserve experiences. ECH is combining oral history work, which is their key tool, with its social, cultural and educational potential. Their motivating factor is their belief in the power of history: 'we believe that history empowers people and we seek to promote civic pride, greater harmony between people and to provide widespread historical research' (Eastside Community Heritage 2010, 1). This statement establishes the project as embedded in community concerns and as motivated by the belief in the restorative power of history-based work. Accounts of recent projects are provided online, at a website entitled 'Hidden Histories', conveying its interest in those histories frequently lost to view or excluded from the dominant narrative. In most cases these are histories of people growing up in east London, experiences of minority groups and the disabled. Collecting oral history accounts from such groups is the mainstay of ECH and has resulted in a rich archive of material for future work and an impressive web presence, which is an inspiration for other groups (Eastside Community Heritage 2010).

A recent initiative led by this London-based group was 'Ireland: What was that about', an oral history project undertaken by young people at a local school based upon collecting personal biographies of the Troubles from people living in England. The project brought together personal testimonies of former members of the British Army, who served in Northern Ireland between 1967 and 2007, as well as members of the British-based Troops Out Movement, which campaigned against British Army presence in the region. The school group used the project as a means to learn about the conflict and the end product was an exhibition displayed in the Tower Museum in Derry for three months in 2010 and a booklet (Bell 2010), which is a copy of the exhibition text. The exhibition combined biography with autobiography: the young people constructed a narrative of the experiences based entirely upon extracts from their interviews with the individuals concerned. In visitor feedback the immediacy of the oral extracts was described as 'brave', 'an excellent insight into the past', and as introducing 'different perspectives in one platform' (Tower Museum 2010). These autobiographical extracts were organised by ECH as a means to combine diverse experiences and attitudes to the Troubles. Former soldiers described personal experiences in Northern Ireland, their attitudes to the task they were set and what they have done since. Protestors explained their motivations. From the perspective of impact, the critical factor is the difference between experiencing this biographical text in a museum space in comparison to accessing the same material in the book format. Rather than on the two-dimensional page, the accounts are displayed in the three-dimensional space of the museum. The importance lies in the fact that the museum is a shared space, where people must read the words and view the images with others. Rather than the privacy of the home and personal space, where books are read, the museum is a social space where people have to acknowledge others and negotiate the space around themselves and others to read the exhibition, and are invited to interact. The disturbing personal accounts provided in this exhibition challenges war and warfare, and the accounts of tragedies make for awkward reading. The visual images have greater impact when enlarged for exhibition panels and draw people to the text. Viewing the content with others, rather than in isolation, establishes an immediate community of viewers and awareness of shared experiences. This is creating an obviously collective experience and has the potential to intensify the experience of biography.

## COMMUNITY BIOGRAPHY AND CHANGE

All autobiography is a process of construction: 'we are the stories we tell ourselves' (Fivush 2010, 88). Through the shared processes of the community engagement described in this chapter, memories are made and are motivated by the contemporary context. Olick and Robbins (1998) refer to Halbwachs, who distinguishes between history (the remembered past, with which we have no relationship), autobiographical memory (that which we have experienced), historical memory (archives/records), and collective memory (the active past). This usefully distinguishes the different layers of historical memory and the different ways it can manifest or be considered. In the projects described above each of the four are employed in an intricate interplay of past, present and future ideas. Autobiographical memory, that we have experienced, is given contemporary relevance, is made active and is encapsulated in archives to become historical memory. This means it has the potential to become history rather than being forgotten in the personal or private realm. Oral histories, photographs and community artefacts, which may otherwise be described as 'everyday form[s] of collective memory' (Assman 1995, 127), are, in this new situation, highly prized. When mediated to become public history or public memory, in the form of archives, exhibitions and websites, they are transformed from the everyday to something more unique. The change in how those memories are valued and used is so fundamental that Assman describes it as the 'concretion of identity' – because the group is now deriving significance from those memories and may later reconstruct them and feel obliged to them.

This is the consequence of creating community history and collective identities. The construction of community biography is a public event and is concerned with creating a collective story, a common history and shared memories. Wulf Kansteiner describes the concept of collective memory as 'not history, though it is sometimes made of the same material'; instead, 'it is a collective phenomenon but it only manifests itself in the actions and statements of individuals. It can take hold of historically and socially remote events but it often privileges the interests of the contemporary. It is as much a result of conscious manipulation as unconscious absorption and it is always mediated' (Kansteiner 2002, 180). The community exhibitions described in this chapter are mediated memories, which are selected, structured and represented in a social setting where they have collective relevance (Kansteiner 2002, 190). In doing so, events of the past are selected and remade in a contemporary context in order to provide a new focus on meaning.

The diversity of motivations, histories and organisation underpinning these different engagements with community histories reveal the complexity of community archives and the danger in making any attempt to generalise about their character. This observation is in accordance with the analysis of London-based archives provided by Andrew Flinn and colleagues (Flinn *et al* 2009). Within the range of archives they reviewed, each quite different, they describe two key commonalities: the archives reflect the founding ideals and motivations of a few key individuals and the decision to constitute an archive is often a reaction to the lack of representation of the community concerned within the dominant culture and formal heritage organisations (Flinn *et al* 2009, 78). This account also reflects the establishment in the UK in 1989 of the African and Asian Visual Artist's Archive,[7] which Stuart Hall puts down to the 'patience and fierce commitment' of an individual who recognised the 'systematic marginalisation' of this genre (Hall 2001, 89). So, despite being a community endeavour, which suggests collective ownership and participation, the initiative of one person will drive the project. This individual must have either the skill to recognise what a group of people need, or the following to be able to tell them. Like any leader, they must have the ability to recognise the moment and the capacity to match it to the opportunities available. The community archive that results represents the desires of those motivated to forge community. Over time, these motivations change, as the group achieves its goals and its sights change. Stuart Hall has commented on the life stages of community archives: their beginnings as 'random collections' that later become 'something more ordered'. The collections begin as 'creative innocence' and later, when established as an archive, enter 'a new stage of self-consciousness' (Hall 2001, 89). Many community history projects start with an awareness of being at the fringe. When the marginalised enters the dominant frame, what happens? Does it challenge and change those structures or will it fall foul of them? An independent community project will change when it later forges a connection with the dominant cultural processes that the initial project may have been a reaction to. This will change the relationship a community has with its biography and may even alter the story.

Analysis of these examples of community history projects from the perspective of the construction of auto/biography is valuable because it throws new light on the creation of community as well as the form and function of auto/biography. These examples reveal the importance of narrative to a community – a community must have its origin myth, its collective stories and shared concepts to draw upon. A community needs to be clear about the key people and events of the past. It must be able to unite around common themes and draw purpose from the past for the future. Auto/biography is in this context an applied process, relevant to the needs and aspirations of those who create the narrative. Auto/biography is constructed with this in mind and is a social agent communicating the ideals of its instigators. Awareness of the dynamic of the relationship between community and auto/biography is essential to understanding the significance of the connections between the two.

7 AAVAA was founded in the 1970s and later established as an independent arts organisation in Bristol in 1989. In 2005 it was renamed the Diversity Art Forum and the archive is now held at the University of East London (see: http://www.vads.ac.uk/collections/AAVAA.html).

## ACKNOWLEDGMENTS

I would like to thank Kate Laverty, volunteer facilitator with Shared History Society, for generously sharing information on the work of this group described in this chapter. I would also like to acknowledge Gemma Weir, Community Outreach Officer with Causeway Museums Service for discussing the origins of the Northern Ireland Community Archive with me. Thanks also to Craig McGuicken for sharing with me visitor feedback to the 'Ireland: What was that about' exhibition at the Tower Museum.

## BIBLIOGRAPHY AND REFERENCES

Assman, J, 1995 Collective Memory and Cultural Identity, *New German Critique* 65, 125–33

Bell, G (ed), 2010 *Ireland What was that about? Toms and TOM remember*, Eastside Community Heritage, London

Crooke, E, 2007 *Museums and Community: Ideas, issues and challenges*, Routledge, London

— 2010 The politics of community heritage: motivations, authority and control, *International Journal of Heritage Studies* 16, 16–29

Eastside Community Heritage, 2009 *Eastside Community Heritage Newsletter* 5, Winter/Spring

— 2010 Hidden Histories [online], available from: http://www.hidden-histories.org.uk/wordpress/ [27 June 2010]

Edwards, E, 2009 Photography and the material performance of the past, *History and Theory* 48, December, 130–50

Evans, M, 1993 Reading Lives: how the personal might be social, *Sociology* 27 (1), 5–13

Fivush, R, 2010 Speaking silence: The social construction of silence in autobiographical and cultural narratives, *Memory* 18 (2), 88–98

Flinn, A M, Steven, K, and Shepherd, E, 2009 Whose memories, whose archives? Independent community archives, autonomy and mainstream, *Archival Science* 9, 71–86

Hall, S, 2001 Constituting an Archive, *Third Text* 54, 89–92

Laverty, K, 2010 Personal communication (interview with the author), 9 June

Kansteiner, W, 2002 Finding meaning in memory: a methodological critique of collective memory studies, *History and Theory* 41 (May), 179–97

Northern Ireland Community Archive, 2010 Telling Our Stories [online], available from: http://niarchive.org/trails/ [7 June 2010]

Office of the First Minister and the Deputy First Minister, 2005 *A Shared Future: Policy Strategic Framework for Good Relations in Northern Ireland*, Community Relations Unit, Belfast

Olick, K J, and Robbins, J, 1998 Social Memory Studies: From 'Collective Memory' to the Historical Sociology of Mnemonic Practices, *Annual Review of Sociology* 24, 105–40

Parke, W, 1988 *A Fermanagh Childhood*, Friar's Bush Press, Belfast

Perks, R, and Thomson, A (eds), 1998 *The Oral History Reader*, Routledge, London

Popular Memory Group, 1998 Popular Memory: Theory, Politics, Method, in *The Oral History Reader* (eds R Perks and A Thomson), Routledge, London, 43–53

Rassool, C, 2006 Making the District Six Museum in Cape Town, *Museum International* 58 (1–2), 9–18

Roberts, B, 2004 Biography, Time and Local History-making, *Rethinking History* 8 (1), 89–102

— 2002 Sociological Lives and Auto/Biographical Writing in *Narrative, Memory and Life Transitions* (eds C Horrocks, K Milnes, B Roberts, and D Robinson), University of Huddersfield, Huddersfield, 163–70

Rose, G, 2000 Practising Photography: an archive, a study, some photographs and a researcher, *Journal of Historical Geography* 26 (4), 555–71

Tower Museum, Derry City Council, 2010 Visitor Feedback: 'Ireland: What was all that about' exhibition (unpublished), May–June

Weir, G, 2010 Personal communication (telephone conversation with the author), 8 June

# The Homunculus and the Pantograph, or Narcissus at the Met

Donald Preziosi

> … ideology, roughly speaking, is about what we think we see when we aren't really looking (Bhaba 1998, 48)
>
> *Magnificat anima mea Dominum* (Luke 1:46)

A clear awareness of the reality of our own finitude being a possibly unbearable source of anxiety, we may at times be tempted to actually believe in our own immortality. Autobiographic, biographic and museographic possibilities for after-lives seduce us into imagining the constraints of the real being eliminated if we keep a tense yet measured distance – a coy similitude or a pantographic relationship – toward our (self) image. As epistemological technologies of virtual space, museums and collections keep the real at a manageable distance in the face of anxieties. The ego's habitation in museological space opened up by its mirror image, however, is yet more complicated and tense. On the one hand, the duplication of the self and the distance it presupposes is a necessary condition for reflection and autonomy. Yet on the other hand, the ego, driven by the will to converge with its image, might be tempted (like the ancient patron saint/avatar of the museum-goer, Narcissus) to annihilate that distance. Hence the efficacy of socio-aesthetic institutions such as museums and religions depends on the maintenance of that tension; the maintenance of a consciousness of the artifice of our realities as artifice – even as we masquerade its denial.

This is not an end of our volume but truly a commencement; an opening up. This end-piece is a brief meditation on what I have been reading as one of the more pervasive subtexts of the contributions to our volume, namely the uncanny relationship; the ambivalent juxtapositions between the individual and the museum object, including especially artefacts staged as representing biographical entities or beings. I will not attempt to summarise nor will I directly comment upon the many finely articulated and challenging contributions to this rich collection of observations on museums and biography. Nor will I attempt to give an overview of the many ways in which that relationship has been or could be viewed historically or thematically, including a direct problematising of the rhetorical/onto-theological distinction itself between 'subjects and objects' – although what follows does bear very much indeed upon that issue.[1]

I would like to reckon with these fraught interconnections using a no doubt rather odd and perhaps seemingly counter-intuitive image, that of the *pantograph*, a term which is familiar in

1 A subject taken up at length in my forthcoming Routledge volume, *Enchanted Credulities: Art, Religion and Amnesia.*

two principal ways. It commonly refers to (a) an instrument for copying a drawing or plan at a different and usually larger scale by a system of linked and jointed rods, and (b) a jointed metal framework for conveying a current to a train, tram, or other electrical vehicle from overhead wires. An image made with a pantograph enlarges or magnifies the original. And a pantograph is a conveyer of power to mobile machinery.

I am strangely reminded of how, on the occasion of her visit to her cousin Elizabeth, the pregnant Mary described her feelings *pantographically*, as follows:

> My soul doth magnify the Lord: and my spirit hath rejoiced in God my saviour.
> For he hath regarded: the lowliness of his handmaiden.
> For behold, from henceforth: all generations shall call me blessed.
> For he that is mighty hath magnified me: and holy is his Name.[2]

This is an extraordinary declaration, for (as with our encounter with museum objects) what is portrayed was no simple one-way encounter between the immortal and the mortal, but rather in fact a claim of *mutual magnification.* The text literally says that Mary's soul (*psyche; anima*) *enlarges* (*megalunei; magnificat*) a divine spirit that in turn *magnifies her*. She becomes a vessel for the divine spirit (her 'saviour') so that, in *conveying* that spirit, channelling it, it in turn enlarges her own soul or spirit. By becoming a divine conveyance, she is no longer a mere 'handmaiden' of that spirit, for she will give birth to its *embodiment*, a mortal manifestation of that spirit. From being herself the issue of mere mortals, her own *issue* is to be an embodied divinity.

What is encountered with an object, image, or artefact in the museum is similarly, of course, no simple or direct confrontation, but the mooting of a possible *conveyance* in which encountering subjects are enriched and transformed, and, following the analogy, in that encounter the 'spirit' of the object itself is magnified.

Does this make idolatrous the individual's relationship to museological (or other artefactual) material? In acceding to the power (spirit, soul ...) of the object, is the viewing/using subject in fact attributing agency to it, or attributing a simulacrum of agency; mooting an agency?[3] Also, in doing one or the other, magnifying its assumed spirit, are we (is it) magnifying (or mooting the magnification of) our own spirit(s)? Did T S Eliot's words in *The Waste Land*, 'In the room the women come and go, speaking of Michelangelo', give a hint that *magnification* has just taken place; that the *speaking* constitutes a magnifying and extension of the spirit of the artist? Teachers of art appreciation/art therapy take heed.

Interpretation or verbal articulation, then, as a recasting of the ancient *ars longa, vita brevis* as *ars longa, ergo vita longa* (or even longer)? Interpretation or critique as ceremonial incantation revivifying a palpably mute artefact? Following the analogy may raise some not so easily

2 English Book of Common Prayer, Luke 1:46–9. In the original Greek: 'megalunei he psyche mou ton Kurion, kai hegalliasen to pneuma mou epi to Theo to soteri mou ... oti epoiesen moi megala ho dunatos, kai hagion to onoma autou'.

3 The situation here hinges on distinguishing between equation and adequation or approximation (*aequatio* vs *adaequatio*), echoing the 16th-century dispute over the interpretation of the reality of the *eucharist*. When the priest intones the words *hoc est corpus meum* (this is my body), at and for that very moment is this piece of bread *literally* (Catholic) Christ's body, or is it symbolically and metaphorically, 'representation' (Protestant) of that body? See the text referred to below, n 4.

articulated mootings of relations between artistic and theological agency, if staged (museological) encountering positions the encounterer as an echo chamber amplifying the spirit of the artificer.

It begins to sound like an echo of the stagecraft of the ancient Greek theatre, where you may recall were strategically sited amongst several ascending semicircular rows of stone seats a series of (harmonically calculated) hollow urns which acoustically amplified and passed on the voices of the actors down below on the small circular speaking, singing, and dancing stage, so that those on the uppermost tiers of the theatre could hear the performers as if they were physically closer to the drama's action.

In the quotation from Luke, Mary's *soul (psyche; anima)* magnified the Lord, yet her *spirit* (*pneuma; spiritus*) – an analogous but not exactly the same entity – rejoiced in her saviour-impregnator. Magnifying and rejoicing from the same individual. Magnifying *as* rejoicing perhaps. Is there a window here into resolving the perennial problem of the fetish, or the aesthetic/theological conundrum of idolatry, and by extension the nature of museological staging and encountering? Shall I be a vessel for the soul/spirit of Picasso in my encounter with *Guernica*, and is my bodily encounter with it a vicarious involvement in what is re-presented? Are we not here confronted with the (essentially problematic) nature of museological aims and functions in relation to the expectations and desires for resolution and fixity of sense on the part of the visitor? The establishment of a field of expectations; of the anticipation of interpretation; of a palpable sense of fixing in place a measured/measureable relationship between subjects and objects. A tense space-time of mutual confrontation, solicitation, and seduction. As one of the most widely distributed Anglophone museum bookstore guides to viewing art so aptly put it, 'Do your best at all times to let the work of art speak directly to you with a minimum of interference or distraction' (Finn 1985, 10).

I walked into this gallery a (mere) citizen, perhaps a mere anonymous handmaiden of a great immaterial Spirit dwelling in a sidereal realm presumably 'outside' the museum (if sidereal realms can be situated by GPS-location concretely relative to other realms). But right there, confronted with the *Guernica*, I become an echoing urn for Picasso's spirit – Pablo not only *living on* as echoed in and by me but being aggrandised by my encounter with his artifice. My soul (*psyche*) doth magnify Picasso, and, what's more, my spirit (*pneuma*) rejoices in him. I am indeed bettered by the encounter, by becoming (wilfully or circumstantially) an instrument of the transmission and dissemination and magnification of Pablo's spirit. Of the artistry or artifice of that spirit.

Was Mary bettered by her chat with her cousin, articulating her recent experience? Was Elizabeth herself duly magnified as a result? Was Mary's transformed state the origin or product of her conversation with Elizabeth? Or ambivalently both: sometimes, after all, conversations may indeed be quite literally productive of what is being pronounced. What exactly was John Soane doing in writing a 'history of my house' in Lincoln's Inn Fields, prior to its full habitation and transformation into a museum, and seeing it in ruins as if discovered by antiquarians of the future trying to make sense of what this artefact might have been? (arguably the first 'science fiction' autobiographic novella)[4]

Is my ingestion of Pablo's spirit an instance of techno-lust, or even of *technophagism*?[5] The story of Narcissus reminds us that merging with one's (or any) image is not so much an ultimate

4 Described in detail *passim* in Preziosi 2003, especially chapter 4, 'The Astrolabe of the Enlightenment'.

5 I will assume this to be a technical term for art-consumption, beyond mere eating of the menu.

autobiographic act, perhaps, but anti-autobiographic. Self-ingestion would seem to defeat the purpose of ingestion, namely to maintain or magnify (grow) oneself by assimilating raw material. Narcissus' aims were evidently no more nor less gastronomic than those of other lovers. But what of lovers of imagery? Consumers of museological materials? We are (decorously) entreated to keep such materials at arm's length; but what of biographical matter? Is that a different matter after all? Does being confronted with (auto) biographical material change the nature of the relationship?

We are perhaps inevitably returned to Hegel's definition of art (indebted in all respects to Plato) as the sensible presentation of *Idea* – a definition, as Jean-Luc Nancy nicely put it a decade and a half ago (Nancy 1996, 88f), yet not without a certain (perhaps unappreciated) irony, that *haunts* philosophy – not to speak of all those disciplinary discourses swirling in its wake (museology, art history, aesthetics, archaeology ...) which have been instituted in modern times to make the invisible (Idea) visible, and henceforth *legible*. Legibility, that is, as translation; as embodiment. A thoroughly theological problem, of course – or more specifically the key problem of (monotheist) theologies in the wake of Plato (not to speak of Moses confronted by those (starving?) wasteland worshippers of that gilded bovine) – all permanently confounded by the perennially irresolvable war between iconophilia and iconoclasm, from (before) Byzantium up or down to the present. The West's problem with 'art' (its own invention, after all) *as* a key problem in philosophy/theology. Perhaps theology's/philosophy's central problem. Plato's own ambivalence about this even in the wake of a need to banish (mimetic) art from the city; to insulate the ordinary citizen from the semiotic indeterminacy (promiscuity) and interpretative ambiguities of artifice.[6]

Let us perhaps understand Mary's *issue*, then, as a party to, perhaps even an uncanny mooting of a resolution of that unresolvable conversation; a mooting as mediating the rhetorical/extra-rhetorical distinction between matter and spirit; between the material and immaterial; the visible and invisible; form and content; signifier and signified? The *Magnificat* if you will as the philosopher's stone of artistry where the Platonic/onto-theological juxtaposition between invisible and visible, between Idea and artifice, endures as the necessary condition for reflection on the singularity of the autonomous ego.

A field of forces is mooted in museological space-time. The museum not as a what but as a fielding of relations: an articulation of stage directions putting actor-agents in place relative to what, precisely by their relative positioning, evokes a stage which makes a backdrop to action.

As epistemological technologies of virtual space-time, museums, collections, exhibitions and expositions do indeed expose this relationship as a distance tensely maintained between the ego of the viewing subject and the viewed object, image, or artefact. A distance that needs no external electronic sensing device for alarms to ring if contracted too much: the pantographic maintenance of the socialised ego is sufficient for the distance to be maintained so that the magnifying process may proceed. Yet the effect of this 'accession to the Symbolic'[7] is to keep in

6 As made quite clear by Agamben (1999, 4); see also Preziosi 2008. Simon Critchley makes similar points in his book *Things Merely Are* (2005), through an extended meditation on the poetry of Wallace Stevens.

7 The Lacanian reference is important here; see Nusselder 2009, especially chapter 4, 'The Body in Space', 83–97, and in particular part 4.2.3, 'Affective Avatars', 93, where the author notes: 'The (spatial) differentiation between the body as organism and the body as image constitutes the ego as a necessary alienation from the direct sensory sensations ... The imaginary ego retains strong elements of illusion

place the rhetorical syntax of content, signification, meaning, the very artifice of the opposed poles of 'subjects-and-objects'.

The situation might seem to be too complex to successfully articulate, but in reality it is quite remarkably simple: *Narcissus is held in check by the desire to prolong and maintain his own narcissism, which is precisely what would be drowned if not drawn out and perpetuated in a semi-idolatrous state of suspension.* Maintaining the tension, suspending disbelief, keeping the real at a manageable distance in the face of anxiety about the fragility of the ego's mirror imagery – a fragility that nonetheless makes possible imagining (imaging) its non-fragility and apparent permanence (its avatar) in virtual museological space-time. (Auto) biographical museological matter (perhaps there is no other completely distinct kind, really) is a mooting or reckoning with the question of embodiment, of magnification, of transmission and dissemination, of interpretation. Of the artifice of interpretation.

The pantograph of the vanities (not to speak of the afterlife of vanity itself) is the crux of the issue of the poetic artifice of museums and biographies. At the end of the day – better yet, let us rather say at the end of the *night* (the night of the soul, indeed) – museums permit us to see fiction as fiction, to see the fictiveness or contingency of our world.

## Bibliography and References

Agamben, G, 1999 (1994) *The Man without Content* (trans G Albert), Stanford University Press, Stanford

Bhabha, H, 1998 Dance this Diss around, in *The Crisis of Criticism* (ed M Berger), The New Press, New York

Critchley, S, 2005 *Things Merely Are*, Routledge, London

Finn, D, 1985 *How to Visit a Museum*, Abrams, New York

Nancy, J-L, 1996 (1994) *The Muses* (trans P Kamuf), Stanford University Press, Stanford

Nusselder, A, 2009 *Interface Fantasy: A Lacanian Cyborg Ontology*, MIT Press, Cambridge MA

Preziosi, D, 2003 *Brain of the Earth's Body: Art, Museums and the Phantasms of Modernity*, University of Minnesota Press, Minneapolis and London

— 2008 Enchanted Credulities: Art, Religion and Amnesia, *X-Tra* 11 (1), Fall, 18–25

and lure, but it has powerful effects. It "virtualizes" our direct sensations by making our awareness of them an effect of the imaginary'.

# List of Contributors

**Jeffrey Abt** is an Associate Professor in the James Pearson Duffy Department of Art and Art History, Wayne State University, Detroit, Michigan, USA. Abt's writings include *A Museum on the Verge: A Socioeconomic History of the Detroit Institute of Arts, 1882–2000* (2001) and 'The Origins of the Public Museum' (in *A Companion to Museum Studies* (edited by Sharon Macdonald, 2006). His new book, *American Egyptologist: The Life of James Henry Breasted and the Creation of His Oriental Institute* was published in December 2011.

**Felicity Bodenstein** is a doctoral candidate in Art History at the Université Paris IV-Sorbonne. Her PhD topic is the history of the *Cabinet des médailles* at the National library in Paris. In 2009–10 she was a research fellow at the Getty Research Institute in Los Angeles with a project entitled *Displaying Classical Antiquity in Paris (1800–1930)*. Its aim was to establish a typology of display strategies relating to Classical Antiquity. She is currently working as a research assistant on the EuNaMus project: *European National Museums: Identity Politics, the Uses of the Past and the European Citizen* at the Université Paris 1 Panthéon-Sorbonne.

**Alison Booth** is Professor of English at the University of Virginia. Her publications include the prize-winning *How to Make It as a Woman: Collective Biographical History from Victoria to the Present* (2004), *Greatness Engendered: George Eliot and Virginia Woolf* (1992), and articles in such journals as *Victorian Studies*, *Narrative*, and *Romanticism and Victorianism on the Net.* She is co-editor of *The Norton Introduction to Literature* (through 10th edition), and editor of *Famous Last Words: Changes in Gender and Narrative Closure* and the Longman Cultural Edition of *Wuthering Heights*. Currently resident fellow of the Institute for Advanced Technology in the Humanities, she directs a study of the narrative structure of biographies in networks: http://womensbios.lib.virginia.edu.

**Stuart Burch** is a Senior Lecturer at Nottingham Trent University, where he teaches museum studies, heritage management and public history. He is currently conducting research into national art museums in northern Europe as part of 'Nordic Spaces', a four-year multinational project supported by Riksbankens Jubileumsfond and a consortium of other funders (http://www.nordicspaces.com).

**Lucie Carreau** is a Research Associate on the AHRC-funded Fiji project at the Museum of Archaeology and Anthropology, University of Cambridge. In addition to her doctoral research on the ethnographic collections of Harry Beasley, she has also worked on the collections of early European voyages in Polynesia (1765–1840) as part of the ESRC-funded 'Artefacts of Encounter' project.

**Elizabeth Crooke** is Senior Lecturer in Museum and Heritage Studies at the University of Ulster, where she has been Course Director of the MA Cultural Heritage and Museum Studies since it started in 2001. She is a member of the AHRC Peer Review College, the Northern Ireland

Museums Council, and the Museums and Archives Committee of Heritage Council (Ireland). She is the author of *Museums and Community: Ideas, Issues and Challenges* (2008) and *Politics, Archaeology and the creation of a national museum in Ireland* (2000). She is currently working on areas of memory, material culture and biography.

**Steffi de Jong** has been working as a PhD candidate at the Norwegian University of Science and Technology in Trondheim since October 2008. In her PhD thesis she analyses the representation of the figure of the witness of history in European World War II and Holocaust Museums. She is affiliated to *Exhibiting Europe*, a research project financed by the Norwegian Research Council which analyses the development of a European narrative in museums, collections and exhibitions. She finished her MA in European Studies at Maastrich University and at the Jagiellonian University in Krakow in August 2008 with the thesis 'Europe on Show: Exhibiting European Culture and History in Museums'. She graduated in 2006 from Royal Holloway, University of London, with a BA in English Literature and Drama/Theatre Studies.

**Mark Elliott** is Newton Trust Curatorial Research Fellow at the Museum of Archaeology and Anthropology, University of Cambridge. He has carried out research on museum collections, curatorial practice and visitor engagement in India and the UK, and has co-curated several exhibitions, including 'Assembling Bodies: Art Science & Imagination'.

**Sophie Forgan** spent her academic life at the University of Teesside, and combined teaching the history of architecture with research in the history of science. She has published extensively on the history of learned societies, universities, museums and exhibitions, and scientific culture. Since 1997 she has been involved with the Captain Cook Memorial Museum in Whitby, which has sharpened her interest in the history and development of personality museums.

**Mariana Françozo** is Assistant Professor of Museum Studies in the Faculty of Archaeology at Leiden University, The Netherlands. She received her PhD in Social Sciences in 2009 after defending a dissertation entitled 'From Olinda to Olanda: Johan Maurits van Nassau-Siegen and the circulation of objects and knowledge in the Dutch Atlantic'. She was visiting researcher at the Center for Research and Documentation about Latin America (CEDLA) of the University of Amsterdam, the Netherlands, and at the Department of Anthropology of the University of Aarhus, in Denmark. In 2010, she was Post-Doctoral Fellow of the Fritz Thyssen Stiftung at the Forschungsbibliothek Gotha, Germany. Her research interests include the history of collections, early modern travel and ethnography, and the history of colonial Brazil.

**Laura Gray** is currently studying for a doctorate at Cardiff School of Art (University of Wales Institute Cardiff), which is funded by the Vice Chancellor's Doctoral Scholarship scheme. Her area of research is how the relationship between sculpture and ceramics is revealed in contemporary ceramics practice. Laura also holds an MA in Art Gallery and Museum Studies from the University of Manchester and an MRes in Curatorial Practice from Liverpool School of Art. Before returning to university to study for her PhD in 2009, she was Assistant Keeper of Art at the Harris Museum & Art Gallery, Preston, UK, and Curatorial Officer in Fine and Decorative Art department of the National Army Museum in London.

**Kate Hill** teaches History at the University of Lincoln. She is the author of *Culture and Class in English Public Museums 1850–1914* (2005), and has recently edited a special edition of the Museum History Journal on the collection and display of the British past, c. 1850–1950. She has been working on a project examining women's donations to English museums around the end of the 19th century, which will be published as *Gendered Objects? Material Culture, Domesticity and Museums 1850–1914*.

**Suzanne MacLeod** is a Senior Lecturer in the School of Museum Studies at the University of Leicester. She has published on museum history as well as museum architecture and design and is currently completing a large project which explores how museum architecture gets made through design and use. She is editor of *Reshaping Museum Space: architecture, design, exhibitions* (2005) and is currently editing *Museum Making: narratives, architectures, exhibitions* with Jonathan Hale and Laura Hanks (2012).

**Wallis Miller** has written several articles on architecture exhibitions and museums, including 'Circling the Square' for the exhibition *O M Ungers: Kosmos der Architektur* at the Neue Nationalgalerie in Berlin (2006) and 'Mies and Exhibitions', for the exhibition *Mies in Berlin* at the Museum of Modern Art, New York (2001). Her current project is *Architecture on Display: Exhibitions, Museums, and the Emergence of Modernism in Germany*, a book about how collecting and exhibiting was formative for architecture in the 19th and early 20th centuries. She is the Charles P Graves Associate Professor of Architecture at the University of Kentucky.

**Belinda Nemec** has qualifications in music, museology and Australian studies; her PhD thesis explored 'The Grainger Museum in its museological and historical contexts'. She has worked in curatorial, registration, research and management roles with museums, historic places and collections for more than 20 years and is an Honorary Research Associate with the Australian Centre at the University of Melbourne.

**Donald Preziosi** is Emeritus Professor of Art History at UCLA and former Slade Professor of Fine Art at Oxford. Recent books include *Brain of the Earth's Body: Art, Museums, and the Phantasms of Modernity* (2003); and, with Claire Farago, *Grasping the World: The Idea of the Museum* (2004) and *Art Is Not What You Think It Is* (2011). His *Enchanted Credulities: Art, Religion, and Amnesia* appears in 2012.

**Helen Rees Leahy** is the Director of the Centre for Museology at the University of Manchester. Prior to joining the university, she worked as a museum curator and director. Her current research interests focus on practices of display, interpretation and visitors' embodied experiences of the museum. Her book *Museum Bodies* is forthcoming.

**Linda Sandino** is the CCW Graduate School, University of the Arts London, Senior Research Fellow in Oral History at the Victoria & Albert Museum where she is researching curators' working lives and their narratives of expertise. She developed VIVA (Voices in the Visual Arts: www.vivavoices.org) and manages the Design History Society oral histories. Her recent publications have focused on narrative identities in art, craft and design.

**Julie Sheldon** is Professor of Art History at Liverpool John Moores University. She is the editor of *The Letter of Elizabeth Rigby, Lady Eastlake* (2009) and the co-author (with Susanna Avery-Quash) of *Art for the Nation: The Eastlakes and the Victorian Art World* (2011). Other co-authored publications include (with Pam Meecham) *Modern Art: A Critical Introduction* (2004), *Making American Art* (2008), and she has co-edited (with Bryan Biggs) a book on the arts in Liverpool, *Art in a City Revisited* (2009).

**Alexandra Stara** directs graduate History & Theory and the MA Thinking Building at the School of Architecture & Landscape, Kingston University. She is a qualified architect with Masters Degrees from the Bartlett and the University of Cambridge, and holds a doctorate in the History of Art from the University of Oxford. She has been teaching, lecturing and publishing on the hermeneutics of art, architecture and the modern museum for the past 15 years. Latest projects include: co-editing *Curating Architecture & the City* with Sarah Chaplin (2009); curating *Strange Places: Urban Landscape Photography* at the Stanley Picker Gallery (2009); and the chapter 'Cultivating Architects: History in Architectural Education' in *The Humanities in Architectural Design* (ed S Bandyopadhyay *et al*) (2010). She is currently preparing a monograph on Alexandre Lenoir's Museum of French Monuments and co-editing a collected volume on the art and literature of trauma.

**Louise Tythacott** is a Lecturer in Museology at the University of Manchester. She trained as an anthropologist and undertook fieldwork in Hong Kong on Chinese deity iconography and temple imagery. She has worked in the museum sector for over a decade, latterly as the Head of Asian, African, American and Oceanic collections at the National Museums Liverpool (1996–2003), where she was responsible for curating the Asia section of the World Cultures Gallery, which opened in 2005. She is the author of *Surrealism and the Exotic* (2003) and *The Lives of Chinese Objects: Buddhism, Imperialism and Display* (2011).

**Chris Whitehead** leads the Art Museum and Gallery Studies postgraduate programme at Newcastle University. He has published extensively in the fields of museum history and the theory and practice of museum education and interpretation. He is the author of *The Public Art Museum in Nineteenth-Century Britain: the development of the National Gallery* (2005), *Museums and the Construction of Disciplines: art and archaeology in nineteenth-century Britain* (2009) and *Interpreting Art in Museums and Galleries* (2012).

**Anne Whitelaw** is Associate Professor in the Department of Art History at Concordia University in Montreal, Canada. Her research examines the intersections of art historiography and cultural institutions in Canada, with a particular focus on practices of exhibition and collecting. She has published extensively on the display of Canadian art at the National Gallery of Canada, on the writings of art historian John Russell Harper, and on the integration of Aboriginal art into the permanent displays of national museums. She is co-editor with Brian Foss and Sandra Paikowsky of *The Visual Arts in Canada: The Twentieth Century* (2010). Her current research includes a book on the relationship between federal cultural institutions and art galleries in Western Canada, and an exploration of the work of women's volunteer committees in North American art museums.

# Index

Page numbers in bold type refer to illustrations and their captions

# Heritage Matters

Volume 1: The Destruction of Cultural Heritage in Iraq
*Edited by Peter G. Stone and Joanne Farchakh Bajjaly*

Volume 2: Metal Detecting and Archaeology
*Edited by Suzie Thomas and Peter G. Stone*

Volume 3: Archaeology, Cultural Property, and the Military
*Edited by Laurie Rush*

Volume 4: Cultural Heritage, Ethics, and the Military
*Edited by Peter G. Stone*

Volume 5: Pinning Down the Past: Archaeology, Heritage, and Education Today
*Mike Corbishley*

Volume 6: Heritage, Ideology, and Identity in Central and Eastern Europe: Contested Pasts, Contested Presents
*Edited by Matthew Rampley*

Volume 7: Making Sense of Place: Multidisciplinary Perspectives
*Edited by Ian Convery, Gerard Corsane, and Peter Davis*

Volume 8: Safeguarding Intangible Cultural Heritage
*Edited by Michelle L. Stefano, Peter Davis, and Gerard Corsane*

Volume 9: Museums and Biographies: Stories, Objects, Identities
*Edited by Kate Hill*

Volume 10: Sport, History, and Heritage: Studies in Public Representation
*Edited by Jeffrey Hill, Kevin Moore, and Jason Wood*

Volume 11: Curating Human Remains: Caring for the Dead in the United Kingdom
*Edited by Myra Giesen*

Volume 12: Presenting the Romans:
Interpreting the Frontiers of the Roman Empire World Heritage Site
*Edited by Nigel Mills*

Volume 13: Museums in China: The Politics of Representation after Mao
*Marzia Varutti*

Volume 14: Conserving and Managing Ancient Monuments: Heritage, Democracy, and Inclusion
*Keith Emerick*

Volume 15: Public Participation in Archaeology
*Edited by Suzie Thomas and Joanne Lea*

www.ingramcontent.com/pod-product-compliance
Lightning Source LLC
LaVergne TN
LVHW081256100826
845148LV00005B/893

* 9 7 8 1 8 4 3 8 3 9 6 1 3 *